Jesse D. Mason

History of Amador County, California

With Illustrations and Biographical Sketches of its Prominent Men

Jesse D. Mason

History of Amador County, California
With Illustrations and Biographical Sketches of its Prominent Men

ISBN/EAN: 9783337010324

Printed in Europe, USA, Canada, Australia, Japan

Cover: Foto ©ninafisch / pixelio.de

More available books at **www.hansebooks.com**

HISTORY

OF

AMADOR COUNTY,

CALIFORNIA,

WITH

Illustrations and Biographical Sketches

OF ITS

PROMINENT MEN AND PIONEERS.

OAKLAND, CAL.
THOMPSON & WEST.
1881.

Entered according to Act of Congress, in the year 1881, by
THOMPSON & WEST,
In the Office of the Librarian of Congress at Washington, D. C.

PACIFIC PRESS PUBLISHING HOUSE,
PRINTERS,
STEREOTYPERS AND BINDERS,
OAKLAND, CAL.

TABLE OF CONTENTS.

INTRODUCTION .... 9—10

CHAPTER I.

Scanty Knowledge of the Pacific Coast Fifty Years Since—Story of "Sergas," by Esplandin—Titles to Immense Regions Conferred by the Pope—Expeditions for Discovery and Settlement—Sir Francis Drake's Operations—Expeditions Overland—Marvelous Stories of a Big Cañon—Expedition of Father Escalante .... 11—12

CHAPTER II.

BIG CANON OF THE COLORADO.

Lieutenant Whipple's Expedition—Lieutenant Ives' Expedition—First Attempt to Explore the Cañon—Land Party Organized—One Sight of the River—First Exploration—Unwilling Venture—Consider the Situation—Death of One of the Parties—Three Months in the Cañon—Arrival at Fort Colville—Exploration Made Under the Direction of the Smithsonian Institute—Indescribable Character of the Stream—Loss of Boats and Provisions—Death of a Portion of the Party—Emergence of the Survivors—Geology and Climate .... 12—17

CHAPTER III.

The Exiles of Loreto—Father Tierra's Methods of Conversion—Death of Father Tierra—Arrest of the Jesuits—Midnight Parting—Permanent Occupation of California—Missions in Charge of Franciscon Friars—Character of Father Junipero—Exploring Expeditions—Origin of the name of the Bay—Mission Dolores—Death of Father Junipero.. ....17—20

CHAPTER IV.

THE MISSIONS OF ST. FRANCIS.

Their Moral and Political Aspect—Domestic Economy—The Establishments Described—Secular and Religious Occupations of the Neophytes—Wealth and Productions—Liberation and Dispersion of the Indians—Final Decay .20—23

CHAPTER V.

DOWNFALL OF THE OLD MISSIONS.

Results of Mexican Rule—Confiscation of the Pious Fund—Revolution Begun—Events of the Colonial Rebellion—The Americans Appear and Settle Things—Annexation at Last. ....23—24

CHAPTER VI.

PRIMITIVE AGRICULTURE.

Extent of the Mission Lands—Varieties of Product—Agricultural Implements and means of Working—A Primitive Mill—Immense Herds and Value of Cattle—The First Native Shop................................. ....24—26

CHAPTER VII.

Sir Francis Drake's Discoveries—The Fabulous Straits of Anian—Arctic Weather in June—Russian Invasion—Native Animals—Various facts and Events.........26—29

CHAPTER VIII.

THE AMERICAN CONQUEST.

Fremont and the Bear Flag—Rise and Progress of the Revolution—Commodores Sloat, Stockton, and Shubrick—Castro and Flores Driven out—Treaty of Peace—Stockton and Kearney Quarrel—Fremont Arrested, etc. ..29—31

CHAPTER IX.

SAN JOAQUIN COUNTY FROM THE TIME CAPT. C. M. WEBER FIRST SAW IT IN NOVEMBER, 1841, UNTIL THE CLOSE OF 1847.

Captain C. M. Weber—Expedition to California, 1841—Names of the Party—Sutter's Fort—Hoza Ha-soos—San Jose—French Camp or Weber Grant—Revolutionary Designs of the Foreigners—Treaty between Weber and Ha-soos—How it was observed by Ha-soos—Fremont's Expedition, 1844—David Kelsey—Thomas Lindsay—Policy of the Foreigners—Weber and Michetorena at San Jose—John A. Sutter aids Micheltorena—A Revolutionary Document—The "Bear Flag"—Attempt to Settle the Grant, 1846—Isbel Brothers and Other Early Settlers—Twins, Second Children born in County, 1847—End of Stanislaus City—First Marriage, 1847—Village of "Tuleburg"—William Gann, First Child born in 1847—Wild Horse Scheme—Resume. ..31—39

CHAPTER X.

BIOGRAPHIC SKETCH OF GENERAL SUTTER.

His Nativity—Migration to the American West—Arrival in California—Foundation of Sutter's Fort—Prosperity and Wealth of the Colony—Decline and Ultimate Ruin—Retirement to Hock Farm—Extract from Sutter's Diary. 39—46

CHAPTER XI.

THE KING'S ORPHAN.

His Observations in the Sacramento Valley in 1843—Indications of Gold—Life at Sutter's Fort—Indian Gourmands—Wonderful Fertility of the Land.. ....46—47

CHAPTER XII.

SUTTER'S FORT IN 1846.

Aspect of Sacramento Valley—Sinclair's Ranch—A Lady Pioineer—Captain Sutter at Home—The Fort Described—Condition and Occupation of the Indians—Farm Products and Prices—Dinner with the Pioneer—New Helvetia ..47—49

CHAPTER XIII.

THE HISTORY OF THE DONNER PARTY.

Scene of the Tragedy—Organization and Composition of the Party—Election of George Donner as Captain—Hastings' Cut-off—Ascent of the Mountains—Arrival at Donner Lake—Snow-storms—Construction of Cabins—"Forlorn Hope Party"—Captain Reasin P. Tucker's Relief Party—James F. Reed's Relief Party—"Starved Camp"—Third Relief Party—Heroism and Devotion of Mrs. George Donner—Fourth Relief Party—The Survivors . ...49—51

TABLE OF CONTENTS.

CHAPTER XIV.
THE DISCOVERY OF GOLD.

Early Reports and Discoveries—Marshall's Great Discovery at Sutter's Mill—His Account of the Event—Views of the Newspapers of that Time—Political and Social Revolution—Great Rush to the Mines—Results—General Sutter's Account of the Gold Discovery—Building of Saw-Mill. 51—58

CHAPTER XV.
EARLY CONDITION OF THIS REGION.

Mountains Unexplored by the Spaniards—The Trappers—Fremont's Passage of the Mountains in 1844—Battles with the Snow—The Indian's Warning—A Glimpse of the Valley—Subsisting on Horse Flesh—Arrival at Sutter's Fort—Early Settlements—An Immigrant Party of 1844—Captain Truckee—Truckee River—Alone on the Summit—Death of Captain Truckee—Immigrants in 1846—Discovery of Gold on the Yuba. 58—65

CHAPTER XVI.
AMADOR COUNTY.

Early History—Origin of the Name of Carson Pass—River and Valley—First White Men in the Territory—Sutter's Whipsaw-mill—Discovery of Gold—Organization of Calaveras County—Removal of County Seat from Double Springs to Jackson—Second Removal to Mokelumne Hill—First Set of County Officers—Second Set of County Officers—Members of the Legislature—Miscellaneous Matters in Calaveras—Joaquin's Career—Chased by Indians—Mokelumne Hill in Early Days—Green and Vogan's Line of Stages—Stories of Grizzlies—Bull and Bear Fight. 65—71

CHAPTER XVII.
DOMESTIC HABITS OF THE MINERS.

Exaggerated Accounts of Bret Harte and Joaquin Miller—Cooking and Washing—Hawks, Squirrels, Quails, and Other Game for Food—Getting Supper Under Difficulties—Laundry Affairs—Prevalence of Vermin—The Sanguinary Flea—Miners' Flea Trap—Fleas versus Bed-bugs—Rats and Other Animals—Visits of Snakes—A Romantic Affair Spoiled by a Skunk. 72—76

CHAPTER XVIII.
ORGANIZATION OF AMADOR COUNTY.

Election for or Against Division, June 17, 1854—Proceedings of the Board of Commissioners—Strife for the Possession of the County Seat—The Owl—Sketches of the First Candidates—Courts Established—Efforts to Suppress Disorderly Houses—Amusing Procession—Election in 1854—Condition of Society. 76—83

CHAPTER XIX.
RANCHERIA MURDERS.

Ill-feeling between the Americans and Mexicans—Frequency of Murders—The Band First Seen at Hacalitas—Up Dry Creek—At Rancheria—To Drytown—A Second Time to Rancheria—Slaughter—Departure of the Robbers—Excitement the Next Day—Immense Gathering—Trial and Hanging of the Mexicans—Death of Roberts—Borquitas—Presence of County Officers—Pursuit of the Murderers—Hunt Around Bear Mountain—The Murderers Overtaken—Death of Phoenix—Expulsion and Disarming of Mexican Population—Outrages at Drytown—Burning of the Church—Mass Meeting at Jackson—Review After a Lapse of a Quarter of a Century. 83—88

CHAPTER XX.
POLITICAL PARTIES IN 1855.

Success of the American Party—List of Officers Elected—Rivalry Between Towns—Financial Matters—Efforts to Suppress Gambling—Political Parties in 1856—Names of Officers Elected—Calaveras Indebtedness—Tax Levy in 1857—Disbursements for 1857—Table of Receipts for all Moneys up to 1857—Political Parties in 1857—Officers Elected in 1857—Officers Elected 1858—Tax Levy 1858—Condition of Treasury—Financial Matters in 1859—Condition of Political Parties. 88—92

CHAPTER XXI.
AMADOR COUNTY AT THE BEGINNING OF 1860.

County Officers—Financial Situation—Political Parties—First Appearance of R. Burnell—First Appearance of Tom Fitch—Officers Elected in 1860—Amador Wagon Road Voted On—Names of Amador Mountaineers—Financial Affairs in 1861—Calaveras Indebtedness Denied—Enormous Profits of Officers—Political Parties in 1861—The Amador Wagon Project Renewed—Vote on the Project, May 10, 1862—Rates of Toll—Impeachment of James H. Hardy—Political Parties in 1862—Great Fire in Jackson—Petition of M. W. Gordon—Supervisors Order the Building of a Court House—Political Parties in 1863—French Bar Affair—Officers Elected in 1863—General Vote—Political Parties in 1864—Vote of 1864—Financial Matters—Political Parties in 1865—Arrest of Hall and Penry—Election Returns by Precincts, 1865—Seaton's Defection—Counting the Votes—Clinton Vote—List of Officers Elected in 1865—Death of G. W. Seaton, and Election of A. H. Rose, his Successor—Financial Matters in 1865 92—107

CHAPTER XXII.
END OF THE SECOND DECADE.

Politics in 1866—Financial Matters—Rabolt Declared Ineligible to the Office of Treasurer, and Otto Walther Appointed—Political Parties in 1867—New Registry Law—Election Returns Showing the New Precincts—Judiciary Election—Financial Matters—Financial Matters in 1868—Contest for Supervisor in the First District—Ingalls Declared Unseated—Carroll Installed—Act of the Legislature in Reference Thereto—Wealth and Population—Political Parties in 1868, —Election Returns by Precincts—Politics in 1869—Election Returns by Precincts. 107—110

CHAPTER XXIII.
CONDITION OF THE COUNTY AT THE BEGINNING OF THE THIRD DECADE—1870.

Condition of the County at the Beginning of the Third Decade—Statistics of the Wealth and Indebtedness—Politics in 1870—Financial Condition—Redemption Fund—Condition of Other Counties—The Miners' League—Death of McMenomy and Hatch—Political Parties in 1872—Election Returns by Precincts, 1871—Persons Elected in 1871—Financial Matters 1872—Political Parties in 1872—Election Returns for 1872—Comparison of Vote with Previous Years—Financial Matters, 1873—Political Parties in 1873—John Eagon's Position—Judge Gordon's Stand—J. T. Farley's Position—Election Returns by Precincts—Officers Elected in 1873—Alpine county Left out in the Election—Financial Matters in 1874—The Funding Project—Political Parties in 1874—Financial Matters in 1875—Robbery of the Treasury May 9, 1875—Conclusion of Butterfield Matter in 1877—Political Matters in 1875—Officers elected in 1875 110—119

CHAPTER XXIV.
FINANCIAL MATTERS IN 1876.

Political Parties in 1876—Election Returns by Precincts—Finances in 1877—Political Parties in 1877—Returns by Precincts—Death of the Honorable Robert Ludgate—Financial Matters in 1878—Political Parties in 1878—Vote on the Adoption of the New Constitution—Financial Matters in 1879—Political Matters in 1879—Officers Elected—Effect of the New Constitution on the Judicial System—Financial Matters in 1880—Political Parties in 1880—Amador County Election Returns Nov. 2, 1880—Review from 1870 to 1880. 119—124

CHAPTER XXV.
GEOLOGY OF AMADOR COUNTY.

Strata in Buena Vista Mountain—Carboniferous Clays—Granite Sandstone—Glacial Epoch—Supposed Section of the Mountains—Former Course of the Rivers—Account of the Blue Lead—Stratified Rocks—Serpentine Range—Chromate of Iron. 125—130

CHAPTER XXVI.
GEOLOGY OF AMADOR COUNTY.
BY GEORGE MADEIRA.

Extensive Character of the Subject—Mother Lode—Methods of Vein Deposits—Character of the Veins East of the Mother Lode—Minerals in the Tertiary Rocks—Nature of the Limestones—Gravel Deposits—Nature of the Supposed Photographic Rock—Evidences of Glaciers—Moving Large Rocks—Volcanoes—Origin of the Trap Rock—Origin of the Smaller Quartz Veins—Butte Mountain—Copper—Iron—Gypsum—Asbestos—Marble—Kaolin—Manganese—Agate—Chalcedony—Skeletons of the Megatherium—Other Fossils—Rhinoceros—Hippopotamus—Horse Destruction of the Arcadian Land—Botany........ 136—141

CHAPTER XXVII.
ORIGIN OF MINERAL VEINS.

Plutonic Theory—Ocean Floors—Other Theories Considered—Function of Wall Rock and Gouge—Surface Veins—Probable Depth of Veins—Methods of Deposit—Jurassic Gravel—Course of the Blue Lead.. 141—145

CHAPTER XXVIII.
QUARTZ MINING.

Quartz Mining, Commencement of—Quartz Miners' Convention—Account of the Mother Lode—Sketch of Different Mines—Gwin Mines—Casco—Murphy's Ridge—Huffaker—Moore-Zeile—Description of a Model Mill—Platner Process of Reducing Sulphurets—Hinkley Mine—Montericherd—Kennedy—Tubbs—Oneida—Summit—Hayward—Character of the Same—Railroad—Wildman—Mahoney—Union or Lincoln—Accident in the Lincoln—Mechanica—Herbertville—Spring Hill—Keystone—Consolidation of Granite State and Walnut Hill—Discovery of the Bonanza—Statistics of Same—Big Grab, and Failure to Hold it—Account of the Suit—Original Amador—Bunker Hill—Pennsylvania Gover—Black Hills—Seaton—Potosi—Quartz Mountain—Plymouth Group—Enterprise—Nashville... 145—161

CHAPTER XXIX.
QUARTZ MINING EAST OF THE MOTHER LODE.

Downs Mine—Marklee—Tellurium—Thayer—Clinton Mines—Mace Range of Mines—Pioneer and Golden Gate Mines—Quartz Veins West of the Mother Lode—Kirkendall—Soap-Stone or Steatite Mine—Quartz Mining in the Future—Put Money in Thy Purse—School Cabinets—Copper Mining—General Craze—Country Formed into Districts—Fanny [illegible]—New [illegible]—Chromic Iron—Failure of Meader—Remarkable Discovery—Present Condition of Copper Mining—Newton Mine. 161—167

CHAPTER XXX.
JACKSON.

Capture of the County Seat—Killing of Colonel Collyer—Loss of the County Seat—Bull Fight and Election—Mines—First School—Improvements in 1854—Hanging Tree—Griswold Murder—Great Freshet 1861—Great Fire 1862—Flood and Loss of Life 1878—Big Frolic—Celebration of Admission Day—Mokelumne River—Murphy's Gulch—Hunt's Gulch—Tunnel Hill—Butte Basin—Butte Mountain—Butte City—Marriage in High Life—The Gate—Ohio Hill—Slab City—Clinton—Spaulding's Invention................167—181

CHAPTER XXXI.
IONE VALLEY AND VICINITY.

First White Men in Ione Valley—First House—First Ranches—Judge Lynch—Starkey's Case—First Mill—Fun with Grizzlies—Origin of Name Ione—First School—First Flour Mill—First Brick Store—Methodist Church—Centennial—President's Address—Extracts from Papers—Extracts from Oration—Ione in 1876—Railroad—Stockton Narrow-Guage-Galt Road—Overflows—Fires—Buena Vista—First Settlement—Mining—Arroyo Seco Grant—Dispossession of Settlers—Present Appearance—Buckeye Valley—Irish Hill—Quincy—Muletown—Miners' Court—The Funny Man—Faithful Wife. .... 182—194

CHAPTER XXXII.
LANCHA PLANA AND VICINITY.

Its Early Settlers—Cholera and Diarrhea—Judge Palmer's Bridge—Fires—First School—Notable Homicide—Bluff Mining—Open Sea—Chaparral Hill—Growth of the Town—Bonita Affair—Indian War—Butler Claim—Decline of the Town—Pat's Bar and the Fruit Interest—Overflows—Townerville—Camp Opera—French Camp—Copper Centre. 194—202

CHAPTER XXXIII.
VOLCANO AND VICINITY.

As it Looked in '49—Georgia Claim—Sharp Mining Broker—Rod. Stowell—Agriculture—Society—A Philosopher—Hydraulic Mining—Nature of the Gravel Deposits—China Gulch—Volcano Tunnel—Former Project of Lowering the Outlet—Fires—Largest Fire—Fire of 1865—Year of Fires—Burning of Hanford's Store—Miners' Joke—Nocturnal Visitor—Murder of Beekman—Lynch Law—Stage Robberies—Miners' Library Association—Dramatic Societies—Russel's Hill—Fort John—Upper Rancheria—Aqueduct City—Centreras—Ashland—Grizzly Hill—Wheeler Diggings—Plattsburg—How Named—Hunt's Gulch—Spanish Gulch—Whisky Slide—Large Crystal Caves...... 202—218

CHAPTER XXXIV.
NORTH-WESTERN PART OF THE COUNTY.

Sutter Creek—First Foundry—Knight's Foundry and Machine Shop—Planing Mill—Society at Sutter Creek—Schools and School-Houses—Shipment of Gold—Fires—Incorporation—Future Prospects—Amador—Ministers—Placer Mines—Gold of Lower Rancheria—Oleta—Execution by Lynch Law—Killing of Carter by Doctor Unkles—Home Rule—Fatal Explosion—Bad Case of Erysipelas—Lynch Law Vetoed—The Famous Safe Robbery—First School—Churches—Present Mining Prospects—Sewell's Addition—Cosumnes River—Amusing account of Mining Machinery—Famous Lynching Affair at Jamison's Ranch ....218—229

CHAPTER XXXV.
NORTH-WESTERN PART OF THE COUNTY.

Drytown—Details of Settlement—First Justice of the Peace—Arrival of Families—Scurvy—Great Fire—Farming—Dry Creek—Rattlesnake Gulch—Mile Gulch—Murderers Gulch—First [illegible]—Yankee Hill Diggings—Willow Springs—Central House—Plymouth—Puckerville—Mineral Springs—Fires—Enterprise—Yeomet. ....229—234

CHAPTER XXXVI.
EASTERN PART OF AMADOR COUNTY.

Elevation Above Tide-water—Ione, Jackson, Volcano—Pine Grove—Dentzler's Flume House—Claiborne Foster's—Antelope Springs—Hipkins & Wiley's Station—Ham's Station—Mud Springs—Stevens' Lumber Yard—Emigrant's Pass—Amount of Timber Remaining—Climatic Effect of the Loss of Timber—Summer Pasture—As a Summer Resort—Practical Jokes—Salt Springs—Mammoth Quartz Vein—Trout Fishing—Silver Mines—Sunset from the Sierras—Climate—Droughts—Freshets—Rain Table for Amador County, as Compiled by Frank Howard—Rain Table for Sacramento, corrected for Sutter Creek........................ 234—242

CHAPTER XXXVII.
ARROYO SECO GRANT.

Claim Rejected—Claim Confirmed on Appeal—Character of Grant—Matters of Record—Letter from T. A. Hendricks, Attorney General—Final Survey—Daring Hancock Agency—Proposed Settlement—Sale to J. Mora Moss & Co.—Memorial to President Lincoln—Dispossession—Settlers' League—Shooting of Herman Wohler—Last Effort—Memorial to Congress............ 242—250

AMADOR COUNTY COURT HOUSE, JACKSON, CAL.

HISTORY
—OF—
AMADOR COUNTY, CALIFORNIA.

BY J. D. MASON.

INTRODUCTION.

CICERO says that, "it is the first law of history that the writer should neither dare to advance what is false nor suppress what is true; that he should relate the facts with strict impartiality, free from ill-will or favor; that his narrative should distinguish the order of time, and, when necessary, the description of places, that he should unfold the motives of men, and, in his account of the transactions, or the events, interpose his own judgment; should relate what was done, how it was done, and what share rashness, prudence, or judgment had in the issue; that he should give the character of the leading men, their weight and influence, their passions, principles, and conduct through life."

A good history is a growth; the first attempts to collate the facts bearing on the settlement and development of a country are necessarily imperfect. Many things will creep in which were better left out, and others of importance are omitted. Some matters will receive undue importance, and few will be accurately related. Not until edition after edition has been brought before the public will the prominent events receive due notice, or the doubtful ones have justice done them. A thousand eyes will be sharpened to criticise the narrative. A thousand new witnesses will arise to contradict, affirm, or correct. The publishers hope that the public will make due allowance for errors unavoidable in the first attempt to collect the facts pertaining to the early history of the county. In many instances the testimony, even of eye-witnesses, is very conflicting. This is true of the affairs of August, 1855. Hardly any two agree in their narratives of the circumstances. In this, as in other matters, the most probable statements are recorded. Nothing has been set down in malice, and some things have been left out as being too much like tales told out of school; as far as possible consigning them to oblivion.

Having resided over a quarter of a century in the county, and acted a part, though a humble one, in many of the circumstances narrated, the writer has drawn largely on his own memory for many of the incidents.

The chapters on geology and mining, will, it is hoped, furnish interesting and profitable reading to all, especially those engaged in mining. The facts and theories are the result of years of observation, and many miles of travel, and are not retailed at second hand from Whitney or other scientists. The observations on mining have been compiled from the statements, opinions and experiences, of hundreds of intelligent miners. Thanks are due to all the superintendents, especially to those of the Amador Consolidated, the Keystone, the Oneida, the Empire, the Downs and the Zeilo mines for valuable information on gold mining, and to Edward Johnson of the Newton mine, for statistics and methods of copper mining.

The habits of the early miners will be read with interest. The writer hopes that some of the false impressions, produced by Bret Hart, Joaquin Miller, and other writers, regarding early Californians, will be dissipated by a true description thereof. The stories of the "Yuba Dam," "Tuolumne Debating Society" and others of that kind, have truth enough for a hint to a lively imagination and no more; and those who, in after years, judge California by those things, will be wide of the mark. The writer, having been a resident of the State since 1850, has an interest in the good reputation of the pioneers, and is glad to enter his protest to such absurdities being recorded as history. With him, the work has been one of love, and a design to do justice to our countrymen, with no desire to hold them up to derision.

The publishers intended to give statistics of the growth of the mining and agricultural industries, but found the published returns entirely worthless. In some instances, the estimations were utterly absurd. In 1877, the yield of wheat in Amador county was estimated at 236 bushels to the acre, this estimato being copied without remark into all the works on statistics. In 1866, the number of grape-vines was estimated at 557,773; in 1867, at 1,140,000; 1868, at 683,623. The estimates in many instances were mere guess work. The values of real and personal property as a basis for taxation, are the only estimates that approximate the truth. These have been given from year to year, in the continuous history of the county.

The history of the Arroyo Seco Grant has been exhaustively treated. The facts in regard to this, the most important event in the history of the county, were fast sinking into obscurity, and it was deemed best to collect and preserve them, that our children might know the great wrong that was perpetrated under cover of the law. Valuable assistance in this was rendered by J. A. Forbes (now deceased), who was familiar with the whole history of the grant system.

The chapter on the Colorado Canon will be found interesting, and worthy of being preserved with the other facts bearing on the discovery and settlement of California.

The article on the Dead Rivers of California, copied from the *Overland Monthly*, is well worth preservation in connection with the geology of the county, and will be welcomed by all who are interested in the ancient river system.

In making up this work, many authorities have been consulted; Forbes' History of California, written in 1835; Farnham's History of the Period of the Arroyo Seco Grant; Annals of San Francisco and California, by Frank Soulé; Tuthill's History of California; History of the Pacific School System, by John Swett; Cronise's Natural Wealth of California; Hittel's Resources of California; Bayard Taylor's El Dorado; Scenes in El Dorado in 1849–50, by S. C. Upham; Raymond's work on the Mines of the Pacific Coast, and others too numerous to mention. The Odd Fellows' libraries of Oakland and San Francisco, the school library of Alameda county, and mercantile library of San Francisco, as well as private collections, have been frequently visited. The files of the *Alta Californian*; *Spirit of the Times* (M. D. Boruck's paper), and other city papers have often been consulted, as well as files of the county papers, the *Ledger*, *Sentinel*, *News* and *Dispatch*. To the proprietor of the *Dispatch* especially, are many thanks due. The county papers published previous to August 23, 1862, were mostly destroyed in the great fire. The loss is irreparable, though it is said the *hermit* at the Gate, J. G. Farrar, has complete files of all the papers ever published in the county, but the author was unable to get access to them.

To point out all the sources of information, or to name all the persons giving us valuable assistance would be impossible. It had to be gathered from a thousand sources, and thousands of notes compared. Valuable assistance was rendered by Hon. H. A. Carter in matters of the Arroyo Seco Grant, Robert Reed, James Bagley, D. Stewart, H. F. Hall, Hon. R. B. Swift, Hon. L. Brusie, J. M. F. Johnson, Mrs. J. T. Henley, J. W. Surface, W. H. Fox, J. P. Martin, P. Scully, William Cook, John Fitzsimmons, Hon. I. B. Gregory, A. Thompson, Hon. J. W. D. Palmer, Isaac Waddell, Hon. William Waddell, William Maroon, J. C. Fithian, R. W. Palmer, George W. Porter, James M. Porter, Thomas Love, Louis Teller, Ellis Evans, A. Askey, Mrs. Ellis Evans, J. D. Davis, James Meehan, George Durham, Hon. M. W. Gordon, Hon. John A. Eagon, Hon. A. C. Brown, J. C. Shipman, Thomas Jones, William Lowry, John Vogan, H. Goldner, J. A. Butterfield, C. J. Nickerson, C. A. Purinton, P. N. Peek, Wilmer Palmer, William Pitt, E. R. Yates, J. E. Reaves, R. Robinson, J. T. Wheeler, A. P. Clough, Jacob Cook, J. C. Ham, Edmund Wise, S. Loree, James Henry, L. Ludikens, L. McLaine, D. S. Boydston, A. Petty, F. M. Whitmore, F. Mace, James Hall, J. A. Foster, W. Q. Mason, A. Jerome, S. Petty, R. Fry, Isaac E. Eastman (who was here in 1848), James Hall, E. Genochio, L. J. Fontenrose, County Clerk, C. H. Turner, A. Cammetti, District Attorney, B. Ross, Hon. J. T. Farley, Thomas Frakes, C. Gossum, T. B. Greenhalgh, J. F. Gould, C. J. Garland, C. B. Goodrich, W. H. Harmon, W. E. Huey, Henry Kutchenthall, James Livermore, S. S. Mannon, James McCauley, I. G. Nute, I. N. Randolph, W. T. Wildman, William Jennings, J. C. Williams, Frank Henderson, S. B. Boardman, H. H. Towns, Superintendent of Amador Canal, James Morgan, J. O. Bartlett, R. T. Bisbee, Wm. O. Clark, M. B. Church, T. A. Chicizola, A. K Dudley, Jacob Emminger, Dan. Worley, John Marchant, Wm. Moon, T. J. Phelps, A. S. Putnam, B. S. Sanborn, E. A. Smith, W. Southerland, Silas Tubbs, J. Northup, Leroy Worden, Hon. Chapman Warkins, and many others.

Many old residents have been interviewed in San Francisco and Oakland, and valuable information gained: John Hanson first Sheriff of Calaveras, John Burke, Dr. Henry M. Fisk, Dr. W. Ayer, J. W. Paugh, J. G. Severance, J. A. Robinson, N. W. Spaulding, Dr. Louis Soher, Hon. E. D. Sawyer, A. J. Houghtaling, W. C. Pratt, (the last three being members of the Legislature at the time of the Act providing for the organization of the county), Hon. W. W. Cope, Hon. Wm. Higby, Hon. Wm. B. Ludlow, B. S. E. Williams, Hon. J. W. Bicknell, Alvinza Hayward, A. W. Richardson. Hon. J. D. Stevenson (commander of the famous Stevenson regiment), J. Alexander Forbes, James Foley, who established Post-offices in Amador, and others names not recalled.

The author may be permitted to say in conclusion that the labor has been a source of constant pleasure; that the memories of the many reunions with the pioneers will remain pleasant as long as life lasts. He hopes the patrons of the work will manifest the same good spirit in reading the work, passing lightly over the unavoidable imperfections, and remembering only that which is good.

CHAPTER I.

Scanty Knowledge of the Pacific Coast Fifty Years Since—Story of "Sergas," by Esplandin—Titles to Immense Regions Conferred by the Pope—Expeditions for Discovery and Settlement—Sir Francis Drake's Operations—Expeditions Overland—Marvelous Stories of a Big Cañon—Expedition of Father Escalante.

THOSE who studied geography forty or fifty years since, recollect how little was known of the "Great West," "Lewis and Clarke's Expedition to the Rocky Mountains and Oregon," contained about all that was known of the Pacific coast; and hundreds of persons now living, remember that that portion of the map now marked California and Arizona, was occupied with a table of distances from Washington to our larger cities. The Rocky Mountains were represented as a single range, running from the Isthmus of Darien to the North Pole. More facts concerning the Pacific slope were learned in the first fifty years after the discovery of the New World, than in the following two hundred. The deserts of Arizona and the "Great Cañon," shut off exploration and settlement from this direction, though rumors of a country rich in gold, had circulation among the hordes that overran Mexico soon after its conquest by Cortez and his followers. On such rumors, was founded the story of "Sergas" by Esplandin, the son of Amadis of Gaul, which contained "the story of a country called California, very near to the terrestrial paradise, which was peopled by black women without any men among them, because they were accustomed to live after the manner of the Amazons. They were of strong and hardened bodies, of ardent courage, and great force. The island was the strongest in the world, from its steep and rocky cliffs. Their arms were all of gold, and so were the caparisons of the wild horses they rode."

At that time, the world was filled with rumors of wonderful discoveries, by land and by sea. Some, like De Soto, set off in quest of the "spring of eternal youth," which it was confidently asserted was just on the other side of a certain range of mountains. It was easier to believe in a land of gold, than in a spring of eternal youth. This exciting book, written to satisfy the literary market of that age, was universally read in Spain; and, it is highly probable, was partly the cause for the expedition which afterwards, under the charge of Hernando Grijalva, actually discovered "California very near to the Terrestrial Paradise;" so that it is probable that a dreamy old romancer in Seville, Spain, suggested the name of the country that was to upheave new continents in the commercial world.

IMMENSE REGIONS GRANTED BY THE POPE.

Cortez had achieved the conquest of Mexico with but a handful of men, in 1519; and nine years after returned to Spain, laden with the spoils of an empire larger and richer, and, perhaps, more civilized than Spain herself; also with accounts of countries still richer and larger, to the north-west of Mexico. He was received with distinguished honors by Charles V., and rewarded by many royal concessions, among which were the right to one-twelfth of all the precious metals he could find, and a perpetual viceroyalty for himself and heirs, over all the countries he should discover. It must be remembered that the Pope, in consideration of the dissemination of the "True Faith," had granted to the Emperor of Spain all lands that his subjects might discover; so the title seemed to be *fee simple* in Cortez, who, from being a piratical, roving vagabond, bounded into royal honors.

EXPEDITIONS OF DISCOVERY AND SETTLEMENT.

Returning to Mexico, he immediately set about the expedition; but, delayed by the difficulty of building and fitting out ships on the western coast, he did not get off until 1535. Having landed on the lower peninsula of California, he found the country so barren and uninviting, that he abandoned the expedition, and returned to Mexico in 1537. On his return, he heard of the De Soto expedition, which, like all the other expeditions, had nearly, but not quite, reached the land where arms, as well as trappings for horses, were made of *pure gold*. This led to the fitting out of another expedition in 1542, under José R. Cabrillo, who sailed northward as far as Cape Mendocino, which he named Cape Mendoza, in honor of his friend, the Viceroy of Mexico. Keeping within sight of the coast the greater part of the way, he discovered the Farallone Islands, also some of the more southern groups; but, like his predecessor, failed to see the future Golden Gate. In an English work printed in 1839, Mr. James Alexander Forbes states that two out of the three vessels, composing this expedition, with some twenty men, were lost in the Gulf of California, in consequence of a mutiny and a difficulty with the natives, near La Paz.

These expeditions were so unsatisfactory, that Cortez resolved upon exploring the coast himself. Three vessels were fitted out at Tehuantepec, he marching overland with a large body of soldiers, slaves, settlers, and priests. Cortez explored the Gulf of California, proved that California was not an island, but part of the main land. For some time the Gulf of California was known as the Sea of Cortez. It was also called The Red Sea (El Mar Rojo), from having a reddish color from the wash of the Colorado river, which empties into the gulf at the head. Cortez returned to Acapulco, but continued to employ others in the explorations, which were confined mostly to lands in the vicinity of the gulf. Several attempts were made to settle the land, but, as it was very barren and poor, the colonies made little progress. The natives were destitute of means and character, both sexes going nearly or quite naked.

SIR FRANCIS DRAKE'S OPERATIONS.

Sir Francis Drake reached the Pacific ocean in 1578, through the Straits of Magellan, thirty-six years after Cabrillo named the Cape of Mendocino, and, not having heard of the former expeditions, took possession of the whole country in the name of Queen Elizabeth. It has been claimed for him that he entered the Bay of San Francisco; but the latitude in which he located it (37° 59′ 5″), proves it to have been some miles north, at a place now called Drake's bay, though most of the old geographies give the present sea-port as "The Bay of Sir Francis Drake." It is strange that, having much intercourse with the natives, he should have failed to discover the great harbor which was in sight from some of the surrounding hills. The real discovery of the Bay of San Francisco, was made by Portala, in an overland expedition. What a vision, when he stood on the top of some of the low ranges of mountains surrounding, and saw the rich valleys reposing in a perpetual Indian Summer, stretching to the northward sixty miles. Little did the Spaniard, or those who came after him, suppose that the rivers flowing into the bay ran over golden sands, or that the hills near the outlet would be covered by a city larger than any of the cities of magnificent Spain.

It is now time to turn to the attempts to explore the country in other ways.

EXPEDITION OVERLAND—MARVELOUS STORIES.

The ill success attending the expeditions up the coast, induced explorations by land, especially as marvelous reports of rich walled cities in the far north, occasionally reached the capital of Mexico. In less than fifty years from the discovery of America, soldiers and priests had explored the Colorado river for a considerable distance above its mouth. The stories of a gigantic people, walled towns, and impassable cañons a mile or more in depth, were consigned to the same fate as the stories of mermaids and other sea monsters. Cervantes in Spain, and Dean Swift in England, had poured unsparing ridicule on the fabulous stories and achievements of the age succeeding the discovery of America. Since the exploring expedition sent out by the United States, the accounts of the great Colorado river have been overhauled and read with avidity, and what was then deemed a pleasant after-dinner fiction of some bibulous priest, has proved to be substantially correct, though the Mojaves, who, doubtless, are the persons described as giants, do not quite come up to their ancestors of three hundred and fifty years ago.

As early as 1540 the Viceroy of New Spain, interested in the stories of a San Franciscan monk who had seen some of the territory, sent out an expedition under the command of Vasquez de Coronado. When they struck the river, a party of twenty-five was detached and sent to the westward. They explored the river to the mouth, and from this point was sent the expedition which eventually succeeded in discovering the bay. Another of Coronado's captains, named Cardinas, reached the pueblos of the Moquis, and from these towns made a visit, under Indian guides, to a portion of the river some hundreds of miles above the explorations of previous parties. The history states that after a march over a desert of twenty days, they came to a river, the banks of which were so high that they seemed to be three or four leagues in the air. The most active of the party attempted to descend, but came back in the evening, saying they had met with difficulties which prevented them from reaching the bottom; that they had accomplished one-third of the descent, and from that point the river looked very large. They averred that some rocks, which appeared from above to be the height of a man, were higher than the tower of the cathedral of Seville. This is the earliest notice in any work of the celebrated cañon of the Colorado, the most astonishing of all mountain gorges, and which may, without doubt, be reckoned the greatest wonder of the world.

EXPEDITION OF FATHER ESCALANTE.

About one hundred years ago, Father Escalante visited the region north of New Mexico, keeping along the head-waters of the Colorado to Salt Lake, thence south-west to the Colorado river at a point nearly opposite that reached by one of Coronado's captains over two hundred years before. This meager account of the great cañon is about all that is on record previous to the acquisition of Arizona by the United States, though trappers and hunters sometimes related incredible stories of a country where great rivers ran in cañons so deep that daylight never reached the bottom. As this river forms a part of the boundary of California, and was, to a great extent, from its unapproachable character, a barrier to the early settlement of this coast, thus perhaps preserving it for its present occupants, and as it has recently become a center of interest on account of the mines in its vicinity, a somewhat extended account of this remarkable and, even now, little known wonder may be justifiable, and will be incorporated into the work in a separate chapter.

CHAPTER II.

BIG CANON OF THE COLORADO.

Lieutenant Whipple's Expedition—Lieutenant Ives' Expedition—First Attempt to Explore the Cañon—Land Party Organized—One Sight of the River—First Exploration—Unwilling Venture—Consider the Situation—Death of One of the Parties—Three Months in the Cañon—Arrival at Fort Colville—Exploration Made Under the Direction of the Smithsonian Institute—Indescribable Character of the Stream—Loss of Boats and Provisions—Death of a Portion of the Party—Emergence of the Survivors—Geology and Climate.

LIEUTENANT WHIPPLE'S EXPEDITION.

In the Spring of 1854 Lieutenant Whipple in command of an expedition for the exploration and survey of a railroad route near the 35th parallel, reached the Colorado at the mouth of Bill Williams' Fork, and

AMADOR COUNTY HOSPITAL, JACKSON, AMADOR CO.,
LOOKING TOWARDS BUTTE MOUNTAIN.

BIG CANON OF THE COLORADO.

ascended the river from that point about fifty miles and reported the country as mostly impassable. From an elevated point a view of an apparent valley or course of a river could be seen, which seemed to be a net-work of impassable cañons. This partial exploration still further intensified the interest in this region. That any portion of the United States was unapproachable was too absurd to credit.

LIEUTENANT IVES' EXPEDITION.

It was not until 1857 that an appropriation became available for further exploration. A small steamer was constructed for the purpose of ascending the river and shipped to San Francisco in parts, and thence reshipped to Fort Yuma, where it was put together. When loaded it drew somewhat less than two feet of water, and the river was ascended four hundred and fifty miles above Fort Yuma. Sometimes the little craft was nearly overwhelmed in the treacherous currents and sometimes the men were obliged to tow the steamer over shoals where it would touch bottom continually. Bands of natives would follow the boat, hugely amused with the puffing, snorting canoe that was, apparently, so helpless and good for nothing. At length the party came in sight of the much talked of cañon, of which so little was known and so much conjectured. The enormous, perpendicular walls of rocks, hundreds of feet high, which had formed the banks of the rivers in many places, had prepared them for wonders, but they did not expect to see a large river come out of a gate-way two thousand feet high and only a few feet across. If the ancients had known of this place they would have added new horrors to their infernal regions.

FIRST ATTEMPT TO EXPLORE THE CAÑON.

The attempt to navigate the cañon with the steamer without a previous reconnoissance was thought too hazardous and a boat expedition was organized Lieutenant Ives with three or four men entered the dark gateway. With much labor they worked their way, sometimes rowing and sometimes dragging the boat over rapids. Night coming on, the party took advantage of a small shingle beach for a camping place. Some drift-wood lodged in a cleft of rocks furnished material for a camp fire. There was no need of sentinels. Eternal silence reigned; not even the chirping of an insect broke the low murmur of the waters as they wound their tortuous way through the dark depths. We quote freely from his report to the Secretary of War :—

"March 10, 1858. * * * Darkness supervened with surprising suddenness. Pall after pall of shade fell, as it were in clouds, upon the deep recesses about us. The line of light through the opening above at last became blurred and indistinct, and, save the dull red glare of the camp fire, all was enveloped in a murky gloom. Soon the narrow belt again brightened as the rays of the moon reached the summits of the mountains. Gazing far upwards upon the edges of the overhanging walls we witnessed the gradual illumination. A few isolated turrets and pinnacles first appeared in strong relief upon the blue band of the heavens. As the silvery light descended and fell upon the opposite crest of the abyss, strange and uncouth shapes seem to start out, all sparkling and blinking in the light, and to be peering over at us as we lay watching them from the bottom of the profound chasm. The contrast between the vivid glow above and the black obscurity beneath, formed one of the most striking points in the singular picture. This morning as soon as the light permitted, we were again on the way. * * * The cañon continued to increase in size and magnificence. No description can convey an idea of the peerless and majestic grandeur of this water-way. Wherever the river makes a turn the entire panorama changes, and one startling novelty after another appears and disappears with bewildering rapidity. Stately façades, august cathedrals, amphitheatres, rotundas, castellated walls and rows of time-stained ruins surmounted by every form of tower, minaret, dome and spire have been moulded from the cyclopean masses of rock that form the mighty defile. The solitude, the stillness, the subdued light and the vastness of every surrounding object, produced an impression of awe that ultimately became almost painful. As hour after hour passed, we began to look anxiously for some kind of an outlet from the range, but the declining day only brought fresh piles of mountains, higher apparently than any before seen. We had made up our minds to pass another night in the cañon and were searching for a spot large enough for a resting place, when we came into a narrow passage between two mammoth peaks that seemed to be nodding across the stream, and unexpectedly found at the upper end the termination of the 'Black Cañon,' and we came into rather of an extensive valley, without a trace of vegetation however; but the hills and mountains around were in parti-colors and prevented the scene from being monotonous. The length of the Black Cañon is about twenty-five miles. It was evident that the river could be navigated no farther. Climbing a mountain nothing but a confused mass of volcanic rocks piled in confusion upon each other came to view. * * * Farther to the east could be seen the course of the river where it formed the Big Cañon."

LAND PARTY ORGANIZED.

The exploring party returned to the steamboat and organized an expedition to explore the river on the south side towards the Rocky Mountains, and the boat was sent back to Fort Yuma. In a few days they struck the lofty plateau, through which the Colorado river with its numerous tributaries, or companion rivers, carry the waters formed from the melting snows of the Rocky Mountains. Scarcely any rain falls on this elevated plain, and the banks of the rivers remain as sharp as they were millions of years ago when the channels were first eroded. Century after century the work of deepening the channel goes on. Before the children of Israel went down into Egypt; before the building of the Pyramids; before the rude ancestors of the Egyptians found the Nile valley; even before the Nile valley itself was formed the Colorado rivers had done the most of their work. It was out of the question to explore the river. They could only approach it at one point. Only the bird that could wing its way for hundreds of miles, could make its way over these cavernous depths that marked the course of the river and all its branches. From elevated points they could see table-land, rising base on base, height on height, with impassable cañons between. As the limits of this work will permit only an abbreviated description of the interesting exploration, an account of one *attempt* to reach the river, giving nearly the author's own words, which cannot be condensed without doing injustice to the subject, will close the story of this expedition.

ONE SIGHT OF THE RIVER.

"Our altitude is very great. During the last march the ascent was continuous, and the barometer shows an elevation of nearly seven thousand feet. The Colorado is not far distant, and we must be opposite to the most stupendous part of the 'Big Cañon.' The bluffs are in view, but the intervening country is cut up by side cañons and cross ravines, and no place has yet been found that presents a favorable approach to the gigantic chasm. * * * The snow-storm (this was in the Winter) had extended over but little area, and the road, at first heavy, in a mile or two became dry and good. The pines disappeared and the cedars gradually diminished * * * Each slope surmounted disclosed a new summit similar to that just passed, till the end of ten miles, when the highest part of the plateau was attained, and a sublime spectacle lay spread before us.

"Toward the north was the field of plateaus and cañons already mentioned, and shooting out from these a line of magnificent bluffs, extending eastward an enormous distance, marked the course of the cañon of the Little Colorado. Farther south, eighty miles distant, towered the vast pile of the San Francisco mountain, its conical summit covered with snow and sharply defined against the sky. Several other peaks were visible a little to the right, and half way between us and this cluster of mighty and venerable volcanos was the 'Red Butte,' described by Lieutenant Whipple (1853), standing in isolated prominence upon the level plain. * * *

"The sun was oppressively warm, and every place whose appearance gave promise of water was searched, but without success. Ten miles beyond us to the head of a ravine, down which there was a well-beaten Indian trail. There was every prospect therefore that we were approaching a settlement, similar to that of the Hualpais, on Diamond river. The descent was more rapid than the former had been, and in the course of a few miles we had gone down into the plateau one or two thousand feet, and the bluffs on either side had assumed stupendous proportions. Still no signs of habitations were visible. The worn-out and thirsty beasts had begun to flag when we were brought to a stand-still by a fall one hundred feet deep in the bottom of the cañon. At the brink of the precipice was an overhanging ledge of rock, from which we could look down, as if into a well, upon the continuation of the gorge far below. The break reached completely across the ravine and the side walls were nearly perpendicular. There was no egress in that direction, and it seemed a marvel that a trail should lead to a place where there was nothing to do but return. A closer inspection showed that the trail still continued along the cañon, traversing horizontally the face of the right-hand bluff. A short distance of it seemed as though a mountain goat could scarcely keep its footing upon the slight indentation that appeared like a thread attached to the rocky wall, but a trial proved that the path, though narrow and dizzy, had been cut with some care into the surface of the cliff, and afforded a foot-hold, level and broad enough both for men and animals. I rode upon it first, and the rest of the party and the train followed—one by one—looking very much like a row of insects crawling upon the side of a building. We proceeded for nearly a mile along this singular pathway, which preserved its horizontal direction. The bottom of the cañon meanwhile had been rapidly descending, and there were two or three falls where it dropped a hundred feet at a time, thus greatly increasing the depth of the chasm. The change had taken place so gradually that I was not sensible of it, till, glancing down the side of my mule, I found that he was walking within three inches of the edge of the brink of a sheer gulf a thousand feet deep; on the other side, nearly touching my knee, was an almost vertical wall rising to an enormous altitude. The sight made my head swim, and I dismounted and got ahead of the mule, a difficult and delicate operation, which I was thankful to have safely performed. A part of the men became so giddy that they were obliged to creep upon their hands and knees, being unable to walk or stand. In some places there was barely room to walk, and a slight deviation in a step would have precipitated one into the frightful abyss. I was a good deal alarmed lest some obstacle should be encountered that would make it impossible to go ahead, for it was certainly impracticable to return. After an interval of uncomfortable suspense, the face of the rock made an angle, and just beyond the angle was a projection from the main wall with a surface fifteen or twenty yards square that would afford a foot-hold. The continuation of the wall was perfectly vertical, so that the trail could no longer follow it, and we found that the path descended the steep face of the cliff to the bottom of the cañon. It was a desperate road to traverse, but located with a good deal of skill, zigzagging down the precipice, and taking advantage of every crevice and fissure that could afford a foot-hold. It did not take long to discover that no mule could accomplish this descent, and nothing remained but to turn back. We were glad to have even this privilege in our power. The jaded brutes were collected upon the little summit, where they could be turned around, and then commenced to return from the hazardous journey. The sun shone directly into the cañon, and the glare reflected from the walls made the heat intolerable. The disappointed beasts, now two days without water, with glassy eyes and protruding tongues, plodded slowly along, uttering the most melancholy cries. The nearest water, of which we had any knowledge, was almost thirty miles distant. There was but one chance of saving the train, and after reaching an open portion of the ravine the packs and saddles were removed, and two or three Mexicans started for the lagoons, mounted upon the least exhausted animals and driving the others loose before them. It was somewhat dangerous to detach them thus from the main party but there was no help for it. Some of the mules will give out before the night march is over, but the knowedge that they are on the road to water will enable the most of them to reach it in spite of their weariness and the length of the way.

"It was estimated that, at this point which was within a few miles of the main cañon, about one-half of the original plain had been cut away by the action of the river and its branches.

"A party was made up to explore the cañon. The distance to the precipice where the mules were turned back was about five miles. The precipice was descended without difficulty, though in one or two places the path traversed smooth, inclined plains that made the footing insecure and the crossing dangerous. The bottom of the cañon which from the summit looked smooth, was found to be covered with small hills thirty or forty feet high. Along the middle of the cañon started another one with low walls at the starting point, which became lofty precipices at the base of the new ravine sunk deeper and deeper into the earth. Along the bottom of this gorge we followed the trail, distinctly seen when the surface was not composed of rocks. Every few minutes low falls and ledges were met with, which we had to jump or slide down, till a formidable number of obstacles were to be met in returning. Like other cañons this was circuitous, and at each turn we expected to find something new and startling. We were deeper in the bowels of the earth than we had ever been before, and surrounded by walls and towers of such imposing dimensions that it would be useless to attempt describing them; but the effects of magnitude had begun to pall, and the walk from the foot of the precipice was monotonously dull; no sign of life could be discerned above or below. At the end of thirteen miles from the precipice an obstacle presented itself that there seemed to be no possibility of overcoming. A stone slab, reaching from one side of the cañon to the other, terminated the plain which we were descending. Looking over the edge it appeared that the next level was forty feet below. This time there was no trail along the side of the bluffs, for these were smooth and perpendicular. A spring of water rose from the cañon above and trickled over the precipice, forming a beautiful cascade. It was supposed that the Indians must have come to this point merely to procure water; but this theory was not satisfactory and we sat down to consider the situation.

"Mr. Egloffstein lay down by the side of the creek, and projecting his head over the ledge to watch the cascade discovered a solution to the mystery. Below the shelving rock, and hidden by it and the fall, stood a crazy-looking ladder, made of rough sticks bound together with thongs of bark. It was almost perpendicular and rested upon a bed of angular stones. The rounds had become rotten from the incessant flow of the water. Mr. Egloffstein, anxious to have the first view of what was below, scrambled over the rock and got his feet upon the first round. Being a solid weight, he was too much for the insecure fabric, which commenced giving away. One side fortunately stood firm, and holding on to this with a tight grip he made a precipitate descent. The other side and all the rounds broke loose and accompanied him to the bottom in a general crash, effectually cutting off the communication. Leaving us to devise means of getting him back he ran to the bend to explore. The bottom of the cañon had been reached. He found that he was at the edge of a stream ten or fifteen yards wide fringed with cottonwoods and willows. The walls of the cañon spread out for a short distance leaving room for a narrow belt of bottom-land on which were fields of corn and a few scattered huts. It was impossible to follow the stream to its union with the main river, which was not far off. Nor could a situation be found where a complete view of the great cañon might be obtained; at one spot the top could be seen, at another the bottom. Measurements were taken which showed the walls of the cañon to be over six thousand feet in height."

Notwithstanding all the efforts backed by money and government the great cañon was not entered, at least from the side. The parties safely made their way out of the chasm, and resumed their journey towards Fort Defiance, finding on their way the towns of stone houses which the early Spanish explorers saw and which had since remained unknown and mostly forgotten.

FIRST EXPLORATION—UNWILLING VENTURE.

Some of my readers may inquire whether this cañon has never been explored? Twice only of which any record has been found. Some time in the sixties, three men, prospecting on the head-waters of the river in the Colorado Territory, fell into a difficulty with the Indians. Two succeeded in reaching their boats, and escaped by rowing swiftly down the stream, the swift current and bold banks facilitating their flight. When they had gone so far as to feel secure from pursuit, and took time to consider the situation, they found themselves floating in a stream, so swift as to prevent their return, even if they desired it, and with banks so precipitous as to make escape in that direction impossible. The stream became swifter and the banks or walls of the cañon higher every hour.

THEY CONSIDER THE SITUATION.

A council of war was held, and all evidence attainable was considered. The questions put forth in one of Addison's essays a hundred and fifty years ago, "Where am I? What sort of place do I inhabit?" seemed particularly applicable to the situation. As to the first question, they could only say, we are in "Uncle Sam's" dominion, and as to the last, it is a " hell of a place." One of them remembered of hearing some old trappers, while sitting around a camp fire near Salt Lake, tell a story of a great river that was lost in a range of mountains and flowed hundreds of miles under ground. Another said that it did not flow under ground, but in a narrow channel thousands of feet in depth, so deep that daylight never reached the bottom. None of them, however, had ever seen the river under those circumstances. The Indians believed, some of them at least, that the deep gorge led to Heaven, and others thought it led to Hell! It was certain that the route to the blessed regions would not go through any such country as they were passing; and as to the latter place, had not Beecher knocked the bottom out of it? So they concluded to go on ; in fact, there was no other alternative. About the third day they heard a great roaring of falling water, and before they had time to consider were plunged over a cataract, that proved not a very high one, for though the boat was smashed, they saved their lives by swimming to an island at the foot of the falls, and were able to save most of their provisions. They now constructed a raft of dry, cotton-wood logs, which they found lodged high up on the island, and continued their voyage.

DEATH OF ONE OF THE PARTIES.

Falls and rapids being now frequent, and the plunges often throwing them off their craft, they imprudently lashed themselves to it. Passing the next cataract the raft was upset, and one of the two was lost. The survivor found himself on the raft, now bottom side up, though entirely ignorant as to how he succeeded in disengaging himself while under the water.

Day after day, week after week, until the weeks became months, he floated down the river, encountering many obstacles but escaping with his life. The river was destitute of fish or animals, but in places he found the mesquite bean which would sustain life. Months afterward a soldier at Fort Colville saw a log floating in the river appearing to have come out of the cañon. The unusual circumstance caused him to turn a telescope upon it. "My God!" said he, "there is a man on that log!!" A boat was dispatched, and the man was brought ashore, nearly famished, speechless, naked, and his body covered with sores. After some nourishment had been taken, he was able to say that he had come through the *great cañon*. The man recovered, and for many years afterward drove a stage in Arizona.

EXPLORATION UNDER THE DIRECTION OF THE SMITHSONIAN INSTITUTE.

The Government of the United States during these years had enough business on hand without attending to expeditions in the cause of science, for, so far, the river had no value. But the Smithsonian Institute undertook the exploration of the river. Lieutenant Powell, an eminent scientist and explorer, was sent out to gather all the information about it that was possible. The trans-continental railroad now made the matter easier. He interviewed the trappers and hunters at Salt Lake and Fort Bridger; visited Arizona, and heard all that the stage-driver could remember, and went East to make preparations for the descent of the river. The scientific public were now aroused, and many were anxious to accompany the expedition. Several boats were made in water-tight compartments, so contrived as to float though they might be stove. Provisions, instruments and all necessary articles were inclosed in water-tight, rubber bags. On the 24th of May, 1869, he left the line of the Union Pacific Railroad at the Green River Station. Those who love to read of the grand, the picturesque, the terrible, will find their satisfaction in reading "Powell's Explorations of the Colorado Cañon." The limits of this book will only permit a short account of the trip which was full of dangers as well as pleasure. They passed safely down the upper waters. Some hundred miles below the starting-point, the labor commenced. Sometimes the river would zigzag between metamorphic slates and granite spurs, making a channel like a line of saw teeth; then it would leave the granite and cut a vast amphitheatre in the sandstone, miles across and thousands of feet high. Towers, domes, castles, minarets, and all the forms of ancient and modern architecture seemed anticipated. Even sculpture was not forgotten, for in many places gigantic figures seemed to be guarding the great cañon, and threatening to overwhelm all who should dare to invade the ancient solitude. For months the party continued their voyage. Notwithstanding their ample preparations, it was nearly a failure. They lost their boats and most of their provisions, as well as their scientific instruments. They were uncertain whether the cañon was three, four, or five hundred miles long. When nearly through it was proposed to leave the river and try to ascend its banks. It was urged that more rapids on the junction of the granite and slate would end the expedition. Part of the men determined to try to scale the walls. They were given a part of the scant provisions, and also a copy of the records of the trip. Both parties bid each other "goodbye," with the firm belief that the other was destined to certain destruction. Powell remained with the party to continue down the river, hoping that if he perished some record of their trip would be picked up on the lower river or the Gulf of California. His judgment proved the best. August 30th he emerged from the cañon, in somewhat better plight than the stage-driver did, having witnessed undoubtedly the greatest wonder of the world. Nothing was heard of the other party for years. A prospector brought the news that they scaled the walls of the cañon, but were soon afterwards killed by the Indians, being mistaken for a party of white men who had committed an outrage on an Indian woman

GEOLOGY AND CLIMATE.

The Colorado river drains a territory of three hundred thousand square miles. A portion of this, eight hundred miles in extent, resting on the Rocky Mountains, is fed by snows, and has numerous rivers which, with all their branches, form cañons—one leading into another and all finally merging into the grand gorge, six thousand feet deep and three hundred miles long. The lower part of the Colorado for one thousand miles runs through an almost rainless country. There is no wearing away of the banks into the rounded, graceful forms so usual in the vicinities of rivers. The channels of the rivers being so deep the country is thoroughly drained of water, and very few springs emerge from the surface. The soil is consequently destitute of vegetation. There are evidences, however, of an extensive alluvial deposit, of a time when the river meandered through fertile plains like the Mississippi. The elephant, the mastodon, and their contemporaries wandered in herds over suitable pastures where now desolation reigns.

It is difficult to estimate the influence which this strange system of rivers has exerted over California. Had not the early explorers when in search of gold met this obstruction, our mines would have been discovered and worked, and California would have

been cursed with the blight that has covered all the Spanish possessions. It was reserved for a more vigorous race to develop.

The climatic influence is also great. It is now believed that our dry, desiccating north winds find their way from the Arizona deserts, and that the particles of red dust with which our summer atmosphere is loaded, is finely-pulverized Arizona soil.

CHAPTER III.

The Exiles of Loreto—Father Tierra's Methods of Conversion—Death of Father Tierra—Arrest of the Jesuits—Midnight Parting—Permanent Occupation of California—Missions in Charge of Franciscan Friars—Character of Father Junipero—Exploring Expeditions—Origin of the name of the Bay—Mission Dolores—Death of Father Junipero.

It was the custom of the Spanish Government to send out a certain number of Christian missionaries with each expedition, whether for discovery or conquest. When the conquerors took possession of a new territory, in the name of the King of Spain, the accompanying Fathers also claimed it for the spiritual empire of the Holy Church, and in this manner California became, at once, the possession of both Church and State, by right of discovery and conquest.

As before stated, California was discovered in 1534, by an expedition which Cortez had caused to be fitted out in the inland seas of Tehuantepec. From that time, during a period of one hundred and fifty years, some twenty maritime expeditions sailed successively from the shores of New Spain to the coast of California, with the object of perfecting its conquest; but none of them obtained any satisfactory result, beyond an imperfect knowledge of the geographical situation of the country. The barren aspect of the coast, and the nakedness and poverty of the savages, who lived in grottoes, caves, and holes in the ground, clearly indicated that they had scarcely advanced beyond the primitive condition of man, and discouraged the adventurers, who were in search of another country like Mexico, abounding in natural wealth, and the appliances of a rude civilization. After the expenditure of immense sums of both public and private wealth, the permanent settlement of California was despaired of. The Spanish Government would advance no more money, private enterprise was turned in another direction, and it was decided to give over the, so far, fruitless experiment to the Fathers of the church. Many attempts had been made to Christianize the natives of the Pacific coast. Cortez is said to have had several ecclesiastics in his train, though there is no account of their having attempted to convert the natives, or even of landing among them. The first recorded attempt was made about the beginning of the year 1596 by four San Francisco friars, who came with Viscaino's expedition. During their stay of two months at La Paz, they visited many of the Indians, who thought them children of the sun, and treated them

very kindly. Three Carmelite friars also came with Viscaino's third expedition in 1602, two Jesuit missionaries in 1648, two Franciscans in 1688, and three Jesuits in 1683, the latter with the expedition of Admiral Otondo. The celebrated Father Kübno was one who came with the latter expedition. Once, when attempting to explain the doctrine of the resurrection to the savages, he was at loss for a word to express his meaning. He put some flies under the water until they appeared to be dead, and then exposed them to the rays of the sun, when they revived. The Indians cried out in astonishment, "I bimuhucite! I bimuhucite!" which the Fathers understood as "they have come to life," the expression he wanted, and applied it to the resurrection of the Redeemer.

No substantial success was, however, achieved until about 1675. Then appeared the heroic apostle of California civilization, Father John Salva Tierra, of the Society of Jesus, commonly called Jesuits.

Father Tierra, the founder, and afterwards visitadore of the missions of California, was a native of Milan, born of noble parentage and Spanish ancestry, in 1644. Having completed his education at Parma, he joined the order of Jesuits, and went as a missionary to Mexico in 1675. He was robust in health, exceedingly handsome in person, resolute of will, highly talented, and full of religious zeal. For several years he conducted the missions of Sonora successfully, when he was recalled to Mexico in consequence of his great ability and singular virtues, and was employed in the chief offices of the provinces. After ten years of ineffectual solicitation, he obtained permission of the Viceroy to go to California, for the purpose of converting the inhabitants, on condition that the possession of land should be taken in the name of the King of Spain, without his being called on to contribute anything towards the expenses of the expedition. Tierra associated with himself the Jesuit Father, Juan Ugarte, a native of Honduras. On the 10th of October, 1697, they sailed from the port of Yaqui, in Sonora, for Lower California, and, after encountering a disastrous storm, and suffering partial shipwreck on the gulf, landed, on the 19th of that month, at San Bruno, at Saint Dennis bay. Not finding that place suitable for their purpose, the Fathers removed to St. Dyonissius, afterwards named Loreto, and there set up the sign of civilization and Christianity on its lonely shore. Thus Loreto, on the east side of the peninsula, in latitude 25° 35' north of the equator, may be considered the Plymouth Rock of the Pacific coast. This historic and memorable expedition consisted of only two ships and nine men, being a corporal, five private soldiers, three Indians, the captain of the vessel, and the two Fathers.

On the 19th of October, 1697, the little party of adventurers went ashore at Loreto, and were kindly received by about fifty natives, who were induced to kneel down and kiss the crucifix.

METHODS OF CONVERSION.

It is said of Father Ugarte that he was a man of powerful frame. When he first celebrated the ceremonials of the church before the natives they were inclined to jeer and laugh over solemnities. On one occasion a huge Indian was causing considerable disturbance, and was demoralizing the other Indians with his mimicry and childish fun. Father Ugarte caught him by his long hair, swung him around a few times, threw him in a heap on the floor, and proceeded with the rites. This argument had a converting effect, as he never rebelled again. As the conversion of the natives was the main object of the settlement, and a matter of the greatest importance to the natives at least, no means were spared to effect it. When the natives around the mission had been Christianized, expeditions inland were undertaken to capture more material for converts. Sometimes many lives were taken, but they generally succeeded in gathering in from fifty to a hundred women and children, the men afterwards following. Two or three days' exhortation (confinement and starvation) was generally sufficient to effect a change of heart, after which the convert was clothed, fed, and put to work. Father Ugarte worked with them, teaching them to plant, sow, reap, and thresh, and they were soon good Christians.

The imposing ceremonies and visible symbols of the Catholic church are well calculated to strike the ignorant savage with awe. Striking results were often attained with pictures. When moving from one mission to another, and especially when meeting strange Indians, the priests exhibited a picture of the Virgin Mary on one side of a canvas, and Satan roasting in flames on the other side. They were offered a choice, to become subjects of the Holy Mother, or roast in the flames with Satan, and generally accepted the former, especially as it was accompanied with food.

DEATH OF TIERRA.

After twenty years of earnest labor, privation, danger, and spiritual success, Father Tierra was recalled to Mexico by the new Viceroy, for consultation. He was then seventy years old; and, notwithstanding his age and infirmities, he set out on horseback from San Blas for Tepic, but, having fainted by the way, he was carried on a litter by the Indians to Guadalajara, where he died July 17, 1717, and was buried with appropriate ceremonies behind the altar in the chapel of our Lady of Loreto.

The historic village of Loreto, the ancient capital of California, is situated on the margin of the gulf, in the center of St. Dyonissius' Cove. The church, built in 1742, is still in tolerable preservation, and, among the vestiges of its former richness, has eighty-six oil paintings, some of them by Murillo, and other celebrated masters, which, though more than a hundred years old, are still in a good condition; also some fine silver work, valued at six thousand dollars. A great storm in 1827 destroyed many of the buildings of the mission. Those remaining, are in a state of decay. It was the former custom of the pearl-divers to dedicate the products of certain days to Our Lady of Loreto; and, on one occasion, there fell to the lot of the Virgin a magnificent pearl, as large as a pigeon's egg, of wonderful purity and brilliancy. The Fathers thought proper to change its destination, and presented it to the Queen of Spain, who gratefully and piously sent Our Lady of Loreto a magnificent new gown. Some people were unkind enough to think the queen had the better of the transaction.

ARREST OF THE JESUITS.

The Jesuits continued their missionary work in Lower California for seventy years. On the second day of April, 1797, all of the Order throughout the Spanish dominions, at home and abroad, were arrested by order of Charles III., and thrown into prison, on the charge of conspiring against the State and the life of the king. Nearly six thousand were subjected to that decree, which also directed their expulsion from California, as well as all other colonial dependencies of Spain. The execution of the despotic order was intrusted to Don Gaspar Portala, the Governor of the province. Having assembled the Fathers of Loreto on the eve of the nativity, December 24th, he acquainted them with the heart-breaking news. Whatever may have been the faults of the Jesuits in Europe, they certainly had been models of devoted Christians in the new world. They braved the dangers of hostile savages, exposed themselves to the malarious fevers incident to new countries, and had taken up their residences far from the centers of civilization and thought, so dear to men of cultivated minds, to devote themselves, soul and body, to the salvation of the natives, that all civilized nations seemed bent on exterminating. It is probable that the simple-minded son of the forest understood little of the mysteries of theology; and his change of heart was more a change of habit, than the adoption of any saving religious dogma. They abandoned many of their filthy habits, and learned to respect the family ties. They were taught to cultivate the soil, to build comfortable houses, and to cover their nakedness with garments. They had learned to love and revere the Fathers, who were ever kind to them.

MIDNIGHT PARTING.

After seventy years of devoted attention to the savages; after building pleasant homes in the wilderness, and surrounding themselves with loving and devoted friends, they received the order to depart. They took their leave on the night of February 3, 1768, amidst the outcries and lamentations of the people, who, in spite of the soldiers, who could not keep them back, rushed upon the departing Fathers, kissing their hands, and clinging convulsively to them. The leave-taking was brief, but affecting. "Adieu, my dear children! Adieu, land of our adoption! Adieu, California! It is the will of God!" And then, amid the sobs and lamentations, heard all along the shore, they turned away, reciting the litany of the Blessed Mother of God, and were soon no more.

For one hundred and sixty years after the discovery of California, it remained comparatively unknown. It is true that many expeditions were fitted out to explore it for gold and precious stones. The first was fast locked in mountains of the Sierras, which were occupied by bands of hostile and warlike Indians; and the last have not yet been found. The circumstances attending the discovery of the great bay, will always be of interest, and deserve a place in every record; for up to 1769, no navigator ever turned the prow of his vessel into the narrow entrance of the Golden Gate.

On the expulsion of the Jesuits from Lower California, the property of the missions, consisting of extensive houses, flocks, pasture lands, cultivated fields, orchards, and vineyards, was intrusted to the College of San Francisco in Mexico, for the benefit of the Order of St. Francis. The zealous scholar, Father Junipero Serra, was appointed to the charge of all the missions of Lower California.

FATHER JUNIPERO, as he was called, was born of humble parents in the island of Majorca, on the 24th of November, 1713. Like the prophet Samuel, he was dedicated to the priesthood from his infancy, and having completed his studies in the Convent of San Bernardino, he conceived the idea of devoting himself to the immediate service of God; and went from thence to Palma, the capital of the province, to acquire the higher learning necessary for the priesthood. At his earnest request, he was received into the Order of St. Francis, at the age of sixteen; and, at the end of one year's probation, made his religious profession, September 15, 1731. Having finished his studies in philosophy and theology, he soon acquired a high reputation as a writer and orator, and his services were sought for in every direction; but, while enjoying these distinctions at home, his heart was set on his long projected mission to the heathen of the New World. He sailed from Cadiz for America, August 28, 1749, and landed at Vera Cruz, whence he went to the City of Mexico, joined the College of San Fernando, and was made President of the missions of Sierra Gorda and San Saba. On his appointment to the missions of California, he immediately entered upon active duties, and proceeded to carry out his grand design of the civilization of the Pacific coast. Acting under the instructions of the Viceroy of Mexico, two expeditions were fitted out to explore and colonize Upper or Northern California, of which little or nothing was known, one of which was to proceed by sea, and the other by land; one to carry the heavy supplies, the other to drive the flocks and herds. The first ship, the *San Carlos*, left Cape St. Lucas, in Lower California, January 9, 1769, and was followed by the *San Antonio* on the 15th of the same month. A third vessel, the *San Jose*, was dispatched from Loreto on the 16th of June. After much suffering, these real pioneers of California civilization, reached San Diego; the *San Carlos*, on the 1st of May; the *San Antonio*, on the 11th of April, 1769, the crews having been well nigh exhausted by scurvy, thirst, and starvation. After leaving Loreto, the *San Jose* was never heard of more.

EXPLORING EXPEDITIONS.

The overland expedition was divided into two divisions; one under command of Don Gaspar de Portala, the appointed Military Governor of the New Territory; the other, under Capt. Rivera Y. Moncado. Rivera and his company, consisting of Father Crespi, twenty-five soldiers, six muleteers, and a party of Lower California Indians, started from Villacota on the 24th of March, and reached San Diego on the 14th of May, 1769. Up to that time, no white man had ever lived in Upper California; and then began to rise the morning star of our civilization.

The second division, accompanied by Father Junipero, organized the first mission in Upper California on the 16th of July, 1769; and there the first native Californian was baptized on the 26th of December, of that year. These are memorable points in the ecclesiastical history of this coast.

On the 14th of July, 1769, Governor Portala started out in search of Monterey, as described by previous navigators. He was accompanied by Fathers Juan Crespi and Francisco Gomez; the party consisting of fifty-six white persons, including a sergeant, an engineer, and thirty-three soldiers, and a company of emigrants from Sonora, together with a company of Indians from Lower California. They missed their course, and could not find the Bay of Monterey, but continued on northward, and, on the 25th day of October, 1769, came upon the great Bay of San Francisco, which they named in honor of the titular saint of the friar missionaries.

ORIGIN OF THE NAME OF THE BAY.

It is said that, while on this expedition, a regret was expressed that no mission was as yet named after the patron of the Order. Says Portala, "Let the saint guide us to a good harbor, and we will name a mission for him." When they came in sight of the bay, Father Gomez cried, "There is the harbor of San Francisco," and thus it received its name.

Father Junipero Serra was not of this illustrious company of explorers, and did not visit the Bay of San Francisco for nearly six years after its discovery. The honor belongs to Fathers Crespi and Gomez, Governor Portala, and their humbler companions. The party then returned to San Diego, which they reached on the 24th of January, 1770, after an absence of six months and ten days. Six years thereafter, on the 9th of October, 1776, the Mission of San Francisco de los Dolores, was founded on the western shore of the great bay, the old church remaining in tolerable preservation to the present time, the most interesting landmark of our present civilization.

MISSION DOLORES.

One may retire from the noise and bustle of the city, and spend a pleasant hour among the quaint surroundings of the old church. The adobe walls, the columns of doubtful order of architecture, the bells hung with rawhide which called the dusky converts to worship, all were doubtless objects of wonder and mystery to the simple-minded natives. From 1776 to 1881, what changes on either side of the continent. A hundred years is much in the life of men, little, except in effect, in the life of a nation.

Father Junipero, who founded these missions, and under whose fostering care they reached such unexampled prosperity, reposes in the old church-yard at Monterey. His life reads like a romance.

CHURCH HISTORY.—It is related of him as illustrating his fiery zeal, that, while on his way to found the mission of San Antonio de Padua, he caused the mules to be unpacked at a suitable place, and the bells hung on a tree. Seizing the rope he began to ring with all his might, regardless of the remonstrations of the other priests, shouting at the top of his voice, "Hear! hear, O ye Gentiles! Come to the Holy Church! Come to the faith of Christ!" Such enthusiasm will win its way even among savages.

FATHER JUNIPERO'S DEATH.

At length having founded and successfully established six missions, and gathered into his fold over seven thousand wild people of the mountains and plains, the heroic Junipero began to feel that his end was drawing near. He was then seventy years old; fifty-three of these years he had spent in the active service of his master in the New World. Having fought the good fight and finished his illustrious course, the broken old man retired to the Mission of San Carlos at Monterey, gave the few remaining days of his life to a closer communion with God, received the last rites of the religion which he had advocated and illustrated so well, and on the 29th of August, 1784, gently passed away. Traditions of the "boy priest" still linger among the remnants of the tribes which were gathered under his care.

CHAPTER IV.*

THE MISSIONS OF ST. FRANCIS.

Their Moral and Political Aspect—Domestic Economy—The Establishments Described—Secular and Religious Occupations of the Neophytes—Wealth and Productions—Liberation and Dispersion of the Indians—Final Decay.

CERTAIN writers upon the early history of California, have taken an unfavorable view of the system under which the missionary friars achieved their wonderful success in reducing the wild tribes to a condition of semi-civilization. The venerable Fathers are accused of selfishness, avarice and tyranny, in compelling the Indians to submission, and forcibly restraining them from their natural liberty, and keeping them in a condition of servitude. Nothing could be more unjust and absurd. It were as well to say that it is cruel, despotic, and inhuman to tame and domesticate the wild cattle that roam the great plains of the continent. The system of the Fathers was only our modern reservation policy humanized and Christianized; inasmuch as they not only fed and clothed the bodies of the improvident natives, but likewise cared for their imperishable souls. The care of Indian souls was the primary object of the friar enthusiasts; the work required of the Indians was of but few hours' duration, with long intervals of rest, and was only incidental to the one great and holy purpose of spiritual conversion and salvation. Surely, "No greater love hath any man than that he lay down his life for his friend;" and it is a cruel stretch of sectarian uncharity to charge selfishness and avarice to the account of self-devoting men who voluntarily went forth from the refinements, pleasures, and honors of European civilization, to traverse the American wilderness in sandals, and with only one poor garment a year, in order to uplift the degraded and savage tribes of Paganism from the regions of spiritual darkness, and lead them to the heights of salvation; nay, even to starve and die on the "coral strand" of California in helpless and deserted age. In 1838, the Rev. Father Sarria actually starved to death at the Mission of Soledad, after having labored there for thirty years. After the mission had been plundered through the perfidy of the Mexican Government, the old man, broken by age and faint with hunger, lingered in his little church with the few converts that remained, and one Sunday morning fell down and died of starvation before the altar of his life-long devotion. O, let not the Christian historian of California, who is yet to write for all time to come, stain and distort his pages by such cruel and unworthy charges against the barefooted paladins of the Cross.

To entirely comprehend the system and proceedings of the friars, it will be essential to know the

---

*This and Chapters V, VI, VII, VIII, X, XI, XII, XIII, XIV and XV are taken from the History of Sacramento County, and Chapter IX from the History of San Joaquin County, these works being among those published by Thompson & West.

meaning of certain descriptive terms of their institutions of settlement. These were—
  1st. Presidios.
  2d. Castillos.
  3d. Pueblos.
  4th. Missions.

The *presidios* were the military garrisons, established along the coast for the defense of the country and the protection of the missionaries. Being the head-quarters of the military, they became the seats of local government for the different presidencies into which the country was divided. There were four of these *presidios* in Upper California—at San Diego, Santa Barbara, Monterey, and San Francisco. They were uniform in structure, consisting of adobe walls twelve or fourteen feet high, inclosing a square of three hundred feet on each side, defended at the angles by small bastions mounting eight twelve-pounder, bronze cannon. Within were the barracks, store-house, a church for the soldiers, and the commandant's residence. On the outside they were defended by a trench, twelve feet wide and six feet deep, and were entered by two gates, open during the day, and closed at night. The number of soldiers assigned to each *presidio* was limited to two hundred and fifty; but rarely were there so many at any one station. In addition to the duty of guarding the coast, small details of four and five men, under a sergeant, accompanied the Fathers when they went about to establish missions, or on other business. A certain number of troops were also assigned to each mission, to keep order and defend the place against the attacks of hostile natives. They dressed in buckskin uniform, which was supposed to be impervious to arrows, and the horses, too, were encased in leather armor, like those of the knights of old.

The *castillo* was a covered battery, near the *presidio*, which it was intended to guard. It was manned and mounted with a few guns, and though but a slight defense against a powerful enemy, it served to intimidate and keep off the feeble and timorous Gentiles.

The *pueblo* was a town, inhabited originally by discharged soldiers who had served out their time at the *presidio*. It was separate from the *presidio* and mission, the lands having been granted by the Fathers. After a while other persons settled there, and sometimes the inhabitants of the *pueblo*, or independent town, outnumbered those of the neighboring mission. There were only three of those *pueblos* in Upper California—Los Angeles, San Jose, and Branciforte, the latter near Santa Cruz. San Francisco was not a *pueblo*. There were three classes of these settlements in later times—the *pueblo* proper, the *presidial*, and the mission *pueblo*. The *rancherias* were King's lands, set apart for the use of the troops, to pasture their cattle and horses.

The *mission* was the parent institution of the whole. There the natives resided, under religious treatment, and others were not allowed to inhabit the place except for a very brief time. This was to prevent the mingling of whites and natives, for it was thought that the former would contaminate and create discontent and disorder among the natives. The missions were all constructed on the same general plan. They were quadrangular, adobe structures, two stories high, inclosing a court-yard ornamented with fountains and trees; the whole consisting of a church, Father's apartments, store-houses, barracks, etc. The four sides of the building were each about six hundred feet in length, one of which was partly occupied by the church. Within the quadrangle or court, a gallery or porch ran round the second story, opening upon the workshops, store-rooms, and other apartments.

The entire management of each mission was under the care of the friars; the elder attended to the interior, and the other the out-doors administration. One large apartment, called the monastery, was occupied exclusively by Indian girls, under the watchful care of the matron, where they were instructed in such branches as were deemed necessary for their future condition in life. They were not permitted to leave the monastery till old enough to be married. In the schools, such children as manifested adequate capacity, were taught vocal and instrumental music, the latter consisting of the flute, horn, and violin. In the various mechanical departments, the most ingenious and skillful were promoted to the foremanship.

The daily routine of the establishment was usually as follows: At sunrise they all arose and repaired to the church, where after morning prayers, they assisted at the mass. The morning religious exercises occupied about an hour. Thence they went to breakfast, and afterwards to their respective employments. At noon they returned to the mission, and spent two hours at dinner and in rest; thence to work again, continuing until the evening angelus, about an hour before sundown. Then, all betook themselves to church, for evening devotions, which consisted usually in ordinary family-prayers and rosary, but on special occasions other devotional exercises were added. After supper, they amused themselves in various games, sports, and dances till bedtime, when the unmarried sexes were locked up in separate apartments till morning. Their diet consisted of good beef and mutton, with vegetables, wheaten cakes, puddings, and porridges, which they called *atole* and *pinole*. The men dressed in linen shirts, pants, and a blanket, the last serving for an overcoat; the women had each two undergarments, a new gown, and a blanket every year. When the missions had grown rich, and in times of plenty, the Fathers distributed money and trinkets among the more exemplary, as rewards for good conduct.

The Indians lived in small huts grouped around, a couple of hundred yards away from the main building; some of these dwellings were made of adobes, and others were of rough poles, conical in shape, and thatched with grass, such as the people had been accustomed to in their wild state. Here the married Indians resided with their families. A tract of land, about fifteen miles square, was apportioned to each mission, for cultivation and pasturage. There is a wide distinction between the signification of the terms "Mission" and "Mission lands;" the former referred to the houses, vineyards, and orchards, in the immediate vicinity of the churches, and also included the cattle belonging to the establishment; while mission lands, assigned for grazing and agriculture, were held only in fief, and were afterwards claimed by the Government—against the loud remonstrance of the Fathers, however. The missions were originally intended to be only temporary in duration. It was contemplated that in ten years from the time of their foundation they should cease, as it was then supposed that within that period the Indians would be sufficiently prepared to assume the position and character of citizens, and that the mission settlements would become *pueblos*, and the mission churches parish institutions, as in older civilizations; but having been neglected and undisturbed by the Spanish Government, they kept on in the old way for sixty years, the comfortable Fathers being in no hurry to insist on a change.

From the foregoing, derived chiefly from Gleeson's valuable work, "History of the Catholic Church in California," it will be inferred that the good Fathers trained up their young neophytes in the way in which they should go. Alexander Forbes, and other historians, say that during church-time a sort of beadle went around with a long stick, and when he perceived a native inattentive to the devotions or inclined to misbehave, gave him or her an admonitory prod, or a rap over the *cabeza!* But all authorities, both Catholic and Protestant agree concerning the gentleness and humanity of the Fathers, who were absolute in authority and unlimited in the monarchy of their little kingdoms. Not that there was never any application of severe and necessary discipline; there were among the Indians, as well as in civilized society, certain vicious and turbulent ones, incapable of affection and without reverence for authority, and these were soundly whipped, as they no doubt deserved, as such crooked disciples now are at San Quentin. Occasionally some discontented ones ran away to the hills, and these were pursued and brought back by the mission cavalry. They generally returned without much trouble, as they had an idea that, having been baptized, something dreadful would happen to them if they stayed away.

While modern sentimentalists may lament that these poor people were thus deprived of their natural liberty and kept in a condition of servitude, it must be admitted that their moral and physical situation was even better than the average poor in the European States at that time. Their yoke was easy, and their burdens were light; and if, in the Christian view of things, their spiritual welfare be taken into account, the Fathers, instead of being regarded as despots and task-masters, must be viewed as the substantial benefactors of the swarthy race.

The wealth created by some of the missions was enormous. At its era of greatest prosperity, the Mission of San Gabriel, founded in 1771, numbered three thousand Indians, one hundred and five thousand cattle, twenty thousand horses, forty thousand sheep; produced, annually, twenty thousand bushels of grain, and five hundred barrels of wine and brandy. Attached to this mission were seventeen extensive ranches, farmed by the Indians, and possessing two hundred yoke of oxen. Some of the old fig and olive trees are still bearing fruit, and one old Indian woman still survives, who is said to have reached the incredible age of one hundred and forty years. In 1836, the number of Indians at the Mission of Upper California was upwards of thirty thousand. The number of live-stock was nearly a million, including four hundred thousand cattle, sixty thousand horses, and three hundred thousand sheep, goats, and swine. One hundred thousand cattle were slaughtered annually, their hides and tallow producing a revenue of nearly a million of dollars, a revenue of equal magnitude being derived from other articles of export. There were rich and extensive gardens and orchards attached to the missions, ornamented and enriched with a variety of European and tropical fruit trees, including bananas, oranges, olives, and figs, to which were added productive and highly cultivated vineyards, rivaling the richest grape-fields of Europe. When the missions were secularized and ruined by the Mexican Government, there were above a hundred thousand piasters in the treasury of San Gabriel.

But, evil times were coming. In 1826, the Mexican Congress passed an Act for the liberation of the mission Indians, and the demoralization and dispersion of the people soon ensued. Eight years thereafter, the number of Christian Indians had diminished from thirty thousand six hundred and fifty, to four thousand four hundred. Of the eight hundred thousand head of live-stock, only sixty-three thousand remained. Everything went to rack and ruin, and what had been a land of abounding life and generous plenty, reverted to silence and desolation. At the Mission of St. John Capistrano, of the two thousand Christian population, only one hundred remained; of the seventy thousand cattle, but five hundred were left; of the two thousand horses, only one hundred survived; and of the ten thousand sheep, not one remained.

And then, after sixty years of cheerful and successful labor, and from happy abundance in which they had hoped to die at last, went forth the downcast Fathers, one after another; some in sorrow to the grave, some to other and rougher fields of missionary labor, and others to be dispersed among the widespread retreats of the Brothers of St. Francis. And the swarthy neophytes—the dark-eyed maidens of San Gabriel, whither went they? Back to the savage defiles of the mountains, down to the depths of barbarism, to wander in the lonely desert, to shiver in the pitiless storm, and to perish at last under the ponderous march of a careless and unfeeling civilization.

CHAPTER V.
DOWNFALL OF THE OLD MISSIONS.

Results of Mexican Rule—Confiscation of the Pious Fund—Revolution Begun—Events of the Colonial Rebellion—The Americans Appear and Settle Things—Annexation at Last.

IN 1822, Mexico declared independence of Spain, and immediately the old missions began to decline. Four years afterwards the Christian Indians were removed from under the control of the Fathers, their manumission having been ordered by the Mexican Government. They were to receive certain portions of land, and to be entirely independent of the friars. The annual salaries of the Fathers, which had been derived from interest on the Pious Fund, were withheld and appropriated by the Government, and soon after the fund itself was confiscated by the Mexican Congress, and used for the purposes of state. The Pious Fund was the aggregated donations of the Catholic world for the maintenance of missions in Lower and Upper California, the interest being about fifty thousand dollars annually, which went for the support of the Fathers. This large sum, principal and interest, amounting in 1817 to one million two hundred and seventy-three thousand dollars, the beggarly Mexican Government meant to steal. Professor Gleeson, writing in defense of the Fathers, makes out a fearful bill of damages against the perfidious Government, amounting to no less than twelve millions two hundred thousand dollars, which will probably never be paid by that rather shaky republic. The missions were thus practically ruined. Following the rapacious example set by Government, the white settlers laid violent hands on the stock and lands belonging to the missions, and, having returned to their mountain fastnesses, the Indians instituted a predatory warfare against the settlers, carrying off their goods, cattle, and sometimes their wives and children. The whites retaliating in kind, villages were destroyed, and the whole country, highlands and lowlands, was kept in a state of apprehension, rapine, and spoliation, resembling the condition of Scotland in the times of the Jacobites.

In the meantime in 1836, a revolt against the Mexican Government was projected by the white settlers who seized upon Monterey, the capital, and declared the country independent. Thirty American riflemen, under Isaac Graham from Tennessee, and sixty mounted Californians, under General Castro, composed the entire insurgent army, Alvarado being the generalissimo. They advanced on and took the territorial capital in November, Governor Gutierrez and his seventy men having valiantly shut themselves up in the fort, where they ignominiously surrendered at the very first gun. Gutierrez with his officials was deported to Lower California, and Alvarado had himself appointed Governor in his stead. Don M. G. Vallejo was appointed military Commandant-General, and Don Jose Castro was created Prefect of Police. The country was then formally declared a free and independent State, providing that in the case the then existing Central Government of Mexico should be overthrown and a federal constitution adopted in its stead, California should enter the federation with the other States. The people of Los Angeles and Santa Barbara refused to acknowledge the new territorial administration, but Alvarado marched upon Los Angeles, where he was met by Castello, and instead of a bloody battle, it was agreed that Alvarado should recognize the existing Central Government of Mexico, and be proclaimed political chief of California, pro tem., while Castello was to proceed to Mexico as deputy to Congress, with a salary of three thousand piasters a year. The Government of Mexico declined to confirm the arrangement, and appointed Don Carlos Carillo Governor of the Territory. Alvarado again went to war, and with a small company of Americans and Californians, marched against Carillo, the new Governor at Santa Barbara. The valiant Carillo, having a wholesome dread of the American sharp-shooters, retired from the field without a battle, leaving Alvarado master of the situation. The pusillanimous character of the then existing Mexican Government is illustrated by the fact that Alvarado was confirmed as Constitutional Governor of California, notwithstanding he had been the leader of the rebellion.

Then ensued a succession of spoliations which destroyed the laborious enterprise of sixty years, and left the old missions in melancholy ruins.

Alvarado bestowed upon his English and American followers large grants of land, money and stock confiscated from the missions. Graham, the captain of the band, obtained a great landed estate and two hundred mules. To the commandant, General Vallejo, fell the goods and chattels of the missions of San Rafael and Solano; Castro, the Prefect of Monterey, received the property of the San Juan Bautista, while Governor Alvarado himself appropriated the rich spoil of the missions of Carmelo and Soledad.*

In the meantime a conspiracy against Alvarado

---

* Authorities differ on this matter. Some well-informed persons say that Alvarado had promised Bates, and others, large tracts of land, if they would assist him in establishing himself as ruler; that after succeeding in his ambitious desires, he turned traitor to his friends, and undertook to destroy them on the pretence of a contemplated insurrection. There was no fair fight. Alvarado captured the men, over a hundred in number, by sending armed parties to their homes in the night, or by luring them to Monterey on pretence of important business, and putting chains on them as fast as they came into his presence, otherwise they would have made short work of deposing him.—[EDITOR.

was set on foot by certain of his English and American compatriots, the object being the admission of California to the American Union. The conspirators were forty-six in number, twenty-five English and twenty-one Americans, under command of Graham. Alvarado soon heard of the design, and sent a party of soldiers, under Castro, to Monterey, surprised the revolutionists in their hut, and poured in a volley of musketry disabling many of them; the balance were taken prisoners, and afterwards deported to San Blas and thence to Tepic, where they were treated as convicts. The Americans and English in California appealed to the Mexican Government, and President Bustamente became alarmed at the danger of war with England and the United States, and ordered the exiled prisoners to be sent back to California, and that they should be indemnified for their loss of time at the rate of three piasters a day. The returned prisoners, immediately on their arrival, resumed their design with greater energy than before, having determined to be revenged on Castro and Alvarado for the outrages they had inflicted.

In 1841 other Americans arrived, and the revolutionary party was considerably increased. Alvarado demanded reinforcements from Mexico, but the only assistance he received was that of three hundred convicts from the Mexican prisons. At this juncture, Santa Ana, the new President, removed Governor Alvarado from office, appointing Micheltorena in his stead, and when the latter arrived, Monterey, the capital, had previously fallen into the hands of the American Commodore Jones, although then in the possession of the Mexicans. Commodore Catesby Jones, having heard that war had been declared between the United States and Mexico, hastened to Monterey, took possession of the city, and hoisted the American colors, but learning his serious mistake on the following day, he lowered his flag and made a becoming apology. This extraordinary incident occurred on the 20th of October, 1842, and it was then obvious that the distracted country must soon fall into the hands of the United States, or some other foreign nation.

One of the first acts of the new Governor, Micheltorena, was the restoration of the missions to the friars, after a turbulent interregnum of six years. But this act of policy and justice came too late; the missions were ruined beyond the possibility of resuscitation. The Indians had been dispersed, many of them living by brigandage, and others had become wandering vagabonds. After two years' exertion by the Fathers things began to improve; some of the Indians had returned, and the lands were being re-cultivated, when the Government again interfered, and ordered Governor Pio Pico, in 1845, to dispose of the missions either by sale or rental, to the white settlers. Thus, at length, the last of the property which the Fathers had created by sixty years of patient labor, passed into the possession of private individuals, many of the Fathers were reduced to extreme poverty, humiliation, and distress, and the missions went down, never to rise again. The destruction of the missions was almost immediately succeeded by the war between the United States and Mexico, and the long vexed territory passed to the American Union.

CHAPTER VI.
PRIMITIVE AGRICULTURE.

Extent of the Mission Lands—Varieties of Product—Agricultural Implements and means of Working—A Primitive Mill—Immense Herds and Value of Cattle—The First Native Shop.

UP to the time of the American conquest the productive lands of California were chiefly in the hands of the missionaries. Each of the missions included about fifteen miles square, and the boundaries were generally equi-distant. As the science of agriculture was then in a very primitive condition in Spain, the monks of California could not be expected to know much about scientific farming. They knew nothing about the utility of fallows, or the alternation of crops, and their only mode of renovating exhausted soil, was to let it lie idle and under the dominion of native weeds, until it was thought capable of bearing crops again. Land being so abundant, there was no occasion for laborious or expensive processes of reeuperation.

The grains mostly cultivated were Indian corn, wheat, barley, and a small bean called *frijol*, which was in general use throughout Spanish America. The beans, when ripe, were fried in lard, and much esteemed by all ranks of people. Indian corn was the bread-staple, and was cultivated in rows or drills. The plow used was a very primitive affair. It was composed of two pieces of wood; the main piece, formed from a crooked limb of a tree of the proper shape, constituting both sole and handle. It had no mould-board, or other means for turning a furrow, and was only capable of scratching the surface of the ground. A small share, fitted to the point of the sole, was the only iron about the implement. The other piece was a long beam, like the tongue of a wagon, reaching to the yoke of the cattle by which the plow was drawn. It consisted of a rough sapling, with the bark taken off, fixed into the main piece, and connected by a small upright on which it was to slide up or down, and was fixed in position by two wedges. When the plowman desired to plow deep, the forward end of the tongue was lowered, and in this manner the depth of the furrow was regulated. This beam passed between the two oxen, a pin was put through the end projecting from the yoke, and then the agricultural machine was ready to run. The plowman walked on one side, holding the one handle, or stilt, with his right hand, and managing the oxen with the other. The yoke was placed on the top of the cattle's heads close behind the horns, tied firmly to

the roots and to the forehead by thongs, so that, instead of drawing by the shoulders and neck, the oxen dragged the plow by their horns and foreheads. When so harnessed the poor beasts were in a very deplorable condition; they could not move their heads up, down, or sidewise, went with their noses turned up, and every jolt of the plow knocked them about, and seemed to give them great pain. Only an ancient Spaniard could devise such a contrivance for animal torture. When Alexander Forbes suggested to an old Spaniard that perhaps it might be better to yoke the oxen by the neck and shoulders, "What!" said the old man, "can you suppose that Spain, which has always been known as the mother of the sciences, can be mistaken on *that* point?"

The oxen were yoked to the carts in the same manner, having to bear the weight of the load on the top of their heads, the most disadvantageous mechanical point of the whole body. The ox-cart was composed of a bottom frame of clumsy construction, with a few upright bars connected by smaller ones at the top. When used for carrying grain, it was lined with canes or bulrushes. The pole was large, and tied to the yoke in the same manner as with the plow, so that every jerk of the cart was torture to the oxen. The wheels had no spokes, and were composed of three pieces of timber, the middle piece hewn out of a log, of sufficient size to form the nave and middle of the wheel, all in one; the middle piece was of a length equal to the diameter of the wheel, and rounded at the ends to arcs of the circumference. The other two pieces were of timber naturally bent, and joined to the sides of the middle piece by keys of wood grooved into the ends of the pieces which formed the wheel. The whole was then made circular, and did not contain a particle of iron, not even so much as a nail.

From the rude construction of the plow, which was incapable of turning a furrow, the ground was imperfectly broken by scratching over, crossing, and re-crossing several times; and although four or five crossings were sometimes given to a field, it was found impossible to eradicate the weeds. "It was no uncommon thing," says Forbes in 1835, "to see, on some of the large maize estates in Mexico, as many as two hundred plows at work together. As the plows are equal on both sides, the plowmen have only to begin at one side of the field and follow one another up and down, as many as can be employed together without interfering in turning round at the end, which they do in succession, like ships tacking in a line of battle, and so proceed down the same side as they come up."

Harrows were unknown, the wheat and barley being brushed in by a branch of a tree. Sometimes a heavy log was drawn over the field, on the plan of a roller, save that it did not roll, but was dragged so as to carry a part of the soil over the seeds. Indian corn was planted in furrows or ruts drawn about five feet apart, the seed being deposited by hand, from three to five grains in a place, which were slightly covered by the foot, no hoes being used. The sowing of maize, as well as all other grains in Upper California, commenced in November, as near as possible to the beginning of the rainy season. The harvest was in July and August. Wheat was sown broadcast, and in 1835 it was considered equal in quality to that produced at the Cape of Good Hope, and had begun to attract attention in Europe. All kinds of grain were threshed at harvest time, without stacking. In 1831, the whole amount of grain raised in Upper California, according to the mission records, was 46,202 *fanegas* —the fanega being equal to 2½ English bushels. Wheat and barley were then worth two dollars the fanega; maize, a dollar and a half; the crop of that year at the several missions being worth some eighty-six thousand dollars.

The mills for grinding grain consisted of an upright axle, to the lower end of which was fixed a horizontal water-wheel under the building, and to the upper end a millstone. As there was no intermediate machinery to increase the velocity of the stone it could make only the same number of revolutions as the water-wheel, so that the work of grinding a grist was necessarily a process of time. The water-wheel was fearfully and wonderfully made. Forbes described it as a set of *cucharas*, or gigantic spoons, set around its periphery in place of floats. They were made of strong pieces of timber, in the shape of spoons, with the handles inserted in mortises in the outer surface of the wheel, the bowl of the spoons toward the water, which impinged upon them with nearly its whole velocity. Rude as the contrivance was, it was exceedingly powerful— a sort of primitive turbine. There were only three of these improved mills in the country in 1835, and the possession of such a rare piece of machinery was no small boast for the simple-hearted Fathers, so far away from the progressive mechanical world. It was not a primitive California invention, however, as Sir Walter Scott, in his romance of "The Pirate," describes a similar apparatus formerly in use in the Shetland Islands.*

Before the advent of foreigners, neither potatoes nor green vegetables were cultivated as articles of food. Hemp was raised to some extent, and flax grew well, but its culture was discontinued for want of machinery for manufacture. Pasturage was the principal pursuit in all Spanish colonies in America. The immense tracts of wild land afforded unlimited ranges, but few men and little labor were required, and the pastoral state was the most congenial to the people. The herds were very large; in the four jurisdictions of San Francisco, Monterey, Santa

---

*This form of water-wheel was common in the Eastern States during the earlier part of this century, and was known as the tub or spur wheel. Even the mounting of the mill-stones was in the manner described.—[EDITOR.

Barbara, and San Diego, there were in 1836 three hundred thousand black cattle, thirty-two thousand horses, twenty-eight thousand mules, and one hundred and fifty-three thousand sheep. Great numbers of horses ran wild, and these were hunted and killed to prevent their eating the grass. There was hardly such a thing as butter or cheese in use, butter being, in general, an abomination to a Spaniard.

In the earlier times immense droves of young bulls were sent to Mexico for beef. The cattle being half-wild, it was necessary to catch them with the lasso, a process which need not be here described. The process of milking the cows was peculiar. They first let the calf suck for a while, when the dairyman stole up on the other side, and, while the calf was still sucking, procured a little of the milk. They had an idea that the cow would not "give down" milk if the calf was taken away from her. The sheep were of a bad breed, with coarse wool; and swine received little attention. The amount of the annual exports in the first few years after the opening of the ports to foreign vessels, was estimated at thirty thousand hides and seven thousand quintals of tallow; with small cargoes of wheat, wine, raisins, olives, etc., sent to the Russian settlements and San Blas. Hides were worth two dollars each, and tallow eight dollars per quintal. Afterwards the exportation of hides and tallow was greatly increased, and it is said that after the Fathers had become convinced that they would have to give up the mission lands to the Government, they caused the slaughter of one hundred thousand cattle in a single year, for their hides and tallow alone. And who could blame them? The cattle were theirs. Notwithstanding all this immense revenue these enthusiasts gave it all to the church, and themselves went away in penury, and, as has been related heretofore, one of them actually starved to death.

In 1836 the value of a fat ox or bull in Upper California was five dollars; a cow, five; a saddle-horse, ten; a mare, five; a sheep, two; and a mule ten dollars.

The first ship ever constructed on the eastern shores of the Pacific was built by the Jesuit Father, Ugarte at Loreto, in 1719. Being in want of a vessel to survey the coast of the peninsula, and there being none available nearer than New Spain or the Philippine Islands, the enterprising friar determined to build one. After traveling two hundred miles through the mountains suitable timber was at last found, in a marshy country; but how to get it to the coast was the great question; this was considered impossible by all but the stubborn old friar. When the party returned to Loreto, Father Ugarte's ship in the mountains became a ghostly joke among his brother friars. But, not to be beaten and laughed down, Ugarte made the necessary preparations, returned to the mountains, felled the timber, dragged it two hundred miles to the coast, and built a handsome ship, which he appropriately named The Triumph of the Cross. The first voyage of this historic vessel was to La Paz, two hundred miles south of Loreto, where a mission was to be founded.

CHAPTER VII.

Sir Francis Drake's Discoveries—The Fabulous Straits of Anian—Arctic Weather in June—Russian Invasion—Native Animals—Various facts and Events.

For many years it was supposed and maintained in England that Sir Francis Drake was the original discoverer of San Francisco bay; but it is now considered certain that he never found the entrance to that inland sea. Drake was a buccaneer, and, in 1579, was in the South Seas looking for Spanish ships to plunder, under the pretext of existing war between England and Spain. He had two other purposes to subserve in behalf of the English Government; to discover a new route from Europe to the Indies, and to find a new territory northward that would rival the Spanish-American possessions in natural wealth. A rich trade had sprung up between the Philippine Islands and Spain; every year a Spanish galleon from the Malayan Archipelago crossed the Pacific to Acapulco, freighted with the richest merchandise, and this, Captain Drake was on the watch for, and did eventually capture.

At that time navigators universally believed that the American and Asiatic continents were separated only by the Straits of Anian, which were supposed to lead eastward to the Atlantic, somewhere about Newfoundland. This long-sought northwestern passage Drake was in search of. In the autumn of 1578 Drake brought his little fleet of three vessels through the Straits of Magellan, and found the Pacific ocean in a stormy rage, and, having been drifted about Cape Horn a couple of months, he concluded that the continent was there at an end; that the Atlantic and Pacific oceans there united their waters; and he very naturally came to the conclusion that a similar juncture of seas would be found at the north. Having captured the great Spanish galleon, and finding himself overburdened with rich treasure, Drake wanted to return to England. He did not care to encounter the stormy waters of Cape Horn, and expecting to find a hostile Spanish fleet awaiting him at the Straits of Magellan, he determined to make his way home by a new and hitherto unknown route, the north-eastern passage. On the 17th of June, 1579, he entered what the historian of the expedition called a "faire, good bay within thirty-eight degrees of latitude of the line." That exactly corresponds with what is now known as Drake's Bay, behind Point Reyes. There, although it was in the month of June, his men "complained grievously of the nipping cold." Drake having given up the perilous north-eastern passage by way of the fabulous Straits of Anian, sailed away for England by way of the Philippine Islands and the Cape of Good Hope. It is probable that while off the north-west coast, Drake saw the snowy crest of Mount Shasta and some of the Oregon peaks, and concluded that he had got near enough to the North Pole. At any rate, it is clear enough that he never passed through the Golden Gate, or rested on the magnificent waters of San Francisco bay.

The Reverend Fletcher, chaplain of Drake's expedition, must have been a terrible old story-teller. He says that when off the coast of Oregon, in the month of June, "The rigging of the ship was frozen stiff, and the meat froze as it was taken off the fire." Moreover, saith the same veracious parson, "There is no part of earth here to be taken up, wherein there is not a reasonable quantity of gold and silver." These arctic regions and golden treasures were found along the ocean shore between San Francisco and Portland.

Another English buccaneer, Thomas Cavendish, appeared on the Pacific coast in 1586, and plundered the Philippine galleon of 122,000 pesos in gold, besides a valuable cargo of merchandise. The pirate ran the vessel into the nearest port, set her on fire, liberated the crew and made his escape to England.

It is supposed that one of the extensive Smith family was the first white man who crossed the Sierra Nevada from the States, but this fact is not altogether certain. In the Summer of 1825 Jedediah S. Smith, the head of the American Fur Company, led a party of trappers and Indians from their camp, on Green river, across the Sierra Nevada and into the Tulare valley, which they reached in July. The party trapped for beaver from the Tulare to the American river, and had their camp near the present site of Folsom. On a second trip Smith led his company further south, into the Mojave country, on the Colorado, where all except himself and two companions were killed by the Indians. These three made their way to the Mission of San Gabriel, near Los Angeles, which they reached in December, 1826. In the following year Smith and his party left the Sacramento valley for the settlements on the Columbia river, but at the mouth of the Umpqua they were attacked by Indians, and all killed except Smith and two Irishmen, who, after much suffering, reached Fort Vancouver. Smith returned to St. Louis in 1840, and the following year was killed by Indians, while leading an expedition to Santa Fé. His history is no less adventurous and romantic than that of the famous Captain John Smith, of Virginia.

In 1807 the Russians first appeared on the coast of California. The Czar's ambassador to Japan came down from Sitka, ostensibly for supplies, and attempted to establish communication between the Russian and Spanish settlements. The better to effect his purpose he became engaged in marriage with the Commandante's daughter, at San Francisco, but on his way back to obtain the sanction of his Government he was thrown from his horse and killed. The lady assumed the habit of a nun, and mourned for her lover until death. In 1812 a hundred Russians and as many Kodiac Indians came down from their northern settlements and squatted at Bodega, where they built a fort and maintained themselves by force of arms until 1841, when they sold the establishment to Captain Sutter and disappeared.

In 1822 Mexico declared her independence of Spain, and established a separate empire. When the Indians at San Diego heard of it they held a great feast, and commenced the ceremonies by burning their chief alive. When the missionaries remonstrated, the logical savages said: "Have you not done the same in Mexico? You say your King was not good, and you killed him; well, our captain was not good, and we burned him. If the new one is bad we will burn him too."

The State of California was originally divided into twenty-seven counties. The derivation of the several terms adopted is given by General Vallejo:

San Diego (Saint James) takes its name from the old town, three miles from the harbor, discovered by Viscaíño, in 1602.

Los Angeles county was named from the city (Ciudad de Los Angeles) founded by order of the Viceroy of New Spain, in 1780.

Santa Barbara was named after the town established in 1780 to protect the five adjacent missions.

San Luis Obispo, after its principal town, the site of a mission founded in 1772 by Junipero Serra and Jose Cavaller.

Monterey, after the chief town, which was so named by Viscaíño in honor of his friend and patron, the Viceroy, Count of Monterey.

Santa Cruz (the Holy Cross) was named from the mission on the north side of the bay.

San Francisco, named in honor of the friars' patron saint.

Santa Clara, named from the mission established there in 1777.

Contra Costa (the opposite coast) is the natural designation of the country across the bay from San Francisco.

Marin county, named after a troublesome chief whom an exploring expedition encountered in 1815. Marin died at the San Rafael Mission in 1834.

Sonoma, named after a noted Indian, who also gave name to his tribe. The word means "Valley of the Moon."

Solano, the name of a chief, who borrowed it from his missionary friend, Father Solano.

Yolo, a corruption of an Indian word *yoloy*, signifying a place thick with rushes; also, the name of a tribe of Indians on Cache creek.

Napa, named after a numerous tribe in that region, which was nearly exterminated by small-pox in 1838.

Mendocino, named by the discoverer after Mendoza, Viceroy of New Spain.

Sacramento (the Sacrament). Moraga gave the main river the name of Jesus Maria, and the principal branch he called Sacramento. Afterwards, the great river came to be known as the Sacramento, and the branch, Feather river.

El Dorado, the appropriate name of the district where gold was discovered in 1848.

Sutter county, named in honor of the world-renowned pioneer, John A. Sutter.

Yuba, a corruption of Uva, a name given a branch of Feather river in 1824 by an exploring party, on account of the great quantities of wild grape vines growing on its banks.

Butte, the common French term for a mound, in allusion to three symmetrical hills in that county; so named by a party of the Hudson Bay Company hunters.

Colusa, from Coluses, the name of a numerous tribe on the west side of the Sacramento. Meaning of the word is unknown.

Shasta, the name of a tribe who lived at the base of the lofty peak of same name.

Calaveras, so named by Captain Moraga, on account of an immense number of skulls in the vicinity of a stream, which he called "Calaveras, or the River of Skulls." This is the reputed site of a terrible battle between the mountain and valley Indians, over the fishing question.

San Joaquin, after the river, so named by Captain Moraga, in honor of the legendary father of the Virgin.

Tuolumne, a corruption of an Indian word, signifying a cluster of stone wigwams.

Mariposa signifies butterfly. So called by a party of hunters, who camped on the river in 1807, and observed the trees gorgeous with butterflies.

Trinity, called after the bay of that name, which was discovered on the anniversary of Trinity Festival.

When first visited by the Spaniards, California abounded in wild animals, some of which are now extinct. One of these was called *Berendo* by the Spaniards, and by the natives, *Taye*. "It is," says Father Venegas, "about the bigness of a calf a year and a half old, resembling it in figure, except the head, which is like that of a deer, and the horns very thick, like those of a ram. Its hoof is large, round, and cloven, and its tail short." This was the *Argali*, a species intermediate between the goat and the sheep, living in large herds along the bases of the mountains, supposed to be a variety of the Asiatic argali, so plentiful in Northern and Central Asia. In his journey from Monterey to San Francisco, Father Serra met with herds of immense deer, which the men mistook for European cattle, and wondered how they got there. Several deer were shot, whose horns measured eleven feet from tip to tip. Another large animal, which the natives called cibolo, the bison, inhabited the great plains, but was eventually driven off by the vast herds of domestic cattle. When Langsdorff's ship was lying in the Bay of San Francisco in 1804, sea-otter were swimming about so plentifully as to be nearly unheeded. The Indians caught them in snares, or killed them with sticks. Perouse estimated that the Presidency of Monterey alone could supply ten thousand otter skins annually. They were worth twenty dollars and upwards apiece. Beechey found birds in astonishing numbers and variety, but their plumage was dingy looking, and very few of them could sing respectably.

The name California was first given to the Lower Peninsula in 1536, and was afterwards applied to the coast territory as far north as Cape Mendocino. There has been much learned speculation concerning the probable derivation of the word, but no satisfactory conclusion has been reached. The word is arbitrary, derived from some expression of the Indians.

The province, as it formerly existed under the Viceroys, was divided into two parts; Peninsular, or Lower and Old California, and Continental, or Upper and New, the line of separation running near the 32d parallel of latitude, from the northern extremity of the Gulf of California, to the Pacific ocean.

The Gulf of California—called also the Sea of Cortez, and the Vermilion Sea—is a great arm of the Pacific, which joins that ocean under the 23d parallel of latitude, and thence extends north-westward inland about seven hundred miles, where it receives the waters of the Colorado and Gila rivers. It is a hundred miles wide at the mouth, widens further north, and still further on contracts in width, till its shores become the banks of the Colorado. The Peninsular, or California side of the Gulf, was formerly celebrated for the size and beauty of its pearls, which were found in oysters. They were obtained with great difficulty, from the crevices at the bottom, by Indian divers, who had to go down twenty or thirty feet, and frequently were drowned, or devoured by sharks. In 1825, eight vessels engaged in the fishing, obtained, altogether, five pounds of pearls, which were worth about ten thousand dollars. Sometimes, however, a single magnificent pearl was found, which compensated for years of labor and disappointment. Some of the richest in the royal regalia of Spain, were found on the California gulf.

Peninsular, or Lower California, lying between the gulf and the ocean, is about 130 miles in breadth where it joins the continent at the north, under the 32d parallel, and nearly in the same latitude as Savannah in Georgia. Thence it runs south-eastward, diminishing in breadth and terminating in two points, the one at Cape San Lucas, is nearly the same latitude as Havana, the other at Cape Palmo, 60 miles north-east, at the entrance of the gulf.

Continental California extends along the Pacific

HIRAM C. MEEK.
(AT 93 Y'S OF AGE.)

from the 32d parallel, where it joins the peninsula, about seven hundred miles, to the Oregon line, nearly in the latitude of Boston. The Mexican Government considered the 42d parallel of latitude as the northern line of California, according to a treaty with the United States in 1828.

Greenhow, writing in 1844, says: "The only mine as yet discovered in Upper California is one of gold, situated at the foot of the great westernmost range of mountains, on the west, at the distance of twenty-five miles from Angeles, the largest town in the country. It is said to be of extraordinary richness."

The animals originally found in California were buffalo, deer, elk, bear, wild hogs, wild sheep, ocelots, pumas, beavers, foxes, and many others, generally of a species different from those on the Atlantic side. Cattle and horses were introduced from Mexico, and soon overrun the country, and drove out the buffalo and other of the large animals. One of the worst scourges of the country was the *chapul*, a kind of grasshopper, which appeared in clouds after a mild winter, and ate up every green thing.

Little or no rain fell during the years 1840 and 1841, in which time the inhabitants were reduced to the verge of starvation.

It is a remarkable fact, that the Golden Gate is nearly in the same latitude as the entrance of Chesapeake bay and the Straits of Gibraltar.

In 1844, the town of Monterey, the capital of Upper California, was a wretched collection of mud, or adobe houses, containing about two hundred inhabitants. The castle and fort consisted of mud walls, behind which were a few worthless guns, good for nothing but to scare the Indians.

In 1838, the Russian settlements at Ross and Bodega contained eight or nine hundred inhabitants, stockaded forts, mills, shops, and stables, and the farms produced great abundance of grain, vegetables, butter, and cheese, which were shipped to Sitka. The lazy Spaniards were bitterly hostile to the industrious Muscovites, but durst not meddle with them. At last, having maintained their independent colony thirty-one years, they sold out to Captain Sutter, and quietly moved away.

CHAPTER VIII.

THE AMERICAN CONQUEST.

Fremont and the Bear Flag—Rise and Progress of the Revolution—Commodores Sloat, Stockton, and Shubrick—Castro and Flores Driven out—Treaty of Peace—Stockton and Kearney Quarrel—Fremont Arrested, etc.

IN the Spring of 1845, John C. Fremont, then a brevet-captain in the corps of United States Topographical Engineers, was dispatched on a third tour of exploration across the continent, and was charged to find a better route from the Rocky Mountains to the mouth of the Columbia river.

This was his ostensible business, but there is reason to believe that he had other and private instructions from the Government concerning the acquisition of California, in view of the pending war with Mexico. Fremont reached the frontiers of California in March, 1846, halted his company a hundred miles from Monterey, and proceeded alone to have an interview with General Castro, the Mexican Commandante. He wanted permission to take his company of sixty-two men to San Joaquin valley, to recruit their energies before setting out for Oregon. To this Castro assented, and told him to go where he pleased. Immediately thereafter the perfidious Castro, pretending to have received fresh instructions from his Government, raised a company of three hundred native Californians, and sent word to Fremont to quit the country forthwith, else he would fall upon and annihilate him and his little band of adventurers. Fremont sent word back that he should go when he got ready, and then took position on Hawk's Peak, overlooking Monterey, and raised the American flag. At this time neither party had heard of any declaration of war between the United States and Mexico.

Fremont's party consisted of sixty-two rough American borderers, including Kit Carson and six Delaware Indians, each armed with a rifle, two pistols, a bowie-knife, and tomahawk. Castro maneuvered round for three days with his cavalry, infantry and field pieces, but, with true Mexican discretion, kept well out of rifle shot; and, on the fourth day, Fremont, perceiving that there was no fight in the gascon, struck his camp and moved at his leisure toward Oregon.

At Klamath lake, Lieutenant Gillespie, of the United States army, overtook Fremont's party, with verbal dispatches, and a letter from the American Secretary of State, commending the bearer to Fremont's good offices. That was all; what the verbal dispatches were is still unknown. Fremont returned to the Sacramento valley, and encamped near the Marysville Buttes. He found the American settlers greatly alarmed by Castro's war-like proclamations, and had no difficulty in raising a considerable company of volunteers, a party of whom marched on the post of Sonoma, captured nine brass cannon, two hundred and fifty stand of small arms, and made prisoners of General Vallejo and two other persons of importance. Eighteen men were left to garrison the place, under William B. Ide. Castro fulminated another proclamation from his head-quarters at Santa Clara, calling on the native Californians to "rise for their religion, liberty, and independence," and Ide issued another at Sonoma, appealing to the Americans and other foreigners to rise and defend their rights of settlement, as they were about to be massacred or driven out of the country. The settlers responded numerously and with alacrity; and, after one or two skirmishes, repaired to Sonoma, declared an independent State, and raised the now celebrated

Bear Flag. That historic standard consisted of a piece of cotton cloth, with a tolerable likeness of a grizzly bear, done with a blacking brush and berry-juice, and now belongs to the California Society of Pioneers.

In the meantime Fremont was organizing a battalion at Sutter's Fort, and having heard that Castro was moving in force on Sonoma, he made a forced march to that point with ninety riflemen. Thence Fremont, Kit Carson, Lieutenant Gillespie, and a few others, crossed to the old fort at San Francisco, made prisoner the Commandante, spiked all the guns, and returned to Sonoma. There, on the 5th of July, 1846, he called his whole force of revolutionists together, and recommended an immediate declaration of independence. This was unanimously assented to, and the bear party was merged into the battalion, which now numbered one hundred and sixty mounted riflemen. Next day it was determined to go in pursuit of the proclaiming Castro, who was said to be entrenched at Santa Clara with four hundred men; but when the battalion had crossed the Sacramento at Sutter's Fort, they learned that Castro had evacuated the Santa Clara country and fled to Los Angeles, whither they resolved to follow him, five hundred miles away. At this point news was received that the American flag had been raised at Monterey, and that the American naval forces would co-operate with the mounted riflemen in the effort to capture Castro. Then the Bear Flag was hauled down, giving place to the stars and stripes, and Fremont and his men set out overland for Los Angeles, after the declamatory but fugacious Castro, who will live in history as the "Captain Bobadil" of that brief but stirring revolution. Up to this time nothing had been heard of a declaration of war between Mexico and the United States.

On the 2d of July, 1846, Commodore Sloat had arrived at Monterey in the United States frigate, *Savannah*, his whole fleet consisting of one frigate and five smaller vessels. He had no intelligence of a declaration of war between the United States and Mexico, but was aware that hostilities were impending, and was in doubt what to do. The British Rear-Admiral, Sir George Seymour's flagship, was lying in the harbor of San Blas while Sloat was at Mazatlan, and eight other British ships were on the coast watching the American movements, and ready to take possession of California. When Sloat sailed from Mazatlan Seymour put out from San Blas, each ship spreading every sail in a race for Monterey, but the American Commodore out-sailed the British Admiral, and, when the latter rounded the Point of Pines at Monterey, he found the Americans in full possession. On the 7th of July Commodore Sloat sent Captain Mervine, with two hundred and fifty marines and seamen, on shore, hoisted the American flag over Monterey, the capital of Upper California, and issued a proclamation declaring the province henceforth a portion of the United States. He had previously dispatched a messenger to San Francisco to Commander Montgomery, and on the 8th of that month the stars and stripes waved over Yerba Buena. On the 10th Montgomery sent an American flag to Sonoma, which the revolutionists received with great joy, pulled down their Bear Flag, and hoisted the Union standard in its stead, and thus ended the dominion of the revolutionary Bear Flag in California, having played a conspicuous and important part in the conquest.

Sloat then organized a company of volunteer dragoons to take possession of certain arms and stores at San Juan; but, when they arrived, Fremont and his battalion had been there from Sutter's Fort, and captured nine pieces of cannon, two hundred muskets, twenty kegs of powder, and sixty thousand pounds of cannon shot.

When Fremont reported himself upon Sloat's order, at Monterey, a misunderstanding occurred between the Commodore and the Pathfinder, and the former refused to co-operate with the latter in the further prosecution of the war, and while the dispute was pending Commodore Stockton arrived to supersede Sloat, who had been too slow and hesitating to suit the authorities at Washington.

Sloat having retired, Stockton and Fremont worked harmoniously. The former assumed command of the land forces, and invited Fremont and Gillespie to take service under him with their battalion. On the 23d, Stockton dispatched Commodore Dupont with the *Cyane*, to convey Fremont and his battalion to San Diego, and soon afterwards himself sailed for San Pedro, the sea-port of Los Angeles. At Santa Barbara he went ashore and took possession unresisted. There he learned that Castro and Pico were at Los Angeles with fifteen hundred men, and also that Fremont had reached San Diego. After drilling his seamen in the land service, Stockton, with his three hundred men, took up his march for Los Angeles, but, on his arrival, Castro had decamped and fled to Sonora. Stockton at once took possession of the place, and was soon after joined by Fremont, and, having received official notice of existing war between the United States and Mexico, he proclaimed California a territory of the United States, organized a temporary government, and invited the people to meet on the 15th of September and elect officers of their own. He then returned to Yerba Buena, or San Francisco, where the people of the neighboring country gave him a public reception.

After Stockton had left Los Angeles, General Flores re-organized the scattered forces of the Mexicans, retook the place, and proclaimed expulsion or death to the Americans; so the conquest had to be made again. Stockton returned to San Diego, and, after various events which cannot be here related in detail, was joined by General Kearney, who had marched across the country from Santa Fe, and, on the 29th of December, commenced his march of one hundred and thirty miles to Los Angeles. He found

SAN JOAQUIN COUNTY FROM 1841 TO 1847.   31

the enemy, a thousand or twelve hundred strong, drawn up in battle array on the bank of the San Gabriel river; a battle ensued, in which the Mexicans were defeated by Stockton and Kearney, and fled towards Los Angeles, and, after three ineffectual attempts to make a stand, they scattered in confusion. On the 10th of January Stockton re-entered Los Angeles, and restored the American flag to the eminence which it still maintains. Flores, after having made a much better fight than Castro, fled to Sonora. The treaty of Couenga ensued, restoring peace to the country and completing the American conquest.

Immediately after the conquest a dispute arose between Commodore Stockton and General Kearney as to precedence in the territorial Government. Kearney was authorized to establish a civil Government in California, provided he should conquer it, as he did New Mexico; Stockton and Fremont maintained that the conquest was accomplished before he arrived. Fremont decided to report officially to Commodore Stockton, who thereupon commissioned him as Governor of the Territory. Thus Fremont obtained the ill-will of General Kearney, who, combining with Commodore Shubrick, in the absence of Stockton, abrogated the treaty of Couenga, and proceeded to oust Fremont from the Governorship. In the meantime Colonel Stephenson arrived with his regiment of New York volunteers, and sided with Kearney. Mason was installed as Governor, and Fremont was ordered to report at Monterey within twelve days; this he failed to do, and Kearney refused him permission to join his regiment, sold his horses, and ordered him to repair to Monterey, where be compelled him to turn over his exploring outfit to another person. When Kearney was ready to go East he compelled Fremont to accompany him, and at Fort Leavenworth Fremont was arrested for insubordination, conveyed to Fortress Monroe, tried by Court-martial, found guilty of mutiny, disobedience, and disorderly conduct, deprived of his commission, but recommended to the clemency of the President. Having suffered these outrageous indignities solely in consequence of a quarrel between Commodore Stockton and General Kearney, Fremont declined to avail himself of executive clemency, and quit the service.

The people of the country generally considered that Fremont had been ungenerously used by the Government, and, a few years after, his popularity having been greatly enhanced through the influence of his magnificent wife, the daughter of Senator Thomas H. Benton, he was nominated for the Presidency by the Republican party.

CHAPTER IX.*

SAN JOAQUIN COUNTY FROM THE TIME CAPT. C. M. WEBER FIRST SAW IT IN NOVEMBER, 1841. UNTIL THE CLOSE OF 1847.

Captain C. M. Weber—Expedition to California, 1841—Names of the Party—Sutter's Fort—Hoza Ha-soos—San Jose French Camp or Weber Grant—Revolutionary Designs of the Foreigners—Treaty between Weber and Ha-soos—How it was observed by Ha-soos—Fremont's Expedition, 1844— David Kelsey—Thomas Lindsay—Policy of the Foreigners— Weber and Micheltorena at San Jose—John A. Sutter aids Micheltorena—A Revolutionary Document — The "Bear Flag"—Attempt to Settle the Grant, 1846—Isbel Brothers and Other Early Settlers—Twins, Second Children born in County, 1847—End of Stanislaus City—First Marriage, 1847 —Village of "Tuleburg"—William Gann, First Child born in 1847—Wild Horse Scheme—Resume.

CAPT. C. M. WEBER was born at Hombourg, Department of Mont Tonnerre, under the Emperor Napoleon I., on the 16th day of February, 1814. His parents were German. This province, about a year later, became a part of the Kingdom of Bavaria. His father was a minister, and held the position which in America would be called County School Superintendent. The Captain received an academic education—but not relishing an outlook that presented the ministry in the future, his education was cut short at the threshold of the classic, and a mercantile horoscope was cast for the years "that were not yet."

Being of an adventurous disposition, the land where Washington had fought and De Kalb had fallen held to his youthful imagination an irresistible attraction; and at the age of twenty-two he crossed the ocean, landed at New Orleans in the latter part of 1836, and for five years was a resident of Louisiana and Texas, when in the Spring of 1841, under medical advice, he visited St. Louis. In the meantime he had read in the newspapers the glowing descriptions of California given by Dr. John Marshe, a resident of the San Joaquin valley, and which were attracting considerable consideration in the States. The Captain—knowing that a trip across the plains, over the mountains of the west, and down into the California valleys would benefit his health, and, at the same time give him an opportunity to see this comparatively unknown country—decided to join an expedition then fitting out in that city for a trip to the Pacific slope, intending in the following Spring to continue his journey to Mexico, through that country, and ultimately, in that way, reach Louisiana, his final destination, having no intention of stopping in California longer, at the farthest, than through the ensuing Winter. But "the best laid schemes o' mice and men gang aft agley."

The party to which the Captain attached himself was a combination of emigrants for three different points: One party was destined for Oregon; another was a company of Jesuit priests going to the western wilds

*The portion of the history of San Joaquin is intimately connected with that of Amador, forming the connecting link between the Spanish and American settlement.

on a mission to the Indians, hoping to Christianize the tribes of Oregon and Idaho, their immediate destination was the missions of Cœur d' Alene and Pen d' Oreille, Father P. J. DeSmet, S. J., was the leading spirit, and his efforts in that field have been written, a brief page in history. and the red man still scalps his foes. The third was the California wing of the little emigrant army, and numbered among its party men whose subsequent acts helped materially to shape the destinies of the State which has since become a golden star in the galaxy of the Republic.

There were thirty-six in that party. One only was a woman—the first American lady, probably, who ever entered California—certainly the first to reach it from over the plains. Her name was Mrs. Nancy A. Kelsey. She was the wife of Benjamin Kelsey, and they had a little daughter named Ann. This family commenced their march then, and, like the wandering Jew, have never since found a place to stop and rest. The beauties of California could not keep them,—they moved away to the forests of Oregon, and then returned again to the El Dorado of the coast; but no sooner had they settled there than the spirit of unrest came whispering "move on," and over the plains again they started; they were attacked by the Camanches in Texas, lost everything, and their little girl was scalped by the savages. Stopping for a time, they once more started for California and now are possibly moving to some new scene.

The men of the party were:—

CAPT. J. B. BARTELSON; Captain of the party; returned to Missouri; is now dead.
JOHN BIDWELL; lives at Chico.
JOSEPH B. CHILES; still alive.
JOSIAH BELDEN; lives at San Jose and San Francisco.
CHARLES M. WEBER; died in Stockton, May 4, 1881.
CHARLES HOPPER; lives in Napa county.
HENRY HUBER; lives in San Francisco.
MITCHELL NYE; had a ranch at Marysville; probably now alive.
GREEN MCMAHON; lives in Solano county.
NELSON MCMAHON; died in New York.
TALBOT H. GREENE; returned East.
AMBROSE WALTON; returned East.
JOHN MCDONEL; returned East.
GEORGE HENSHAW; returned East.
ROBERT RYCKMAN; returned East.
WM. BETTY or BELTY; returned East by way of Santa Fe.
CHARLES FLUGGE; returned East.
GWIN PATTON; returned East; died in Missouri.
BENJIMAN KELSEY; was within a few years in Santa Barbara county, or at Clear Lake, Lake county.
ANDREW KELSEY; killed by Indians at Clear Lake.
JAMES JOHN or LITTLEJOHN; went to Oregon.
HENRY BROLASKY; went to Callao.
JAMES DOWSON; drowned in Columbia river.
MAJ. WALTON, drowned in Sacramento river.
GEORGE SHORTWELL; accidentally shot on the way out.
JOHN SWARTZ; died in California.
GROVE COOK; died in California.
D. W. CHANDLER; went to Sandwich Islands.
NICHOLAS DAWSON; dead.
THOMAS JONES; dead.
ROBERT H. THOMES; died in Tehama county, California, March 26, 1878.
ELIAS BARNET.
JAMES P. SPRINGER.
JOHN ROWLAND.

They left Independence, Missouri, May 8, 1841 and all traveled together as far as Fort Hall, near Salt Lake, where Capt. J. B. Bartelson's party, as named above, separated from the rest and started for California, without a guide, by the way of Mary's (now Humboldt) river, they went to Carson river, and from the latter, to the main channel of Walker's river, up which they went to near its source, from which point they commenced their passage of the Sierra Nevada, descending its western slope between the Stanislaus and Tuolumne rivers, reaching the San Joaquin valley and passing down along the Stanislaus, crossed the San Joaquin river and arrived at the Dr. Marshe ranch, near the eastern base of Mount Diablo; on the 4th of November, 1841, having been six months, lacking four days, on the way. Here the company rested for a number of days, and then disbanded, each going to the point in the country which his interests demanded. The Captain and a friend started for Sutter's Fort, having letters of introduction to Captain Sutter. They passed through the country now known as San Joaquin county, and beheld for the first time the land that the result of his own labors was to people within his life-time with thirty thousand souls.

The Winter of 1841–2 was spent by the Captain at Sutter's Fort, occupying his time by acting as overseer and assistant for Captain Sutter. While at the fort he found a quantity of seeds which had been laid away and apparently forgotten. They had been sent to Sutter by Wm. G. Ray, of the Hudson Bay Company, as a friendly expression of good will. The Captain, desiring to try an experiment, had the land around the fort prepared by Indians, and planted the seeds. Among them were three kinds of tobacco, a number of varieties of flowers, and some vegetables. The experiment proved a grand success, and in the Spring Sutter's Fort seemed like an enchanted fortress built in the midst of perennial gardens.

During the winter of 1841–2 José Jesus (pronounced Ho-za Ha-soos), the celebrated chief of the Si-yak-um-na tribe, visited the fort, at which time the Captain first met him. In after years there sprang up a warm friendship between these two men, that had much to do with the peaceable manner in which the country was afterwards settled by the whites. The Captain learned, in his intercourse with foreigners in the country, that there was germinating a principle or feeling which was in some localities freely

talked of, to eventually Americanize California; and, concluded with that prospect to look forward to, that he was fully warranted in casting his destinies with the other venturesome spirits who had decided to make Alta California their future home.

In the Spring he visited San Jose, and concluded to make that the point of his future business operations, until the time should come, if ever, when it would become necessary to wrest from Mexico a portion of the country, over which to hoist a flag with the "lone star."

We do not wish to be misunderstood in this matter. The intention of the leading pioneers of California, those who came here previous to June, 1846, with the intention of making this their home, without regard to their nationality, was to work a political change in the country, "peaceably if they could, forcibly if they must;" and this was to be done not because of any desire to injure the native Californians, nor in a spirit of conquest, but because it was evident to those clear-headed Argonauts that to make the country a prosperous one, (one that would warrant occupation by a people of progressive civilization), necessitated a radical change in the manner of administering the affairs of State.

This change they proposed to effect in connection with the native inhabitants, if they could; and if this could not be done, to eventually, when they became strong enough, wrest a portion of the territory from Mexico, and form a government of their own.

Captain Weber formed a copartnership with Guillermo Gulnac, and soon established a credit which enabled the firm to do a very large business. They were the first parties in that portion of the State to build a flouring mill and manufacture flour, combining with the business the manufacture of sea-biscuit or crackers, this mill having been erected and flour made in 1842. They also entered quite largely into the manufacture of soap and American shoes, being the first manufacturers of the latter in California.

In 1843, July 14th, Guillermo Gulnac petitioned Manuel Micheltorena, the Governor of California, for a grant of eleven square leagues, or forty-eight thousand acres of land, to be located in the vicinity of French Camp, in the San Joaquin valley. Captain Weber was the real party, the power behind the throne; Mr. Gulnac's name being used because he was a Mexican citizen, as only such could obtain grants. About this time the commercial partnership was dissolved, the Captain becoming the successor to the business, and Mr. Gulnac, his eldest son, Jose, and Peter Lassen, with several vaqueros, took the cattle belonging to them and Captain Weber, and proceeded to take possession of the applied-for grant, at first making their head-quarters where Stockton now is; but owing to the fact that the Hudson Bay trappers had left for the summer, they became alarmed for their personal safety among the Indians and moved their camp up to the Cosumnes river, so as to be in reach of Sutter's Fort for protection. Mr. Gulnac visited Captain Sutter, and was presented by that officer with a swivel gun such as the navy used in those days when attacking an enemy in small boats, mounting the swivel in the bow. This "young cannon" was to be used by Mr. Gulnac as a warning to the Indians to "flee from the wrath to come." It would make a "heap big noise" when fired, and was respected accordingly by the aborigines.

A statement will probably come in no place more opportune than here, of the reason which caused Captain Weber to desire the location of his proposed grant on the "up country side of the San Joaquin river." We have already given the political intentions of those pioneers which in 1843 had assumed so definite a form as to have caused the question to be discussed among them of where the division line was to be drawn between the Mexican provinces and the territory to be taken from them, in case it should result in that extreme measure; and the conclusion had been tacitly arrived at that the San Joaquin river and the bays of San Francisco, San Pablo and Suisun were to form the line of division. It will therefore be seen that a strong reason for choosing a locality north of the San Joaquin was to secure land where he could gradually concentrate his property within the limits of the country to be acquired. Another reason, for selecting this special locality, was the facilities it would give him for dealing with the Hudson Bay trappers, who made their head-quarters every winter at French Camp, from whom, in exchange for fur, he obtained ammunition, blankets, clothing, etc., of a better quality and at lower figures than could be obtained elsewhere at that time.

The attempt to settle the expected grant had failed because of the fears of Gulnac, and the Captain obtained a passport from the Alcalde of San Jose, and proceeded to visit Sutter's Fort, with a view of seeing the Indian chief, Ila-soos, and making a treaty of peace with him, if possible. After arriving in the country, an Indian runner was sent to find the chief, and ask him to meet the Captain at a given time and place. A meeting was arranged, and at the appointed time the two men, representatives of their races in the country, met. Captain Weber explained his plans to the Indian, stating that he was desirous of settling on land in the San Joaquin valley; that the Americans were desirous of being his allies and friends; that they were not coming to injure nor rob, but as friends to aid and benefit his tribe; that he wished to settle here to be beyond the reach of the Spaniards, in case of trouble between the Americans and native Californians, against whom this celebrated chief was waging an endless war. The result was a friendly alliance that remained unbroken to the end. The chief advised the building of the American village at the point where it was located, the present site of Stockton, and agreed to provide all the help necessary in the tilling of the soil, and to furnish a war party when called upon to defend the settlers' property against either Indians or Mexicans. The Captain was generous in his presents, and a friendship was started at the interview that lasted during the life of Ha-soos, and the Captain now remembers the Si-yak-um-na chief as one of his most reliable and valued friends of early days.

The inhabitants of to-day can little appreciate the importance at the time, and the immediate advantage accruing to the foreign population of the country resulting from that treaty. One may pass through the County of San Joaquin and ask the old settlers what they know of Ha-soos and his connection with this country in early days, and may find five persons in his travels that will remember the chief, and that he was friendly to the Americans; but they, with *one* exception, that of Capt. C. M. Weber, will give him no credit for being so, supposing that it was forced or indolent friendship. It has become popular with the historian, as well as the men of 1849 and later, to place the California Indians, in the scale of creation, but one step above the African gorilla. Whatever may have been the general rule, there certainly was an exception in favor of the aborigines occupying the territory between the Tuolumne and Mokelumne rivers. These Indians were divided up into rancherias or villages, each village having its chief and name. Consequently there was a number of petty chiefs, but all acknowledge an indefinite but undisputed supremacy and authority in the chief of the Si-yak-um-nas, Ho-za Ha-soos, who had made himself a terror to the Spanish inhabitants of North California. His name was to the native population what Osceola's was to the Floridians, except that the former chief was less brutal than the latter. He did not scalp his victims, like the Seminole, nor seek the midnight massacre of isolated persons.

He believed that he and his people had been wronged by the Spanish, and he would never smoke the pipe of peace with them. He would swoop down upon the plains and carry off their stock, taking it to his stronghold in the foot-hills of the Sierras; and if the missions or settlers of those valleys saw fit to attempt a rescue, he fought them, and was universally victorious. The San Joaquin river divided his territory from the Californians, and when east of that stream he was upon his native heath; and it was rare indeed that the pursuers followed him into his own country. They had learned better in their battle on the banks of the Stanislaus in 1829, when "Estanislao," the former chief of the Si-yak-um-nas, defeated their combined San Jose and Yerba Buena forces.

It will be seen that Ho-za Ha-soos was so circumstanced as to receive favorable advances from a people who gave as one of their reasons for desiring his friendship the probable hostility that might in the future exist between them and the Spanish people of the country. He believed that he was strengthening himself against his old foe. It will also be observed that the line beyond which the native Californians, even in armed parties, found it dangerous to pass, was the San Joaquin river. Beyond this it was considered and understood by them to be savage and inhospitable wilds. Ha-soos had made them respect that river as the *practical* north boundary line of their territory. Hence the propriety or policy of the foreign population in selecting this river as the south boundary of the country they proposed, under certain circumstances, to make into an independent state, along the borders of which they would have a picket line of Indian allies.

In this connection we will mention two instances in which Ha-soos demonstrated his good will to the Americans, carrying out, on his part, the spirit of the alliance he had made with Captain Weber; and we mention these with some hesitancy, not because of any doubt of the facts, but because it is hitherto unwritten history that may be questioned. The incidents referred to were related to us by Captain Weber, who says that when Captain Sutter passed through the country, in the Winter of 1844, to join and aid Manuel Micheltorena against the revolutionary General, Jose Castro, Ha-soos joined him with a number of warriors. And later, when Gen. J. C. Fremont passed through the San Joaquin valley south, to help take this country from Mexico, that this chief was again on hand, and accompanied him to San Jose, to fight his old foes, in the interest of his friends, the Americans. Whether he actually performed any military act of hostility to the enemy on either occasion does not appear, but that he was ready so to do was demonstrated by his presence with his warriors.

On the 13th of January, 1844, the Governor of California complied with the petition of Mr. Gulnac, and issued to him the grant of land known as "El Rancho del Campo de los Franceses," which in English means "The French Camp Ranch." After the issuing of the grant, the next event worthy of note in the county was the passage through it of Capt. J. C. Fremont, who, on the 25th of March of that year, camped over night at the place since known as the village of Liberty, on the south side of Dry creek. It was in his memorable first expedition to the Pacific coast. He had been at Sutter's Fort recruiting and had started south on his way through the San Joaquin valley en route for the States. The following taken from the published history of his expedition, will have peculiar interest to the residents of this county:—

"March 25th—We traveled for twenty-eight miles over the same delightful country as yesterday, and halted in a beautiful bottom at the ford of the *Rio de los Mukelemnes*, receiving its name from another Indian tribe living on the river. The bottoms on the stream are broad, rich, and extremely fertile; and the uplands are shaded with oak groves. A showy *lupinus* of extraordinary beauty, growing four or five feet in height, and covered with spikes in bloom, adorned the banks of the river, and filled the air with a light and grateful perfume.

"On the 26th we halted at the *Arroyo de los Calaveras* (Skull creek), a tributary to the San Joaquin—the previous two streams entering the bay between the San Joaquin and Sacramento rivers. This place is beautiful, with open groves of oak, and a grassy sward beneath, with many plants in bloom; some varieties of which seem to love the shade of the trees, and grow there in close, small fields. Near the river, and replacing the grass, are great quantities of *ammole* (soap plant), the leaves of which are used in California for making, among other things, mats for saddle cloths. A vine with a small white flower (*melothria*) called here *la yerba buena*, and which from its abundance, gives name to an island and town in the bay, was to-day very frequent on our road—sometimes running on the ground or climbing the trees.

"March 27th—To-day we traveled steadily and rapidly up the valley; for with our wild animals any other gait was impossible, and making about four miles an hour. During the earlier part of the day, our ride had been over a very level part of prairie, separated by lines and groves of oak timber, growing along dry gullies, which are filled with water in seasons of rain; and, perhaps, also by the melting snows. Over much of this extent, the vegetation was sparse; the surface showing plainly the action of water, which, in the season of flood, the Joaquin spreads over the valley. At one o'clock we came again among innumerable flowers; and a few miles further, fields of the beautiful blue flowering *lupine*, which seems to love the neighborhood of water, indicated that we were approaching a stream. We have found this beautiful shrub in thickets, some of them being twelve feet in height. Occasionally three or four plants were clustered together, forming a grand bouquet, about ninety feet in circumference, and ten feet high; the whole summit covered with spikes of flowers, the perfume of which is very sweet and grateful. A lover of natural beauty can imagine with what pleasure we rode among these flowering groves, which filled the air with a light and delicate fragrance. We continued our road for about half a mile, interspersed through an open grove of live-oaks, which, in form, were the most symmetrical and beautiful we had yet seen in the country. The ends of their branches rested on the ground forming somewhat more than a half sphere of very full and regular figure, with leaves apparently smaller than usual. The Californian poppy, of a rich orange color, was numerous. To-day, elk and several bands of antelope made their appearance.

"Our road was now one continued enjoyment; and it was pleasant, riding among this assemblage of green pastures with varied flowers and scattered groves, and out of the warm, green Spring, to look at the rocky and snowy peaks, where lately we had suffered so much. Emerging from the timber we came suddenly upon the Stanislaus river, where we hoped to find a ford, but the stream was flowing by, dark and deep, swollen by the mountain snows; its general breadth was about fifty yards.

"We traveled about five miles up the river, and encamped without being able to find a ford. Here we made a large *corral*, in order to be able to catch a sufficient number of our wild animals to relieve those previously packed.

Under the shade of the oaks, along the river, I noticed *erodium cicutarium* in bloom, eight or ten inches high. This is the plant which we had seen the squaws gathering on the Rio de los Americanos. By the inhabitants of the valley, it is highly esteemed for fattening cattle, which appear to be very fond of it. Here, where the soil begins to be sandy, it supplies to a considerable extent the want of grass.

"Desirous, as far as possible, without delay, to include in our examination the Joaquin river, I returned this morning down the Stanislaus, for seventeen miles, and again encamped without having found a fording-place. After following it for eight miles further the next morning, and finding ourselves in the vicinity of the San Joaquin, encamped in a handsome oak grove, and, several cattle being killed, we ferried over our baggage in their skins. Here our Indian boy, who probably had not much idea of where he was going, and began to be alarmed at the many streams we were putting between him and the village, deserted.

"Thirteen head of cattle took a sudden fright, while we were driving them across the river, and galloped off. I remained a day in the endeavor to recover them; but finding they had taken the trail back to the fort, let them go without further effort. Here we had several days of warm and pleasant rain, which doubtless saved the crops below."

In August, 1844, David Kelsey, with his wife and two children, a boy and a girl, settled at French Camp, and built a tule-house. Mr. Gulnac, who was stopping at the Cosumnes river, had offered to give Mr. Kelsey a mile square of land if he would stop at that place, and live one year; he turned over to him the "swivel" that Sutter had given him. Every night Mr Kelsey threw this piece of ordnance "into battery," and fired an evening gun; which he did to frighten the Indians, on the same principle that a boy sometimes whistles as he is going through the woods after dark. At that time there was only one other house in the county, also constructed of tule, occupied by Thomas Lindsay, at Stockton.

Mr. Kelsey remained for several months at that place, and after his family had been obliged to live for two months on boiled wheat, meat, milk, and mint tea, gathered along the banks of the creek, he buried the swivel and removed temporarily to San Jose, where he first saw Captain Weber. While at that place he unfortunately went to see a sick Indian who had the small-pox, just before returning to French Camp. After returning he was immediately taken sick, and Mrs. Kelsey desired to take him to Sutter's Fort, where he could have medical assistance, not knowing that he had the small-pox. When they reached Stockton, Mr. Lindsay induced them to stay over night, and while there a man by the name of James Williams gave him some medicine that caused the disease to break out. Lindsay immediately vacated the premises, giving, as he left, advice that has a twang of barbarism in it; he told them if the old man died to leave his body where the coyotes would devour it. In about six days the father died, the mother and boy were prostrated with the same disease, and little America, a girl eleven years of age, was left alone with her sick mother and brother, to administer to their wants, while her dead father lay unburied in the hut; a sad introduction to the first American girl who ever saw the place where Stockton now stands, and a sadder one to the first white woman that visited the place, for the mother became blind from the effects of the disease, beholding that delirious, weird scene of pestilence and death as the last, to haunt the memory through the coming years of darkness; a hideous phantom, a scene of desolation, was that last look of the mother upon the surroundings of that little child nurse.

Some herders chanced to come that way, who, after considerable hesitation, assisted little America in burying her father. One of them, Geo. F. Wyman, afterwards became the husband of America. The reason why they hesitated in coming to her assistance was a double one,—they feared the contagion and Captain Sutter, who had said he would have any man shot who brought small-pox to the fort, or went among the Indians who had it. The father was buried near where Col. Thos. R. Moseley's house now stands, and in a few days the little nurse was stricken down with the dread disease, but recovered so as to be able to leave for Monterey in about six weeks. In about two weeks after they left, Thomas Lindsay returned to his house on Lindsay's Point, in Stockton, and was killed by the Luck-lum-na Indians, from Ione valley, in Amador county, who fired the tule-house with their victim's body in it, and drove off all the stock. A party of whites, Mexicans and friendly Indians, went in pursuit of the band who had committed the depredations, and overtook them at the place called the "Island," near the foot-hills, where a conflict occurred, resulting in the burning of the Indian rancheria, with what provisions and property they had, the killing of a few of the warriors of the hostile tribe, and the capture of one Indian boy by William Daylor, of Daylor's ranch; one Mexican by the name of Vaca, a member of the Vaca family, formerly of Solano county, was killed by the Indians in the fight. After this defeat they retreated into the mountains, where they were followed, but not overtaken."

*Since the foregoing was written in 1879, some further facts have come to our knowledge, which not only puts this matter in a different light but also demonstrates the difficulty of making the first attempt at writing history successful.

D. T. Bird, who, at one time, was an officer in the California battalion under Fremont, during the hostilities that succeeded the Bear Flag war, says that he was one of the parties that pursued the Indians who murdered Lindsay at Stockton, and he takes the poetry all out of the conclusion given to that expedition. Instead of the Luck-lum-na Indians of Ione valley being chastised, they whipped the pursuing party (about thirty strong, half whites and half friendly Indians), who were under the command of Captain Merritt, of Bear Flag fame. Captain Sutter organized the pursuing party, and among the white men accompanying it, were Captain Merritt, D. T. Bird, Charles Heath, Vaca (a Spaniard), Hicks and Gillespie. The fight was a short one, resulting in Vaca's receiving a mortal wound from an arrow

The small-pox and the breaking out of the Micheltorena war, combined, had depopulated the county.

There had been, in the latter part of 1844, and Spring of 1845, a serious departure by the foreign population of the country from their understood policy, in their intercourse with the natives of California; which was a policy of non-intervention between opposing factions of the country, that had been decided upon and agreed to between the leading men, as being the best calculated to produce the final result at which they were aiming. Let the Spanish population quarrel to their hearts' content, let civil war sweep over the country, and array the opposing factions against each other on the battle field; it helped to prepare the people of all classes, foreign and native, for a change; but in every emergency the American, the German, the Englishman, the immigrant, whatever his native land was to hold himself aloof, reserving his strength to be used as one man for the general good of all, when the proper time should come to act. All over California, from Los Angeles to Monterey, and from Monterey to Sutter's Fort, the foreign population were few in numbers, one and two, sometimes a half-dozen in a place, so scattered and so isolated that a false move on the part of a few might prove fatal to many; it consequently was important at that time that the policy of non-interference should be pursued. Yet, as we have previously mentioned, a serious departure from that policy was inaugurated in the Micheltorena war, without, apparently, any general consultation or plan on the part of immigrants, those of each section or country marking out their own line of action, regardless of the probable consequent injury that might result to those of a different locality.

The first instance was that forced upon Capt. C. M. Weber, consequent from the loss of control, by Micheltorena, over the outlaws called soldiers, whom he commanded in 1844. The Captain was in business at the Pueblo of San Jose when the war broke out, and was acquainted with and personally friendly to both Micheltorena and Castro. He had a very large stock of goods in the place, and was anxious on account of it. He knew that the soldiers under Micheltorena were mostly convicts, turned loose from the prisons in Mexico, and were dependent upon the meager revenue derived from forced loans and plunder for their pay. His goods

that entered his side. In attempting to draw it from his body, the arrow-head was broken from the shaft, and in an hour the unfortunate man was dead. Up to the time of his death they managed to hold their position, when, finding the enemy too strong for them, the body of the dead Spaniard was laid upon a pile of brush and burned, to prevent its falling into the hands of the savages; after which they stole away in the darkness, and reached Sutter's Fort without unnecessary delay.

would be a rich prize, and if they once entered San Jose, they would be sure to help themselves to what he had; consequently all his interests were opposed to the occupation of the town by such a body of men. As Micheltorena advanced, Jose Castro became alarmed, and, leaving San Jose to its fate, retreated up the valley towards Oakland with his forces; whereupon Captain Weber addressed a communication to the commander of the advancing forces, stating that Castro had left San Jose, and asked him if he would not pass to one side of the pueblo, and not enter it with his troops. Micheltorena replied that he found it necessary to pass through San Jose in his pursuit of Castro. In the meantime the Captain received prompt information to the effect that the Governor had lost control of his soldiery, who insisted on entering the village for plunder; whereupon the Captain caused the tocsin of war to be sounded through the streets. The people assembled, and the Captain presented the position of affairs, and told them that he believed, with a force composed of the citizens and foreigners in the place, the advancing army could be checked, and forced to take a different route in their line of march after Castro. A company was immediately formed, placed under his command, and moved out to meet the enemy, a handful against a host. Sending a courier in advance to meet Micheltorena, advising him of what he was doing, and that it was done, not in a spirit of opposition to him personally, or the cause which he represented, but with a determination to protect their homes from plunder. The forces met some twelve miles out from the village, and for several days the entire army, numbering several hundred, was held in check by this little band of brave men under Captain Weber. Castro, hearing of the fact, became ashamed of himself, turned back from his retreat, joined the Captain with his forces, took command of the army, and forced Micheltorena to surrender, and, finally, to agree to leave California and return to Mexico. For the time this ended the war. It was again revived by Micheltorena, who failed to comply with his agreement when he learned that Capt. John A. Sutter could be relied upon for assistance. Sutter, wishing to retain the old régime until his land titles were perfected, in December, 1844, marched to the lower country with his deluded followers, being met on the way, at the residence of Dr. John Marshe, by J. Alex. Forbes, of the Hudson Bay Company, who tried to dissuade him from proceeding further with the enterprise, but without avail, telling the Captain at the same time that in General Castro's army was a large number of Americans, and that his act was arraying the foreign-born population against each other. Sutter's reply to all was that he had gone too far to withdraw without discredit to himself. He pushed on towards the south, and his men, suspecting something wrong, began to desert until but few remained. Finally, when the hostile armies stood face to face, a parley was insisted upon, and it was found that the foreigners were fighting in the ranks of both armies; after which, Sutter had, practically, no followers, and fell, finally, into the hands of Castro, who, but for the strong intervention of friends, would have had him shot.

This unfortunate proceeding was the second breach in the policy of non-intervention; and it came so near becoming disastrous, that it called forth an expression of disapprobation for the course pursued; such a policy continued would Mexicanize the Americans, not Americanize the Mexicans. The result was that the narrow escape demonstrated the necessity of an organized plan of action, so that in future they might be well advised of all contemplated movements, and act together as a body and thus make themselves felt, instead of expending their force against each other. With a view of accomplishing this object, and thus pave the way for the future segregation of California from Mexico, a call was written, subscribed and circulated. * * * *

For various causes there was not as formidable a gathering as was desired at the time designated,* and the meeting only included those within easy reach of San Jose; there was consequently nothing of importance accomplished, and there was a failure to obtain a general organization; but the purposes of the foreign population remained unchanged, and culminated, finally, in the hoisting of the "Bear Flag," which, but for the United States taking the struggle off their hands, would have proved to be what it was in fact, a premature move. It was entered upon without general consultation or matured plan, and but for the occupation of the country by the United States, which occurred a little later, would have proved disastrous to many foreigners living farther south, who were wholly unadvised in regard to the movement. Had the organization been made as was contemplated by the signers of the instrument, the Bear Flag would never have been raised, but without the intervention of the United States it would have resulted in taking the country from Mexico, making San Joaquin one of the frontier counties of the State.

It is not the purpose of this work to give a State history, therefore we return to the march of events in San Joaquin, having followed those occurrences outside only which had a direct bearing upon the history of this county.

On the third day of April, 1845, C. M. Weber purchased of Mr. Guinac the remaining interest in the French Camp Grant, Mr. Weber becoming its sole owner; but no further attempt was made at settlement until 1846, when he induced a number of settlers, under the leadership of Napoleon Schmidt, to locate. They had no sooner become settled in their new homes than the war-cloud burst, which had been hanging over the country, and the settlers

* July 4, 1845.

again scattered to locations where they would be less isolated in case of an attack by the Mexicans.

In November, 1846, the Isbel brothers took up land on the Calaveras, that stream dividing their ranches or claims; Dr. I. C. Isbel occupying the north, and his brother James the south side of the "river of skulls," where Fremont had crossed it in 1844. The doctor erected a log cabin near the river, which is still standing. It is the oldest house in the county, in fact the oldest in the San Joaquin valley, and should be preserved as a relic of the past. The same month and year, Turner Elder erected a cabin on Dry creek, where the village of Liberty was afterwards laid out. Mr. Elder was a married man, and had brought his wife and three little children with him to this country. On the opposite, or north side of the creek, and a little further down, his father-in-law, Thomas Rhodes, located. Thomas Pyle settled at what is now known as Staples' Ferry, in the same year and month, with his family—a wife and two children. It was during the month of November, 1846, that Samuel Brannan established his colony on the Stanislaus, about one and one-half miles above its mouth, calling the place "Stanislaus City."

It will be observed that during this year, two distinct colonies were established, and four ranches taken up in San Joaquin county, at the points where the old Spanish trail, between Sutter's Fort and San Jose, crossed the several streams in the county. This was a strong demonstration toward settlement. Weber's party had left at the first notes of alarm ; Samuel Brannan's colony remained until the following Spring, and then all left, except Buckland—leaving only the ranchers on the Spanish trail and Buckland, as the inhabitants to dispute possession of the county with the Indians. The five settlers remaining were Dr. I. C. Isbel, and his brother, James, on the Calaveras; Thomas Pyle, on the Mokelumne; Turner Elder, on Dry creek; and Buckland, on the Stanislaus.

* Dr. Isbel retained his claim until 1848, when he sold to the Hutchinson brothers, and they in turn to Mr. Dodge.

Thomas Pyle abandoned his place in 1848, and moved to Coyote creek, near San Jose, where he was shot through the head and killed, about 1855, by a young Spaniard. A man by the name of Smith took up the place, claiming a grant, and sold to John F., the brother of Thomas Pyle, and John W. Laird, who had married one of his sisters. These parties sold to Staples, Nichols & Co., in February, and moved from there in April, 1850. Mr. Laird died near Grayson, in May, 1878; and J. F. Pyle is still living on his ranch, near Weldon, on Kern river, California.

Turner Elder lived at Dry creek about one

* Dr. Isbel is mentioned in another part of the history in connection with a mob affair in the western part of the county (Amador). He resided in Volcano, in 1855.

year, and then moved on to the north bank of the Mokelumne river, at the place afterwards known as the "Benedict Ranch," and, while there, on the fifth day of November, 1847, his wife *presented him with a pair of twins*, a boy and girl, who were named John and Nancy. These were the second children born of white parents in the county. Soon after the birth of these children, on account of the unprotected position, Mr. Elder abandoned his place and joined his brother-in-law Daylor, of the Daylor ranch, in Sacramento county. He afterwards made money in placer mining, and returned to Ray county, Missouri, in 1849, where he now lives. The children are both living; the girl in Ray county, as the wife of a Dr. Reese; and the boy, now married, at Emigrant's Ditch, in Fresno county, California—his post-office address being " Kingsbury Switch."

Mr. Buckland, of Stanislaus City, moved from there to Stockton, in the fall of 1847. Assisted by William Fairchilds, he afterwards built the Buckland House, in San Francisco. Of the Stanislaus City settlers, the only ones known to be living now are Samuel Brannan, of San Francisco, John M. Horner, near San Jose, and —— Nichols, of San Leandro.

When, in the Fall of 1847, Turner Elder left his log-house and claim at Dry creek, Mrs. Christina Patterson, his aunt, moved into it—her husband having died of mountain fever while crossing the mountains in 1846. She was soon after married to Ned Robinson. This was the *first marriage ceremony performed in the county*. Mr. Robinson, in turn, abandoned the place when gold was discovered, in January, 1848, and in 1878 they were stopping at French Camp, for the Winter, on their way to the northern country.

Captain Weber, in the meantime, had been living at San Jose from 1842 to 1847, following his business of merchandizing, and not giving personal attention to the settlement of his grant. During the year 1847 he sold his stock of goods, and in August of that year, with a number of men, two hundred horses and four thousand cattle, moved to the San Joaquin, and founded a settlement which became permanent; Stockton being the point and result of his efforts. In the Fall, the grant was surveyed and sectionized by Jasper O'Farrell, through his deputy, Walter Herron; a village site being at the same time laid out for settlers' homes, which received the name of "Tuleburg." Coming events had not yet "cast their shadows before." The village plat of Tuleburg, and the name, both passed out of existence at the same time, when, in 1848, after the gold discovery, the place was re-surveyed and laid out for commercial purposes by Captain Weber, who gave it the name of Stockton, after Com. Robert Stockton, of the United States navy.

In October, 1847, a company of overland immigrants arrived at the place, on their way to the lower country. Mr. Weber persuaded them to stop for a time and look over the valley, to see if they would not consider it to their advantage to remain. W. H. Fairchilds, County Supervisor in 1878, was of this party, as well as Nicholas Gann and his wife, Ruth, who, while they were camping on the point where Weber's house now stands, in October, gave birth to a son, to whom they gave the name of William. This was the first child born of white parents in the county. With the exception of Mr. Fairchilds, the parties all decided to move farther south. Mr. Nicholas Gann now lives not far from Gilroy, in Santa Clara county, California.

It was during that year that Capt. Charles Imus undertook to carry out a "wild horse scheme." He selected a point on the San Joaquin river, where San Joaquin City now stands, which he considered favorable, and then went to the mountains west of the valley and commenced cutting timber, to build a corral, into which he proposed driving wild horses, and there to capture them; when Pico, on whose grant he was cutting the timber, put a stop to his visions of corralling the "untamed steeds of the desert;" by singing to him the pathetic song of "Woodman, Spare that Tree," and the Captain, not caring to verify the old saw of "a nod is as good as a kick for a blind horse," folded up his tent like the Arab, and departed into the lower country. Captain Imus was the leader of the party that crossed the plains in 1846, of which the Pyles, Isbels, Elders, and Rhodes were members.

The history of San Joaquin county, up to the close of 1847, has been given in the preceding pages as completely as it is possible to get it from the memory of the participants who still survive. The only occupants of this section of country, up to that time, had first been the Indians, then the American trappers, followed by the Hudson Bay Company, who were succeeded in turn by the Americans, who came from the States, with a view of making for themselves and families permanent homes.

But a change, absolute and radical, lay hid in the near future. On the line that separated the year 1847, and what had preceded it, from "the future that was not yet," stands a mile-post that "Time," set by the wayside, which marks the beginning of a year, in which was wrought a change as absolute, in the march of human events, and the destinies of this coast, as would ordinarily have occurred in the passing of a century.

CHAPTER X.

BIOGRAPHIC SKETCH OF GENERAL SUTTER.

His Nativity—Migration to the American West—Arrival in California—Foundation of Sutter's Fort—Prosperity and Wealth of the Colony—Decline and Ultimate Ruin—Retirement to Hock Farm—Extract from Sutter's Diary.

THE following sketch of the life and adventures of General John A. Sutter is from Oscar T. Shuck's "Representative Men of the Pacific." The facts were derived directly from the famous old pioneer, and are, perhaps, the most complete and accurate that have ever been published. Mr. Shuck says:—

"General John A. Sutter was born March 1, 1803, in the Grand Duchy of Baden, where his early boyhood was passed. His father, who was a clergyman of the Lutheran church, afterwards removed to Switzerland, and settled there with his family. He purchased for himself and heirs the rights and immunities of Swiss citizenship, and there the subject of our sketch received a good education, both civil and military.

"Early in life he married a Bernese lady, and was blessed with several children. At the age of thirty-one he determined to gratify a desire he had long cherished to immigrate to the United States. Not knowing whether or not he should settle permanently in the Great Republic, he concluded to leave his family behind him, and arrived at New York in July, 1834. After visiting several of the Western States he settled in Missouri, and there resided for several years. During his residence in Missouri he made a short visit to New Mexico, where he met with many trappers and hunters who had returned from Upper California, and their glowing descriptions confirmed his previous impressions, and excited an ardent desire to behold and wander over the rich lands and beautiful valleys of that then almost unknown region. Upon returning to Missouri he determined to reach the Pacific coast by joining some one of the trapping expeditions of the American or English Fur Companies. But great obstacles were to be surmounted, and long years were to intervene before his feet would rest upon the virgin soil of California. On the 1st of April, 1838, he was enabled, for the first time, to connect himself with a trapping expedition. On that day he left Missouri with Captain Tripp, of the American Fur Company, and traveled with his party to their rendezvous in the Rocky Mountains. There he parted with the expedition, and with six horsemen crossed the mountains, and, after encountering the usual dangers and hardships, arrived at Fort Vancouver, on the Columbia river.

"Having learned that there was no land communication with California from the valleys of the Columbia or Willamette in Winter, and there being then a vessel of the Hudson Bay Company ready to sail for the Sandwich Islands, General Sutter took passage, hoping to find at the islands some means of conveyance to California. Only one of the men who had remained with him thus far consented to accompany him to the strange land. On reaching the islands he found no prospect of conveyance, and, after remaining five months, as the only means of accomplishing his purpose, he shipped as supercargo, without pay, on an English vessel bound for Sitka.

"After discharging her cargo at Sitka, and, with the authority of the owners, he directed the vessel southward, and sailed down the coast, encountering

heavy gales. He was driven into the Bay of San Francisco in distress, and, on the second day of July, 1839, anchored his little craft opposite Yerba Buena, now San Francisco.

"He was immediately waited upon by a Mexican official with an armed force, and ordered to leave without delay, the officer informing him that Monterey was the port of entry. He succeeded, however, in obtaining permission to remain forty-eight hours to get supplies.

"A few days later, upon arriving at Monterey, General Sutter waited upon Governor Alvarado, and communicated to him his desire to settle in Upper California, on the Sacramento. Governor Alvarado expressed much satisfaction upon learning his visit or a wish, particularly when he understood his desire to settle on the Sacramento, saying that the Indians in that quarter were very hostile, and would not permit any whites to settle there; that they robbed the inhabitants of San Jose and the lower settlements of horses and cattle. He readily gave Sutter a passport, with authority to settle on any territory he should deem suitable for his colony, and requested him to return to Monterey one year from that time, when his Mexican citizenship would be acknowledged, and he would receive a grant for the land he might select. Thereupon, he returned to Yerba Buena and chartered a schooner, with some small boats, and started upon an exploring expedition on the Sacramento river.

"Upon inquiry he could not find any one at Yerba Buena who had ever seen the Sacramento river, or who could describe to him where he should find its mouth. The people of that place only professed to know that some large river emptied into one of the connected bays lying northerly from their town. General Sutter consumed eight days in the effort to find the mouth of the Sacramento river.

"After ascending the river to a point about ten miles below where Sacramento City now stands, he encountered the first large party of Indians, who exhibited every sign of hostility save an actual attack. There were about two hundred of them, armed and painted for war. Fortunately there were among them two who understood Spanish, and with whom the General engaged in conversation. He quieted them by the assurance that there were no Spaniards in his party, and that he wished to settle in their country and trade with them. He showed them his agricultural implements and commodities of trade, which he had provided for the purpose, and proposed to make a treaty with them. Pleased with these assurances, the Indians became reconciled; the crowd dispersed, and the two who spoke the Spanish language accompanied Sutter and his party as far as the mouth of Feather river, to show him the country. All other parties of Indians seen fled at the sight of the vessel and boats.

"Parting with his two Indian interpreters and guides at the mouth of Feather river, he ascended the latter stream to a considerable distance, when a few of his white men became alarmed at the surrounding dangers and insisted upon returning, which he was constrained to do.

"On his descent he entered the mouth of the American river, and on the 15th day of August, 1839, landed at the point on the south bank of that stream, where he afterwards established his tannery within the present limits of Sacramento. On the following morning, after landing all his effects, he informed the discontented whites that all who wished to return to Yerba Buena could do so; that the Kanakas were willing to remain, and that he had resolved to do so, if alone. Three of the whites determined to leave, and he put them in possession of the schooner, with instructions to deliver the vessel to her owners. They set sail for Yerba Buena the same day.

"Three weeks thereafter General Sutter removed to the spot upon which he afterwards erected Fort Sutter. In the early days of the settlement he encountered many troubles with the Indians, who organized secret expeditions, as he afterwards learned, to destroy him and his party, but he contrived to defeat and frustrate all their machinations, and those of the Indians who were at first his greatest enemies, came to be his best and most steadfast friends. He now devoted himself energetically to agriculture, and became very wealthy and prosperous.

"In the Fall of the year 1839, he purchased of Señor Martinez three hundred head of cattle, thirty horses, and thirty mares. During the Fall eight more white men joined his colony. When he commenced the improvements that resulted in the erection of Sutter's Fort and his establishment there, he had much trouble in procuring suitable lumber and timber. He floated some down the American river from the mountains, and was compelled to send to Bodega, on the sea-coast, a distance of several hundred miles.

"In August, 1840, Sutter was joined by the five men who had crossed the Rocky Mountains with him, and whom he had left in Oregon. His colony now numbered twenty-five men, seventeen whites and eight Kanakas. During the Fall of that year the Mokelumne Indians became troublesome, by stealing the live-stock of the settlers, and compelled General Sutter, by their acts and menaces, to make open war against them. He marched with his forces thirty miles, in the night time, to the camp of the Indians, where they were concentrating large forces for a movement against him, some two hundred warriors, and attacked them with such great effect that they retreated, and being hotly pursued, they sued for peace, which was readily granted, and ever afterwards mutually maintained.

"Shortly after this encounter, Sutter purchased one thousand more head of cattle, and seventy-five horses and mules. His colony continued to increase fast, by the addition of every foreigner who came into the country; they sought his place as one of security. The trappers he furnished with supplies, and purchased their furs; the mechanics and laborers he either employed or procured them work.

"In June, 1841, he visited Monterey, the capital, where he was declared a Mexican citizen, and received from Governor Alvarado a grant for his land, under the name of New Helvetia, a survey of which he had caused to be made before that time. Thereupon he was honored with a commission as 'representante del Governo en las fronter as del norte y encargado de la justicia.'

"Soon after his return to his settlement he was visited by Captain Ringgold, of the United States Exploring Expedition under Commodore Wilkes, and about the same time by Alexander Rotchoff, Governor of the Russian Possessions, Ross and Bodega, who offered to sell to General Sutter the Russian Possessions, settlements, and ranches at those places.

"The terms were such as induced him to make the purchase, for thirty thousand dollars. The live-stock consisted of two thousand cattle, over one thousand horses, fifty mules, and two thousand sheep, the

greater part of which were driven to New Helvetia. This increase of resources, together with the natural increase of his stock, enabled him the more rapidly to advance his settlement and improvements.

"In the year 1844 he petitioned Governor Micheltorena for the grant or purchase of the *sobrante*, or surplus, over the first eleven leagues of the land within the bounds of the survey accompanying the Alvarado grant, which the Governor agreed to let him have; but, for causes growing out of existing political troubles, the grant was not finally executed until the 5th of February, 1845; during which time he had rendered valuable military services and advanced to the Government large amounts of property and outlays, exceeding eight thousand dollars, to enable it to suppress the Castro rebellion; in consideration of all which he acquired by purchase and personal services the lands called the Sobrante, or surplus.

"At that time he also secured from Governor Micheltorena the commission of 'Commandante militar de las fronteras del norte y encargado de la justicia.' After this time the war between the United States and Mexico came on, and although General Sutter was an officer under the Mexican Government, and bound to it by his allegiance, yet, upon all occasions, such was his respect towards the citizens and institutions of the United States, that whenever any party of American citizens, civil or military service, visited him, his unbounded hospitalities were uniformly and cordially extended to them; and when the country surrendered to the American forces, the General, who had been for some time convinced of the instability of the Mexican Government, upon request, did, on the 11th of July, 1846, hoist the American flag with a good heart, accompanied with a salute of artillery from the guns at the fort. Soon after this Lieutenant Missoon, of the United States Navy, came up and organized a garrison for Sutter's Fort, principally out of his former forces of whites and Indians, and gave to General Sutter the command, which he maintained until peace returned. He was then appointed by Commodore Stockton Alcalde of the district, and by General Kearney Indian Agent, with a salary of seven hundred and fifty dollars a year; but a single trip in discharge of his duty as Indian Agent cost him one thousand six hundred dollars, and he resigned the office.

"General Sutter was now in the full tide of prosperity. His settlement continued to grow and his property to accumulate, until the latter part of January, 1848. He had then completed his establishment at the fort; had performed all the conditions of his grants of land; had, at an expense of at least twenty-five thousand dollars, cut a race of three miles in length, and nearly completed a flouring-mill near the present town of Brighton; had expended towards the erection of a saw-mill, near the town of Coloma, about ten thousand dollars; had sown over a thousand acres of land in wheat which promised a yield of forty thousand bushels, and had made preparations for other crops; was then the owner of eight thousand head of cattle, over two thousand horses and mules, over two thousand sheep, and one thousand head of hogs, and was in the undisturbed, undisputed and quiet possession of the extensive lands granted by the Mexican Government. But a sad change was about to take place in the affairs of the old pioneer; a grand event was about to transpire, which, while it would delight and electrify the world at large, was destined to check the growth of the settlement at Sutter's Fort. General Sutter's mills were soon to cease operations; his laborers and mechanics were soon to desert him; his possessions, his riches, his hopes were soon to be scattered and destroyed before the impetuous charge of the gold-hunters. The immediate effect was that Sutter was deserted by all his mechanics and laborers, white, Kanaka and Indian. The mills thus deserted became a dead loss; he could not hire labor to further plant or mature his crops, or reap but a small part after the grain had ripened. Few hands were willing to work for even an ounce a day, as the industrious could make more than that in the mines. Consequent of the gold discovery there was an immense immigration, composed of all classes of men, many of whom seemed to have no idea of the rights of property. The treaty between the United States and Mexico guaranteed to the Mexican who should remain in the country a protection of his property, and Sutter regarded himself as doubly entitled to that protection, either as a Mexican or a citizen of the United States, and that he held a strong claim upon his country's justice. His property was respected for a season; but when the great flood of immigration, which poured into the country in 1849-'50, found that money could be made by other means than mining, many of the new-comers forcibly entered upon his land, and commenced cutting his wood, under the plea that it was vacant and unappropriated land of the United States. Up to the first of January, 1852, the settlers had occupied all his lands capable of settlement or appropriation, and the other class had stolen all his horses, mules, cattle, sheep and hogs, save a small portion used and sold by himself. One party of five men, during the high waters of 1849-'50, when his cattle were partly surrounded by water near the Sacramento river, killed and sold enough to amount to sixty thousand dollars.

"Having seen his power decline and his riches take wings, General Sutter removed to the west bank of Feather river, and took up his residence at Hock farm. Here, in the midst of his family, who had recently arrived from Europe, he led the quiet life of a farmer in the county that bears his name."

The following *verbatim* copy of notes in General Sutter's own handwriting, we insert, notwithstanding there are some repetitions of facts given in the former part of this chapter:—

[The following rough notes of narrative, in the handwriting of the venerable General Sutter, the discoverer of gold in California, were found amongst the papers of an eminent citizen of this State, recently deceased, through the kindly courtesy of whose widow we are enabled to give them to the public. As a relation of incidents in the life of a man held in respect by every Californian, these hasty and imperfect memoranda will, it is believed, have a double interest and a lasting value. We have thought it best to preserve as nearly as was practicable, the quaint phraseology, erroneous orthography, and imperfect punctuation of the manuscript; giving, in our judgment, an added charm to the narrative.—*San Francisco Argonaut.*]

"Left the State of Missouri (where I has resided for a many years) on the 1th a April, 1838, and travelled with the party of Men under Capt Tripps, of the Amer. fur Compy, to their Rendezvous in the Rocky Mountains (Wind River Valley) from there I travelled with 6 brave Men to Oregon, as I considered myself not strong enough to cross the Sierra Nevada and go direct to California (which was my intention from my first Start on having got some informations from a Gent'n in New Mexico, who has been in California.

"Under a good Many Dangers and other troubles I have passed the Different forts or trading posts of the Hudsons Bay Compy. and arrived at the Mission at the Dalls on Columbia River. From this place I crossed right strait through thick & thin, and arrived to the great astonishment of the inhabitants. I arrived in 7 days in the Valley of the Willamette, while others with good guides arrived only in 17 days previous my Crossing. At fort Vancouver I has been very hospitably received and invited to pass the Winter with the Gentlemen of the Company, but as a Vessel of the Compy was ready to sail for the Sandwich Islands, I took a passage in her, in hopes to get Soon a Passage from there to California, but 5 long Months I had to wait to find an Opportunity to leave, but not direct to California, except far out of my Way to the Russian American Colonies on the North West Cost, to Sitka the Residence of the Gov'r, (Lat. 57) I remained one Month there and delivered the Cargo of the Brig Clementine, as I had Charge of the Vessel, and then sailed down the Coast in heavy Gales, and entered in Distress in the Port of San Francisco, on the 2d of July, 1839. An Officer and 15 Soldiers came on board and ordered me out, saying that Monterey is the Port of entry, & at last I could obtain 48 hours to get provisions (as we were starving) and some repairings done on the Brig.

"In Monterey I arranged my affairs with the Custum House, and presented myself to the Gov'r Alvarado, and told him my intention to Settle here in this Country, and that I have brought with me 5 White Men 8 Kanacas (two of them married) 3 of the Whitemen were Mechanics, he was very glad to hear that, and particularly when I told him, that I intend to Settle in the interior, on banks of the river Sacramento, because the Indians then at this time would not allow white Men and particularly of the Spanish Origin to come near them, and was very hostile, and stole the horses from the inhabitants near San Jose. I got a General passport for my small Colony and permission to select a Territory where ever I would find it convenient, and to come in one Years time again in Monterey to get my Citizenship and the title of the Land, which I have done so, and not only this, I received a high civil Office.

"When I left Yerbabuena (now San Francisco) after having leaved the Brig and dispatched her back to the S. I. I bought several small Boats (Launches) and Chartered the Schooner "Isabella" for my Exploring Journey to the inland Rivers and particularly to find the Mouth of the River Sacramento, as I could find Nobody who could give me information, only that they Knew some very large Rivers are in the interior.

"It took me eight days before I could find the entrance of the Sacramento, as it is very deceiving and very easy to pass by, how it happened to several Officers of the Navy afterwards which refused to take a pilot. About 10 miles below Sacramento City I fell in with the first Indians which was all armed & painted & looked very hostile, they was about 200 Men, as some of them understood a little Spanish I could make a Kind of treaty with them, and the two which understood Spanish came with me, and made me a little better acquainted with the Country. all other Indians on the up River hided themselves in the Bushes, and on the Mouth of Feather River they runned all away so soon they discovered us. I was examining the Country a little further up with a Boat, while the larger Crafts let go their Ankers, on my return, all the white Men came to me and asked me, how much longer I intended to travell with them in such a Wilderness.

"The following Morning I gave Orders to return, and entered in the American River, landed at the farmer Tannery on the 12th, Augt. 1839. Gave Orders to get every thing on Shore, pitch the tents and mount the 3 Cannons, called the white Men, and told them that all those which are not contented could leave on board the Isabella, next Morning, and that I would settle with them imediately, and remain alone with the Canaca's, of 6 Men 3 remained, and 3 of them I gave passage to Yerbabuena.

"The Indians was first troublesome, and came frequently and would it not have been for the Cannons they would have Killed us for the sake of my property, which they liked very much, and this intention they had very often, how they confessed to me afterwards, when on good terms. I had a large Bull Dog which saved my life 3 times, when they came slyly near the house in the Night, he got hold of them and marked most severely, in a short time removed my Camps on the very spot where now the Ruins of Sutters fort stands, made acquaintance with a few Indians which came to work for a short time making Adobes, and the Canacas was building 3 grass houses, like it is customary on the Sandwich Islands. Before I came up here, I purchased Cattle & Horses on the Rancho of Señor Martinez, and had great difficulties & trouble to get them up, and received them at least on the 22d October 1839. Not less than 8 Men, wanted to be in the party, as they was afraid of the Indians, and had good reasons to be so.

"Before I got the Cattle we was hunting Deer & Elk etc and so afterwards to safe the Cattle as I had then only about 500 head, 50 horses & a manada of 25 mares. One Year that is in the fall 1840, I bought 1000 head of Cattle of Don Antonio Sañol and many horses more of Don Joaquin Gomez and others. In the fall 1839 I have built an Adobe house covered with Tule and two other small buildings which in the middle of the fort, they was afterwards destroyed by fire. At the same time we cut a Road through the Woods where the City of Sacramento stand, then we made the New Embarcadero, where the old Zink house stands now. After this it was time to make a Garden, and to sow some Wheat &c we broke up the soil with poor California ploughs, I had a few Californians employed as Baqueros, and 2 of them making Cal. Carts & stocking the ploughs etc.

"In the Spring 1840, the Indians began to be troublesome all around me, Killing and Wounding Cattle stealing horses, and threatening to attack us en Mass, I was obliged to make Capaigns against them and punish them severely, a little later about 2 a 300 was aproching and got United on Cosumne River, but I was not waiting for them. left a small Garrison at home, Canons & other Arms loaded, and left with 6 bravo men & 2 Baquero's in the night and took them by surprise at Day light, the fighting was a little hard, but after having lost about 30 men, they was willing to make a treaty with me, and after this lecon they behalved very well, and became my best friends and Soldiers, with which I has been assisted to conquer the whole Sacramento and a part of the San Joaquin Valley.

"At the time the Communication with the Bay was very long and dangerous, particularly in open Boats, it is a great Wonder that we got not swamped a many times, all time with an Indian Crew and a Canaca at the helm. Once it took me (in December 1839,) 16 days to go down to Yerba buena and to return, I went down again on the 22d Xber 39, to Yerba buena and on account of the inclemency of the Weather and the strong current in the River I need a whole month (17 days coming up) and nearly all the provisions spoiled.

"On the 23d Augt, 1841. Capt. Ringold of Comadore Wilkes Exploring Squadron, arrived on the Embarcadero, piloted by one of the Launches Indian crew, without this they would not have found so easy the entrance of the Sacramento. They had 6 Whaleboats & 1 Launch 7 Officers and about 50 men in all, I was very glad indeed to see them, sent immediately saddled horses for the Officers, and my Clerk with an invitation to come and see me, at their arrival I fired a salut, and furnished them what they needed. they was right surprised to find me up here in this Wilderness, it made a very good impression upon the Indians to see so many whites are coming to see me, they surveyed the River so far as the Butes.

"September 4th 1841. Arrived the Russian Govr Mr. Alexander Rottibeff on board the Schooner Sacramento, and offered me their whole Establishment at Bodega & Ross for sale, and invited me to come right off with him, as there is a Russian Vessel at Bodega, and some Officers with plein power, to transact this business with me, and particularly they would give me the preference, as they became all acquainted with me, during a months stay at Sitka. I left and went with him down to the Bay in Company with Capt. Ringold's Expedition, what for a fleet we thought then, is on the River. Arriving at Bodega, we came very soon to terms, from there we went to fort Ross where they showed me everything and returned to Bodega again, and before the Vessel sailed we dined on board the Helena, and closed the bargain for $30,000, which has been paid. And other property, was a separate account which has been first paid.

"On the 28th of September I dispatched a number of men and my Clerk by Land to Bodega, to receive the Cattle, Horses, Mules & Sheep, to bring them up to Sutter's fort, called then New Helvetia, by crossing the Sacramento they lost me from about 2000 head about 100, which drowned in the River, but of most of them we could safe the hides, our Cal. Banknotes at the time.

"March 6, 1842. Captain Fremont arrived at the port with Kit Carson, told me that he was an officer of the U. S. and left a party behind in Distress and on foot, the few surviving Mules was packed only with the most necessary, I received him politely and his Company likewise as an old acquaintance. the next Morning I furnished them with fresh horses, & a Vaquero with a pack Mule loaded with Necessary Supplies for his Men. Capt. Fremont found in my Establishment every thing what he needed, that he could travell without Delay, he could have not found it so by a Spaniard, perhaps by a great Many and with loosing a great deal of time. I sold him about 60 Mules & about 25 horses, and fat young Steers or Beef Cattle, all the Mules & horses got Shoed, on the 23d March, all was ready and on the 24th he left with his party for the U States.

"As an officer of the Govt. it was my duty to report to the Govt. that Capt. Fremont arrived, Genl. Micheltorena dispatched Lieut. Col. Telles (afterwards Gov. of Sinalo) with Capt., Lieut., and 25 Dragoons, to inquire what Captain Fremonts business was here; but he was en route as the arrive only on the 27th, from this time on Exploring,

Hunting & Trapping parties has been started, at the same time Agricultural & Mechanical business was progressing from Year to year, and more Notice has been taken, of my establishment, it became even a fame, and some early Distinguished Travellers like Doctor Sandells, Wasnesensky & others, Captains of Trading Vessels & Super Cargos, & even Californians (after the Indians was subdued) came and paid me a visit, and was astonished to see what for Work of all kinds has been done. Small Emigrant parties arrived, and brought me some very valuable Men, with one of those was Major Bidwell (he was about 4 Years in my employ). Major Reading & Major Hensley with 11 other brave men arrived alone, both of these Gentlemen has been 2 Years in my employ, with these parties excellent Mechanics arrived which was all employed by me, likewise good farmers. we made imediately Amer. ploughs was made in my Shops and all kind of work done, every year the Russians was bound to furnish me with good iron & Steel & files, Articles which could not be got here likewise Indian Beeds and the most important of all was 100 lb of fine Rifle & 100 lb of Canon powder and several 100 lb of Lead (every year) with these I was careful like with Gold.

"June 3d 1846. I left in company of Major Reading, and most all of the Men in my employ, for a Campaign with the Mukelemney Indians, which has been engaged by Castro and his Officers to revolutionize all the Indians against me, to Kill all the foreigners, burn their houses, and Wheat fields etc. These Mukelemney Indians had great promesses and some of them were finely dressed and equiped, and those came apparently on a friendly visit to the fort and Vicinity and long Conversations with the influential Men of the Indians, and one Night a Number of them entered in my Potrero (a kind of closed pasture) and was Ketching horses to drive the whole Cavallada away with them. The Sentinel at the fort heard the distant Noise of these Horses, and gave due notice, & imediately I left with about 6 well armed Men and attacked them, but they could make their escape in the Woods (where Sac. City stands now) and so I left a guard with the horses. As we had to cross the Mukelemney River on rafts, one of these rafts capsized with 10 Rifles, and 6 prs of Pistols, a good supply of Amunition, and the clothing of about 24 Men, and Major Reading & another Man nearly drowned.

"June 16th 1846. Merritt & Kit Carson arrived with News of Sonoma beeing occupied by the Americans, and the same evening arrived as prissoners Genl. Vallejo, Don Salvador Vallejo, Lt. Col. Pradon & M. Leese, and given under my charge and Care, I have treated them with kindness and so good as I could, which was reported to Fremont, and be then told me, that prissoners ought not to be treated so, then I told him, if it is not right how I treat them, to give them in charge of somebody else.

"Capt. Montgomery did send an Amer. flag by Lieut. Revere than in Command of Sonoma, and some dispatches to Fremont, I received the Order to hiss the flag by Sunrise from Lt. Revere, long time before daybreak, I got ready with loading the Canons and when it was day the roaring of the Canons got the people all stirring. Some them made long faces, as they thought if the Bear flag would remain there would be a better chance to rob and plunder. Capt. Fremont received Orders to proceed to Monterey with his forces, Capt. Montgomery provided for the upper Country, established Garrisons in all important places, Yerba buena, Sonoma,

San Jose, and fort Sacramento. Lieut. Missroon came to organize our Garrison batter and more Numbers of white Men and Indians of my former Soldiers, and gave me the Command of this Fort. The Indians have not yet received their pay yet for their services, only each one a shirt and a pre. of pants, & abt. 12 men got Coats. So went the War on in California. Capt. Fremont was nearly all time engaged in the lower Country and made himself Governer, until Genl. Kearney arrived, when an other Revolution took place. And Fremont for disobeying Orders was made prisoner by Genl. Kearney, who took him afterwards with him to the U. States by Land across the Mountains. After the War I was anxious that Business should go on like before, and on the 28th May 1847, Marshall & Gingery, two Millwrights, I employed to survey the large Millraise for the Flour Mill at Brighton.

"May 13th, 1847. Mr. Marshall commenced the great work of the large Millraise, with ploughs and scrapers.

"July 20th, 1847. Got all the necessary timber and frame of the millbuilding.

"Augt. 25th. Capt Hart of the Mormon Battaillon arrived, with a good many of his Men on their Way to great Salt Lake, they had Orders for Govt. Horses, which I delivered to them, (War Horses) not paid for yet. They bought provisions and got Blacksmith work done. I employed about Eighty Men of them, some as Mechanics, some as laborers, on the Mill and Millraise at Brighton, some as laborers at the Sawmill at Columa.

"Augt. 28th. 1847. Marshall moved, with P. Wisners family and the working hands to Columa. and began to work briskly on the sawmill.

"Septr. 10th. Mr. Saml Brannan returned from the great Salt Lake, and announced a large Emigration by land. On the 19th the Garrison was removed, Lieut't Per Lee took her down to San francisco.

"Novr. 1th. Getting with a great deal of trouble and with breaking wagons the four Runs of Millstones, to the Mill Sit (Brighton) from the Mountains.

"December. 22. Received about 2000 fruit trees with great expenses from Fort Ross, Napa Valley and other places, which was given in Care of men who called themselves Gardeners, and nearly all of the trees was neglected by them and died.

"January 28th, 1848. Marshall arrived in the evening, it was raining very heavy, but he told me that he came on important business, after we was alone in a private Room he showed me the first Specimen of Gold, that is he was not certain if it was Gold or not, but he thought it might be; immacdiately I made the proof and found that it was Gold, I told him even that most of all is 23 Carat Gold; he wished that I should come up with him immediately, but I told him that I have to give first my orders to the people in all my factories and shops.

"February 1th. Left for the Sawmill attended by a Baquero (Olimpio) was absent 2d, 3d, 4th, & 5th. I examined myself everything and picked up a few Specimens of Gold myself in the tail race of the Sawmill, this Gold and others which Marshall and some of the other laborers gave to me (it was found while in my employ and Wages) I told them that I would a ring got made of it so soon as the Goldsmith would be here. I had a talk with my employed people all at the Sawmill. I told them that as they do know now that this Metal Is Gold, I wished that they would do me the great favor and keep it secret only 6 weeks, because my large Flour Mill at Brighton would have been in Operation in such a time, which undertaking would have been a fortune to me, and unfortunately the people would not keep it secret, and so I lost on this Mill at the lowest calculation about $25,000.

"March 7th. The first party of Mormons, employed by me for washing and digging Gold and very soon all followed, and left me only the sick and the lame behind. And at this time I could say that every body left me from the Clerk to the Cook. What for great Damages I had to suffer in my tannery which was just doing a profitable and extensive business, and the Vatts was left filled and a quantity of half finished leather was spoiled likewise a large quantity of raw hides collected by the farmers and of my own killing. The same thing was in every branch of business which I carried on at the time. I began to harvest my wheat, while others was digging and washing Gold, but even the Indians could not be keeped longer at Work, they was impatient to run to the mines, and other Indians had informed them of the Gold and its value; and so I had to leave more as ⅔ of my harvest in the fields.

"April 18th, 1848, more curious people arrived bound for the Mountains. I left for Columa, in Company with Major P. B. Reading and Mr. Kembel (Editor of the Alta California) we were absent 4 Days. we was prospecting and found Silver and iron ok in abundance.

"April 28th. A great many people more went up to the Mountains. This day the Saw mill was in Operation and the first Lumber has been sawed in the whole upper Country.

"May 1th. Saml Brannan was building a store at Natoma, Mormon Islands, and have done a very large and heavy business.

"May 15th. Paid of all the Mormons which has been employed by me, in building these Mills and other Mechanical trades, all of them made their pile, and some of them became rich & wealthy, but all of them was bound to the great Salt Lake, and spent there their fortunes to the honor and Glory of the Lord !

"May 19th. The great Rush from San Francisco arrived at the fort, all my friends and acquaintances filled up the houses and the whole fort, I had only a little Indian boy, to make them roasted Ripps, etc, as my Cooks left me like every body else, the Merchants, Doctors, Lawyers, Sea Captains, Merchants, etc. all came up and did not know what to do, all was in a Confusion, all left their wives and families in San Francisco, and those which had none locked their Doors, abandoned their houses, offered them for sale cheap, a few hundred Dollars House & Lot (Lots which are worth now $100,000 and more; some of these men were just like greazy. Some of the Merchants has been the most prudentest of the whole, visited the Mines and returned immediately and began to do a very profitable business, and soon Vessels came from every where with all Kind of Merchaudize, the whole old thrash which was laying for Years unsold, on the Coasts of South & Central America, Mexico, Sandwich Islands etc. all found a good market here.

"Mr. Brannan was erecting a very large Warehouse, and have done an immense business, connected with Howard & Green, S. Francisco.

"May 21th. Saml Kyburg errected or established the first Hotel in the fort in the larger building, and made a great deal of Money. A great Many traders deposited a great deal of goods in my Store (an Indian was the Key Keeper and performed very

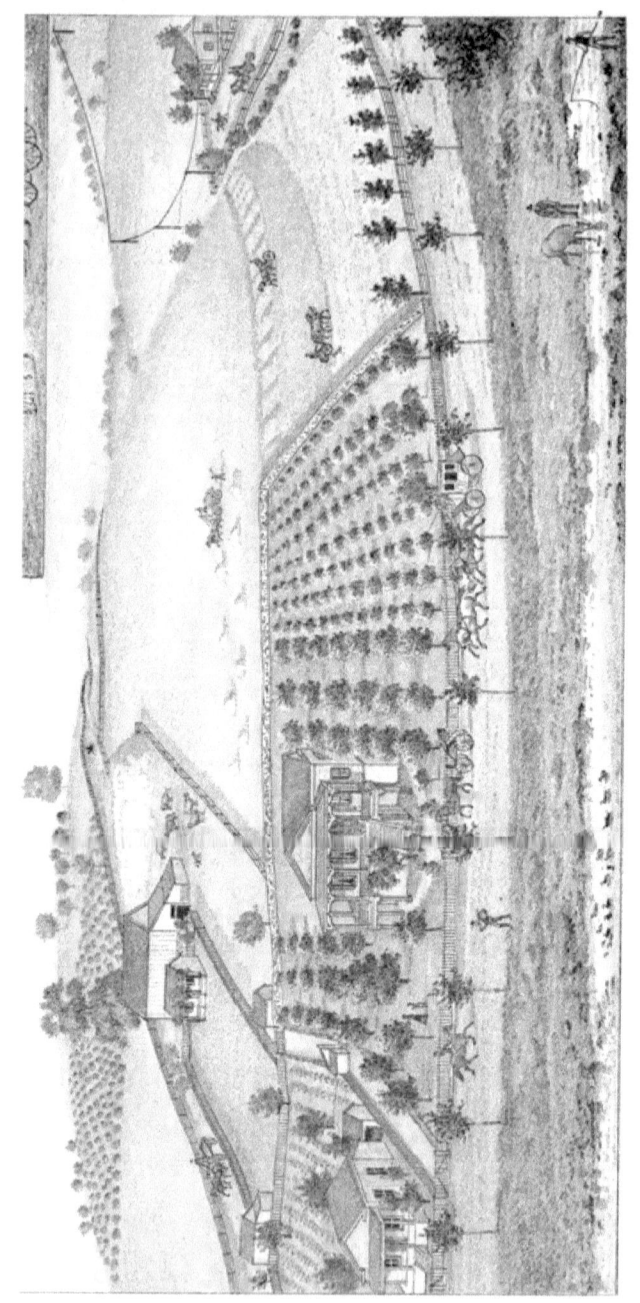

well) afterwards every little Shanty became a Warehouse and Store, the fort was then a veritable Bazaar. As white people would not be employed at the Time I had a few good Indians attending to the Ferry boat, and every night came up, and delivered the received Money for ferryage to me, after deduction for a few bottles of brandy, for the whole of them, perhaps some white people at the time would not have acted so honestly.

"May 25th. The travelling to the Mines was increasing from day to day, and no more Notice was taken, as the people arrived from South America. Mexico, Sandwich Islands, Oregon etc. All the Ship-Crews, and Soldiers deserted. In the beginning of July, Col. Mason our Military Governor, with Capt Sherman (Secretary of State) Capt. Folsom Quartrmstr, and an Escort of which some deserted, and some other Gentlemen, travelled in Company with the Governor.

"As we wanted to celebrate the 4th of July we invited the Governor and his suite to remain with us, and he accepted. Kyburg gave us a good Diner every thing was pretty well arranged. Pinkett was the Orator. It was well done enough for such a new Country and in such an excitement and Confusion. And from this time on you know how every thing was going on here. One thing is certain that the people looked on my property as their own, and in the Winter of 1849 to 1850. A great Number of horses has been stolen from me, whole Manadas of Mares driven away and taken to Oregon etc. Nearly my whole Stock of Cattle has been Killed, several thousands and left me only a very small Quantity. The same has been done with my large stock of Hogs, which was running like ever under nobodies care and so it was easy to steal them, I had not an Idea that people could be so mean, and that they would do a Wholesale business in Stealing.

"On the Upper Sacramento, that is, from the Butte downward to the point or imputh of feather River, there was most all of my Stock running and during the Overflow the Cattle was in a many bands on high spots like Islands, there was a fine chance to approach them in small Boats and shoot them, this business has been very successfully done by one party of 5 Men (partners) which had besides himsl people, and Boats Crew's which transported the beef to the Market at Sacramento City and furnished that City with my own beef, and because these Men was nearly alone, on account of the Overflow, and Monopolized the Market.

"In the Spring of 1850, these 5 men divided their Spoil of $60,000 clear profits made of Cattle, all of them left for the Atlantic State; one of them returned again in the Winter from 1850 to 51, hired a new band of Robers to follow the same business and kill of the balance of the few that was left. My Baqueros found out this Nest of thiefs in ther Camp butchering just some head of my Cattle. on their return they informed me what they have seen, in the neighborhood of the same Camp they saw some more cows shot dead, which the Rascal then butchered. Immediately I did send to Nicolaus for the Sheriff (Jas Hopkins) as then at the time we had laws in force?!? after all was stolen and destroyed the Sheriff arrived at Hock farm I furnished him a Posse of my employed Men. they proceeded over on the Sacramento to where the thiefs were encamped. as the Sheriff wanted to arrest them they just jumped in their Boats and off they went, the Sheriff threatened them to fire at them, but they was all, and laughing they went at large.

"One day my Son was riding after Stock a few miles below Hock farm, he found a Man (his name was Owens) butchering one of our finest milch Cows (of Durham stock of Chile, which cost $300.) He told the Man that he could not take the Meat, that he would go home and get people, and so he has done, and he got people and a Wagon and returned to the Spot, but Owens found it good to clear out. Two brothers of this Man, was respectable Merchants in Lexington, Mo. and afterwards in Westport well acquainted with me, he came one day in my house and brought me their compliments, I received him well, and afterwards turned out to be a thief. How many of this kind came to California which loosed their little honor by crossing the Istmus or the plains. I had nothing at all to do with speculations, but stuck by the plough, but by paying such high Wages, and particularly under Kyburg' management, I have done this business with a heavy loss as the produce had no more the Value like before, and from the time on Kyburg left I curtailed my business considerable, and so far that I do all at present with my family and a few Indian Servants. I did not speculate, only occupied my land, in the hope that it would be before long decided and in my favor by the U. S. Land Commission; but now already 3 years & two months have elapsed, and I am waiting now very anxiously for the Decision. which will revive or bring me to the untimely grave.

"All the other Circumstances you know all yourself, perhaps I have repeated many things which I wrote in the 3 first sheets, because I had them not to see what I wrote, and as it is now several months I must have forgotten. well it is only a kind of memorandum, and not a History at all. Only to remember you on the different periods when such and such things happened.

"I need not mention again, that all the Visitors has allways been hospitably received and treated. That all the sick and wounded found always Medical Assistance, Gratis, as I had nearly all the time a Physician in my employ. The Assistance to the Emigrants that is all well known. I dont need to write anything about this.

"I think now from all this you can form some facts, and that you can mention how thousends and thausands made their fortunes from this Gold Discovery produced through my industry and energy, (some wise merchants and others in San francisco called the building of this Sawmill, another of Sutter's folly) and this folly saved not only the Mercantile World from bankruptcy, but even our General Govt. but for me it has turned out a folly, then without having discovered the Gold, I would have become the richest wealthiest man on the Pacific Shore.

J. A. SUTTER."

James C. Ward, who visited Gen. Sutter in 1848, says of him :—

"A Swiss by birth, he held during the reign of Charles X. the rank of captain in the French army. He purchased the buildings at Ross, just north of Bodega, of the Russians, and as he proposed to settle the wilderness to the north of the Bay of San Francisco with European immigrants, the Mexican Government made him a grant of eleven leagues of land on the Sacramento river. After landing he camped, surrounded by hostile savages, in the open plain where the fort was afterward built, and the next morning, after dressing in full uniform, he went, accompanied by his Indian servant, both well armed, to the Indian village in the woods near by. The savages were informed through the interpreter that he came to them as a friend, and if they would help him a little with their labor, he would make them presents.

"The Indians were set to work to make adobes, of which the fort was built. It is a parallelogram in form, with two bastions. In the middle of the square is a building two stories high, containing four rooms, and a counting-room upstairs. A blacksmith shop, mill for grinding corn, scrape manufactory and dwelling are around it, built against the walls of the fort. At one time he had a well-drilled force of thirty Indians within its walls, with guards posted night and day for its defense. No one reached it without being fed and lodged.

"I passed the evening of my arrival, after supper, in his company. His manners are polished, and the impression he makes on every one is very favorable. In figure he is of medium height, rather stout, but well made. His head is round, features regular, with smiling and agreeable expression; complexion healthy and rosente. He wears his hair cut close, and his moustache trimmed short, *a la militaire*. He dressed very neatly in frock coat, pantaloons and cap of blue, and with his gold-headed malacca in hand, you would rather suppose him prepared for a saunter on the Boulevards than a consultation with Simplon, his Indian alcalde, about hands required for the day's work, or ox-teams to be dispatched here and there."

CHAPTER XI.

THE KING'S ORPHAN.

His Observations in the Sacramento Valley in 1843—Indications of Gold—Life at Sutter's Fort—Indian Gourmands—Wonderful Fertility of the Land.

IN 1843 a young Swedish scholar visited Sutter's Fort, and made observations which are now highly interesting. He had been educated at a Government institution, and, on that account, was known as one of the "King's Orphans." One of the requirements of the school was that the pupil, after receiving a gratuitous education, should travel in foreign lands, write out his observations and discoveries, and deposit them in the library of the institution. In pursuance of that duty, the young Swede found his way to California, made drawings of the Golden Gate, the town of Yerba Buena, and the old Presidio, visited and described Sutter's Fort, and, on his way home, died at New Orleans. His papers fell into the hands of Col. T. B. Thorpe, who reported them to the Associated Pioneers of the Territorial Days of California. While examining the country surrounding Sutter's Fort, in 1843, the "Orphan" wrote:—

"The Californias are rich in minerals. Gold, silver, lead, oxide of iron, manganese, and copper ore are met with throughout the country, the precious metals being the most abundant."

Describing Sutter's establishment, the Swedish traveler said:—

"It has more the appearance of a fort than a farming establishment. It is protected by a wall ten feet high, made of adobes, or sun-dried brick, having a turret with embrasures and loop-holes for fire-arms. Twenty-four pieces of cannon of different sizes, can be brought to defend the walls. Against the walls on the inside are erected the store-houses of the establishment; also, a distillery to make spirits from the wheat and grapes, together with shops for coopers, blacksmiths, saddlers, granaries, and huts for the laborers. At the gate-way is always stationed a servant, armed as a sentinel. I arrived at the establishment in the morning, just as the people were being assembled for labor by the discordant notes of a Mexican drum. I found Captain Sutter busily employed in distributing orders for the day. He received me with great hospitality, and made me feel on the instant, perfectly at home under his roof. The magical sound of the drum had gathered together several hundred Indians, who flocked to their morning meal preparatory to the labors of the day, reaping wheat. The morning meal over, they filed off to the field in a kind of military order, armed with a sickle and hook.

"Breakfast was by this time announced for the family, which was served up in an out-house adjoining the kitchen. It consisted of wholesome corn-bread, eggs, ham, an excellent piece of venison, and coffee. In the rear of the fort is a large pond, the borders of which are planted with willows and other trees. This pond furnishes water for domestic use, and for irrigating the garden. The want of rain is the greatest evil that befalls the country. In the front of the fort there are inclosures for horses and cattle, and places to deposit corn and wheat. The manner of threshing was conducted on a most patriarchal plan, the grain being strewn upon the floor and then trodden out by horses or cattle, which causes it to be much broken and mixed with the earth, and almost impossible to clean.

"The raising of wheat, corn, horses, and cattle, constitutes the principal business of Captain Sutter; but he has realized considerable income from the salmon fisheries of the rivers, the fish being unequaled in flavor, and found in the greatest abundance. He also organized extensive hunting and trapping expeditions for the skins of the beaver, otter, elk, deer, and antelope, but in this he was greatly interfered with by the Hudson Bay Company, who sent their hunters upon his grounds. He complained to the proper authorities, but they paid no attention to the matter. His enemies, not content with thus injuring him, informed the suspicious Mexican Government that Captain Sutter was concocting revolutionary plans, and that he encouraged deserters and other disorderly persons to live at his settlement. Captain Sutter replied to these charges by stating that he had received the grant of his lands on condition that he should obtain settlers, the principal portion of whom he expected from Europe. To make amends, he had encouraged the stragglers in the country to flock to his central position, and they being chiefly unmarried men, and some rather lawless spirits from the mountains, they soon formed a very independent set of men, and were quite competent to defend themselves.

"The Government at Monterey was not satisfied with this explanation, and urged on by envious neighbors, it was prompted to send to Captain Sutter a committee of investigation. The Captain was so enraged at the indignity that he treated the committee with great contempt, and said he could defend himself against any force that might be employed against him. Whereupon the Government at Monterey threatened to send a military force, but thought better of the matter when they learned the character of the men Sutter had about him, and the Russian armament he had mounted on the walls of the fort;

but they annoyed him with lawsuits, and, after a great deal of difficulty, he was acquitted of any treasonable designs against the Government.

"The Hudson Bay Company having destroyed his trade in furs, he retaliated upon them by erecting a large distillery, with the product of which he secretly purchased from the hunters of the Company the greater part of their furs, and managed to make more by the operation than if he had kept up a large hunting establishment of his own.

"Mr. Sinclair, a partner with Captain Sutter in farming pursuits, and a Mr. Grimes, have large and productive farms on the American Fork. Mr. Sinclair is from Scotland, is a very interesting gentleman in conversation, and possesses great enterprise in business. He was a hunter for many years among the Rocky Mountains, acting as a clerk to one of the Hudson Bay Company's expeditions. He treated me to a rural breakfast, and, in accordance with his old habits, broiled his meat on a ramrod stuck up before the fire. The limpid and beautiful river near which his home is situated, is made doubly attractive when compared with the sultry plains in the vicinity, upon which good water is not always to be obtained."

The "Orphan" explains the process of Indian signal-fires:—

"A hole is dug in the ground much wider at the bottom than at the top; this hole is filled with combustibles and set on fire; once well ignited the hole is nearly closed at the opening. By this means the smoke rises to a considerable height in a column, and thus information is conveyed to different tribes of the approach of an enemy or friend, and whether they are coming in large or small bodies."

The gluttonous habits of the Indians are described:

"The Indians that constituted the crew of the schooner, having been rather stinted of food for a day or two, determined on a feast as a recompense for their previous fasting. They presented on that occasion a spectacle I had never before witnessed of disgusting sensual indulgence, the effect of which on their conduct, struck me as being exceedingly strange. The meat of the heifer, most rudely cooked, was eaten in a voracious manner. After gorging themselves they would lie down and sleep for a while, and get up and eat again. They repeated this gluttony until they actually lost their senses, and presented in their conduct all the phenomena peculiar to an over-indulgence in spirituous liquors. They cried and laughed by turns, rolled upon the ground, dozed, and then sprang up in a state of delirium. The following morning they were all wretchedly sick, and had the expression peculiar to drunken men recovering their reason after a debauch."

The great fertility of the soil in parts of the Sacramento valley is referred to as follows :—

"Vegetables of all kinds can be raised in the greatest abundance, frequently two or three crops a year. Wormwood and wild mustard abound as weeds. Oats grow wild, and the cultivated grow to an enormous height. Wheat crops sown in the Fall, early the following year have yielded one hundred and fourteen bushels to the acre. At the Mission of St. Joseph it was ascertained that the yield was one hundred and twenty bushels to the acre, and the spontaneous crop the following year was sixty bushels to the acre. The wheat of Taos has six distinct heads. Clover and the grasses are extraordinarily fine and productive. Indian flax grows wild all over the country. Horses, cattle, sheep, and hogs thrive well, and are possessed in greater or less numbers by all the inhabitants, and are tended by herdsmen."

CHAPTER XII.
SUTTER'S FORT IN 1846.

Aspect of Sacramento Valley—Sinclair's Ranch—A Lady Pioneer—Captain Sutter at Home—The Fort Described—Condition and Occupation of the Indians—Farm Products and Prices—Dinner with the Pioneer—New Helvetia.

THE following interesting and accurate description of Sutter's Fort, before the gold discovery, is from Edwin Bryant's work, "What I Saw in California," published in 1849. Mr. Bryant, with a party of nine persons, left Independence, Missouri, on the 1st of May, 1846, and reached Sutter's Fort about midsummer, when he took the following observations :—

"Sept. 1, 1846. A clear, pleasant morning. We took a south course down the valley, and at 4 o'clock P. M. reached the residence of John Sinclair, Esq., on the Rio de los Americanos, about two miles east of Sutter's Fort. The valley of the Sacramento, as far as we have traveled down it, is from thirty to forty miles in width, from the foot of the low benches of the Sierra Nevada to the elevated range of hills on the western side. The composition of the soil appears to be such as to render it highly productive, with proper cultivation, of the small grains. The ground is trodden up by immense herds of cattle and horses, which grazed here early in the Spring, when it was wet and apparently miry. We passed through large evergreen oak groves, some of them miles in width. Game is very abundant. We frequently saw deer feeding quietly one or two hundred yards from us, and large flocks of antelopes.

"Mr. Sinclair, with a number of horses and Indians, was engaged in threshing wheat. His crop this year, he informed me, would be about three thousand bushels. The soil of his rancho, situated in the bottom of the Rio de los Americanos, just above its junction with the Sacramento, is highly fertile. His wheat-fields are secured against the numerous herds of cattle and horses, which constitute the largest item in the husbandry of this country, by ditches about five feet in depth, and four or five feet over at the surface. The dwelling-house and outhouses of Mr. Sinclair are all constructed after American models, and present a most comfortable and neat appearance. It was a pleasant scene, after having traveled many months in the wilderness, to survey this abode of apparent thrift and enjoyment, resembling so nearly those we had left in the far-off country behind us.

"In searching for the ford over the Rio de los Americanos, in order to proceed on to Sutter's Fort, I saw a lady of a graceful, though fragile figure, dressed in the costume of our own countrywomen. She was giving some directions to her female servants, and did not discover me until I spoke to her, and inquired the position of the ford. Her pale and delicate, but handsome and expressive countenance, indicated much surprise, produced by my sudden and unexpected salutation. But, collecting herself, she replied to my inquiry in vernacular English, and the sounds of her voice, speaking our own language, and her civilized appearance, were highly pleasing. This lady, I presume, was Mrs. Sinclair; but I never saw her afterwards.

"Crossing the Rio de los Americanos, the waters

of which, at this season, are quite shallow at the ford, we proceeded over a well-beaten road to Sutter's Fort, arriving there when the sun was about an hour and a half high. Riding up to the front gate, I saw two Indian sentinels pacing to and fro before it, and several Americans, or *foreigners* (as all who are not Californians by birth are here called), sitting in the gateway, dressed in buckskin pantaloons and blue sailor shirts, with white stars worked on the collars. I inquired if Captain Sutter was in the fort. A very small man, with a peculiarly sharp red face and a most voluble tongue, gave the response. He was probably a corporal. He said, in substance, that perhaps I was not aware of the great changes which had recently taken place in California;—that the fort belonged to the United States, and that Captain Sutter, although he was in the fort, had no control over it. He was going into a minute history of the complicated circumstances and events which had produced this result, when I reminded him that we were too much fatigued to listen to a long discourse, but if Captain Sutter was inside the walls, and could conveniently step to the gate a moment, I would be glad to see him. A lazy-looking Indian with a ruminating countenance, after some time spent in parleying, was dispatched with my message to Captain Sutter.

"Captain S. soon came to the gate, and saluted us with much gentlemanly courtesy and friendly cordiality. He said that events had transpired in the country, which, to his deep regret, had so far deprived him of the control of his own property, that he did not feel authorized to invite us inside of the walls to remain. The fort, he said, was occupied by soldiers under the pay of the United States, and commanded by Mr. Kern. I replied to him that, although it would be something of a novelty to sleep under a roof, after our late nomadic life, it was a matter of small consideration. If he would supply us with some meat, a little salt, and such vegetables as he might have, we neither asked nor desired more from his hospitality, which we all knew was liberal, to the highest degree of generosity.

"A servant was immediately dispatched with orders to furnish us with a supply of beef, salt, melons, onions, and tomatoes, for which no compensation would be received. We proceeded immediately to a grove of live-oak timber, about two miles west of the fort, and encamped within a half a mile of the Sacramento river. * * * *

"He [Captain Sutter] planted himself on the spot where his fort now stands, then a savage wilderness, and in the midst of numerous and hostile tribes of Indians. With the small party of men which he originally brought with him, he succeeded in defending himself against the Indians, until he constructed his first defensive building. He told me that, several times being hemmed in by his assailants, he had subsisted for many days upon grass alone. There is a grass in this valley which the Indians eat, that is pleasant to the taste, and nutritious. He succeeded by degrees in reducing the Indians to obedience, and by means of their labor erected the spacious fortification which now belongs to him.

"The fort is a parallelogram, about five hundred feet in length, and one hundred and fifty in breadth. The walls are constructed of adobes or sun-dried bricks. The main building, or residence, stands near the center of the area, or court, inclosed by the walls. A row of shops, store-rooms, and barracks, are inclosed within, and line the walls on every side. Bastions project from the angles, and ordnance, mounted in which, sweep the walls. The principal gates on the east and the south are also defended by heavy artillery, through port-holes pierced in the walls. At this time the fort is manned by about fifty well-disciplined Indians, and ten or twelve white men, all under the pay of the United States. These Indians are well clothed and fed. The garrison is under the command of Mr. Kern, the artist of Captain Fremont's exploring expedition.

"The number of laboring Indians employed by Captain Sutter during the seasons of sowing and harvest, is from two to three hundred. Some of these are clothed in shirts and blankets, but a large portion of them are entirely naked. They are paid so much per day for their labor, in such articles of merchandise as they may select from the store. Cotton cloth and handkerchiefs are what they most freely purchase. Common brown cotton cloth sells at one dollar per yard. A tin coin issued by Captain Sutter circulates among them, upon which is stamped the number of days that the holder has labored. These stamps indicate the value in merchandise to which the laborer or holder is entitled.

"They are inveterate gamblers, and those who have been so fortunate as to obtain clothing, frequently stake and part with every rag upon their backs. The game which they most generally play is carried on as follows: Any number which may be concerned in it seat themselves cross-legged on the ground, in a circle. They are then divided into two parties, each of which has two champions or players. A ball, or some small article, is placed in the hands of the players on one side, which they transfer from hand to hand with such sleight and dexterity that it is nearly impossible to detect the changes. When the players holding the balls make a particular motion with their hands, the antagonist players guess in which hand the balls are at the time. If the guess is wrong, it counts one in favor of the playing party. If the guess is right, then it counts one in favor of the guessing party, and the balls are transferred to them. The count of the game is kept with sticks. During the progress of the game, all concerned keep up a continual monotonous grunting, with a movement of their bodies to keep time with their grunts. The articles which are staked on the game are placed in the center of the ring.

"The laboring or field Indians about the fort are fed upon the offal of slaughtered animals, and upon the bran sifted from the ground wheat. This is boiled in large iron kettles. It is then placed in wooden troughs standing in the court, around which the several messes seat themselves, and scoop out with their hands this poor fodder. Bad as it is, they eat it with an apparent high relish, and no doubt it is more palatable and more healthy than the acorn mush, or *atole*, which constitutes the principal food of these Indians in their wild state.

"The wheat crop of Captain Sutter, the present year [1846], is about eight thousand bushels. The season has not been a favorable one. The average yield to the acre, Captain S. estimated at twenty five bushels. In favorable seasons this yield is doubled; and if we can believe the statements often made upon respectable authority, it is sometimes quadrupled. * * * * The wheat-fields of Captain S. are secured against the cattle and horses by ditches. Agriculture, among the native Californians, is in a very primitive state, and although Captain S. has introduced some American implements, still his ground is but imperfectly cultivated. * * *

"Wheat is selling at the fort at two dollars and

fifty cents per fanega, rather more than two bushels English measure. It brings the same price when delivered at San Francisco, near the mouth of the Bay of San Francisco. It is transported from the Sacramento valley to a market in launches of about fifty tons burden. Unbolted flour sells at eight dollars per one hundred pounds. The reason of this high price is the scarcity of flouring-mills in the country. The mills which are now going up in various places will reduce the price of flour, and probably they will soon be able to grind all the wheat raised in the country. The streams of California afford excellent water-power, but the flour consumed by Captain Sutter is ground by a very ordinary horse-mill.

"I saw near the fort a small patch of hemp, which had been sown as an experiment, in the spring, and had not been irrigated. I never saw a ranker growth of hemp in Kentucky. Vegetables of several kinds appeared to be abundant, and in perfection.

* * * * * * * *

"Captain Sutter's dining-room and his table furniture do not present a very luxurious appearance. The room is unfurnished, with the exception of a common deal table standing in the center, and some benches, which are substitutes for chairs. The table, when spread, presented a correspondingly primitive simplicity of aspect and of viands. The first course consisted of good soup, served to each guest, in a china bowl, with silver spoons. The bowls, after they had been used for this purpose, were taken away and cleaned by the Indian servant, and were afterwards used as tumblers or goblets, from which we drank our water. The next course consisted of two dishes of meat, one roasted and one fried, and both highly seasoned with onions. Bread, cheese, butter, and melons, constituted the dessert.

* * * * * * * *

"Such has been the extortion of the Government in the way of import duties, that few supplies which are included even among the most ordinary elegancies of life, have ever reached the inhabitants, and for these they have been compelled to pay prices that would be astonishing to a citizen of the United States or of Europe, and such as have impoverished the population. As a general fact, they cannot be obtained at any price, and hence those who have the ability to purchase are compelled to forego their use from necessity.

"The site of the town of Nueva Helvetia, which has been laid out by Captain Sutter, is about a mile and a half from the Sacramento. It is on an elevation of the plain, and not subject to overflow when the waters of the river are at their highest known point. There are now but three or four small houses in this town, but I have little doubt that it will soon become a place of importance.

"Near the Embarcadero of New Helvetia is a large Indian 'sweat-house,' or temescal, an appendage of most of the *rancherias*."

CHAPTER XIII.

THE HISTORY OF THE DONNER PARTY.

Scene of the Tragedy—Organization and Composition of the Party—Election of George Donner as Captain—Hastings' Cut-off—Ascent of the Mountains—Arrival at Donner Lake —Snow-storms—Construction of Cabins—"Forlorn Hope Party"—Captain Reasin P. Tucker's Relief Party—James F. Reed's Relief Party—"Starved Camp"—Third Relief Party—Heroism and Devotion of Mrs. George Donner— Fourth Relief Party—The Survivors.

THREE miles from Truckee, and resting in the green lap of the Sierras, lies one of the loveliest sheets of water on the Pacific coast. Tall mountain peaks are reflected in its clear waters, revealing a picture of extreme loveliness and quiet peace. Yet this peaceful scene was the amphitheatre of the most tragic event in the annals of early California. "The Donner Party" was organized in Sangamon county, Illinois, by George and Jacob Donner and James F. Reed, in the Spring of 1846. In April, 1846, the party set out from Springfield, Illinois, and by the first week in May had reached Independence, Missouri, where the party was increased until the train numbered about two or three hundred wagons, the Donner family numbering sixteen; the Reed family, seven; the Graves family, twelve; the Murphy family, thirteen; these were the principal families of the Donner party proper. At Independence, provisions were laid in for the trip, and the line of journey taken up. In the occasional glimpses we have of the party, features of but little interest present themselves, beyond the ordinary experience of pioneer life. A letter from Mrs. George Donner, written near the junction of the North and South Platte, dated June 16, 1846, reports a favorable journey of four hundred and fifty miles from Independence, Missouri, with no forebodings of the terrible disasters so soon to burst upon them. At Fort Laramie a portion of the party celebrated the Fourth of July. Thereafter the train passed, unmolested, upon its journey. George Donner was elected captain of the train at the Little Sandy river, on the 20th of July, 1846, from which act it took the name of "The Donner Party."

At Fort Bridger, then a mere trading post, the fatal choice was made of the route that led to such fearful disasters and tragic death. A new route, *via* Salt Lake, known as Hastings' Cut-off, was recommended to the party as shortening the distance by three hundred miles. After due deliberation, the Donner party, of eighty-seven souls (three having died) were induced to separate from the larger portion of the train (which afterwards arrived in California in safety) and commenced their journey by way of Hastings' Cut-off. They reached Weber river, near the head of the cañon, in safety. From this point, in their journey, to Salt Lake, almost insurmountable difficulties were encountered, and instead of reaching Salt Lake in one week, as anticipated, over thirty days of perilous travel were consumed in making the trip—most precious time in view of the dangers imminent in the rapidly approaching storms of Winter. The story of their trials and sufferings, in their journey to the fatal camp at Donner lake, is terrible; nature and stern necessity seemed arrayed against them. On the 19th of October, near the present site of Wadsworth, Nevada, the destitute company were happily reprovisioned by C. T. Stanton; furnished with food and mules, together with two Indian vaqueros, by Captain Sutter, without compensation.

At the present site of Reno it was concluded to rest. Three or four days' time was lost. This was the fatal act. The storm-clouds were already brewing upon the mountains, only a few miles distant. The ascent was ominous. Thick and thicker grew the clouds, outstripping in threatening battalions the now eager feet of the alarmed emigrants, until, at Prosser creek, three miles below Truckee, October 28, 1846, a month earlier than usual, the storm set in, and they found themselves in six inches of newly-fallen snow. On the summit it was already from two to five feet deep. The party, in much confusion, finally reached Donner lake in disordered fragments. Frequent and desperate attempts were made to cross the mountain tops, but at last, baffled and despairing, they returned to camp at the lake. The storm now descended in all its pitiless fury upon the ill-fated emigrants. Its dreadful import was well understood, as laden with omens of suffering and death. With slight interruptions, the storm continued for several days. The animals were literally buried alive and frozen in the drifts. Meat was hastily prepared from their frozen carcasses, and cabins rudely built. One, the Schallenberger cabin, erected November, 1844, was already standing, about a quarter of a mile below the lake. This the Breen family appropriated. The Murphys erected one three hundred yards from the lake, marked by a large stone twelve feet high. The Graves family built theirs near Donner creek, three-quarters of a mile further down the stream, the three forming the apexes of a triangle; the Breen and Murphy cabins were distant from each other about one hundred and fifty yards. The Donner brothers, with their families, hastily constructed a brush shed in Alder Creek valley, six or seven miles from the lake. Their provisions were speedily consumed, and starvation, with all its grim attendant horrors, stared the poor emigrants in the face. Day by day, with aching hearts and paralyzed energies, they awaited, amid the beating storms of the Sierras, the dread revelation of the morrow, "hoping against hope" for some welcome sign.

On the sixteenth day of December, 1846, a party of seventeen were enrolled to attempt the hazardous journey over the mountains, to press into the valley beyond for relief. Two returned, and the remaining fifteen pressed on, including Mary Graves and her sister, Mrs. Sarah Fosdick, and several other women, the heroic C. T. Stanton and the noble F. W. Graves (who left his wife and seven children) at the lakes to await in vain his return) being the leaders. This was the "Forlorn Hope Party," over whose dreadful sufferings and disaster we must throw a veil. A detailed account of this party is given from the graphic pen of C. F. McGlashan, and lately published in book form from the press of Crowley & McGlashan, proprietors of the *Truckee Republican*, to which we take pleasure in referring the reader. Death in its most awful form reduced the wretched company to seven—two men and five women—when suddenly tracks were discovered imprinted in the snow. "Can any one imagine," says Mary Graves in her recital, "the joy those foot-prints gave us? We ran as fast as our strength would carry us." Turning a sharp point they suddenly came upon an Indian rancheria. The acorn-bread offered them by the kind and awe-stricken savages was eagerly devoured. But on they pressed with their Indian guides, only to repeat their dreadful sufferings, until at last, one evening about the last of January, Mr. Eddy, with his Indian guide, preceding the party fifteen miles, reached Johnson's ranch, on Bear river, the first settlement on the western slope of the Sierras, when relief was sent back as soon as possible and the remaining six survivors were brought in next day. It had been thirty-two days since they left Donner lake. No tongue can tell, no pen portray, the awful suffering, the terrible and appalling straits, as well as the noble deeds of heroism that characterized this march of death. The eternal mountains, whose granite faces bore witness to their sufferings, are fit monuments to mark the last resting-place of Charles T. Stanton, that cultured, heroic soul, who groped his way through the blinding snow of the Sierras to immortality. The divinest encomium—"He gave his life as a ransom for many"—is his epitaph, foreshadowed in his own noble words, "I will bring aid to these famishing people or *lay down my life*."

Nothing could be done, in the meantime, for the relief of the sufferers at Donner lake, without securing help from Fort Sutter, which was speedily accomplished by John Rhodes. In a week, six men, fully provisioned, with Captain Reasin P. Tucker at their head, reached Johnson's ranch, and in ten or twelve days' time, with provisions, mules, etc., the first relief party started for the scene at Donner lake. It was a fearful undertaking, but on the morning of the 19th of February, 1847, the above party began the descent of the gorge leading to Donner lake.

We have purposely thrown a veil over the dreadful sufferings of the stricken band left in their wretched hovels at Donner lake. Reduced to the verge of starvation, many died (including numerous children, seven of whom were nursing babes) who, in this dreadful state of necessity, were summarily disposed of. Rawhides, moccasins, strings, etc., were eaten. But relief was now close at hand for the poor, stricken sufferers. On the evening of the 19th of February, 1847, the stillness of death that had settled upon the scene was broken by prolonged shouts. In an instant the painfully sensitive ears of the despairing watchers caught the welcome sound. Captain Tucker, with his relief party, had at last arrived upon the scene. Every face was bathed in tears, and the strongest men of the relief party melted at the appalling sight, sat down, and wept with the rest. But time was precious, as storms were imminent. The return party was quickly gathered. Twenty-three members started, among them several women and children. Of this number two were compelled to return, and three perished on the journey. Many hardships and privations were experienced, and their provisions were soon entirely exhausted. Death once more stared them in the face, and despair settled upon them. But assistance was near at hand. James F. Reed, who had preceded the Donner party by some months, suddenly appeared with the second relief party, on the 25th of February, 1847. The joy of the meeting was indescribable, especially between the family and the long-absent father. Re-provisioned, the party pressed on, and gained their destination after severe suffering, with eighteen members, only three having perished. Reed continued his journey to the cabins at Donner lake. There the scene was simply indescribable; starvation and disease were fast claiming their victims. March 1st (according to Breen's diary) Reed and his party arrived at the camp. Proceeding directly to his cabin, he was espied by his little daughter (who, with her sister, was carried back by the previous party) and immediately recognized with a cry of joy. Provisions were carefully dealt out to the famishing people, and immediate steps were taken for the return. Seventeen comprised this party. Half-starved and completely exhausted, they were compelled to camp in the midst of a furious storm, in which Mr. Reed barely escaped with his life. This was "Starved Camp," and from this point Mr. Reed, with his two little children and another person, struggled ahead to obtain hasty relief, if possible.

On the second day after leaving "Starved Camp," Mr. Reed and the three companions were overtaken by Cady and Stone, and on the night of the third day, reached Woodworth's camp, at Bear valley, in safety. The horrors of "Starved Camp" beggar all description, indeed, require none. The third relief party, composed of John Stark, Howard Oakley, and Charles Stone, were nearing the rescue, while W. H. Foster and W. H. Eddy (rescued by a former party) were bent on the same mission. These, with Hiram Miller, set out from Woodworth's camp on the following morning after Reed's arrival. The eleven were duly reached, but were in a starving condition, and nine of the eleven were unable to walk. By the noble resolution and herculean efforts of John Stark, a part of the number were borne and urged onward to their destination, while the other portion was compelled to remain and await another relief party. When the third relief party, under Foster and Eddy, arrived at Donner lake, the sole survivors of Alder creek were George Donner, the captain of the company, and his heroic and faithful wife, whose devotion to her dying husband caused her own death during the last and fearful days of waiting for the fourth relief. George Donner knew he was dying, and urged his wife to save her life, and go with her little ones, with the third relief, but she refused. Nothing was more heart-rending than her sad parting with her beloved little ones, who wound their childish arms lovingly around her neck and besought her with mingled tears and kisses to join them. But duty prevailed over affection, and she retraced the weary distance to die with him whom she had promised to love and honor to the end. Such scenes of anguish are seldom witnessed on this sorrowing earth, and such acts of triumphant devotion are among her most golden deeds. The snowy cerements of Donner lake enshrouded in its stilly whiteness no purer life, no nobler heart than Mrs. George Donner's. The terrible recitals that close this awful tragedy we willingly omit.

The third relief party rescued four of the last five survivors; the fourth and last relief party rescued the last survivor, Lewis Keseberg, on the 7th of April, 1847. Ninety names are given as members of the Donner party. Of these forty-two perished, six did not live to reach the mountains, and forty-eight survived. Twenty-six, and possibly twenty-eight, out of the forty-eight survivors are living to-day—several residing in San Jose, Calistoga, Los Gatos, Marysville, and in Oregon.

Thus ends this narrative of horrors, without a parallel in the annals of American history, of appalling disasters, fearful sufferings, heroic fortitude, self denial and heroism.

CHAPTER XIV.
THE DISCOVERY OF GOLD.

Early Reports and Discoveries—Marshall's Great Discovery at Sutter's Mill—His Account of the Event—Views of the Newspapers of that Time—Political and Social Revolution—Great Rush to the Mines—Results—General Sutter's Account of the Gold Discovery—Building of Saw-Mill.

FROM the first discovery of California by the Spaniards the impression prevailed that the country was rich in silver, gold, and precious stones. When setting out on his northern expedition, the object of Cortez was to find another country like Mexico, inhabited by a semi-civilized people, whose rich treasures he might appropriate; and afterwards there existed among the inhabitants of New Spain a strong belief in the great riches of the new province, both in gold and precious stones. The first published report of gold in California is found in Hakluyt's account of Sir Francis Drake's expedition to this coast in 1579. The historian of the voyage says: "There is no part of the earth here to be taken up wherein there is not a reasonable quantity of gold or silver."

It is not related that any of Drake's men penetrated into the interior of the country or made any search for these metals, and since neither gold nor silver is found in the neighborhood of Drake's or San Francisco bay, it is to be inferred that this statement was a falsehood, uttered for the purpose of giving importance to Drake's supposed discovery.

There is no further account of gold or silver discoveries for two hundred and twenty-three years, until 1802, when it is said that silver was found at Alizal, in Monterey county, but the mine never produced anything of consequence. Manfras says that gold was found in San Diego county in 1828; but as the discovery had not been heard of by Alexander Forbes, the historian of California, in 1835, it could not have been of any importance. On the contrary, Forbes, in his book of that date, says: "No minerals of particular importance have yet been found in Upper California, nor any ores of metals." In another place, referring to Hijar's migration to California in 1833, he says: "There were goldsmiths in the party proceeding to a country where no gold existed." Mr. Forbes was then the British Vice-Consul at Monterey, and was doing all in his power to interest the English Government in the country; it is therefore certain that up to that time—1835—no mineral discoveries of any consequence had been made in the province.

The first mine to produce any noticeable amount of precious metal was the gold placers in the cañon of the San Francisquito creek, forty-five miles northwest of Los Angeles. It was discovered about the year 1838, and was worked continuously for ten years, when it was deserted for the richer discoveries in the Sacramento basin. Its total yield was probably not over sixty thousand dollars or about six thousand dollars a year.

In 1842, James D. Dana, the geologist and mineralogist with Wilkes' Exploring Expedition, traveled from the northern frontier through the Sacramento basin to the Bay of San Francisco, and afterwards published a work in which he said: "The gold rocks and veins of quartz were observed by the author in 1842, near the Umpqua river, in southern Oregon, and pebbles from similar rocks were met with along the shores of the Sacramento, in California, and the resemblance to other gold districts was remarked, but there was no opportunity of exploring the country at the time." Mr. Dana's professional knowledge enabled him to perceive certain indications of gold, but no practical discoveries were made.

On the 4th of May, 1846, Thomas O. Larkin, then United States Consul at Monterey, wrote to the Secretary of State as follows: "There is said to be black lead in the country at San Fernando, near San Pedro. By washing the sand in a plate, any person can obtain from one to five dollars per day of gold that brings seventeen dollars per ounce in Boston. The gold has been gathered for two or three years, though but few persons have the patience to look for it. On the south-west end of the Island of Catalina there is a silver mine from which silver has been extracted. There is no doubt that gold, silver, quicksilver, copper, lead, sulphur and coal mines are to be found all over California, and it is equally doubtful whether, under their present owners, they will ever be worked." Till May, 1846, no productive mines were in operation, except the one on San Francisquito creek, in what is now Los Angeles county.

It was reserved for James W. Marshall to make the great discovery, on the 19th of January, 1848, at Sutter's mill, on the South Fork of the American river, near the present town of Coloma, in El Dorado county.

No account of the memorable event can be so interesting as that of Mr. Marshall himself, who in a letter of January 28, 1856, says:—

"Towards the end of August, 1847, Captain Sutter and I formed a copartnership to build and run a saw-mill upon a site selected by myself (since known as Coloma). We employed P. L. Weimer and family, to remove from the fort (Sutter's Fort) to the mill-site to cook and labor for us. Nearly the first work done was the building of a double log cabin, about half a mile from the mill-site. We commenced the mill about Christmas. Some of the mill hands wanted a cabin near the mill. This was built, and I went to the fort to superintend the construction of the mill irons, leaving orders to cut a narrow ditch where the race was to be made. Upon my return, in January, 1848, I found the ditch cut as directed, and those who were working on the same were doing so at a great disadvantage, expending their labor upon the head of the race instead of the foot.

"I immediately changed the course of things, and upon the 19th of the same month, January, discovered the gold near the lower end of the race about two hundred yards below the mill. William Scott was the second man to see the metal. He was at work at a carpenter's bench near the mill. I showed the gold to him. Alexander Stephens, James Brown, Henry Bigler, and William Johnston, were likewise working in front of the mill, framing the upper story. They were called up next, and, of course, saw the precious metal. P. L. Weimer and Charles Bennett were at the old double log cabin (where Hastings & Co. afterwards kept a store), and, in my opinion, at least half a mile distant.

"In the meantime we put in some wheat and peas, nearly five acres, across the river. In February, the Captain (Captain Sutter) came to the mountains for the first time. Then we consummated a treaty with the Indians, which had been previously negotiated. The tenor of this was that we were to pay them two hundred dollars yearly in goods at Yerba Buena prices, for the joint possession and occupation of the land with them; they agreeing not to kill our stock, viz.: horses, cattle, hogs or sheep, nor burn the grass within the limits fixed by the treaty. At the same time, Captain Sutter, myself, and Isaac Humphrey, entered into a copartnership to dig gold. A short time afterwards, P. L. Weimer moved away from the mill, and was away two or three months, when he returned. With all the events that subsequently occurred, you and the public are well informed."

The following additional particulars of the discovery appeared in the Coloma *Argus* in the latter part of the year 1855, and were evidently derived from Weimer himself:—

"That James W. Marshall picked up the first piece of gold, is beyond doubt Peter L. Wimmer (Weimer), who resides in this place, states positively that Mr. Marshall picked up the gold in his presence; they both saw it, and each spoke at the same time, 'What's that yellow stuff?' Marshall being a step in advance picked it up. This first piece of gold is now in the possession of Mrs. Wimmer, and weighs six penny-weights, eleven grains. The piece was given to her by Marshall himself. * * * The dam was finished early in January, the frame for the mill also erected, and the flume and bulk-head completed. It was at this time that Marshall and Wimmer adopted the plan of raising the gate during the night to wash out sand from the mill-race, closing it during the day, when work would be continued with shovels, etc. Early in February—the exact day is not remembered—in the morning, after shutting off the water, Marshall and Wimmer walked down the race together to see what the water had accomplished during the night. Having gone about twenty yards below the mill, they both saw the piece of gold mentioned, and Marshall picked it up. After an examination, the gold was taken to the cabin of Wimmer, and Mrs. Wimmer instructed to boil it in saleratus water; but, she being engaged in making soap, pitched the piece in the soap-kettle, where it was boiled all day and all night. The following morning the strange piece of stuff was fished out of the soap, all the brighter for the boiling it had received. Discussion now commenced, and all expressed the opinion that perhaps the yellow substance might be gold. Little was said on the subject; but every one each morning searched in the race for more, and every day found several small scales. The Indians also picked up many small thin pieces, and carried them always to Mrs. Wimmer.

"About three weeks after the first piece was obtained, Marshall took the fine gold, amounting to between two and three ounces, and went below to have the strange metal tested. On his return, he informed Wimmer that the stuff was gold. All hands now began to search for the 'root of all evil.' Shortly after Captain Sutter came to Coloma, when he and Marshall assembled the Indians, and bought of them a large tract of country about Coloma, in exchange for a lot of beads and a few cotton handkerchiefs. They, under color of this Indian title, required one-third of all the gold dug on their domain, and collected at this rate until the Fall of 1848, when a mining party from Oregon declined paying 'tithes,' as they called it.

"During February, 1848, Marshall and Wimmer went down the river to Mormon Island, and there found scales of gold on the rocks. Some weeks later they sent a Mr Henderson, Sydney Willis, and Mr. Fifield, Mormons, down there to dig, telling them that that place was better than Coloma. These were the first miners at Mormon Island."

In a little work entitled "Mining in the Pacific States," published by H. H. Bancroft & Co., in 1861, Mr. John S. Hittell presents the following interesting facts concerning the great discovery:—

"Marshall was a man of an active, enthusiastic mind, and he at once attached great importance to his discovery. His ideas, however, were vague; he knew nothing about gold-mining; he did not know how to take advantage of what he had found. Only an experienced gold-miner could understand the importance of the discovery, and make it of practical value to all the world. That gold-miner, fortunately, was near at hand; his name was Isaac Humphrey. He was residing in the town of San Francisco, in the month of February, when a Mr. Bennett, one of the party employed at Marshall's mill, went down to that place with some of the dust to have it tested; for it was still a matter of doubt whether this yellow metal really was gold. Bennett told his errand to a friend whom he met in San Francisco, and this friend introduced him to Humphrey, who had been a gold-miner in Georgia, and was therefore competent to pass an opinion upon the stuff. Humphrey looked at the dust, pronounced it gold, at the first glance, and expressed a belief that the diggings must be rich. He made inquiries about the place where the gold was found, and subsequent inquiries about the trustworthiness of Mr. Bennett, and on the 7th of March he was at the mill. He tried to induce several of his friends in San Francisco to go with him; they all thought his expedition a foolish one, and he had to go alone. He found that there was some talk about the gold, and persons would occasionally go about looking for pieces of it; but no one was engaged in mining, and the work of the mill was going on as usual. On the 8th he went out prospecting with a pan, and satisfied himself that the country in that vicinity was rich in gold. He then made a rocker and commenced the business of washing gold; and thus began the business of mining in California. Others saw how he did it, followed his example, found that the work was profitable, and abandoned all other occupations. The news of their success spread, people flocked to the place, learned how to use the rocker, discovered new diggings, and, in the course of a few months, the country had been overturned by a social and industrial revolution.

"Mr. Humphrey had not been at work more than three or four days before a Frenchman, called Baptiste, who had been a gold-miner in Mexico for many years, came to the mill, and he agreed with Humphrey that California was very rich in gold. He, too, went to work, and being an excellent prospector, he was of great service in teaching the new-comers the principles of prospecting and mining for gold, principles not abstruse, yet not likely to suggest themselves, at first thought, to men entirely ignorant of the business. Baptiste had been employed by Captain Sutter to saw timber with a whip-saw, and had been at work for two years at a place, since called Weber, about ten miles eastward from Coloma. When he saw the diggings at the latter place, he at once said there were rich mines where he had been sawing, and he expressed surprise that it had never occurred to him before, so experienced in gold-mining as he was; but afterwards he said it had been so ordered by Providence, that the gold might not be discovered until California should be in the hands of the Americans.

"About the middle of March, P. B. Reading, an American, now a prominent and wealthy citizen of the State, then the owner of a large ranch on the western bank of the Sacramento river, near where it issues from the mountains, came to Coloma, and after looking about at the diggings, said that if similarity in the appearance of the country could be taken as a guide, there must be gold in the hills near his ranch; and he went off, declaring his intention to go back and make an examination of them. John Bidwell, another American, now a wealthy and influential citizen, then residing on his ranch on the bank of Feather river, came to Coloma about a week later, and he said there must be gold near his ranch, and he went off with expressions similar to those used by Reading. In a few weeks news came that Reading had found diggings near Clear creek, at the head of the Sacramento valley, and was at work there with his Indians; and not long after, it was reported that Bidwell was at work with his Indians on a rich bar of Feather river, since called Bidwell's Bar."

Although there were two newspapers, the *Californian* and *Star*, published in San Francisco, they do not seem to have been either very credulous or very enterprising. They did not hear of the discovery till some weeks after the great event; or, if they did hear of it, they did not credit the report. The first published notice of the gold discovery appeared in the *Californian* on the fifteenth of March, nearly two months after the event, and was as follows:—

"GOLD MINE FOUND.—In the newly-made raceway of the saw-mill recently erected by Captain Sutter, on the American fork, gold has been found in considerable quantities. One person brought thirty dollars' worth to New Helvetia, gathered there in a short time. California, no doubt, is rich in mineral wealth; great chances here for scientific capitalists. Gold has been found in almost every part of the country."

Three days afterwards the *Star* made the following brief allusion to the subject:—

"We were informed a few days since that a very valuable silver mine was situated in the vicinity of this place, and again, that its locality was known. Mines of quicksilver are being found all over the country. Gold has been discovered in the northern Sacramento district, about forty miles above Sutter's Fort. Rich mines of copper are said to exist north of these bays."

The *Star* of March 25th says: "So great is the quantity of gold taken from the new mines recently found at New Helvetia, that it has become an article of traffic in that vicinity."

It was three months after Marshall's discovery, before the San Francisco papers announced that gold mining had become a regular and profitable business. The *Californian* of April 26th says:—

"GOLD MINES OF THE SACRAMENTO.—From a gentleman just from the gold region, we learn that many new discoveries have very recently been made, and it is fully ascertained that a large extent of country abounds with that precious mineral. Seven men, with picks and spades, gathered nine thousand six hundred dollars within fifteen days. Many persons are settling on the lands with the view of holding preemptions, but as yet every person takes the right to gather all he can, without any regard to claims. The largest piece yet found is worth six dollars."

The *Star* of April 1, 1848, contained an elaborate article on the resources of California, giving due credence and importance to the great event which was so soon to vitalize the sluggish province, in which the writer said:—

"It would be utterly impossible at present to make a correct estimate of the mineral wealth of California. Popular attention has been but lately directed to it. But the discoveries that have already been made will warrant us in the assertion that California is one of the richest mineral countries in the world. Gold, silver, quicksilver, iron, copper, lead, sulphur, saltpetre, and other mines of great value have already been found. We saw, a few days ago, a beautiful specimen of gold from the mine newly discovered on the American fork. From all accounts the mine is immensely rich, and already we learn the gold from it, collected at random and without any trouble, has become an article of trade at the upper settlements. This precious metal abounds in this country. We have heard of several other newly-discovered mines of gold, but as these reports are not yet authenticated we shall pass over them. However, it is well known that there is a placer of gold a few miles from the ciudad de Los Angeles, and another on the San Joaquin."

The *Californian* of August 14, 1848, contained an article descriptive of the process and implements of gold-mining at that time, and having related the particulars of the discovery at Sutter's mill, the writer continues:—

"It soon began to attract attention, and some persons discovered gold in the river below, and for some distance above the mill, in large quantities; so much so that persons who only gave credit to one-third of what was said about it left their homes and went to work in the mines. It was the work of but a few weeks to bring almost the entire population of the Territory together, to pick up the precious metal. The result has been that in less than four months, a total revolution has been effected in the prospects and fate of Alta California. Then, the capital was in the hands of a few individuals engaged in trade and speculation; now, labor has got the upper hand of capital, and the laboring men hold the great mass of the wealth of the country—the gold.

"There are now about four thousand white persons, besides a number of Indians, engaged in the mines; and from the fact that no capital is required, they are working in companies, on equal shares, or alone, with their baskets. In one part of the mine, called the dry-diggings, no other implement is necessary than an ordinary sheath-knife, to pick the gold from the rocks. In other parts, where the gold is washed out, the machinery is very simple, being an ordinary trough made of plank, round on the bottom, about ten feet long, and two feet wide at the top, with a riddle or sieve, at one end, to catch the larger gravel, and three or four small bars across the bottom, about half an inch high, to keep the gold from going out with the dirt and water at the lower end. This machine is set upon rockers, which give a half-rotary motion to the water and dirt inside. But far the largest number use nothing but a large tin-pan, or an Indian basket, into which they place the dirt, and shake it about until the gold gets to the bottom, and the dirt is carried over the side in the shape of muddy water. It is necessary, in some cases, to have a crowbar, pick, or shovel, but a great deal is taken up with large horns, shaped spoon-fashion at the large end.

THE DISCOVERY OF GOLD. 55

"From the fact that no capital is necessary, a fair competition in labor, without the influence of capital, men who were only able to procure one month's provisions have now thousands of dollars of the precious metal. The laboring class have now become the capitalists of the country.

"As to the richness of the mines, were we to set down half the truth, it would be looked upon in other countries as a Sinbad story, or the history of Aladdin's lamp. Many persons have collected in one day, of the finest grade of gold, from three to eight hundred dollars, and for many days together averaged from seventy-five to one hundred and fifty dollars. Although this is not universal, yet the general average is so well settled, that when a man with his pan or basket does not easily gather from thirty to forty dollars in a day, he moves to another place; so that taking the general average, including the time spent in moving from place to place and in looking for better diggings, we are of the opinion that we may safely set down an ounce of pure gold, or sixteen dollars per day, to the man. Suppose there are four thousand persons at work, they will add to the aggregate wealth of the Territory about four thousand ounces, or sixty-four thousand dollars a day.

"Four months ago, flour was sold in this market (San Francisco) for four dollars per hundred; now it is sixteen. Beef cattle were then six; now they are thirty. Ready-made clothing, groceries, and other goods, have not risen in the same proportion, but are at least double their former cost. If we make bread and meat the standard by which to determine the value of gold, then it is worth only one-fourth of what it is elsewhere. But if gold and silver be the standard, then the bread and meat is worth four times what it was. But, the relative value of the grain-gold, compared with gold and silver coin, can only be changed by the action of Government; for, however abundant the gold may be, it must produce its relative value in coin; and, while a five-dollar gold-piece will be received at the Treasury as five dollars, so long must an ounce of gold be worth sixteen dollars.

"As to the future hopes of California, her course is onward, with a rapidity that will astonish the world. Her unparalleled gold mines, silver mines, iron ore, and lead, with the best climate in the world, and the richest soil, will make it the garden-spot of creation."

The *Californian*, of September 23, 1848, gives the following graphic account of the grand rush to the gold mines:—

"It would seem that but little doubt was entertained of its being the *Simon-pure* staff; for operations immediately ceased at the mill, and all hands commenced searching for gold. It was soon found that gold abounded all along the American fork, for a distance of thirty miles. But little credit however was given the report, though occasionally a solitary gold-hunter might be seen stealing down to the launch, with a pick and shovel, more that half-ashamed of his credulity. Sometime during the month of May a number of credible persons arrived in town from the scene of operations, bringing specimens of the ore, and stating that those engaged in collecting the precious metal were making from three to ten dollars per day. Then commenced the grand rush. The inhabitants throughout the Territory were in a commotion. Large companies of men, women, and children could be seen on every road leading to the mines; their wagons loaded down with tools for digging, provisions, etc. Launch after launch left the wharves of our city (San Francisco) crowded with passengers and freight, for the Sacramento. Mechanical operations of every kind ceased. Whole streets, that were but a week before alive with a busy population, were entirely deserted, and the place wore the appearance of a city that had been suddenly visited by a devastating plague. To cap the climax, the newspapers were obliged to stop printing, for want of readers.

"Meantime, our mercantile friends were doing an unwonted stroke of business. Every arrival from the mining district brought more or less gold-dust, the major part of which immediately passed into the hands of the merchants, for goods. Immense quantities of merchandise were conveyed to the mines, until it became a matter of astonishment where so much could be disposed of. During the first eight weeks of the golden times, the receipts at this place (San Francisco) in gold-dust amounted to two hundred and fifty thousand dollars. For the eight weeks ending at this date (Sept. 23, 1848), they were six hundred thousand dollars. The number of persons now engaged in gold-hunting will probably exceed six thousand, including Indians, and one ounce per day is the lowest average we can put for each person, while many collect their hundreds of dollars for a number of days in succession, and instances have been known where one individual has collected from fifteen hundred to eighteen hundred dollars worth of pure gold in one day. Explorations have been progressing, and it is now fully ascertained that gold exists on both sides of the Sierra Nevada, from latitude forty-one degrees north, as far south as the head-waters of the San Joaquin river, a distance of four hundred miles in length and one hundred in breadth. Farther than this has not been explored; but from the nature of the country beyond the sources of the San Joaquin, we doubt not gold will also be found there in equal abundance. The gold region already known is sufficiently extensive to give profitable employment to one hundred thousand persons for generations to come. The ore is in a virgin state, disseminated in small doses, and is found in three distinct deposits—in sand and gravel beds, in decomposed granite, and intermingled with a kind of slate."

In April, 1848, Mr. Jonas Spect, an enterprising pioneer, gave the following interesting account of gold discoveries:—

"Up to this time there had been little excitement about the gold diggings; but at Knight's Landing we were overtaken by Spaniards, who were on their way to Sutter's mill to dig gold, and they reported stories of fabulously rich diggings. After discussing the matter, we changed our course to the gold mines and hurried on, arriving at the mill on the thirtieth day of April. It was true that several rich strikes had been made, but the miners then at work did not average two and a half dollars per day. Marshall and Sutter claimed the land and rented the mines. Every one supposed gold was confined to that particular locality. We did not engage in mining, and concluded to resume our journey across the plains. On our return trip we learned that gold had been found on Mormon Island. But we took no further notice of gold, and on the 12th of May arrived at Johnson's ranch. We found one man there waiting our arrival, but we expected many others in a short time. We waited until about the 25th, when we learned that there was another rush to the mines, and then vanished all prospect of any company crossing the mountains that Summer. My partner left for the American river, and I proposed to Johnson that we should prospect for gold on Bear river. We went some distance up the stream and spent three days in the search without any satisfactory result. I then suggested to Johnson that he should send his Indian with me, and I would prospect the Yuba river, as that stream was about the size of the South Fork of the American river. We prepared the outfit, and on the 1st of June, we struck the Yuba near Long Bar. After a good deal of prospecting, I succeeded in raising 'color.' That night I camped in Timbuctoo ravine, a little above where we first found the gold. The next day, June 2d, I continued prospecting up the stream, finding a little gold, but not enough to pay. The Indian was well acquainted, and he piloted me up to the location of Rose's Bar, where we met a large number of Indians, all entirely nude and eating clover. I prospected on the bar, and found some gold, but not sufficient to be remunerative. Greatly discouraged, I started on my return home. When I arrived at a point on the Yuba river, a little above Timbuctoo ravine, I washed some of the dirt and found three lumps of gold worth about seven dollars. I pitched my tent here on the night of June 2d, and sent the Indian home for supplies. In about a week I moved down on the creek, and remained there until November 20th, when I left the mines forever. June 3d, the next day after the location of my camp, Michael C. Nye and William Foster came up the creek prospecting for gold."

The discovery of gold on the American river led Mr Nye and party to start out on a prospecting trip. In the Summer—the exact date is not known—they found paying diggings on Dry creek, near its junction with the Yuba, and commenced working on an extensive scale. The discoveries by Mr. Spect and Mr Nye's company were nearly contemporaneous, and as the parties started from different localities, and without any knowledge of the acts of the other, due credit should be given to each.

GENERAL SUTTER'S ACCOUNT OF THE GOLD DISCOVERY.

The following extracts are from an article communicated, in his own handwriting, by General Sutter to *Hutchings' California Magazine* for November, 1857. As a part of the history of the great event referred to, and as the personal narrative of one of the chief actors in the golden drama, it is one of the most interesting records of the time. General Sutter says:—

"It was in the first of January, 1848, when the gold was discovered at Coloma, where I was building a saw mill. The contractor and builder of this mill was James W. Marshall, from New Jersey. In the Fall of 1847, after the mill site had been located, I sent up to this place Mr. P. L. Wimmer, with his family, and a number of laborers from the disbanded Mormon Battalion, and a little later I engaged Mr. Bennett, from Oregon, to assist Mr. Marshall in the mechanical labors of the mill. Mr. Wimmer had the team in charge, assisted by his young sons to do the teaming, and Mrs. Wimmer did the cooking for all hands.

"I was very much in need of a saw-mill to get lumber to finish my flouring-mill, of four run of stones, at Brighton, which was commenced at the same time, and was rapidly progressing; likewise, for other buildings, fences, etc., for the small village of Yerba Buena, now San Francisco. In the City Hotel (the only one) this enterprise was unkindly called 'another folly of Sutter's,' as my first settlement at the old fort, near Sacramento City, was called by a good many 'a folly of his,' and they were about right in that, because I had the best chances to get some of the finest locations near the settlements; and even well-stocked ranches had been offered me on the most reasonable conditions. But I refused all these good offers, and preferred to explore the wilderness, and select a territory on the banks of the Sacramento.

"It was a rainy afternoon when Mr. Marshall arrived at my office, in the fort, very wet. I was somewhat surprised to see him, as he was down a few days previous, when I sent up to Coloma a number of teams with provisions, mill irons, etc. He told me then that he had some important and interesting news which he wished to communicate secretly to me, and wished me to go with him to a place where we should not be disturbed, and where no listeners could come and hear what we had to say. I went with him to my private rooms; he requested me to lock the door, I complied, but told him at the same time that nobody was in the house except the clerk, who was in his office in a different part of the house.

"After requesting of me something which he wanted, which my servants brought and then left the room, I forgot to lock the door, and it happened that the door was opened by the clerk just at the moment when Marshall took a rag from his pocket, showing me the yellow metal. He had about two ounces of it; but how quick Mr. Marshall put the yellow metal in his pocket again, can hardly be described. The clerk came to see me on business, and excused himself for interrupting me; and as soon as he had left, I was told, 'Now, lock the door. Didn't I tell you that we might have listeners?' I told him he need fear nothing about that, as it was not the habit of this gentleman; but I could hardly convince him that he need not be suspicious.

"Then Mr. Marshall began to show me this metal, which consisted of small pieces and specimens, some of them worth a few dollars. He told me that he had expressed his opinion to the laborers at the mill that this might be gold; but some of them laughed at him and called him a crazy man, and could not believe such a thing.

"After having proved the metal with aqua fortis, which I found in my apothecary shop, likewise with other experiments, and read the long article 'Gold,' in the *Encyclopedia Americana*, I declared this to be gold of the finest quality, of at least twenty-three carats. After this Mr. Marshall had no more rest or patience, and wanted me to start with him immediately for Coloma, but I told him I could not leave, as it was late in the evening, and nearly supper-time, and that it would be better for him to remain with me till the next morning, and I would then travel with him. But this would not do; he asked me only, 'Will you come to-morrow?' I told him yes, and off he started for Coloma in the heaviest rain, although already very wet, taking nothing to eat. I took this news very easy, like all other occurrences, good or bad, but thought a great deal during the night about the consequences

THE DISCOVERY OF GOLD.

which might follow such a discovery. I gave all the necessary orders to my numerous laborers, and left the next morning at seven o'clock, accompanied by an Indian soldier and a vaquero, in a heavy rain, for Coloma. About half-way on the road, I saw at a distance a human being crawling out from the brushwood. I asked the Indian who it was. He told me, 'the same man who was with you last evening.' When I came nearer I found it was Marshall, very wet. I told him he would have done better to remain with me at the fort, than to pass such an ugly night here; but he told me that he went to Coloma, fifty-four miles, took his other horse and came half-way to meet me. Then we rode up to the new El Dorado.

"In the afternoon, the weather was clearing up, and we made a prospecting promenade. The next morning, we went to the tail-race of the mill, through which the water was running during the night, to clear out the gravel which had been made loose for the purpose of widening the race; and after the water was out of the race, we went in to search for gold. This was done every morning. Small pieces of gold could be seen remaining on the surface of the clean-washed bed-rock. I went into the race and picked up several pieces of this gold; several of the laborers gave me some which they had picked up, and from Marshall I received a part. I told them I would get a ring made of this gold as soon as it could be done in California; and I have had a heavy ring made, with my family's coat-of-arms engraved on the outside, and on the inside of the ring is engraved: 'the first gold discovered in January, 1848.' Now if Mrs. Wimmer possesses a piece which had been found earlier than mine, Mr. Marshall can tell, as it was probably received from him. I think Mr. Marshall could have hardly known himself which was exactly the first little piece, among the whole.

'The next day I went with Mr. Marshall on a prospecting tour in the vicinity of Coloma, and the following morning I left for Sacramento. Before my departure, I had a conversation with all hands; I told them I would consider it a great favor if they would keep this discovery secret only for six weeks, so that I could finish my large flour-mill at Brighton, which had cost me already about twenty-four or twenty-five thousand dollars. The people up there promised to keep it secret so long. On my way home, instead of feeling happy and contented, I was very unhappy, and could not see that it would benefit me much; and I was perfectly right in thinking so, as it came just precisely as I expected. I thought, at the same time that it could hardly be kept secret for six weeks; and in that I was not mistaken, for, about two weeks later, after my return, I sent up several teams, in charge of a white man, as the teamsters were Indian boys. This man was acquainted with all hands up there, and Mrs. Wimmer told him the whole secret; likewise the young sons of Mrs. Wimmer told him that they had gold, and that they would let him have some, too; and so he obtained a few dollars' worth of it, as a present. As soon as this man arrived at the fort, he went to a small store in one of my outside buildings, kept by Mr. Smith, a partner of Samuel Brannan, and asked for a bottle of brandy, for which he would pay the cash. After having the bottle he paid with these small pieces of gold. Smith was astonished, and asked if he meant to insult him. The teamster told him to go and ask me about it. Smith came in, in great haste to see me, and I told him at once the truth—what could I do? I had to tell him all about it. He reported it to Mr. S. Brannan, who came up immediately to get all possible information, when he returned and sent up large supplies of goods, leased a larger house from me, and commenced a very large and profitable business. Soon he opened a branch house at Mormon Island.

"So soon as the secret was out, my laborers began to leave me, in small parties at first, but then all left, from the clerk to the cook, and I was in great distress. Only a few mechanics remained to finish some necessary work which they had commenced, and about eight invalids, who continued slowly to work a few teams, to scrape out the mill-race at Brighton. The Mormons did not like to leave my mill unfinished; but they got the gold-fever, like everybody else. After they had made their piles they left for the Great Salt Lake. So long as these people have been employed by me, they have behaved very well and were industrious and faithful laborers; and when settling their accounts, there was not one of them who was not contented and satisfied.

"Then the people commenced rushing up from San Francisco and other parts of California, in May, 1848. In the former village (San Francisco,) only five men were left to take care of the women and children. The single men locked their doors and left for 'Sutter's Fort,' and from thence to the El Dorado. For some time the people in Monterey and further south, would not believe the news of the gold discovery, and said it was only a 'ruse de guerre of Sutter's, because he wanted to have neighbors in his wilderness.' From this time on I got only too many neighbors, and some very bad ones among them.

"What a great misfortune was this sudden gold discovery to me! It has just broken up and ruined my hard, industrious, and restless labors, connected with many dangers of life, as I had many narrow escapes before I became properly established. From my mill buildings I reaped no benefit whatever; the mill-stones, even, have been stolen from me. My tannery, which was then in a flourishing condition, and was carried on very profitably, was deserted; a large quantity of leather was left unfinished in the vats, and a great quantity of rawhides became valueless, as they could not be sold. Nobody wanted to be bothered with such trash, as it was called. So it was in all the other mechanical trades which I had carried on; all was abandoned, and work commenced, or nearly finished, was left, at an immense loss to me. Even the Indians had no more patience to work alone, in harvesting and threshing my large wheat crop; as the whites had all left, and other Indians had been engaged by some white men to work for them, and they commenced to have some gold, for which they were buying all kinds of articles at enormous prices in the stores, which, when my Indians saw this, they wished very much to go to the mountains and dig gold. At last I consented, got a number of wagons ready, loaded them with provisions and goods of all kinds, employed a clerk, and left with about one hundred Indians and about fifty Sandwich Islanders, which had joined those which I brought with me from the Islands. The first camp was about ten miles from Mormon Island, on the South fork of the American river. In a few weeks we became crowded, and it would no more pay, as my people made too many acquaintances. I broke up the camp and started on the march further south, and located my next camp on Sutter creek, now in Amador county, and thought that I should there be alone. The work was going on well for awhile, until three or four traveling grog-shops surrounded me, at from one-half to ten miles distance from the camp. Then, of course, the gold was taken to these places, for drinking, gambling, etc., and then the following day they were sick and unable to work, and became deeper and more indebted to me, particularly the Kanakas. I found it was high time to quit this kind of business, and lose no more time and money. I therefore broke up the camp and returned to the fort, where I disbanded nearly all the people who had worked for me in the mountains digging gold. This whole expedition proved to be a heavy loss to me.

"At the same time, I was engaged in a mercantile firm at Coloma, which I left in January, 1849, likewise with many sacrifices. After this, I would have nothing more to do with the gold affairs. At this time the fort was the great trading-place, where nearly all the business was transacted. I had no pleasure to remain there, and moved up to Hock farm, with all my Indians, who had been with me from the time they were children. The place was then in charge of a major-domo.

"It was very singular that the Indians never found a piece of gold and brought it to me, as they very often did other specimens found in the mountains. I requested them continually to bring me some curiosities from the mountains, for which I always recompensed them. I have received animals, birds, plants, young trees, wild fruits, pipe-clay, red ochre, etc. but never a piece of gold. Mr. Dana, of the Wilkes Exploring Expedition, told me that he had the strongest proof and signs of gold in the vicinity of Shasta mountain, and further south. A short time afterwards Dr. Sandels, a very scientific traveler, visited me, explored a part of the country in a great hurry, as time would not permit him to make a longer stay. He told me likewise that he found some signs of gold, and was very sorry that he could not explore the Sierra Nevada. He did not encourage me to attempt to work and open mines, as it was uncertain how it would pay, and would probably be only profitable for a Government. So I thought it more prudent to stick to the plow, notwithstanding I did know the country was rich in gold and other minerals. An old, attached Mexican servant, who had followed me from the United States as soon as he knew that I was here, and who understood a great deal about working in placers, told me he found sure signs of gold in the mountains on Bear creek, and that we would go right to work after returning from our campaign in 1845; but he became a victim to his patriotism, and fell into the hands of the enemy near my encampment, with dispatches for me from General Micheltorena, and he was hung as a spy, for which I was very sorry. J. A. SUTTER."

CHAPTER XV.

EARLY CONDITION OF THIS REGION.

Mountains, Unexplored by the Spaniards—The Trappers—Fremont's Passage of the Mountains in 1844—Battles with the Snow—The Indian's Warning—A Glimpse of the Valley—Subsisting on Horse Flesh—Arrival at Sutter's Fort—Early Settlements—An Immigrant Party of 1844—Captain Truckee—Truckee River—Alone on the Summit—Death of Captain Truckee—Immigrants in 1846—Discovery of Gold on the Yuba.

THE native Californians never penetrated into the heart of the mountains that skirt the Sacramento valley on the east; gazing from a distance upon their snow-clad crests, they had named them Sierra Nevada, the "snowy mountains," but beyond this they remained *terra incognita* to them. The bold and adventurous trappers of the American Fur Company, and the Hudson Bay Company, passed over them several times on their way to and from the choice trapping grounds in the valley. The celebrated trapper, Stephen H. Meek, claims to have been the first white man who gazed upon the Truckee river, on which stream he set his traps in 1833. The river did not receive its name, however, until eleven years later, as will appear further on. The Yuba and Bear rivers, having been explored by the Spaniards in 1822, in the valley, had been named at that time, the one Rio de las Uva (Grape river) and the other Rio de los Osos (Bear river), but as to their source and direction in the mountains nothing whatever was known. To them were unknown lakes Donner, Tahoe, and the scores of lesser lakes that are the pride of the mountains. A few miserable Digger Indians lived in huts, and subsisted on acorns, grass, rabbits, etc., and were sovereign lords of the beautiful Sierras.

The valleys of California were, during the early part of this century, occupied and traversed by bands of trappers in the employ of the many American and foreign fur companies. The stories of their wanderings and experiences are mostly related in the form of sensational novels, whose authenticity and accuracy must be taken with a great degree of allowance. Few records concerning these fur-hunters remain which are within the reach of the historian, and the information given has been gleaned in part from personal interviews with those whose knowledge of the subject was gained by actual experience, or by a personal acquaintance with those who belonged to the parties. In many cases their stories differ widely in regard to facts and names.

As early as 1820, the Tulare, San Joaquin, and Sacramento valleys were occupied by trappers, who had wandered there while searching for the Columbia river. Captain Sutter, in 1834, while in New Mexico, heard from these California trappers of the Sacramento valley, which afterwards became so reputed as his home. The disputes arising in regard to the occupation of the northern part of the Pacific coast trapping region, in Oregon, led the American hunters to occupy the territory in and about the Rocky Mountains. In 1815, Congress, at the earnest request of the people of the West, passed an Act driving out British traders from the American territory east of the Rocky Mountains. Immediately the employes of the old North American Fur Company, still under charge of John Jacob Astor, began to trap and hunt in the region of the head waters of the Mississippi and Upper Missouri. In 1823, Mr. W. H. Ashley, of St. Louis, an old merchant in the fur trade, at the head of a party, explored the Sweetwater, the Platte, the South Pass, and the head-waters of the Colorado, returning in the Summer. In 1824 he extended his explorations to Great Salt Lake, near which, on a smaller lake named

Lake Ashley, he built a fort and trading post, which was occupied for three years by his men. In 1826 (or 1827) Mr. Ashley disposed of his business, including the fort, to the Rocky Mountain Fur Company, under the leadership of Jedediah Smith, David Jackson and William Sublette.

During the Spring of 1825, Smith, with a party of forty trappers and Indians, started from the headquarters on Green river, traveling westward, crossed the Sierra Nevada mountains, and in July entered the Tulare valley. The country from the Tulare to the American fork of the Sacramento river was traversed in trapping for beaver. They found at the fork another party of American trappers encamped, and located their own rendezvous near the present town of Folsom. In October, Smith, leaving the remainder of the party at the camp, returned to the company's head-quarters on Green river. In May, 1826, Smith again set out for the new trapping region, taking a route further south than on the first trip, but when in the Mohave settlements, on the Colorado, all the party except Smith, Galbraith, and Turner, were killed by Indians. These three escaped to San Gabriel Mission, and December 26, 1826, were arrested as spies or filibusters. They were taken to the presidio at San Diego, where they were detained until the following certificate from Americans then in San Francisco was presented:—

"We, the undersigned, having been requested by Capt. Jedediah S. Smith to state our opinion regarding his entering the Province of California, do not hesitate to say that we have no doubt but that he was compelled to, for want of provisions and water, having entered so far into the barren country that lies between the latitudes of forty-two and forty-three west, that he found it impossible to return by the route he came, as his horses had most of them perished for want of food and water; he was therefore under the necessity of pushing forward to California, it being the nearest place where he could procure supplies to enable him to return.

"We further state as our opinion, that the account given by him is circumstantially correct, and that his sole object was the hunting and trapping of beaver and other furs.

"We have also examined the passports produced by him from the Superintendent of Indian affairs for the Government of the United States of America, and do not hesitate to say we believe them perfectly correct.

"We also state that, in our opinion, his motives for wishing to pass by a different route to the Columbia river, on his return, is solely because he feels convinced that he and his companions run great risk of perishing if they return by the route they came.

"In testimony whereof we have hereunto set our hand and seal, this 20th day of December, 1826.
 WILLIAM G. DANA, Captain of schooner *Waverly*.
 WILLIAM H. CUNNINGHAM, Captain of ship *Courier*.
 WILLIAM HENDERSON, Captain of brig *Olive Branch*.
 JAMES SCOTT.
 THOMAS M. ROBBINS, Mate of schooner *Waverly*.
 THOMAS SHAW, Supercargo of ship *Courier*."

Smith was liberated, and during the Summer of 1827, with his party, left the Sacramento valley, journeying toward the Columbia river. While encamped at the mouth of the Umpqua river, near Cape Arago, the Indians attacked them, and, with the exception of Smith, Richard Laughlin, and Daniel Prior, killed the entire party. These three escaped to Fort Vancouver, where they received a cordial reception and kind treatment. Some writers state that Smith then went directly to St. Louis, while others claim that, with a party of the Hudson Bay Company's men, he returned to the scene of his last battle, and meeting no opposition, journeyed on and down the Sacramento valley until he reached the junction of the Sacramento and Feather rivers, near which a camp was located. This party, under command of a Scotchman named McLeod, was the first of the Hudson Bay Company to occupy California. If the latter version is correct, then Smith soon after left the party and returned to the trapping grounds of his own company.

In the Spring of 1832, Capt. B. L. E. Bonneville, an officer in the United States Army, on furlough, at the head of a company of one hundred men, with wagons, horses, mules, and merchandise, crossed the Rocky Mountains, leading parties of men into the Colorado, Humboldt and Sacramento valleys.

Ewing Young, who had trapped with parties on the upper part of the Del Norte, the eastern part of the Grand and the Colorado rivers, pursuing the route formerly traversed by Smith, in the Winter of 1829-30, entered the San Joaquin valley, and hunted on Tulare lake and the adjacent streams. During the last part of 1832, or early in 1833, Young, having again entered the San Joaquin valley and trapped on the streams, finally arrived at the Sacramento river, about ten miles below the mouth of the American. He followed up the Sacramento to the Feather river, and from there crossed over to the coast. The coast-line was traveled till they reached the mouth of the Umpqua, where they crossed the mountains to the inland. Entering the upper portion of the Sacramento valley, they proceeded southerly till they reached the American river. Then they followed down the San Joaquin valley, and passed out through the Tejon pass, in the Winter of 1833-4. Besides these parties and leaders mentioned, during this period there were several trappers or "lone traders," who explored and hunted through the valleys.

The attention of the officers of the wealthy and powerful Hudson Bay Company was first specially called to the extent and importance of the fur trade in California by Jedediah Smith, in 1827 or 1828. The first expedition sent out by them was that under the command of McLeod. A short time after the departure of this company, a second one was sent out under the leadership of Mr. Ogden, which followed up the Columbia and Lewis rivers, thence southerly over Western Utah, Nevada, and into the San Joaquin valley. On their return they trapped on the streams in Sacramento valley, and went out at the northern limit in 1830. About the middle of 1832 another band of trappers, under Michael Laframboise, came into the Sacramento valley from the north, and until the next Spring spent the time in trapping on the streams flowing through the great valley. The Hudson Bay Company continued sending out its employes into this region until about the year 1845. Their trappers in California belonged to the "Southern Trapping Party of the Hudson Bay Company," and were divided into smaller parties composed of Canadians and Indians, with their wives. The trapping was carried on during the Winter, in order to secure a good class of furs. The free trappers were paid ten shillings sterling for a prime beaver skin, while the Indians received a moderate compensation for their services. The outfits and portions of their food were purchased from the company. The Hudson Bay Company employed about ninety or one hundred men in this State. The greater part of the Indians were fugitives from the Missions, and were honest and peaceably inclined, from the fact that it was mainly to their interest to be so. From 1832 the chief rendezvous was at French Camp, about five miles south of Stockton. About 1841 the company bought of Jacob P. Leese the building he had erected for a store in San Francisco, and made that their business center for this territory. The agents were J. Alex. Forbes, and William G. Ray, both of whom were intelligent, dignified, and courteous gentlemen. Mr. Ray, who was very sensitive, and given slightly to dissipation, when some complaint of a trivial character was made in reference to his acts, committed suicide in 1845. His death, and the scarcity of beaver and otter caused the company to wind up their agency and business in the territory. Mr. Forbes was, for a long series of years, the British Consul at San Francisco, and by his genial manners, superior culture, and finished education, made a good record, which places him among the noted men of the State. This gentleman now resides in Oakland, and although seventy-five years of age, his faculties are as strong as ever. His memory is wonderful, and this power of retention, with the vast fund of knowledge possessed, has been of great service to the historian. He has the honor of being the first English historian of California, his "California," published in London in 1839, being written in Mexico four years previous to the date of its publication."

During the months of January and February, 1844, John C. Fremont, then Brevet Captain of Topographical Engineers, on his return from his first exploring expedition to Oregon, passed down the east side of the Sierras, and crossed the snow-covered summit of New Helvetia (Sacramento), suffering many privations and hardships. His experiences are so clearly related in his report to the Chief of Engineers, that the portion relating to this stage of his journey is here given to show the character of

*Mr. Forbes had twenty of heart disease.

the mountains, the nature of the inhabitants, and the scarcity of knowledge of the Sierras, although the passage was made in El Dorado county. Passing by the account of his journey southward from the Dalles we take up his narrative on the evening of January 31, 1844, upon reaching the Upper Truckee river, south of Lake Tahoe.

"In the course of the afternoon, one of the men had his foot frost bitten; and about dark we had the satisfaction of reaching the bottom of a stream timbered with large trees, among which we found a sheltered camp, with an abundance of such grass as the season afforded, for the animals. We saw before us, in descending from the pass, a great, continuous range, along which stretched the valley of the river, the lower parts steep, and dark with pines, while above it was hidden in clouds of snow. This we felt satisfied was the central ridge of the Sierra Nevada, the great California mountain, which now only intervened between us and the waters of the bay. We had made a forced march of twenty-six miles, and three mules had given out on the road. Up to this point, with the exception of two stolen by Indians we had lost none of the horses which had been brought from the Columbia river, and a number of these were still strong, and in tolerably good order. We had now sixty-seven animals in the band. (The party consisted of twenty-five persons.)

"* * * We gathered together a few of the more intelligent of the Indians, and held this evening an interesting council. I explained to them my intentions. I told them that we had come from a very far country, having been traveling now nearly a year, and that we were desirous simply to go across the mountain into the country of the other whites. There were two who appeared particularly intelligent—one, a somewhat old man. He told me that before the snows fell, it was six sleeps to the place where the whites lived, but that now it was impossible to cross the mountain on account of the deep snow; and showing us, as the others had done, that it was over our heads, he urged us as strongly to follow the course of the river, which, he said, would conduct us to a lake (Tahoe), in which there were many large fish. There, he said, were many people; there was no snow on the ground, and we might remain there until the Spring. From their descriptions, we were enabled to judge that we were encamped on the upper water of the Salmon Trout river. It is hardly necessary to say that our communication was only by signs, as we understood nothing of their language; but they spoke, notwithstanding, rapidly and vehemently, explaining what they considered the folly of our intentions, and urging us to go down to the lake. Tah-ve, a word signifying snow, we very soon learned to know, from its frequent repetition. I told him that the men and horses were strong, and that we would break a road through the snow; and spreading before him our bales of scarlet cloth and trinkets, showed him what we would give for a guide. It was necessary to obtain one, if possible, for I had determined here to attempt the passage of the mountain. Pulling a bunch of grass from the ground after a short discussion among themselves, the old man made us comprehend that if we could break through the snow, at the end of three days we would come down upon grass, which he showed us would be about six inches high, and where the ground would be entirely free. So far, he said, he had been in hunting for elk; but beyond

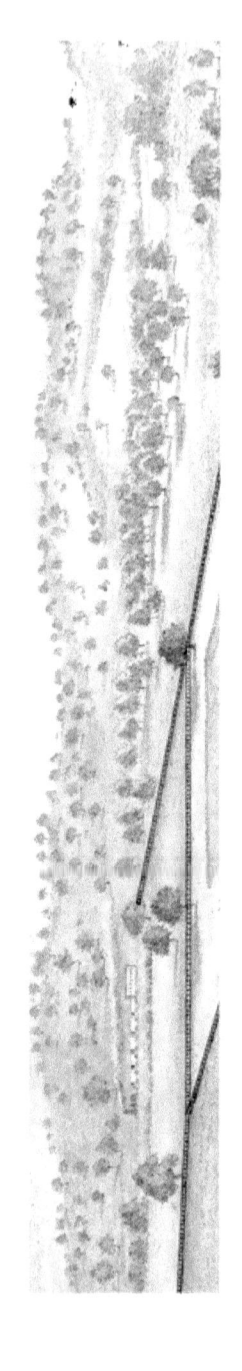

that (and he closed his eyes) he had seen nothing; but there was one among them who had been to the whites, and, going out of the lodge, he returned with a young man of very intelligent appearance. Here, said he, is a young man who has seen the whites with his own eyes; and he swore, first by the sky, and then by the ground, that what he said was true. With a large present of goods, we prevailed upon this young man to be our guide, and he acquired among us the name Melo—a word signifying friend, which they used very frequently. He was thinly clad and nearly bare-footed, his moccasins being about worn out. We gave him skins to make a new pair, to enable him to perform his undertaking to us. The Indians remained in the camp during the night, and we kept the guide and two others to sleep in the lodge with us—Carson (Kit Carson) lying across the door, having made them acquainted with the use of our fire-arms. The snow, which had intermitted in the evening, commenced falling again in the course of the night, and it snowed steadily all day. In the morning I acquainted the men with my decision, and explained to them that necessity required us to make a great effort to clear the mountains. I reminded them of the beautiful valley of the Sacramento, with which they were familiar from the descriptions of Carson, who had been there some fifteen years ago, and who, in our late privations, had delighted us in speaking of its rich pastures and abounding game, and drew a vivid contrast between the Summer climate, less than a hundred miles distant, and the falling snow around us. I informed them (and long experience had given them confidence in my observations and good instruments) that almost directly west, and only about seventy miles distant, was the great farming establishment of Captain Sutter—a gentleman who had formerly lived in Missouri, and, emigrating to this country, had become the possessor of a principality. I assured them that from the heights of the mountain before us, we should doubtless see the valley of the Sacramento river, and with one effort place ourselves again in the midst of plenty. The people received this decision with the cheerful obedience which had always characterized them, and the day was immediately devoted to the preparations necessary to enable us to carry it into effect. Leggins, moccasins, clothing—all were put into the best state to resist the cold. Our guide was not neglected. Extremity of suffering might make him desert; we therefore did the best we could for him. Leggins, moccasins, some articles of clothing, and a large green blanket, in addition to the blue and scarlet cloth, were lavished upon him, and to his great and evident contentment. He arrayed himself in all his colors, and, clad in green, blue and scarlet, he made a gay looking Indian; and, with his various presents, was probably richer and better clothed than any of his tribe had ever been before.

" * * * The river was forty to seventy feet wide, and now entirely frozen over. It was wooded with large cottonwood, willow and grain de bœuf. By observation, the latitude of this encampment was 38° 37′ 18″.

"February 2d. It had ceased snowing, and this morning the lower air was clear and frosty; and six or seven thousand feet above, the peaks of the Sierra now and then appeared among the rolling clouds which were rapidly disappearing before the sun. Our Indian shook his head as he pointed to the icy pinnacles, shooting high up into the sky, and seeming almost immediately above us. Crossing the river on the ice, and leaving it immediately, we commenced the ascent of the mountain along the valley of a tributary stream. The people were unusually silent, for every man knew that our enterprise was hazardous, and the issue doubtful. The snow deepened rapidly, and it soon became necessary to break a road. For this service a party of ten was formed, mounted on the strongest horses, each man in succession opening the road on foot, or on horseback, until himself and his horse became fatigued, when he stepped aside, and, the remaining number passing ahead, he took his station in the rear. Leaving this stream, and pursuing a very direct course, we passed over an intervening ridge to the river we had left. On the way we passed two huts, entirely covered with snow, which might very easily have escaped observation. A family was living in each, and the only trail I saw in the neighborhood was from the door-hole to a nut-pine near, which supplied them with food and fuel. We found two similar huts on the creek where we next arrived, and traveling a little higher up, encamped on its banks, in about four feet of snow. To-day we had traveled sixteen miles, and our elevation above the sea was six thousand seven hundred and sixty feet.

"February 3d. Turning our faces directly towards the main chain, we ascended an open hollow along a small tributary to the river, which, according to the Indians, issues from a mountain to the south. The snow was so deep in the hollow that we were obliged to travel along the steep hill-sides, and over spurs, where wind and sun had lessened the snow, and where the grass, which appeared to be in good quality along the sides of the mountain, was exposed. We opened our road in the same way as yesterday, but only made seven miles, and encamped by some springs at the foot of a high and steep hill, by which the hollow ascended to another basin in the mountain. The little stream below was entirely buried in snow. * * * We occupied the remainder of the day in beating down a road to the foot of the hill, a mile or two distant; the snow being beaten down when moist, in the warm part of the day, and then hard frozen at night, made a foundation that would bear the weight of the animals the next morning. During the day several Indians joined us on snow-shoes. These were made of a circular hoop, about a foot in diameter, the interior space being filled with an open net-work of bark.

"February 4th. I went ahead early with two or three men, each with a led horse, to break the road. We were obliged to abandon the hollow entirely, and work along the mountain side, which was very steep, and the snow covered with an icy crust. * * * Towards a pass which the guide indicated, we attempted in the afternoon to force a road; but after a laborious plunging through two or three hundred yards, our best horse gave out, entirely refusing to make any further effort; and, for a time, we were brought to a stand. The guide informed us that we were entering the deep snow, and here began the difficulties of the mountain; and to him, and almost to all, our enterprise seemed hopeless. I returned a short distance back, to the break in the hollow, where I met Mr. Fitzpatrick. The camp had been all the day occupied in endeavoring to ascend the hill, but only the best horses had succeeded, not having sufficient strength to bring themselves up without the packs; and all the line of road between this and the springs was strowed with camp stores and equipage, and horses floundering in snow. I therefore immediately encamped on the ground with my own mess, which was in **advance, and** directed Mr. Fitzpatrick to encamp at the springs, and **send all the animals, in** charge of Taban, with a strong guard, back to **the** place where they had been pastured the night before. * * * Two Indians joined our party here; **and** one of them, an old man, immediately began **to** harangue us, saying that ourselves and animals would perish in the snow; and that if we would go back, he would show us another and a better way across the mountain. He spoke in a very loud voice, and there was a singular repetition of phrases and arrangement of words, which rendered his speech striking, and not unmusical. We had now begun **to** understand some words, and, with the aid of signs, **easily comprehended the** old man's simple ideas. '**Rock upon rock—rock upon rock—snow upon snow— snow upon snow,'** said he; 'even if **you get over the snow you will not be able to get down from the mountains.** He made us the sign of precipices, and showed us how the feet of the horses would slip, and throw them off from the narrow trails that led along their sides. Our Chinook, who comprehended even more readily than ourselves, and believed our situation hopeless, covered his head with his blanket and began to weep and lament. 'I wanted to see the whites,' said he; 'I come away from my own people to see the whites, and I wouldn't care to die among them, but here,' and he looked around into the cold night and the gloomy forest, and, drawing his blanket over his head, began again to lament. Seated around the tree, the fire illuminating the rocks and the tall bolls of the pines around about, and the old Indian haranguing, we presented a group of very serious faces.

"February 5th. The night had been too cold to sleep, **and** we were up very early. Our guide was standing by the fire with all his finery **on**; and seeing him shiver in the cold, I threw on **his shoulders** one of my blankets. We missed him **a few minutes** afterwards, and never saw him again. He had deserted. His bad faith and treachery **were in** perfect keeping with the estimate of Indian character, which a long intercourse with this people had gradually forced upon my mind. While a portion of the camp were occupied in bringing up **the baggage** to this point, the remainder were busy in **making sledges** and snow-shoes, I had determined to **explore the** mountain ahead, and the sledges **were to be used in** transporting the baggage. * * *

"February 6th. Accompanied by Mr. Fitzpatrick, I set out to-day with a reconnoitering party, on snowshoes. **We** marched all in single file, tramping the snow **as** heavily **as** we could. Crossing the open basin, **in** a march of about **ten** miles we reached the top of one of the peaks, to the **left of** the pass indicated by our guide. Far below us, dimmed by the distance was a large snowless valley, bounded on the western side, **at** the distance of about a hundred miles, by a low range of mountains, which Carson recognized with delight as the mountains bordering the coast. 'There,' said he, 'is the little mountain (Mt. Diablo)—it is fifteen years ago since I **saw it;** but I am just as sure **as** if I had seen it **yesterday.'** Between us, then, and **this** low coast range, **was the** valley of the Sacramento; and **no** one who **had not** accompanied us through the incidents of our **life for** the last few months could realize the delight **with** which we at last looked down upon it. At the distance of apparently thirty miles beyond us **were distinguished** spots of prairie, and a dark line, **which** could be traced with the glass, was imagined **to be** the course of the river; but we were evidently **at a** great **height** above **the valley, and** between us and the plains extended **miles of** snowy fields and broken ridges of pine covered mountains. * * * All our energies **were now** directed to getting our animals across **the snow; and** it was supposed that, after all the baggage **had** been drawn with the sleighs over the trail we had made, it would be sufficiently hard to bear our animals. * * * With one party drawing sleighs loaded with baggage, I advanced to-day about four miles along the trail, and encamped at the first grassy spot, where **we** intended to bring our horses. Mr. Fitzpatrick, with another **party,** remained behind, **to** form **an** intermediate station between us and the animals. * * *

"February 8th * * * Scenery **and** weather, combined, must render these mountains beautiful in Summer; the purity and **deep-blue color** of the sky are singularly beautiful; **the days are sunny and** bright, and even warm in the noon hours; and if we could be free from the many anxieties that oppress us, even now we would be delighted here; but our provisions are getting fearfully scant. Sleighs arrived with baggage about ten o'clock; and leaving a portion of it here, we continued on for a mile and a half, and encamped **at the foot of a long hill on this** side of the open bottom. * * *

"February 9th. During **the** night **the weather** changed, the wind rising **to** a gale, and commencing to snow before daylight; before morning the trail was covered. We remained quiet in camp all day, in the course of which the weather improved. Four sleighs arrived toward **evening,** with the bedding of the men. We suffer much from want of salt, and all the men are becoming weak from insufficient food.

"February 10th. Taplin was sent back with **a few** men to assist Mr. Fitzpatrick, and continuing on with three **sleighs** carrying a part **of the** baggage, we had the **satisfaction** to encamp within two and a half miles of the head of the hollow, and at the foot of **the last mountain ridge.** Here two large **trees** had been **set on fire, and** in the holes, where the **snow** had been melted away, we found a comfortable **camp.** Putting **on our** snow-shoes, we spent the **afternoon** in exploring **a** road ahead. The glare of the snow combined with great fatigue, had rendered many of the people nearly blind, but we were fortunate in having some black silk handkerchiefs, which, worn **as veils,** very much relieved the eyes.

"February 11th. High **wind** continued, **and our trail this** morning was **nearly** invisible—here and there indicated by a little ridge **of** snow. Our situation became tiresome and dreary, requiring a strong exercise of patience and resolution. In the evening I received a message from Mr. Fitzpatrick, acquainting me with the utter failure of his attempt to get our mules and horses over the snow—the half-hidden trail had proved entirely too slight to support them, and they had broken through, and were plunging **about** or lying half buried in the snow. * * * I wrote him **to** send the animals immediately back to their old pastures, and after having made mauls and **shovels, turn in all** the strength of his party to open **and beat a road** through the snow, strengthening it with branches and boughs of the pines.

"February 13th. **We** continued to labor on the road; **and** in **the** course of the day had the satisfaction to see the people working down the face of the opposite hill, about three miles distant. * * * The **meat** train did not arrive this morning, and I gave **Godey** leave to kill our little dog (Tlamath), which he prepared in Indian fashion, scorching off the hair, and washing the **skin with** soap and snow, and then cutting it up in pieces, which were laid on the snow. Shortly afterward, the sleigh arrived with a supply of horse meat; and we had to-night an extraordinary dinner—pea soup, mule and dog. * * *

"February 16th. We had succeeded in getting our animals safely to the first grassy hill; and this morning I started with Jacob on a reconnoitering expedition beyond the mountain.

"We traveled along the crest of narrow ridges, extending down from the mountain in the direction of the valley, from which the snow was fast melting away. On the open spots was tolerably good grass; and I judged that we should succeed in getting the camp down by way of these. Toward sun-down we discovered some icy points in a deep hollow, and, descending the mountain, we encamped at the head-water of a little creek, where at last the water found its way to the Pacific. * * * We started again early in the morning. The creek acquired a regular breadth of about twenty feet, and we soon began to hear the rushing of the water below the ice-surface, over which we traveled to avoid the snow; a few miles below we broke through, where the water was several feet deep, and halted to dry our clothes. We continued a few miles farther, walking being very laborious without snow-shoes. I was now perfectly satisfied that we had struck the stream on which Mr. Sutter lived; and, turning about, made a hard push, and reached the camp at dark. * * *

"On the 19th, the people were occupied in making a road and bringing up the baggage; and, on the afternoon of the next day, February 20, 1844, we encamped with the animals and all the material of the camp, on the summit of the pass in the dividing ridge, one thousand miles by our traveled road from the Dalles of the Columbia. The people, who had not yet been to this point, climbed the neighboring peak to enjoy a look at the valley. The temperature of boiling water gave for the elevation of the encampment nine thousand three hundred and thirty-eight feet above the sea. This was two thousand feet higher than the South Pass in the Rocky Mountains, and several peaks in view rose several thousand feet still higher. * * *"

From the summit the party passed down the western slope of the Sierras, following the general course of the stream, and suffering many hardships and privations, encountering much deep snow and sustaining life on none too juicy mule meat. The stream whose course was being followed was the south fork of the American river. Describing the happy termination of this perilous journey by an advance party of eight, Mr. Fremont says:—

"March 6th. We continued on our road through the same surpassingly beautiful country, entirely unequaled for the pasturage of stock by anything we had ever seen. Our horses had now become so strong that they were able to carry us, and we traveled rapidly—over four miles an hour; four of us riding every alternate hour. Every few hundred yards we came upon little bands of deer; but we were too eager to reach the settlement, which we momentarily expected to discover, to halt for any other than a passing shot. In a few hours we reached a large fork (North Fork of the American river), the northern branch of the river, and equal in size to that which we had descended. Together they formed a beautiful stream, sixty to one hundred yards wide, which at first, ignorant of the nature of the country

through which that river ran, we took to be the Sacramento. We continued down the right bank of the river, traveling for a while over a wooded upland where we had the delight to discover tracks of cattle. * * * We made an acorn meal at noon and hurried on. Shortly afterwards we gave a shout at the appearance on a little bluff of a neatly built adobe house with glass windows. We rode up, but, to our disappointment, found only Indians. There was no appearance of cultivation, and we could see no cattle, and we supposed the place had been abandoned. We now pressed on more eagerly than ever; the river swept round in a large bend to the right; the hills lowered down entirely; and, gradually entering a broad valley, we came unexpectedly into a large Indian village, where the people looked clean, and wore cotton shirts and various other articles of dress. They immediately crowded around us, and we had the inexpressible delight to find one who spoke a little indifferent Spanish, but who at first confounded us by saying there were no whites in the country; but just then a well-dressed Indian came up and made his salutations in very well-spoken Spanish. In answer to our inquiries, he informed us that we were upon the *Rio de los Americanos* (the river of the Americans), and that it joined the Sacramento river about ten miles below. Never did a name sound more sweetly! We felt ourselves among our countrymen; for the name of *American*, in these distant parts, is applied to the citizens of the United States. To our eager inquiries he answered, 'I am a vaquero (cow herd) in the service of Captain Sutter, and the people of this *rancheria* work for him.' Our evident satisfaction made him communicative; and he went on to say that Captain Sutter was a very rich man, and always glad to see his country people. We asked for his house. He answered that it was just over the hill before us, and offered, if we would wait a moment to take his horse and conduct us to it. We readily accepted his civil offer. In a short distance we came in sight of the fort; and passing on the way the house of a settler on the opposite side (a Mr. Sinclair), we forded the river; and in a few miles were met a short distance from the fort by Captain Sutter himself. He gave us a most frank and cordial reception—conducted us immediately to his residence—and under his hospitable roof had a night of rest, enjoyment, and refreshment, which none but ourselves could appreciate."

Gen. Fremont the next day started back with provisions and horses to meet and relieve the main body of the party, who were several days in the rear. He met them near the forks of the river, "Each man, weak and emaciated, leading a horse or mule as weak and emaciated as himself." Of sixty-seven horses and mules, only thirty-three had survived that terrible journey across the mountains. Many of them had been killed for food, while others had died of starvation or exhaustion or lay at the bottom of rocky cañons, down which they had plunged from the precipitous heights above. Many valuable specimens, collected during the long journey were lost.

It was in the few years prior to the discovery of gold that the genuine pioneers of California braved the unknown dangers of the plains and mountains, with the intention of settling in the fair valley, of which so much was said and so little known, and building a home for themselves and their children. Many of these immigrants crossed the mountains by nearly the same route pursued by the Central Pacific Railroad, except that they followed down Bear river to the plains. The first settlement reached by them was that of Theodore Sicard, at Johnson's Crossing, on the Placer county side, and a few miles below Camp Far West. This settlement was made in 1844, and was the first point reached by the members of the ill-starred Donner Party in 1847. Opposite Sicard's settlement was Johnson's ranch, owned by William Johnson and Sebastian Kyser, who settled there in 1845. Johnson's Crossing was for years a favorite landmark and rallying point.

The next Winter after Fremont made his perilous crossing of the Sierras, another party, a band of hardy pioneers, worked their laborious way through the drifting snow of the mountains, and entered the beautiful valley, one of them remaining in his snow-bound camp at Donner lake until returning Spring made his rescue possible. The party consisted of twenty-three men: John Flomboy; Captain Stevens, now a resident of Kern county, Cal.; Joseph Foster; Dr. Townsend; Allen Montgomery; Moses Schallenberger, now living in San Jose, Cal.; G. Greenwood, and his two sons, John and Britt; James Miller, now of San Rafael, Cal., Mr. Calvin, William Martin; Patrick Martin; Dennis Martin, Martin Murphy, and his five sons; Mr. Hitchcock, and son. They left Council Bluff, May 20, 1844, en route to California, of the fertility of whose soil and the mildness of whose climate glowing accounts had been given. The dangers of the plains and mountains were passed, and the party reached the Humboldt river, when an Indian named Truckee presented himself, and offered to guide them to California. After questioning him closely, they employed him as their guide, and as they progressed, found that the statements he had made about the route were fully verified. He soon became a great favorite among them and when they reached the lower crossing of the Truckee river, now Wadsworth, they gave his name to the beautiful stream, so pleased were they by the pure water and abundance of fish to which he had directed them. The stream will ever live in history as the Truckee river, and the fish, the famous Truckee trout, will continue to delight the palate of the epicure for years to come.

From this point the party pushed on to the beautiful mountain lake, whose shores but two years' later witnessed a scene of suffering and death unequaled in the annals of America's pioneers. Here, at Donner lake, it was decided to build a cabin and store their goods until Spring, as the cattle were too exhausted to drag them further. The cabin was built by Allen Montgomery, Joseph Foster, and Moses Schallenberger, all young men used to pioneer life, and who felt fully able to maintain themselves by their rifles upon the bears and deer that seemed so plentiful in the mountains. The cabin was built of pine saplings, with a roof of brush and rawhides; it was twelve by fourteen feet and about eight feet high, with a rude chimney, and but one aperture for both a window and door; it was about a quarter of a mile below the foot of the lake, and is of peculiar interest, as it was the first habitation built by white men within the limits of Nevada county, the entering wedge of civilization that in a few years wrested these beautiful hills with their wealth of gold from the hands of the barbarous Digger, and brought one more country under the dominion of intelligence.

The cabin was completed in two days, and the party moved on across the summit, leaving but a few provisions and a half-starved and emaciated cow for the support of the young men, who had undertaken a task, the magnitude of which they little dreamed. It was about the middle of November when the party left Donner lake, and they arrived at Sutter's Fort on the 15th of December, 1844, the journey down the mountains consuming a month of toil and privation. The day after the cabin was completed a heavy fall of snow commenced and continued for several days, and while the journeying party were plunging and toiling through the storm and drifts, the three young men found themselves surrounded by a bed of snow from ten to fifteen feet deep. The game had fled down the mountains to escape the storm, and when the poor cow was half consumed the three snow-bound prisoners began to realize the danger of their situation. Alarmed by the prospect of starvation, they determined to force their way across the barrier of snow. In one day's journey they reached the summit, but poor Schallenberger was here taken with severe cramps, and was unable to proceed the following day. Every few feet that he advanced in his attempt to struggle along, he fell to the ground. What could they do? To remain was death, and yet they could not abandon their sick comrade among the drifting snows on the summit of the Sierras. Foster and Montgomery were placed in a trying situation. Schallenberger told them that he would remain alone if they would conduct him back to the cabin. They did so, and providing everything they could for his comfort, took their departure, leaving him, sick and feeble, in the heart of the snow-locked mountains.

A strong will can accomplish wonders, and a determination to live is sometimes stronger than death, and young Schallenberger by a great exertion was soon able to rise from his bed and seek for food. Among the goods stored in the cabin he found some steel-traps, with which he caught enough foxes to sustain himself in his little mountain cabin, until the doors of his prison were unlocked by the melting rays of the vernal sun, and a party of friends came to his relief. On the 1st of March, 1845, he, too, arrived at Sutter's Fort, having spent three months

in the drifting snows of the "Snowy Mountains"—the Sierra Nevada.

The after history of the Indian Truckee, whose name so many objects bear, is an interesting one. Passing down the mountains, he arrived at Sutter's Fort with the main party, and remained until the breaking out of the war in 1846, when he joined Fremont's Battalion, and was ever afterwards known as Captain Truckee. He was quite a favorite with Fremont, who presented him with a Bible with the donor's autograph on the fly leaf. This with a copy of the *St. Louis Republican*, Captain Truckee jealously preserved until the time of his death. After the American conquest, Truckee returned to his people, east of the Sierras, and when the rich silver discoveries in the Washoe region brought thousands of white men there, he became their fast friend and a universal favorite among the miners. The Indian camp where he lived was in the Palmyra District, Lyon county, Nevada, about a mile from Como, and near the spring where the town of Palmyra was subsequently built. One day in 1860, Captain Truckee went to the mining camp at Como to ask the men what remedy he should use for a large swelling on his neck. The men thought he had been bitten by a tarantula and advised him to apply a slice of bacon. Poor Captain Truckee died that night, his last request being to be buried by the white men and in the white man's style. The miners dug a grave near Como, in the croppings of the old Goliah lodge, and good Captain Truckee was laid away to rest, the Bible and the paper he had cherished so long lying by his side.

The terrible sufferings of the Donner party have been already portrayed. The groans of the starving, and the wails of the dying, crazed with hunger, will ever haunt the shores of Donner lake, and the winds as they moan among the drooping branches of the pines, will whisper tales of suffering such as few have seen, and the most vivid imagination fails to realize. The two cabins built by the Donner party near that of Schallenberger, and which formed the camp of the Breens, Graves, and Murphys, were the second monuments of civilization in Nevada county. About two weeks before the Donner party found the way across the summit barred by the snow, another immigrant train passed in safety. Among these immigrants were Claude Chana, who now lives at Wheatland, Yuba county, and Charles Covillaud, one of the original proprietors of Marysville, and who married Mary Murphy, a member of the Donner party, from whom the name Marysville was derived. The widely different experiences of these two parties in crossing the mountains, but illustrate the changes that can there be wrought by a few days of snow. This party also followed down Bear river to Johnson's ranch, from which point the relief parties were sent to Donner lake. The years 1846, 7 and 8, saw many trains of immigrants on their way to Oregon and California, those for this State crossing the mountains by several routes, though most of them came by way of Truckee river.

CHAPTER XVI.
AMADOR COUNTY.

Early History—Origin of the Name of Carson Pass—River and Valley—First White Men in the Territory—Sutter's Whipsaw-mill—Discovery of Gold—Organization of Calaveras County—Removal of County-Seat from Double Springs to Jackson—Second Removal to Mokelumne Hill—First Set of County Officers—Second Set of County Officers—Members of the Legislature—Miscellaneous Matters in Calaveras—Joaquin's Career—Chased by Indians—Mokelumne Hill in Early Days—Green and Vogan's Line of Stages—Stories of Grizzlies—Bull and Bear Fight.

A GENERAL history of the State has been given, in which but little mention has been made of that portion of the territory out of which Amador county was afterwards carved. It is probable that some trappers occasionally visited the lower portions of Mokelumne river, though not often, for the Indians, who inhabited that portion of the country, watched with jealous eye the intrusion of strangers for any purpose whatever. The Hudson's Bay Company had a trail from French Camp to Oregon, which was most of the way through the tules, and of course far to the west of the present limits. The "Arroyo Seco" grant purports to have been made in 1840, but it is quite certain that no Mexican had ever set his foot on the hills, or had ever seen them except far away, from the Diablo range of mountains. Those persons who accompanied General Sutter in his campaign against Mikelkos in 1843, might have seen the Lyons mountains twenty miles to the east. As early as 1840, according to James Alexander Forbes, then the agent for the Hudson Bay Company in Alta California, all attempts to raise cattle on the east side of the San Joaquin, had been an utter failure, the Indians invariably driving off the stock and destroying the ranches.

CARSON PASS, VALLEY, AND RIVER.

The impression is generally prevailing that Carson discovered the pass bearing his name. In the famous trip across the mountains Fremont and Carson traveled northward from Walker's river, crossing the river bearing Carson's name in their course, making the crossing of the summit by way of Truckee and Lake Tahoe. The river was then named in honor of Carson, the pass and valley being named from the river, so that it is quite probable that Carson never crossed the mountains at that point until 1853, when he came through with a division of U. S. troops under Colonel Steptoe.

The first authentic report of the presence of white men in the county was in 1846, when Sutter, with a party of Indians and a few white men, sawed lumber for a ferry-boat in a cluster of sugar pines on the ridge between Sutter and Amador creeks, about four miles above the towns of Amador and Sutter. In 1849 the remains of the timbers and the sills over

HISTORY OF AMADOR COUNTY, CALIFORNIA.

the pit were in good preservation though showing indications of being older than the gold-hunting immigration. The partially filled-up pit may still be seen.

At this time the country was one unbroken forest from the plains to the Sierra Nevadas, broken only by grassy glades like Ione valley, Volcano flats and other places. The tall pine waved from every hill, the white and black oak alternating and prevailing in the lower valleys. The timber in the lower foothills and valleys, though continuous, was so scattering that grasses, ferns, and other plants grew between, giving the country the appearance of a well-cared-for park. The quiet and repose of these ancient forests, seemed like the results of thousands of years of peaceful occupation, and at every turn in the trails which the immigrants followed, they half expected to see the familiar old homestead, orchard, ciderpress and grain fields, the glories of the older settlements in the Eastern States. These things, after thirty years' residence, are beginning to appear, but this settlement is the subject of our history, and must not be anticipated. How much the ancient sylvan gods were astonished and shocked at the irruption of the races that tore up the ground and felled the woods, the poets of some other generation will relate.

DISCOVERY OF GOLD IN AMADOR COUNTY.

In the latter part of March, 1848, a man arrived in Stockton, then called Tuleburgh, bringing with him specimens of scale-gold, from Sutter's mill. He informed the people there of the recent discoveries on the American river, the specimens confirming his report; whereupon, Captain Weber, catching a spark from the flame, fitted out a prospecting party, consisting of settlers on his grant, some strangers that chanced that way, and a force of Si-yak-um-na Indians, and commenced the exploration of the country east of Stockton, beginning at the Stanislaus, and working north. The fever was on them; haste and nuggets their watchwords; inexperience their companion, and failure the result, until they had reached Mokelumne river, where the Captain decided to make a more deliberate search, the result of which was the discovery by him, on that river, of the first gold found in the section of country, that was afterwards known as the Southern mines. Owing to their more careful search and added experience, gold was found north from this river, in every gulch and stream to the American river. Arriving at Sutter's mill, it was decided to commence mining at what was called afterward Weber's creek, near Placerville. As soon as he had got work on Weber creek well under way, he returned to Stockton, and organized a party to explore the country south of the Mokelumne river. In a short time they returned with finer specimens than had been found at Coloma. A mining company was formed, which afterwards gave name to Wood's creek, Murphy's creek, Angel's Camp, and other places. Then commenced the general working of the "Southern mines," the rush of miners, the immigration which built up the flourishing counties of Amador, San Joaquin, Calaveras, Tuolumne, and the changing of the world's commerce.

The Mokelumne river, the gulches at Drytown, Volcano, and Ione, were mined extensively in 1848. General Sutter and party tried it near the town of Sutter, but he was disgusted with the opening of a saloon near his works, and left the mines, never to return. The emigration from the Eastern States, by way of the plains and the Horn, brought a large accession to the population, and brought about the necessity of some political organization. El Dorado county was organized with Dry creek as its southern boundary, Calaveras, with Dry creek as its northern limits. From these two territories, Amador was afterwards carved, first in 1854, by setting off the territory north of the Mokelumne from Calaveras, and in 1856-57, by the addition of the strip from El Dorado lying south of the Cosumnes, the boundaries farther east being rather indefinite, as will be hereafter seen. A short account of the organizations of these two counties, will suffice for this work. Calaveras county was organized in the session of the Legislature, in 1849-50. It is said that it took its name from an immense number of skulls found on that river. The story was that a great number of Indians coming down from the Sierras to fish for salmon, were all slaughtered. There is a probability that they were the result of the fearful mortality, before mentioned, occurring among all the valley tribes, from the head waters of the Sacramento to those of the San Joaquin, in 1830. The county took its name from the river.

The first officers were William Fowle Smith, County Judge; John Hanson, Sheriff; Colonel Collyer, County Clerk; A. B. Mudge, Treasurer; H. A. Carter, Prosecuting Attorney. Pleasant Valley, better known as Double Springs, was designated as the county seat. The courts were held in a long tent, eight or ten feet wide, imported from China. The first Grand Jury held its sessions under a big tree. According to all accounts, justice was anything but a blind goddess. Very contradictory reports are current in regard to the characters of the officers. "Fowle Smith," an Eastern man, was represented by some as a miserable concentration of all meanness that was supposed to characterize that kind of men; stinginess, cowardice, and "all that sort of thing." Others say that he was honest, and would not countenance Colonel Collyer's peccadillos, hence, their mutual dislike. He has since taken to preaching, and is said to be causing great revivals in some of the Eastern States.

Colonel Collyer, according to the same authority, was a southern man, with southern virtues in excess; pompous, portly, genial, brave, and reckless, with a habit of calling everybody, who crossed his will, a d——d son of a ——, and threatening to cut his heart out; a treatment he had applied to Judge Smith, until the latter was seriously afraid the Colonel was in earnest. Among the peculiarities of Collyer, was the pocketing of all fees received in his official capacity, leaving Judge Smith to collect his salary, or extras, as he might. Collyer is said to have naturalized sixty foreigners in one day, charging them one ounce each, all of which he applied to his own benefit. Mudge may be described in a few words, as putting all the money received into his own pocket, and decamping when it became too heavy to carry around. John Hanson, Sheriff, now engaged in business in San Francisco, was a native of Maine, and, probably by attending strictly to his business, made no extraordinary history. The same may be said of H. A. Carter, the Prosecuting Attorney, a native of New York. He now resides in Ione valley.

CHANGE OF COUNTY SEAT.

According to the laws of the sessions of the Legislature of 1849–50, whenever a majority of the voters of any county petitioned for an election fixing the county seat, the Judge might order an election on thirty days' notice. In accordance with this provision an election was held in 1850, the two contesting places being Jackson and Mokelumne Hill. When the first count or estimate was made up, Mokelumne Hill was said to have been the successful town, and a team was sent to Double Springs to remove the archives; but a subsequent count by Judge Smith made Jackson the county seat. Smith was openly charged with fraud in the second counting. The whole affair was probably as near a farce as elections ever got to be. The manner of changing the archives from Double Springs will be more fully set forth in the township history of Jackson. The seat of justice remained at Jackson until 1852, when it was transferred by election to Mokelumne Hill. The general vote in 1851 was: Democratic, 1,780; Whig, 1,267.

County officers, 1852: Sam. Booker, District Attorney; A. Laforge, Treasurer; Jo. Douglass, County Clerk; Ben. Marshall, Sheriff; C. Creaner, District Judge.

1852—Pierce, 2,848; Scott, 2,200.

1853—The officers of Calaveras county were: Treasurer, A. Laforge; County Clerk, Jo. Douglass; Sheriff, Ben Marshall; Prosecuting Attorney, Wm. Higby; County Judge, Henry Eno.

Members of the Legislature: Senators—E. D. Sawyer, Charles Leake. Assemblymen—A. J. Houghtaling, Martin Rowen, W. C. Pratt, C. Daniels vice Carson, deceased.

The vote for Governor was: John Bigler (Democrat) 2,545; William Waldo (Whig) 2,212.

JOAQUIN'S CAREER IN AMADOR.

This renowned bandit commenced his career in this county. His exploits are notorious, and like all events of that kind, are multiplied and exaggerated until the clearest sight can no longer distinguish the true from the fabulous. Whether he was induced to commence a career of murder and robbery on account of being flogged at Jamison's ranch, will always remain an uncertainty. His first operations were to mount himself and party with the best horses in the country. Judge Carter, in 1852, had a valuable and favorite horse which for safety and frequent use was usually kept staked a short distance from the house. One morning the horse was missing. Cochran, a partner in the farming business, started in pursuit of the horse and thief. The horse was easily tracked, as in expectation of something of this kind the toe corks on the shoes had been put on on a line with the road instead of across it. The track led Cochran across Dry creek, across the plains and thence toward the mines several miles, where the rider seemed accompanied by several other horsemen. Coming to a public house kept by one Clark, he saw the horse with several others, hitched at the door. Going in he inquired for the party who rode his horse, saying that it had been stolen. He was told he was a Mexican, and was then at dinner with several others. Clark, who was a powerful and daring man, offered to arrest him, and suiting the action to the word, entered the dining-room in company with Cochran, and, placing his hand on Joaquin's shoulder—for it was he—said: "You are my prisoner." "I think not," said Joaquin; at the same time shooting Clark through the head, who fell dead. A general fusilade ensued, in which one of the Mexicans was shot by the cook, who took part in the affair, Cochran receiving a slight wound. The Mexicans mounted their horses and escaped, leaving Carter's horse hitched to the fence.

VISIT TO SUTHERLAND'S RANCH.

Jack Sutherland, now residing on King's river, had in early days a ranch on Dry creek, below Ione, and also one near Plymouth. Soon after moving to the former place, Billy Sutherland, then seventeen or eighteen, who had charge of the place in the absence of his father, sold a band of cattle for several thousand dollars in gold. After the purchasers had gone with their property, he took a notion to count the money again, before putting it away in the safe, which, in this instance, was a hole in a log, and emptied the sack on the table. While piling it up in hundreds and thousands, a shadow darkened the door. Looking up, who should he see but Joaquin, the famous bandit. To say that he was not afraid would be incredible, for Joaquin usually traveled with a band, which, probably was not far off; but he immediately conceived a plan to save his money and life. Resistance was out of the question; for he was alone, and no houses within miles. He politely invited Joaquin to alight, and in answer to the question whether he could stay all night with his party, replied in the affirmative. Joaquin called to his party, in Spanish, that he had found some friends, telling them to unsaddle. They were fierce and sullen looking fellows, but he trusted to out-maneuver them. He pretended not to know his guests, and set about getting their suppers After eating, the leader asked young Sutherland if he was not afraid to stay alone with so much money in the house; and inquired what he would do if Joaquin should come around? Sutherland replied that Joaquin was a gentleman, and would not harm his friends; that he and his father were acquainted, and referred to some transactions which had occurred, in which his father had benefited Joaquin. "Are you Jack Sutherland's son?" says Joaquin. "I am," says Sutherland. After some further conversation, they laid down on their saddle blankets, and slept until morning. At parting, Joaquin paid his bill, remarking that if any persons coming along during the day should inquire for a party answering their description, it would be as well for him to remember nothing about their having been there. Young Sutherland thought so also.

During the latter part of October, 1852, Joaquin was prowling around the northern part of Calaveras, in the vicinity of Oleta (Fiddletown). One day, one of the Mexican women told an American that Joaquin was in the town. As it was a common thing for Mexicans to ride from one camp to another, the presence of strangers caused no remark. His name, however, was sufficient to raise a storm, and in a few minutes he was being hunted. He was dressed in the usual Spanish style, with wide-brimmed hat, serape, white drawers, and pantaloons opening up the sides. When he found he was betrayed, he jumped on a table in a gambling room, flourished a pistol around his head, said he was Joaquin, and defied the town to take him. This bravado may have been necessary to ensure his retreat, for he and his party left immediately, with half the town in pursuit. As it was, he came near being surrounded, and had to force his way out. "Am. Parks" had hold of his bridle, but was induced to let loose by a shot in his face, which, however, only grazed the skin. The party of three or four left, amid a shower of bullets from revolvers, none of them taking effect, except, perhaps, on the horses; either this or the party were not well mounted, for in the pursuit which took place, the footmen kept well up, some Indians, who joined in the chase, being in the advance. Joaquin took the trail towards Slate creek, and thence across Dry creek towards Lower Rancheria. Fresh men joined the pursuers at every gulch. To get rid of the Indians, the Mexicans stripped themselves first of serape, spurs, and everything that could be thrown off hastily. At the crossing of Dry creek, a half mile below Dead Man's creek, a long-legged Missourian with a still longer rifle, came up within forty or fifty yards, but was afraid to fire on account of that terrible revolver of Joaquin's, which never missed. The Missourian never will get out of the range of ridicule, that has been heaped on him ever since.

The Mexicans left their horses, and escaped in the thick chaparral on the divide between Rancheria and Dry creeks. That night they made their way into Lower Rancheria, accounting for their demoralization by saying they had been chased by Indians which was true.

CHASED BY INDIANS.

In the Winter of 1850-51 a party of four or five men, of whom A. Askey, now of Jackson, was one, were hunting deer in the mountains a few miles above Volcano. Venison being worth fifty cents a pound they could afford to take some risks. One day, while following a wounded deer, Askey discovered a party of Indians, whom, by their dress, he judged to be Washoes, who had the reputation of being much better fighters than the California Indians. They saw him about the same time, and, coming up, professed to be very friendly, wanting to shake hands, which he prudently declined. A conference, mostly by signs, ensued, in which both parties agreed to pursue the deer, Askey taking one side of the hill, the Indians the other. He did not follow the deer far, but made the very best time to the camp that his short legs would admit of. In the morning, reinforced by his companions, he made a *reconnoissance* in force, and, as he expected, found that the Indians had made an effort to cut him off, the tracks in the snow showing that they had followed him until they sighted the camp. The following day an old Indian came peering about, and, by signs, intimated that the bark and wood set around the hut would keep out arrows. Suspecting him of being a spy, they thought best to detain him until morning, when he was dismissed with an application of a number ten boot to his rear that accelerated his departure.

MOKELUMNE HILL IN EARLY DAYS.

In early days Mokelumne Hill was reputed one of the liveliest places in the mines. It had the misfortune to be settled by a heterogenous population—Yankees, Westerners, and Southerners, from the United States; and French, German, and Spanish, from Europe, and Chilenos and Mexicans. Death by violence seemed to be the rule. For seventeen successive weeks, according to Dr. Sober, of San Francisco, a man was killed between Saturday night and Sunday morning. Five men were once killed within a week. The condition of things became so desperate that a vigilance committee was resolved upon, which, however, did not continue in existence long. One man, who was hung for stealing, confessed, just before his death, to having committed eight murders between Mokelumne Hill and Sonora. He was a Mexican, of powerful physique and desperate character. Shooting was resorted to on the most trivial occasions. Two strangers sat quietly taking a dinner at a restaurant, and talking with each other. A gambler seated near, fancying that he heard his name mentioned, drew his revolver and shot one

man dead. The conversation proved to be about mining matters which did not concern the gambler. A year after, to a day, the surviving man, who was talking with the person slain, had occasion to pass through the town, and remembering the former shooting of his partner, concluded not to stop, but a roysterer saw him, and disliking something in his appearance, drew a bead on him and fired; the aim was spoiled by some one throwing up the pistol at the moment of the explosion. The stranger thought it a curious country; his partner was killed a year before for some harmless talk; he was shot at while quietly passing along the streets.

THE MINES.

The gulches around the hill were very rich, and in the Winter of 1850-51 the leads were traced into the hills. The yield was enormous, even fabulous. The hill is supposed to be a continuation of the same wash that made Tunnel Hill rich.

THE FRENCH WAR.

A party of Frenchmen opened a hole in the richest part of the hill. Some Americans mining near them conceived the plan of driving them out, on the score of their not being citizens. The Frenchmen resisted, and the Americans raised the cry that the French had hoisted a French flag and defied the Government, and called on everybody to arm and drive them out. One Blankenship was foremost in the matter. The Frenchmen lost their claim. During the time of the difficulty, hundreds of persons jumped into the hole, which was about fifty feet square, and carried away dirt which would pay from fifty to one hundred dollars per sack. The Frenchmen had camped in the hole, cooking, eating, and sleeping there, to prevent other parties stealing the dirt or jumping the claim. Though the people generally united to drive the original holders out, none can now be found to justify the expulsion, which is now looked upon as a downright robbery.

STAGING—GREEN AND VOGAN'S LINES.

Charles Green and John Vogan commenced the business in 1853, running from Jackson, through Drytown, to Sacramento in one day. The line proving profitable, it was extended through Mokelumne Hill to Sonora, making the whole distance in one day, through fare being twenty dollars. The cost of stocking a line was enormous. None of the horses cost less than three hundred dollars each, and some of them twice that. Concord wagons cost from six hundred to one thousand dollars, and Troy coaches twenty-five hundred to three thousand dollars. A good driver was worth one hundred and fifty dollars per month; hostlers one hundred dollars. Hay and barley were also high, sometimes one hundred dollars per ton. Notwithstanding these expenses, the line was profitable, the coaches generally being loaded to their utmost capacity. Staging then and now were quite different affairs.

Then there were no roads, the coaches following the trails, or zigzaging around the dust-holes in Summer, and mud-holes in Winter. There were no bridges, and sometimes driver and horses were lost. During the Summer season the trip was rather pleasant, but when the coach stuck in a raging stream of water four or five feet deep, the situation made a timid man pray and a wicked one swear. The highwaymen occasionally levied tribute on the passengers, who, though armed, would find themselves unexpectedly confronted with a pistol in such close proximity that it was useless to resist. The line was afterwards consolidated with the California Stage Company, which proved to be a losing concern.

MYSTERIOUS SICKNESS.

In early days N. W. Spaulding, since Mayor of Oakland, and Judge Thompson, of Mokelumne Hill, now a resident of San Francisco, were living in the same cabin, and both had a kind of rash or breaking out on the skin, which was very annoying, causing an intolerable itching. Dr. Soher, an eminent physician, was consulted in the matter. He said it was produced by a feverish condition of the blood, induced by a change from the cool air on an ocean voyage to the dry atmosphere of California, and recommended laxative medicines, which they took for several weeks without any beneficial effects. The matter became rather serious. A closer inspection revealed the cause of the sickness to be an army of greybacks, who had taken up all the available ground on their bodies, and were doing their best to work it out, their operations being, happily, on the surface, however, tunnel mining not having been discovered. The clothing and cabin, even, were swarming with the vermin. A three days' campaign with boiling water, supplemented with a little unguentim, expelled the trespassers. The matter was considered too disgraceful to speak of publicly, and they paid the doctor's bill, sixty-five dollars each, without grumbling. Thirty years' silence over so good a thing having become painful, mutual threats of exposure brought out the story at a recent meeting of the San Francisco Pioneer Society, amid shouts of laughter. They were not the first or last persons thoroughly astonished at the unexpected presence of grey-backs in overwhelming numbers.

ADVENTURE WITH A GRIZZLY NEAR VOLCANO.

A genuine grizzly was discovered in a ravine a mile or two from town, and a valiant party, armed with axes, knives, pistols, and a few guns, started after him. When the huge fellow, curious to see what all the fuss was about, raised himself up on his quarters to look around, all wisely ran but one man, who had faith in his rifle, which carried a ball about as large as a pea. He fired and hit the bear, only to enrage him however, for the ball hardly more than stung him. He soon came up with the man, caught his head in his mouth, tearing off nearly the whole scalp, and otherwise lacerating the man, who surrendered at discretion, leaving the bear to make his own terms. By remaining entirely passive, the man induced his bearship, Ursa, the terrible, to suspend farther punishment. After the bear left, the man contrived to crawl towards his home. A short time after a party better armed pursued the bear and killed him. Curious to see what effect the pea rifle had on the bear, they examined his hide, and found that the ball penetrated it and lodged against the shoulder-blade, without injuring the animal at all. The bear was a monster. When loaded into an ordinary wagon-bed, eleven feet long, his legs stuck out behind fully three feet, making his total length not far from fourteen feet. He was poor and tough, and was not considered fit for food. When discovered he was feeding on carrion.

THE JOHNSTONS' ENCOUNTER WITH A GRIZZLY.

This occurred near the El Dorado county line. The bear had been seen several times and was known to frequent a patch of thick chaparral. A party of ten or twelve persons, among whom were the Johnstons, Jim and Jack, started out to find him. They succeeded in getting a fatal shot at *his majesty* the bear, which contrary to all expectation, retreated into the thick brush. From the amount of blood along his trail they judged that he was too severely wounded to be dangerous, and they imprudently followed him. The infuriated animal charged upon the Johnstons, who were foremost, and brought one of them to the ground, his gun during the encounter being thrown out of reach. The other fired when the opportunity presented itself to do so without endangering his brother's life, again wounding the bear, which left the first one to pursue the other. It does not seem that they succeeded in loading again, but each endeavored to draw the bear away from the other by pounding him over the head with the gun, when the animal would get the other down and commence again gnawing and lacerating his arms, head and body. It was a desperate fight now to get away. The balance of the party had deserted them at the first sight of the animal, when he made his charge, leaving the two to their fate. Jack's arms were now so useless from the repeated crushings, that he could no longer raise the gun to strike the bear, but still intent to get his brother away, he pushed his shoulder against the animal, which would leave the other for a moment. The creature was a monster in size, his back being nearly on a level with Jack's shoulder. The struggle seemed hopeless, but at the last moment the bear, becoming exhausted or subdued by the severe wounds, gave a kind of snarl and again beat a retreat. One of the men was now utterly helpless and the other one not much better, he however, succeeded in dragging his brother out of the brush to the open ground. He was taken away in a wagon and cared for, and recovered after several months. The crippled hand and arm, and terrible scars all over his person, attest the severity of the contest. After their recovery they revisited the place. They found the skeleton of the bear, which was of unheard-of dimensions. The stories of bears weighing fifteen hundred pounds, to those who have seen only the bears of two or three hundred pounds weight, which frequent the mountains of the Eastern States, seem utterly absurd. Making allowance for the exaggeration natural under some circumstances, there can be no doubt of their occasionally reaching to a monstrous size, perhaps weighing seventeen or eighteen hundred pounds.

KILLING A GRIZZLY.

In 1850 grizzlies were occasionally met with, and they hardly ever gave the road, though not apt to attack man unless provoked. It was Mr. Spaulding's good fortune to have one of the most thrilling adventures with one, that is recorded. At that time he was in charge of a saw-mill and had occasion to visit Mokelumne Hill late in the day. The trail led through a deep, shadowy glen which the animals sometimes visited, trampling down the brush and leaving tracks twice as large as a Hoosier's. As a matter of prudence he took his rifle promising himself to "fight it out on that line" if he met one. The daylight trip was well enough, no "bars" putting in an appearance, but on his return after night-fall, as he descended into the cool, shadowy part of the glen, he heard the ominous cracking of the brush, and the sound of footfalls along the trail. Nearer and nearer came the animal that was never known to give the road. To turn back was contrary to our hero's principles. Pierpont's

> "Stand!
> The ground's your own, my braves.
> Will ye give it up to slaves?
> Look ye for greener graves?"

From the old school reader, flashed through his mind, and he stood! With gun cocked and hair on end, he waited the onset. As the outline of the animal came dimly into view he took as good aim as possible and fired. An unearthly growing was succeeded by the monster's tumbling, rolling and tearing down the trail to the bottom of the deep ravine. It was evident the animal was severely wounded, and like all grizzlies, would be then most dangerous, even if the wound was mortal. To go down into the dark and thick woods and fight the grizzly alone, would be dangerous, perhaps fatal to him, for had not the grizzly proved a match for many men even when fatally wounded? Life was bright before him; hopes of meeting—well, no matter whom, and renewing the tender relations; hopes of wealth, of political success, of honor—were not these worth more than the chance of killing a grizzly? He went back on the trail, and making a wide circuit, reached the camp at a late hour, exhausted with the excitement and his long walk. After hearing his adventures the men made up a company to visit the ravine the next morning and finish the monster. All the guns were heavily loaded, and plans laid for approaching the animal with the least danger. The most vulnerable parts of the grizzly were duly discussed, some contending for an eye shot, others a side shot, at the heart, etc. Cautiously they descended into the deep ravine, avoiding clumps of trees or chaparral. At the bottom they found signs of the conflict—blood and broken brush. One, bolder than the rest, followed the trail, and—a great roar of laughter, with "Darned if it aint Dr. Herschner's old jackass," changed the sentiment of the party. The poor, patient old fellow had packed many a load of grub to the miners, and would, when relieved of his burden, return home alone, but he had made his last trip. Forty dollars paid for the animal, but many forties would not pay for the liquors and cigars at Spaulding's expense; and the end is not yet, for a mention of hunting grizzlies will still bring out the best in the house.

BULL AND BEAR FIGHT.

In the days when Calaveras and Amador were one, the population of the ancient capital were wont to amuse themselves with bull and bear fights. Sunday, by custom, was the day set apart for these exhibitions, for, on that day, everybody came to town. A large portion of the population was Spanish, and anything pertaining to the fighting of bulls would draw out the full Mexican population, señors señoras, and señoritas. Spanish cattle were plentiful, and there were plenty of men who had been trained to handle them; but bears, real grizzlies, were not so easily caught and handled. They were valued all the way from one to four thousand dollars; consequently, when a real grizzly was caught and caged, he was generally given an unfair advantage. The bull was lassoed just before the fight, his horns sawed off, and the fight pretty well taken out of him before he was turned into the ring. On one occasion, the miners, and other spectators, got rampant over the way in which a steer was sacrificed, "without any fight at all worth speaking of." Unfortunately, for the exhibitors, the bull-pen close by had several fierce, untamed, and undaunted steers, any one of which felt amply able to avenge their slaughtered companion. One of them especially attracted the notice of the spectators. He would have filled the old Mosaic requirements, being perfect in all his parts. Lithe as a cat, his horns long and slender, he commenced bounding around his limited arena as soon as he heard the bellowings of his less able compañero, that was being chawed and clawed in the hug of the grizzly.

The vaqueros were ordered to turn the anxious steer into the pen, a hundred revolvers being drawn to enforce the request. The proprietors knew that business was on hand, unless the request was acceded to, as the grizzly was sure to be shot, and, perhaps, some of their own number, too. There was no alternative, and they turned the anxious fellow in, though

they expected the bear would be slain in a short time. The bull came in, proud and defiant, gave a snort of contempt, whirled his tail high in the air, lowered his head, and made a charge. His majesty seemed not to be aware of any unusual company, and looked as placid and serene as though he had just made an ample dinner of young and tender pig, and was going to take his daily afternoon nap. He received the bull with his usual affectionate hug, the bull's horns passing each side of his body. He caught the bull by the back of the neck with his mouth, and with the aid of his forepaws, held him firmly to his bosom, using his hind feet with terrible effect on the bulls neck and sides. One ear was stripped off in a twinkling. Every dig of those terrible claws left gaping wounds, while the bull seemed utterly powerless to inflict any damage on the bear. About five minutes of this kind of one-sided fighting, served to convince the bull that he was not so invincible after all. His bellowings of defiance changed to notes of rage, and then to terror, and finally to cries for mercy; the last howls being so loud as to be heard a mile away. After punishing the bull for a while, the bear, entertaining no malice, magnanimously let the bull loose, which, blinded by blood and rage, made a charge at the picket-fence, which separated him from the spectators, and went through it, scattering the crowd in every direction, like a whirlwind. A dozen *vaqueros* mounted their horses and started after him. Down through the town went the bull, charging with his bloody head at every gathering of men, until he got to the clothing stores, kept by the Jews. The bright red shirts attracting his attention, he demolished these places one after another, monarch of all around, until the *vaqueros* succeeded in getting their lariats around his horns and legs, curbing the further exhibition of his varying moods of temper. It is unnecessary to say that the several acts of the exhibition were highly satisfactory to the crowd, the general verdict being, "*That thar bar's some, you bet.*"

It was not always the case that the bear whipped the bull. In early days, a bear and bull fight was advertised to come off at Coloma. No Spanish bulls being at hand, a lazy, good-natured old fellow, that crossed the plains some years previously, and had since lounged around the streets at will, was selected to fight the bear, much to the disgust of the assembled multitude. The fight was very short, the bull killing the bear in two or three minutes, by goring him through. In this instance, as in the one before related, the victory was won by the cool and wary, the victorious bull retiring from the contest, seemingly unconscious of any unusual event.

CHAPTER XVII.

DOMESTIC HABITS OF THE MINERS.

Exaggerated Accounts of Bret Harte and Joaquin Miller—Cooking and Washing—Hawks, Squirrels, Quails, and Other Game for Food—Getting Supper Under Difficulties—Laundry Affairs—Prevalence of Vermin—The Sanguinary Flea—Miners Flea Trap—Fleas versus Bed-bugs—Rats and Other Animals—Visits of Snakes—A Romantic Affair Spoiled by a Skunk.

For the satisfaction of curious women who wish to know how their fathers and brothers managed housekeeping, we have added this chapter. Men who never tried pioneer life, and have no prospect or necessity of trying it, may omit reading this altogether, or forever hold their peace. Many exaggerated stories are in circulation concerning the habits and characters of our early settlers. Bret Harte, Joaquin Miller, and a score of other writers, have taken some odd sample of humanity, added some impossible qualities, and set him up to be laughed at, or perhaps admired; when the fact is, the caricature is about as near the original as the Indian maiden of romance is to the filthy squaw that would eat the raw entrails of a horse or bullock without adding anything to the dirt, that already ornamented her hands and face. The '49er is represented as having pounds of dust loose in his pockets, which he passed out by the handful for whisky or whatever struck his fancy; as carrying an arsenal of knives and revolvers which he was wont to use on the slightest provocation—"rough but generous, brave, and kind." While it is true that an ideal '49er occasionally made an appearance in those days—for it is almost impossible to draw a monster, physical, moral, or intellectual, that has not some familiar features—the fact is, that the mass of the people had no resemblance to the ideals of Bret Harte or Joaquin Miller. They were sober, industrious, and energetic men, who toiled as men with ambition and strength can toil. The labor these men performed in damming and turning rivers, or tunneling mountains, was not the spurt of enthusiasm born of whisky. Many of the men had families at home whose letters were looked for with the most eager interest. The younger men, who had no families, had ties perhaps equally as strong. The exceptions, which have given such a false character to the '49er, were unprincipled adventurers from every State and nation, gamblers in bad repute, even among their own kind, frontiersmen who acknowledged no law, and fugitives from justice everywhere. This was the class that made a vigilance committee necessary in San Francisco in 1850 and 1856, which occasionally aroused the wrath of the mass of miners by robbing or killing a peaceable citizen. The description of this class is not the object of this chapter; they have already, in the hundred books which have been written of them, had more notice than they deserved. The substantial, honorable, and industrious must now claim our attention.

When the lucky prospector had found a paying claim, the next thing was to set up his household. From two to four was the usual number of the mess. The Summers were long and dry, and there was no discomfort in sleeping out of doors. But even in Summer a house, though humble it might be, had many advantages over a tent for comfort and security. A stray horse or ox would sometimes get into the flour-sack or bread-sack, upset the sugar, or make a mess of the table-ware. Wandering Indians would pilfer small things, or take away clothing which might be left within reach; but in a cabin things were tolerably secure from depredation. A site for a cabin was selected where wood and water were abundant. These things, as well as the presence of gold, often determined the location of a future town. Bottle Spring (Jackson), Double Springs, Mud Springs, Diamond Springs, and Cold Springs, at once suggest their origin. In the earlier days, log-cabins were soon put up, for suitable logs were found everywhere. Though these cabins are in the dust—passed into history—there is no need of describing them, as the books are full of the "settlers' log cabin," and no boy of the present generation, who has arrived to the age of ten, would need instruction in building one.

In the western settlements a floor made of hewn timbers (puncheons) was usual, but the ground served for a floor, and was considered good enough for a man. The sleeping places were as various as the minds of men. Sometimes a kind of dais, or elevation of two or three feet, was made on one side of the cabin, where the men, wrapped in their blankets, slept with their feet to the fire. Generally, bunks were made by putting a second log in the cabin at a proper elevation and distance from the sides, and nailing potato or gunny sacks across from one to the other, making in the same way a second tier of bunks, if necessary. Some fern leaves or coarse hay on these sacks, with blankets, made a comfortable bed. A good fire-place was necessary. Most of the mining was in water, necessarily involving wet clothes. A rousing fire, especially in Winter, was necessary to "get dried out." Some of these fire-places would be six feet across, and built of granite or slate rocks, as each abounded. There was not much hewing done to make them fit. When the structure had been carried up four or five feet, an oak log was laid across as a mantle-piece, and on this the chimney, generally made of sticks or small poles plastered with mud, was built. A couple of rocks served for rests for the backlog and forestick. A shelf or two of shakes, or sometimes an open box in which pickles or candles had come around the Horn, would serve for a cupboard to keep a few tin plates, and cups, and two or three cans containing salt, pepper, and soda. A table of moderate size was also made of shakes, sometimes movable, but oftener nailed fast to the side of the house. Those who crossed the plains would often take the tail gate of

Charles Green   Mrs Charles Green

the wagon for this purpose. A frying-pan, coffee-pot, Dutch-oven, and water-bucket completed the list of household utensils. As the miners became prosperous, a soup-kettle for boiling potatoes, and also for heating water to wash their clothes on a Sunday was added. Somewhere in a corner was a roll of paper, with pen and ink, with which to correspond with the folks at home. Cooking was sometimes done turn-about for a week, and sometimes seemed to fall to the lot of the best-natured one of the crowd, the others bringing wood and water by way of offset. Not much attempt was made at neatness, and oftentimes one had to console himself with eating only his own dirt, for there were camps where the dishes were not washed for months. Sometimes a little hot coffee turned on a plate would take off the last-formed dirt; but washing dishes—the everlasting bane of woman's housekeeping—was, if possible, more repugnant to man, and was *frequently* omitted; it made the gold-pan greasy (the miner's prospecting-pan served for washing dishes as well as gold, also as a bread-pan, and wash-tub on Sunday); there was no time to stop after breakfast, and they worked so late that they could not delay supper for the dishes to be washed, and so they were left from day to day. The cooking was a simple matter, boiling potatoes, making coffee, frying slap-jacks and meat, being the usual routine. Bread?—yes, I am going to tell you about that. All sorts of bread but good bread, were made at first. The miners knew that their wives and mothers put in soda, so they put in soda. Some of them brought dried yeast across the plains, and undertook to make raised bread, but as a general thing miners' bread was but sorry, sad stuff. The most successful plan was to keep a can of sour batter (flour and water mixed), with which to mix the bread, neutralizing the excess of acid with soda. Some of the miners became quite expert with this, judging to a nicety the exact amount of soda required. Dough mixed in this way and set in the sun, would soon raise, and, if the soda was rightly proportioned, was palatable and wholesome. The sour batter was splendid for *slap-jacks*. The old story that a California miner could toss his slap-jack up a chimney, run out doors, and catch it as it came down, right side up, is too old to be repeated; but it is a fact that they would turn the slap-jacks with a dexterous *flip flop* of the frying-pan, though when the batter was made stiff enough to stand this kind of usage, the cake would answer for half-soling a boot. The better way was to have two frying-pans, and turn the cakes by gently upsetting the contents of one into the other. Thirty years' experience and observation suggest no improvement on this method.

Practice made many of the miners expert cooks. New methods of cooking were sought out, and new dishes invented. Think of using a dry-goods box for an oven, and baking a pig or shoulder of pork in it! No trick at all. Drive down a stake or two,

and on them make a small scaffold, on which to place your roast; now build a very small fire of hard wood, at such a distance away that a moderate sized dry-goods box will cover it all, and your arrangements are complete. The fire will need replenishing once or twice, and in two or three hours, according to the size of the roast, you may take it out, done in a rich gold color, with a flavor unattainable by any other method. Steaks were roasted before a fire, or smothered, when sufficiently fried by the ordinary process, in a stiff batter, and the whole baked like a batch of biscuit, making a kind of meat pie. Game sometimes entered into the miner's bill of fare. Quails, rabbits, hares, coons, squirrels, and hawks, were all converted into food, as well as deer and bear. Some Frenchmen in 1852, during a time of scarcity, killed and eat a coyote, but their account of his good qualities was not such as to induce others to try the experiment. In 1851, some miners getting out of both money and meat, shot a young and fine-looking hawk. He was fat, and, the flesh looking toothsome, they cooked him, and reported that "*he was better nor a chicken.*" Some neighbors tried the same experiment, but, unfortunately, killed the old fellow that was preserved from drowning a great many years ago, through the kindness of one of our forefathers. His flesh was about the color and consistency of sole-leather, and after boiling him for three days in the vain attempt to reduce his body to an eatable condition, he was cast away. Even the rice with which he was boiled acquired no hawk flavor, which induced one of the miners to remark, "*They's much difference 'a hawks as 'n women*". A second trial resulted in a splendid dish, and after that hawks learned to avoid that settlement. On Christmas-day, 1852, a company of miners got up a big dinner. They put a fine large hawk in the center of a Dutch-oven, about twenty quails around it, and around them, potatoes. Some slices of salt pork on the hawk and quails, seasoned the birds, and tempered the upper heat of the oven. The hawk was pronounced the best of all. The Winter of 1852-53, was perhaps the roughest time ever seen in California. The long spell of high water utterly prevented the transportation of provisions from the cities, and there was much want, though no actual cases of starvation. Many men lived for weeks on boiled barley. Beans, without even a ham-bone to season them, furnished, in some cases, the only food for weeks. At one camp, a pork rind was borrowed from one house to another, to grease the frying-pan for slap-jacks.

A narrative of personal experience of one who lived on the south branch of Dry creek, in 1852, will give an idea of the troubles of that year:—

"It had been raining for about six weeks, and our claim had been four feet under water for a month. There were no gulches there that would pay, and we had been waiting for the rain to cease until every bit of provision of any description was gone, as well as money or dust. Something had to be done, even if the rain was coming down in torrents. There were four of us, one Yankee, two young married men from Illinois, and a man who had served in the United States army in the Seminole war, and, also as a volunteer in the Mexican war. We shouldered our pick, shovel, and rocker, and started up towards Indian gulch. After going a short distance, one of the Illinoisians got to thinking of his young wife, and the pleasures of home compared with this country, and, overcome by his feelings, burst into a blubber of despair, and started on the run for the cabin, where he was found at night hovering over the cold ashes of the fire-place, the fire totally extinguished by his floods of tears.

"At the head of Indian gulch we found some paying dirt. We went to work, and by dint of ground sluicing, rocking and panning, about four o'clock we had, probably, an ounce of dust. With this I started to Fiddletown to buy a supper for the boys. An ounce of gold dust, in 1881, will buy almost a year's provisions for a man, but in 1852 (flour at one hundred dollars per barrel, and meat seventy-five cents per pound), it was not much. After standing and aheming awhile, I remarked that I thought the rain would hold up shortly, so that provisions would get cheaper; believed that I would buy but a small quantity to-night, etc. Mr. Wingo, the gentlemanly trader, did not seem to notice my embarrassment, but politely sold me the little dab of flour and a piece of meat, which went down into the corner of the sack out of sight. I started for the cabin, darkness coming rapidly on, and the rain still falling. The creeks were now nearly waist deep, but I safely got through them all until I got to Dry creek. The log on which I crossed in the morning was gone, and the water was running high over the banks. Two or three hundred yards away was the cabin, and I knew, by the bright light shining through the cracks of the door, that a big fire had been built to cook our suppers, out of the proceeds of our day's work, and to dry our clothes, soaked by twelve hours' rain. A council of war was called, and all attainable information regarding roads, bridges, and ferries, called for. The creek was nowhere fordable; that proposition was disposed of without delay. One witness, or member of the council, had an indistinct recollection of having seen a tree across the creek a mile or two below, some days since, but could not vouch for its being there at present. This being the only information attainable, the commander ordered a change of base, to the possible bridge. Down the creek, in utter darkness, over rocks and bushes, stumbling and falling, and after an hour's hard work, the bridge was found. It was a cedar tree, the butt resting on the stump, the large top reaching to the opposite shore, and the middle sagged down so that the water was running, perhaps, two feet deep over the trunk, and threatening every moment to sweep the tree off its moorings; for, standing on its upper end, I could feel it swaying to the movement of the water. But the submerged part had limbs standing up out of the stream, and a charge in force across the bridge was ordered, with this caution, 'My boy, if you go overboard, the boys will go without their suppers.' The opposite bank was gained in safety, by feeling the way and holding to the limbs; and, an hour later, some bread and fried pork, and a roaring fire, brought us to a comfortable condition, and gave us the spirit to laugh at all our troubles."

LAUNDRY AFFAIRS.

Necessity compelled every man to do some kind of cooking. The calls of a ravenous stomach three or four times a day could not be disregarded with impunity; but the matter of having clean shirts and beds, though quite as necessary, was not so forcibly called for, and the washing was postponed from one Sunday to another until the traditional washing-day, in many camps, was well-nigh forgotten. A clean shirt was hauled over a dirty one, until the accumulations of sweat and red clay would afford a study for a geologist. The blankets, too, were slept in for months, for no minor ever dreamed of having clean sheets, and as for pillows, his boots tucked under his blankets served as a support to his head. When a shirt was changed, the cast-off garment was laid aside, or left in his bunk to be washed at a more convenient time—which never came. No wonder then that the gray-backed lice, the genuine army vermin, colonized every blanket and shirt. For months respectable men, who would as soon have been accused of stealing as being lousy, went scratching around without a suspicion of the trouble. Poison oak, hives, change of climate, and a hundred other things were supposed to produce the intolerable, persistent itching. When the true cause became known, for sooner or later the discovery was sure to come, the conduct of the victims became amusing. Some would swear, some would cast their clothing away, or perhaps bury it, and purchase an entire new outfit—but the fact was the louse had taken possession of the whole country; like the angel of the apocalypse, he had a foot on the sea and on the dry land; in the store as well as in the cabin. A vigorous war with hot water, on everything that would scald, would exterminate him, though some lazy, and consequently lousy, miners contended that hot water would not kill them. The louse eventually abandoned the country; but whether from the neater habits of the miners, or the coming of the avenger,

THE FIERCE SANGUINARY FLEA,

Is still an open question. Between 1851 and '53, contemporaneous with the irruption of the rat, the flea fought his way into every camp, and held the fort, too, against all enemies. If unwashed shirts and blankets were favorable to the existence of myriads of gray-backs, not less so was the swarming lice for the flea, for he made meat and drink of them. Hot water had no terrors for the flea; he was out and off before a garment would go into the water. During the day he made his home in the dust floor of the cabin, and at night sallied out of his lair, thirsting for blood. And he must be a good sleeper indeed, who could close his eyes in slumber, while hundreds of lancets were puncturing his cuticle. Sometimes a cabin was abandoned on account of them. A person happening to come in would have hundreds crawling on his pants in a few minutes.

Sometimes a man would leave his cabin and blankets and sleep on the naked ground on the outside to get rid of his persistent bed-fellows.

THE MINERS' FLEA-TRAP.

If necessity is the mother of invention, the flea-trap was a sure corollary. It was a simple and effective affair. It was known that fleas would gather around a light; taking advantage of this habit, the miners would set a lighted candle on the floor, and around it set their pans with a small quantity of slippery soap-suds in each. The flea would fall in, struggle vigorously for awhile to get out, and finally drown. A tablespoonful of the rascals in the morning was considered a satisfactory catch. Later the bed-bugs drove out, to some extent, the flea, and still hold the land. The good housewife is often reduced to despair by the persistence of these unwelcome tenants of her rooms, who neither pay rent nor vacate.

The following article, from the *Oakland Times*, is commended to the attention of housekeepers who are still in the thick of the doubtful and unequal contest:—

"Stockton is celebrated for its mosquitoes, Sacramento for its bed-bugs, San Francisco for its rats, and Oakland for its fleas. They are larger and there are more of them; they can jump further and higher, bite oftener and deeper, than any fleas in the world. They are more persistent than a book agent, and hold with a tighter grip than a money-lender. They swarm everywhere—in the streets, the stores, and the public places. Everybody 'has 'em bad.' The young and the old, the tender and the tough, alike are meat for them. If you wish to say a complimentary thing to a lady, ten to one a flea will bite you where it is impossible to scratch, while, likely, the lady, troubled in the same way, will manifest impatience. Do not misjudge her, or be discouraged.

"You may fancy that your neighbor in the cars has the itch; no such thing; only the irrepressible flea. Flea catching is one of the accomplishments of our belles. They never disrobe without taking a hunt, and boast of the numbers they slay. Even the sanctuary is invaded by them; in fact, the church flea is the most ravenous of all. Starved during the week, he has an extraordinary appetite when the Sabbath comes. No bells calling a laboring man to his dinner ever brought such joy as the Sunday chimes do to the fasting flea. How he rushes to the attack as the people take their seats! How the victims writhe and squirm as the flea plunges his jaws into them! Preachers unaccustomed to the phenomenon, imagine it to be the sword of the spirit bringing sinners to a lively sense of their condition, and they lay on and spare not. Fleas, reverend sir; nothing more.

"Those who have studied phlebotomy think they can distinguish the bites of the different denominations. There is the flea of the gushing Methodist, that is gentle and affectionate; of the iron-bound Presbyterian, that bounces you like a bull-dog; but for downright, hard work, take the flea of the hard-shell Baptist. Raised amidst difficulties, like the Scotchman among his crags, and the New Englander among the granite boulders, he is fitted for every possible emergency in a race for life. None but the hardiest survive, which proves Darwin's theory of the survival of the fittest.

"The fleas are not without their benefits, however. Half of the success of our business men is supposed to be due to the irritation of the fleas, who never let them rest, day nor night. And then—now housekeeper listen—no bed-bugs can live where such a race of fleas has taken the land. To use the words of a noted housekeeper, "the fleas eat 'em up." Not a bed-bug is known in all Oakland. What a blessing these fleas would be in our interior towns, where the bed-bugs have had possession for a quarter of a century. How the sangrados would riot in blood! What consternation among the respectable, aldermanic old bugs, as the bloodthirsty flea, his jaws reeking with gore, dashed in among them! The irruption of the hordes of Alaric into Rome, or the contemplated raid of Kearney's hoodlums into Chinatown, could not compare with it.

"If our country neighbors want some of these fleas, I think the Oaklanders would be willing to spare them. Though usually anxious to drive a good bargain, in the sale of fleas they would be generous. They will help you catch them. You have only to sleep a night or two in the churches, and you will have enough. Negotiations may be opened with our Mayor or any of the city officers."

RATS AND OTHER VERMIN.

Rats have been mentioned as coming in with the fleas. The mild climate, exposed condition of eatables, and absence of cats and dogs, the natural enemies of rats, caused them to multiply with extraordinary rapidity. They were as much at home in the country as in the town, and a miner, camping in the hills away from the town, soon received visits from the rats, who thenceforth managed to have a share of all he brought into his camp. After he had retired to his blankets, the rats in troops would run over his body, making it the jumping-off place in their playful gambols. They left their tracks on his butter, gnawed holes into his flour-sack, danced cotillions on his table, and kicked up a fuss generally. Nothing but boxes of tin or heavy lumber would keep them from eating, destroying, or dirtying every article of food around the cabin. It will be borne in mind that the houses or cabins were made of logs daubed with mud, without floors or windows, and were accessible to all kinds of vermin, as well as rats. Rattlesnakes sometimes crawled into the interstices of the logs, and first made their presence known by the sharp rattle or perhaps the deadly thrust of their poisonous fangs into the sleeper's limbs. A young man living on the Slate-creek side of American hill, near Oleta, was bitten in this way without any warning on the part of the snake. He felt the sting, felt the deadly paralysis coming over him, and, in company with two or three companions, started for town, but sunk helplessly to the ground before getting there, dying shortly after. The following morning an examination of the bed revealed the presence of a young and vigorous rattlesnake, three feet or more in length. A Frenchman in the vicinity, was bitten about the same way, though he was living alone and was unable to reach the town, perishing on the way, being found in the trail some days afterwards without any visible wound. A rattlesnake, dead on the floor of his cabin, indicated the cause of his death. The long, yellow chicken snake would sometimes crawl into the cabin and create consternation among the rats and lizards, as well as among the miners. As the miners got to building their cabins of sawed lumber and elevating them above the ground, snakes, rats, mice, and skunks, became less frequent visitors. When dogs and cats were called in as friends and protectors, men, and women as well, could sleep without fear of disturbance. Since skunks have been mentioned, the reader may feel an interest in the adventures of a young and romantic miner with an animal of this kind, which, possibly, exerted a great influence in shaping his destiny:—

"I had been mining on the South fork, in the Summer of '52, and came down to Dry creek in the Fall, a little the worst-busted individual you ever saw. Save some old, worn-out shovels and picks, I had nothing, not even a decent pair of pants. About that time two or three families had settled on Dead Man's creek, a little above my camp. I had seen a slender, willowy form flitting in and out of a cabin, and all the powers of my imagination were summoned to describe her charms. 'Young and fair with bright golden hair,' was not then written, but I thought it though, as well as many other fine things, and spent some days in composing compliments to her musical ability, sweet voice, beautiful eyes, mouth, teeth, feet, 'and all that sort of thing.' I worked like a Trojan 'panning-out,' to get money enough to buy raiment fit to appear in her presence. At length, one Saturday evening, the task was performed, and I hung the suit up by my bed and slept—tondly dreaming—etc. I was awakened in the night by a scratching on the logs above my head, which I supposed was by the rats. Now, they had annoyed me so often in that way, that I had lost all patience with them, and resolved to 'fix 'em.' A gun was standing by my side, and I proceeded to gently draw out a ramrod, with which to kill some of them, for, from the scratching I concluded there must be a dozen or two, at least. I succeeded in getting the rod out without alarming my visitors, and suddenly whipping it into the corner over my head, did my best to kill the whole of them. There were three other persons sleeping in the cabin. Hearing the racket, they all roused up with: 'WHE—W!' 'WHAT IN H—L!!' 'OH, JE—RUSALEM!' We all leaped into the middle of the floor, and, hastily stirring the coals in the fire place, raised light enough to see our friend crawling out of a hole in the unfinished gable of the cabin. He did not take the atmosphere with him. Clothing, blankets, provisions, boots and shoes, and even the very logs of the cabin, were saturated with the essence of all that is villainous. Months afterwards when the scent had become so diffused that we could no longer perceive it, I made a visit to Fiddletown (Oleta). There was a ball going on, and I stepped into the ball-room to get a glimpse, once more, of a woman's face. Several persons made the remark that somebody must have killed a skunk. I did not tell them that the skunk was not killed, but quietly retired. Somebody else got that girl.'"

CHAPTER XVIII.

ORGANIZATION OF AMADOR COUNTY.

Election for or Against Division, June 17, 1854—Proceedings of the Board of Commissioners—Strife for the Possession of the County Seat—The Owl—Sketches of the First Candidates—Courts Established—Efforts to Suppress Disorderly Houses—Amusing Procession—Election in 1854—Condition of Society.

JACKSON and Mokelumne Hill had been rival towns. When Calaveras county was organized, Double Springs became the county seat; for a short time only, however, for it was captured by a coup de main, and transferred to Jackson, where it remained for nearly two years. From that place it was transferred to Mokelumne Hill, as the result of a choice, by election, of the people, called in accordance with an Act of the Legislature of 1851–2, the particulars of which will be set forth more particularly in the township histories. The politicians never rested contentedly under this change. They asserted that men on the south side of the Mokelumne river got the offices, and they went to work to convince the people that their interests would be better served by having a new county organized. By this time (1853) there were several ambitious towns that were willing to take charge of the county seat and furnish grub and whisky, particularly the latter, to all who were rich enough to indulge in the luxury of going to law. It was also urged, with too much reason to be disputed, that the taxes were being wasted at Mokelumne Hill; that no money was paid into the State Treasury; more that the officers wasted the county funds on loose women. It was asserted that whenever you wished to see an official on business, you must look for him in one of the half-dozen dance-houses that ornamented and conserved the morals of that high-toned town.

In 1853–4 the Legislature passed an Act calling for the vote of the people in regard to a division, fixing the 17th of June following as the day, and appointing W. L. McKimm, E. W. Gemmill, A. G. Sneath, Alexander Boileau, and Alonzo Platt as Commissioners, to organize the new county in case the people voted for a division. The bill was drawn by E. D. Sawyer, one of the Senators from Calaveras, Charles Leake being the other Senator. The name originally given in the bill for the new county was Washington, but the name Amador was substituted in the Assembly, and concurred in by the Senate. The bill was read three times, and passed the same day—the motive for this hurry being expected opposition. A delegation from Mokelumne Hill had arrived to oppose the measure, but they had been wined until all ideas of county seats were obliterated so a bill was hurried through before the drunk was off, lest convincing arguments should be urged against it when they returned to their senses.

The prospect of having a county seat enlisted a great many in the matter who otherwise would have been utterly indifferent. Ione was beginning

G₁º C. WELLER.

C. WELLER.

Mʳˢ C. WELLER.

RESIDENCE of CONRAD WELLER,
JACKSON, AMADOR COUNTY, CAL.

to flourish on the sale of water-melons, vegetables, hay, and barley, to the miners; had plenty of level ground on which to build a town, and had no difficulty in proving that it was the proper place for dispensing justice and the disbursement of the peoples' money. Sutter Creek was growing from the development of the quartz mining, which was likely to be permanent. It claimed to be the town *par excellence*, having a high-toned, moral people, where no dance-houses or kindred institutions, were likely to demoralize the public officers, as at Mokelumne Hill. The latter reason was a sly thrust at Jackson, which had early supported several of these resorts. There was also a good place for a picturesque town, the hills closing together around the place like an amphitheater. Volcano—well—it could not urge many reasons except that it wanted the benefit of a county seat. It was true that it was on the outside of the county to be created, or any possible county for that matter; it was down in a deep hole where people had to be hoisted up to get out; the roads beyond Volcano went to no place but the deep caves, or some place still deeper; the town was hot in the Summer, and muddy in the Winter, but it was growing rapidly, had plenty of men to vote, and might get the county seat any way. So Volcano became interested. Jackson had been the county seat, and had had a taste of the profits and pleasures. It had the old jail; that might be repaired and used again, and had many reasons to urge for a new organization. Every town, too, had a set of candidates for the offices—men who were willing to sacrifice their own business for the public good.

On the south side of the river some towns conceived the idea that in case the county was divided, the seat of justice might be moved from Mokelumne Hill, so the interest in favor of division became general.

On the day appointed the election came off, resulting in a majority, though a small one, for the division. But Mokelumne Hill was not to be taken that way. The law required that the returns should be transmitted, sealed, to the Board of Supervisors. When the returns were handed in, it was found that all from the north side of the river were opened—had been tampered with! They were consequently rejected. Here was a dilemma. The matter was investigated, and it was found that the returns from Mokelumne Hill had also been opened, though afterwards sealed again. Several persons, among whom was J. T. Farley, had seen the returns from Mokelumne Hill, and knew that they had been opened also. The fact was, all of them had been opened as soon as they were received, and the party in power had resolved to take advantage of their own mistakes. A deputy Clerk was induced to make out the certificates of the election, and the Board of Commissioners resolved to organize the county notwithstanding the decision of the officers. The proceedings are copied in full from a small book, the first of the records of Amador county. The phraseology and quaint style have been preserved, believing that the original form will be most interesting. Tucker's ranch mentioned, has since been known as the T Garden, and was situated at the junction of the Sutter Creek, Ione, Jackson, and Volcano roads, and was selected both for convenience and because it was not likely to give umbrage to any of the aspiring towns.

"Be it remembered that on the third day of July, in the year of Our Lord one thousand eight hundred and fifty-four, the Board of Commissioners appointed under an Act granting to the electors of Calaveras county the privilege to vote for or against a division of said county, and to organize the county of Amador—Approved May the Eleventh A. D. 1854. Met at the house of Martin Tucker in said county of Amador present William L. McKimm, E. W. Gemill, A. G. Snoath, Alexander Boileau and Alonzo Platt; And on motion of Alonzo Platt seconded by E. W. Gemill William L. McKimm was chosen President of the Board. And on motion of Alexander Boileau, Alonzo Platt was chosen Secretary of the Board:

"The President then called for the reading of the Law appointing the Board of Commissioners and defining their duties and the same was read by the Secretary; and having been considered by the Board, it was on motion resolved by the Board to proceed to establish Election Precincts in and for the county of Amador.

"And thereupon the Board having considered the matter and being fully advised in the premises directed the Secretary to enter the following Order on the Record:

"*Ordered*, By the Board of Commissioners that there shall be twenty-one Election Precincts in the county of Amador and that they shall be known and designated as follows, to-wit: Dry Town, Upper Rancheria; New York Ranch, Grass Valley, Rancheria, Amador, Lancha Plana, Gales Ranch, Butte City, Russell's, Volcano, Jackson, Plattsburgh, Port John Streeter's Ranch, Q Ranch, Ione City, Clinton, Sutter, Armstrong's Mill, White's Bar.

"And on motion the Board proceeded to consider the matter of the application for an Election Precinct at 'Whale Boat Ferry,' on the Moquelumne River; and proof being introduced and heard, it appearing to the satisfaction of the Board that 'Whale Boat Ferry' was not two miles from Butte City, another election precinct; It was by the Board

"*Ordered*, That the application for an Election Precinct at 'Whale Boat Ferry' be not allowed, and the Board then proceeded to consider the matter of the appointment of Inspectors and Judges of Election in the several Election Precincts established by them; it was

"*Ordered*, That In Dry Town Precinct Chas. W. Fox be appointed Inspector, and J. T. King and J. D. Cross Judges of Elections.

"Upper Rancheria—Samuel Loree, Inspector; Dr. Cartmill and Mr. Votaw, Judges.

"New York Ranch—S. Spears, Inspector; John Elkins, John Decks, Judges.

"Grass Valley—Abner P. Clough, Inspector; J. O'Neal, G. Shoemaker, Judges.

"Rancheria—Wm. Snediker, Inspector; S. Neese, Andrew Onstott, Judges.

"Amador—J. M. Scott, Inspector; M. M. Glover, G. W. Taylor, Judges.

"Lancha Plana—J. W. D. Palmer, Inspector; J. Bullard, G. Wagner, Judges.

"Gates Ranch—E. J. Martin, Inspector; William Moon, J. Albertson, Judges.

"Butte City—John Reno, Inspector; J. Northup, William Young, Judges.

"Russell's—William Foster, Inspector; Harrison Freals, D. Robinson, Judges.

"Volcano—C. B. Woodruff, Inspector; J. K. Payne, M. K. Boucher, Judges.

"Q Ranch—L. C. Patch, Inspector; A. R. Phillips, A. K. Sexton, Judges.

"Ione City—Robert Reed, Inspector; T. Rickey, J. E. Hunt, Judges.

"Clinton—F. M. McKenzie, Inspector; Thomas Lochr, S. L. Robinson, Judges.

"Sutter—William Loring, Inspector; Herbert Bowers, N. Harding, Judges.

"Jackson—T. Hinkley, Inspector; E. C. Webster, Ellis Evans, Judges.

"Plattsburgh—J. A. Dunn, Inspector; F. B. Case, A. S. Richardson, Judges.

"Fort John—P. Vaughn, Inspector; L. Schon, — Gilbert, Judges.

"Streeter's Ranch—Wm. Porter, Inspector; Thos. Jones, Wm. Amick, Judges.

"Armstrong's Mill—John Howlett, Inspector; J. McDonough, Goff Moore, Judges.

"White's Bar—J. E. Weeks, Inspector; James Gregg, — ——, Judges.

"And the Board then proceeded to consider the form of the proclamation ordering an election on the seventeenth day of July instant, for county officers and the location of the seat of justice of the county of Amador, and it was

"*Ordered*, That the Secretary propose a form and submit the same to the Board for their consideration.

"The Secretary submitted to the Board a form for an election notice with an appendix of instructions, and the Board having considered the same, it was

"*Ordered*, By the Board that the following form of an "Election Notice" for the county of Amador be adopted, and that the President of this Board be authorized and instructed to procure the same to be printed together with the appendix of instructions, and that he be further authorized to name one or more executive officers, and appoint them to post (in pursuance of the law) in the several election precincts in this county at least ten days before said election the said election notice, to-wit:

"Election Notice Amador county.—The undersigned, a Board of Commissioners appointed to organize the county of Amador under the authority and by virtue of 'An Act granting to the electors of Calaveras county the privilege to vote for or against a division of said county, and to organize the county,' Approved May 11th, A. D. 1854, do hereby order an election to be held by the qualified electors at the several precincts, hereinafter named, on Monday the seventeenth day of July instant, for the election of the following officers, to-wit: One County Judge, one County Clerk, one District Attorney, one Sheriff, one Assessor, one Treasurer, one Coroner, and one Public Administrator, and do hereby, under said law, appoint the persons whose names are placed opposite to each said precinct. And we do further order under said law, that on said day and at each of said precincts, the qualified electors do also vote for a place for the location of the seat of justice of said county of Amador. The election precincts are established and the inspectors and judges of election appointed as follows:

[Here follows a list of the officers of the election, already mentioned on a former page.]

"Given under our hands and seals at Tucker's ranch, in the county of Amador, on Monday, the third day of July, A. D. 1854.

(Signed) W. L. McKimm,
E. W. Gemmill,
A. G. Sneath,
A. Boileau,
Alonzo Platt.

"Appendix of Instructions: Inspectors, judges and clerks of election should be sworn by a Justice if one is present; if not, the Inspector will swear the judges and clerks, and one of the judges then swear the Inspector.

"The returns should be securely sealed with wax wafer or paste, so that the envelope cannot be removed.

"The returns may be made to either one of the Board of Commissioners, but with all the requirements of the law in the revised statutes in relation to sending, forwarding or delivering election returns to the County Clerk with the exception of returning to one of the Board; the returns must by the law, organizing the County of Amador, be made within five days.

"The votes for county officers and seat of justice are to be on one ballot.

"If the inspectors and judges are not present to conduct the election the voters will appoint them.

Wm. L. McKimm,
President of the Board of Commissioners.

Alonzo Platt, *Secretary.*

"It was

"*Ordered*, That the President be authorized and required to notify the inspectors and judges of their appointments. It was

"*Ordered*, That when this Board adjourn it adjourn to meet at Jackson, in the County of Amador, on Saturday, the twenty-second day of July, A. D. 1854, to canvass the votes and proceed to a final discharge of their duties as Commissioners.

"There being no further business before the Board the motion to adjourn having been made and seconded, it was ordered that the Board of Commissioners now adjourn.

(Signed) W. L. McKimm,
E. W. Gemmill,
A. G. Sneath,
A. Boileau,
Alonzo Platt.

"Be it remembered that on the twenty-second day of July in the year of our Lord one thousand eight hundred and fifty-four, the Board of Commissioners appointed by law to organize the County of Amador, met in pursuance to their adjournment at Jackson in the county of Amador.

"Present—W. L. McKimm, President of the Board; A. G. Sneath, E. W. Gemmill, Alexander Boileau and Alonzo Platt, Secretary.

"The record of the last meeting of the Board was read and approved and signed by all the Board, and the Board proceeded to open the returns from the several precincts and draw up a statement thereof; and the said statement having been compared with said returns and read and examined was approved, and the President was ordered to file the said statement with the County Clerk of the County of Amador.

"It was then ordered that the President and Secretary forward a transcript of the same certified by

ORGANIZATION OF AMADOR COUNTY.

them officially, to the Secretary of the State of California and to the Governor thereof. It was then

"*Ordered*, That a statement of the whole number of votes received by each person for each office, and by each place for county seat, be entered on the records of this Board.

"Which statement is here entered and is as follows, to-wit:—

"For County Seat: Briggs Ranch, 1 vote; Upper Rancheria, 1; Jackson City, 2; Jackson, 1002; Sutter Creek, 539; Ione Valley, 496; Volcano, 937; Drytown, 3; Ione, 2; Fort John, 1; Amador Creek, 1; Rancheria, 1; Amador Mills, 1.

"For County Judge: James F. **Hubbard, received** 1354 votes; M. W. Gordon, 1484.

"For County Clerk: Chas. Boynton, received 1447 votes; James C. Shipman, 1779.

"For Sheriff: Wm. A. Phœnix received 1500 votes; James Harnett, 1410.

"For Treasurer: James T. Farley **received 1384** votes; W. L. McKimm, 1522.

"District Attorney: W. W. **Cope received 1372** votes; S. B. Axtell, 1528.

"Assessor: James L. Halstead received 1345 votes; H. A. Eichelberger, 1579.

"Public Administrator: **J. T. King received 1316** votes; E. B. Harris, 1569.

"Coroner: Wm. M. Sharp received 1350 votes: G. I. Lyon, 1553.

"The whole number of votes polled in said county was 3021."

The following persons were declared elected—being the first persons elected to these offices in the county of Amador:—

M. W. Gordon, Judge; William A. Phœnix, Sheriff; James C. Shipman, County Clerk; W. S. McKimm, Treasurer; S. B. Axtell, District Attorney; H. A. Eichelberger, Assessor; E. B. Harris, Public Administrator; G. S. Lyons, Coroner.

The Judges, Inspectors, and Clerks, at this election were allowed eight **dollars** per day for services, many of **them** receiving sixteen dollars each for the day and night.

It will be seen that the county seat question was one of the principal elements in **the election, the** results among the contestants being: For Ione, 496 **votes**; for Sutter Creek, 539 **votes**; for Volcano, 937 votes; for Jackson, 1,002 votes.

The following table will give **an idea of the comparative size of the several towns:—**

FIRST ELECTION HELD IN AMADOR COUNTY, JULY 17, 1854. LIST OF VOTES BY PRECINCTS.

	Clinton	Butte City	Drytown	Sutter Creek	Jackson	Lancha Plana	Volcano	Grass Valley	Patterson's	Gale's Ranch	New York Ranch	Ione City	Armstrong's Mill	Fort John	Russell's Diggings	Upper Rancheria	White's Bar	Lower Rancheria	Amador	Q. Ranch	Totals
COUNTY SEAT.																					
Jackson	132	47	33	5	675	28	19	11	9	14	2	14			1				4		10	1,002
Sutter Creek	6	23	7	275	6	9	22	5	9	1	4	6	7	6	1	42	27	30	50	3	539
Ione Valley	2		31	2	11	146	9	2				228	25				1	3	61	496
Volcano	13	3	22	2	4	1	646	82	13	16	35	6		38	24	6				1	937
COUNTY JUDGE.																					
James F. Hubbard	103	18	58	164	234	41	369	54	18	16	29	123	6	16	18	28	7	9	29	36	1,354
M. W. Gordon	47	48	40	111	445	130	281	46	12	7	5	124	22	29	4	19	19	13	26	47	1,484
COUNTY CLERK.																					
Chas. Boynton	110	30	40	36	443	55	105	40	13	8	32	131	6		12	20		9	28	45	1,447
James C. Shipman	41	30	52	235	242	125	582	60	18	19	2	121	22	45	11	29	26	21	28	31	1,779
SHERIFF.																					
W. A. Phœnix	119	42	30	107	408	45	372	73	19	21	32	98	6	15	18	29	4	8	27	27	1,500
James Harnett	34	24	65	166	285	155	312	26	12	8	2	153	24	31	5	20	27	26	22	42	1,410
TREASURER.																					
James T. Farley	66	41	36	103	319	31	450	6	15	20	33	114	6	42	16	17		9	24	32	1,384
Wm. L. McKimm	91	27	62	172	373	148	215	94	16	9	1	140	23	2	5	25	26	21	28	45	1,522
DISTRICT ATTORNEY.																					
W. W. Cope	106	40	78	106	281	44	364	44	14	16	32	99	5	29	18	25	1	9	30	33	1,372
S. B. Axtell	35	20	21	170	407	135	318	55	16	12	3	150	20	17	5	24	25	26	25	44	1,528
ASSESSOR.																					
James L. Halstead	89	20	41	103	278	42	428	50	15	17	7	118	5	15	18	31		7	28	32	1,345
H. A. Eichelberger	61	45	57	173	414	139	256	49	16	12	26	132	25	28	5	18	26	26	28	44	1,579
PUBLIC ADMINISTRATOR.																					
Jerry T. King	83	36	69	101	282	44	346	50	15	19	19	119	4	16	18	26		9	28	35	1,316
E. B. Harris	66	29	28	175	411	134	337	50	16	12	16	121	24	30	5	24	26	21	28	42	1,569
CORONER.																					
W. M. Sharp	86	36	42	103	319	41	351	55	15	16	31	113	5	16	18	26		9	29	39	1,350
L. G. Lyon	60	29	57	173	374	138	323	45	16	12	3	138	23	29	5	23	26	21	27	31	1,553
NUMBER OF VOTES CAST.	154	73	99	284	696	181	696	100	31	31	41	254	32	46	26	50	27	35	56	77	2,989

Immediately after the determination to organize, the activity became remarkable.

Sutter Creek offered to give towards county buildings ten thousand dollars; Jackson ten thousand dollars, and Ione about six thousand dollars. Volcano offered nothing, but ridiculed the offers of money as all *bosh*, that Jackson would probably donate the old county jail, which was made of logs so small that a man could cut his way out in an hour or two with his jack-knife, and, moreover, the logs were so rotten that an enterprising pig would root his way out. Volcano relied upon votes, and it is probable with a little outside exertion would have carried the matter for itself, as it only lacked sixty or seventy votes of the selection. Real estate in Volcano and Jackson went up with a boom. Town-lots were staked off everywhere, and, until the evening of the election, people were in a high financial fever. Volcano patients soon recovered, but the Jackson unfortunates were afflicted for some years.

It will be noticed that the candidates at this election were mostly men of ability. Some of them will have biographies in the chapter devoted to lawyers. Others have become lawyers since leaving the county.

M. W. GORDON remained in the county, occupying many times stations of honor.

JAMES F. HUBBARD was originally a surveyor; studied law, practiced awhile in Amador county, moved to San Francisco, and has drifted out of sight.

CHAS. BOYNTON, the brilliant editor and poet, will be mentioned again in connection with newspapers.

JAMES C. SHIPMAN, several times elected County Clerk, was from Virginia—one of the genuine, old stock. His honor and integrity have never been questioned even by his political opponents—enemies he never had.

W. A. PHOENIX was a young man of energy, integrity, and ability. He was killed in the unhappy Rancheria affair, in which account he will be further mentioned.

JAMES HARNETT was a farmer of good standing in Ione valley. He returned to the East and has drifted out of sight.

JAMES T. FARLEY is our present United States Senator, and will have further mention in the proper place.

W. L. McKIM, the first Treasurer, occupied many positions of honor and profit; was Government Surveyor, and was employed to settle disputes in regard to lines, having the confidence of all parties. He was killed by being thrown from a buggy, while descending the hill south of Jackson, in company with the Hon. John A. Eagen.

W. W. COPE, now resident of San Francisco, once a Judge of the Supreme Court will have further mention.

S. B. AXTELL, since member of Congress from the First District, Governor of Salt Lake and New Mexico, will be further mentioned.

JAMES L. HALSTEAD farmed in the early days on Volcano Flat, has since been a member of the Legislature from Santa Cruz, and is now a prominent lawyer in that county.

H. A. EICHELBERGER was a trusted citizen of Amador county several years; went to Nevada in the beginning of the mining excitement, and was accidentally killed while trying to prevent a quarrel between two of his friends. His remains lie in the cemetery of Ione.

J. T. KING has drifted out of sight.

DOCTOR HARRIS acted quite a prominent part in the early settlement of Amador county. He was a successful physician as well as miner. He built and ran for some time the Newton Hotel; was largely instrumental in the organization of Amador county; found time to help build up the State Agricultural Society; mingled in politics; taught singing, and did many things to help build up society. He was among the foremost who went to the Washoe mines, put up a custom mill, and made thirty thousand dollars before other men had time to look around. When the civil war broke out, he joined the Union army, and was made Assistant Surgeon General, where his known skill as a surgeon, his great executive ability, and energy, were invaluable. Though genial and social in his habits, he never, either by his presence or conversation, promoted or countenanced gambling, drinking, and other vices, that swept into the vortex of ruin so many brilliant and talented young men in early days. At present he is practicing medicine in Nevada.

DOCTOR SHARP was an able and successful physician for many years in Jackson.

DOCTOR LYONS was a farmer and physician in Ione. He was unfortunate in his domestic relations, in being connected, by report at least, in the drowning of his wife, which happened in a well in his own yard. He was acquitted by the jury of the charge of murder, and soon after left the country.

"THE OWL."

This was a paper published occasionally in the early days of Jackson—a sort of bubbling or frothing over of wit that was too lively to be bottled up. A reproduction of some of its articles will recall many incidents, in connection with the county seat, long forgotten:—

In Snoozerville's romantic bay
A gallant bark at anchor lay,
Whose banner bore this strange device:
Inquire at Logan's for the price
Of passage up Salt river.

The Owl, upon its office door,
The following flaming placard bore:
"Here Logan, agent of the line,
From four o'clock till half-past nine,
Sells tickets for Salt river."

At four o'clock, the anxious crew,
With vacant looks and pockets, too,
Crowded around the sanctum door
Of him, who oft had made before,
The passage up Salt river.

RANCH & RESIDENCE of WILLIAM H. PROUTY, Jackson Valley, Amador County, Cal.

RESIDENCE of EDGAR BISHOP, Ione City, Amador County, Cal.

ORGANIZATION OF AMADOR COUNTY. 81

Towering above the cast was seen
A stove-pipe hat* of doubtful mien;
Battered and bruised, and crushed, it looked
As if its owner had been booked
Already for Salt river.

The poem had eighteen verses of this kind, filled with allusions to noted persons. Snougerville was a name given to what is now called Water street. One of its citizens was nicknamed Snouger—hence, Snouger bay.

From the *Owl*, August 25, 1854:—

There was a sound of revelry by night,
And our new county seat had gathered then
Her miners, and her merchants; and the light
Of tallow candles shone on drunken men.
A dozen hats had bricks in them; and when
Some jolly fellow, tighter than the rest,
Invited the whole crowd to drink again,
Not one among them needed to be pressed;
But hush! hark! a deep sound strikes every guest.
Did ye not hear it? No, 'twas but the wind,
Or some damned jackass braying in the street.
Give us our drinks—let joy be unconfined;
Nor part till morn—we've got the county seat.
What fellow was it offered to stand treat?
But hark! that heavy sound breaks in once more,
As if the walls its echo would repeat,
And nearer, more distinctly than before
It is! it is, ———— to be concluded next week.

COURTS ESTABLISHED.

The first term of the Court of Sessions was held in McKimm's Building, near the present Central House; M. W. Gordon, acting as Judge; O. P. Southwell and William Wagner, as Associate Judges. These last were selected from the Justices of the Peace elect. The names of the first Grand Jury were D. W. Aldrich, C. Derthick, D. L. Wells, W. S. Birdsell, James Beckman, W. P. Jones, A. L. Harding, I. Bell, Leon Sompayrac, Robert Reed, B. S. Sanborn, Simeon Burt, Thomas Jones, Frank Wayne, A. B. Andrews, E. Evans, S. B. Herrick, and J. T. King.

Levi Hanford not appearing in season, and having no satisfactory excuse, was fined twenty five dollars, which he paid.

The first indictment for murder was against John Chapman, for the murder of E. P. Hunter, of Laneha Plana. The case of C. Y. Hammond, who had the previous Summer killed his partner Elliot, as it was alleged, with a blow of his fist, came before them and was dismissed. Indictments for assault with intent to commit murder, were found against one Mexican, and several Chinamen. They also recommended the suppression of the houses of prostitution, so frequent and conspicuous in Jackson, and the other towns; the division of the county into townships, also the purchase of a safe, for keeping the public funds.

The first trial jury was in the case, "The people vs. Domingo Verjara," the names of the jurors being Nathan Coon, John T. Griggs, E. H. Williams, Charles Towles, A. H. Kirby, William Jennings, John Rawley, John McKay, James Creighton, William Horton, J. L. Averill, and B. Ashton.

*Referring to Colonel Platt.

EFFORTS TO SUPPRESS DISORDERLY HOUSES.

The first Grand Jury had called the attention of the authorities to the houses conspicuously kept for the purposes of prostitution. The courts paid little attention to it, perhaps thinking the Puritanic spasm would soon pass away, or that the matter was a dangerous one to touch, on account of so many of the courts' constituents making their living by it. But the second Grand Jury, summoned for December, 1854, took the creature by the horns, and indicted several prominent citizens for renting houses for the purposes of prostitution. The parties were duly arraigned in court. After some skirmishing the charge was dismissed on motion of the District Attorney, S. B. Axtell, on the ground of *want of evidence*. The jury also found true Bills against the town authorities for obtaining money under false pretenses, for licensing the aforesaid places as business houses. On motion of the District Attorney the Court dismissed the charge.

The names of the Grand Jury, which made these efforts at reform: George L. Gale, Foreman; James L. Harnett, T. H. Loehr, Thomas S. Crafts, I. Stewart, J. W. D. Palmer, G. M. S. Matthews, L. L. Robinson, Silvester Streeter, D. C. Ferris, James Johnson, A. D. Follett, James M. Ballard, I. S. Roy, A. Boileau, Scott Cooledge, and Samuel Davis.

Though these efforts miscarried, they showed that the leaven of reform was beginning to work. The practices were not stopped, but the stamp of condemnation was set on them, so that a man seeking office at the hands of the people, made a practice at least of decency. In ——— a man of education and apparent respectability, with M. D. to his name, in the town of Volcano, waited upon a prostitute to a circus. There were numbers of respectable females, young and old, present, and though the doctor had an undoubted right to select his company, the act was looked upon as at war with the better interests of society. The roads were rather muddy, and the portly doctor took the soiled dove in his arms and carried her home, the act being as coolly done in the presence of hundreds, as though the woman was a cherished wife or daughter. The following Autumn he came up as a candidate for Sheriff. He was met with such a rebuff that he withdrew his name, and shortly left the town. In the earlier days persons high in office were often seen in the dance with the frail ones.

AMUSING PROCESSION.

It will be remembered that the several towns anxious to have the honor of being the county seat, Volcano excepted, offered liberal sums for the erection of county buildings. Some of the croakers predicted that the promises would be forgotten after the election. The prediction did not prove true, for Jackson went to work in good faith, and at the end of three or four months presented to the county a nice and comfortable Court House. The county officers had been occupying rooms at the foot of

Broadway, in and around the American Hotel. A procession was formed here to take possession of the new Court House. The order of the procession was as follows:—

BAND,

Consisting of cracked drum and asthmatic clarionet.

[This was as good as the band which escorted Napoleon to his palace on the island of Elba, which, according to Sir Walter Scott, consisted of four wretched fiddles.]

FIREMEN—(In red Shirts).
M. W. GORDON, County Judge,
Flanked by
WM. WAGNER and O. P. SOUTHWELL, Associate Judges; John Phœnix, Sheriff; S. B. Axtell, District Attorney; J. C. Shipman, County Clerk; Wm. L. McKimm, Treasurer;

Followed by Citizens generally.

They marched to the Court House in a body, when, after Court was called, A. C. Brown, in behalf of the citizens of Jackson, presented the building to the county. Judge Gordon accepted it in a neat speech, complimenting the citizens of Jackson on their liberality and public spirit. Some four or five hundred dollars, back on the erection of the building, was made up by subscription, Major Shipman, the recently elected County Clerk, giving fifty dollars towards it. The location of the county seat at Jackson, was supposed to insure the permanent prosperity of the town. In the burst of enthusiasm following the settlement of the matter, the Court, county officers, and citizens generally, were invited to partake of the hospitalities of several of the leading saloons and bars of the town. The procession reformed in the same order as before. The Court being still in session (according to our informant) the officers, jurors and witnesses were compelled to follow, or subject themselves to a fine for contempt! There is no record of any punishment for contumacy or even of failure to partake of the proffered hospitalities, so it is presumed that the arrangement was mutually satisfactory. Our informant, though a juror, and consequently obliged to follow the Court while it was in session, may have been mistaken in thinking the Court was not adjourned, but, as suspecting his veracity would spoil a good story, it is best to give the story the benefit of the doubt.

ELECTION, 1854.

Dwight Crandall (Democrat) was elected Senator and James T. Farley and J. W. D. Palmer (Whigs) were elected Assemblymen. The county was considered Democratic, but the Know-Nothing or Native American party had organized and made itself a power in politics. The campaign was conducted mostly by James T. Farley and Alonzo Platt, the latter, though an old politician, being no match for the young candidate, who, though in his early twenties, showed canvassing powers of the highest order. He did not carry any angular notions into the canvass, but professed to be willing to be governed by the will of the people.

The vote for Governor stood: J. Neely Johnson (Know-Nothing), 2,035; John Bigler (Democrat), 1,719.

FIRST TAX LEVY.

The Legislature of 1853–4 having abolished the office of Supervisors in Calaveras county, the Court of Sessions was empowered to transact the business of the county. August 26, 1854, the Court ordered a tax of fifty cents on each one hundred dollars of property, five cents of which was to be devoted to school purposes, and forty-five to county purposes.

CONDITION OF SOCIETY IN 1854.

The introduction of improved methods of mining brought a great increase of population to Amador, as well as the other counties of California. Along with prosperity came the institutions, the dance-house and the gambling saloons, looked upon then as a peculiar feature in California society, but which is now found to be a natural growth wherever sudden wealth comes to those unacquainted with its proper use. The absence of the family influence also favored a condition of society in which the influence of woman was in the descending scale. The soiled doves were mostly natives of Mexico, "dusky daughters of Montezuma" as the poets termed them, and of Peru. It is said that at one time two hundred of the frail beauties were resident in the town of Jackson. Their daily appearance on the street or dancing during the evening in sight from the street, called forth no remark of disapproval but had come to be regarded as a matter of course. Some respectable citizens made left-handed wives of them, and wealthy men did not hesitate to build houses and rent them for these institutions. Men who had left families in the East were seen in friendly chat, and young men by the score or hundreds rather poured their gold into wanton laps. Some of these women would accumulate ten thousand dollars, or in some instances double that, in a Winter's campaign.

Faro, monte and other games gave the lucky miner a chance to double his money or lose it, the latter being the ordinary result. Many men who now bewail their bad luck in California, turned their earnings into these banks that receive deposits but never pay interest or principal. Whisky, too, had its devotees, and the principle was inculcated that he who would not drink was a mean man. Nearly all social intercourse was based upon "drinks all around." When men met and when they parted, drinks were in order; when they traded, drinks for all were ordered as a matter of course. When a man ran for office, whisky was his trump card. An old politician said to a man about running for office: "If you will not treat, you may as well stay at home and give it up." Another one said:

"Twelve hundred drinks elected me." To decline these social observances was to become to some extent ostracised. There were exceptions it is true; there were men who would shut themselves in their cabins and decline all intercourse rather than indulge in the prevailing vices. These would remain unknown until fortune in the shape of a rich claim smiled on them, and then they were mentioned in no complimentary terms. Every day men might be seen in all stages of intoxication; some crazy with rough fun, others ready for a brawl. One day one man in a cabin was on a spree and requiring the restraint of his companions, the next another. Whether because the whisky was bad or because the hot, dry climate aggravated the ills of the fiery liquors, or both, the effect was disastrous, morally, physically, financially. The men capable of writing a solid article on political or scientific subjects, or of delivering an oration off-hand, could be seen ranting and howling through the streets or sleeping off the effects of a debauch.

CHAPTER XIX.
RANCHERIA MURDERS.

Ill-feeling between the Americans and Mexicans—Frequency of Murders—The Band First Seen at Hacalitas—Up Dry Creek—At Rancheria—To Drytown—A Second Time to Rancheria—Slaughter—Departure of the Robbers—Excitement the Next Day—Immense Gathering—Trial and Hanging of the Mexicans—Death of Roberts—Borquitas—Presence of County Officers—Pursuit of the Murderers—Hunt Around Bear Mountain—The Murderers Overtaken—Death of Phœnix—Expulsion and Disarming of Mexican Population—Outrages at Drytown—Burning of the Church—Mass Meeting at Jackson—Review After a Lapse of a Quarter of a Century.

This affair happened something over a quarter of a century since. Many of the witnesses are dead, others are gone, and many have forgotten some of the important matters. Those who are accustomed to criminal trials, know how contradictory testimony may be among candid, truth telling men, even while the events are fresh in the mind. How much more difficult then to get at the truth when a quarter of a century has rolled over the events, inevitably obliterating much that would be necessary to form a rational opinion of the murders, and the resulting events of the following month. A somewhat retrospective view of the relations between the Mexican population and our own, seems necessary, to get a correct view of the situation.

There never was a good feeling between the native population and the Americans. The indolent native, fond of his *siesta* and cigarette, proud of the smallest quantity of Castilian blood, and holding in utter abhorrence laborious occupations, had, at first, contempt, and then hatred, for the wild Americanos, or Gringos (green-horns), as the Americans were termed, who seemed to be endowed with an infernal energy that tore up all the ordinary routine of life, and made men almost maniacs, in the search for wealth.

This feeling was older than the war in which California was conquered. Years before that Alexander Forbes, an Englishman, now a resident of Oakland, who wrote the "History of California," as early as 1835, speaks of occasional parties of Americans who came from the frontiers of the United States, whom no danger could appall and no difficulty deter; who would be likely in time to take California and hold it as they had taken Texas, if some foreign power did not step in and forestall them. At the time of the war, there were some two hundred Americans who had often made their power felt. Isaac Graham, with some fifty or sixty men, had taken possession of the Capital (Monterey), and made Juan B. Alvarado, Governor. They were always in a *quasi* rebellion. Fremont with his battalion, had gone in force through the country, stubbornly refusing to be whipped. The Mexican Government had an article inserted in the treaty, that the rights of the Mexicans to their property in California should be respected. But this did not prevent the Americans, on the discovery of gold, from taking possession of the best lands, and parceling them out into farms and cultivating them. The native owner was wont to consider himself lucky if he could save even his houses and his herds. The latter, the Americans would drive off and slaughter by the thousand, with hardly a pretense of secrecy. In this way the herds of nearly all the old *dons* were exterminated. The titles to their lands were scarcely ever recognized until they had passed into the hands of the Americans. In the gold mines, they were treated as intruders, and the discovery of a placer was sure to bring a swarm of men about, who believed in "Americans ruling America." This ill-feeling often culminated in murder and robbery. Particular roads frequented by parties of Mexicans, were found to be dangerous to travel. Several persons had been murdered on the road between Drytown and Cosumnes. Murderer's gulch, north of the town, had witnessed several murders, which, as the people believed, had been traced to the native population. Several attempts had been made to banish them from the country, but when driven from one camp they would go to another. As the miners were roving about and the population changing, the expulsion was soon forgotten, and the natives would return embittered and sullen. Joaquin's raids through the country had not been forgotten, and when the news of the slaughter of six or seven persons at Rancheria had spread over the county, it is not strange that the community should be terribly excited, and should be moved to deeds which were afterwards looked upon with regret.

The murders were committed by twelve men, one of whom seemed to be white, and one a black man, the rest appearing to be of the ordinary Mexican type. Some of these were men of education, others had been *vaqueros* in the valleys; and all perhaps felt that they had some grievance to avenge, for we cannot account for their subsequent career on any other hypothesis. They were first heard from at Hacalitas (hard camp) not far from the Q ranch, on the night of the 5th of August, 1855, where they stayed all night.

The following morning, Monday, August 6th, they left the camp and made their way towards Drytown, first robbing a China camp, leaving the Chinamen tied. They passed some white men without disturbing them, however. It happened that George Durham, foreign tax collector, had started on much the same route and found that all the China camps from there to Rancheria had been robbed. He got a very good description of the numbers and appearance of the men, and found that they had been at Rancheria at Francis' store; also saw their camp just out of the town. He warned Francis against the men, saying that he thought they were the same men who had recently committed some depredations at Tuttle's store in Tuolumne county, and told Francis that he was in danger of being robbed. Durham then went towards Drytown, passing their camp. There seemed to be some difficulty among them, as two were well stripped apparently to fight, but were quieted by a tall, slender man, who seemed to be recognized as a chief. Two of the party followed Durham as if to attack him, but turned back after going a short distance. At Drytown, Durham engaged Cross, the constable, to assist in collecting the tax from the Chinamen at Milton's ranch, as they had dodged him before when he went alone. They got back to Drytown about dark, and went into Mizener's store. While there Judge Curtis came in and said that a Spanish woman had come to his office and told him that the town was full of robbers; that she was afraid that they were all going to be robbed. The description of the party corresponded with the party which had been seen at Rancheria, and Cross and Durham resolved to visit the place on Chile flat where the robbers were taking supper. On coming to the house, they had left, but were found a short distance to the rear. Both parties, as they met, commenced firing, some thirty or forty shots being exchanged. The Mexicans were on an elevation, and Durham and Cross were in a depression; these circumstances as well as the darkness prevented any fatal results, one person only, a Mexican, being wounded. Both parties now withdrew, the Mexicans going to their camp on the hill a half mile away, and Durham and Cross to the American part of the town. It was now evident that no small job was on hand. Twelve desperate men thoroughly armed would take the town. The citizens had heard the firing and many of the bullets had struck the buildings, though without doing any damage to persons. Although this was in 1855, only a few years away from the time that the men crossed the plains each with his rifle in order, but few fire-arms could be found. When these had been gathered up, it was learned that the banditti had decamped and gone toward Rancheria. Whether it was a ruse to draw the armed party away from the town or not was uncertain, but it was now evident that one or both places was to be attacked. It was also evident that, but for the premature alarm, Drytown would have been the first victim, and probably Rancheria afterwards. Two persons, Robert Cosner being one, volunteered to go to Rancheria to inform them of the danger. They avoided the road, going up Rattlesnake gulch; but while the party were discussing the matter the Mexicans had done the work. On the arrival of Cosner and ——, the robbers appeared to be leaving the town on the opposite side. There were no lights and a dreadful silence prevailed. They called aloud several times before they heard any reply. David Wilson was found hiding in a ditch; when he heard their voices he said: "My God! The whole town is slaughtered; my brother Sam is killed, and I don't know how many more." At Francis' store they found Dan Hutchinson, his clerk, dead behind the counter, also Sam Wilson and ——. Francis was missing but was found not far away with both legs broken and several severe wounds, but still alive. It seemed that he had fought them to the last and eventually ran out of the back door on the stumps of his legs. While searching for Francis they found the dead body of an Indian. The safe was blown open and the contents, about twenty thousand dollars, abstracted. At Dynan's Hotel they found Mrs. Dynan dead, shot through the body, and Dynan wounded. Mrs. Dynan seemed to have been shot while putting her child out of the window. Francis died the next day. One leg was amputated and the other set with the hope of saving his life. After death it was discovered that his back bone was nearly severed, apparently by a blow from an axe. Altogether there were six men, one woman and an Indian killed and two men wounded. It seemed that the party divided, a part going to each house, commencing the attack at about the same moment. At Dynan's a party were playing cards when the house was attacked. Dynan escaped up stairs and through the windows. A man by the name of Foster, the simpleton of the party, had wit enough to throw himself under the table and remain there until the trouble was over and thus saved his life.

THE NEXT DAY

The news rapidly spread. By nine the next morning perhaps five hundred people were present. The atrocious character of the murders, the unprovoked and causeless attack, raised the anger of the people almost beyond control. Some were for an immediate war on all of the Mexican race. Parties were engaged in arresting and bringing in all in the vicinity. It is difficult now to ascertain whether any trial was held or not. There was no organization of the crowd which was continually coming and going. A few elderly men, among whom may be mentioned two Hinksons, acted as a sort of jury, to give a form of deliberation to the affair. Judge Curtis is said

Residence of O. E. MARTIN, Amador City, Amador Co. Cal.

also to have taken part in the proceedings. These men were noted for their moderation and prudence. They probably prevented the crowd from doing much worse than it did. "Let us proceed cautiously; let us be just; let us hang no innocent men," said they. They were men in whom the people had confidence. Some thirty-five men were brought within the rope circle and guarded. A motion was put to hang the whole of them, all but a few voting for it. They were then asked to give the men a trial. This was reluctantly consented to; and a committee—it could not be called a jury—set themselves to ascertain the evidence against the men. All that could be found was that James Johnson, a miner who lived in a cabin near by, and looked out through a crack in the door when the shooting was going on, *thought* he heard a Mexican, called Port Wine (because he was always drunk, or nearly so, on port), shouting for Mexico. Another one had placed a light in the road in front of his house. The third one was seen running around with the banditti during the shooting. This was on the testimony of one man who thought he saw it through a slight opening of his cabin door. The committee reported that this was all that could be found against any of them. It was determined to hang them immediately. Port Wine was a half-witted man, almost incapable of committing a crime. He cried and begged, to no purpose; he was hung while his wife was begging for him, two others being hung at the same time. The jury, whose names it is impossible to learn, must not be blamed in this matter. It is impossible to tell what any one would do until they are tried. Hundreds of exasperated people were clamoring for the death of somebody. It is likely that the hanging of the three appeased, to some extent, the thirst for vengeance. William O. Clark, a well-known citizen of Drytown, made a speech advocating a trial by law, by the Courts, and made an appeal to the people to place themselves, in imagination, in a foreign country, and about to be hung for a crime some of their own countrymen had committed; but the people were in no mood to hear finely constructed sentences, and he was silenced. It was even proposed to hang him for being friendly to the Mexicans. A Mrs. Ketchum was particularly active in creating a sentiment against Clark. The balance of the party arrested were liberated on condition of leaving the camp within four hours.

DEATH OF ROBERTS.

About this time a terrible accident occurred. A man by the name of Roberts, or Robinson, who had been one of the most violent in demanding a wholesale hanging, shot himself in the breast, dying immediately. There are so many conflicting reports that it is with reluctance the subject is mentioned. One person says they were about to go home, and Roberts was taking the gun towards him, neither angry nor intoxicated, when it went off, striking him in the breast. Another one says that Robinson—or Roberts—was violently demanding the death of another prisoner, which was not immediately assented to, whereupon he said he would settle the question himself, snatching up the gun with the result heretofore stated.

BORQUITAS.

William Sutherland, whose veracity no one will question, relates the following circumstances in regard to it: A young Spaniard by the name of Borquitas, General Castro's business agent, happened to be visiting Sutherland's at the time of the murders. Being a well educated man, speaking the English language fluently, he remarked that he might be of assistance in ferreting out the criminals, and would go up to Rancheria. When he got there, he found himself one of the criminals, or, at least, he was reckoned among the criminal class. During the affair, trial it could not be called, he conversed with one of the accused. Becoming convinced of the innocence of the party of any complicity in the murders, he told the people so; whereupon, it was proposed to hang him (Borquitas) also. It was then that Roberts undertook to shoot him, with the result of death to himself. Sutherland then told Borquitas that he could do no good by staying and risking his own life; that he had better leave. Taking the advice of Sutherland, he left in the confusion, caused by the death of Roberts.

It is said that Judge Gordon, S. B. Axtell, District Attorney, Judge Hubbard, and others, were present; but as the hanging took place before noon, and the Court met at ten, as usual, on the morning after the murders, it is almost impossible that they should have witnessed the hanging, though they probably were present during the afternoon.

Port Wine had a good claim, which was considered forfeited at his death. James Robinson, on whose testimony he was hung, taking possession of it the same evening. He worked it for a few days, but finding work a burden, he sold it for two hundred dollars, which he spent in a week's spree, shortly after.

WHERE WERE THE OFFICERS?

Phœnix, and some of his deputies, visited the scene of the disturbance, in the early morning. After looking at the mutilated bodies, he merely said, "Follow me." A party was immediately organized to pursue the banditti, which, as before stated, left Rancheria, taking the road towards El Dorado county. This proved to be a false scent. They went as far as Indian Diggings, and, finding themselves off the trail, returned to Jackson. There they learned that the gang had crossed the Mokelumne at Diamond bar. Phœnix, Cross, Perrin, Sherry, Eichelberger, and Durham, went to Mokelumne Hill that night. They there learned that Sheriff Clark, Paul McCormick, and six-fingered Smith of Camp Seco, had attacked the murderers at Texas bar, on the Calaveras, and had wounded and captured one of the party, who had told the history and names of the others. His name was Manuel Garcia, and he had been a vaquero for Charles Stone, at Buena Vista. He was sent to Jackson with Eichelberger and Perrin. The crowd had assembled to receive him; parting to the right and left, and closing up after him, they escorted the prisoner to the tree, which was already provided with a noose. When his head was placed in it, the buggy was moved along, and the body left dangling. This was the eighth time the tree had borne its fruit.

It was now ascertained that the balance of the party were concealed around Bear mountain. Two days spent in hunting failed to find them; and then the officers went to Jenny Lind where they learned that the Mexicans were camped near Reynold's ferry on the Stanislaus. A large number of Mexicans at Jenny Lind were disarmed, to prevent any assistance reaching the banditti from that settlement, and the pursuit continued, but somebody had given notice of the approach of the officers and the party had left going towards the Tuolumne river. A guard was set at Reynold's ferry, but the robbers did not attempt to cross. The next day the officers visited Tuttletown, Sonora, Campo Seco, and Jamestown. At the latter place they again struck the trail, and found some of the horses, which had been stolen at Rancheria, dying of exhaustion.

The reader will bear in mind that the ground at this season of the year (August) is hard as a rock, receiving scarcely any impression from a hoof or a shoe passing along; and besides the Mexicans traveled in the night time, concealing themselves in the thick chaparral, with which the hills around Bear mountain abound during the day, so that closely following the trail was out of the question; but it was now evident that they were nearing the objects of their search. Chinese Camp and a Mexican camp, at what is called Old Chinese Camp, were visited. At the latter place was a large dance-house near the hills, the thick chaparral coming down close to the house. It was out of the question to get any correct information with regard to the party they were in search of, but they concluded to stop awhile and watch events. Drinks around and the usual hospitalities followed, as a matter of course. While some of the party engaged the señoritas in conversation, others kept a general lookout. A girl at the door was seen making signals to some one in the rear, as if to go away. Durham sprang to the door, and saw some of the men they were in search of. Phœnix was anxious to capture them alive, and to this reluctance to kill them, was due the fatal result; but shooting commenced at once. It is difficult to recall events in their order, in which two or three seconds make a failure or success of a movement; but in the affray Phœnix was the first to fall; his slayer the next—the latter though severely wounded, still kept fighting, being finally dispatched by a blow on the head with an axe. The party dispersed in a short time, the officers holding the ground. A boy, who had witnessed the affair from a distance, told the officers that he had seen a wounded man crawl into a cloth shanty, blood stains indicating the correctness of the statement. The man was told to come out, but as no answer was received, the hut was set on fire, as it was deemed dangerous to follow him in. Not until it was blazing all over, so that it was thought impossible for any living being to be there, did he appear. He rushed out, covered with blood, clothes and hair on fire, with a pistol in each hand, shooting as he came. He was more frightful than dangerous, and was soon quieted. Phœnix was shot through the heart, dying immediately. He was buried by the Masonic order at Sonora. He was, perhaps, thirty years old, of social character, openhearted, holding malice towards none, and was universally esteemed. He was in poor health at the time, hardly fit for such an enterprise, as he took upon himself to lead. On his return from the unsuccessful search in El Dorado, he was urged to rest; was told that, considering the disturbed condition of the county, his presence was needful—which was true. But he replied that if he should decline pursuing the murderers, his courage would be called in question, and he started the same evening. His attempt to capture the men alive, was a fatal mistake. It was no kindness to the party, for, in the excited condition of the people, every one taken was sure to be hung without a trial.

This affair occurred Sunday evening, August 12, 1855.

A day or two after these occurrences, Marshall Wood, of the town of Columbia, telegraphed the party that he had arrested forty or more Spaniards, and thought that some of the men they were in search of, were among them. On visiting Sonora, Durham recognized one of the party, a well-dressed, educated, young man, who had formerly lived at Drytown. At first, he understood no English, knew nothing about the matter, but upon being called by name, Manuel Escobar, and being told that Garcia, the one taken at Camp Seco, had given the names of the whole party, he commenced cursing in *good* English, and did not deny his connection with the murders. He was taken to Jackson, and hung, being the tenth and last hung on the famous tree. A photograph was taken of the scene, and the picture lithographed, some copies of which are still preserved by the people of Jackson.

Shortly after this, an old Mexican from Algerine Camp, told the officers that the man who had killed Phœnix, came to his house wounded in several places, he thought fatally, wanting to be taken care of; that he did not wish to harbor him, as he thought that the Americans would kill him if they found it out, and so told the wounded man, who, however, threatened to kill him if he refused assistance. The old Mexican had put him down a shaft which had a short tunnel connected with it, in which the wounded man was hiding. Durham and his party visited the place, and called upon the man to come out; receiving no answer, some brush was thrown into the shaft and set on fire, shortly after which the report of a pistol was heard. He had shot himself rather than surrender. When the fire had gone out, he was brought out dead. He was shot in five places around the neck, and could hardly have recovered under any circumstances.

EXPULSION AND DISARMING OF THE MEXICAN POPULATION.

The excitement all through the county was such that business was nearly suspended. Extravagant rumors of the intention of the Mexican population to rise and take the county, got into circulation. The same excitability that demanded the hanging of a whole nationality, formed a good material to float impossible stories of an insurrection. The second day after the murders, a great number of people came around Rancheria. The Mexicans had left the day of the hanging. It is said that some of the wives and friends of the executed had hardly time to bury the dead. When the crowd came the second day they destroyed all the huts and houses belonging to the Mexicans. It was then resolved that they should leave the country. A large body of those that had been expelled from Rancheria were encamped in Mile gulch, which runs north into Dry creek, its head being near the town. Thither the party proceeded. An indiscriminate shooting commenced. Some Indians, who seemed to be watching the Spanish, were told to kill all they could. Some were known to be killed—it is hoped, however, not as many as were reported—but the whole people left as rapidly as they could. One Mexican was seen packing two trunks on each side of a donkey. The overloaded animal could not keep up and he was obliged to abandon them. They were broken open and found to be filled with shirts and finery, apparently goods plundered from Francis' store. The Indians drew these on, one over another, until they would have on five or six each. This prevented the Indians from killing many of the fugitives, though when questioned about it afterwards, they said they had killed *ocho*, meaning eight. Some were found dead in holes and shafts, others at springs, where they had dragged themselves after being wounded. Several persons say they have seen the hogs devouring the bodies of the slain. Pork was at a discount during the season, on that account. At Sutter Creek an extravagant rumor got into circulation that five hundred men were coming to take the town. A committee of safety was organized, and some fifty or sixty Mexicans who were mining on Gopher flat, were arrested and brought to town. One man was unfortunate enough to have some connection, in some way, with the Rancheria affair. He was traced into the Mexican camp and a thorough search made for him. It was about to be abandoned when a large pile of clothes, just ironed, lying on a bed, attracted attention. Underneath was found the man. He was dragged out and hung on a gibbet made by lashing wagon-tongues together, forming an A, the wagons being locked to prevent separation. The fifty on Gopher Flat were ordered to leave, which they consented to do provided an escort was given them, for they dared not leave the town disarmed, and alone. They were escorted across the Mokelumne river. At that time nearly the whole of the street below the bridge, was occupied by the Mexican population. They were ordered to leave and *señoras* and *señoritas*, as well as the children (of which there was a considerable number), were seen climbing the hills on their way out of the town. At *Hucalitas*, the camp where the banditti stayed the Sunday night previous to the outrage, the people were disarmed and ordered to leave. One white man was left to make out the passports, the others leaving for a similar duty at another camp. The Mexicans at *Hucalitas* pleaded utter ignorance of any knowledge or participation in the operations of the murderers, but went without making any resistance. A company from Drytown went towards El Dorado county, disarming and driving all the Mexicans away. Men came back with numbers of revolvers and other arms taken from them.

OUTRAGES AT DRYTOWN.

There were but few Mexicans at Drytown, the Spanish population being mostly Chilenos; hence, the name Chile Flat, the portion of the town where they lived. Though speaking the same language, the Chilenos and Mexicans had very little to do with each other; and, consequently, the Chilenos were not charged with any complicity in the outrages at Rancheria, and were generally living on good terms with the people of Drytown.

On the following Sunday, about dark, some fifteen or twenty men on horseback, came into Drytown, and set fire to the Chilenian part of it, and in a few minutes the whole was in a blaze. The people, most of whom were poor, some being women and children, ran in dismay to some of their friends, among the Americans. It is said that William O. Clark's house was filled with crying women and children, who had fled from their burning homes. One man, by the name of Williston, usually called Boston, from his native city, set fire to the Catholic church, which was soon in ashes. The persons engaged in this evening's work, seemed to have had all their plans laid before coming into town, apparently consulted no one, and permitting no interference. Some of the citizens of Drytown have been charged with assisting the rioters, but a thorough investigation fails to connect any one of its citizens with the affair, which was generally condemned as cruel and wanton.

CONVENTION, OR MASS MEETING, AT JACKSON.

A meeting was called to consider the propriety of outlawing all of the Mexican population. Some of the more violent approved of the measure, but the hanging of the men at Jackson and Rancheria, the excesses committed at Mile gulch and vicinity, had caused the more thoughtful to doubt the propriety or necessity of turning all the blood-thirsty loose, with license to kill Mexicans wherever they could be found, for such would be the result of outlawry. R. M. Briggs, especially, violently opposed the measure, and it was abandoned. Most of the Mexicans had left the county, and the necessity of such a measure, was questionable on several grounds. W. O. Clark, who opposed it, perhaps in imprudent words, came near being lynched, his speeches at Rancheria, the day after the murders, being remembered. Many of the Mexicans who fled the county on that occasion, settled near Jenny Lind, in Calaveras county, where they have made peaceable and quiet citizens.

GENERAL FEELING A QUARTER OF A CENTURY AFTER.

There are few, and the number is few, who helped to vindicate justice, as they term it, who are proud of the part they took in the matter. But the more thoughtful look at it as one full of excesses to be regretted. There are many who believe that the three persons hung at Rancheria the day following the outrage were entirely innocent of any complicity in the crimes committed. There appeared to have been two classes of the Mexicans, the *caballeros* or horsemen and the *peons* or laboring class. The first were accustomed here, as they were in Mexico, to help themselves to whatever they wanted of the *peons* who occupied much of the former position of the blacks in the Southern States, having no rights which a *caballero* was bound to respect. It is said that whenever these gentry were known to be in a Mexican camp, or expected, the lights were blown out and everything kept as quiet as possible so as to attract no attention. Old residents say that though a Mexican with a crowbar and *bataya* might steal an axe or a piece of meat, he was never known to commit an outrage. The fact that half a dozen white men would go to a Mexican camp of ten times their number and disarm them does not prove them very belligerent. It would seem that most of the crimes, and they were many, committed by the Mexican population may be justly charged to the *caballeros*, who were generally gamblers and horse-thieves, or worse; who never worked for themselves but appropriated the results of others' industry, not hesitating at murder when necessary to accomplish their object.

CHAPTER XX.
POLITICAL PARTIES IN 1855.

Success of the American Party—List of Officers Elected—Rivalry Between Towns—Financial Matters—Efforts to Suppress Gambling—Political Parties in 1856—Names of Officers Elected—Calaveras Indebtedness—Tax Levy in 1857—Disbursements for 1857—Table of Receipts for all Moneys up to 1857—Political Parties in 1857—Officers Elected in 1857—Officers Elected 1858—Tax Levy 1858—Condition of Treasury—Financial Matters in 1859—Condition of Political Parties.

THE Know-Nothing, or Native American Party, had become the most numerous of any. The almost annihilation of the Whig party in the Presidential contest of 1852, and the subsequent growth of the free soil element into a party, had left the Whigs to form new combinations. As the defeat of the Whigs was largely due to the solid, foreign Democratic vote, it is not strange that the defeated Whigs should organize to control or resist the foreign element. The epithet, " Know-Nothing," seems to have been first given in derision, from a constant assertion, " I know nothing about it," when the members were interrogated about the existence of such an organization, and afterwards partially adopted, or, at least, quietly received by them. The object was a practical exclusion from power of the foreign element. It was urged that a few individuals often controlled hundreds of votes, and could be influenced by improper means; that the foreigners, as a rule, when they come to this country, had no knowledge of the nature of our institutions, and, from having been subjected to unjust laws in Europe, were instinctively opposed to all wholesome restraints; that the percentage of crimes and misdemeanors committed by the foreign element was much greater than their percentage of the population. The meetings, at first, were held secretly, and nearly all the members of the Whig party, as well as many Democrats, were induced to act with them, so that until the day of the election, few men, not belonging to it, were aware of the extent of the organization, and were surprised to find the new party in possession of nearly all the offices, from the Governor down. When the election was over, and concealment no longer necessary, the members showed themselves in processions and public meetings.

RIVALRY BETWEEN TOWNS.

While Volcano was making some pretensions to superior size, the *Sentinel* at Jackson published, as amusing matter, the experience of a Jackson man in Volcano; the latter town being represented as so poverty-stricken, that a five-dollar piece had not been seen for weeks. When our Jackson friend was transacting some little business, he accidentally displayed a ten-dollar piece. The sight was so unusual that a crowd immediately gathered around to admire and wonder. He good-naturedly allowed them to view and handle it, after which he *treated*, paid his bill, and left. The *Sentinel* made quite an amusing article of it; but the Volcano man was to

BLE, STAGE & EXPRESS OFF
VOLCANO.

have his turn now. He acknowledged the story as true in most of the statements. "It was astonishing that a man coming from Jackson should have ten dollars, and still more unusual for a Jackson man to treat; but when he paid his bill before leaving, the astonishment of the people exceeded all bounds; they were still talking about it."

LIST OF OFFICERS ELECTED IN 1855.

Members of the Assembly—J. T. Farley, G. W. Wagner.
Public Administrator—Wm. Jennings.
School Commissioner—J. Goodin.
County Surveyor—David Armstrong.

JUSTICES OF THE PEACE.

Township No. 1—Bruce Husband, Hugh Robinson.
Township No. 2—J. W. D. Palmer, N. C. F. Lane.
Township No. 3—Geo. L. Gale, N. Harding.
Township No. 4—E. B. Howe, W. C. Bryant.
Township No. 5—J. B. King, W. B. Caswell.
Township No. 6—E. R. Yates, James Burt.

E. B. Howe and E. R. Yates were elected Associate Justices to act with M. W. Gordon.

FINANCIAL.

Jan. 1, 1855, the total amount of warrants issued since Sept 14, 1854, was........$41,144.78	
Warrants redeemed during same time	$41,041.29
Total amount outstanding	103.49
Amount on hand	$6,117.07

The second assessment for taxes was as follows:
On personal and real property for county purposes, on each $100..........50c.
For school purposes, on each $100..........10c.
Support of indigent sick,   "   "   ....10c.
Roads and highways,   "   "   ....2c.
State purposes   "   "   ....60c.—$1.32
Poll-tax 3.00

On January 1, 1856, the Supervisors made the following report:—

Jan. 1, 1855, cash on hand	$6,117.07
Received during the year on account of property tax	3,008.24
On account of poll tax	2,270.90
Foreign miners' licenses	10,300.68
County licenses	13,258.75
Fees from Probate Court	61.50
Sale of county property	120.00
Refunded from State treasury	182.18
Total receipts for 1855	$35,957.07
Total disbursements for 1855	34,741.10
Balance on hand Jan. 1, 1856	$1,216.57
Total amount of warrants issued since Sept. 14, 1854, to present	$41,144.78
Amount redeemed	40,041.29
Outstanding	$103.49

EFFORTS TO SUPPRESS GAMBLING.

At the February term, 1856, the Grand Jury made some effort to suppress gambling. Up to this date monte, faro, and other games were openly dealt in many places in the county, demoralizing a great many men. Laws against banking games had been passed a year or two previous, but it was thought to be impossible to enforce them in the mountain towns. All laws are inoperative until sanctioned by public opinion; in this instance only a movement was needed to show that public gambling was not countenanced by the community at large. The names of the Grand Jury that first grappled with this evil are S. G. Hand, who acted as foreman, John Dean, Thos. Luther, Elias Kratzer, Z. Crane, Wm. Cochran, Wm. Goode, David Beach, A. P. Clough, Samuel Folger, Heman Allen, Ellis Evans, Thomas Skidmore, Luther Morgan, Wm. Glenn, D. B. French, B. Davenport, J. H. Young, D. W. Aldrich, E. W. Rice, and S. M. Streeter. Several indictments were found against persons for gaming, also against the owners of houses permitting it. Though gambling never was entirely suppressed it was forced to retire from public sight.

POLITICAL PARTIES IN 1856.

Three parties made their appearance this season: The Democratic party, confident in strength from a sway of nearly a quarter of a century; the Know-Nothing, flushed with a recent victory; and the Republican, having nothing, with everything to hope for. The fact that the Republicans had carried several Eastern States with rapid increase of numbers everywhere, encouraged them to nominate a full county ticket. They first called a general meeting at Drytown on the 4th of October, met in mass meeting numbering about seventy-five, and nominated a full ticket. Col. Baker addressed the meeting in the evening and spoke afterwards at several places in the county. Some little disposition to mob out the Republicans was manifested in several places. At Volcano the sign of the Republican club was torn down and destroyed and a notice served on Mahoney, the owner of the hall, that if the meetings were permitted his hall should be torn down. Leading Democrats hastened to disavow any countenance of the violent proceedings and assured the Republicans that they should not be molested again. At Lancha Plana, M. Frink, a candidate for the Assembly, was torn from the stand, though this was said to have been in consequence of remarks of a personal nature. The fact that mobbing a speaker, however obnoxious his sentiments are, is an argument generally in his favor, is well known and serves to keep the appearance of peace at least.

The Know-Nothings held an imposing convention. J. T. Farley, flushed with the honors of Speaker of the Assembly, acted as president. A huge cannon was fired at intervals of a few minutes through the day, reminding the people for twenty miles around that the Know-Nothing Convention was in session.

The Democratic ticket was elected, the Republicans casting a little over six hundred votes, or about one-sixth part of the entire vote.

The vote for President was: Buchanan (Dem.), 1784; Fillmore (K. N.), 1557; Fremont (Rep.), 637.

OFFICERS ELECTED NOVEMBER, 1856.

Assemblymen—Wm. M. Seawell, James Livermore.
Sheriff—W. J. Paugh.
County Clerk—H. S. Hatch.
District Attorney—S. B. Axtell.
Treasurer—Ellis Evans.
Assessor—H. A. Eicholberger.
Public Administrator—J. B. King.
County Surveyor—James Masterson.
Coronor—A. B. Kibbe.

SUPERVISORS.

District No. 1—J. G. Severance.
District No. 2—E. A. Kingsley.
District No. 3—J. A. Brown.
Superintendent Common Schools—E. B. McIntyre.

JUSTICES OF THE PEACE.

Township No. 1—L. N. Ketchum, Bruce Husband.
Township No. 2—N. C. F. Lane, J. W. D. Palmer.
Township No. 3—A. M. Ballard, Geo. Monkton.
Township No. 4—E. B. McIntyre, D. R. Gans.
Township No. 5—C. N. W. Hinkson, G. W. Haynes.
Township No. 6—Stephen Kendall, I. F. Ostrom.

CALAVERAS INDEBTEDNESS.

When Amador was set off from Calaveras a provision was made that the new county should assume a just proportion of the common debt. As no especial methods of determining this amount was provided, the matter was neglected until Calaveras brought suit, January 27, 1857, against J. C. Shipman, as Auditor of Amador county, to recognize the obligation. James H. Hardy was employed as a lawyer to defend Amador county, and was allowed one thousand dollars as a fee for his services. February 3d there is a minute to the effect that the Board adjourned to meet the Board of Calaveras county to effect an amicable arrangement. The records of the Board of Supervisors do not make mention of the matter again until the 7th of August following, when Alonzo Platt and James F. Hubbard were appointed as a Commission to meet an equal number on the part of Calaveras county, to determine the amount of the indebtedness. This conference resulted in fixing the amount at twenty-six thousand five hundred and seventeen dollars and thirty-two cents. A warrant was issued for this amount, and, as Number 103, became famous in the financial history of the county as the source of evasions, injunctions and lawsuits.

The Board of Supervisors ordered that one-half of the general fund should be set aside for the payment of this warrant. From the records, it appears that an arrangement had been made with the Calaveras authorities, that evidence of Calaveras indebtedness, or "county scrip," might be applied in payment of this debt. George Durham was appointed a broker, to buy up the scrip, sixty-five cents on the dollar being the price he was to be paid for it, "and no more." One thousand dollars was advanced to him, as capital to begin with, and directions made that he should settle as often as once a month. J. C. Shipman, Alvinza Hayward, John C. White, William Sharp, and Wesley Jackson, were his sureties for the faithful performance of the duties. It is to be regretted that the records of the Board of Supervisors are not more complete. The high price of ink, or some other freak of economy, kept them from keeping a full account, and we are obliged to write history out of hints and disjointed *memoranda*. The purchase of scrip does not seem to have been satisfactory, for suit was commenced against Durham on account of the matter. There is a minute to the effect that the District Attorney be directed to suspend the suit against Durham, as long as M. W. Gordon should pay to the County Treasurer fifty dollars a month; that the stay of proceedings should cease whenever the said M. W. Gordon should neglect or refuse to pay the fifty dollars per month.

TAX LEVY OF 1857.

For county purposes, on each $100..............50c.
School purposes,   "   "   ....10c.
Indigent sick,   "   "   ....20c.
Calaveras Fund,   "   "   ....30c.
State taxes,   "   "   ....70c.—$1.80

A poll-tax of $3.00 was ordered on account of roads, and the same also for State and county purposes.

January 1, 1858, the Supervisors made the following report:—

Warrants issued during the year exclusive of the
  famous 103 for Calaveras indebtedness was.....$12,457.27
Outstanding for previous year......................103.49
                                                $12,560.76
Warrants redeemed during the time..............$35,078.40
Warrants outstanding..............................$7,482.36
                                                 26,517.32
Including Calaveras indebtedness................$33,999.68

Inventory of county property.
Delinquent taxes...............................$ 5,881.40
County jail and improvements....................7,017.80
*Court House and lot improvements...............2,379.10
Furniture of clerk's office.......................400.00
Sheriff's and other offices.......................270.00
County hospital...................................200.00

    Total..................................... $16,148.30

September 18, 1857, the Supervisors ordered the Treasurer to make no payment at all to S. L. McGee, the holder of *warrant No. 103*, drawn on account of the Calaveras indebtedness. From this item it would appear that McGee had become the owner of the warrant, and refused to take scrip on it.

The funds set aside for the payment of this warrant accumulated until they amounted, in January, 1859, to $20,198.27, less $605.00, which had been allowed the outgoing Treasurer as percentage.

This concatenation of awkward events was inaugurated by J. G. Severance, E. A. Kingsley, and James A. Brown, acting as the Board of Supervisors.

---

* The Court House having been donated by the town of Jackson, only the improvements are estimated.

POLITICAL PARTIES IN 1857.

ACCOUNTS ALLOWED FROM JANUARY 1, 1857, TO JANUARY 1, 1858.

County Judge	$ 2,500 00
County Clerk and Auditor	3,104 53
District Attorney	1,810 00
Associate Justices	874 00
Assessor	2,653 34
Sheriff	7,406 22
Supervisors	1,095 55
Justice's Fees	624 10
Constable's Fees	1,318 49
Witnesses' Fees	113 50
Jurors	4,384 50
Superintendent and Marshals Common Schools	581 00
Hospital	4,336 61
Officers of Election	568 00
Repairs on Court House and Jail	1,550 92
Stationery	494 92
Scaffold and Execution of Cottle	100 00
Attorneys' Fees in Criminal Cases	135 00
P. M. Examinations and Taking Insane to Asylum	484 30
Attorneys' Fees in County Suits	1,400 00
Supplies for Jail	275 00
Printing	917 00
Roads	12 25
Taxes Refunded	45 24
Miscellaneous	224 80
Total	$37,079 35

Table Showing the Amounts of Money Received into the Treasury to 1857.

COMPILED BY F. McBRIDE, THOMAS H. LOEHR, AND T. G. HOARD, SUPERVISORS.

ON WHAT ACCOUNT.	1854.	1855.	1856.	1857.	TOTAL.
Property Tax	$7501 90	$7172 02	$9034 10	$30444 77	$50932 79
State and County Licenses	6746 50	16061 27	14756 15	14262 65	50925 62
Foreign Miners' Tax	6351 30	2045 72	18284 04	22544 16	7500 24
Poll-Tax	2671 50	4579 30	7414 12	9434 85	19458 89
Fines	300 00	564 55	357 20	626 20	1953 85
Refunded from State	464 40	482 18	1448 44	1352 53	3847 55
Probate Court		61 50	42 00	53 00	156 50
Sale of County Property		150 00	100 00		250 00
School-Tax			1821 00	5030 63	6851 66
Hospital			906 25	5020 41	5926 66
Property Tax (Roads)			161 24		161 24
Jurors' Fees			408 00	45 00	453 00
Calaveras Tax				5841 85	5841 85
Bridge and Ferry Licenses				872 00	872 00
Miscellaneous	45 00		63 00	89 58	197 58
Total	$25020 70	$30870 30	$55112 00	$95855 80	$223100 93

POLITICAL PARTIES IN 1857.

Three tickets were put into the field as usual. The Democrats flushed with the recent Presidential victory, and strong in the possession of the public funds, the other two suffering from overwhelming defeats. R. M. Briggs, of the *moribund* Know-Nothing party, was the only one elected on that ticket in the county, and almost the only one in the State. In the Assembly, "he chewed the bitter cud of Knownothingism, to the end, alone." There was little interest in the election outside of the scramble among the office-seekers. Every town had a full set of candidates for all the positions.

The following list was elected:—

State Senator—L. N. Ketchum.
Assemblymen—R. M. Briggs, Homer King.
County Surveyor—John R. Dicks.
Superintendent Common Schools—E. B. McIntyre.

JUSTICES OF THE PEACE.

Township No. 1—J. M. Douglass, Geo. S. Smith.
Township No. 2—J. T. Poe, J. W. D. Palmer.
Township No. 3—John Doble, Geo. Monkton.
Township No. 4—D. R. Gans, E. B. McIntyre.
Township No. 5—C. N. K. Hinkson, E. B. Styles.
Township No. 6.—Steve Kendall, Hugh Bell.

Vote for Governor—J. B. Weller (Dem.), 1619; G. W. Bowie (K. N.), 997; Ed. Stanley (Rep.), 492.

OFFICERS ELECTED IN 1858.

Assembly—W. W. Cope, J. A. Eagan.
County Judge—M. W. Gordon.
Sheriff—W. J. Paugh.
County Clerk—T. M. Pawling.
District Attorney—J. G. Severance.
Treasurer—C. A. Lagrave.
Assessor—F. P. Smith.
Public Administrator—E. Gallagher.
Superintendent Common Schools—H. H. Rheese.
Coroner—John Vogan.
Surveyor—Albert Moore.

SUPERVISORS.

District No. 1—R. D. Stiles.
District No. 2—Robert Stewart.
District No. 3—Jacob Linzee.

JUSTICES OF THE PEACE.

Township No. 1—Geo. S. Smith, J. W. Hutchins.
Township No. 2—C. English, J. C. Wicker.
Township No. 3—John Doble, A. M. Ballard.
Township No. 4—E. B. Howe, D. R. Gans.
Township No. 5—E. B. Stiles, C. N. W. Hinkson.
Township No. 6—Hugh Bell, B. Nichols.
Township No. 7—Sam Loree, D. Cartmill.

RATES OF TAXES FOR 1858.

For State purposes on each $100 .... 50c.
County purposes, " " .... 50c.
School purposes, " " .... 10c.
Indigent Sick, " " .... 20c.
Calaveras Fund, " " ....
Board purposes, " " .... 15c.—$1.75
Also $3.00 poll-tax for roads, and also the same for general purposes.

There is no report found of the state of the finances at the end of the year. Ellis Evans, the County Treasurer, reports the total indebtedness at $24,409.43. This must have been a balance, as the famous warrant, No. 103, still remained with no portion paid, with accumulated interest. On the first of July, in his second quarterly report, he fixes the amount of outstanding warrants at $46,717.77.

There was in the Treasury credited to the
General Fund .... $ 1,799.02
Hospital Fund 305.73
Road Fund 74.84
Calaveras Fund .... 14,897.45—$17,077.45
Total indebtedness $29,640.63

At the end of 1858 the Calaveras Fund had accumulated until it amounted to $20,198.27, which, less 3 per cent., $605.94, Treasurer's commission, was turned over to the incoming Treasurer, C. A. Lagrave.

FINANCIAL MATTERS IN 1859.

Rates of taxes for State purposes on each $100 ...... 60c.
County purposes, " " ...... 50c.
School purposes, " " ...... 10c.
Calaveras Debt, " " ...... 20c.
Road purposes, " " ...... 5c.—$1.45
Poll-tax, $3.00 for roads, and the same for general purposes.

During the first quarter of the year there was paid on the Calaveras debt (warrant 103) the sum of $19,005.50, leaving due the sum of $19,577.75, of which sum $9,281.05 was interest.

On the 7th of November, Treasurer Lagrave reported the county debt, exclusive of warrant 103, at $6,644.18; Calaveras debt, $9,109.17; making a total of $15,753.35.

This estimate was made after deducting moneys on hand which were as follows:—

General Fund	$7,168.91
Hospital Fund	$2,248.82
School Fund	2,348.42
Road Fund	567.72
Calaveras Fund	3,759.40—$16,091.27

DISBURSEMENTS FROM JULY 1, 1858, TO AUG. 1, 1859.

Salary of County Judge		$ 2,499.96
County Clerk and Auditor		3,234.73
District Attorney, salary and fees		2,175.00
Associate Justices		726.00
Assessor		2,880.00
Sheriff fees in criminal cases	$4,189.95	
" boarding prisoners	3,426.50	
" jailor and assistant	1,886.00	9,502.45
Supervisors per diem and mileage		1,065.95
Hospital expenses and burials		5,596.57
Officers of election		561.00
Supplies for Court House and jail		1,387.07
Stationery		684.63
Attorneys' fees in criminal cases		884.95
Printing		1,585.00
Road purposes		1,367.02
Inquests		268.60
Interpreting		99.00
Collecting county licenses extra per cent		129.47
Deficiences in gold-dust		156.25
Miscellaneous expenses		1,303.19
Total warrants issued		$43,995.86

The interest on the Calaveras debt had accumulated to $9,281.05, making the whole debt $35,798.37 before any payment was made thereon.

CONDITION OF POLITICAL PARTIES.

With the close of the election of 1857, the Know-Nothing party ceased to be a formidable element in politics. The leaders, generally, having been prominent members of the defunct Whig party, now found little difficulty in falling into the ranks of their ancient foemen, the Democrats. Early in the season of 1857, a number of prominent Know-Nothings, J. O. Goodwin of Yuba, and James T. Farley of Amador, being of the number, agreed that, in view of the breaking up of old parties, and the formation of new parties in the East, and the expressed sentiments of President Buchanan in regard to some of the objects sought by the American party, it was not necessary to continue the organization. Farley became a member of the party, working in the ranks, until, as he was wont to say, he had been forgiven. R. M. Briggs also trained with the Democrats until the spring of 1861. W. W. Cope, D. W. Seaton, J. W. Bicknell, and others, old Whigs, also fell into the Democratic ranks. The Republican party was mostly made up of men who did not put themselves forward for office. A lawyer was not often to be found in their ranks, occasioning some trouble to find a suitable candidate for District Attorney. Hearing some Republicans lamenting the want of a suitable man in their ranks to run for attorney, D. W. Seaton remarked: "Never mind. You will have lawyers enough on your side when you come to a majority." During the first four years of the organization, it was in a hopeless minority, with few politicians or orators to meet the attacks of ridicule and sarcasm, always given to the hindmost in the race.

With the breaking up of the Know-Nothing party, and the affiliation of most of the members with the Democratic party, came the distinction "Lecompton" and "Anti-Lecompton," growing out of the attempt of Northern and Southern men to colonize the Territory of Kansas, and bring it in as a free or slave State; one wing of the Democratic party favoring, and the other opposing the admission of Kansas with the Lecompton Constitution, which established slavery.

The vote for Governor, stood as follows: Latham (Democrat), 2,023; John Curry (Anti-Lecompton), 985; Stanford (Republican), 232.

OFFICERS ELECTED IN 1859.

State Senator—J. A. Eagan.
Assemblymen—P. C. Johnson, J. H. Bowman.
Coroner—J. C. Shepherd.

SUPERVISOR.

District No. 1—C. Y. Hammond.

JUSTICES OF THE PEACE.

Township No. 1—J. W. Hutchins, G. S. Smith.
Township No. 2—Chas. English, J. A. Peters.
Township No. 3—John Doble, S. S. Hartram.
Township No. 4—D. R. Gans, H. Wood.
Township No. 5—C. N. W. Hinkson, R. C. Brown.
Township No. 6—H. Bell, B. Nichols.
Township No. 7—Jacob Emminger, Sam Lorce.

About this time the office of Supervisor was made of three years duration and the elections so arranged among the districts that one new member should be elected each year.

CHAPTER XXI.

AMADOR COUNTY AT THE BEGINNING OF 1860.

County Officers—Financial Situation—Political Parties—First Appearance of R. Burnell—First Appearance of Tom Fitch—Officers Elected in 1860—Amador Wagon Road Voted On—Names of Amador Mountaineers—Financial Affairs in 1861—Calaveras Indebtedness Denied—Enormous Profits of Officers—Political Parties in 1861—The Amador Wagon Project Renewed—Vote on the Project, May 10, 1862—Rates of Toll—Impeachment of James H. Hardy—Political Parties in 1862—Great Fire in Jackson—Petition of M. W. Gordon—Supervisors Order the Building of a Court House—Political Parties in 1863—French Bar Affair—Officers Elected in 1863—General Vote—Political Parties in 1864—Vote of 1864—Financial Matters—Political Parties in 1865—Arrest of Hall and Penry—Election Returns by Precincts, 1865—Seaton's Defection—Counting the Votes—Clinton Vote—List of Officers Elected in 1865—Death of G. W. Seaton, and Election of A. H. Rose, his Successor—Financial Matters in 1865.

Up to this period, which seems a natural point in time for a review, Amador county met with unremitting prosperity. The placers were yielding undiminished sums; the quartz mines were beginning to show their inexhaustible treasures; agriculture had assumed a permanent and profitable

RESIDENCE, RANCH AND ORCHARD OF J.W. VIOLETT, IONE VALLEY, AMADOR COUNTY, CAL.

character; schools were established, and in working condition; churches, and other beneficiary institutions were prosperous, proving that society was being built on a healthy basis; and, last though not least, the county finances had been generally economically managed, so that, notwithstanding the inevitable expenses of organization and commencing a government, moderate taxes were sufficient to liquidate all expenses. According to the Assessor's report there were fifteen saw-mills cutting 11,500,000 feet of lumber per year; thirty-two quartz-mills crushing yearly 61,000 tons of quartz; six hundred miles of main canal, besides distributors; 10,000 acres of cultivated land, yielding 6,000 tons of hay, 34,800 bushels of wheat, 46,000 of barley, 28,000 of corn, besides other produce. There were nearly 10,000 head of cattle, 1,700 head of horses, 6,000 swine, 60,000 fruit trees, and 300,000 grape vines.

This condition of affairs would justify a hope that prosperity might continue; but the failure of the placer mines, disastrous fires, injudicious management of county finances, with unfortunate national affairs, so changed the current of events, that Amador came near taking her place among the bankrupt counties of California.

January 1, 1860, found the following persons in office:—

District Judge—Chas. Creanor.
County Judge—M. W. Gordon.
District Attorney—J. G. Severance.
County Clerk and Recorder—T. M. Pawling.
Sheriff—W. J. Paugh.
Treasurer—C. A. LaGrave.
Supervisors—District No. 1, R. D. Stiles; District No. 2, Robert Stewart; District No. 3, J. Linzee.

February 6, 1860, the Supervisors allowed J. C. Shipman one hundred and sixty dollars for acting as Clerk of the Board of Supervisors for twenty days, also seventy-eight dollars for acting as Clerk of the Board of Equalization. These allowances seem but the entering wedge to other and more extravagant appropriations, which followed in the course of a few years.

FINANCES.

Tax levy for 1860, adopted February 9th.

For State purposes, on each $100......... 60c.
County   "   "   "   ....50c.
School   "   "   "   ....10c.
Indigent Sick, "   "   ....20c.
Calaveras indebtedness, on each $100........30c.
Road Fund   "   "   .... 5c.—$1.75

In the following report of the indebtedness of the county the interest seems to have been omitted:—

May 1, 1860—
Warrants outstanding on General Fund.$11,581.44
   "   "   "   Calaveras   "   10,797.57—$22,379.01
Cash on hand—
General Fund.................$2,990.36
Hospital   " 36
School   " 1,797.23
Road   " 19.80
Due from Sacramento County.....   426.85
    "   Calaveras   " 94.38
    "   State to Hospital Fund....156.68—$ 5,485.66

On the 7th of November previous, the Calaveras debt was estimated at $19,577.75, of which sum $9,281.05 was for interest.

July 7, 1860, F. Richling, Geo. L. Gale, and D. L. Triplett, appointed a commission, by Board of Supervisors, to purchase a site for hospital grounds; which was done, for the price of sixteen hundred dollars. The erection of a suitable building on this tract commenced a series of debts which hung over the tax-payers for the next twenty years.

REPORT NOVEMBER 5, 1860.

Calaveras indebtedness, excluding interest..... ....$10,086.05
Other   "   "   " 12,249.51
                Total................$22,335.56
Cash on hand—
  Calaveras Fund....................$4,108.05
  General   " 7,997.47
  Hospital   " 2,575.98
  Road   " 684.56
Due from Sacramento county................. 2,120.00
    "   Calaveras   " 116.00
                Total...............$17,512.06
Total debt, exclusive of interest, and less the amount in
  the treasury..........................$8,823.50½

This method of making reports was not well calculated to give the people any correct idea of the state of the finances. The interest on warrant 103 alone, now amounted to twenty thousand dollars or more; much of it was due, having accumulated to upwards of ten thousand dollars before any portion of principal or interest was paid.

The Supervisors, beginning with September 3d, were:—

District No. 1—C. Y. Hammond.
District No. 2—R. Stewart.
District No. 3—Geo. McWilliams.

The latter taking his seat September 3d, succeeding J. Linzee.

POLITICAL PARTIES IN 1860.

Some of the waves raised by the political storm that was raging in the Eastern States began to be felt in California. The prospect of carrying the Presidential election and sharing the official patronage induced the Republicans to put forth greater efforts, and for the first time in the history of the party, it looked possible to carry some of the county offices. The Democratic party seemed to be disintegrating, having divided into the Douglass and Breckenridge factions, while members of the old Whig party, confident in their principles, thought to rally round them all the conservative elements and quiet the storm which threatened to engulf the nation. There are some questions that are so positive in their nature as to admit of no compromise; all or nothing being the only terms of settlement. The Republicans took strong ground against the extension of slavery, though denying any thought of interfering with it where it then existed. The Douglass Democrats wished to leave it to the Territories and States to determine for themselves whether slavery should or should not exist within their boundaries, thus excluding the matter from Congressional action. The Breckenridge party contended that having been recognized by the Constitution as an element in the social compact of States, it could not be excluded from the Territories either by National or Territorial legislation without manifest injustice to the States wherein slavery existed. Each party endeavored to prove that a true interpretation of the Constitution would justify the proposed measures of exclusion, relegation of the matter to the States and Territories, or general protection and recognition everywhere under the flag. Careful readers of the early history of the United States cannot fail to discover the tenderness, evasion even, with which the subject of slavery was treated. The word slavery had no mention in the Constitution, those opposed to it hoping that it would cease of itself; those in favor of it satisfied with its partial recognition. Able writers on political economy assert that Constitutions are growths of public opinion; that no constitutional enactments can stand long against overwhelming public sentiment; that the courts and government shape the enactment when they execute the law, and, that public sentiment establishes the government. Three large parties accused each other of trying to subvert the Constitution, each professing to see, in the success of either of the others, utter ruin and destruction. We shall see, as history progresses, the truth of the principles alluded to, for the meaning of the Constitution was eventually fixed at a cost of a million of lives and billions of money.

First-class orators, as well as many who were not rated at all, traversed the country, not omitting Amador in their labors. Thousands of documents bearing on the question, were sent through the mails or circulated by means of committees.

R. Burnell, afterwards conspicuous in Amador politics, made his appearance for the first time. He was a lawyer by profession, from the central part of New York. Having accumulated considerable money by raising stock on the plains around Sacramento, he spent a Winter in the capital, took a notion to mingle in political affairs, and made Amador County a starting-point. He was a man of graceful presence, pleasing address, a fluent speaker, with a good training in the New York school of politics, of which Martin Van Buren was the best specimen and *ideal*, whose political gospel was "neither give nor take offense." He rapidly made his way upwards, being first elected to the Assembly, where he was elected Speaker, and afterwards two terms to the Senate. He was also a prominent candidate for Congress.

FIRST APPEARANCE OF TOM FITCH.

This celebrated orator was sent into the country to try his strength of wing in the woods and chaparral. Though he had spoken once or twice on the steamer on which he was a passenger to this State, and again once or twice after landing, the general impression was that he was speaking a piece that some one had written for him. His appearance was boyish in the extreme. His plump and rather girlish face, his lips with the babyish cupid's bow still giving them shape, and his extremely youthful appearance, (not over twenty at least), did not impress one at first sight, or give any indication of his oratorical powers. The first meeting at which he appeared was in Ione. Very few had heard of him, and it was supposed that the State Central Committee had sent, as they often had done before, some troublesome aspirant for oratorical honors, where he would do the least harm. James M. Hanford, M. W. Belshaw and two or three local politicians were announced to speak, and confident in their strength, inquired of Fitch which part of the evening he would prefer, and also how much time he would like to occupy, for it was intended to *give the boy a chance* for success. He rather dignifiedly answered that he would be satisfied with any arrangements that might be made; so he was generously allowed the closing speech! After the several speakers had plodded wearily through the evening, the President introduced Thomas Fitch. The writer of this, who was present, recollects well the shade of disgust that passed over the faces of the audience at the prospect of sitting out another hour of dullness. He bowed dignifiedly to the President and audience. His boyish appearance was already gone, giving place to the ease and self-possession born of conscious strength. He commenced with a few long, Ciceronian sentences, as stately and beautiful in structure as a Grecian temple, and what was more, he kept them up for a full hour, never faltering for a word, never missing a note in the lofty song which he commenced, winding up with a burst of eloquence in favor of universal freedom that Colonel Baker might have equaled, but never surpassed. There was none of the school-boy in the oration. The sentences, ponderous as they were, came out of his mouth as if propelled by an intellectual steam engine. Had the people seen a train of cars dragged by a single pony, going a hundred miles an hour, their astonishment could not have been greater. The following night he spoke at Lancha Plana to a large audience, that had gathered, as much out of curiosity as anything else, to hear the prodigy. Those who had not heard him still contended that he must have repeated what had been written for him by some one else; but a circumstance occurred which set that question at rest. A few minutes before he ascended the stand the news came that Colonel Baker had been elected United States Senator for Oregon—Oregon, the home of Joe Lane, the immovable Democratic State! The subject was one worthy the power of an orator, and Fitch did it justice. "The waves of public opinion, sweeping a continent in their course, are rocking the strongest citadels of slavery." Those who came out of curiosity remained, entranced. Perhaps he was the only man who ever spoke in Amador county that would hold every one of his audience to the close.

Though a born orator, of unsurpassed ability, his

moral qualities were not of corresponding greatness. He sadly disappointed the hopes of his early admirers, and is now only a fourth rate lawyer.

Among the prominent speakers engaged in this campaign was James H. Hardy, candidate for Judge of the Sixteenth Judicial District, who ably supported the Breckenridge side of the question.

The general vote was: Lincoln, 995; Douglass, 1866; Breckenridge, 945; Bell, 178; total, 3984, being the largest vote ever polled in the county.

OFFICERS ELECTED IN 1860.

Judge of 16th Judicial District—J. H. Hardy.
Assemblymen—R. Burnell, Thomas Horrell.
Sheriff—R. Cosner.
Clerk—J. W. Bicknell.*
Treasurer—C. A. LaGrave.
District Attorney—J. Foot Turner.
Assessor—F. McGrath.
Public Administrator—E. Gallagher.
Superintendent of Schools—Samuel Page.
Surveyor—J. M. Griffith.
Coroner—W. E. Fifield.

JUSTICES OF THE PEACE.

Township No. 1—H. J. Bostwick, M. J. Little.
Township No. 2—W. C. Pratt, Charles English.
Township No. 3—J. M. Hanford, S. S. Hartram.
Township No. 4—Harvey Wood, D. R. Gans.
Township No. 5—C. W. N. Hinkson, George W. Haines.
Township No. 6—H. Bell, B. Nicholls.
Township No. 7—J. McMurren, S. H. Loree.

AMADOR WAGON ROAD VOTED ON.

The discovery of the Comstock mines gave an increased desire for the building of a wagon road to Carson valley. The Legislature, by an act approved March 23, 1861, required the Board of Supervisors of Amador, to call a special election of the voters of Amador county to submit to them a proposition to issue bonds of said county, not exceeding in the aggregate the sum of forty thousand dollars, to be expended in the construction of a wagon road, commencing at Antelope Springs, in Amador county, on the ridge dividing the waters of the Mokelumne and Cosumnes rivers, and following thence the best practicable route to Hope valley on the eastern slope of the Sierra Nevada Mountains, and for the purpose at the same time of electing one Road Commissioner in each Supervisor District of said county.

The proposition was rejected by the following vote: For building the road, 1495; against, 1683.

A year later the subject was revived and carried through.

*J. W. Bicknell was nominated in the Convention by a bit of sharp practice. Alvinza Hayward, a friend of Bicknell's, went around among the delegates, asking them to give the old gentleman a complimentary vote, saying that he could not get the nomination, but it would please him to get a good vote. When the complimentary vote was counted, it was found to be the requisite number to nominate him. There was no chance to retreat; so the Convention bore the joke as well as they could.

NAMES OF AMADOR MOUNTAINEERS.

Enrolled 1861, for service on the plains, guarding the mail route to Fort Laramie:—

Wm. McMullen, Capt.   A. R. Abbott,
D. B. Haskell, 1st. Lieut. John Davis,
R. M. Crandall, 2d. Lieut. Joseph Willet,
John Parsons, Brev Lieut.   J. Dennis,
W. L. Rhynerson,   F. Robjent,
J. M. Griffith,   John Ennis,
J. H. Bradley,   J. P. Ewing,
A. Allen,   Albert Moore,
W. R. McCormick,   D. B. Trimble,
C. H. Ashby,   J. Hall,
L. D. Winchester,   T. J. Yager,
Geo. Teas,   B. J. Thompson,
John Ferguson,   Geo. Monroe,
I. N. Swan,   John Evans,
F. Brill,   H. R. Brown,
J. Johnson,   John Dickinson,
P. H. Repp,   T. H. Dickin,
John Morris,   Chas. Walton,
Isaac Perrin,   A. Carpenter,
W. S. Cooledge.   P. Brady,
Joseph Alyen,   E. McCaugherty,
A. R. Martin,   W. Kelly,
J. C. H. Wagner.

[The publishers intended to furnish a list of all the volunteers who left the county, but were unable to get their names.]

The Supervisors made the following report of financial matters May 7, 1861:—

Amounts of all warrants drawn on Treasury from Nov. 5, 1860, to May 7, 1861, on General Fund.....................$22,991.26
Total receipts for same time exclusive of Calaveras and School Funds......... 31,365.81
Total amount of indebtedness exclusive of interest on outstanding warrants and Calaveras debt..................... 4,936.05
Calaveras indebtedness including interest on same...................... 5,769.69—$10,754.74
Assets—County buildings and furniture.. 14,500.00
Cash on hand including solvent debts .. 6,955.86—$21,455.86
Above indebtedness................... 810,701.06

RATE OF TAXES FOR 1861.

For State purposes on each $100................60c.
County purposes,   "   "   ....50c.
School purposes,   "   "   ....10c.
Indigent sick,   "   "   ....20c.
Calaveras debt,   "   "   ....30c.
Road purposes,   "   "   ....5c—$1.75

Also $6.00 poll-tax for State and County purposes.

CALAVERAS INDEBTEDNESS DENIED.

At a meeting of the Board of Supervisors, December 26, 1861, the following proceedings were had:—

"WHEREAS, By the quarterly financial report of the Auditor and Treasurer of Amador county, submitted to the Board on the first Monday of December, 1861, it appears that there was, upon that day, in the hands of said Treasurer, the sum of six thousand one hundred and fifty-five dollars and four cents, credited to a fund known as the Calaveras County Fund; and,

"WHEREAS, It is the opinion of this Board that the object for which said fund was created, no longer exists (the debt formerly due from Amador county to said Calaveras county, having been fully paid.)

"It is therefore ordered that the said Treasurer of Amador county be, and is hereby directed, to transfor from the said Calaveras County Fund to the General Fund of Amador county, the sum of six thousand dollars, and also that all such sum or sums as may be paid into the said Treasury after the said first Monday of December, 1861, upon said Calaveras County Fund, be credited to the General Fund of Amador county."

From the records of the Board of Supervisors, it appears that on the second day of December, 1861, they entered into an agreement with J. Foot Turner, by which the said Turner agreed to evade or satisfy the payment on the part of Amador county, of the sum of six thousand one hundred and fifty-eight dollars, then on hand and in the treasury, due to the county of Calaveras as a part of the Calaveras indebtedness on warrant 103, which he seems to have done, as he was allowed the commission of ten per cent. on the same, at a meeting of the Board September 1, 1862. Subsequently, however, the matter came before the District Court. In the suit of Boals, the holder of warrant No. 103, against the Supervisors of Amador county, in 1864, the records showed that a writ of *mandamus* was issued from the District Court, S. W. Brockway presiding, to the Board of Supervisors of Amador county, requiring them to levy a special tax for the payment of the balance of the Calaveras indebtedness, amounting to $7,556.16, in accordance with a law approved April 27, 1855. The matter was appealed to the Supreme Court, where the decision of Judge Brockway was confirmed. The amount of the warrant when drawn, was $26,517.32; up to 1865, $31,292.83 had been paid on it when the county, by the advice of J. Foot Turner, refused to pay anything further. The judgment given by Brockway, $7,556.16, was avoided until it amounted to $11,000, making over $40,000 in all that was paid on the warrant, the costs, and attorneys' fees, swelling it to at least $50,000, before the demand was settled.

ENORMOUS PROFITS OF THE OFFICE-HOLDERS.

It is said that the offices of Sheriff and County Clerk were worth from fifteen to twenty thousand dollars per year. The latter was also Recorder of Deeds, and acted as the Clerk of the Board of Supervisors and Equalization; also, as Auditor of Accounts, for all of which he drew high pay. At a meeting of the Board of Supervisors, February 6, 1861, present, James H. Allen and George McWilliams, it was ordered that the Auditor, J. W. Bicknell, be paid, as salary, two hundred and forty dollars per month, in quarterly installments; though October 9th, following, his salary was reduced to one hundred and sixty-five dollars per month. The following items from the records of the Board of Supervisors will show how the money went:—

November 18, 1861—Allowed J. W. Bicknell $300 for making assessment roll; also, $58 as Clerk to the Board of Equalization.

October 3, 1862—$100 per month for signing poll-tax receipts, and foreign miners' licenses.

October 3, 1862—(Page 435, Vol. B, minutes of Board of Supervisors.) Allowed J. W. Bicknell quarterly salary as Auditor, $495; quarterly salary as Clerk of Board of Supervisors, $167.50.

October 8th—Recording bonds of county officers, $153.

November 8th—Allowed for acting as Clerk of Supervisors, $96. Each of the Board also allowed themselves, November 8, 1862, $48, as members of the Board of Equalization.

July 1, 1861—George F. Tripp, allowed fees in criminal cases, $2,155, a fourth claim—$810—being rejected. For a few minutes' services as interpreter, involving no loss of time worth mentioning, $5.00 was allowed. $24 was allowed for moving a person twelve miles.

February 14, 1863—Treasurer LaGrave allowed three per cent., amounting to $64, for apportioning School Fund.

June 2, 1862—C. Y. Hammond and other Supervisors allowed each $32 for services on the wagon-road election, which services should have been included in the ordinary duties of Supervisor. The Chairman was allowed $25 per month for signing road receipts.

July 7, 1863—Board of Supervisors allowed themselves $8.00 per day for twenty-three days, for acting as members of the Board of Equalization.

July 7, 1863—Allowed fees to Sheriff for month of June, $549.53; also, for copying summons to Jurors, $339.

March 3, 1863—Allowed County Treasurer $143 for signing licenses; same date, J. W. Bicknell $330 for acting as County Auditor.

April 8, 1863—Treasurer allowed $88.40 for apportioning School Fund; June 6th, for same, $119.34.

January 6, 1863—For printing blank road receipts, $150.

April 8, 1863—Allowed $251 for printing county blanks; also, June 2d, for same, $120.

June 6, 1863—Quarterly salary of $495 allowed J. W. Bicknell as Auditor.

September 9th—$285 rent allowed for county buildings for month of August.

September 9, 1863—$627 allowed as Sheriff's fees for last month.

September 21, 1863—Supervisors allowed themselves $8.00 a day as canvassers of the election returns.

October 7, 1863—J. W. Bicknell allowed $200 for making out duplicate military list.

December 16, 1863—County Auditor allowed $495 as quarter's salary.

All services rendered seemed to be the subject for special fees. It is not strange that candidates should spend a thousand or two in trying to get a nomination when a nomination was equivalent to an election, or as much when the result of the election was doubtful.

POLITICAL PARTIES IN 1861.

Soon after the election of Lincoln, the old landmarks, which had stood for many years as guides to the various political crafts, went down out of sight. Men who had for a quarter of a century anchored to the Whig or Democratic doctrines, found themselves without soundings. Professed politicians, who were accustomed to weigh public opinion and move accordingly, were now unable to tell where the surging waters and contrary currents would permit

RESIDENCE of D. B. SPAGNOLI, JACKSON, AMADOR COUNTY, CAL.

SPRINGDALE: RESIDENCE and FARM of A. CAMINETTI, FOUR MILES N.E. of JACKSON, AMADOR COUNTY, CAL.

secure anchorage. When everything is in confusion, it sometimes happens that a single commanding voice will turn a wavering crowd to its own course. The steady disruption of the Southern States, the boldness of their friends in California, who certainly evinced no fear of consequences, made the prospect of cutting out California from the Union, quite imminent. The newspapers, usually, are but the mouth-pieces of public sentiment. During this uncertain condition of affairs, the *Ledger*, which, since 1856, had been acting with the Democratic party, while speaking of the breaking off from the Union of Southern States, remarked: "*For the present the interests of California seem to be, to remain with the old Union.*"

This sentiment prevailed to a great extent among the politicians. Among the first to raise the alarm of danger, was R. M. Briggs, a Douglass Democrat, who called public meetings in different parts of the county, and proclaimed to the people the designs of some of the ultra-Breckenridge Democrats to carry California out of the Union. He made speeches in his peculiar style of oratory, in several of the larger towns; introduced strong Union resolutions, with no uncertain sound, which were usually adopted. At Ione he was met with a solid Union club of one hundred, from Muletown, headed by the president, Jack Miller, who pledged his company to the maintenance of the Union, though some of his political friends persuaded him afterwards that he was a little premature in his promises. There is no doubt that these demonstrations, made previous to the firing on, and surrender of, Fort Sumter, helped to shape public sentiment, so that when the time came for an expression of public opinion, it was overwhelmingly in favor of the perpetuity of the Union. The Fourth of July celebrations in the different towns of the county were hearty and enthusiastic—nearly the whole population participating.

The Douglass Democratic Convention at Sacramento, which met to nominate a candidate for Governor, took strong Union grounds, denouncing hesitation as cowardice, and doubt as treason.

The three parties put forward full sets of candidates. All professed to be in favor of union. The Republicans favored the maintenance of the Union by prosecuting the war until all rebellion was crushed out, at whatever expense; the Douglass Democrats, by conducting the war according to the Constitution, with Democratic generals under a Democratic admin-

ELECTION RETURNS BY PRECINCTS—1861.

PRECINCTS.	GOVERNOR.			LT. GOVERNOR.			MEMBERS OF CONGRESS.								ASSEMBLYMEN.					
	John Conness, D. D.	John R. McConnell, A. D.	Leland Stanford, R.	Richard Irwin.	Jasper O'Farrell.	J. F. Chellis, R.	H. E. Edgerton.	J. C. McKibbon.	H. P. Barbee.	D. O. Shattuck.	T. G. Phelps, R.	A. A. Sargent.	F. F. Low.	J. R. Gatehel.	G. W. Seaton.	W. A. Waldrif.	C. B. Smith.	James A. Brown.	T. C. Boucher.	M. W. Belshaw.
Amador	11	51	73	10	50	64	10	10	51	51	64	62	63	1	18	22	48	52	65	63
Arkansas	10	1	11	10	1	11	10	10	1	1	11	11	11		12	11			9	10
Badger's Store	16	12	25	14	14	25	14	14	14	14	25	25	25		17	12	9	14	24	26
Boston Store	18	11		18	11		18	18	11	11					9	18	20	11		
Buena Vista	23	21	14	25	22	12	26	25	22	22	12	11	11		24	24	19	9	11	13
Butte City	17	28	45	21	28	42	23	22	28	28	40	41	37		20	30	48	48	35	41
Clinton	27	53	8	26	53	9	26	26	53	53	9	9	9		17	29	51	52	9	10
Drytown	46	14	68	48	14	64	49	49	15	15	63	62	63		81	49	15	13	38	50
Fiddletown	45	101	73	46	101	71	48	46	102	102	72	68	8		48	30	98	103	63	83
Foster's Ranch	2	14	16	5	14	15	4	4	14	14	15	15			5	3	14	14	13	14
Forest Home	17		32	20		29	20	20			29	29	29		18	21			27	28
Iowa Flat	33	12	8	33	12	8	30	30	12	12	8	8	8		30	33	12	12	11	8
Ione City	117	66	128	121	67	112	139	136	66	66	108	109	109		111	127	65	64	107	112
Jackson	306	97	117	232	97	103	328	328	98	98	97	96	5		275	329	95	100	118	108
Lancha Plana	61	38	48	62	38	47	67	66	38	38	42	42	5		58	80	29	31	42	40
Martin's Ranch	4	8	4	6	7	2	6	6	7	8	3	2	2		6	6	8	8	2	2
Middle Bar	7		25	8		24	8	8			24	24	19		1	8			31	24
Muletown	35	12	4	33	12	4	37	37	12	12	2	2	2		35	36	12	12	2	2
New York Ranch	15	8	21	30	8	6	31	30	7	8	6	6			29	30	7	8	7	5
Rich Bar	24		9	25		8	25	25			8	8	8		21	25			7	12
Pine Grove	25	6	27	26	6	25	36	6	6		25	24	24		35	35	7	7	23	24
Putt's Bar	26		18	24		20	26	25			18	19	18		23	24			19	19
Ranch	28	21	35	33	21	30	33	31	21	21	30	27	26		32	38	23	21	25	27
Sutter Creek	34	82	186	112	84	106	113	112	84	81	103	107	72	26	106	119	85	99	99	102
Upper Rancheria	22	53	39	21	55	38	28	25	54	55	33	35	35		41	32	50	50	19	26
Volcano	201	95	236	236	100	195	241	241	102	101	189	189	179		231	233	165	101	188	195
Willow Springs	34		6	35		5	37	36		1	3	3	3		29	35		1	6	6
White's Bar						15					15	15	15						15	15
Yeomet	3	22	7	2	22	9	2	2	22	22	8	8			2	2	21	21	8	8
French Bar	43	1	1	43	1	1	45	43	1	1	1	1			36	43	1	1	1	1
Totals	1258	827	1299	1448	838	1009	1487	1478	841	844	1063	1058	843	27	1370	1477	819	826	1024	1083

13

istration, believing that genuine Democracy was a cure for all the ills that could befall a State. The Breckenridge Democrats were supposed to be, to some extent, in sympathy with the Rebellion, but they confined their arguments mostly to charging the Administration with numerous faults, and a systematic violation of the Constitution. Axtell, Farley, and Eagan were able speakers, and represented the Nation as having been hurried into a needless war by the infatuation of half-crazy fanatics, who, unless prevented, would ruin everything to give liberty to a race that was little above the beasts of the field in intellectual and moral development. It was their object generally to represent the South as the aggrieved party, that was willing, even anxious, to return to the Union when their rights were secured to them. Occasionally a speaker, like the Hon. A. B. Dibble, of Nevada, would take up the old story of negro equality, and draw a lively picture of a

"Nigger in the bed
With your sister wed."

But the more thoughtful knew that two opposing civilizations had met in the "irrepressible conflict;" the one based on the rights of all men to pursue their own substantial happiness; the other, on the customs which made privileged classes of kings, nobility, and hereditary masters, with the concomitants of subjects and slaves. It must be confessed that in the history of the ages that have gone before, the privileged classes have usually won the field.

The relative strength of the parties, as manifested by the vote for Governor, was: For Stanford (Republican), 1,299; Conness (Douglass Democrat), 1,258; McConnell (Breckenridge Democrat), 827.

The following persons were elected in Amador county:—

State Senator—R. Burnell.
Assemblymen—G. W. Seaton, W. A. Waddell.
Supervisor, District No. 3—James H. Allen.

JUSTICES OF THE PEACE.

Township No. 1—J. S. High, G. S. Smith.
Township No. 2—Chas. English, J. A. Peters.
Township No. 3—H. T. Barnum, John Doble.
Township No. 4—J. S. Hill, H. Wood.
Township No. 5—R. C. Brown, E. B. Styles.
Township No. 6—Green Aden, B. Nichols.
Township No. 7—S. H. Loree, N. Vipon.

AMADOR WAGON ROAD REVIVED.

The increasing importance of the Nevada mines, the discovery of the veins at Markleeville, Silver City, and other places in the eastern part of Amador county, the transportation of enormous quantities of goods over the Placerville route, and the consequent prosperity of that portion of El Dorado county, traversed by the road, induced the friends of an Amador tramontane road, to make another effort. Accordingly, in answer to the requests of a large number of petitioners, the Legislature granted a second trial, specifying how the road should be built, in case the people voted for it. An election was held May 10, 1862. About sixty per cent. of the population voted, the measure being carried by less than half the voters in the county. Towns along the proposed line of the road, or connected with it, voted nearly unanimously for it. Towns outside, like Lancha Plana, were equally opposed to it. The question was decided by a vote of 1,307 for, and 542 against.

VOTE BY PRECINCTS.

For or Against the Amador Wagon Road, May 10, 1862.

PRECINCTS.	For the Road and Issuance of Bonds	Against the Road and Issuance of Bonds
Amador	14	54
Sutter Creek	117	29
Badgers Store	40	8
Forest Home	34	1
Fiddletown	209	....
Drytown	18	80
Arkansas	19	....
Aqueduct City	30	5
Fosters Ranch	24	....
Upper Rancheria	50	13
Pine Grove	64	1
Volcano	416	7
Butte City	22	9
Clinton	21	7
Lancha Plana	....	126
Q. Ranch	25	3
New York Ranch	26	9
Jackson	97	101
French Bar	15	1
Ione City	65	64
Iowa Flat	1	24
Total	1307	542

A. J. Potter, Wm. Crangle, and W. C. Jennings were chosen a Board of Commissioners to build the road.

The franchise for building this road was granted to C. D. Burleson, James Tullock, E. B. Wooley, Geo. Johnson, R. M. Briggs, David Coblentz, M. Tynan, and Leroy Worden. The county was permitted, by Act of the Legislature, to assist these parties to the extent of twenty-five thousand dollars in bonds bearing twelve per cent. interest per annum, payable in one, two, three, four and five years from date. In case the county donated these bonds, the road was to be finished by the 1st of October of the same year, or the franchise was to be forfeited. The road was to be sixteen feet wide, and the maximum grade eighteen feet to the hundred. Tolls were permitted as follows:—

For each loaded wagon, one dollar; for each animal attached, twenty-five cents; loaded pack-animals, each twenty-five cents; pleasure carriages and buggies, one dollar; empty freight wagons and unladen pack-animals, half rates. The tolls were to be reduced twenty per cent. at the end of five years.

The route was divided into five sections, beginning at Antelope Springs, thence to Tragedy Springs, which formed section No. 1; thence to the crossing of the outlet of Silver lake, which formed section No. 2; thence to Carson Spur, No. 3; to Summit lake, No. 4; and Hope valley, No. 5; the road at the latter place intersecting the Big Tree and Carson Valley road. The payment of the bonds was provided for by taxes as follows, levied on all property:—

1862—Twenty-five cents on each $100.
1863—Fifty cents on each $100.
1864—Forty-five cents on each $100.
1865—Forty cents on each $100.
1866—Thirty-five cents on each $100.
1867—Thirty cents on each $100.

When the vote was found to be in favor of the road, quite a rush was made to get favorable locations for public houses, and several fine buildings were erected at different points along the road. Saw-mills were constructed with the expectation of supplying both the Washoe mines and the Sacramento market. On completion of the road a stage line, in connection with the Sacramento and Stockton lines, took passengers to Silver Lake and other way places. Quite a trade sprang up over the road, the farmers carrying their fruit and produce to Washoe. The travel had to be abandoned as winter came, on account of the snow, which fell to the depth of from three to twenty feet, the last named being the usual depth at Silver Lake. The deep snow very often crushed the houses and destroyed the furniture. A fine house near Corral Flat, owned by Goldsworthy and Mayo, was destroyed in this way. The road did not answer the expectations of the public. The trade was not diverted from the Placerville road, and, on the completion of the railroad to Nevada, both roads fell into comparative disuse. The lower portion of the road is used to take lumber from the mountains, and, in Summer, a few visitors to Silver Lake give a little life to the higher portion.

IMPEACHMENT OF JAMES H. HARDY.

Hardy was Judge of the Sixteenth Judicial District comprising the counties of Amador and Calaveras. He was a man of undisputed talents, great independence of character, amounting to recklessness. Like all men of that character, he took no middle course, was always in one extreme or the other, and made hosts of friends as well as enemies. Early in the contest he took the side of the South; often boasted of being a rebel, expressed the opinion that the Government had gone to hell, drank to the success of the Southern Confederacy, and conducted himself generally in a way hardly suitable to the position he occupied. Early in the session of the Legislature of 1862, Judge Campbell of Calaveras, prepared articles of impeachment, numbering some twenty or more, charging him with malfeasance in office on divers occasions; one specification being a charge of violating his oath of office in procuring the discharge of David S. Terry, on his trial for killing Broderick. The article alleged that a change of venue had been made to Marin county, where Hardy was holding Court; that, with his knowledge and consent, the clock had been put forward; that he opened Court at ten according to the clock, although it was much earlier by the true time; that the trial was hastily and indecently hurried through, without giving time to get the witnesses on the part of the State; that, although the important witnesses were then on the way from San Francisco, and, even in sight on the bay, being detained by contrary winds (there then being no steam-ferry), he refused to continue the Court, and ordered the jury in the absence of the witnesses, to find for the acquittal of Terry, setting him free. On this charge, the Assembly, sitting as a High Court of Impeachment, was evenly divided, standing eighteen to eighteen. On the charge of uttering disloyal sentiments, and using language unbecoming his high position, he was found guilty, and suspended from performing the duties of the office.

Judge W. H. Badgely, afterwards unanimously elected to the position, was appointed to fill the unexpired portion of the term.

POLITICAL PARTIES IN 1862.

The disruption of the Douglass Democracy, became apparent early in the season. The efforts put forward by the South to maintain the Confederacy, and, by the Administration to break it down, convinced the most skeptical that peace could come only by the utter defeat of one or the other. The Democracy now assumed a stronger tone. The *Dispatch*, their ably edited organ, did not hesitate to avow its sympathy for the Rebellion, and kept in its columns the Kentucky resolutions of 1798, which held to the right of each State to judge of any infraction of the *compact* by any other State, as well as the right to choose it own remedy therefor, meaning that each and every individual of the family of States had a right to step out, at its will or convenience. About this time, the "Knights of the Golden Circle" were organized in different parts of the county. Their meetings were generally held in out-of-the-way places, and as quietly as possible. The object of the organization was probably made known to but few of the members even, the design being to have the material well in hand to use in case an opportunity offered, rather than the execution of any well-digested plan of aiding the Rebellion, or carrying the State of California out of the Union. A hundred and twenty-eight men had monthly meetings in the hills west of the Blue Ridge, near where Stony creek comes into Jackson creek; though, it is said, that a few meetings were held near Buena Vista. The organization was met by another, the "Loyal League," and also by the organization of the "Home Guards," who were supplied with guns and ammunition by the Government. The fact that the population of California was composed of people from all the States, rendered it quite certain that an insurrection would be attended with a fearful destruction of life and property. Property is always a powerful conservator of the peace; and it is much harder to arouse the people into a war of ideas than it would have been ten years before, when the farms, residences, and valuable stores, had not yet made their appearance; and no insurrection occurred.

When the Republican Convention met, a petition, signed by three hundred Douglass Democrats, was handed in, asking the Convention to drop the name "Republican," disorganize, and form a Union party. As there was nothing in a name, and the objects of the two were essentially the same, the request was acceded to. It will be remembered that the Douglass Democrats in the county, only a year before, had a much larger number of votes than the Breckenridge Democrats, the relative numbers of the parties on the vote for Governor being for Stanford, 1,299; Conness, 1,258; McConnel, 827.

They had swept all the county offices by majorities from three to eight hundred.

The vote for State Senator in 1861 was: For Burnell, 1,546, Farley, 1,029; Hanford, 753.

Mr. Burnell joined the Union party. The movement seems to have been preconcerted throughout the State, as from this date the Douglass party disappeared. The Democratic party ceased to wear any qualifying prefix, and became, thenceforth, the "Simon Pure." The old and well-known war horses, Farley, Gordon, Axtell, and Eagan, still held their places as leaders in the ranks; but Porter and Briggs were now found with the Republicans. It will be seen that Wm. H. Badgely, who had been appointed to fill the unexpired term, made vacant by the impeachment of James H. Hardy, received the unanimous vote of all parties.

ELECTION RETURNS IN 1862.
(Showing the relative standing of parties.)

	VOTES.
State Supt. Public Instruction.	
John Swett (Rep.)	1497
J. D. Stevenson (Dem.)	1327
O. P. Fitzgerald (A. D.)	391
District Judge.	
Wm. H. Badgely [vice Hardy impeached] received the entire vote of	3067
Assembly.	
A. B. Andrews (Dem.)	1563
E. M. Simpson (Rep.)	1550
Edward Gallagher (Dem.)	1496
J. G. Severance (Rep.)	1524
County Judge.	
M. W. Gordon (Dem.)	1595
J. M. Porter (Rep.)	1560
County Clerk.	
James W. Bicknell (Dem.)	1712
C. C. Belding (Rep.)	1464
County Recorder.	
A. Day (Dem.)	1692
Isaiah Heacock (Rep.)	1501
Sheriff.	
R. Cosner (Dem.)	1765
S. F. Dexter (Rep.)	1431
District Attorney.	
S. B. Axtell (Dem.)	1657
R. M. Briggs (Rep.)	1505
County Treasurer.	
F. McGrath (Dem.)	1609
Antonio Arata (Rep.)	1556
Superintendent of Public Instruction.	
Samuel Page (Dem.)	1790
E. B. McIntyre (Rep.)	1403
Public Administrator.	
Geo. W. Beers (Dem.)	1668
Wm. Pitt (Rep.)	1510
Coroner.	
Louis Wentzel (Dem.)	1670
J. Shumer (Rep.)	1506
Surveyor.	
Geo. Kress (Dem.)	1633
J. M. Griffith (Rep.)	1500
Supervisor, District No. 1.	
I. B. Gregory (Dem.)	769
G. W. Withington (Rep.)	502
Township System.	
For 327 Against	2075

THE GREAT FIRE

On the 23d of August, 1862, will be more particularly described under the head of "Jackson," in the township histories. The principal interest at this point of our view is the destruction of the county buildings. It will be remembered that the town of Jackson donated the Court House, costing some ten thousand dollars, to the county, the jail being afterwards added at an expense of more than six thousand dollars. On the morning of the 24th, the county was without a place of meeting for the Courts. Rooms were hired in different places for transacting the county business, at high rates—one hundred dollars per month being paid for the use of a hall in which to hold Court. The offices of Sheriff, County Clerk, Treasurer, and District Attorney, were kept from necessity in inconvenient and improper places. These circumstances induced Judge Gordon to set forth the necessity of erecting county buildings, and the powers of the Supervisors in the premises, in the following petition:—

PETITION OF M. W. GORDON.

"*To the Board of Supervisors, of Amador county, California:* Your petitioner, a resident citizen and tax-payer of said county, respectfully represents to said Board, that, by article eleven, section five, of the Constitution of said State, the Legislature thereof "have power to provide for the election of a Board of Supervisors in each county, and that these Supervisors, shall jointly and individually perform such duties as may be prescribed by law." Your petitioner states, that, in pursuance of said law, the said Legislature, at its sixth session, by an Act approved March 20, 1855, did create and establish, in each of the counties of this State, a Board of Supervisors.

"Your petitioner says, that, both by the said Constitutional provision and by the provisions of said law, the *sole power* over the property of each county, is given to the Board of Supervisors, and is prohibited to the Legislature of the State, the Legislature having the power to provide *only* for the election of a Board of Supervisors, who shall perform such duties as may be prescribed by law.

RESIDENCE AND RANCH OF JAMES W. SHEALOR.
6 MILES E. FROM VOLCANO, AMADOR COUNTY, CAL.

RESIDENCE AND SAWMILL OF F. M. WHITMORE.
ANTELOPE CREEK, NEAR VOLCANO, AMADOR COUNTY, CAL.

"Your petitioner says that amongst the duties prescribed by law, to be performed by said Board, (Wood's Digest, page 692, section 91), is the duty "To cause to be erected and furnished a Court House, jail, and such other public buildings as may be necessary, and to keep the same in repair." It is true, that section 16, page 696, says: "The Board of Supervisors shall not, for any purpose, contract debts or liabilities, except those fixed by, or in pursuance of law; and whenever debts or liabilities shall have been created, which, added to the salaries of county officers and other estimated liabilities fixed by law for the remainder of the year, will equal the revenue of the county for current expenses, no allowance whatever shall be made of any account; nor shall any expense be incurred other than the salaries and fees expressly prescribed by, or in pursuance of, the law." But it will be observed that the erection and furnishing of a Court House and jail are fixed by law in section 91, clause 11.

"Your petitioner says that the granting of the powers in said Act to the Board of Supervisors by the Legislature, and the specification of the duties to be performed by said Board excludes the Legislature from all power over the : airs of each and every county in the State, and ..xes those duties exclusively on the Board of Supe ..isors.

"Your petitioner says that, by article 514, section 2, page 127, Wood's Digest, Ja: son is the county seat of Amador county; and that, by article 670, section 59, page 154, the Court House must be situated at the county seat.

"Your petitioner says that the Court House and county jail of Amador county was destroyed by fire on the 23d of August, 1862; that these public buildings are necessary for the conducting of the civil and criminal business of the county, and that the public business cannot be transacted without them; that, as already shown, it is the duty of the Board of Supervisors to proceed, as soon as practicable, to erect and furnish a Court House and jail at Jackson, for the use of said Amador county.

"Your petitioner, therefore, moves the Honorable the Board of Supervisors of Amador county, on the 3d of October, A. D. 1862, to hear this petition, to examine the law and the facts in said petition alleged; and upon the allegations herein being proved, that said Board will decide upon erecting, as soon as practicable, a Court House and county jail, on the site of the late Court House and jail, not to exceed in cost the sum of twenty thousand dollars.

September 15, 1862.   M. W. GORDON."

Board of Supervisors—District No. 1, J. B. Gregory; District No. 2, H. B. Bishop; District No. 3, J. H. Allen.

On the 4th of October the Supervisors invited proposals for the building of a Court House and jail, according to plans presented, but on opening the bids at the following session they were found too indefinite for acceptation, and new ones were called for, according to a plan presented by S. D. Mandell, architect of the M. E. Church of Ione. It will be seen that during this year the debts were made which hung over the county for twenty years, bonds being issued for Amador wagon road, twenty-five thousand dollars; for Court House and jail an indefinite sum; for hospital, also uncertain.

October 3d, the Commissioners reported the completion of the wagon road, and the full amount of the bonds authorized to be issued was paid over to the contractors.

POLITICAL PARTIES IN 1863.

The doubtful result of the war, the loss of friends and relatives on one side or the other by nearly all, begat an ill-feeling between the two parties that, at times, looked like the forerunner of hostilities. The *Ledger* and *Dispatch* now flung terms of reproach, more true than polite, perhaps, but bitter and unrelenting. It was difficult to tell whether national issues, personal animosity, or desire for office, was the greatest motive in the conduct of the campaign. Men would be found first on one side and then on the other, as one or the other of those motives prevailed, and, it would seem, buried all doubts by an increased or simulated enthusiasm for the side adopted. An old politician expressed the sentiment that each side accused the other of all kinds of venality, and knew themselves guilty of it. Every technicality was used to further the interests of the different individuals.

Some men were bold enough to throw technicalities to the winds, and fix up ballots by the hundred. The famous

FRENCH BAR AFFAIR

Occurred this season. At night the poll list numbered twenty-six, but, during the counting, it swelled to one hundred and thirty-eight, with votes in the ballot-box to correspond. Jim Saultry was credited with planning and executing this brilliant raid on the enemy's ranks, which, however, failed to elect anybody. The names were said to have been taken from a Panama passenger list.

The eastern part of the county, up among the pine trees, had rather uncertain boundaries, and pleasure parties, or others could, according to the existing law, get up a precinct almost anywhere, and shape or influence elections. When the temptations for fraud were so great, and the opportunities so frequent, nothing less than divine strength would take the just course, and we have to look in century-old annals for politicians of that character.

Complaints, that the collecting of taxes by the Sheriff gave too much importance to that office, having become general, the Legislature provided for township Assessors and Collectors; and for six years, from 1863 to 1869, the latter method was in use.

At the election for Supervisors, held in 1863, quite a contest occurred as to the boundaries of Amador County in the vicinity of the Summit. The following extract from the *Ledger* will show the *animus* of the affair:—

"Out of curiosity, however, and for the purpose of branding Copperhead demagogues with the eternal and ineffaceable stamp of burning infamy and disgrace which of right belongs to them, the recount *was* made, and that same count did disclose and fasten upon the so-called Democratic party of Amador county, the most disgraceful, hellish, diabolical, and deep-dyed villainous scheme to commit a crime upon the body politic that ever disgraced the criminal calendars of the whole world. The bare thought of what he has done to the "tool" employed to execute it, must be a coal of fire in his brain, an enraged adder in his heart. He must feel as if every hair of his head were a serpent, like the hair of Eumenides, and his aids and abettors, the devil's scanty leavings, over whom, in their last hours, black despair shall sit, with carrion birds and secesh owls hovering over their heads."

As the article does not give any clue to the *crime*, it may be explained that tampering with the votes was suspected.

Having given a sample of the editorial style of the *Ledger*, the *Dispatch* must be equally favored. In the edition of June 4, 1864, referring to Lincoln, it said:—

"Is it possible that this long-shanked, flop-eared, jimber-jawed, mule-countenanced, backwoods, rail-splitting boor is wiser, purer, more far-seeing, and understands better the powers of the Government than the great Father of his country, who presided over the deliberations of the Convention that made it?"

OFFICERS ELECTED IN 1863.

State Senator—R. Burnell.
Members of Assembly—Wm. B. Ludlow, A. C. Brown.
County Judge—J. Foot Turner.
District Attorney—R. M. Briggs.
County Clerk—E. S. Hall.
Recorder—H. Wood.
Sheriff—B. B. Redhead.
Treasurer—Otto Walther.
Surveyor—J. M. Griffith.
Supt. Schools—D. Townsend.
Public Administrator—H. Robinson.
Coroner—C. H. Kelly.

From the minutes of the Board of Supervisors it appears that some doubt existed as to who was elected Supervisor from District No. 3. E. B. Woolley and E. A. Kingsley both appeared and claimed the seat. The latter had acted as Supervisor one month, and drawn pay therefor. On the 22d of November, Bishop and Gregory recognized E. B. Woolley as the member, Kingsley filing a protest thereto. The latter appeared for several days as a claimant to the seat. November 6th, he was allowed thirty-seven dollars salary and mileage, Woolley retaining his position.

GENERAL RESULT IN 1863.

Governor.
F. F. Low (Rep.) 2,245
J. G. Downey (Dem.) 2,046
Congress.
T. B. Shannon (Rep.) 2,258
Wm. Higby (Rep.) 2,256
C. Cole (Rep.) 2,257
John B. Weller (Dem.) 2,042
John Bigler (Dem.) 2,043
N. E. Whitesides (Dem.) 2,044

County Ticket.
Senator.
R. Burnell (Rep.) 2,165
J. T. Farley (Dem.) 2,022
Assemblymen.
W. B. Ludlow (Rep.) 2,166
A. C. Brown (Rep.) 2,182
—— Woodburn (Dem.) 1,908
—— Lon (Dem.) 1,948
Sheriff.
B. B. Redhead (Rep.) 2,153
R. Cosner (Dem.) 2,043
County Clerk.
E. S. Hall (Rep.) 2,152
J. W. Bicknell (Dem.) 2,036
Treasurer.
Otto Walther (Rep.) 2,184
Francis McGrath (Dem.) 2,008
District Attorney.
R. M. Briggs (Rep.) 2,210
S. B. Axtell (Dem.) 1,869
Public Administrator.
H. Robinson (Rep.) 2,196
—— Beers (Dem.) 2,009
Surveyor.
J. M. Griffith (Rep.) 2,185
—— Kress (Dem.) 2,003

This estimate includes the vote of the territory afterwards incorporated into the territory of Alpine.

TOWNSHIP ELECTIONS, 1863.

No. 1—John Burke, Collector; J. G. High, C. Y. Hammond, Justices of the Peace.
No. 2—J. Farnsworth, Collector; H. M. Roberts, Chas. English, Justices of the Peace.
No. 3—T. A. Goodwin, Collector; H. T. Barnum, J. H. Bradley, Justices of the Peace.
No. 4—Thomas Dunlap, Collector; J. S. Hill, J. S. Porter, Justices of the Peace.
No. 5—Chas. D. Smith, Collector; W. W. Swadley, R. C. Brown, Justices of the Peace.
No. 6—A. P. Wood, Collector; J. T. Phelps, B. Nichols, Justices of the Peace.
No. 7—M. B. Oliver, Collector; W. H. Jones, Jacob Emminger, Justices of the Peace.
No. 8—S. A. Hawkins, Collector; O. Bonney, J. B. Marshall, Justices of the Peace.
No. 9—D. N. McBeth, Collector; Geo. J. Newman, J. C. Ransom, Justices of the Peace.

TAXES FOR 1863 BY TOWNSHIPS.

Township No. 1 .... $11,349.11
    "   " 2 (for '63–'64)... 24,681.41
    "   " 3 .... 10,252.30
    "   " 4 .... 10,389.33
    "   " 5 .... 6,674.34
    "   " 6 .... 7,219.63
    "   " 7 .... 1,034.91

TAXES ASSESSED FOR 1863.

For State purposes, on each $100 .... 62c.
Federal Tax   "   "   .... 62c.
Road Fund   "   "   .... 10c.
School purposes "   "   .... 20c.
Hospital   "   "   .... 25c.
Sierra Wagon road "   "   .... 50c.—$2.29

During this season the Court House, which was to cost $18,000, was swelled into a $50,000 structure, by the changes from the original plan, involving stone basement and water tables, and stone steps in front and rear.

March 3, 1863.—"Ordered (by the Supervisors) that the steps to the Court House be made of stone instead of brick, as specified in the original plan; also, that the balustrade of the steps be made of stone, and that the top step be made four feet wide." A special superintendent, Francis McGrath, was employed to measure and examine the work.

February 3, 1864.—The Supervisors ordered a warrant to be drawn for $9,174.76, in favor of Mat. Canavan, assignee of Epley, Canavan, and Meloney, he having obtained a judgment in the District Court to that amount, as a balance due on the Court House contract. Farley and Armstrong, attorneys for the county, were allowed $500.00 as fees.

During 1863, townships eight and nine were organized east of the Sierra Nevadas, out of territory that was afterwards incorporated into Alpine county; also the election precincts of Silver Mountain, Mogul, Mineral City, and Markleeville. The uncertainty of the boundaries of these precincts, especially on the Calaveras side, was the source of much trouble until the final separation of the territory from Amador county. Communication could only be maintained in the Summer months. In the Spring of 1864, the delegates attending the Conventions for nominating delegates to the Electoral Convention, came over by way of Placerville. The county of Alpine was created March 16, 1864, by Act of the Legislature, out of territory of El Dorado, Amador, and Calaveras. By this Act, the eastern boundary of Amador county was fixed at Hope valley, Kirkwood's house being just within Amador. Alpine county was to issue two warrants in favor of Amador, for $5,000 each, payable out of the general fund, and bearing interest at the rate of six per cent. per annum, payable in one and two years, as her part of the common debt. The two counties were made one district, for choosing Legislative officers.

POLITICAL PARTIES IN 1864.

Biennial instead of annual sessions of the Legislature having been established, and the election of members of the Legislature made to correspond in time with that of the county officers, there were no local interests to fan politics into the usual white heat; but the great questions of union and freedom, which had convulsed the nation for years, were still in abeyance and proved ample enough to arouse the highest feeling and bring out a full vote. The habitual leaders, having no inducements to accommodate their sentiments to those of the public, were comparatively candid in expressing their opinions. At the Convention held to elect delegates to the Electoral State Convention, John Eagan, J. T. Farley, R. Stewart, Long Primer Hall, and A. H. Rose,

opposed the prosecution of the war as unjust, unconstitutional, and inexpedient under any circumstances. The sentiment, afterwards incorporated into the National Democratic platform, that "four years of war having demonstrated the impossibility of conquering the South, hostilities should cease, with a view of peaceable separation, if satisfactory terms of union could not be agreed upon," was generally advocated. M. W. Gordon, however, was opposed to acknowledging the independence of the Confederacy, under any circumstances, but believed the Union could be restored, only by employing Democratic generals, under a Democratic Administration, with a Democratic President. He would prefer Thomas H. Seymour, of Connecticut, for President, but would accept Grant, McClellan, or Sherman.

These sentiments did not suit the majority of the Convention, but M. W. Gordon was a man of too much talent and influence to be slighted or left out in the cold, and J. T. Farley, with his usual skill and tact, advocated his having a place in the delegation. James Meehan, J. T. Farley, M. W. Gordon, and R. Cosner, were sent from the county at large, and T. D. Wells, —— Lanning, Gerhard Sphon, Robert McLellan, —— Dickinson, and J. W. Leslie, from the several townships.

Those of our readers who are not old enough to remember the famous campaigns of "Tippecanoe and Tyler too," of 1840, may form some idea of that memorable affair, by the processions, bon-fires, and illuminations of this season. Every town had its turn, but, as usual in all such excitements, the active, the aggressive, swept the conservative away, and the Union demonstrations were the most brilliant and noisy. Long processions, with all trades and employments in active operation, were the usual beginnings of a political meeting. Rail-splitting, tailoring, shoe-making, blacksmithing, weaving, printing, and everything that could be done on a house, were made parts of the display. Abraham Lincoln split a lot of rails once, and the three or four stalwart men swinging the mauls, were sure to bring out the enthusiasm. There was a touch of the humorous in these displays, which would have been enjoyable, but for the solemn fact, that a million of our noblest and best, were, at the moment, locked in a death struggle. The whole nation went on a frolic in 1840, but no such shadows of death rested on the people as in 1864. But, as a politician expressed it, the party that could do the most of this work, would get the *bulge*, and it was done.

VOTE OF 1864.

Presidential ticket—Republican, 1392; Democratic, 1200.

Congressional ticket—Higby (Rep.), 1390; Coffroth (Dem.), 1200.

TOWNSHIP COLLECTORS AND JUSTICES OF THE PEACE.

Township No. 1.—John Burke, Collector; J. G. High and T. Masterson, Justices of the Peace.

Township No. 2—J. Farnsworth, Collector; J. Bowen and C. English, Justices of the Peace.

Township No. 3—T. A. Goodwin, Collector; H. T. Barnum and H. Cook, Justices of the Peace.

Township No. 4—I. N. Randolph, Collector; H. Wood and J. S. Hill, Justices of the Peace.

Township No. 5—F. (or N.) King, Collector; J. W. Morgan and R. C. Brown, Justices of the Peace.

Township No. 6—A. P. Wood, Collector; J. W. Whitaker and B. Nichols, Justices of the Peace.

Township No. 7—M. B. Oliver, Collector; R. Saunders and A. J. Lucas, Justices of the Peace.

At the judicial election in the Autumn of 1863, the average Republican majority was seven hundred, in a total vote of about three thousand.

FINANCIAL MATTERS, 1864.

The rate of taxation for all purposes, made May 7th, was three dollars and twenty-five cents on each hundred dollars.

On the 7th of June, the Treasurer reported outstanding warrants over and above sums in the Treasury to apply on General Fund, $74,159.42; on Sierra Wagon Road Fund, $15,125.00; on Road fund, $1,467.35; making a total of $90,751.77.

This estimate does not include interest, which would swell the amount to $100,000. The extravagance of the two previous years, laid a foundation for the permanent debt.

The following December the amount of the debt, exclusive of interest, was estimated at $111,139.94. Before the taxes were collected, it was apparent that the levy was insufficient to meet current expenses, and a new schedule was made out, as follows:—

For State purposes	on each $100	92c
County "	" "	200c
" General Fund	" "	100c
" Hospital "	" "	25c
" School "	" "	20c
Sierra Nevada Wagon Road	" "	45c
Redemption Road Fund	" "	10c—84.92

TAXES ASSESSED BY TOWNSHIPS.

Township No. 1		$ 9,597.71
"	" 2 (for 1863–64)	24,681.41
"	" 3	4,947.48
"	" 4	9,701.93
"	" 5	6,879.10
"	" 6	6,844.26
"	" 7	1,014.24
"	" 8 } afterwards }	9,627.72
"	" 9 } Alpine Co. }	3,030.46

POLITICAL PARTIES IN 1865.

This, the last year of the bitter strife, witnessed the most exciting scenes of all. The year opened with the defeat of the rebel armies in all quarters, and soon saw the surrender of the last of them. Whether from indiscreet rejoicing on the part of the Republicans, or embittered feelings on the part of the Democrats, or both, the Democratic newspapers became more bitter and vituperative than ever. Public opinion was in a highly excited condition in consequence, and when the news of the assassination of Lincoln was flashed across the Continent, the danger of riots, and destruction of life and property, was imminent. Human nature is much the same the world over. It is but two hundred years since our ancestors thought it expedient and right to burn, slay, destroy, torture, and harass, all who differed with them, either religiously or politically, and, notwithstanding all our boasted improvement, the desire to do so is still an active element in our characters. The animus of the parties may best be shown by extracts from the papers.

Dispatch, March 5, 1865:—

"The first act of Lincoln's administration was stained by falsehood, and shortly afterwards by deliberate, palpable, tongue-blistering, soul-damning perjury." * * *

"The first officer under our Government, whose moral conduct should reflect the virtues and dignity of a great country, and be an example for all classes of people to imitate, stands before the world with the brand of perjury upon his brow!"

"The rebels fight for the priceless boon of liberty as did their fathers of the Revolution; the mercenaries of the federal army, for Government greenbacks."

March 12, 1865:—

"If to sympathize with a brave and gallant people who are struggling to throw off the yoke of a merciless despot, * * * be secessionism, then we are secessionists."

March 26, 1865:—

"Abraham Lincoln, the self-confessed perjurer; * * * the buffoon; the vulgar joker; the spiritualist; the abolitionist; the man who believes the negro his equal."

ARREST OF L. P. HALL AND W. M. PENRY.

A company of cavalry had been stationed in Ione valley to eject settlers from the Arroyo Seco grant. After the assassination of Lincoln, persons were arrested in different parts of the State for sympathy with the Rebellion, or for treasonable expressions. The *Dispatch* had been one of the ablest and most outspoken Democratic papers in the State, and although not coming within the boundaries of giving "substantial aid and comfort to the enemy," it had advocated the right, if not the policy, of secession, had eulogized the President and officers of the Confederate States; had abused the Union President in severe terms, and had, in fact, been a magazine of Southern ideas and arguments, on Northern soil. Some of the ablest articles in defense of the South had come out in the *Dispatch*; in fact, there was no writer in the county, on the Union side of the question, that was a match for the editor of the *Dispatch*. It was quite natural that the wrath of the Union men should seek victims in the editors and writers of the paper, though it was not charged that it had ever sanctioned the assassination of Lincoln. On the morning of the 8th of May, about daylight, the persons mentioned awoke to find themselves surrounded by a troop of cavalry under the command of Captain Starr, acting presumably, under the command of General McDowell, at San Francisco. The printing office was closed up, and two or three hours

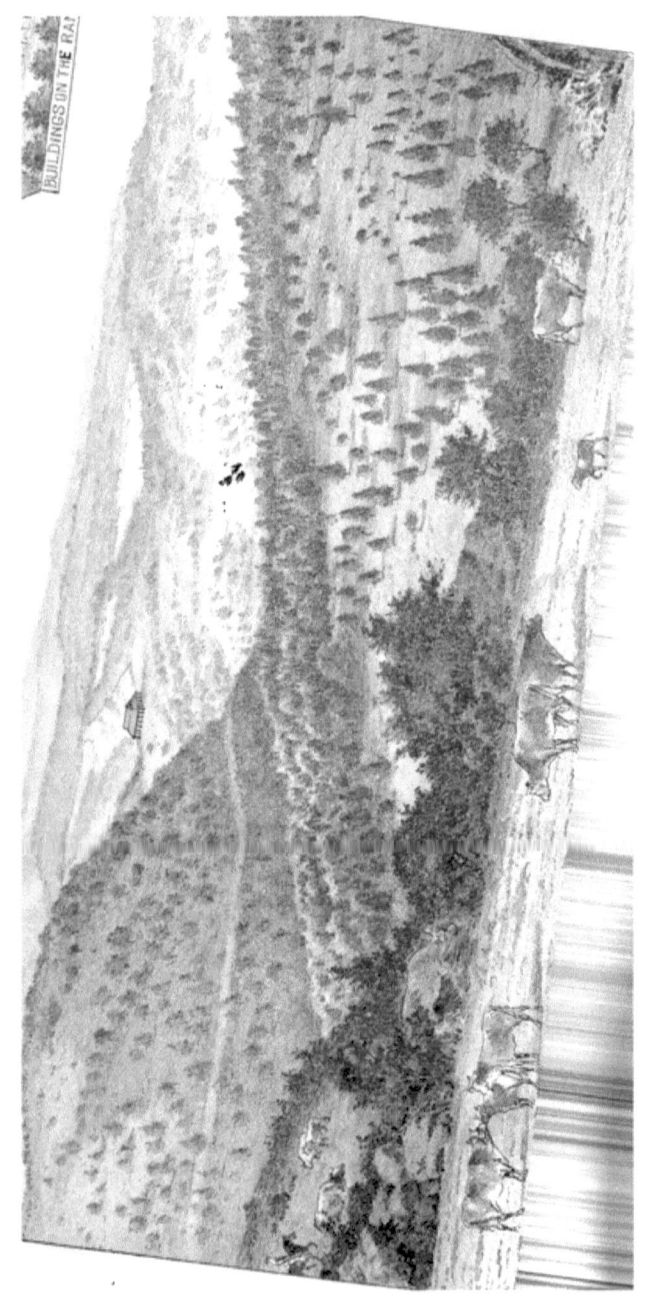
BUILDINGS ON THE RA[NCH]

afterwards the entire party left for Camp Jackson, in Ione valley, our friends walking through the hot sand, with the thermometer at 100° in the shade. From thence they were taken in irons to Fort Alcatraz, where an eighteen-pound ball with chain, was attached to the legs of each man. They had the choice of hard labor on the works, under guard, or confinement in the sweat-box, and wisely chose the former. They were kept here, in company with other sympathizers, until about the middle of the following month, when peace, law, and order were so far established, that it was considered safe for them to be at large. It is said that neither of the men ever had the remotest suspicion of the cause of their incarceration!

In justice to the *Dispatch* and its conductors, it must be said that they picked up the cudgels of warfare at the place where they dropped them at the time of the arrest, and when they resumed the publication of the paper, which they did on the 23d of September following, it had lost none of the vigor which characterized it through the four years of the great Rebellion.

L. P. Hall, who was arrested with Penry, was one of the most original men ever connected with the press in Amador county, or, perhaps, in the State. He was able to stand up to the case and set up his most vituperative articles without manuscript, a feat that few editors or printers are capable of. He was thoroughly aggressive in his character, and if he had been on "Southern Soil" at the time of the breaking out of the Rebellion, his temperament would have been as likely to have carried him into the opposition as anywhere. He was previously the editor of the *Equal Rights Expositor*, at Visalia, a paper as pronounced in its disloyal sentiments as the *Dispatch*. It was suppressed by the order of General McDowell, and the editor, and three others arrested with him, set free on taking the following oath:—

STATE OF CALIFORNIA, }
County of Tulare.   }

We, L. P. Hall, ———— of Tulare, State of California, Citizens of the United States, do solemnly swear that we will support the Constitution and Government of the United States against all enemies, whether foreign or domestic, and that we will bear true faith and allegiance, and loyalty to the same, any ordinance, resolution, or any State Convention or law of any Legislature to the contrary, notwithstanding; that we will give no aid, assistance or encouragement, by word or act, to any person or persons, or pretended Government, engaged in rebellion against the Government of the United States. And further, that we will do this with a full determination, pledge, and purpose, without any mental reservation whatsoever, so help us God.

(Signed) L. P. HALL, *

Subscribed and sworn to before me, this fifth day of January, 1863.   M. A. McLAUGHLIN,
Cap'tain 2d Cavalry, C. V., Commanding.

Whatever difference of opinion may have existed with regard to his course as an editor, there was none with regard to his ability.

*There were three other signatures.

John Gaver, of Sutter Creek, who had written many of the articles in the *Dispatch*, was arrested about the same time, and subjected to the same treatment. He was charged with rejoicing over the assassination, which, however, he denied, or asserted, that if he did, he was drunk, and unconscious of what he said. He was arrested on complaint of O. L. Chamberlain, F. Tibbetts, and T. Frakes.

After the assassination of Lincoln, more than one Union meeting was held to consider the expediency of demolishing the *Dispatch* establishment, but better counsels prevailed. It is quite likely, however, that the arrest of Penry and Hall, and the suppression of the paper for awhile, saved the material from destruction. The excitement gradually wore away, and better feeling began to prevail.

SEATON'S DEFECTION.

There was a full set of county officers, as well as members of the Legislature, to elect, and the politicians set about arranging these matters. The national question having to some extent been settled, personal ambitions and antipathies began to be more manifest. When the Republican Convention met, R. Burnell was nominated, after some opposition, as candidate for Senator. G. W. Seaton, who had been acting with the Republican party for years, arose and denounced Burnell as having tried to throw the State into the hands of the secessionists, by voting for giving the seat to a Democrat in a contested election case. This affair had happened some years before, and, if true, Burnell was only voting to decide who was elected, the politics of the man, properly, having nothing to do with his right to a seat. It is likely that personal antipathy was the ruling motive, for Mr. Seaton had supported Burnell in Convention and on the stump, after the occurrence of the contested election case; but, at any rate, he announced his intention of defeating Mr. Burnell if it cost ten thousand dollars. As he had a very rich quartz vein just then to draw on for funds, the threat was very serious. He immediately announced himself as an independent candidate for Senator, and took the stump. The Democrats left the nomination for the Senatorship vacant, with the understanding that Seaton's name was to be used. The contest of course was very spirited, Seaton's gold mine being a powerful influence in his favor. It is not supposed that votes were directly purchased, but money, which Seaton had in abundance, would purchase fire-works, *orators*, music, gun-powder, and whisky, which certainly have the power of moving many people in their political opinions.

It is generally believed too, that in the early days the Italian vote was practically purchasable, that is to say, that from fifteen hundred to twenty-five hundred dollars would buy the influence of one or two men, who would control the greater portion of the Italian vote, which was numerous enough to decide, in many cases, the election. (It is said, now, by those best acquainted with the Italians, that that condition no longer exists; that individual independence is becoming as common with them as with other nationalities.) When the contest was over, Seaton was elected. Amador and Alpine had remained one district for the election of members of the Legislature, Alpine being allowed one member and Amador the other three. O. F. Thornton and Harvey Lee were candidates by the respective parties, Republican and Democratic of Alpine county—Lee being elected. The following table of the returns will be interesting, as not only showing the names and popularity of the different candidates, but also as showing the names of many precincts which were abolished when the registry law was established, this election being the last held under the old law:—

ELECTION RETURNS BY PRECINCTS, SEPTEMBER 6, 1865.

Offices	Names	Aqueduct	Amador	Avery's Lumber Yard	Alabama House	Badger Steps	Butte City	Bartolotti's Ranch	Buena Vista	Clinton	Copper Hill	Dry Town	Fiddletown	Foster's Ranch	French Hill	Ione City	Jackson	Lancha Plana	New York Ranch	Pine Grove	Sutter Creek	Volcano	U Rancheria	Willow Springs	Yeomet
Senators	E. Burnell	12	53	15	27	25	21	33	28	6	19	55	92	13	28	25	145	163	60	18	43	122	8	157	17	33
	G. W. Seaton	29	100	15	8	21	22	4	11	61	19	112	104	13	29	24	63	221	30	10	35	120	26	147	23	55
	M. Frink	12	40	17	26	24	22	30	28	6	23	50	88	13	28	30	113	159	78	16	44	133	8	162	24	34
Assemblymen	O. F. Thornton	13	41	17	26	25	21	29	27	6	25	50	80	14	27	16	116	154	60	17	44	131	8	162	24	34
	Harvey Lee	29	104	14	8	21	22	7	12	64	16	105	104	11	14	30	88	235	30	13	32	112	26	109	17	56
	A. C. Brown	29	105	14	8	21	24	7	12	64	17	107	99	13	12	26	99	236	18	14	32	107	26	107	13	56
	I. N. Randolph	11	59	13	23	25	14	25	25	7	24	71	80	14	24	15	89	155	49	18	33	145	8	143	25	44
Sheriff	R. Cosner	35	85	20	17	21	22	20	18	66	13	97	116	12	20	32	129	261	32	16	44	101	26	130	17	53
County Clerk	J. A. Robinson	15	41	14	23	26	21	27	28	20	24	71	90	14	27	16	118	176	49	18	42	133	8	158	29	38
	J. C. Shipman	31	103	17	17	21	23	20	13	55	15	97	115	12	17	32	98	223	32	16	35	114	26	116	10	59
Recorder	M. J. Goodrich	12	40	17	16	24	22	30	28	7	25	57	99	18	27	16	118	160	36	18	45	14	8	171	26	34
	A. C. Hinkson	32	105	15	14	23	22	16	13	66	14	111	114	11	17	32	99	246	51	18	34	124	26	107	13	61
Treasurer	Otto Walther	13	39	19	27	23	22	30	28	10	25	75	88	15	26	16	125	160	36	18	45	14	8	188	27	33
	L. Rabolt	33	103	13	13	25	22	17	13	63	14	95	115	11	23	32	93	227	45	17	32	132	26	85	13	64
District Attorney	R. M. Briggs	16	29	19	25	24	30	28	8	25	75	86	14	28	14	97	25	63	18	44	137	8	164	30	32		
	J. A. Eagon	30	107	13	15	23	20	17	13	64	14	94	116	14	16	33	112	170	34	16	33	110	26	119	10	65
Supt. Schools	D. Townsend	15	40	16	26	25	22	28	28	7	25	72	96	14	27	16	121	159	60	17	45	137	8	161	30	34
	S. G. Briggs	33	103	16	14	21	22	17	13	66	14	96	110	11	17	32	96	238	39	17	32	109	26	113	10	63
Pub. Administ'or	H. Robinson	15	40	16	25	25	22	29	28	14	25	68	89	9	27	16	121	171	60	17	44	138	8	165	29	34
	M. Tynan	33	103	16	13	21	22	17	13	56	17	98	114	17	16	32	95	228	39	17	33	107	26	109	11	62
Surveyor	J. M. Griffith	15	40	16	26	25	22	27	28	6	25	72	90	14	27	16	122	169	60	17	45	136	8	165	30	34
	T. C. Stowers	33	105	16	14	21	22	16	13	66	14	97	115	11	17	32	95	230	40	17	30	109	26	107	10	63
Coroner	V. Stacy	15	40	16	25	25	22	29	28	7	25	78	89	14	30	10	118	157	32	18	44	135	8	163	30	34
	C. Boarman	33	103	16	6	21	22	18	16	66	14	96	115	11	14	32	93	243	46	16	33	110	26	109	10	62
Sup. Dist. No. 1	C. Ingalls				25		17		25	25								12	119	163	40	18				
	James Carroll				14		15		14	15							36	98	199	50	16					

COUNTING THE VOTES.

It is difficult to gather the facts in the matter of the counting of the votes. There was much ill-feeling about it, and many charges of fraud, and much filing and counter-filing of protests. Judge Badgely asked that the Supervisor votes for District No. 1 be canvassed, which was refused. The two candidates were James Carroll and C. Ingalls. The custom had prevailed, whether lawful or not, of holding elections in the camps in Arizona and Utah, where the volunteers from Amador were stationed, and returning their votes as from a precinct. Though these soldiers were known to be of both parties, the returns were generally all one way. It was alleged by the Democrats that no fair election was held; that the officers made out the returns to suit themselves. The Democrats further urged that voting in Arizona for officers in Amador, was carrying the doctrine of constructive residence a little too far; that it was unconstitutional. The Republican arguments in favor of counting their votes, were rather necessity and expediency, than law. They showed the absurdity of the Union men all going to the war, and having no voice in the choice of officers, and leaving the secessionists in the rear to rule; and the votes were counted, though protests were filed by D. Worley, John Eagon, A. C. Brown, Henry Lee, James Carroll, R. M. Bradshaw, and John Surface.

There were also other irregularities. At Clinton, D. B. Spagnoli acted both as Inspector and Clerk. There was no appearance of fraud in the matter, though the proceeding was evidently illegal. Here was a chance for a contest. The vote was generally six Republican, and sixty-four Democratic, making a difference of fifty-eight votes. If the soldiers' vote was rejected and Clinton accepted, most of the Democrats would be elected, otherwise, most of the Republicans. J. W. Armstrong, now a noted lawyer in Sacramento, then a young man, taking his first flights in law and logic, contended for the legality of the Clinton proceeding, and asserted the principle, that the statute permitted what it did not prohibit. The returns from Lower Rancheria having no certificate attached, were rejected.

LIST OF OFFICERS ELECTED IN 1865.

State Senator—G. W. Seaton.
Members of Assembly—M. Frink, H. Lee.
Sheriff—R. Cosner.
County Clerk—J. C. Shipman.
Recorder—A. C. Hinkson.
Treasurer—Otto Walther.
County Surveyor—T. C. Stowers.
District Attorney—R. M. Briggs.
Superintendent of Schools—S. G. Briggs.
Coroner—J. Boarman.
Public Administrator—M. Tynan.
Supervisor District No. 1—C. Ingalls.

TOWNSHIP ELECTIONS.

No. 1—John Burke, Collector; E. Turner, Thomas Jones, Justices of the Peace.
No. 2—J. W. Surface, Collector; Wm. H. Scudder, Wm. Shelley, Justices of the Peace.
No. 3—R. M. Bradshaw, Collector; H. T. Barnum, George S. Fake, Justices of the Peace.
No. 4—Thomas Dunlap, Collector; C. K. Johnson, P. Cook, Justices of the Peace.
No. 5.—D. Worley, Collector; R. C. Brown, G. Devore, Justices of the Peace.
No. 6—A. P. Wood, Collector; W. W. Swadley, H. D. Ford, Justices of the Peace.

DEATH OF G. W. SEATON AND ELECTION OF HIS SUCCESSOR.

This was caused by the explosion of the steamer *Yo Semite*, October 12, 1865, between Sacramento and San Francisco, W. A. Rogers, of Jackson, being killed at the same time. A more particular account of his life will be given in the account of the Amador Bar. This accident necessitated the calling of another election, which was fixed on the 2d of December. A. H. Rose was nominated by the Democrats and O. N. Morse by the Republicans.

Quartz again, as was said, influenced the election. Rose had money to loan where it would do him good. The M. E. Church Society at Ione borrowed some $1,500. It was not charged that this purchased any votes, but having shown a disposition to accommodate the church, he was a good man and ought to be supported. He also obtained quite a support from the recently ejected settlers in Ione, inducing them to think that Congress could be persuaded to remunerate them by a memorial which he promised to get through the Legislature. His part of the contract he fulfilled; the memorial, containing a concise, well-written history of the Arroyo Seco grant, being transmitted to Congress with the official seal of the State on it. These things are not related to cast reflections on Mr. Rose's method of conducting the canvass, but to show, as a soldier would, how battles are lost and won.

The returns showed the following result: A. H. Rose, 1,342; O. H. Morse, 1,099.

H. Lee, the member from Alpine county, was killed some months after by being thrown from a buggy.

Miner Frink's seat was contested by A. C. Brown, who received but two or three votes less in the election than Frink. Brown proved that two or three illegal votes were cast for Frink, and obtained the seat.

Frink afterward got a position in the office of Internal Revenue, but a year or two later, was found dead in his bed at the hotel, in San Francisco.

FINANCIAL MATTERS.

The tax levy for 1865 was—

For State purposes	on each $100	......	$1	15
General Fund	" "	......	1	00
Amador Wagon Road	" "	......		40
Hospital Fund	" "	......		25
School Fund	" "	......		30
Redemption Road Fund "	" "	......	10—	$3.20

In February, the outstanding warrants were reported as being—

On General Fund............	$74,308.18
Hospital Fund,...........	11,619.71
Wagon Road Fund.	9,918.55
Redemption Fund,........	185.27—$96.031.71

This did not include interest which was then accumulating at the rate of about ten thousand dollars per year, which would have carried the debt up to about one hundred and thirty thousand dollars.

This season the famous warrant, No. 103, was liquidated, the balance due being $7,556.16.

REPORT OF AN EXPERT, 1865.

E. G. Hunt was appointed to examine the state of the finances, and reported receipts from all sources, from March, 1864, to December, 1865, as follows:

Credited to General Fund......	$61,907.48		
"	State	"	...... 58,751.63
"	School	"	...... 17,643.39
"	Hospital	"	...... 16,905.04
"	Road	"	...... 3,328.28
"	Sierra W. R.		...... 13,906.57—$166,442.39

Taxes assessed in 1864 amounted to $75,753.20; delinquent, $15,072.26; making a net of $60,680.94.

CHAPTER XXII.
END OF THE SECOND DECADE.

Politics in 1866—Financial Matters—Rabolt Declared Ineligible to the Office of Treasurer, and Otto Walther Appointed—Political Parties in 1867—New Registry Law—Election Returns Showing the New Precincts—Judiciary Election—Financial Matters—Financial Matters in 1868—Contest for Supervisor in the First District—Ingalls Declared Unseated—Carroll Installed—Act of the Legislature in Reference Thereto—Wealth and Population—Political Parties in 1868, —Election Returns by Precincts—Politics in 1869—Election Returns by Precincts.

The year 1866 opened with little attention to politics. No elections occurring this season, the strife was over the far away subjects of reconstruction, taxing bonds, and negro suffrage, which did not immediately concern the people.

June 2d, the Treasurer reported outstanding warrants as follows:—

On General Fund........................$83,343.93
Hospital Fund....................... 13,342.40
Road Fund 3,569.31
To this must be added the bonds of the
  Sierra Nevada Wagon Road, amount-
  ing to............................   6,000.00—$106,255.64

This does not include interest, which, since 1863, has been steadily accumulating, at the rate of ten thousand dollars yearly.

December 1st, the outstanding warrants were reported as—

On General Fund......................$92,229.30
Wagon Road Fund....................   4,860.86
Hospital Fund .... 14,698.00—$111,788.16

No mention made of interest.

The assessment roll was reported at $1,874,817.75, taxes on same, $58,685.70.

L. Rabolt, who had been elected Treasurer the previous season, was declared ineligible to the position, on the ground that he was not a citizen; and the office being vacant, Otto Walther was appointed to fill it.

POLITICAL PARTIES IN 1867.

The election of State and county officers, as well as members of Congress, caused the politicians to set their standards early in the field.

H. H. Haight was nominated for Governor by the Democrats, and George C. Gorham, by the Republicans. Higby and Coffroth, both representative men from the mines, were put forth by the Republicans and Democrats respectively, for Congress. The failure to impeach Andrew Johnson, which project was a Republican measure, had given the Democrats courage everywhere in the county, State, and nation. The Democrats had, to some extent, adopted his financial views about the payment, or rather, non-payment of the national debt; and the traveling orators, including Farley and Coffroth, roundly asserted, not only the right, but the expediency of taxing national bonds, while Edgerton, and other Republican speakers, as roundly denied it, and referred to numerous decisions of the Supreme Court, establishing the non-taxability of national securities. The bitterness of war times was evidently passing away. The discussion of financial questions involved figures rather than feelings; and not every one was capable of entering into the spirit of large numbers. Bloated bondholders and prospective negro suffrage, all could understand, and a general interest, rather than the intense bitterness of former years, marked the campaign.

The following table will show the relative strength of the parties, and the names of the new polling places under the registration law, which, though somewhat difficult to put into operation, worked to the general satisfaction of the public. Under the old form of election, any out-of-the-way place could get up a precinct. A poll list was kept, it is true, but so loosely, that a man might vote in several places, or several times a day, without detection. Unnaturalized foreigners were voted in some places, by the dozens. Men were chosen for judges and inspectors, who could hardly read; and it was possible to make up a general result only by condoning a multitude of mistakes and irregularities.

ELECTION RETURNS—1867.

OFFICES.	NAMES.	Jackson	Volcano	Forest Home	Dry Town	Fiddletown	Lancha Plana	Sutter	Total
Governor	H. H. Haight, (D.)	409	147	280	18	69	160	45	
	Geo. C. Gorham, (R.)	296	128	237	32	96	80	42	
Lieut. Governor	Wm. Holden, (D.)	401	144	257	17	73	164	44	
	John P. Jones, (R.)	253	137	245	30	96	105	45	
Congressman	J. W. Coffroth, (D.)	392	143	286	17	59	164	44	
	Wm. Higby, (R.)	360	135	218	33	99	105	46	
Assemblyman	J. B. Gregory, (D.)	403	134	290	17	59	158	45	
	Geo. M. Payser, (D.)	405	134	286	17	64	164	47	
	Chas. D. Smith, (R.)	255	131	248	43	113	105	43	
	William Pearson, (R.)	248	129	245	30	106	96	42	
Sheriff	Geo. Durham, (D.)	397	142	297	26	73	158	45	
	Samuel Smith, (R.)	250	141	235	37	99	116	47	
County Clerk	A. C. Brinkers, (D.)	411	142	286	17	55	165	46	
	A. F. Northrup, (R.)	246	135	240	35	82	114	47	
Recorder	D. B. Spagnoli, (D.)	396	135	256	16	82	156	46	
	Ph. Seibenthaler, (R.)	267	135	198	36	100	125	45	
Treasurer	James Meehan, (D.)	366	134	294	11	74	164	45	
	Henry Giouochio, (R.)	287	137	236	36	96	164	47	
District Attorney	H. L. Waldo, (D.)	392	145	286	19	73	146	47	
	R. M. Briggs, (R.)	262	137	189	31	94	109	46	
Surveyor	A. Speer, (D.)	392	145	293	17	75	162	44	
	Sam Love, (R.)	256	134	248	35	96	105	47	
Coroner	Chas. Boarman, (R.)	409	145	287	17	76	163	45	
	W. L. Fifield, (R.)	246	136	249	35	92	108	46	
Public Administ'r	W. A. Few, (D.)	387	144	291	17	71	164	45	
	G. L. Brady, (R.)	257	134	215	33	96	105	47	
Supt. Schools	S. D. Briggs, (D.)	403	134	291	17	74	166	45	
	J. D. Mason, (R.)	253	147	241	35	96	100	45	

The entire Democratic ticket was elected with the exception of Seibenthaler, for County Clerk, who was chosen by a small majority. It was currently reported, and believed by many, that Otto Walther, who became acting County Clerk, owed his election to a commercial transaction rather than to political preferences. If it was so, it was so quietly done that no member of a Grand Jury ever got an inkling of it.

The Collectors and Assessors for 1867 were—

Township No. 1—N. M. Bowman.
Township No. 2—J. W. Surface.
Township No. 3—J. Foster.
Township No. 4—Thomas Dunlap.
Township No. 5—J. T. Maffitt.
Township No. 6—F. L. Sullivan.

At the judiciary election, J. Foot Turner, Republican, was re-elected over J. T. Phelps, Democrat, by a large majority. This apparent change in the political cast of the vote was explained by the fact that Judge Turner never was an active politician, and was supported by persons of both parties.

FINANCIAL MATTERS IN 1867.

January, 1867, the reported outstanding warrants, over and above the funds on hand to meet them, was—

On General Fund..................$94,761 74
Hospital Fund .... 13,691 53—$108,453 27

The Wagon Road Fund was $122.19 in excess of liability. This did not take into account the fifth bond which matured during the year, as the next report mentions it with the accrued interest, amounting to $5,510. In this estimate no mention is made of the interest which is steadily increasing.

RESIDENCE AND RANCH OF CAPT. M. J. LITTLE, JACKSON, AMADOR COUNTY, CAL.

RESIDENCE OF R. C. DOWNS, SUTTER CREEK, AMADOR COUNTY, CAL.

END OF THE SECOND DECADE.

TAX RATE FOR 1867.

For State Fund, on each $100		$1 13
General Fund "		1 00
Wagon Road Fund "		30
Hospital Fund "		25
School Fund "		25

In March the total indebtedness, exclusive of interest, was reported at $84,110.01. How it was reduced $24,000 since January does not appear.

March 12, 1867, John Burke, Collector of Township No. 1, was declared defaulter to the amount of nine hundred and eighty-three dollars, by A. C. Hinkson, County Auditor, for which act, as well as other improper transactions, he was removed, and J. M. Griffith appointed in his place. Among other things, Burke was charged with making out receipts with pencil, and collecting money thereon, and afterwards procuring the receipts again for a trifle, erasing the name and amount, and using them again, or returning them to the Board of Supervisors as unused.

FINANCIAL MATTERS IN 1868.

Rate of taxes for State purposes on each $100			$1.00
General Fund,	"	"	60
Hospital Fund,	"	"	25
School Fund,	"	"	25—$2.50
March 3d, the outstanding warrants were:			
General Fund			$87,074.97
Hospital Fund			11,403.50—$98,478.17
Exclusive of interest!!			

The Supervisors making this report were C. Ingalls, L. McLaine and D. M. Goff. James Carroll was afterward declared by Judge Brockway entitled to the seat occupied by C. Ingalls for nearly three years. Many rumors were in circulation of a bargain between Carroll and Ingalls, that the latter should allow himself to be ousted that the former might draw a salary for the whole term; at any rate, Carroll presented a bill for $1,665.50, salary for the full term, which was allowed by the Supervisors, but payment was stopped by means of an injunction served on the Treasurer by District Attorney Waldo. In 1872 the Legislature ordered the Supervisors of Amador county to draw a warrant for $1,050 as back salary, H. Waldo, John Eagon, and J. T. Farley being members for Amador county. Since the allowance was made by the Supervisors, lines in ink have been drawn through the minutes as if for erasure. Carroll took his seat July 6th; the allowance was made August 3d, following.

THE WEALTH AND POPULATION

According to reports were as follows: Real estate, $962,284; improvements, $247,549; personal property, $527,625; total, $1,737,458. Population, 11,400; registered votes, 2,552.

POLITICAL PARTIES IN 1868.

There being no local officers to elect, this was the off year in politics. The county officers, securely fixed in their seats for a year, rested serenely on their comfortable salaries. Some of the politicians and orators, scenting places in the Custom House or office of internal revenue, put on their armor, loaded their mental guns with the heaviest shot, and plunged into the thickest of the fight, making a great smoke and noise whether they hit anybody or not.

The State had been divided into Congressional Districts so that but a single Congressman was to be voted for. Coffroth and Sargent, Democratic and Republican candidates respectively, stumped the districts, taking Amador county in their course. The questions of payment of the national debt, the taxation of the bonds, and the reconstruction of the Southern States, again came before the people. Grant, the Republican nominee for President, was reviewed, and, as was to be expected, was bitterly assailed and as warmly defended. The danger of electing soldiers to office was held up to view. Many professed to believe that he would, with the aid of the army, make himself Emperor; that in case he was elected he would be the last President the United States would ever have; that in a short time we should have an order of hereditary nobility established. Others professed to think Grant only a lucky fool, who would be the tool of designing politicians; that he was not much of a General anyhow; that Sherman, Thomas, Sheridan, Logan and others whipped the Rebellion. On the other hand Seymour was represented as heartless, treacherous and unworthy. The microscope was turned on him and every possible mistake of his life magnified into a monstrous crime. His treatment of the New York rioters at the time of the draft was made constructive treason. "He ought to have turned loose the dogs of war on the rioters; ought never to have addressed them calling them his friends." Illustrated editions of the New York riots in which brutal Irishmen were slaying defenseless negro orphan children were everywhere circulated; in short, the old, old stories, told every year from the time of Jefferson down, were brought out, colored and re-shaped to suit the times and persons, so that they were almost as good as new. Strangers to our country and its style of conducting a campaign, whether national or local, would imagine that we were on the eve of

ELECTION RETURNS BY PRECINCTS IN 1868.

PRECINCTS.	SEYMOUR	GRANT	COFFROTH	SARGENT
Jackson	320	236	320	223
Ione City	142	127	142	157
Lancha Plana	42	49	42	49
Clinton	70	23	72	21
Volcano	246	222	247	221
Fiddletown	91	81	92	81
Enterprise	54	28	54	28
Sutter Creek	138	188	133	188
Amador	42	48	41	48
Drytown	62	64	62	64
Forest Home	16	42	16	42
Total	1223	1098	1221	1112
Democratic majority	125		110	

anarchy, a general breaking up of all order and industries; but the elections pass away, the people, satisfied with masquerading, return to their avocations and prosperity continues.

POLITICAL PARTIES IN 1869.

A full set of county officers to be elected, set things to going early. The interest was the most intense in the Democratic party as being the most likely to win, though much of the work was given to obtaining the nominations.

The railroad question began to be agitated this year, the question of regulating fares and freights having become an element in politics. To what extent, if any, candidates were supplied with the material for making a successful campaign, by pledging themselves, will always be a matter of mystery. The Democrats, as usual, elected their whole ticket. It will be observed that the township system was discontinued, a County Assessor and Collector being chosen.

ELECTION OF JUSTICES OF THE PEACE, 1869.

Township No. 1—E. Turner, J. S. Campbell.
Township No. 2—Charles Walker, William Shelby.
Township No. 3—Louis Miller, Louis Ludiken.
Township No. 4—C. K. Johnson, U. Nurse.
Township No. 5—M. B. Church, C. D. Smith.
Township No. 6—E. R. Yates, F. Shearer.

ELECTION RETURNS—1869.

CHAPTER XXIII.

CONDITION OF THE COUNTY AT THE BEGINNING OF THE THIRD DECADE—1870.

Condition of the County at the Beginning of the Third Decade—Statistics of the Wealth and Indebtedness—Politics in 1870—Financial Condition—Redemption Fund—Condition of Other Counties—The Miners' League—Death of McMenomy and Hatch—Political Parties in 1872—Election Returns by Precincts, 1871—Persons Elected in 1871—Financial Matters 1872—Political Parties in 1872—Election Returns for 1872—Comparison of Vote with Previous Years—Financial Matters, 1873—Political Parties in 1873—John Eagon's Position—Judge Gordon's Stand—J. T. Farley's Position—Election Returns by Precincts—Officers Elected in 1873—Alpine county Left out in the Election—Financial Matters in 1874—The Funding Project—Political Parties in 1874—Financial Matters in 1875—Robbery of the Treasury May 9, 1875—Conclusion of Butterfield Matter in 1877—Political Matters in 1875—Officers elected in 1875.

ACCORDING to the reports of the Assessor the value of all property, personal and real, was $2,241,070. The county debt had been estimated as being less than $100,000, but as was written in the previous chapters of the history, it was constantly increasing, the sums paid not being equal to the interest, and consequently no portion was applied to the payment of the principal. At the beginning of this decade the debt was nearly, if not quite, $200,000. It seems to be the fate of political organizations, as well as of individuals, to go into extravagant and wasteful expenditure in prosperous times, and pay up when times are hard. At the beginning of 1860 we found placer mining remunerative to a high degree; quartz mining established on a paying basis and agriculture and horticulture profitably employing a great number of men. The farms on the Mokelumne river, in Jackson, Ione and Dry Creek valleys, as well as on the heads of the latter creeks, with their waving fields of grain, orchards, and vineyards, were all that could be desired.

Many causes combined to arrest this tide of prosperity. The Frazer river excitement drew away a great many miners. Still later the discovery of the Washoe mines caused another outflow of hundreds of able, industrious men. The copper excitement took a great many away from moderately profitable work; and, when copper failed in the subsequent years to prove remunerative, at least five hundred men were set adrift, most of whom left the county in search of some more promising place. During the years of 1861-64, the price of cattle of all kinds went down with a panic, so that many, who considered themselves well fixed, became poor men. The wine business, which promised so much, had proved an utter failure, every attempt to market the wine in the East resulting in loss; so that many persons were induced to tear up their vineyards and give up the business. The orchards, which produced a great quantity of the finest fruit, were also poor property; for the emigration of many of the miners left no market for such products. The quartz mining alone saved the county from comparative poverty. The mines along the mother lodes, as well as in the eastern part of the county, on the Volcano range, gave employment to perhaps one thousand men. Some of the mines, such as the Lincoln, Mahoney and Hayward at Sutter Creek, and others at Drytown, Amador, and Plymouth, took out sums varying from ten thousand to sixty thousand dollars per month. Large quantities of wood and lumber were required, which furnished labor to as many more men as were engaged in the mines.

With all this there was little increase in the population and prospective wealth. The vote, which in 1860 had closely reached four thousand, in ten years was reduced to about two thousand, though there was no decrease in population in proportion to the vote, as the roving part was composed mostly of men without families.

The gradual improvement in financial standing, through wise management, and a gradual and healthy growth in all the business industries of the county will appear as the third decade passes away.

A FEW STATISTICS

As to the comparative wealth and population will be interesting:—

PRECINCTS.	Population in 1870.					Population in 1860.*		
	Total.	Native	Foreign.	White.	Colored.	Chinese.	Total.	White.	Colored.	Chinese.
Jackson	2408	1179	1325	1988	3	417	1344	1322	17	505
Ione	1779	1094	685	1330	24	425	2742	2008	21	539
Volcano	1357	840	517	1218	2	137	1345	1527	5	113
Sutter	1966	1157	809	1858	36	7	1214	1022	13	179
Drytown	853	486	367	640	2	211	1559	852	18	689
Oleta	1219	702	517	849	5	365	1191	824	6	361
Rancheria							478	382	1	95
Total	9582	5449	4223	7883	72	1627	10090	8527	81	2535

In making these estimates the Government gave the township the name of the largest town.

	1870	1860
Assessed value of Real Estate	$1,167,525	
Farm Property	785,419	
Total	$1,952,944	$2,395,684
True value	$4,428,490	
State Taxes	$19,944	$28,855.90
County Taxes	$29,293	
Total	$48,237	
County Debt	$165,000	$4,823.50
Improved Land (in acres)	41,534	38,483
Unimproved " "	19,782	
Cash value of Farms	8486,400	
" " Farm Impl'ts	45,015	
" " Orchard Products	43,350	
" " Farm	363,983	
" " Market Gardens	11,665	
" " Manufactories	26,000	
" " Animals for Food	62,232	
" " Live Stock	280,587	
Number of Horses	1,686	1,749
" Mules	141	
" Milch Cows	1,471	
" Working Oxen	68	9,633
" Other Cattle	2,497	

* There is a slight discrepancy in the census returns.

Number of Sheep	23,914	3,990
" Swine	5,380	
Bushels of Wheat raised	16,678	39,000
" Corn "	36,370	19,000
" Barley "	51,815	31,175
" Potatoes "	9,988	9,200
" " Sweet "	1,060	
Pounds of Wool	73,010	
Gals. Wine made	54,165	
Pounds of Butter	43,700	
" Cheese	950	
Gals. Milk sold	1,000	
Tons Hay raised	5,908	3,000
Pounds of Hops	12,050	
" Honey	2,520	
Quartz Mills	33	27
Tons of Rock crushed	61,736	70,360

POLITICAL PARTIES IN 1870.

This was a year of quiet, as neither national, State, or county officers were to be elected. The mutterings of the storm, that was prevailing in the East, were but little heeded in the off years. It took the loaves and fishes of the county offices to arouse the politicians to a full sense of the dangers impending over our Constitution, our country or our race. No livery teams were hired to carry the men, ambitious to serve their country in easy, lucrative offices, around to alarm the people. No twenty-dollar pieces were left at the saloons to pay for beer doled out where it would do the most good. In fact, everything was distressingly dull, and the people were allowed to attend quietly to their business.

FINANCIAL CONDITION OF THE COUNTY.

Nobody knew exactly how it stood. It is true that quarterly returns were made by the Sheriff, Auditor, Treasurer, and Supervisors, and occasionally the Grand Jury would have a spasm of economy and make an inquiry into the financial condition; but who among the Grand Jurors had time to look over the status of the outstanding warrants to see for what purpose, or when they were drawn, or how much interest had accumulated, or whether even the interest had been paid! A few persons were conscious of the painful uncertainty and to these the county is indebted for the arrangements which not only brought the accumulating debt to view, but provided means for its gradual liquidation.

REDEMPTION FUND.

As early as February 7th the Supervisors, L. McLaine, Henry Peek, and D. M. Goff, took the matter under consideration and recommended a plan which, however, was said to have been first suggested by James Meehan, the Treasurer, that sixty cents on each one hundred dollars should be raised to be used as a sinking fund for outstanding registered warrants. Meehan went to Sacramento and personally solicited the support of the members not interested in the matter, his position as Treasurer enabling him to explain the necessity of some such measure, to prevent the county from becoming bankrupt. Messrs.

Farley and Brown, Senator and Assemblyman respectively, ably supported the Bill, and on the 12th of March it became a law. It provided a sinking fund of sixty cents on each one hundred dollars which was sacred for this purpose; also that no warrant should be drawn unless there was money to meet it; a certificate of indebtedness, bearing no interest, being given when occasion demanded. Though the sum specially assessed was sufficient to check the accumulation of interest, and also assisted materially in bringing to light the different items, it was not until December 3, 1872, that the full amount of liabilities was known and reported, the debt having been estimated at one hundred and sixty-five thousand dollars. To anticipate the result it was then reported that the outstanding warrants

On General Fund with interest was ...$157,126 02
On Hospital Fund,   "   " ... 38,007 33
On New Certificates not bearing interest 13,755 23—$208,884 58.

CONDITION OF OTHER COUNTIES.

About this time, general attention was attracted towards some of the older mining counties, which, in former years, had contained much the largest share of the population. At one time, El Dorado county, now numbering less than ten thousand inhabitants, had fifty thousand. Tuolumne, Calaveras, and some others, also showed a great reduction. In Calaveras, the condition was much worse than in Amador. The population reduced to less than ten thousand; the assessment roll yearly decreasing; the debt, principal and interest, constantly accumulating, so that five per cent. taxes was hardly sufficient to meet current expenses, was a condition calculated to depress and crush out all industrial energy. It was known that stock-men, who grazed their flocks in the mountains of Calaveras, would hold them in other counties, where the rates of taxation were lower, until the time for assessing was past, before they would drive them to their pastures. A tax rate as high as five per cent. was considered as a mortgage for all the property was worth. Things were looking so serious that the Legislature felt called upon to investigate the matter before the question of State responsibility for county indebtedness, should meet them in the shape of a judgment.

In making these investigations, Amador was considered one of the counties possibly requiring the aid of the State. Happily, it has passed any such probable contingency.

THE MINERS' LEAGUE.

Any history of Amador county which failed to give an account of the Miners' League, would be lamentably deficient. This Society organized as a kind of mutual benefit association. It does not appear that any unlawful measures were at first contemplated; but organization gave the members an idea of strength and influence. Merchants joined the league, for fear of losing the trade of the miners; politicians, to make a few votes; and the lawless and desperate, to work against law and order in society. In Sutter Creek, it numbered about three hundred members, composed of Irish, Cornishmen, Austrians, and Italians, and had a membership of perhaps as many more in other parts of the county. They built a large hall, costing several thousand dollars. Luke Burns, who had had some experience in similar associations in Virginia City, was President, and L. J. Marks, Secretary.

The immediate cause of the outbreak was the reduction of twenty-five cents a day on the wages of the hands working on the surface, in the Consolidated Amador mine. After much discussion a general strike was agreed upon, also a determination to enforce it everywhere, and not permit the working of the mines unless at the proposed rates. The schedule of wages demanded by the Miners' League made very little advance over the existing rates, but the right to make even a small advance implied a right to control the working of the mines, and the mine owners refused to accept the rates. Members of the league to the number of two hundred visited the different mines, and ordered the stopping of the work. They carried no arms that were in sight, though according to some reports they supplied themselves with clubs from the wood piles of the mills. It is now contended by some that no threats or force was used; that the miners went rather as a committee of conference than as a menacing party. They would not permit any work to be done, not even allowing an engine to be run to keep the water out. John Eagon, since State Senator, and James Meehan, as well as other prominent men, were members of the league. The former person accompanied the body of miners to the mills, as he asserted, to prevent them from committing any excesses, though others say, that having raised a storm he could not control he was swept along in the whirlwind. The mills at Amador, Sutter, and Oneida were all stopped. It is true that some of these mines, like the Keystone, Consolidated, Amador, and others, were paying mines, and could have paid higher wages and dividends also; but other mines like the Oneida had never paid dividends, but had always been worked at a loss. The wages paid varied from two dollars and a half a day for top hands, to four dollars for underground men. There was no plea that the wages were insufficient to support the families, or less than were paid in other laborious occupations, but it was intended to raise them to the Virginia and Gold Hill standard, where the expenses of living were much higher. The daily threats of destruction of life and property showed the existence of so much ill-feeling that the Governor was invoked for aid, and a body of volunteers, under General Cazenau, came from San Francisco and camped on the hill near the old Wolverine shaft. They had several pieces of artillery, and formed a regular military camp, sending out and

RESIDENCE OF JUDGE GEORGE MOORE, JACKSON, AMADOR COUNTY, CAL.

relieving guards every evening for the different mines. Correspondents from the cities accompanied the troops, and reported the conditions every day.

Never, at any time in the history of the county, was the apprehension of danger to life and property so strong. The members of the league were men who were accustomed to danger, for what does a man care for life who risks it every day as a miner does. And then the mass of the miners felt amenable to no laws but their own. There is no class of people who have so little intercourse with the outside world, who have their own codes of ethics and modes of thought, as the professional miners. The threats of life and property, extended to other parts of the county. It seemed that the officers of justice were paralyzed. The newspapers of the county said little about it, as if fearful that a word might bring destruction upon them.

The result was a general prostration of business. The towns around the quartz mines had been the principal market for produce for some years, and when a thousand or more men were thrown out of employment and the money which was usually paid as wages ceased to circulate, the depression in business was universal, producing in some instances actual distress.

The soldiers remained in the county for several weeks, and prevented any destruction of property. Some kind of concession was made which terminated the siege, and the soldiers left, although the ill-feeling engendered by the operation remained for some time. The damage to the county by this affair can hardly be estimated. The mines of gold and copper, as well as other minerals, require the aid of capital to be made profitable. Capital must be protected, or it silently shuts itself up. In subsequent years, the memory of the Amador war diverted many thousands of dollars from investment in the county.

DEATH OF M'MENEMY AND HATCH.

Several altercations grew out of the matter, one resulting in the death of two men and the wounding of a third. The following from the *Dispatch* of July 29, 1871, gives the only account of the matter to be found:—

"The wounds received by Hatch and McMenemy have both proved fatal. Both of the wounded men were attended by the best of medical aid, but human effort proved of no avail. McMenemy lingered until half-past twelve P. M., on Wednesday, when he died; Mr. Hatch, till half-past four the same afternoon, when he breathed his last. He was conscious to the last, but unable to speak for some hours before his death.

"We will not attempt to give any of the particulars of this truly melancholy affair, as there are so many conflicting statements and rumors afloat that it is almost impossible to arrive at the truth of the matter. The immediate cause of the shooting, however, grew out of an attack made on Mr. Hatch the Friday night previous, at a concert given in Sutter Creek. The result has created much feeling and excitement in our county. Where it will end no one can now tell."

Hatch was the confidential clerk of the Amador Consolidated Co. Bennet was his friend, who took up the quarrel that was forced on Hatch. He was obliged to leave the county. Hatch left a young wife to mourn her loss.

Wrigglesworth, an engineer, who persisted in running an engine for pumping, after notice to quit, was set upon in the streets, and escaped through the kindness of a woman in the Exchange Hotel, who hid him away while the crowd was searching for him. He also had to leave the county.

The reign of terror gradually passed away, though the influence of the Miners' League was felt in political matters sometime after.

POLITICAL PARTIES IN 1871.

A full set of county and State officers was to be elected and, consequently, the politicians began early to take advantageous positions and set their forces in the field. There were no great national issues to arouse public interest, but a combination, or perhaps a bidding for the vote of the Miners' League, heretofore mentioned, gave a great deal of interest to the campaign. John Eagon, a member of the League, was supposed to control three hundred votes, which number would ensure the election of any one nominated by either party. Few of the better citizens of either party would countenance the proceedings of the League, but as one old politician said, three

ELECTION RETURNS—1871.

CANDIDATES.	Jackson.	Clinton.	Ione City.	Lancha Plana.	Volcano.	Sutter Creek.	Amador.	Drytown.	Forest Home.	Fiddletown.	Kentucky.
GOVERNOR.											
H. H. Haight (D.)	202	105	103	30	187	118	66	36	14	92	40
Newton Booth (R.)	209	24	125	61	186	238	68	70	36	89	31
LIEUTENANT GOVERNOR.											
R. J. Lewis (D.)	270	105	101	31	185	158	76	36	15	94	47
R. Pacheco (R.)	208	24	135	59	187	210	54	66	35	81	30
CONGRESSMAN.											
Coffroth (D.)	273	108	100	30	185	149	73	38	14	93	46
Sargent (R.)	204	22	140	51	180	211	58	69	36	80	31
ASSEMBLYMEN.											
Waldo (D.)	214	85	107	22	109	97	59	30	15	62	45
Johnson (D.)	23	107	100	24	187	100	70	58	14	83	46
Coleman (R.)	164	23	130	55	153	179	60	68	35	85	31
Eagon (Ind.)	180	45	113	62	158	211	66	69	29	79	24
Swift (Ind.)	14		15		4	52	4	1		2	
SHERIFF.											
John Vogan (D.)	310	104	117	36	189	161	47	72	14	78	46
H. Kelly (R.)	151	23	123	46	184	264	87	70	36	93	31
COUNTY CLERK.											
Spagnoli (D.)	277	117	97	25	188	137	71	18	2	68	32
Richtmyer (R.)	190	11	147	56	187	234	80	88	48	108	45
TREASURER.											
Meehan (D.)	306	30	55	29	180	126	67	36	17	89	43
Bullou (R.)	169	99	180	51	203	218	59	67	36	86	28
DISTRICT ATTORNEY.											
Turner (D.)	278	75	98	19	186	97	68	35	14	70	45
Briggs (R.)	185	52	140	62	195	257	60	67	34	89	28
ASSESSOR.											
Surface	220	109	150	25	134	108	58	47	17	119	50
Mullen	180	20	80	54	137	252	73	58	32	54	28
SUPERINTENDENT SCHOOLS.											
Briggs	230	101	102	27	205	154	78	38	11	70	38
Keff	184	23	130	52	63	215	54	68	39	99	29
SURVEYOR.											
Rentro	285	104	100	25	188	129	76	40	15	86	46
McKimm	180	25	130	56	187	211	55	66	36	87	31
PUBLIC ADMINISTRATOR.											
Yoak	319	106	104	27	189	172	76	36	10	85	45
Wininger	155	22	136	54	184	229	57	68	39	83	31
CORONER.											
Bearman	282	105	100	33	188	147	75	41	16	85	46
Sharp	185	23	134	45	190	236	59	65	35	87	31

15

hundred votes were hard to pick up, so the three hundred were treated with distinguished consideration. What diplomatic feats were performed; what promises made and broken none will tell. The election returns form the best history of the transaction.

OFFICERS ELECTED IN 1871.

District Judge—A. C. Adams.
County Judge—T. M. Pawling.
Assemblymen—H. A. Waldo, J. A. Eagon.
District Attorney—R. M. Briggs.
County Clerk—B. F. Richtmyer.
Sheriff—H. B. Kelley.
Treasurer—O. Button.
Surveyor—D. D. Reaves.
Assessor—J. W. Surface.
Superintendent of Schools—S. G. Briggs.
Coroner—Charles Boarman.
Public Administrator—A. Yoak.

JUSTICES OF THE PEACE.

Township No. 1—J. C. Shipman, Hugh Robinson.
" " 2—L. Brusie, L. M. Earle.
" " 3—S. F. Mullen, L. Ludekin.
" " 4—P. Cook, J. S. Hill.
" " 5—M. B. Church, D. Worley.
" " 6—E. R. Yates, James Gregg.

FINANCIAL MATTERS IN 1872.

This may be distinguished as the year of waking up, when every cranny and pigeon hole was ransacked to find the amount of the county debt. In February the Treasurer estimated the debt as $179,265.47. On the sixth day of June the report indicated outstanding warrants on—

General Fund with interest.........$153,551.00
Hospital Fund "   " 36,995.68
New Certificates....................... 1,979.64—$192,526.32

The following note is appended to the report:—

"Upon a thorough examination of the registration of outstanding warrants against the redemption and hospital funds of the county, as the same appears on the books of the County Treasurer, it appears that the reports made of the indebtedness of the county for the past years have been incorrect, the true indebtedness being much greater than reported. The presumption is, the error was committed by reporting the interest paid as a reduction of the principal to that amount, when in fact it did not reduce it at all."

The last quarterly report, December 3, 1872, was outstanding warrants on—

General Fund....................$157,121.02
Hospital Fund.................... 38,007.33
New General Fund................ 13,756.23—$208,884.58

The Assessor, J. W. Surface, catching some of the economic spirit, doubled the assessment roll and astonished the people with the amount of wealth in the county.

Assessment roll for 1872:—
Real Estate ....$ 359,133
Improvements................ 269,165
Town Lots..................   90,965
Improvements thereon........ 279,800
Mining Claims............... 1,226,200

Improvements................... 150,350
Telegraph...........................   800
Water Ditches.................... 82,950
Personal Property.......... 3,027,119—$5,556,442
Rate of taxation, $2.35 on each $100.
Taxes assessed, including special school taxes, $77,531.17.

TAX RATES.

Sinking Fund....70c.   Producing..$22,307 25
General Fund....45c.   "   .. 14,340.37
School Fund....30c.   "   .. 9,560.25
Hospital Fund...40c.   "   .. 6,373.50
State Fund......50c.—$2.35 "   .. 15,933.75—$74,888.62

Considering that the population of the county was something less than ten thousand, government was quite a luxury, costing about $8.00 per capita.

POLITICAL PARTIES IN 1872.

This year furnishes an apt illustration of the often repeated assertion that the desire for office was at the foundation of the enthusiasm generally prevalent during elections. There were no county offices to fill, and it was difficult to kindle any interest in the mass of voters. The Presidential election was a far away matter in the chances to get a public appointment, and few took any interest on that account. Then the nominations were singular. Grant, the Republican nominee for President, in former days, was considered a Democrat, and Greeley, the Democratic nominee never was a Democrat; on the contrary, he had been during his whole life, fiercely aggressive on them; had charged them with all kinds of sins, individually and collectively—sins political, moral and intellectual; but Greeley had quarreled with the administration, and he was thought a suitable candidate to make an inroad in the Republican ranks. A great many, who were former admirers of Greeley, were known to be disaffected, and, it was thought, would leave the Republican party. The Democrats had now conceded the payment of the national debt and the validity of the Constitutional amendments, so that there was really little difference of opinion, on national questions, to keep the people apart. The old Democrats reluctantly fell into the ranks with

ELECTION RETURNS FOR 1872.

PRECINCTS.	Grant (R.)	Greeley (D.)	Page (R.)	Coggins (D.)
Jackson...........	173	172	159	188
Clinton...........	65	20	65	21
Ione City.........	115	92	88	119
Lancha Plana......	35	38	25	46
Volcano...........	165	155	135	188
Sutter Creek......	155	80	135	132
Amador............	53	85	30	106
Drytown...........	47	26	43	31
Forest Home.......	34	12	12	24
Fiddletown........	52	45	11	89
Enterprise........	15	25	12	26
Plymouth..........	55	22	29	46
Total.............	964	772	744	1016

Greeley at the head of the column. It was a decided case of self-sacrifice for the benefit of the country. The younger Democrats suspended the *rule* and voted as they pleased. As might have been expected the vote was very light. Even the vote for Congressman was far short of the usual numbers.

A comparison of the vote with that of 1868 will be of interest as showing the want of interest in the election:—

1868.	1872.
Grant (R.).....1,109	Grant (R.)..... 946
Seymour (D.)...1,223	Greeley (D.).... 772
Total........2,332	Total........1,718

Decrease in vote, 614.

CONGRESSIONAL VOTE.

1868.	1872.
Sargent (R.)....1,102	Page (R.) ......744.
Coffroth (D.)...1,222	Coggins (D.).....1,016
Total........2,324	Total........1,760

Decrease in vote, 564.

Page's vote was two hundred and two less than Grant's, and Greeley's vote two hundred and forty-eight less than Coffroth's. It is evident that many men of both parties failed to vote, and that personal preferences, with many Democrats as well as Republicans, were stronger than party ties; also, that National questions were considered of less moment than the election of the right kind of men for county officers, as the whole vote fell short of the vote of the previous year as follows:—

County Clerk—Spagnoli, 1,002; Richtmyer, 1,194; total, 2,196. Presidential vote, 1872—1,718. Difference, 478.

Vote for County Clerk in 1873—Stevens, 1,087; Richtmyer, 1,017; total, 2,104. Difference, 386.

FINANCIAL MATTERS IN 1873.

From this time, there seems to have been an earnest effort to pay off the debt, as well as to check county expenditures. The effort to make the prospective value of the mines an item on the assessment roll, failed. The mine owners succeeded in evading it, sometimes by a technicality. In other instances, the Supervisors abated part of the tax, to avoid a doubtful and expensive lawsuit. The Keystone mining property was assessed in bulk, the taxes amounting to nine thousand dollars, which the company refused to pay, whereupon, J. W. Surface, the collector, proceeded to sell the property. In the suit which followed, the Court decided, that, though the property was principally owned by one company, it should have been described and assessed as three separate properties; that, in consequence of this, the collector be restrained from selling it.

The assessment roll was reduced, to $3,186,750, and $18,176.90 taxes were reported as delinquent. The total indebtedness July 31st, was reported at—

Outstanding warrants on Gen. Fund.. $141,768.08
"   "   Hospital Fund. 34,044.36
Certificates not bearing interest....... 13,991.09—$189,803.53

October 3d, it was reported—

Outstanding warrants on Gen. Fund.. $143,894.39
"   "   Hospital Fund . 34,736.46
Certificates not bearing interest....... 17,774.65
New Hospital Fund...............   1,032.85—$197,438.35

POLITICAL PARTIES IN 1873.

Early in the season, it was evident that a nomination by the Democratic party was equivalent to an election, and the strife was principally in the primaries. Nearly every town had a full set of candidates, who undertook to effect a combination which should have their own names on the slate. When the primaries were over, the successful operators went into the Convention, each with his list of delegates, which he could trade or bestow on any other candidate as a consideration for votes given to himself. Some sturdy, independent men, finding themselves valued, labeled and consigned to certain parties, will rebel and fret, but a skillful manipulator will manage to conciliate them with the promise of a nomination another year, or something equally delusive, and so, year after year, a smart manager wriggles himself into office; and the man who studies political economy instead of men, who knows less of primaries and more of the science of government, is left in the rear in the race. It may be said, however, in defense of this kind of political economy, that the best governments are the result of organizations which harmonize conflicting elements into a force working for the general good; that he who cannot lead, and is unwilling to follow, must stand aside.

This season showed a change of positions of some of the leaders. John Eagon, one of the old Democratic war horses, who was wont to fall into the front line when a charge was sounded, now ranged himself with the Republicans. When he made his intention known, he excused, or rather justified, himself with the remark of a Roman orator: "*Tempora mutantur, mutamur,*" which may be translated, *Times change, we change*. In a rather lengthy address, the sentiment, above quoted, was elaborated into something like the following: "Fellow-citizens: I honestly defended slavery, not that I believed it advantageous to States or to the nation, but because I found it recognized in the national compact as an existing institution. I opposed the attempt to coerce the States who refused to submit to the election of of a President, and the establishment of an administration hostile to the institution of slavery, not because I justified secession, but because I believed that reunion could be safely left to time and opportunity. The nation thought otherwise. Slavery has been abolished by the court of last resort; the Union has been re-established, though at a fearful price. I do not believe in prolonging a useless strife. I am willing to accept the verdict, and abide the judgment of the Court. I am willing to forget the past, and join with any party to cultivate peace and friendship between the two sections, and repair the waste and desolations of the war."

Judge Gordon also took the stump for the Republican party. He had been longer a member of the Democratic party, because an older man; had been a Murat in the thickest of the fight, where his intellectual sword was sure to cleave a broad way through opposing ranks. Though his judgment might have caused him to submit to, and advocate the new order of political economy, his heart did not respond to the new slogan. His speeches lacked the usual fire and vim, and, in a few years after, he concluded to give his old age to the party of his youth.

James T. Farley, who had quietly taken the bitter pill of defeat during the years of the war, was now in front. He had been prudent during the years of bitter strife, had tried to soften the asperity and vindictiveness of both parties. He had remained with the Democrats when sure defeat awaited them. His uniform consistency won the confidence of the community. He also accepted the results of the war, and wished to cultivate peace and amity.

In this campaign was the beginning of that continuous wave of popularity which carried him into the United States Senate.

The comparison of the vote with that of 1861, when he received less than one-third of the votes, must be to him a source of satisfaction.

ELECTION RETURNS—SEPTEMBER, 1873.

CANDIDATES	Jackson	Clinton	Ione City	Lancha Plana	Volcano	Sutter Creek	Amador	Drytown	Forest Home	Fiddletown	Kirkwoods	Totals
HARBOR COMMISSIONER.												
John W. Boot, (R.)	235	64	121	34	207	171	98	42	7	58	17	94 1195
Paul Neumann, (D.)	176	41	104	2	106	16	30	37	30	30		56 667
SENATOR.												
J. T. Farley, (D.)	229	73	141	46	222	180	111	50	31	78	23	105 1285
John A. Fagan, (R.)	100	31	77	24	80	148	3	40	12	45	4	65 945
ASSEMBLYMEN.												
W. H. Stowers, (R.)	241	69	154	34	221	206	117	52	12	92		20 199 1234
J. M. Johnson, (D.)	218	56	97	79	78	175	94	34	14	42	8	83 999
L. Miller, (R.)	229	52	107	3	236	1	5	59	39	30	79	32 91 1171
J. A. Taggard, (R.)	171	40	07	26	73	121	35	39	27	2	41	69 700
SHERIFF.												
Peter Fagan, (D.)	170	48	69	30	136	179	109	43	14	64	15	73 935
J. Farnsworth, (R.)	189	55	142	31	169	18	74	47	303	12	33	52 727
L. S. Randolph, (Ind.)	69	4	13	7	61	146	31	3	1	11	4	45 408
TREASURER.												
J. A. Butterfield, (D.)	251	13	149	45	241	199	85	43	13	60		24 103 1232
S. G. Spagnoli, (R.)	174	36	89	23	64	141	62	14	30	2	7	64 812
CLERK.												
J. B. Stevens, (D.)	290	69	115	34	199	165	90	30	3	39	14	98 1087
B. F. Richtmyer, (R.)	139	24	110	33	124	117	68	69	42	85	1	119 1017
DISTRICT ATTORNEY.												
T. J. Phelps, (D.)	224	62	100	30	196	161	99	39	13	111	22	95 1185
M. W. Gordon, (R.)	197	44	124	36	100	146	53	56	30	12	9	78 899
ASSESSOR.												
J. W. Surface, (D.)	289	62	150	38	18	299	109	38	22	9	30	80 1266
S. C. Wheeler, (R.)	139	42	73	27	120	123	42	5	22	2	10	92 787
SURVEYOR.												
W. L. McKimm, (D.)	231	67	122	35	199	217	105	40	8	36	17	80 1317
H. C. Meek, (R.)	191	33	105	30	105	18	41	49	31	32	12	76 735
SCHOOL SUPERINTENDENT.												
S. G. Briggs, (D.)	237	67	92	33	209	143	98	49		7	10	82 128
H. L. Gould, (R.)	120	40	115	23	110	160	50	44	42	45	14	92 872
CORONER.												
D. Myers, (D.)	201	50	115	25	179	220	91	38	15	80	17	91 1214
J. S. Hill, (R.)	211	47	109	31	120	114	62	52	30	4	12	42 994

OFFICERS ELECTED IN 1873.

State Senator—James T. Farley (D.)
Assemblymen—W. H. Stowers (D.), Louis Miller (R.)
District Attorney—T. J. Phelps (D.)
County Clerk—J. B. Stevens (D.)
Sheriff—Peter Fagan (D.)
County Treasurer—J. A. Butterfield (D.)
County Surveyor—Wm. L. McKimm (D.)
Assessor—J. W. Surface (D.)
Superintendent of Schools—S. G. Briggs (D.)
Coroner and Public Administrator—D. Myers (D.)

JUSTICES OF THE PEACE.

Township No. 1—J. C. Shipman, Hugh Robinson.
Township No. 2—L. Brusie, L. M. Earl.
Township No. 3—L. McLaine, L. Ludekins.
Township No. 4—J. A. Brown, C. K. Johnson.
Township No. 5—M. B. Church, R. S. Hinkson.
Township No. 6—S. Cooledge, L. G. Lewis.

ALPINE COUNTY LEFT OUT IN THE ELECTION.

When Alpine county was organized, in 1864, it was joined to Amador as a Legislative district, which was allowed one Senator and two Assemblymen. It was a mutual understanding that Alpine should have one Assemblyman, and Amador the other, and the Senator. This arrangement was observed for two Legislative terms, but in 1871 and 1873 the bargain was forgotten in the *hurly burly* of election, and Amador got the whole delegation. It happened, in this way, that Louis Miller, a Republican, was elected to the Assembly, though the party to which he belonged was in the minority. In 1874 Alpine was joined to El Dorado for election purposes, and had no further political connection with Amador.

FINANCIAL MATTERS IN 1874.

January 31st the outgoing Treasurer, O. Button, made the following report:—

Cash in Treasury School Fund	$10,338 19
" " General Fund	13,964 36
Outstanding Warrants on General Fund with interest	134,694 39
Outstanding Warrants on Hospital Fund with interest	33,183 34
Certificates on Current Expense Fund, no interest	6,622 31
Certificates on New Hospital Fund	735 00—$174,599 57
Cash to Apply	13,964 36
Total Indebtedness	$160,504 21
Value of Taxable Property	$2,738,970 00
Rate of Taxation	2 65
Amount of Taxes	72,582 70
Delinquent for 1873	7,162 74

ASSESSMENT ROLL FOR 1874.

Real Estate and Improvements	$1,724,140 00
Personal Property	830,415 00
Mines	503,780 00
Improvements on same	194,310 00
Ditches	61,080 00
Telegraphs	900 00—$3,314,625 00

CONVENTION TO CONSIDER THE FUNDING PROJECT.

The Grand Jury which met at the February term, C. C. Belding, foreman, recommended a serious effort to put the finances on a better basis; proposed a general reduction of the salaries of officers, and a funding of the county indebtedness at a lower rate of interest, and proposed a general mass-meeting on

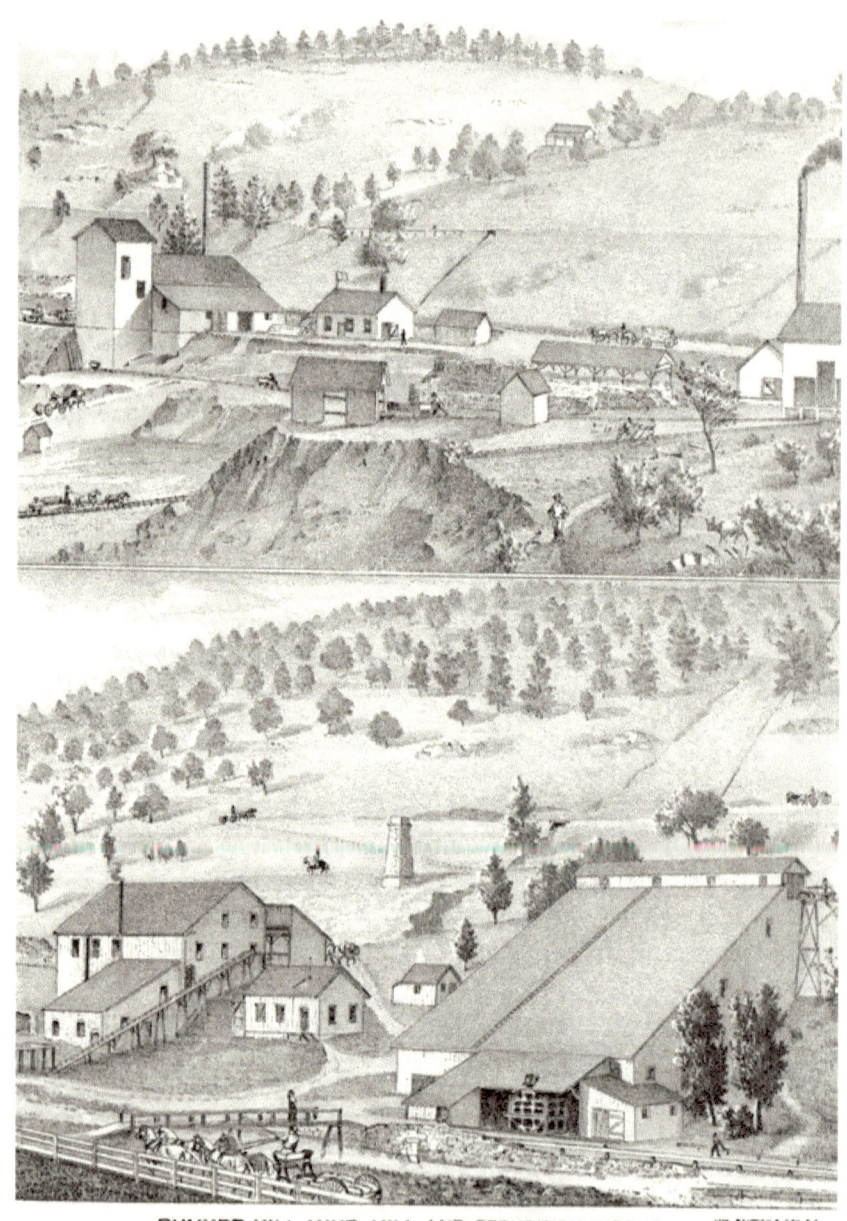

BUNKER HILL MINE, MILL AND REDUCTION WORKS.
ISRAEL W. KNOX, PRES.   NEAR AMADOR CITY, AMADOR CO. CAL.

the 21st instant to consider the situation. The call for a convention was responded to by only a few individuals, who did not seem to have very clear ideas of how refunding the whole debt and issuing bonds bearing interest should lessen the taxes of the county, when a considerable portion of the indebtedness was not bearing interest. The movement was scouted by some as a measure in the interest of the bond-holders, and by others advocated as an economical measure. Nothing resulted from it.

POLITICAL MATTERS OF 1874.

As there were neither national, State, or county elections during this year, the chapter on political matters will be much like the one said to have been written by Dean Smith on the snakes of Ireland, which consisted of the single line, "*There are no snakes in Ireland.*" No momentous events occurred to disturb the serenity of those who were comfortably seated at their desks in the Court House. The newspapers kept up the usual rattle of squibs and fire-crackers, and continued to take in the cash for Sheriff's sales, patent medicines, and "new goods for sale cheaper than ever at the old stand."

FINANCIAL MATTERS, 1875.

March 1st.—J. A. Butterfield, County Treasurer, reported the outstanding warrants with interest—

On Redemption Fund............... $105,436 46
Hospital   " 21,130 58
Certificates not bearing int. rest... 2,342 42—$128,909 46

The assessment roll for this year, was—

Real Estate.................... $977,188 00
Improvements.................. 766,810 00
Personal Property.............. 799,787 00
Money .... 25,138 00—$2,568,913 00

Taxes were assessed on each one hundred dollars—

For State Fund....................... 60c
    General Redemption Fund.......... 65c
    Current Expense Fund.............. 74c
    Hospital Redemption Fund......... 10c
    Hospital Current Expense Fund.... 16c
    School Fund...................... 20c
    Road Fund........................ 5c—$2 60

ROBBERY OF THE COUNTY TREASURY.

This occurred on the night of the 9th of May, 1875. The following account is made up from the files of the *Dispatch* of May 15, 1875:—

Sometime in the night, the residence of the Treasurer (Mr. Butterfield) was entered, and his pants rifled of the key to the inner lock of the safe, the outer one being a Bussey combination lock. The robbers then went to the Court House, unlocked the office door, opened the safe, and took out fifteen thousand two hundred and forty-eight dollars, most of which belonged to the School Fund, consisting of fourteen thousand dollars in gold coin, one thousand two hundred and eight dollars in silver coin, and forty dollars in gold notes. The safe and room were then re-locked, and the prize carried away. There were two checks amounting to one thousand dollars, and some four or five hundred dollars in gold notes, which were not taken. When Mr. Butterfield awoke in the morning, he was affected with dizziness and a sickness of the stomach, and did not get up until after his usual hour of rising, and did not miss the loss of the pants until five o'clock.

When Mr. Butterfield discovered the loss of the key, he suspected that a robbery had been committed, and called upon several citizens to go to the Court House with him to examine the safe. They found the door of the office locked as usual; the safe was also in its usual condition, the outer door being locked, and apparently undisturbed. It yielded to the usual combination, but the larger portion of the money, amounting to fifteen thousand two hundred and forty-eight dollars, was missing. Some spots of candle-grease on the floor, were the only marks of disorder perceptible.

A meeting of the Board of Supervisors was called to consider the matter. A reward of three thousand dollars was offered for the recovery of the treasure, and one thousand dollars for the conviction of the robbers. Some professional detectives were employed to make a thorough investigation into all the circumstances connected with the matter. They decided that it was next to impossible for any one, not acquainted with the combination, to open the door without breaking the lock, or to shut it when opened. On inquiry, it was found that the combination was the one in use during the term of office of his predecessor, Mr. Button; that several persons besides the Treasurer knew the combination; James B. Stevens, the County Clerk, had once opened the safe during a temporary illness of the Treasurer, the combination having been written on a slip of paper for that purpose; that it was called off by another person in the hearing of several others—Mr. Stevens turning the handle to correspond with the letters called.

The detectives were of the opinion that no robbery was committed on the night in question; that it had been abstracted at a time, or at different times, previous to the 9th and 10th of May, by parties who were familiar with the combination. The wildest rumors were immediately afloat concerning the loss of the money. It was said that a syndicate of Court House officers with some outside friends, had been using the funds to speculate in stocks, which, at the time, were making and breaking fortunes for hundreds of lucky or unlucky men. As ten thousand dollars or more of the school funds were frequently left in the safe for months, the use of it in a *certain* venture would do the county no harm. The abstraction of the money with the intention of returning it, was not stealing. All this and much more was put forward as probable excuses for abstracting the public funds. In fact, it was confidently stated that a fortunate speculation was once made by a former Treasurer in that same way.

The Treasurer had erected a costly residence soon after coming into office. He was the owner of a saw-mill and could erect several houses, if necessary, without taxing the mill above its powers, but he had to bear a share of the public rumors. The using of the old combination, which was known to several persons, was a matter which merited blame, and suspicion must necessarily rest upon all who were familiar with the combination and had access to the safe.

Some of the efforts to find the money were ludicrous enough to set the public on the grin. Dr. Randall of Ione, who is a firm believer in his power to call spirits up, or down, from the ethereal deep, and gather knowledge from their more than human wisdom, announced his ability to find the missing money, but the sibyls either knew nothing about it, or set him to digging in the wrong places, for its location is still a mystery—to the public.

June 17, 1875.—At a special meeting of the Board of Supervisors, to consider the loss of the county funds, it was ordered that proceedings be immediately commenced against the Treasurer and bondsmen, for the missing funds.

It may be as well to anticipate the result, and make a connected history of the affair. At the close of Mr. Butterfield's term of office, two experts, employed to investigate the accounts, reported as follows:—

*Cash on hand, March 2, 1874, on taking possession of the office	$ 19,058 50
Amounts received during two years as taxes on property	131,446 01
Poll-taxes	6,834 45
Licenses	6,311 81
State apportionment	24,297 87
Fines in Justices Courts	374 07
Bonds forfeited	43 00
Sales of lumber	10 00
Sales of school lands	2,202 06
Total receipts for two years	$190,592 83
DISBURSEMENTS.	
Warrants redeemed	$132,905 55
Paid State Treasurer	26,653 91
Treasurer's Mileage	154 00
Auditor's allowance	606 07
Cash on hand, March 6	7,030 00
Amount stolen	15,248 00
Accounts otherwise short	4,834 70—$190,592 83
The deficit being	20,142 76

This was incorporated into the judgment, which was obtained against the Treasurer and bondsmen, which, with costs, amounted to twenty-two thousand two hundred and ninety-two dollars and forty-six cents.

"In the District Court, Eleventh Judicial District for the county of Amador.

"Amador county, plaintiff, vs. J. A. Butterfield, et. al., defendants.

"It was held by the Court that the custodian of the county funds was responsible to the county for them in all cases, except by acts of God, or a public enemy, in which cases there might be a doubt. As these conditions were not included in the plea of the defendants, they would not be considered. The Court ordered judgment to be entered against defendants for full amount of loss and costs, amount-

*These figures are copied from newspaper reports, and are evidently incorrect.

ing to twenty-two thousand two hundred and ninety-two dollars and forty-six cents."

The following sureties were included in the judgment, for the sums set opposite their names:—

F. H. Hoffman	$ 4,000	Thos. Carpenter	$ 1,000
Joseph Samuels	3,000	James Adams	2,000
F. Rocco	1,000	P. A. Clute	5,000
A. Chicizola	1,000	Joseph Cuneo	2,000
James Mechan	14,000	R. F. Fry	2,000
E. Muldoon	5,000	A. Rossi	1,000
E. C. Palmer	4,000	J. Coleman	5,000
E. Genochio	2,000	John Vogan	3,000
F. M. Whitmore	1,000	J. W. Surface	3,000
L. McLaine	4,000	R. Ludgate	3,000
L. Cassinelli	4,000	J. P. Surface	3,000
Hiram Beigle	5,000	J. P. Martin	10,000
Chas. Steckler	2,000	F. Hutner	5,000
John Miller	5,000		

CONCLUSION OF THE BUTTERFIELD MATTER, 1877.

At a meeting of the Board of Supervisors in the early part of 1877, to take into consideration the Butterfield judgment for twenty-two thousand seven hundred and one dollars and thirty-one cents, it was ordered that the proposition of the defendants' attorneys, Farley and Porter, to pay the sum of six thousand dollars, in three annual installments without interest, be accepted, the payments to commence April 1, 1877. This compromise was considered best because the sureties resisted the payment of the full amount, and a long and costly suit being the alternative. It was further said: "If we compel the sureties to pay the deficit, no future Treasurer could ever get bonds!"

Mr. Butterfield undertook to work the matter out without loss to the bondsmen, and, though his health was much shattered by the unfortunate affair, it is nearly settled. Public opinion, much against him at first, has become nearly unanimous that he was more sinned against than sinning; a victim rather than a criminal. No clue has yet been obtained to the missing money, though it is generally thought to have gone into Flood and O'Brien's bank, through stock speculations.

POLITICAL MATTERS IN 1875.

The uniform success of the Democratic party during recent years, left the struggle principally for the nominations. Personal popularity was the basis for success in the Convention. Although the national questions were discussed to some extent on the stump, it was done rather in obedience to custom than for any particular interest the people took in the matter. Judge Carter, Democratic nominee for the Assembly, was noted for suavity and pleasing address, and in his progress through the county, mostly let politics alone and dealt in personal reminiscences. Dunlap was a merchant in Sutter Creek, and though not a speaker, had the confidence of the community. Greenwell, his adversary in Sutter Creek, and Brown of Jackson, though men of eloquence and ability, failed to make any inroad on the solid Democratic vote. Brown was in charge of the Amador ditch, and was expending much money in the county. Peck and Aitken, candidates for County Clerk, were both good men, who stood high in the community; also in the societies to which they both belonged. Vogan! who does not know his bland face, twinkling with humor, which has carried sunshine along all the stage-roads since '49? There were no personal objections to the candidates on either side, and when the vote was counted the results were not unexpected.

OFFICERS ELECTED IN 1875.

Assembly—H. A. Carter, Thomas Dunlap.
Sheriff—John Vogan.
District Attorney—T. J. Phelps.
Treasurer—James Meehan.
Surveyor—W. L. McKimm.
Assessor—J. J. Jones.
Superintendent of Schools—W. H. Stowers.
Coroner and Public Administrator—D. Myers.

JUSTICES OF THE PEACE.

Township No. 1—H. Goldner, H. Robinson.
" " 2—L. Brusie, L. M. Earle.
" " 3—L. McLaine, L. Ludekins.
" " 4—C. K. Johnson, L. B. Maxey.
" " 5—M. B. Church.
" " 6—E. R. Yates, S. G. Lewis.

CHAPTER XXIV.
FINANCIAL MATTERS IN 1876.

Political Parties in 1876—Election Returns by Precincts—Finances in 1877—Political Parties in 1877—Returns by Precincts—Death of the Honorable Robert Ludgate—Financial Matters in 1878—Political Parties in 1878—Vote on the Adoption of the New Constitution—Financial Matters in 1879—Political Matters in 1879—Officers Elected—Effect of the New Constitution on the Judicial System—Financial Matters in 1880—Political Parties in 1880—Amador County Election Returns Nov. 2, 1880—Review from 1870 to 1880.

On taking his seat, the Treasurer made a thorough examination of the records of the Treasury. It was found, notwithstanding the losses, that the finances were in a healthy condition.

The outstanding warrants on the—

General Fund	$67,533 94
Hospital Fund	16,713 46
Certificates on Current Expense Fund	4,191 48
Interest Estimated at	38,963 73—$127,402 61

Expenses for year ending March 1, 1875—

Amount allowed on Current Expense Fund	$21,319 17
Amount allowed on Hospital Expense Fund	4,654 32—$25,973 49

Expense for year ending March 4, 1876—

Amount allowed on Current Expense Fund	$21,019 22
Amount allowed on Hospital Expense Fund	3,944 02—$24,963 24
Total for two years	$50,936 73

The Treasurer made a calculation that, the taxes remaining the same, outstanding warrants on the General Fund would be redeemed in four years; the warrants on the Hospital Fund, in eight years.

POLITICAL PARTIES IN 1876.

All parties had heartily united in celebrating the Centennial. Whatever their differences of opinions as to the means of preserving the Union, there were none as to its value. War Democrats, peace Democrats, as well as Republicans, spoke from the same stand, with the same flag floating over them. No one, in listening to the orations, and judging from their tenor alone, would suppose that a few years previous, they had accused each other of treason, and all imaginable crimes. Talk is cheap. If professions of love and devotion to the Constitution and the country are cheap, so are charges of treason and corruption. People do not mean all they say, or say all they mean.

It was evident that a close contest for the Presidency was impending. A few votes in Amador county might decide the vote of the State, and that of the State might decide the Presidential question. Four votes in the city of New York elected a Congressman, whose vote on the thirty-sixth ballot, made Thomas Jefferson President. John Quincy Adams was made President by a small number of votes in the same way. Though disagreeing little on Constitutional matters, and the payment of the national debts, the parties diverged widely as to details. Some were in favor of an unlimited amount of paper money. The Whig doctrines of 1836-40, were revived; only the advocates were found among the members of the hard money party of that day, while most of the Whigs, who, in former times, advocated paper money, were found in the ranks of Republicans, who were generally favorable to a gold and silver currency. Almost every one, old enough to have remembered those days when Jackson and Clay were the leaders of the opposing hosts, might have said with the Roman orator, "Times change, and we change;" for almost every one had changed positions.

As usual, vituperations and accusations, charges of dishonesty and peculations, were made a large element in the campaign. Although Governor Tilden was instrumental in breaking up one of the most gigantic municipal rings that ever controlled a city government, and plundered the people, he was represented as the incarnation of dishonesty, while the Republican party was charged with being the abettor of frauds, running through all the civil service. The administration, from the President down to tide-waiters, was represented as corrupt and dishonest. The "Solid South" was born in this campaign. The Democrats were charged with interfering with the freedom of elections in the Southern States, of traveling around the country in disguise, and whipping, maiming, and even killing, negroes who dared to vote the Republican ticket. According to the Republican orators, no one could enjoy life or property in the old slave States, without conforming to their political creeds. It is not our purpose to write a history of the United States, or to discuss the political issues of that or any other day; but it may be permissible to remark, that a little of the good feeling, manifested in the Fourth of July celebration, carried into the canvass would have done neither party any harm, in votes or otherwise. It is quite probable, first, that scarcely anybody meant all they said, and second, that few men changed their minds or votes in consequence of mutual criminations.

ELECTION RETURNS BY PRECINCTS.

PRECINCTS.	Tilden (D.)	Hayes (R.)	Brown (D.)	Kenfield (R.)	Carpenter (D.)	Page (R.)
Jackson	273	185	273	185	272	185
Clinton	51	32	51	32	51	32
Ione	157	160	157	160	156	160
Lancha Plana	39	44	38	44	38	45
Volcano	162	131	162	131	161	132
Ham's Station	21	11	21	11	21	11
Sutter Creek	173	204	173	204	169	208
Amador City	172	80	172	80	172	79
Drytown	66	81	66	81	64	83
Forest Home	20	37	20	37	19	38
Plymouth	99	136	99	136	87	147
Fiddletown	70	68	70	68	70	68
Enterprise	12	3	12	3	12	3
Total	1315	1172	1314	1172	1292	1191

It may be mentioned as a remarkable occurrence, that the vote at this election approximated the usual vote on county officers, falling only one hundred short of the vote the following year.

FINANCES IN 1877.

The Supervisors reported, March 1, 1877—

Total receipts for three years as $169,055 48
Cash on hand at the beginning of the
  Term 1874 .... 23,767 19—$192,825 67
Disbursements during same time $167,513 36

On hand $46,312 31

October 1st the Treasurer reported—

Outstanding warrants on
  General Fund $52,689 23
  Hospital Redemption Fund 14,502 39
  Current Expense Fund 11,351 84
  Hospital Expense Fund 1,016 21
  Unclassified 89 86
  Deficiency .... 65 80—$79,715 33

This does not include interest. It is not probable that any accurate estimate of interest had been made up to this date, as it was considered the work of several weeks to go over the outstanding warrants and estimate the interest due; hence the apparent contradictions in annual reports. In other instances reports, made before and after the collections of the annual tax, showed a great reduction of the debt when, considering the whole year, no reduction had been made. In March, Judge Williams, of the District Court, decided that the warrants only bore seven per cent. interest, this applying to all that were issued previous to 1858, as well as since.

POLITICAL PARTIES IN 1877.

The occurrence of the county election again brought out a new crop of aspirants. This season Amador was joined with San Joaquin as a Senatorial District, the later county being entitled to one for itself, and another jointly with Amador. James T. Farley, who had been Senator for two successive terms, was now a candidate for the U. S. Senate, and declined a re-election. Frank Brown, who had had some experience in a former canvass as candidate for the Assembly, was nominated a joint Senator with San Joaquin. Dunlap, the former member, and R. Ludgate of Ione, a popular man, were nominated for the Assembly by the Democrats, Judge Carter having declined a re-election. Eagon, who was now working well in the Republican ranks, and James Johnston of Ione, a pioneer and universally liked, were nominated by the Republicans for the same positions. Vogan, incumbent, was re-nominated for Sheriff, running against Frank Howard of Sutter Creek. Meehan, Treasurer, was also re-nominated. Caminetti, a young and active lawyer, popular with everybody in general, especially the ladies, received the nomination of District Attorney at the hands of the Democrats against J. S. Hill, a well-known pioneer, nominated by the Republicans. Henry Peck, County Clerk, was re-nominated by the Democrats. Tom Chicizola receiving the Republican nomination. The men were all popular in their respective precincts, and were expected to make large inroads into the votes of their opponents. Brown and Eagon did the heavy speaking for the Republicans, Caminetti doing similar service for the Democrats. Mr. Farley, however, though not on the ticket, as usual led the Democratic forces. The matter of electing a delegation to the Legislature favorable to his aspirations to the Senatorship, was an important element in the canvass, which was remarkable for the good feeling and absence of the usual vituperation and abuse.

ELECTION RETURNS---1877.

CANDIDATES.	Jackson	Ione City	Lancha Plana	Volcano	Amador Creek	Sutter Creek	Forest Home	Drytown	Plymouth	Fiddletown	Enterprise	Total
SENATOR.												
Cullahan (D.)	227	49	118	45	19	199	176	166	27	85	108	83	13 1249
Brown (R.)	244	57	154	26	39	129	193	71	31	105	157	75	3 1346
ASSEMBLYMEN.												
Ludgate (D.)	282	57	142	44	39	230	165	164	24	54	108	69	18 1354
Dunlap (D.)	268	6	136	8	27	209	155	206	24	55	98	3	1 1245
Eagon (R.)	229	42	118	33	26	119	198	78	28	106	170	71	5 1297
Johnston (R.)	189	42	15	30	33	121	99	165	31	106	172	67	4 1272
SHERIFF.												
Vogan (D.)	300	58	169	48	45	188	173	131	28	99	115	70	10 1469
Howard (R.)	174	42	102	30	14	128	192	253	25	100	155	68	3 1180
CLERK.												
Peck (D.)	298	59	165	44	45	194	173	167	28	6	111	83	13 1477
Chicizola (R.)	165	41	109	29	16	129	96	231	25	94	136	46	2 1106
DISTRICT ATTORNEY.												
Caminetti (D.)	314	75	136	41	26	197	154	169	35	50	109	84	18 1396
Hill (R.)	155	25	133	31	31	129	115	204	36	110	164	81	4 1237
TREASURER.												
Meehan (D.)	312	64	153	42	35	193	171	199	27	51	93	80	13 1506
Potter (R.)	158	37	140	30	22	128	102	192	31	109	206	83	3 1977
CORONER.												
Freeman (D.)	273	57	136	42	36	179	173	165	27	36	101	63	15 1375
Gibson (R.)	199	43	138	30	31	115	108	198	31	109	180	65	4 1241
SCHOOL SUPT.												
Norton (D.)	300	57	136	44	27	181	151	166	25	45	109	6	14 1721
Eblager (R.)	175	45	133	29	28	135	144	231	30	115	163	75	4 1395
SURVEYOR.												
W. L. McKinney (R.)	397	45	132	21	31	130	160	304	37	102	173	68	4 1202

RESIDENCE OF JOHN VOGAN, JACKSON

MOUNTAIN SPRINGS, RANCH AND TOLLHOUSE OF JOHN VOGAN.
IONE & JACKSON ROAD. AMADOR COUNTY, CAL.

JUSTICES OF THE PEACE ELECTED 1878.

Township No. 1—S. G. Spagnoli, H. Goldner.
Township No. 2—L. Brusie, L. M. Earlo.
Township No. 3—L. Ludekin, L. Huey.
Township No. 4—J. Gundry, J. B. Maxey.
Township No. 5—M. B. Church.
Township No. 6—S. G. Lewis, S. Cooledge.

The list of returns is well worth a study. It will be seen that each candidate made large inroads into his opponent's vote in his own district, also, that when the vote was counted, there was a great uniformity in the majorities.

DEATH OF THE HON. ROBERT LUDGATE.

This occurred February 15, 1878, while in Sacramento attending, as far as his failing health would allow, to his duties as Legislator. He was born in the county of Waterford, Ireland, and was forty-four years old at the time of his death. He came to the United States in 1850, and a year later to California, settling in Ione valley, where he built up a home. He was a man of warm feelings, active temperament, strong convictions, and undoubted integrity, winning the respect and esteem of all with whom he became acquainted. His death was not unexpected, as he had been suffering for many years from a pulmonary disease. A committee of both houses was appointed to escort his remains to Ione, and assist in the funeral ceremonies.

FINANCIAL MATTERS IN 1878.

Rates of taxes:—

For State Fund	.55 c.
Gen. Redemption Fund	.57½c.
Current Expense "	.65 c.
Hospital Red'ption "	.15½c.
Hospital Current Expense Fund	.20 c.
School Fund	.24 c.
Road "	.13 c.—$2.50

November 4th, the Treasurer reported outstanding warrants on Current

Expense Fund	$10,947 68	
Hospital Current Expense Fund	224 83	
Salary "	2,530 15	
General Redemption "	43,032 74	
Hospital "	10,138 63—	$66,874 33

This does not seem to include interest, which two years before was estimated at $38,063.73.

This would carry the debt to upwards of $100,000.

POLITICAL PARTIES IN 1878.

The usual political problems were postponed to consider the matter of framing a new Constitution. For once in our history the people were engaged in discussing the first principles of government. The overshadowing growth of the great railroad company, which had extended its Briarian arms, so as to bring every industry, whether mercantile, agricultural, or mechanical, under its influence; the growth of the gas and water companies in the cities; the appropriation of the streams flowing from the mountains by the ditch and water companies; the holding of large tracts of land, amounting in some instances to one hundred thousand acres, for purely speculative purposes, as well as many other similar institutions, caused a general fear in the State, that a few were soon to have the wealth, and that poverty was to be the inheritance of the workers. In the cities the agitation was greatest among the day laborers, who beheld a favored few—unjustly favored in the minds of the laborers—rolling along the streets in easy carriages, while they, who had built the houses, worked the mines, and made the property, were working for barely enough to obtain the merest necessaries of life. In San Francisco, Sacramento, and Stockton, socialistic sentiments prevailed to a great extent, and at one time, when Kearney was organizing the workers, as well as those who never did nor would work, into a voting party, the prospect of a forcible distribution of property was quite imminent. Hundreds of fierce, brutal faces hung on his words and listened for the expected order to help themselves to all they wanted, and, also, take satisfaction for past sufferings and injuries.

During the working of the placer mines, when any one who would work could make three dollars or more per day, thousands wasted their earnings on cards, whisky, or women. A stream of gold flowed to the cities, building up stores, dwellings, and big bank accounts, leaving the worked-out gulches and hills, and the old, worn-out, dilapidated miners as the heritage of the country that furnished the wealth. Many of these demoralized miners drifted towards the cities, following the wake of their departed means, and, homeless, hopeless, and useless, joined the city vagrants in their efforts to compel the restitution of their wasted wealth, their sole political aim being to "give old money-bags hell."

In the country, especially in Amador county, the agitation was on a different basis. Here were numerous small proprietors, owning ten to one hundred acres of land stocked with a few cattle and sheep, who did their own work, and who, by industry and close economy, could make both ends of saving and expenditure meet at the end of the year. Every year the Assessor came around and made a note of every pig, chicken, or cow that was about the place. The land, as well as improvements, was assessed up to full value. If, in consequence of sickness or a failure of crops, the farmer had been compelled to mortgage his home to keep things going, the taxes remained unabated. It was known that men with large sums of money loaned out at high interest, paid nominal taxes. When money could be made to pay two or three per cent. per month it was forthcoming, but when taxes were assessed it was a *nonentity*. It was like the little joker under Lucky Bill's* fingers: now you could see it, but when the thimble was lifted it was not there.

It was known that large tracts of land that were held for purely speculative purposes, paid only a

---

*William Thornton (Lucky Bill) made a hundred dollars or more in Placerville, in 1850, with a piece of sponge, which he dexterously played under two or three thimbles. He indeed thousands of men to bet a hundred on finding it, generally taking in the money.

nominal tax. It was believed that the producing class bore the brunt of taxation, while corporated companies and dealers in stocks virtually escaped.

The subject of taxation was discussed at every fireside in the county. The farmers and gardeners had no feelings in common with the socialist or communist. Dennis Kearney could not have raised a corporal's guard who would indorse his theory of political economy. But the feeling of distrust towards capitalists, for a short time, united the most antipodal extremes, and found the farmers voting with city *proletariats*. This was manifested less in the election of delegates than in the vote to adopt the Constitution afterwards framed. The non-partisan ticket prevailed, Wm. H. Prouty, a farmer of Jackson valley, and John A. Eagon, a lawyer, being elected delegates to the Constitutional Convention. The selection of these two was evidently a compromise or union of the solid parts of both Republican and Democratic parties, as a measure of defense against the wild theories of the Kearney party in the cities.

THE VOTE ON ADOPTION OF THE NEW CONSTITUTION

Showed a preponderance of the farming interest for the Constitution, and of the mining interest against it, Ione City, which was the center of the farming population, giving seventy-one majority for the Constitution, while Amador, Plymouth, Drytown and Volcano were as decidedly against, the former town giving nearly ten to one. This overwhelming opposition was ascribed to the influence of the mine owners, who induced the workmen to believe the mills would stop under the new Constitution.

	For.	Against.
Amador	20	190
Clinton	34	28
Drytown	21	115
Enterprise	1	14
Forest Home	15	31
Ham's Station	8	5
Ione City	174	103
Jackson	207	207
Oleta	62	45
Lancha Plana	32	53
Plymouth	70	166
*Sutter Creek	224	133
Volcano	140	171
Total	1008	1261

Majority for adoption, 253.

FINANCIAL MATTERS IN 1879.

Tax rates:—

For State Purposes	62½c.
General Redemption Fund	57½c.
Expense Fund	67½c.
Hospital Redemption Fund	15½c.
Hospital Current Expense Fund	50c.
School Fund	24c.
Road Fund	13c.—$2 60

*Sutter Creek seemed to have voted differently from the other mining towns. This was owing to a partial resuscitation of the Miners' League.

ASSESSMENT ROLL.

Real Estate	$925,400 00	
Improvements	979,110 00	
Personal Pr'perty	661,369 00	
Money	12,183 00	$2,578,071 00
Taxes on the same	67,307 78	
State Portion	16,179 75	
County Portion	51,128 03	$67,307 78

TREASURER'S REPORT, OCTOBER 31, 1879.

Outstanding Warrants on—

Current Expense Fund	$7,057 66½
Hospital Expense Fund	1,536 48
Salary Expense Fund	8,150 95
General Redemption Fund	41,812 34
Hospital Redemption Fund	8,606 38—$67,463 81½
Cash in treasury to apply	24,847 61
Total Indebtedness	$42,611 20½

As this report was made previous to the application of the current year's revenue, it shows an undue amount of debt.

January 31st, following—

The indebtedness, exclusive of interest	$69,493 76
Cash in Treasury to apply	61,060 31
Leaving	$8,433 45

POLITICAL MATTERS IN 1879.

The election following the Constitutional Convention, would naturally partake of the peculiar character of the previous year's canvass; but it seemed that the reaction setting in over the State, was felt also in Amador county. The impracticability of righting all wrongs by statute law, became manifest as the Convention set about the work, so that the fierce and positive opinions became considerably modified in the course of a few months. The election of most of the old officers was a natural result. Where new ones were substituted, men of moderate opinions were chosen. Dr. Brusie, an old resident of the county, and a highly esteemed man, never had been active in politics, and was elected more for his personal popularity, than for any speeches he had made on the stump. The same might be said of R. C. Downs, who had resided in the county for thirty years. He had been engaged in quartz mining most of the time, in which vocation he had been eminently successful, having opened and developed some of the richest mines in the county, as early as 1851. Fontenrose, the new County Clerk, was a young man, born of Italian parents, and educated in the county. He received the full Republican vote, and also many of the votes of Democratic Italians. This class of foreign citizens formerly voted the Democratic ticket unanimously, but the solidarity is being broken up, and in a few years they are likely to divide on all political questions.

Judge Moore, elected to the position of Superior Judge, is a young and promising lawyer, and fills the position with honor to himself, and satisfaction to all who bring business before him.

It will be observed that B. F. Langford, State Senator, is a resident of San Joaquin county, which, three years before, was joined to Amador as a joint Senatorial District, for one Senator. As Amador had the nomination of the first Senator on that plan, the second fell to San Joaquin.

OFFICERS ELECTED.

Superior Judge—Geo. Moore.
State Senator—B. F. Langford.
Assemblymen—L. Brusie, R. C. Downs.
District Attorney—A. Caminetti.
County Clerk—L. J. Fontenrose.
Sheriff—John Vogan.
Treasurer—James Meehan.
Surveyor—J. A. Brown.
Assessor—A. Petty.
Superintendent Schools—L. Miller.
Coroner and Public Administrator—H. Schacht.

THE NEW CONSTITUTION AND THE JUDICIAL SYSTEM.

At the general election held in the month of September, 1879, the people adopted the new Constitution, which took effect on the first day of January succeeding.

By the provisions of this instrument the entire *judicial system* of the State was revolutionized, and new courts succeeded to the powers and jurisdiction of the old ones. Prior to January, 1880, Hon. George E. Williams, of El Dorado county, was the Judge of the District Court, embracing within its territorial boundaries, the counties of Amador, Calaveras, and El Dorado; and Hon. A. C. Brown was the Judge of the County Court of Amador county.

By the new Constitution the *combined jurisdiction* of these two tribunals in this county, was merged into one court—called the "Supreme Court of the County of Amador," with *one Judge*, who was elected at the general election in 1879, and took his seat on the first Monday in January, 1880.

At that time, Hon. George Moore, of Jackson, was elected to the position of "Superior Judge," for a term of five years. Judge Moore is a native of Kentucky, a regular graduate of Centre College, and at the date of his elevation to the bench was about thirty years of age, being one of the youngest Superior Court Judges in the State.

This new judicial system, which establishes and keeps open at all times, a court of general common law, equity, and criminal jurisdiction in each county of the State, would, it was thought, greatly facilitate the speedy trial of causes, and prove more economical in every way, both to litigants and tax-payers.

Having now watched its workings for one year, we are satisfied that these expectations are being fully realized. In this, and indeed in every county throughout the State, we find that it is daily growing in popularity with both bar and bench, as well as with the people. We no longer hear from any quarter, the many complaints in reference to the delay and expense incident to litigation under the old system; but all who are best posted touching these matters, unite in saying that the change was one much needed, and one which will promote the best interests of the entire State.

FINANCIAL MATTERS IN 1880.

At the close of the fiscal year the Treasurer reported outstanding warrants on—

Current Expense Fund	$10,101 71	
Salary Fund	7,344 41	
Hospital Expense Fund	456 57	
Redemption Fund, excluding interest	41,812 54	
Hospital Redemption Fund	8,601 38	$60,493 76
Cash in Treasury to apply		61,060 31
Indebtedness exclusive of interest		$8,433 45

It would have been more satisfactory to have known the exact amount, but the calculations of interest seem to be repulsive to most persons except those who are to receive it. The most careless reader will perceive that the debt is being gradually extinguished, however, forming a pleasing contrast to the end of the previous decade, when the principal was one hundred thousand dollars, and the interest as much more, amounting to two hundred and eight thousand dollars, with habits of careless extravagance to add to the burden.

POLITICAL PARTIES OF 1880.

With the return of the Presidential campaign came the resort to abuse. It looks like folly to recur so often to these things. Those who, for the first time, vote the Presidential ticket might imagine that it was possible that a rascal had wriggled into the nomination. Those whose memory extends back a half century, or whose reading extends over the hundred years of our national existence, will know that this personal abuse is peculiar to no age, no Presidential campaign, no year; that it does not depend upon malaria in the atmosphere or dyspepsia prevailing in the national stomach, but is incidental to a free discussion of political matters, whether by a mob of Athenians, a body of dignified Senators, or a crowd of sand-lot political economists. No man, however exalted his character, can expect to escape. Washington, Jefferson, Jackson, and Lincoln, men whom a grateful posterity have enshrined, felt the bitterness of vindictive misrepresentation. At the close of Washington's administration, a resolution approving his administration and recommending his successors to follow in his footsteps, met the fiercest opposition. Mr. Giles, Senator from Virginia, Washington's own State, remarked: "I do not consider his administration an able one; on the contrary, I think it is to his imbecility and cowardice that we owe all our misfortunes." Probably no President ever received severer language on the floor of Congress. Quite a number of men voted against the resolution, among the number being Andrew Jackson, then a Senator by appointment from the recently admitted State of Tennessee. The *Philadelphia Aurora*, a leading Republican paper, commenced an article, on the day spoken of, in this wise:—

"'Lord lettest thou now thy servant depart in peace, for mine eyes have seen the glory of thy salvation.' If ever any nation had reason to utter this, it is this nation. If any people ever had occasion to utter it, it is this people, for this day the author of all our woes retires to private life. Let him go to that retirement which he so much desires."

And much more of the same sort. Volumes could be filled with the written and spoken abuse of our best men; but it is not the province of this work to contain a history of the United States. The vituperation, the charges of treason, cowardice, dishonesty, and everything else conceivable that is bad, that were hurled at the distinguished men who were candidates for the Presidency, are the subjects of mystery. That Garfield should have sold himself for three hundred and twenty-nine dollars, or that Hancock contemplated handing his army over to the rebels, is, now that the campaign is over, too absurd to deserve a thought. How people can bring themselves to such a mental condition is mysterious, but it is probably the same faculty of imagination which induced a man to think he had married an angel and then induced him to larrup her within an inch of her life in less than a week from the wedding day. The election passed off, and as the sun went down so did the passions and anger which the occasion had engendered, the smoke of the jubilee bonfires and powder being the last of it.

ELECTION RETURNS—1880.

CANDIDATES	Jackson	Clinton	Ione	Lancha Plana	Volcano	Dhan's Station	Amador	Sutter Creek	Drytown	Forest Home	Plymouth	Fiddletown	Total
PRESIDENT.													
Hancock (D.)	309	58	145	47	210	17	166	192	63	37	132	73	1411
Garfield (R.)	27	23	145	49	193	11	136	218	60	39	188	74	1343
CONGRESS.													
J. R. Glascock (D.)	293	51	157	47	210	17	163	193	48	37	153	74	1339
H. F. Page (R.)	277	29	145	49	195	11	139	214	65	39	189	73	1348
ASSEMBLYMEN.													
Thomas Dunlap (D.)	381	58	146	47	220	16	149	204	44	39	123	71	1377
C. D. Swift (D.)	290	55	16	48	199	17	157	193	48	25	123	78	1333
J. A. Eagon (R.)	280	24	12	48	184	17	86	160	90	40	176	59	1242
Chapman Watkins (R.)	275	27	139	49	195	11	147	215	60	39	198	59	1400

The careful reader will see that the average Democratic majority has been decreasing for some years, being less than one hundred where it was formerly three hundred. The two persons elected to the Legislature were new men. Swift, a man of reading and culture, had modestly kept in the background until forced to accept a nomination. Watkins is a professional miner, who has studied the structure of veins, wall rocks, dips, and strikes, more than tariffs and taxes. He is a man of mature judgment and inflexible integrity, and is not likely to be bribed or led into the support of vicious legislation.

REVIEW FROM 1870 TO 1880.

At the beginning of this decade the county was two hundred and eight thousand dollars in debt; the population was decreasing; the placer mines had become comparatively exhausted; the population, being made up largely of women and children, instead of the stalwart, healthy men who settled the country, had become less self-sustaining, and a general decline in all industrial industries seemed imminent. The towns of Sutter and Amador alone seemed to be in a flourishing condition. These towns furnished the best market for lumber, wood, and agricultural products, and in one way and another contributed towards sustaining every industry. We have seen the effect of economy in county expenditures, which, without increasing the rate of taxation, has so worn away the public debt that it is expected to call in the last outstanding warrant by the first of January, 1884. Though quartz mining has mostly ceased in Sutter Creek, where its annual productions once reached millions, it has been placed on a paying basis in several places (notably Volcano and Plymouth), where it was not profitable before, and largely increased in other places, as Amador and Jackson. New mines are being opened at several places which bid fair to rival, in richness and permanency, the once rich mines of Sutter Creek. Agriculture has received a new impetus, and small vineyards, orchards, and farms, are appearing on the hill-sides and valleys, which are made to teem with life by means of the water from the mining ditches. The population is increasing in numbers, the census returns showing an increase of one thousand seven hundred and forty since 1870, being nearly twenty per cent. More permanent buildings are being erected, and more extensive farming operations contemplated. The population have less expectation of getting rich suddenly, and are more willing to labor for a fair compensation. Better school-houses are being erected and the attendance is more constant, showing better results in every way.

The once common vices of gambling and drinking with the usual accompaniments of lewdness and obscenity, are vanishing before a healthy public opinion, a sense of self-respect taking the place of the recklessness of early days. Most of the surroundings are conducive to the building up of peaceful, honorable industries, and an industrious and virtuous community.

NOTE.—Those who undertake to verify the statistics of the last two chapters, will discover many inaccuracies. They have been compiled from newspapers, the official reports not being accessible. Only professional statisticians, like DeBow or Walker, can handle large columns of figures without confusing them. Though imperfect in detail, the general results are substantially correct. The publishers give them as the best attainable.

CHAPTER XXV.
GEOLOGY OF AMADOR COUNTY.

Strata in Buena Vista Mountain—Carboniferous Clays—Granitic Sandstone—Glacial Epoch—Supposed Section of the Mountains—Former Course of the Rivers—Account of the Blue Lead—Stratified Rocks—Serpentine Range—Chromate of Iron.

SOME account of its geology seems absolutely necessary in connection with the extensive mining interests; yet it is rather dangerous ground to step on. Every day is bringing some discovery, which sweeps away an old and well-established opinion. To write an opinion of its geology may subject one to the fate experienced by Dr. Lardner, who wrote a very copious book, demonstrating beyond a doubt the impossibility of crossing the ocean by steam. About the time the book was well out, a steamer crossed the ocean, without paying any attention to the *impossibility*. It would be of little use to the majority of the readers of this book to tell them that the slates were what is called *hypogene schistose*, by some authors, to signify that they might have come from the earth in an injection between the vertical rocks; or *metamorphic* slates by others, to signify that they had been altered by heat, or other causes; that these slates were generally metaliferous, and that veins of ores of all kinds might be found in such rocks. These matters are known to scientific readers, and are but the skeleton parts, which must be clothed with a thousand accompanying facts to make geology a living, interesting topic. The limits of this work will not permit a full treatise of the geology of this county, even if the author were fully able, which is not the case. Only the most obvious and important matters, with the proofs that can be seen without much trouble or expense, will be noticed.

A large volume might be written on the subject, without exhausting it; and years, aye, a life-time, might be spent in the study of geology, and still only penetrate the outer precincts of the science. A distinguished geologist, who had given a quarter of a century to the study, said if one could live a thousand years he might know something about it. While the author disclaims any pretensions to profound knowledge of this subject, in justice to himself and readers, he claims to have given it much thought. Twenty-five years' residence in the county, close and careful observation, with perhaps as much reading as generally falls to a laboring man, has given him an opportunity to appreciate, if not to master, the difficulties of some of the problems in *geology*. As scarcely one of the subscribers to this work will claim or acknowledge any skill in this science, the writer may be excused for treating it in a popular manner. If some one of our young readers may be induced to give the subject his attention, if only one Hugh Miller, is kindled with a desire to be able to read the records of creation, as told by the rocks, and shall give a score of years of active, vigorous life, to the examination of the subject, so as to be able to give the world a *true geology*, the writer will have been a thousand times remunerated.

TIME.

In treating of geology, I must ask my readers to make a free use of *time*. Let thousands, aye, hundreds of thousands of years enter into our calculations without fear of using up that part of the material, for Nature is never pressed for time. No matter how small the yearly progress, time will accomplish great changes. Those who have given chronology thorough study, think they can trace the creation back *six hundred millions of years*. Let us consider too that change, if not life, is the inherent quality of all matter; that no form is permanent; that the "eternal hills" is true not for a day even; that the loftiest mountain, buttressed with granite, was once sleeping beneath the sea, and will again; that the deep sea holds mountain chains in her bosom, that will, in their own good time, emerge to the light.

As all stratified rocks, or at least such as we are likely to meet with, were once horizontal, let us go back in imagination to the time when the deep sea was rolling over our own Sierra Nevadas. We must not hesitate in the cause of science, to sink also the Utah basin, and even the Rocky Mountains. It matters not that some of our sarcastic friends tell us that we have no ground to stand on; that will appear presently. We have now the sea, deep as the Atlantic, rolling over the future Great West. Only a portion of the continent, perhaps the White Mountains and Apalachian range, are yet out of the sea. It is during these immensely long periods that the slates and the rocks, the future sources of mineral wealth, are deposited in the deep sea. Age after age (time is no object) the deposit goes on, perhaps the thousandth part of an inch a year. Minerals, suspended or in solution in the water, may be brought and deposited, either by precipitation or by gravity, and compounded into the mass. Every one has seen how iron is precipitated by a small particle of sea-weed along the shore, the iron in turn uniting with something else—lime, salt, magnesia, potash, silex, alumina, and, perhaps, gold and silver, through chemical changes that are constantly intermingling, changing, and forming new compounds. The coral insect goes to work, and, laying hold of each particle of lime that comes along, incorporates it into a solid reef—the future limestone ranges of the continent that is forming. The smallest insect, the infusoria, finding the water charged with silex, lays hold of the atoms, builds its tiny shells so small that a thousand millions would not make an inch, and patiently, year after year, age after age, piles up the little shells, until five, ten, perhaps fifty feet of infusorial earth forms the material for the quartz veins of our continent yet to be. Ten thousand, twenty thousand, and sometimes fifty thousand feet of various minerals may be deposited in this way, all this matter being slowly worn away from some pre-existing land, which perhaps has had a birth in a former cycle. As the material accumulates and acquires depth, the internal heat of the earth, which is manifested in all deep mines, by an increase of temperature of one degree for each sixty feet or thereabouts, begins to facilitate and perhaps produce chemical changes in the first formed strata, which soon lose their former texture and become our future metamorphic, or, as they were formerly called, the *hypogene schistose* rocks. Allowing an increase of one degree for each sixty feet, we have for a depth of forty thousand feet a heat of six hundred or more degrees, and making allowance for rents and seams permeating the mass, probably much greater in places. And now for some unknown reason, the great mass, so long quiet, slowly arises out of the water, not all at once, but in long, parallel reefs, one preceding the other perhaps by ages; low and marshy at first, but soon, geologically speaking, assuming shape. Whether from a greater force of upheaval or from a weakness or want of cohesion, some of these ranges, or axes of elevation, break for great distances, and granite is erupted, forming mountains, down whose sides water begins to run, carrying the *detritus* or decay into the new valleys. The mineral matters, having undergone great changes in the depth of the earth, appear, perhaps, concentrated into veins.

Now, let us consider for a moment the appearance of these different strata. At first horizontal and existing in floors and parallel layers, they are now distorted, bent in places into the shape of a "U," in others into a "V" shape, the lower parts being still down thousands of feet in the earth, subject to the six hundred or more degrees of heat, which were before referred to. If we could see the strata in its shape where the mountain chains are being elevated, it would present an appearance something like a hundred or more layers of cloth pressed edgewise together, thus:—

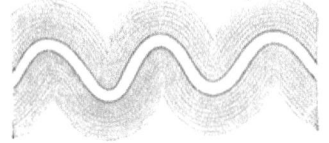

The reader will not for a moment consider that the different layers of rock will hold together like cloth; we have supposed the breakage to take place where the greatest strain occurred, which would be on the top of the bends or bights. We must also consider these bends, anywhere from ten to twenty miles apart, or at least twice the thickness of our deposit in the sea, though these mountain elevations may be hundreds or even thousands of miles apart, in which case we might have a valley like the space between the Alleghany and Rocky Mountains, or with unequal elevations, we might have a valley like the space between the Sierra Nevada and Rocky Mountains with short ranges interspersed.

We have presumed upon the tops of these bights or axes of upheaval, breaking so as to expose the lower lying strata. In fact, denudation would set in and the tops of these elevations would be cut off nearly to the line of the primitive or granitic rocks. It is now evident that the lower or first formed rocks, being the hardest or most highly metamorphosed, would form the tops of the ridges, even where the granite had not cropped out.

The formation of mountain ranges is a thing of past ages, but is a product of forces still in operation. Slowly the Coast Range is emerging from the sea, and along the base of the Sierra Nevada Mountains, as well as the Coast Range, are indisputable marks of a former sea-shore, when both ranges of mountains and the intervening valley were some hundreds of feet lower than at present. How many of these axes of elevation occur in the Sierra Nevadas, may not be determined, but it is quite certain that the higher mountains were, so to speak, in active operation while the foot-hills, where the principal mines are, were still the floor of the ocean. It is also certain that the older or higher ranges had auriferous quartz veins, while the present worked veins were either unformed or slumbering in the depths of the sea. Those who have never studied the rocks, except to learn their economic value, can form but little idea of the history of their creation, which their texture, quality and locality relate. A boy who picks up a rounded quartz pebble considers it a good article with which to pelt a dog or knock a squirrel out of a tree; a gravel miner would consider it an indication of a hill deposit, and forthwith would commence a shaft on the top of the nearest hill; while a railroad man would think a deposit would make splendid material to ballast his road. A geologist would immediately ask, "Where is the river which rounded this pebble? for every rounded pebble is the result of pluvial action. Where is the quartz vein from which this has been torn?" A bed of boulders on the top of a hill marks the bed of an ancient river, though the present stream runs some hundred feet below. He will tell you that in by-gone ages the river was *up there;* that the valleys had been made by erosion. So every rock, every pebble, has its history. The placers which were worked in an early day—Tunnel Hill, Butte Basin, Prospect Hill, American Hill at Oleta, as well as Loafer Hill—all speak of a system of rivers, and of course a system of quartz veins from which the gold was filched. The vast masses of sand, gravel, and clay, with which the San Joaquin valley is filled, as well as the eroded valleys, ancient rivers, and lava-capped hills, all testify of the forces that have helped to make our present abode.

A history of the denudation may be read in the layers of potter's clay, gravel, sand, and lava, that form the foot-hills and the bed of the San Joaquin valley. The Buena Vista mountain is, perhaps, from its exposure on several sides, a convenient book of reference. Standing on the top of this, one may see many parts of the original plain, of which this mountain formed a part, that once rested on the valleys of Ione, Buena Vista, and Buckeye, from three hundred to six hundred feet thick, sloping to the edge of the former sea-shore, which was forced farther away as the masses of matter carried down by the rivers filled the valley or basin, precisely as the *debris* or *slickens* is now filling up the low places. The top of this mountain is about six hundred feet above the valley, and seems to have formed a part of the same plain which extended east past Jackson, Sutter, and Amador, though at these last-named places the plain was some hundreds of feet higher than at Buena Vista. Marks of this plain can be seen around the base of Butte mountain, which stood, like Thomas H. Benton, "solitary and alone," while the shallow rivers fumed and fretted at its feet, depositing beds of auriferous gravel to be scrambled for in after ages. Let us see what the

BUENA VISTA MOUNTAIN

Is composed of. Commencing at the top, we find indurated volcanic ash, or what may be termed trachyte, with some indications of columnar cleavage............ 80 feet.
Coarse fragments of lava, not hardened, forming a loose, porous soil. This is the sloping portion, below the bold part of the hill.................................. 100 feet.
Bed of volcanic and quartz gravel, containing some gold .... 50 feet.
(This, on the surrounding hills, is the bed upon which is generally superimposed the *breccia*, or unwashed lava, not having been rounded by the action of water.)
Sandstone, resembling granite, suitable for building purposes.................... 40 feet.
(In some of the surrounding hills this becomes of a fine red color, owing to the presence of sesquioxide of iron. The balustrade of the steps of the Court House in Jackson are made of this stone.)
Clays of different kinds, containing, in places, iron ore, sometimes white, sometimes composed of sand, white as snow, supposed to be mostly from volcanic material, as in corresponding strata; farther west, pieces of pumice-stone of fine quality abound......................... 200 feet.
Carboniferous clays and sandstones, containing impressions of vegetation, mostly of the kinds now growing, such as alder, ash, pine, cedar, spruce, with some of leaves resembling the palm. The feathers of birds are also converted into coal, and preserved in the seams of clay......... 100 feet.
(These clays are the matrices of the coal beds, which vary in thickness from a mere stain to several feet.)
Ferruginous clay, containing spheroidal concretions, from a foot to six feet in diameter, with impressions of leaves and plants. The discovery of an old well, with cut stone walls, proved to be the lower half of a concretion, the shell of which bore much resemblance to a stone wall.................................... 40 feet.
Coarse clay and beds of sand, with some vegetable remains half converted to coal. These veins furnish water for the artesian wells; when traced to the mountains they become auriferous gravel-beds (*)... 150 feet.

These strata all have a descent to the west of about one hundred feet to the mile, and correspond nearly with the ascending beds of the ancient east and west rivers; thus, continuing the line east at Jackson, the elevation of the plain would be about twelve hundred feet; at Volcano twenty-five hundred. This plain terminates in the present Sacramento or San Joaquin plain, about five or six miles west. The lava flow may be seen in several places dipping into the ground, or into the level that was once a sea-shore line, as at Whipples, near the Poland House on the Mokelumne river; on the mountain west of J. P. Martin's lower ranch, where it forms the crest of the mountain; on the hills south of the Newton mine, and, perhaps, in a hundred other places in the county.

I have deemed it necessary to particularly notice the formation of the foot-hills, because here we have a record of the denudation that has gone on in the mountains, the separate layers each telling its story. Let us examine the lowest formation, which here rests on the hardest and most highly metamorphosed slate we meet with in the whole series of the foot-hills, the slaty structure being very hard to trace. These reefs of rocks form the dividing lines, and frequently, the boundaries of the valleys; as, for instance, the hill near the junction of Dry creek with Jackson creek, and the same class of rocks north and south of Jackson valley. In looking at these one can easily believe they have been a mass of boulders, partially melted and fused together. You can easily pick out rocks of different kinds, which seemed to have formed the original mass, yet the geologists tell us that they were never melted; that this apparent fusion occurred when the rocks were in a plastic state, and that the boulder appearance is due to the tendency to spheroidal concretion, manifested by all plastic substances. The long reefs of rocks, smoothed as if with a plane, show the wash of a surf for an indefinite period of time, and the subsequent burying by matter, held in suspension, indicates a calm, sheltered bay, where the tides and currents were gentle.

---
*These figures are in round numbers. The depth or thickness of the strata constantly varies.

If we examine the gravel at the base of the slate hills, we shall find no volcanic matter; quartz, slate, and granite boulders only. This would indicate a considerable period of erosion, of denudation of the hills before any eruption of lava. The next deposit is mostly destitute of volcanic matter, but contains much iron, indicating a breaking down of ledges or rocks containing iron and sulphur, as secondary sulphurets are frequent; in fact, much of the gravel of this age is cemented by sulphurets; for instance, in the lower beds of gravel in Mat Murray's claim, at Lancha Plana.

THE CARBONIFEROUS CLAYS.

These contain a great deal of volcanic matter which seems to have been carried into the rivers as ashes, pumice-stone and scoriæ. In many places the pumice-stone, as in the hills west of Ione, is found in considerable quantities. The streams depositing this were apparently running in broad, shallow channels, with but small depression, the layers being regular, and sometimes so thin that hundreds of different deposits may be found in the thickness of a foot. The length of this period seems to have been immense. We can conceive something of the number of years necessary to fill up a valley, even like that of the Sacramento or San Joaquin with running rivers, bankfull of mud, gravel, and sand; but to calculate the time a gentle current, perhaps only discolored with clay, would require to fill an open sea, or bay, a hundred feet or more deep, makes quite a draft on our stock of time. In this deposit we find the coal-beds which seem to be nothing more than masses of drift-wood, of the kinds now growing on the surrounding hills, such as cedar, pine, oak, manzanita, and alder, the latter being particularly abundant, inclosed in the tight clays, and imperfectly carbonized. This part of the subject will be treated more fully under the head of coal.

If a heavy draft on time was necessary for the deposite of the carbonaceous strata, a much heavier one is necessary for the overlying clays, which are, in places, two hundred feet thick. In some places they are alternate with beds of infusorial earth, which could have been deposited only in clear water holding silex, not in suspension, but in solution, as a hundredth, or perhaps a thousandth part of an inch of mud would have destroyed the insects which build these little shells.

These clays have an economic value, as fine pottery is being made from them, and it is quite probable that porcelain will, at no distant day, be manufactured, using the clays and quartz of the higher ranges.

GRANITIC SANDSTONE.

There is little volcanic matter in this. The deposit shows a breaking down of granitic rocks, and a more vigorous wash of the streams, indicating an increased altitude of the mountains, and consequently a greater carrying power to the water.

BOULDER FORMATION.

For the first time in our record, we find a volcanic boulder in the drift. The volcanoes now disgorge lava, solid rock, instead of ashes and scoriæ, and are evidently in full operation, the streams being all at work. In many places the lava deposits quite hide the rock-beds heretofore traversed by the streams, as the drift is composed wholly of volcanic boulders which cover thousands of acres, in fact, half the hills of the county seem capped with them. They are hard, almost indestructible, and, wherever a mass has been deposited, effectually protect the ground from erosion.

Breccia, or lava, is found still higher than the boulders, and sometimes has completely filled the channels, turning the rivers into entirely new courses. These masses of lava flowing red hot to the sea, must have presented a magnificent sight to man, if he existed. Boulders of considerable size are found in the lava, but were probably formed by spheroidal concretion, or by being rolled or crowded along while in a partially melted state. This formed the climax of volcanic action. But for the presence of volcanic ash on the breccia, or lava, we might conclude that the volcanoes ceased their working after the terrific outpour of lava, but it would seem that they quieted down gradually, perhaps were in their old age for centuries. Extensive as the flow was, Amador county was only on the outer edge of the volcanic action; farther north the whole country, for thousands of square miles, was covered so deeply that no rivers have cut their way through it. If it buried gold mines, they are still there. This outflow of lava and boulders pushed the shore-line of the bay some seven or eight miles farther out, burying the drift-wood hundreds of feet deep. If we could have seen Amador county at this time, it would have presented the appearance of a vast plain with a few peaks, like the Butte mountain, and a few of the higher points west of the quartz belt, standing above the mass of lava and boulders. It could have had no vegetation, any more than the Modoc lava-bed. What a few acres are now, barren and sterile, the whole county was then. It could have sustained no vegetation. Some of the places are left, especially in the upper parts of the county.

It must not be inferred that a uniform mass of lava covered the county. The same water-shed as now sent its streams to the sea, meandering upon the plain, piling up here gravel and there sand, changing their courses frequently. Nearly all the strata, described in this chapter as belonging to the Buena Vista mountain, thin out as we strike the slates, and many are entirely lost; a few of the more extensive, like the lava boulder and clay formations, have their representatives in the more elevated parts of the county.

GLACIAL EPOCH.

A new actor comes upon the scene. From being covered with streams of melted lava, flowing in a

JOHN A BROWN

GEOLOGY OF AMADOR COUNTY.

fiery stream to the sea, the ice king throws his mantle over it, and claims it for his own. As in all the rest of North America, or at least the northern part of it, the falling snows accumulated thousands of years, until, compacted into ice, they were miles in depth. There is not room here to prove the glacial theory. One must read it for themselves, or look for its track in our mountain cañons, or on our long sloping plains. They must see, as the author has seen, the piles of rock, miles in extent, heaped up by them, and the vast surfaces worn away, smoothed down as with a gigantic plane, which it is; then the track of a glacier will be recognized, as easily as the track of a land-slide. These glaciers reached to the sea-line, though the heaviest work was done towards the summits. These great masses of ice move, slowly it is true, twenty or thirty feet in a year, forcing along everything in their way that is movable. Granite boulders, twenty feet in diameter, are held in the ice as in a vice, and cut their way through lava, through slate, and through granite, leaving the powdered *debris* to be carried off in the melting stream, in the shape of clay. How long these streams continued is uncertain; long enough to erode deep cañons in the hardest rocks. Silver lake is a glacial erosion, for —— years it moved down the cañon below Silver lake, down the American river, cutting its way with irresistible force; but the glacial epoch had its time, and the ice king slowly surrendered his dominions, retreating up the mountain sides, stubbornly contesting each foot of ground. At Silver lake, he made a last stand before a complete surrender. The ice could get no farther than the outlet of the lake, and melted at that point. Here were accumulated the broken and worn-out tools, used in the excavation, piled up in a great mass across the lower end of the lake. These dams, or piles of rocks, so well known to geologists, are called moraines and always mark the retreat of a glacier. The outlet of the lake has not yet worn much below the channel, left at the melting of the great mass. Those who are curious enough to examine them, may find several small glaciers, a few acres in extent, around the lake. We may well believe that a mass of ice a couple of miles in depth, forced along by several miles more upon the mountain sides, could scoop out a basin like Silver lake, or even like Tahoe lake, which is also a glacier erosion. The basin of Volcano is also a glacial erosion, the glacier melting and leaving a lake nearly a hundred feet deep, which shrunk away as the waters cut the cañon deeper. The limestone, sometimes smoothed as if hammered and polished, and then, again, honey-combed by the streams flowing from the melting mass of ice, have kept a faithful record of the matter. Butte basin is also another glacial erosion, with this difference, however, it was filled up within a short time after the melting of the ice. The long sloping valleys around Jackson, Sutter, Amador, and Plymouth,

have the same origin. As a general thing, a valley with the bed-rock near the surface, worn smoothly away, without regard to the character of the rock, is the result of glacier erosion, as is also a long, straight, or nearly straight, channel of a creek. A crooked channel, dodging the hard places, is a water erosion. The present channels of the streams are below the channels eroded by the glaciers, from one hundred to four hundred feet, so that the track of the glaciers must be looked for on higher ground.

If we could take a section a few miles in depth, out of the mountains between Ione and Volcano, the appearance would be something like the following rough drawing:—

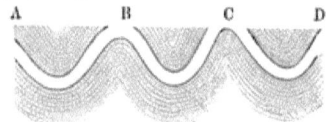

We will suppose "A" to be in the vicinity of Ione; "B" to represent the serpentine range which passes the Mountain Spring House; "C" to be the ridge west of Jackson, Sutter Creek, Amador, and Plymouth, and "D" to be the ridge west of Volcano and the principal marble range, these points being the axes of elevation, no attempt being made to preserve the relative distances. Further examination might show another axis of elevation between the Mother Lode, as it is called, and the limestone range, but the present diagram is accurate enough to illustrate the theory of denudation, the mineral veins and the ancient valleys. It will be seen from this that a great portion of the elevation is gone. It may have been, probably was, miles in depth, for the limestones that now form such prominent objects in many parts of the county are destitute of fossils, with a high crystalline formation, which changes could have been accomplished only under the pressure of a superincumbent mass of perhaps, miles in depth. The same pressure was requisite to obliterate the fossils of the metamorphic rocks constituting the summits of the hills at the axes of the elevations. If any one should object to this as involving too great a removal of earth, a question as to the source of the material forming the San Joaquin and Sacramento valleys might prepare his mind to assent to the denudation.

FORMER COURSE OF THE RIVERS.

The present rivers intersect these ridges or former mountain ranges, yet there are many facts showing a system of rivers running parallel with these lines of elevation. Looking at these mountains in a clear day, from an elevated point on the Sacramento plains, one may easily trace the course of these rivers by their banks which have been only partially obliterated. From Bear Mountain in Calaveras to the ridges west of the lower end of Indian creek, in the northern part of the county, and the ridges west of the quartz mines of Nashville and Aurum City, the marks of an ancient valley are unmistakable. The other valleys, though not so prominent, may be easily traced. The gravel beds also furnish another incontestible proof of the existence of these valleys. The glacial erosion did not wholly obliterate the beds of the ancient rivers. Beginning with Tunnel hill, where we find a large deposit, we pass northward, passing Jackson, which we find to be in the track of a glacier, to the hills east of the Gate, when we again come upon the river bed. North of the Gate it passes under the lava ridge, shows itself on the east side of the town of Sutter Creek in several places, though it is somewhat obscured where the east and west streams intersect it. An examination of the gravel will generally determine the age of the stream. As the stream we are following existed previous to the volcanic era, we shall find few or no boulders of that formation. East of Amador and Plymouth the traces are nearly obliterated. Snake Flat, east of the Gover mine, probably is a relic of the river. East of Volcano we also find the same evidence of former streams. Prospect hill, now overgrown with pines, Humbug hill, and the hills in the vicinity of Spanish gulch, the hills farther up the forks of Sutter Creek, Mason's claim, Hall's claim, the Italian claim,—all belong to that age of deposit. The streams must not be confounded with the subsequent rivers which intersected all that we are speaking of. The rivers of the first instance were shallow, meandering along valleys of considerable width, following no certain direction and frequently changing their channels. The quartz boulders abounding in these channels do not indicate a powerful stream but rather a steady wear; furthermore, the boulders, especially the heavy ones, were not moved far from the veins, which usually may be found within a short distance. It is highly probable that the actual elevation of these rivers was much less than at present. Perhaps at this time a description of the great lead of California may be introduced as showing the character of the rivers existing previous to the volcanic era. This description is taken from the *Overland Monthly*, and is worthy the attention of all desirous of a knowledge of the former systems of rivers. We propose to show in a future chapter the possible continuation of the river into this county, all traces of it having been, according to our best authorities, lost.

THE DEAD RIVERS OF CALIFORNIA.

"What is a dead river?"

"The simplest reply to this natural question would be, that a dead river is one which formerly existed, but exists no longer. In volcanic regions it sometimes happens that the liquid lava, seeking the lowest ground, fills up the beds of rivers which would die, and are replaced by water courses running in other channels, and in different directions. These dead streams are so few and of little importance elsewhere, that as yet, no class-name has been given them; but in California they are among the chief sources of its mineral wealth, and among the most remarkable features of its geological formation. They take us back to a remote era, before the time of Rome, or Greece, or Egypt, far back beyond the origin of history or tradition, before our coast had taken its present shape; before the Sierra Nevada had risen to its present elevation; before Shasta, and Lassen, and Castle Peaks, had poured out their lava floods; before the Sacramento river had its birth, and while, if not before, the mastodon, the elephant, the rhinoceros, the horse, the mammoth bull, the tapir, and the bison, lived in the land. They are indeed among the most remarkable discoveries of the age, and among the greatest wonders of geology. They deserve some common name, and we have to choose between 'extinct' and 'dead.' We speak of 'extinct volcanoes,' and of 'dead languages,' and as the latter is Saxon and short, we prefer it. They had been called 'old channels,' but this name does not convey the proper idea, since a channel is not necessarily a river, and an old channel is not necessarily a dead one. A dead river is a channel formerly occupied by a running stream, but now filled up with earthy or rocky matter, and is not to be confounded with a channel that is open and remains dry during the greater part of the year because of a lack of water, or that has been abandoned by the stream for a deeper channel elsewhere. A dry river bed is not a dead river.

"The dead rivers of California, so far as known, are on the western slopes of the Sierra Nevada, from five hundred to seven thousand feet above the sea. They are auriferous, and therefore they have been sought for and examined. They have yielded probably $300,000,000 in all; they now produce perhaps $8,000,000 annually. They are not less interesting, therefore, to the miner than to the geologist, not less important to the statesman than to the antiquarian.

"The largest dead river is known as 'the Big Blue Lead,' and has been traced from Little Grizzly, about latitude thirty-nine degrees and forty-five minutes, in Placer county, a distance of sixty-five miles. The course is south-south-east, the position about thirty miles west of, and parallel with, the main divide of the Sierra Nevada. The elevation is five thousand feet above the sea at Little Grizzly, and two thousand eight hundred at Forest Hill, showing an average fall of thirty-three feet per mile. The live rivers of the Sierra Nevada run at right angles to the course of the range, and have cut cañons from fifteen hundred to three thousand feet deep, and they are separated by ridges which are from three to six miles apart, and are as high as the cañons are deep. The Blue Lead runs across these ridges from two hundred to one thousand feet below their summits. The traveler does not see any signs of a dead river in these ridges, which are as high and have the same general appearance at the Blue Lead as at other places. I shall presently tell how the miner discovers the lead, but before coming to that, I want to give you a clear idea how the dead river crosses the ridges. Take a piece of common ruled cap paper; put your pen on a line, draw it up at an angle of forty-five degrees to the second line above, then down the first line at the same angle, and so on until the line made by your pen looks like eight rectangular saw-teeth, which are about an inch high. Consider those teeth as the ridges of the Sierra Nevada on the line of the Blue Lead in Sierra county, and the intervals between them as the cañons. Write over the first cañon to the left, 'Cañon creek;' over the next, 'Goodyear's creek,

GEOLOGY OF AMADOR COUNTY.

and over the others consecutively, 'North Fork of the Yuba river,' 'Rock creek,' 'Oregon ravine,' 'West ravine,' and 'Middle Yuba.' Now draw a horizontal line across all the ridges, a quarter of an inch from their tops. That line is the Blue Lead. The diagram made as directed, represents a perpendicular section of the ridges and cañons of the Sierra Nevada, on the line of the Big Blue Lead in Sierra county as seen from the west.

"I have said that the traveler would see no sign of a dead river in riding over the country. The ridges are as high on its line as elsewhere; the cañon sides present the same appearance. Years elapsed before the miners discovered the existence of the ancient channel. But it required only a few months for the discovery that the live rivers were very rich in gold up to a certain point; that the abundance and size of the particles increased as they ascended up to that point; and that beyond or east of that point the streams were poor. Those points on the different streams were nearly on a line. Just there the ravines on the sides of the cañons were very rich, and they were comparatively poor elsewhere. The miners followed up the ravines, washing the dirt in their beds, and the dirt where the ravines were not too steep was a foot or two deep over the slate rock. At last, when the miners got near the top of the ridge, they found that the narrow, shallow rock-bed of the ravine suddenly disappeared, and the body of the hill was composed of gravel, which had a peculiar blue color, and part of it, a horizontal stratum about half a mile wide from east to west, and five feet thick, was very rich in gold. They looked after the metal and paid little attention to anything else. As the stratum ran across the ridges from north to south, the miners followed it in with adits, or tunnels, and in more than one place the tunnels met; and a few years ago it was customary for footmen passing between Monticello and Excelsior to go under ground a distance of a mile rather than to climb over the hill six hundred feet high, by a path nearly two miles long. In the same manner Forest City and Alleghany were connected by a continuous tunnel, but the timbers have rotted, the roof has fallen in, and the passage is now closed.

"The auriferous deposit is gravel, mixed with boulders, clay, and sand, ranging from a hundred to three hundred feet in depth; in strata, distinguished from one another by differences in color, in the size of the boulders and gravel, and in the number and size of the particles of gold. The predominant color is bluish-gray, dark at the bottom and lighter above, with a reddish tinge in those places that have long been exposed to the air, showing the presence of iron. The material of the boulders, gravel and sand, is almost exclusively quartz. In the whole length of the river, as traced for a distance of sixty-five miles, assuming that the deposits of gravel average half a mile wide and two hundred feet deep, there were, counting in the portions which have been washed away by the live rivers, six hundred and sixty million cubic yards of quartz and clay, and the quartz alone must have measured five billion cubic yards. In the live rivers, quartz forms only a small portion of the gravel.

"Whence came all the quartz of the Big Blue? How did it happen that no granite, slate, porphyry, basalt or sandstone was buried in its bed? If all the quartz veins now known in California were cleaned out to a depth of one hundred feet, they would not supply so much as is found in sixty-five miles of a river that must have run for many hundreds of miles.

The gravel is all water-worn, and rounded by long attrition. It came from far north. A piece of rough quartz, while being carried five hundred miles in the fiercest of our mountain streams, would not be worn so smooth as is every pebble in the Blue Lead. And the immense size of the boulders implies a mighty current. Those in the lowest stratum average, in some places, a ton, and many are found of twenty tons. These are worn as smooth as the pebbles. They are not found scattered here and there as though they had tumbled down the banks of the river near the spot where they are found; but they are evenly distributed in a stratum of equal thickness across the whole bed, and for miles in length. Above that may be a stratum of larger ones. The great river handled these masses of rock with as much apparent ease, and spread them out as evenly, as if they had been no larger than pigeons' eggs.

"The particles of gold are larger in size, and contain more silver at the bottom than at the top. The smaller pieces are in the upper strata and as they have a larger surface proportionately, the silver is eaten out by the sulphurous acid which is developed in the gravel by the oxidation of pyrites. If a double eagle and twenty one-dollar pieces are thrown into a solution of vitriol and left there for several weeks, the small pieces will, at the end of that time, contain a larger proportion of gold than the large one; and for a similar reason the surface placer gold is finer chemically than that obtained from the deeper strata. As a general rule, the deep gold is nine hundred fine, or is worth eighteen dollars and sixty cents per ounce, and the surface gold is nine hundred and twenty fine, and is worth nineteen dollars in the Big Blue Lead. The gold and gravel are deposited as in the live rivers, in the banks, bars, eddies, ripples and rapids.

"The richest places have contained as much as fifty dollars to the cubic yard of the lower stratum, or if the large boulders were left out of the estimate, to two or three cubic feet. The space between the boulders is filled with sand, clay, and gravel, which contains the gold. In the upper strata there are from fifty cents to two dollars to the cubic yard. The bed is of slate rock, and the banks are from fifty to three hundred feet high; but there are few places where they have been examined, for nowhere has all the gravel been washed away across the channel.

"But how was it possible that the bed of a large river could be filled three hundred feet deep with gravel? When the miners in 1850 to 1852, flumed the live rivers of California, and took the gold from their beds, they found a deposit of gravel that did not average more than five feet deep on the bed rock, in streams that ran in cañons one thousand feet deep; and it is strange that the Big Blue should have filled its bed with gravel. Yet this filling is not without an analogue of our day. Under the influence of hydraulic washing, Bear river and Yuba river have, within the last fifteen years, begun to fill up with gravel, and their beds have, for miles, risen seventy feet or more above the levels of 1853. This gravel is auriferous, and it is deposited in strata, and the arrangements and general appearance resemble those of the Big Blue Lead. The filling up began down in the valley, and as it ascended the current became less rapid, and lost the power to carry away the gravel. In Bear river, below Dutch Flat, the bed rises two feet per month during the chief washing season, from February to September, and in the remaining months it falls on account of the stoppage of washing and of the Winter floods, which carry off perhaps half of the accumulation of the Summer.

"Some persons claim that various camps on parts of dead rivers in Plumas county, are on the Big Blue Lead, and others think that portions of a dead river, near Placerville, belong to the same stream. I do not accept these theories, but if they are true, the Big Blue river has been traced about one hundred and ten miles. In the northern part of Plumas county, the river is buried under deep beds of lava and basalt, and south of Placerville it is probably below the level of the live streams, and thus cannot be found by any system of mining or mode of prospecting now in use. Even in places where it is above the level of the live streams, it may be covered on the sides of the cañons by slides of rock or barren dirt or gravel, and the miner might spend thousands of dollars in a vain search for treasures not ten feet from his drift, as many have done, and some accident, luck, or perseverance, afterwards proved the proximity of the rich deposit. In several cases the lead was found by calculation. The miner took his position on a hill-side, on a level with other camps, and in a few days he found a fortune; and others have spent years working on a similar plan without success. The river must have taken bends on the north side of Rock creek and Oregon ravine, and twelve years of searching have not revealed the position of the bends.

"But why did the Big Blue river die, and leave nothing but its gravel and its gold to tell the story of its greatness? The main cause must have been the subsequent rise of the Sierra Nevada. Suppose that a range of mountains, seven thousand feet high were upheaved thirty miles east of the Mississippi; that the bed of the stream were on the mountain side, three thousand feet above the sea, and that thirty miles west the country retained its present level; the result would be that the present Mississippi would soon be a dead river; it would be cut across by streams running down the mountain side, and pouring into a new Mississippi, thirty miles or more west of the present one. We know that the Sierra Nevada has been upheaved; that a large stream ran on what is now the mountain side; and that it has been succeeded by a new river farther west; and we must infer that the death of the old and the birth of the new river was caused by the upheaval.

"Many of the hills crossed by the Big Blue are capped with lava or basalt, which covered much of the country from near the summit of the range to about three thousand feet above the sea. It seems then that the river filled its bed with gravel; the mountains began to rise, and volcanoes broke out along the divide; the lava ran down and covered the land to the line of the dead river and beyond it; the mountains rose still higher, and the waters running down their sides cut through the lava and made deep cañons, and washed away two-thirds of three-fourths of the dead river, and scattered its gold among the living waters.

"The descent of thirty-three feet per mile observed between Little Grizzly and Forest Hill would make a terrific current in a stream half a mile wide. The Sacramento is a lively river, yet its grade is only five feet in a mile. But no ordinary current could have carried the large quartz boulders of the Big Blue Lead from distant regions and distributed them evenly over the river bed. It is possible, however, that in the lifting up of the mountains the relative elevations have been altered, and that the present grade differs from that of the Big Blue while it was alive.

"A question suggests itself whether the great dead river was the predecessor of any living stream; but to this no satisfactory answer can now be given; and it is doubtful whether time and research will ever furnish one. The Big Blue was parallel to the Sacramento and has to a certain extent been succeeded by it; but it drained a much larger district than the Sacramento does, or the rain-fall of the country was much greater in the era of its existence. The Sacramento does not carry one-fourth of the water which ran in the Big Blue—probably not one-tenth. If we could ascertain that the quantity of rain had not altered, then we should be justified in presuming that the Columbia river, which would just about fill the bed of the Big Blue, instead of turning westward at Walla Walla, originally continued southward, until the lifting up of Shasta and Lassen, and the adjacent ridges, stopped its course, and compelled it to break through the Cascade range at the Dalles. With our present limited knowledge, we are not justified in calling the Big Blue river either the dead Sacramento or the dead Columbia.

"Some persons have argued that the Big Blue Lead never was a river, but only a lacustrine or alluvial deposit. This theory, however, is untenable. The Big Blue Lead has all the marks which a dead river should have. It has a long course; a width nearly uniform, a course nearly straight, some bends with eddies on the inner side, a peculiar quartz unlike any found in the neighboring ridges, or in the streams to the eastward, an abundance of quartz, which no place now known to us could have supplied, and which came, probably, from a distant northern region now covered with lava; water-worn gravel, which must have been carried far; flat stones pointing down stream, as a current would place them; strata of coarse and fine gravel, which must have been deposited in a stream; a uniform, descending grade; the coarse particles of gold, which could not have been distributed so evenly over a wide channel except in a strong current; an immense quantity of gold, which required ages to scatter through a deposit three hundred feet deep; drift-wood unmistakably water-worn; trunks of trees with the butts up stream; tributary brooks, and a number of other evidences which would require more space for their description and explanation than I could spare. To say that the Big Blue is not a dead river, is equivalent to saying that the bones of the mastodon never belonged to a living animal, but were formed under geological influences exclusively.

"If this were the only dead river in the State, the proof would be less conclusive, but there are a dozen others. One which runs south-westwardly, and may be called the dead Brandy river, appears at La Port, Brandy City, Camptonville and North San Juan, and is marked by the same general characteristics, save that the gravel is finer, the pebbles in the upper strata being generally not larger than a pigeon's egg.

"In Tuolumne and Calaveras counties we have the dead Stanislaus, or Tuolumne table mountain, which runs from near Silver mountain, in Alpine, to Knight's Ferry, and there disappears. It is covered by a bed of basalt, which flowed as lava from a volcano, and filled up the ancient bed, and this basalt has resisted the elements, and now stands as a mountain forty miles long, a quarter of a mile wide, and eight hundred feet high, the softer adjacent slate rock having been wasted and washed away. Under this mountain lies a dead river, rich in gold. A similar table mountain of basalt, covering an auriferous dead river, which I call the dead Cherokee,

JOSEPH WOOLFORD.

after its chief mining camp, extends seventy miles, from Lassen's Peak to Oroville. At Bangor, in Butte county, is a small dead river, seventy feet below the general surface of the ground, and covered with ordinary soil and gravel. There are also dead rivers at Smartsville, Mokelumne Hill and San Andreas. The Big Blue and dead Brandy are distinguished by the depth of their gravel, and by the absence of pebbles of eruptive origin in it. The others have either short courses or shallow deposits of gravel; and the quartz forms a much smaller percentage of the gravel. In the dead rivers at Cherokee, Bangor, and Smartsville, a large proportion of the boulders and pebbles is of lava and basalt, as if the stream had been formed after the commencement of the volcanic era. But different as is the material of the gravel, the fluvial origin of the deposits is similar and indubitable in all of them, when they are studied together."

It may be presumptive to offer any suggestion as to the source of the immense stream which formed or deposited this lead. The suggestion that it might have been the Columbia river before it had broken its way through the Dalles, is perhaps worth considering. Another suggestion may be permitted. Those who have crossed the Utah basin, will have noticed the water lines far up on the sides of the mountains, showing that it was formerly an inland sea, or lake, larger than any now on the continent, which might have had its outlet through some of the passes in the Sierra, ere its waters were lapped up by the desiccating winds. This suggestion is made for the benefit of the future geologist. The question may be decided when the great lava bed, which buried up the supposed channel of the river, shall have been explored, and its secrets laid bare. For the present we may lay this question aside, as one too momentous for our present limited information. How long these rivers pursued their course, where they emptied, and into what waters, are also matters for future investigation. The deposits of clay which marked this era, indicated an almost interminable period. We may be inclined to ask, Of what use was the earth at this time?

RIVERS FLOWING TO THE WEST.

But there came an end to this sleepy, easy flow of events. The volcanoes, which had so long sent forth only mud and ashes, now took on an industrious fit, and commenced pouring out lava without stint, choking up the former channels, and, in some instances, burying them under three or four hundred feet of lava. It is probable that previous to this, many, or perhaps all, of these rivers had worn a way through the low mountains which hemmed them in, and found their way to the sea; but the lava forced them to form channels in a new direction. The low mountain barriers were overflowed. The rivers, running with an increased velocity, now swept along great boulders of lava, granite, slate, or whatever came in their way. On a ridge between Amador and Sutter, some miles below the towns, may be seen boulders ten feet in diameter, which appear to have been left at the foot of a long descending portion of the river. Many times the new rivers would choke up, compelling the water, again and again, to seek new channels. These channels, in many places, occupy the ridges between the present river beds, sometimes at a height of six hundred feet.

STRATIFIED ROCKS.

The surface having been considered, the stratified rocks may next claim attention. These all dip into the ground at various angles, sometimes with pitch to the east, and sometimes to the west. In these stratified rocks are found our valuable metals; and any theory of vein formation, to be of value, must consider them as a unity. Commencing at the foot of the mountains, at the lowest formation visible, at Ione, Lancha Plana, and the corresponding places farther north, we find the strata in the following order. I have set the names of the strata to correspond somewhat with the position of the rocks named, and also have elevated, and otherwise noted, the metamorphic rocks which formed the summits of the ancient valleys.

HISTORY OF AMADOR COUNTY, CALIFORNIA

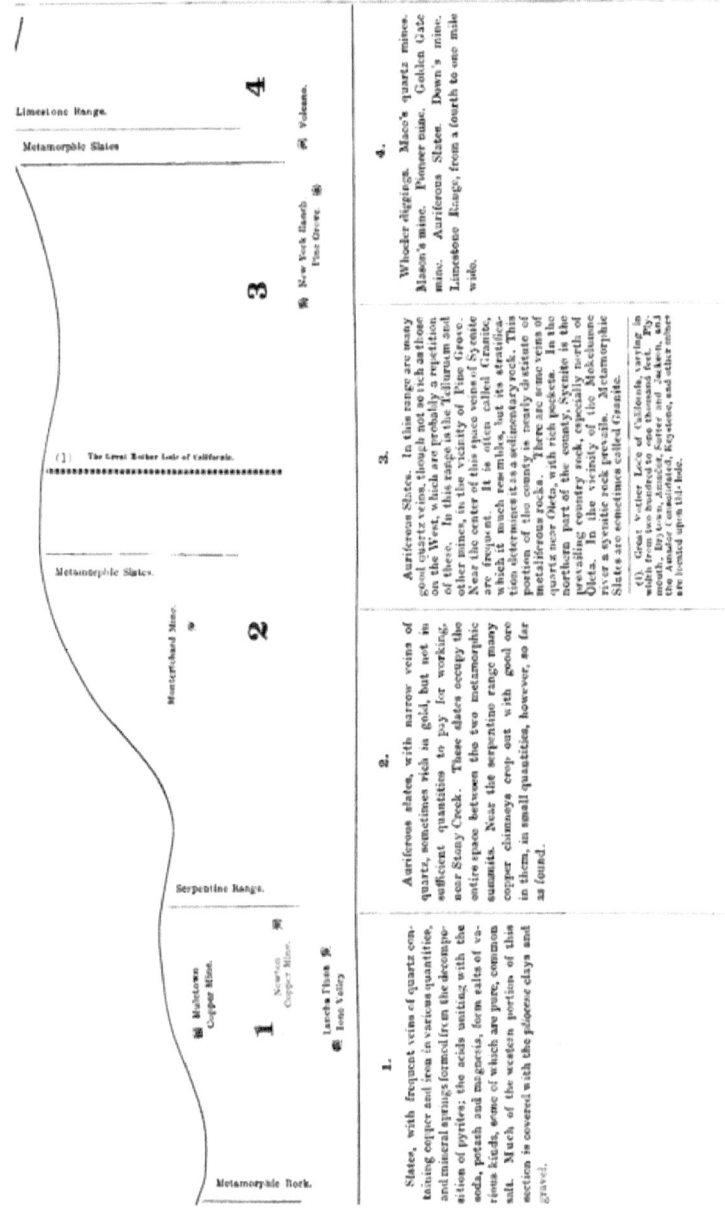

Limestone Range.

Metamorphic Slates

4. ⓦ Volcano.

3. ⓦ New York Ranch ⓦ
Pine Grove.

[ ] The Great Mother Lode of California.

Metamorphic Slates.

2. ⓦ Muletophand Mine.

Serpentine Range.

1. ⓦ Muletown
Copper Mines.
ⓦ Newton
Copper Mines.
ⓦ Lancha Plana ⓦ
Ione Valley.

Metamorphic Rock.

---

1. Slates, with frequent veins of quartz containing copper and iron in various quantities, and mineral springs formed from the decomposition of pyrites; the acids uniting with the soda, potash and magnesia, form salts of various kinds, some of which are pure, common salt. Much of the western portion of this section is covered with the pliocene clays and gravel.

2. Auriferous slates, with narrow veins of quartz, sometimes rich as gold, but not in sufficient quantities to pay for working, near Stony Creek. These slates occupy the entire space between the two metamorphic summits. Near the serpentine range many copper chimneys crop out with gold ore in them, in small quantities, however, so far as found.

3. Auriferous Slates. In this range are many good quartz veins, though not so rich as those on the West, which are probably a repetition of these. In this range is the Tellurium and other mines, in the vicinity of Pine Grove. Near the center of this space veins of Syenite are frequent. It is often called Granite, which it much resembles, but its stratification determines it is a sedimentary rock. This portion of the county is nearly destitute of metaliferous rocks. There are some veins of quartz near Oleta, with rich pockets. In the northern part of the county, Syenite is the prevailing country rock, especially north of Oleta. In the vicinity of the Mokelumne river a syenitic rock prevails. Metamorphic Slates are sometimes called Granite.

(1) Great Mother Lode of California, varying in width from two hundred to one thousand feet. Plymouth, Hayward, Amador, Sutter and Jackson, and the Amador Consolidated, Keystone, and other mines are located upon this lode.

4. Whocker diggings. Mace's quartz mines. Mason's mine. Former same. Golden Gate mine. Auriferous Slates. Down's mine. Limestone Range, from a fourth to one mile wide.

GEOLOGY OF AMADOR COUNTY.

It must not be supposed that any stratum preserves a uniform character for any distance. Only a few of the great veins or ranges like the serpentine and the other metamorphic can be traced in this way. Whether from currents in the ocean depositing different materials previous to the upturning of the slates, or from subsequent change by translation of minerals, or both, the slates change in character every mile or two. The black slate will change to gray, then to quartzose, or perhaps to syenite. The metamorphic is often thinned out by other rocks. In some place the serpentine is two miles wide, in others nearly wanting, so that a description of rocks at Ione might not fully apply to the rocks four or five miles further north.

The metamorphic rocks near Ione, Lancha Plana and Buena Vista, which have been referred to before, may be taken as a starting-point. These do not form a continuous reef, but here stand as detached masses probably eroded as before mentioned by the waves of the sea. Along the junction of this with the black slate are some of the largest quartz veins in the county. One of them may be seen near Randal's ranch near Ione, one at Mrs. Nichol's place near Buena Vista, and at several other places. That one on Randal's ranch has been sunk on some eighty feet or more without finding anything of value. Where these veins have been subjected to sea wash, as at Muletown, and, perhaps, the Arkansas diggings, they have made good placer mining. Irish Hill was enriched by a mountain stream, as the gravel is composed of entirely different rocks from that of Muletown. The hill east of Ione is probably sea wash, of the same age as the Muletown deposit. The seashore line may be easily traced by the bench-like erosions.

Near the foot-wall of this belt are the Cosumnes, the Arroyo Seco, Lancha Plana, and other copper mines. On the opposite side of this belt is the Newton copper mine, as well as several others of promise. The reader is requested to note the fact of paying mines being found in the vicinity of these hard slates, though these slates themselves scarcely ever contain any mineral of value. In the intermediate space are many veins containing copper and other minerals in small quantities. Near the Boston ranch some small veins of quartz are estimated to have five dollars to the ton, but they seem to thin out and ramify through the ground so as to be unprofitable to work, though many ravines have been enriched by them. Some veins of steatite (soap-stone) have considerable gold in them visible to the eye, but no one, as yet, has been able to separate it. The gulches running from this range have been rich. Near Irish Hill is the Kirkendall district which was thought to be rich in quartz veins, but the expectations have not been realized.

SERPENTINE RANGE.

This is a striking formation of metamorphic rock, so twisted, contorted and scraggy, that it has been considered by many as of volcanic origin. The point between Jackson and Stony Creek was thought to be an old crater. A close investigation shows it to be slate, and the ragged, contorted appearance to be the result of the substitution of magnesia for potash in the composition of the rock. Chromate of iron abounds in it, a vein of it near the Westfalls' ranch being nearly three feet thick. Hundreds of small quartz veins, as well as other ore chimneys, may be seen within a mile or two while walking along this range. Vogan has used many of these veins for road material. When sunk on they often turn to clay, and many of them are known by being sinks in the ground, or sometimes pot-holes of clay. Silver, gold, and copper are all found in these chimneys in small quantities. They were formerly explored for copper. These ore deposits may be a continuation of those found on the west side of the lower metaliferous range. Farther east are many small quartz veins with considerable gold, though the veins are too narrow to be worked with profit. Limestone is found in many places on this range. Not far from the Filmer ranch is a large deposit which burns into good lime; though many of the deposits contain too much silica or magnesia for that purpose, being perhaps a kind of dolomite. It is too dark colored and too hard for ornamental purposes. On the Mokelumne river, near the head of the Lancha Plana ditch, is a curious formation of lime, resembling a frozen waterfall. It is somewhat obscured by the dirt which has fallen over it, but is well worth an examination.

A short distance below is an iron spring, a good illustration of an active ore deposit, a formation of iron ore constantly going on, which is every year carried away by the high waters of the river. The ore is probably the result of the percolation of water through decomposing sulphurets not far away. Passing east we strike another belt of metamorphic slates in places two miles in width. This may be considered the great foot-wall of the Mother Lode, also the most prominent indication of the largest valley, following the ranges of mountains, that existed in this county. As the Mother Lode has been, and is now, perhaps, the source of more gold than any space of the same width and length in the world, and, from its having been worked deeper and better than any other place, furnishes more material for a scientific account of the formation of quartz veins, the consideration of it will be deferred to another chapter. It may be said of it that it probably furnished the gold with which the streams once running parallel to it were enriched, as well as the streams which now cross it, also the larger part of the gold that enriched the gravel diggings at the foothills. It is probable that the stream debouched into the Mokelumne or through that depression for a long time before the volcanic era, as there are no large deposits of gravel along the foot-hills near the outlet of the present streams that are of sufficient amount to have been produced by its wash.

East of the Mother Lode, which must be considered never less than two hundred, and sometimes two thousand, feet wide, there is little quartz that has any value. We find veins of slate and syenite alternating with each other. Some of the gulches are enriched by the wash of the great streams of gravel that resulted in the breaking up of the first system of rivers. Nearly half of the ground around Pine Grove seems to be a relic of this wash; streams of gravel, some rich and some nearly barren, traversing the hills in all possible directions. The quartz veins near the last metamorphic range spoken of are probably connected by a sort of geological, umbilical cord with the Mother Lode, though vastly inferior to it in wealth. The veins have not regularity of pitch or strike, sometimes breaking through the slate across the rift and frequently losing themselves in extensive ramifications. In places they are very rich, thirty or forty dollars per ton not being uncommon.

CHAPTER XXVI.
GEOLOGY OF AMADOR COUNTY.
BY GEORGE MADEIRA.

Extensive Character of the Subject—Mother Lode—Methods of Vein Deposits—Character of the Veins East of the Mother Lode—Minerals in the Tertiary Rocks—Nature of the Limestones—Gravel Deposits—Nature of the Supposed Photographic Rock—Evidences of Glaciers—Moving Large Rocks—Volcanoes—Origin of the Trap Rock—Origin of the Smaller Quartz Veins—Butte Mountain—Copper—Iron—Gypsum—Asbestos—Marble—Kaolin—Manganese—Agate—Chalcedony—Skeletons of the Megatherium—Other Fossils—Rhinoceros—Hippopotamus—Horse Destruction of the Arcadian Land—Botany.

[The following chapter on technical geology, by a professional mining expert, will please the more scientific of the readers of this work. The writer is amply competent to write an extended and exhaustive treatise on the subject of geology or practical mining.—Editor.]

To the geologist and mining explorer, Amador county offers the most interesting field of research to be found in the State, containing, as it does within its limits, the most extensive quartz deposits to be found on the western slope of the Sierras. The great Mother Lode passes entirely across the county in a northerly and southerly direction. At the Keystone mine (Amador) the course of the vein is, south forty-two degrees, twenty-six minutes east; north forty-two degrees, twenty-six minutes west. Inclination of east wall of fissure, fifty degrees; the east hanging wall is a metamorphic silicious slate; and what is known, along the lode, as the west wall rock, or foot-wall, is a blue-black, laminated slate. These laminated slates on the west may not be the true foot-wall, as we find, one-fourth of a mile to the west, a similar parallel wall of metamorphic slate, although it does not contain the silica found in the east wall rock.

Between these widely divided parallel walls of metamorphic slates, we find numerous stringers of quartz, from the width of a knife-blade to many feet. The main Mother Lode, however, is found running along the east hanging-wall rock, but in some instances it leaves the same and varies to the west. In the Keystone, at Amador, the vein leaves the east wall, and, for a space of four hundred feet, does not return to it. In the same mine we find the entire width of the quartz deposit, as far as penetrated to the west, nearly one hundred and fifty feet. At the Empire mine, Plymouth, the vein is seventy-five feet in width. At the Zeile mine, one-half mile south of Jackson, the vein is thirty to forty feet at its greatest width.

Stringers and feeders, from the country rock in geological times, carried the silicious waters to the main fissure, where it deposited its lode of silica that went to form the vein. This lode gives indubitable evidence of the manner in which it was formed, to wit: by infiltration from the country rock, mostly from the east. The east hanging-wall, in many places along the line of the fissure, is a crystalline, metamorphic slate, which has been changed by heat and pressure into a near approach to diorite. These slates are silicious rather than talcose, and frequently pass into rock closely resembling diorite or trap, and are difficult to distinguish from the intrusive or eruptive rocks. They, at times, assume a porphyritic structure, and may be taken for eruptive rocks.

As we pass to the west, we find the slates gradually change from metamorphic, to laminated, then to conglomerate slate,* a series of fragmental rocks. These conglomerate slates have caused much comment among explorers, other than geologists, as to their origin, and as they are abundant to the west of the great Mother Lode, but are not found to the east of it, we will give their origin.

These slates are made up of quartz pebbles, fragments of slate, mica, and feldspar. They appear as stratified gravel deposits, and gold has been found in them. These strata were formed on the bottom of a jurassic sea, and are the cemented fragments torn from older rocks. In the upheaval of the Sierras, these slates escaped the pressure that was brought to bear on those further to the east, and hence we find them to-day a series of conglomerate slate and sandstone. It is interesting to pass over these slates, eastward, and see them pass gradually into the metamorphic slates, and trace the outlines of the quartz pebble in the firm silicious slate along the great fissure that contains the Mother Lode.

At some period, after the jurassic era, the upheaval of the Sierra fissured the western slope, as it is known to have fissured the eastern, with numerous large and small openings. Along the line of the then base of the Sierras, volumes of steam and streams of silicious waters poured from the great fissure, which now contains the Mother Lode. The

*May be seen in quantity near Drytown.

GEOLOGY OF AMADOR COUNTY.

heated waters deposited their loads of silica, and, the ascending vapors their metalic deposit. From near Berranda, on the South Pacific Railroad, to Trinity on the north, spouting geysers and steaming solfataras, ladened the air with vapors, and marked the site of the gold deposits of to-day.

East of the Mother Lode, from one to three miles, a ridge of feldspathic rock runs parallel with the lode across the county. In some places, it is a compact granite; in others, a gneissoid granite. It is traversed in places by dikes of trap and large veins of barren quartz. At Quartz mountain, on the line of this granitic ridge, is an immense deposit of quartz, low grade ore. The auriferous slates of the county are arenaceous, argillaceous, and quartzose, sometimes changing in a few rods, from magnesian to aluminous, or to hard, blue metamorphic slates. These slates further change as we go west, and at the Newton copper mine we find them an argillaceous shale.

When excavations are made in the alum slates, a deposit of that mineral forms on the damp walls, and waters flowing from tunnels in the slates, are sometimes heavily charged with alum from decomposing pyrites of iron. These slates, as has been determined from fossils, found further north in Plumas county, belong to the upper triassic and jurassic epoch.

The auriferous slates on either side of the great Mother Lode are of the same age as the Jura Alps, and hence jurassic. They have a width of about thirty miles from east to west. Five miles from Jackson, on the Volcano road, we find these slates divided by an immense ridge of granite; and three miles east of the town of Volcano, the granite rocks commence and extend, with slight interruptions, to the summit of the great chain of the Sierras. All the country rock, between these granite ridges, which runs the county in a northerly direction, is occupied by the auriferous slates—except where the carboniferous limestone divides it. There are several strata or formations of the limestone which cross the county in the same general direction that the quartz veins do. These limestones mark the near shore-line of a carboniferous ocean, and are the work of the coral polyps that once existed on the golden shores of Amador. It is a well-known fact that the coral insect does not live and work at a greater depth than one hundred feet; and at the period when these limestones were formed, the land lay at the bottom of a shallow sea; or the rising Sierras shifted the receding shore-line continually to the west. Hence we find the greatest deposit of the limestones on the east of Volcano, where they have a width of three thousand feet. Between Volcano and Sutter, we find two narrow strata of limestone; and three or four miles to the west of Sutter, we find the last, or most western, strata of the carboniferous limestones.

These limestones do not contain a fossil of the coral polyps, who built them; not even with the microscope can they be detected. The strata has been so metamorphosed and changed by pressure, as to destroy the form, and change its beautiful coral formations (as found in the limestones of the same age in Shasta county), into crystalline marble. This limestone is a white, crystalline, saccharoidal marble of fine and coarse texture, with veinings of oxide of iron and black oxide of manganese. It is traversed, in many places, by heavy and light trap-dikes.

Previous to the deposition of the gold-bearing gravel upon it the rock has been worn by the action of the elements into the most fantastic shapes. By the removal of the auriferous gravel covering the limestones, domes and spires, monuments and towers, of dark-veined marble have been exposed to view, presenting an imposing appearance. It is full of pot-holes formed by the action of water, and deep, curiously eroded cavities, once filled with gold-bearing gravel.

Caves, caverns, and long, sinuous galleries have been formed by the eroding waters carrying the carbonate of lime in solution, depositing it at different parts of the deposit, in many instances decorating the roofs and floors of the caverns with beautiful stalagmite and stalactite formations. The limestone belt is crossed by quartz veins of small size. Layers of flint, or chert, possibly formed from the cast-off shells of diatoms, are found along the line of the marble and slaty beds of the same rock. The gravel deposits, which at Volcano have been extensively worked for gold, rest on the auriferous slates as well as the limestones. Beneath the limestones the slates are not found.

In the ridge north of the town (Volcano) the auriferous gravel is overlain by horizontal beds of white and pink tufa or volcanic materials, consisting of ashes and pumice cemented and stratified by water. Upon these horizontal strata rests a mass of trachyte, broken into rounded forms on the surface. Under this massive volcanic ridge, the entire auriferous belt plunges, re-appearing on the opposite side, at Fort John.

Between the Volcano basin and the Mokelumne river is another high ridge of volcanic materials, under which the auriferous belt passes in a southerly direction.

These volcanic ridges—which may be met with all along the western slopes of the main chain, extending in parallel courses from the summits of the high Sierras to the low tertiary foot-hills, which in many instances they cap with a shallow deposit—extend in a continuous line to the summit of the Sierra Nevada.

These ridges push out in detached masses to the confines of the Sacramento valley, where, becoming thinner and thinner, they have finally stopped, and are found on the summits of the low tertiary hills around Ione valley.

Near the surface in some of these tufa deposits, may be found beautiful specimens of what are called photographic rock—dendritic formations; generally resembling delicate tracery of trees and shrubs.

Some of the pictures are ideal landscapes, with hill, valley, and lake; the lake in the foreground, bordered by grass and ferns, the low hills in the background with palmate and branching trees, delicate as sea mosses. They are not, as supposed, nature's photographs, but are formed by waters, holding black oxide of manganese in solution, percolating through the fissures in the rock. These formations are abundant in the claims of McLaughlin & Co., on Union Flat, and Whitney & Co., on the same range near Volcano.

The jurassic and carboniferous strata are overlain by the strata of the tertiary and post-pliocene, with boulder or glacial drift and aluvium deposits. The volcanic deposits cap the whole, and are consequently the latest formations.

GLACIAL EVIDENCES.

On the summits of many of the high ridges, both exposed and under the lava flow, are deposits of glacier drift, in places rich in gold. The question with many is, how these immense polished boulders have been left on the summits.

The solution of the question is that they were carried there in the glacial period, after having been torn from the numerous quartz, and other ledges, over which the glacial flow passed, carrying them over valley and hill—as they are known to have traveled —from a northerly direction. The great body of ice, possibly two or three miles in thickness, acted as a mighty arastra, grinding down the quartz lodes, pulverizing the mass, polishing the boulders, and depositing the gold in the drift (to be concentrated afterwards by the flowing streams from the melting ice), wearing down the slates, and leaving the auriferous gravel in the beds of the rivers and gulches, filling the great valley of the Sacramento to an unknown depth. The Stockton artesian well, sunk to a depth of eleven hundred feet, did not go through the deposit, nor the well at the Sacramento sugar refinery, two thousand two hundred feet in depth, the auger bringing up gold, quartz, and wood, at a depth of two thousand feet. We mention these deep sinkings in the valley to show that the debris, for countless ages, has been pouring into the valleys, and must for countless ages to come. Three miles west of the town of Amador we find evidences of glacial deposit. On the summit of one of the volcanic ridges, mingled with the huge, rounded trachyte boulders, are fifteen granite glacier-polished boulders. The largest is thirteen feet long by seven and one-half feet wide; the part above ground is five feet high. It contains fifty tons of rock, and has the ovid or sheep-back form peculiar to glacial boulders. The others, all similar in appearance, are much smaller. There is no granite of the same character nearer than twenty miles north-east, in an air line. We followed the line of the glacier drift over the volcanic ridges, and down the deep cañons, to near Upper Rancheria, where we again came upon the same character of granite boulders, but distant from the first mentioned by ten or twelve miles. They are from five to thirty tons weight. They mark the line of the glacial flow, and their polished sides show the action of the moving ice.

VOLCANOES.

There are no well-defined volcanoes, with the exceptions of Butte mountain, near Jackson, and one west of Tragedy Springs, near Silver lake. At the last-mentioned point, there are evidences of the most stupendous volcanic outbursts, and from this point the lava ridges may be traced for forty miles or more, toward the valley of the Sacramento. These lava rivers in the volcanic epoch, flowed down the lowest places, or river beds. As the ages rolled on, the eroding waters and high mountain glaciers, wore the softer slates away, and left those ridges, as we find them to-day, the most elevated portion of the county. That portion of the county to the east of the great Mother Lode, is traversed, to a greater or less extent, by igneous rocks, mostly trap and diorite. These dikes cut through all formations, and are found extending to the boulder drift and aluvium deposits. (According to Clarence King, United States geologist, they were erupted in the cretaceous, or chalk period.) They are from a few inches in width to many (sometimes five hundred) feet wide. We have traced many of them for a distance of two miles, through several formations. They are, in many instances, intimately connected with the formation of quartz lodes; and where they cut a ledge or intersect it, deposits of rich ore are often found. In the Pioneer district, five miles east of Volcano, the small quartz lodes in the granite, owe their origin to these trap-dikes; they are what is known as segregated lodes, that is, drawn from the granite by the heat of the ascending dike.

Trap-dikes cross the basin on which the town of Volcano is located, in almost all directions. The richest placer deposits have been found in close proximity to these erupted dikes, on one or the other side. They appear to have acted as gigantic riffles during the glacial period, and held the gold as it was ground out of the abundant quartz lodes, much as is common in a sluice at the present time. A large dike of doleritic trap rock, with large crystals of augite, malacolite, and sablito, of a dingy green color, passes just above the falls on Indian gulch, near Volcano, and through which a tunnel has been driven. This heavy dike of igneous rock changed the inclosing limestones to a coarse crystalline carbonate of lime, some of the crystals an inch square. Some very good marble has been formed in the same way, at various places on the limestone belt. This great dike, in a few hundred feet, frays out into numerous small dikes; some of them cutting small quartz veins, in the here silicious limestones, which show gold where the trap passes through the quartz.

Butte mountain gives indubitable evidence of having been erupted on the spot, the molten matter coming up through an opening in the slates. We find the conical mountain composed of volcanic rocks and ashes, resting on the auriferous slates. This mountain is a conspicuous figure in the landscape, and the view from its summit, extensive and grand.

COPPER.

What is known as the copper belt, and on which the Newton copper mine is located, passes across the county five or six miles to the west of the great Mother Lode. The slates in this section are the magnesian and argillaceous. Large ledges and strata of serpentine rocks cross and cut these slates in all directions. The ore obtained at the Newton mine is the sulphuret, known as chalcopyrite, the yellow oxide of copper. There is some iron pyrites mixed with the ore to a greater or less extent, which lowers the percentage of the ore correspondingly; red oxide is also obtained in smaller quantities.

The process of working is simple. The ore is roasted, then leached, and the copper precipitated with iron, or rather, collected on iron scraps.

Along this copper belt are numerous croppings and evidences of the existence of other deposits of copper, and the future prospector may yet uncover mines equal to the one described above.

MINERALS.

Iron is abundant; and the day is not distant when the inexhaustible iron deposits of Amador will be profitably worked.

Wood is abundant for the manufacture of charcoal; limestone of the best quality for smelting purposes without limit; and iron ore of a good grade beyond computation. It is on every hand; in the limonite that binds the gravel beds in solid conglomerate to lodes or deposits of great extent; in masses of dark steel-gray hematite, and lodes of magnetic iron ore; in specular iron; in masses of iron and black oxide of manganese; in ocherous earth and jaspery croppings; in stalactites and small beautiful specimens of titanic ore; last but not least, in the blood-red soil of the environing hills.

GYPSUM.

Small deposits of sulphate of lime have been found at various points in the county, but not in paying quantities. The future explorer may develop quantities of the mineral.

ASBESTOS.

Small veins of the above mineral exist all over the county, changing from the fibrous to immense ledges of steatite of a coarse variety.

MARBLE.

Marble of a good quality, and of different shades from blue-veined to crystalline white, is found along the limestone belt. Small quantities of onyx are also found in the same vicinity.

MANGANESE.

Small veins of the above mineral are also met with.

KAOLIN.

A good quality of potter's clay is found in horizontal deposits near Carbondale, and around Ione Valley. A good deposit of the same mineral exists at Aqueduct City.

Accompanying the quartz veins, in many instances forming selvedge or "gouge," as it is called by the miners, is a fair quality of kaolin; formed from decomposed feldspar.

AGATE—CHALCEDONY.

In Soldiers' gulch, back of the town of Volcano, is a quartz vein passing through the gravelly deposit, formed, by the action of water holding silica in solution, since the deposition of the gravel. It is a ferruginous, jaspery vein of geodic chalcedony and agate. Some of the cavities are most beautifully lined with silicious crystalline deposits of these minerals.

About one hundred feet to the north of the above-described curious jaspery formation, is a dike or trap, which, when erupted, baked the clay on either hand for a distance of fifty feet into porcelanite, a species of jasper. Near this dike we found several casts of bones of the megatherium (?)—a gigantic animal that existed in the tertiary period. The casts are of porcelanite, and very large.

In some of the clay slates, all over the county, we found tracks and borings of worms and rain-drop impressions; and in the hard blue slates along the Mother Lode, we frequently find the wave marks left by the receding jurassic sea. In a mining claim (at Volcano) near the junction of the slates and limestones, we found some fine specimens of ferruginous lignite, or in other words, fossil woods changed to iron ore, the fibre of the wood clear and distinct. Here we also found a similar sample of palm wood, the bark still remaining on the wood. The other woods found presented a fibre similar to alder and maple. We also found fossil plants, two in number, all of which probably belonged to the triassic slates. In the high volcanic ridge, known as Shake ridge, about three miles north-east of Volcano, is the tunnel of W. Q. Mason, which has been driven under the volcanic matter or lava, through the channel rim of slates, cutting an ancient river bed, or lacustrine deposit. The thinly laminated clayey deposit, has been formed in still water, as may be determined from the position of the fossil vegetation. Charred wood and ferruginous lignite, or wood changed to iron ore, is abundant. Mr. Mason has a pine cone—a beautiful specimen, changed into sulphuret of iron. Here we found between the thin, clayey layers, the leaves of the following trees: Alder, willow, oak, maple, fig, and a very large leaf we could not determine. These leaves, and what appeared to be the fronds of a species of fern, are abundant, forming a deposit in some places two or three feet thick. They are very fragile, and all attempts to preserve them, even for a few days, were futile.

The fossil plants belong to the tertiary period, and the volanic flow, that ended their existence, carbonized and preserved their varied forms intact. Similar leaves and fossil woods are found, in and around Jackson and Ione valleys, beneath the horizontal clay strata that form the hills.

Fossil remains of the elephant and mastodon have been found at various places in the county by miners and others.

In Jackson valley they have been upturned by the plow. At Grass Valley a tusk of a mastodon, nine feet long, was washed from the auriferous gravel deposits.

At one period of time in the geological history of Amador, the rhinoceros (an animal allied to the hippopotamus), an extinct species of horse, and an animal allied to the camel, wandered through the palm groves and tropical woods of Arcadian Amador; none of these survived the grand catastrophe that swept them from the earth and buried their bones with the destroyed groves through which they wandered under the great lava-covered ridges, in the ancient river beds of to-day.

The feathery palm lifted its proud head to a tropical sun; the wild fig dropped its fruit along the streams, and the maple flourished on the gently rolling hills; gigantic ferns grew in rank luxuriance around the margin of the placid lake; birds of gay plumage winged their flight through flowering groves, and the air was rank with heated vapors.

But a change came over the spirit of the dream; a geological epoch had been accomplished, and the rising Sierras, with their teeming volcanoes, lit up the eastern heavens with a lurid glare, sending down streams of lava and volcanic material, burying the remains of those animals beneath the fiery flood. Later the elephant and the mastodon wandered over the hills and valleys of our county, only to be swept away by the seas of ice, or ground to atoms beneath its accumulated weight, leaving their remains as evidence of their existence.

BOTANY OF AMADOR COUNTY.

Sugar Pine (*Pinus Lambertina*)—The first and grandest tree of the Sierras, which should have been named pinus saccharina, an appropriate and suggestive name. It deposits a sugary mass, similar to the manna of the druggist, but a mild cathartic, although pleasant to the taste.

This majestic tree, with its long horizontal branches and pendant cones of twelve to twenty inches in length, towering high above its fellows, forms a most attractive figure in the landscape. The white pine lumber from this tree is the best met with in the Sierras.

Pitch Pine (*Pinus ponderosa*)—Comes next in value, and immense quantities are sawed into lumber and shipped to the valleys, or floated down the ditches to the mines at Sutter, Amador, and other places.

Arbor Vitæ (*Thugia gigantea*)—Or the noble fir, is found in the deep cañons a few miles east of Volcano.

Red Fir (*Abies Douglasii*)—Is also found on the volcanic ridges, and down the cañons.

Balsam Fir (*Picea grandis*)—Is also met with, and used for economical purposes.

The White Cedar (*Labrocedus ducurens*)—Is a beautiful tree, and many attempts have been made to transplant it to the valley homes, for ornamental purposes, but with only partial success.

Nut or Rock Pine (*Pinus sabiana*)—Is found growing on the rock lands of the western part of the county, and along the carboniferous limestones, bearing a large cone full of edible nuts. The wood is poor, even for fire-wood.

Nutmeg Tree (*Torreya Californica*)—Which grows into a stately tree in the Coast Range, here only reaches a small shrub. The nuts are not like the nutmeg of commerce, except in outside appearance. The meat is edible, but the squirrels usually get it.

Western Yew (*Taxus brevifolia*)—Found in the eastern part of the county, as also the mountain spruce.

Bay Tree, or Mountain Laurel (*Oreodaphne Californica*)—A beautiful, spicy tree, which grows to an immense size in the Coast Range, but here, only to a respectable shrub.

White Oak (*Quercus Lobata*)—Differs from that found east of the Rocky Mountains.

Quercus Agrifolia—Quite plenty on the ridges, and around Ione valley.

Cañon Live-Oak (*Q. Crysolepsis*)—A valuable wood for ship timbers.

California Chestnut (*Castanopsis Chrysophylla*)—A shrubby tree; grows on the rocky lands.

Hazelnut (*Corylus Rostrata*)—In the cañons and north hill-sides; bears nuts in small quantities.

Alder (*Alnus Viridis*)—Found growing along the streams. In the Coast Range is used for powderwood.

Common Willow (*Salix Biglowii*)—Found in large trees along the creeks and streams.

Cottonwood Poplar (*Populus monilifera*)—Large trees; in some instances along the creeks.

Bayberry or Wax Myrtle (*Myrica Californica*)—On moist hill-sides and streams.

Leather Wood (*Dirca palustris*)—A bush six to ten feet high; grows on dry ridges; very tough.

Alder Buckthorn (*Rhamnus Californica*)—From five to ten feet high; called Wild Coffee from the fact the berry contains seeds that resemble coffee, and

have been so used, but it is distinct from the true coffee plant.

Mountain Lilac *(Ceanothus thyrsiflorus)*—Two varieties, blue and white; a fragrant, handsome tree or shrub.

Ceanothus papillosus—Resembles the last; found in the mountains; the body of the tree is full of nobs made by the attacks of insects; used for canes on account of this peculiarity.

ROSE FAMILY.

Wild Cherry *(Prunus ilicifolia)*.

Mountain Holly *(Heteromeles arbutifolia)*—Grows as high as twenty feet, with beautiful red berries, which ripen in January or February; much sought by birds.

Service Berry *(Amelanchier alnifolia)*—Grows high in the mountains.

Chaparral-Chemisal *(Adenostoma fasciculatum)*—Grows from five to twenty feet high; covers the rocky hills to the exclusion of all other trees.

MAPLE FAMILY.

Buckeye Horse-chestnut *(Æsculus Californica)*—A beautiful tree in the Spring when in bloom; nut used by the Indians for food, who soak the poison out with water.

Big Leafed Maple *(Acer macrophyllum)*—Grows into a small tree.

Poison Oak *(Rhustaxico dendron)* and *(Rhus dicersilobus)*—Either variety of which will make the visitor wish he or she had not met with it. This obnoxious shrub grows all over the State.

HEATH FAMILY.

The Madrona or Strawberry Tree of the Spaniards *(Arbutus Menziessii)*—A beautiful tree with orange colored branches and deep green varnished leaves; bears a red berry of which the wild pigeons are fond.

Manzanita *(Arctostaphylos tomentosa)* and *(A. Glauca)*—Two varieties; bears berries, which the Indians gather in large quantities, of which they make a kind of cider.

Flowering Dogwood *(Cornus Nuttallii)*—A beautiful tree when in bloom.

C. Californica—Grows mostly along the streams; another species of Dogwood.

Elder *(Sambucus glauca)*—Bears edible berries.

Californicum Rhododendron—Is found in some parts of the county.

Of plants, we have, lilies, saxifrages, orchides, equisetæ, sedges, etc., ferns in variety, wood mosses, and lichens; there are lupines, orthocarpus; the poppy family is represented by three or four beautiful species, and the lilies by as many.

There are two or three species of violets.

This list might be extended much farther.

CHAPTER XXVII.
ORIGIN OF MINERAL VEINS.

Plutonic Theory—Ocean Floors—Other Theories Considered—Function of Wall Rock and Gouge—Surface Veins—Probable Depth of Veins—Methods of Deposit—Jurassic Gravel—Course of the Blue Lead.

It may seem presumptuous to offer any ideas on the formation of the various metaliferous veins that ramify through our mountains; but between those who think God called all things into existence just as they are, and those who can readily explain everything(?) there is quite room enough for many persons, however different their opinions, to stand without jostling each other. Notwithstanding all the discoveries in science, and they are many and of great importance, we are but on the boundaries of the infinite field, for natural science, in any of its thousands branches, is an illimitable expanse which would require an eternity to explore.

An elaborate treatise on the formation of mineral veins would be out of place in a volume of this kind, even if the writer were capable of such a work; hence only matters pertaining to the industries of the county will find place here. Thirty years' experience in gold and other mining, much of which, for want of knowledge, has been unprofitable, has left many valuable hints, which, like trees blazed by the pioneer through the pathless woods, serve to guide those who come after. An abandoned shaft or mine should tell its tale of warning, and when properly interrogated will probably do so.

PLUTONIC THEORY.

It was formerly held that all mineral veins were the result of internal heat, which out of an immense amount of material always hot, molten, sent some small fragments to the upper earth. Nearly all the rocks were supposed to have the same origin; but the inexplicable difficulties which this theory led to, soon caused its abandonment. The metalic veins were too finely ramified, reticulated through the rock, to admit of that method of deposit. If the metaliferous lodes had been raised to the necessary degree of heat for fusion, the wall rocks or casings would have been destroyed or vitrified; whereas, the slate or other rocks in the vicinity of a vein are frequently unchanged. The ribbon quartz, consisting of parallel layers sometimes not thicker than paper, and extending for hundreds of feet in length and depth, would be impossible by the Plutonic theory. Then again, known eruptive rocks are entirely different from the rocks in which minerals are found. Lava beds contain no gold or silver.

OCEAN FLOORS.

It is now a favorite theory with many that metaliferous veins are deposited in floors of the ocean previous to their upheaval into mountain ranges, and that the metals are precipitated by chemical action; in proof of which we are cited to the precipitation of iron by vegetable matter on a sea-shore. The sea of Sargasso, which is an immense field of seaweeds in mid-ocean, near the tropics, must be, according to this theory, a vast mineral bed, perhaps of gold and silver. We hope no one, in consequence of this suggestion, will get up an expedition to stake off and work this mineral bed, although it might prove fully as profitable as a Cocos island investment. It is certain that nature is a unit in all her works, and that all things work together for final results. We have seen in the deposits at the foot-hills, which probably have an extension into the plains, or former bed of the bay, the deposits of silicious matter in the shape of infusoria, which forms beds several feet in thickness. Mid-ocean, which receives, though slowly, the same material, held in suspension by the water, is consequently reproducing a similar formation in the bottom of the ocean. Let us suppose that the Sacramento valley be buried twenty thousand feet deep,—in *slickens*, if you please,—and that after remaining long enough at that depth for the layers of sand, clay, and gravel, to become indurated or solidified, it begins to slowly emerge as a mountain range. Let us now consider the minerals likely to be found in the rocks. The best statistics of the composition will be a list of the materials which have been dumped into the bay by the rivers. According to the best authorities, *twenty thousand feet*, at least, of rocks have been ground or torn away. Much of this was gold-bearing; indeed, there is much evidence in favor of the opinion that the richest portions of the quartz veins were on the surface. No twenty-five pound lumps have been found in the veins. The gold found in the gulches may have been the coarser particles, rounded by attrition of all this tremendous denudation. How much of the gold was originally coarse? How much of that now found in the quartz veins, if ground in a cañon of rocks like those found in any mountain river, would leave coarse rounded gold? Free gold is usually found in threads and spangles. The Hayward vein, the Keystone, the Plymouth, did not enrich the gulches to any extent. The series of rich surface veins, near Mace's ranch, hardly make a ravine worth working, so fine is the gold. The fine gold of the veins, as well as the particles worn off the sprangly threads, leaving the rounded dust or nuggets, has gone into the valley, and is deposited in an impalpable state in the sand, clay, and gravel, or, perhaps, more finely divided, has gone to sea, to be deposited in the mid-ocean beds of earthy deposits. We may trace it farther than this; some of it may be held in solution. The Platner process of dissolving gold in hydrochloric acid, has shown how it is possible for the sea-water to hold it in solution, and has, perhaps, given us a hint of its possible recovery therefrom. How about the proportion left in the gulches? When one looks at the operations of a glacier, which reduces everything in its grasp to the finest clay; and to such cañons as the American, Mokelumne, or Cosumnes rivers, which take in tons in weight of hard, flinty rocks, reduce them to powder, and send them out on the plains as *slickens*, and asks what has become of the soft gold, it must be answered: It is not destroyed, but not one per cent. of it is left to be mined out in the rivers; not a quarter of one per cent. even. For every million that goes to the mint, more than five hundred has been lost as far as the present race is concerned. It may be worked out when our Sierras and the deep sea shall exchange places, but not before.

To continue the illustration of the formation of quartz veins: the layer of rock over and, perhaps, under the ranges of sand or gravel containing the gold, shall be firm, consistent, holding water, and forming a subterranean channel, such as the water in our artesian wells flows through, these tight floors and roofs becoming the wall rocks of our future vein. When these strata are upheaved so far as to have one portion of the "U" several hundred feet, or perhaps a thousand feet, higher than the other, the lower portion reaches down to depths where the heat may be much above the boiling point, this being reached at the depth of twelve thousand seven hundred and twenty feet, or an increase of one degree for each sixty feet of descent. The iron, sulphur, potash, soda, and other minerals, usually found with all ores, were not mentioned in connection with the gold, supposed to be in the soil of the Sacramento valley, for the reason that they are so common as to be perceptible in every soil. When this arrangement has been completed, the process of depositing mineral veins may be considered to have commenced. It is not essential that more than one end of the "U," or succession of them, shall be exposed. We only stipulate for such an arrangement as will allow the rain-water which falls on the top of the mountain to sink into the earth and carry along whatever mineral it may be able to hold in solution, parting now with a particle of potash or sulphur, taking up a particle of magnesia, silex, or other minerals, until it reaches the alembic, crucible, or laboratory, where heat comes in as a stimulant to its holding or solvent powers. It is impossible to overestimate the capacity of a circulation of this sort. When the water reaches the opposite end of the "U," and again encounters the cooler temperature of the surface, it must gradually part with the greater portion of the mineral which it picked up in its long journey, though not quite all, for every spring contains more or less mineral matter, especially if it emerges in such quantity as to exceed the capacity of the ground for cooling it, as is the case with thermal or hot springs. What would be the consequence of a break or crack in the roof or floor of this channel? Would it not result in the formation of a side or branch vein? An irregularity of upheaval which shall separate the roof of the subterranean channel into numerous parts, would result in setting up new lines of deposit, and a consequent weakening of the main lode. Now, it is a fact, so common in quartz mining as to amount to a certainty, that, without a good hanging-wall not far away, a vein is almost sure to fail. If it were true that the minerals are deposited in veins on ocean floors, this condition would not be so imperious.

A cross fracture in the roof-wall would produce a cross-vein like the Gato vein, the one east of the Zeile mine, and others that might be named. How can such veins be accounted for on the supposition that the precipitation is while the locality is yet a floor? Why should quartz be the vehicle for gathering and retaining gold as well as most other metals? The solution of gold by the Platner process, before referred to, may give us a hint as to the chemical agency of common salt and sulphur in gathering up the gold scattered in impalpable particles through the soil and concentrating it in veins; the precipitation by the sulphuret of iron, tells its own story also, as this form of iron is constantly associated with gold. The free gold and large lumps still remain to be accounted for. Some miners of intelligence believe that gold grows—by accretion—both in quartz and gravel. Possibly it does. Who can tell when, if ever, the particles of matter, even in the hardest rocks, ceased to adjust themselves to each other? J. T. Burke, the oldest and most experienced quartz miner in the county, thinks that the quartz veins are still receiving gold. It is said that the silver mines of Mexico, which were worked three hundred years since, have again become rich from the flowing through them of water containing silver in solution. The copper mines in the lower part of the county are known to be in an active condition, gaining or losing ores all the time.

The mineral belts of Amador county are various and extensive, but there are many reasons for believing they once were one floor. Beginning with the lower veins nearly on a level with the rivers, as the last formed, we have the Arroyo Seco lead near Muletown on the west, and the Newton lead on the east; thence across the axis of elevation (the serpentine range near the Mountain Spring House), we have another extension of the same, but a few miles in width, and by no means continuous from north to south. Some rich quartz is found in this range, and considerable copper, the latter in chimneys of small extent. Next is the Mother Lode, which has been fully described, the upper end or east side of the "U" being near Volcano. East of Volcano is the last one to be considered, for the reason that by denudation the upper and older lines of elevation are nearly erased. Why the lower belt near the foothills should have copper instead of gold; why the middle belt should have the custody of the richest quartz veins; why the upper or Volcano range should have its veins transverse or at angles, varying with the cleavage of the slate, is among the many, very many, mysteries.

So far, we have only taken into account the fissure or true veins, which may be considered as those that reach the bottom, or continue through the inverted syphon. The true fissure vein may be in the shape of a chimney, wide, with a short run north and south, or it may be continuous for hundreds of feet, with about the same thickness; but in either case it may be poor or rich, the essential condition of its wealth being, that it must be located in a gold-bearing soil or lode. A vein of quartz by itself may not be rich in gold any more than a ravine. There are quartz mountains in New Hampshire, as well as in California; but no gold in them that is known.

SURFACE VEINS.

These have an entirely different origin, and in general pinch out at no great distance from the surface. They are probably produced by the precipitation of gold and quartz, held in solution by surface streams. Some surface veins are quite rich; little fortunes are often made out of them. This is the character of many of the veins in the vicinity of West Point. A surface vein is characterized by a nearly total want of *gouge*. What this has to do with a quartz vein, may not be apparent to the general reader. In all fissures of any extent is found a clay, sometimes several inches in thickness, which is said to be produced by the slow grinding or rubbing of the walls against each other. The rocks and clay are striated, the lines showing the directions of these oscillations, which are not necessarily perceivable, in a generation even. There is apt to be a heavier deposit of ore along the gouge, which, as a usual thing, also is a water-course. If the fissure is but temporary, extending down a few hundred feet at most, below which the rock is solid, there can be no grinding or rubbing of the walls together, and, consequently, no *gouge*. These surface veins are in constant formation, though some of them probably are contemporaneous with the true fissure veins. A small quartz vein will sometimes form in a lava bed; also in the coal veins, or beds of lignite, in the foot-hills. They are found in the tertiary or sandstone hills of the Coast Range, some of the veins having considerable gold in them. These hills, by the way, though in some places thousands of feet high, bear marks of a birth long subsequent to the Sierras, and are, probably, in great part composed of the *debris* from the summits of the Sierras, when they had not yet bared their heads of granite. The cement of old buildings sometimes contains thin veins of crystallized quartz. The gold-bearing veins of steatite near Ione, probably were enriched the same way; that is, by surface action. Let our future chemists take a hint from this in the reduction of gold quartz.

PROBABLE DEPTH OF VEINS.

It is well settled that quartz and other mineral veins have no particular connection with the center of the earth, but are surface affairs, extending no deeper than the deposits of rocky matter that in the great cycle of events is now filling up an ocean, and now being lifted to be denuded and sent again to the bottom of the deep sea. If the slope in the Keystone, Gover, and Seaton mines were maintained for a few thousand feet it would be apt to meet the bottom of the "V," or inverted syphon. The wall rock of the Consolidated Amador failed at one thousand seven hundred and fifty feet; other mines may extend to greater depths, but if they could or should be worked down to greater depths, probably the wall rock would be found gradually getting flatter. Indeed, the universal testimony is that after the permanent vein is reached a change in the direction of the vein is always towards a horizontal. The opinion sometimes entertained, that the quartz veins extend to interminable depths is probably erroneous, though the limit may never be reached by any known methods of working deep mines.

METHODS OF DEPOSIT.

An uneducated person, when first shown a piece of crystalized quartz, is apt to form the opinion that it had been melted and run into that shape, but a little observation will convince him that the regular forms must be the result of a general law resulting from the adjustment of the particles to each other. In some specimens of crystals we may see the lines of deposit which are always parallel to the terminal faces. In examining veins of quartz of different localities, we find some in fine layers (like ribbons when viewed edgewise), not thicker than paper. The slightest amount of iron, lime, or other mineral, in solution with the silicious matter, will suffice to mark the lines of deposit. In other veins, which appear to be solid, we may get a hint of the method of deposit by the lines of decomposition or decay, which show an arrangement of particles like melting ice, which does not melt in parallel lines, but in cavities. So a quartz vein will show a deposit of irregular crystals adhering to the sides of a cavity and gradually approaching each other until they unite and become solid. This seems to be a common form of deposit in the recent or surface veins. In other cases the quartz is in nodules or amorphous bunches. This is the case in the Keystone where the bunches are sometimes so large as to contain forty thousand tons of rich milling ore. The Hayward had a *boulder* vein also, though it would scarcely pay for milling. A more thorough investigation may show a uniform and decided difference in the lines of deposit of surface and true fissure veins, by which their character may be determined.

JURASSIC GRAVEL.

Geologists have determined the gold-bearing quartz and adjoining rocks to belong to the jurassic age. This classification is said to rest on the discovery of fossil reptiles, and is probably correct. The point to note in the matter, which seems to have escaped the attention of the professors, is the existence of large bodies of gravel in different portions of the county, in strata parallel to the quartz veins, and probably extending down as far or farther than the quartz veins. These veins of gravel are full of quartz pebbles, as well rounded as any that can be found in creek or river, and are no spheroidal concretions formed when the slates were a plastic mass, but are evidently the product of a rapid stream passing over auriferous quartz. Where is the stream that rounded these pebbles? Where is the system of quartz veins which must antedate the Mother Lode from which these pebbles were torn? Where is the mountain that gave impetus to these streams that rounded them? The beds appear in such quantities and in such places and conditions as to forbid the idea of their having fallen into a fissure in the earth. They have the regular stratification and cleavage of the slate; the layers being separated frequently by thin, delicate lines of slate such as may be seen in any alluvial deposit. The gravel may be seen in nearly all the cañons west of the Mother Lode, but the most decided outcrop is about one thousand feet east of Drytown, where there are two distinct deposits each a hundred feet thick, separated by a strata of the black clay slate, common to the country. This reef extends the whole length of Murderer's gulch on the north, and to the Rancheria hill on the south, a distance of two miles, and from the gold found in the ravine near by, is evidently gold-bearing. What becomes of the Mother Lode theory now? Here is gravel that is as old in its place as the Mother Lode, that presupposes an older lode still, not only that, but a subsequent upheaval. There is but one conclusion in the matter possible; there must have been an older Mother Lode, or grandmother, if such a term is permissible, which existed and was in a mountain or range of mountains ere the upturning of the slates in whose company the gravels rest. As there are some two or three thousand feet of clay slate between this gravel and the Mother Lode, older than the quartz, occupying the inferior position, millions of years were necessary for the slow deposit of the clays afterwards indurated into slate. Reference to evidence of a former mineral region, denuded to the granite rock in a former age has once before been made.

In the northern part of the State where the integrity of the mountain tops has been better maintained, there are large rivers which seem to run towards the south and become lost. The Blue Lead, the largest of these, is said to have been traced to El Dorado county. As this river was far to the east, occupying a much greater altitude, these gravel beds may be the lacustrine termination of the Blue Lead which by a subsequent upheaval, is now tightly inclosed in its coffin of slate. The question, "What has become of the Blue Lead?" may possibly be answered here. The discovery may have no economic value but it will be an interesting leaf to read in the geology of California. This lead of gravel, tracing it by the appearance in places, seems to have taken a south western direction

ARTHUR B. SANBORN.

across the county. It may be seen in Sutter creek about four miles below the town, and again in the southern part of the county near the Mokelumne river. Although the veins have never been worked, a thorough prospecting might prove them to have some economic value.

CHAPTER XXVIII.
QUARTZ MINING.

Quartz Mining, Commencement of—Quartz Miners' Convention—Account of the Mother Lode—Sketch of Different Mines—Gwin Mines—Casco—Murphy's Ridge—Huffaker—Moore—Zeile—Description of a Model Mill—Plattner Process of Reducing Sulphurets—Hinkley Mine—Montechardo—Kennedy—Tubbs—Oneida—Summit—Hayward—Character of the Same—Railroad—Wildman—Mahoney—Union or Lincoln—Accident in the Lincoln—Mechanics—Herbertville—Spring Hill—Keystone—Consolidation of Granite State and Walnut Hill—Discovery of the Bonanza—Statistics of Same—Big Grab, and Failure to Hold it—Account of the Suit—Original Amador—Bunker Hill—Pennsylvania Gover—Black Hills—Seaton—Potosi—Quartz Mountain—Plymouth Group—Enterprise—Nashville.

The intelligent men who worked the gulches and rivers in an early day, soon sought the sources of the gold. Sometimes gold was found with quartz adhering to it, or occasionally a quartz pebble riveted through and through with gold. The veins of quartz seaming the hills in the vicinity of the richest placers, also served to point to that rock as the original source of the gold. At Carson Hill, in Mariposa county, quartz had been found immensely rich; but the expense of blasting the rock out and crushing it was such, that no serious attempts were made, in Amador county, until 1851. The whole country abounded with quartz; in some places there were mountains of it, which had filled the ravines with broken quartz, where no gold was to be found; so that the search for auriferous quartz was a tedious affair until men were put upon the scent.

The first discovery of gold in quartz seems to have been made by a man by the name of Davidson, a Baptist preacher, in February, 1851, on the south side of Amador creek near the spring then used by the miners. Boulders of considerable size were lying on the top of the ground, supposed to have been detached from the vein. Gold was found in some of these, and subsequently, in the vein from which these came. Associated with Davidson were Glover, Herbert, and P. Y. Cool, all ministers; hence the claim was known as the "ministers' claim." Samuel Hill, afterward a resident of Buckeye, was taken in as a capitalist, and the company organized as the Spring Hill Company. About the same time, Thomas Rickey, and his son James, afterward residents of Ione, located the vein on the north side of the creek, since known as the Original Amador. Gold could also be seen in this rock. None of these men had ever seen any quartz mining; in fact, there was none in the world to compare with what may be seen now at any mining town. Hill, of the Spring Hill Company, went to Sacramento and bought a

steam engine, aged and ancient in style, which proved a mine of trouble to them, as it took an enormous quantity of wood to make steam. The main shaft was wood with bearings of round bar iron, two inches in diameter, which were driven in with a hammer, the end of the log being banded with iron. The cams were large spikes of bar iron driven into the shaft and afterward bent. The stamps had wooden stems, and spikes driven into the stems for tappits or projections, against which the cams should play to raise the stamps. The gold was saved, or rather lost, by means of a rocker about eight feet long, worked by the same power as the stamps. The machinery proving a failure, was soon rebuilt with improvements suggested by experience.

The mill on the north side was started about the same time, September 5, 1851, with somewhat better machinery. The shaft was of wood, but had axe-bar iron four inches wide and half an inch thick for cams, the bars being bent after they were put in the shaft. The stamps also had wooden stems with slots in the middle to receive the cams. Dan Fiddler was the master mechanic, and J. T. Berke the superintendent of this mine. It made dividends as well as wages for its owners, who were all workers. Quicksilver was tried, but from some cause failed to give satisfactory results. It was also discovered that much of the gold was lost, being too fine to settle into the ordinary riffles. While experiments were being made to remedy the matter, a German, who had had experience in mining in Peru, proposed to amalgamate with arastras. With his assistance the company took out about seventy-five ounces a week, the German receiving one-thirteenth part for his share. This was the first successful quartz mining in the county.

QUARTZ MINERS' CONVENTION.

The discovery of gold-bearing quartz aroused the whole country. All were looking forward to the time when the gulches and surface claims should be exhausted, and there were numbers of men who thought this was the case as early as 1851. Quartz was now tried everywhere; like any other mining craze it went beyond all reasonable bounds. Possibilities became certainties. A mill had been put up at Quartzburg on the Cosumnes river which was thought to be making fabulous fortunes for its owners, which, however, was far from true. It may as well be told here that the superintendent, Dr. Harris, a native of Nashville, Tennessee, brought out seventeen thousand dollars to work the mine, drew on the company for twenty-eight thousand dollars more, and then abandoned the mine to the hired hands to make their back wages out of it if they could. The lead or Mother Lode, as this system of veins, chutes, or chimneys, has been called, was soon traced to the Cosumnes on the north, and the Mokelumne on the south. All kinds of claims were set up and a harvest of lawsuits seemed impending, when it was resolved to hold a quartz convention and make regulations to ensure the peace and security of quartz mining, which, after a proper notice, was held at Rancheria, that being probably the largest place in the county.

The following is copied from the book of records now in the hands of M. B. Church of Drytown.

"QUARTZ MINING LAWS.

"At a meeting of the miners of Dry Creek, Rancheria Creek, Amador Creek, Sutter Creek, holden near the town of Rancheria, June 7, 1851, in accordance with previous public notice, for the purpose of making rules and regulations for quartz miners, in the mining districts hereinafter described.

"T. J. Lawton was chosen President; Samuel Herbert, Vice-President; Wm. Salter, Jr., Secretary.

"On motion of O. L. Palmer, a committee of three was appointed consisting of O. L. Palmer, Wm. Fenton, of Rancheria, and Hiram B. Platt, of Drytown, to prepare resolutions for the consideration of the meeting. The committee offered the following report, which was accepted.

"*Resolved*, That rules and regulations for the security, peace and harmony of the miners, who are now or who may be hereafter engaged in prospecting and working quartz mines, are positively necessary.

"2.—That in compliance with that necessity, we do hereby ordain and establish the following rules and regulations for the government of the district within the following bounds, to wit: All that portion of the county of Calaveras that lies south of the dividing ridge between Cosumnes river and Dry creek and north of the Mokolumne river.

"3.—That the size of a claim in quartz veins shall be two hundred and forty (240) feet in length of the vein without regard to the width, to the discoverer or company, and one hundred and twenty (120) feet in addition thereto for each member of the company that shall now or may be hereafter organized.

"4.—That no claims, hereafter made, shall be considered good and valid, unless the same shall have been staked off, in conformity with the provisions of Resolution 3, and written notice of the size of the claim, and the number of the men in the company, posted on a stake or tree at each end of the claim, together with the date of the day when the claim was made; and all claims now made shall be staked off in conformity with these resolutions, within five days from the date of the adoption of these resolutions.

"5.—That the size of the claim, the names and number of men composing the company that holds the claim, together with a brief description of the location of the same, so that it may be identified, shall, within ten days after the claim is made, be filed in the office of the Justice of the Peace, in whose district the same may be located. And all persons holding such claims shall file the same within ten days from this meeting, and all persons hereafter making claims (within ten days after the claims are located), or otherwise, said claims shall be forfeited.

"6.—In all cases where claims are held by a company working jointly, they shall not be required to work in more than one place; but where held by individuals, each several claim must be worked.

"7.—Whenever a claim has been abandoned, and such can be clearly proved before the Justice of the Peace, where such filing was made, said claim shall be forfeited to the person or persons establishing such proof.

"8.—That these rules, regulations, and proceedings, be signed by the president and secretary of this meeting, and filed in the Justice's office at Drytown.
"T. J. LAWTON, *Pres.*,
"WM. SALTER, *Sec.*"

The number of talented men in this Convention was noted, although it was not unusual for such bodies, in the early fifties, to be composed of men who might have sat in Legislative halls, with credit to themselves and all concerned.

The Convention was hopeful, and even confident, of success. Some, who were not in possession of satisfactory claims, wished the size to be cut down. It was urged that fifty feet of a vein, which probably had no bottom, was quite enough to satisfy any reasonable man. One thousand dollars a ton was set as the probable value of the quartz. Some of the veins were fifty, and even a hundred feet wide. It was easy to figure up into millions within a short distance of the top on a fifty-foot claim. Some ventured to say that the quartz would not pay a dollar a pound. Mr. Davidson, being a candid, unexcitable man, was called upon to give his opinion as to the value of it. He said that he had no wish to deceive the Convention, but he doubted if the rock would average more than ten cents per pound, or two hundred dollars per ton (he had not then started his mill); and claims were made one hundred and twenty feet, with two extra claims to the discoverer. What would have been the feelings of the Convention if they could have foreseen that one-tenth of the sum named would come to be considered very rich? Scarcely one of all the number who assembled that day, but what retired from quartz mining, bankrupt and discouraged. This, however, is anticipating.

Quartz mining was now fairly inaugurated. In a short time, the Granite State, the Herbertville, the Union, Eureka, Badger, Wolverine (the last three being consolidated in the Hayward mine), Oneida, all came in a short time. The Granite State was the first to put up a mill with iron shaft, tappits and stems. John Conness was a stockholder in this mine. Garfield, afterwards Governor of Washington Territory, invented the stamp with tapering stem and socket, to correspond. Shaking tables were introduced in 1852, and were in use until 1860. The Chile mill, with rotating balls and revolving barrel, was introduced by P. M. Randal. The last is still used. Roasting the ore was tried, but, though it was more easily pulverized, it was soon abandoned as not satisfactory. The sulphurets were saved by means of blankets or rawhides placed along the bottoms of the sluices, and amalgamated in the Chile mill, or revolving barrel.

THE MOTHER LODE.

Perhaps no term more inappropriate could have been selected. The name is inappropriate because there is no principal lode or vein at all, but rather a series or system of veins, chutes or chimneys along a certain range of country, varying in width from two hundred to four thousand, or perhaps eight thousand feet. In some places there are hundreds of veins, as on the Black hills and Murphy's ridge, some of which are mere threads, ramifying in every direction. In other places, the ore-bearing ground is narrowed within walls two or three hundred feet apart, as at the Keystone, Plymouth, and the Hayward mines; though even here, as we shall see, the ore is not concentrated in a single vein. The term *mother*, is also misleading, for it gives the idea that all other veins are connected somehow, and fed from this, than which nothing could be more erroneous. Evidently, the first theorists presumed that all mineral veins came out of the interior regions of the earth, where the fires are always glowing, and that down some thousand feet all the veins of quartz, big and little, would come together in one main lode, extending the whole length of the State, or as far as the gold range extends.

SKETCH OF THE DIFFERENT MINES.

The Gwin mine, though in Calaveras county, is really the beginning of the series of veins which have made Amador the richest county in the State in quartz. This is in Rich gulch, which is supposed to have derived its wealth from the breaking down of the vein matter. The owner, Dr. Gwin, is better known as Duke Gwin, from his having that title conferred on him for valuable aid to the Emperor Maximillian of Mexico. The mine is said to be paying well. The series of veins here is quite wide, several other veins cropping out a thousand feet or more to the east.

The Casco mine is on the north side of the Mokelumne river, and consequently in Amador county. This mine was worked in 1868 by J. R. Hardenburg some eight hundred feet deep, the rock being crushed by a water-mill of twenty stamps, not far from the mine. The owner sunk twenty thousand dollars in the operation. The Casco mine is on the eastern side of the range, which here is quite wide. Abraham McKinney has a mine on the west side of the range, which is yet undeveloped, but which shows some very rich specimens, some of which are of singular appearance, containing gold in crystalline forms in coarse granulated quartz. Persons who entertain an opinion that gold is deposited in a melted state, will find a puzzling problem in these specimens. The rock east of here (hanging-wall) is syenitic or stratified rock, resembling granite, varying in texture and character at every dividing seam. On the west the wall rock (foot-wall) is the hard metamorphic slate sometimes termed by the miners "blue granite."

MURPHY'S RIDGE.

This singular formation is the Mother Lode in its integrity with the foot and hanging-walls washed away and occupied by ravines, Murphy's gulch and Black gulch on one side, and Hunt's gulch on the other. It is likely that the gouge, which is generally a soft, clayey mass, which seems to have been formed by the slow grinding of the walls against the vein, gave direction to the course of the water which finally eroded them away. On the west side of the ridge the miners have followed the gouge down in places to a considerable depth for the gold that lies on the foot-wall. The ravines were, perhaps, the richest ever found in the county, as they were worked with profit for twenty years, one set of miners after another taking away their "piles."

The ridge is a network of small veins which ramify in every direction through a rather soft earthy slate. Some of the seams are immensely rich, four or five hundred dollars being taken out of a bucketful of the rotten rock. Sometimes the gold is found in combination with arsenic, or arsenical sulphurets, which pay a thousand dollars or more to the ton, though the tons are not many, as the veins may not be a half inch in thickness. In places the ridge is being washed down by hydraulic power. As much of the gold is too fine to be saved by this process, much must be lost. In other instances the small veins of quartz are mined out and crushed, paying good wages. "There is millions in it," *i. e.*, the hill or ridge, but how to get it out economically is the question. Isaac N. Dewitt owns twenty acres of this ridge, being a long strip four hundred feet wide along the center.

Many experienced miners think all these veins will come together below, and offer as a reason for this opinion that the wall rocks are converging as they go down. James Morgan, a man with much experience in mining, is of this opinion, and is now running a cross cut some four hundred feet below the summit of the ridge, to test the theory. A shaft sunk four hundred feet on the east side of the ridge, did not expose any workable vein.

HUFFAKER LEAD.

This once very rich mine, some two thousand feet or more to the east of the last-named mine, is not worked at present. It is said that in 1856 the Huffaker brothers and —— Harris, found quartz that would pay twenty thousand dollars per ton. The gold was found in bunches or pockets. Like all pocket veins, this one marred about as many fortunes as it made. James Morgan is now sinking on this lode with good prospects. This vein is believed to have supplied the gold that enriched the hills around the south side of the Butte Basin.

THE MOORE MINE

Is at the head of Hunt's gulch, on the eastern side of the Mother Lode. It is a curiosity, and is worthy of observation. It is a rather thin vein of good looking quartz, with an enormous mass of barren quartzose rock for a foot-wall, the whole mass being considerable out of the range of Murphy's ridge, which is thought to be the main lode. North of Murphy's the quartz seems to be wanting, though a few small veins crop out over a space perhaps half a mile wide, some of these being in the hard, metamorphic slate, which is supposed to have been the axis of elevation when the mountain chains were formed. These veins may be traced along the ridge west of Jackson and the Oneida. Though they contain some gold they *pinch out* at a short distance from the surface, and are avoided by quartz miners.

There has been considerable prospecting in the neighborhood of Jackson, and several times the announcement of the beginning of the quartz mining era was made, but it never came. So many promising mines were discovered that in 1862 the Kearsing brothers erected a four-stamp mill and arastra, run by water-power, for custom work. The mill was afterwards enlarged to ten stamps, but it was not a paying concern. In 1862

THE ZEILE MINE

Was discovered by Leonard Coney, who put up a mill with sixteen stamps, with works to reduce the sulphurets, though the Platner process was not introduced at that time. Some very good runs were made, realizing ten thousand dollars per month. In April, 1866, it was sold by Charles T. Meader, who had been running it, to Dr. Zeile, of San Francisco, for seventy-five thousand dollars. Work was suspended until within the past two years, since which time new hoisting works and mill, with all the latest improvements, have been placed on the mine. As this is considered the model mill of the county, a description of it will be in place. The hoisting works over the shaft have powerful pumps, which can be set in motion without interfering with the other machinery. An air-compressor saves the work of striking the drills, while an automatic dumper does away with the dangerous work of bucket landing, by which so many men have been injured. The rock is carried on a tramway to the upper story of the mill, where a "grizzly" separates the fine from the coarse rock, the latter going into a rock-breaker, which prepares it for the stamps. From the rock breaker the quartz goes to the automatic feeder, a machine that seems almost endowed with life, so closely does it watch the batteries, supplying them with quartz at the moment the stamps begin to strike the bed of the mortar. The action is simple and reliable. The idea originated with James Tullock, of Volcano, who erected the first one some years ago. Several designs have been patented since, but his holds a place yet among quartz-mills. The tappit or collar around the stem of the stamp, by means of which the cam raises the stamp, is the agent employed. It is put in connection with a revolving belt or table, containing the quartz to be fed to the battery, so that when the stamp descends to the bottom of the mortar, the tappit moves the table, and drops some rock into the battery, which it continues to do until the want is supplied. An automatic feeder is required for each battery. When the pulverized quartz has passed through the shaking tables, and other machinery for saving the free gold, it passes to the machine known as the "Frue Concentrator," for saving the sulphurets. This machine is a recent invention, and considered a great improvement over either the Buddle or the Hendy concentrator. The pulp is caught on a wide rubber belt, which, with an oscillating motion, is made to carry the tailings up an incline against a gentle stream of water, which washes away the lighter particles, leaving the sulphurets, which are heavier, to adhere, by their own specific gravity, to the endless belt, which passes into a water-bath, removing the sulphurets, which are thus saved in a very concentrated condition.

THE PLATNER PROCESS

Of reducing sulphurets was introduced into California by a miner by the name of Deakin, and is now in general use. By this process the sulphurets formerly lost are made to pay from fifty to six hundred dollars per ton, amounting in some instances to twenty per cent. of the entire gold product. The "chlorination works" is a long building with a furnace some forty feet long, and sixteen feet wide with arched roof from one to three feet above the floor. There are several openings along the sides to put in and withdraw the charge, (which, in a furnace of the above size, would be about three tons,) also to observe the progress of the work. The first heat is moderate and is intended to expel the moisture, after which the heat is increased and the sulphur is set on fire. This burns for some hours, keeping the mass at a dull red heat; after the sulphur has burned out the fire must be increased so as to drive off the arsenic and other base metals. Too much heat will now volatilize the gold, which will be found gilding the roof of the arch. Too little fire leaves the fine particles of gold coated with a metal that would prevent the last and most important process (to be described hereafter), so that constant watchfulness is requisite, though a trusty man, without being a chemist, soon learns the necessary treatment. The mass, after being roasted from twenty-four to thirty-six hours, is allowed to cool off, and is then place in tubs five or six feet wide and two feet high with tight-fitting covers, where it is subjected for thirty-six hours to the action of chlorine gas which dissolves the gold, forming the chloride of gold which is soluble in water. The process of making gold soluble is particularly described, because it may be necessary to remember this when we consider the origin of the gold deposits in the quartz veins. The chlorine gas is obtained by the action of sulphuric acid on common salt and oxide of manganese, all cheap articles. It is a corrosive gas eating up other metals as well as gold, and also destroys animal matter, purifying the atmosphere of offensive odors. Water is now turned into the tubs and the gold comes out as a greenish-brown liquid; in fact, gold is of a green color, notwithstanding the ordinary opinion, as may be seen by looking through a very thin film of gold, which will appear of a beautiful green. Water is run through the mass until no green tinge is left. Sulphate of iron (copperas) is now added to the solution and in a short time the gold begins to settle in the shape of a brown powder, which, upon being put in the crucible, melts into gold 995. fine, worth twenty dollars per ounce. The cost of reducing sulphurets this way is about seventeen dollars per ton. It is expected that the cost of extracting and reducing ore at this mill will fall below two dollars per ton. If this can be accomplished, it will, perhaps, cause many other mines of low grade ore to be worked. The works, with the powerful and massive machinery, form a wonderful contrast to the mills at Amador thirty years ago.

THE HINKLEY MINE

Is a pocket mine and was discovered in 1863 while the owner was digging a post hole. Some four thousand dollars were taken out in a few days. The vein is two and a half feet thick at the surface; at a depth of forty feet it was five feet thick; turned from a perpendicular to a horizontal for thirty feet, and then ran down nearly vertically again. It has produced eighteen thousand dollars at an expense of six thousand dollars. It has many times made its owner happy, but the rock when away from a pocket is distressingly poor. Mr. Hinkley owns about four hundred feet of the vein.

A few hundred yards east of the Zeile mine is a slash vein, so called, running nearly at right angles with the ordinary course. At the Gate is another of great width and nearly a thousand feet long. They are seen occasionally in other parts of the county, and, although they have never been worked to any extent, they are important as throwing considerable light on the formation of quartz veins.

The Monterichard is a cross vein in the hard metamorphic slate about two miles west of Jackson. It was discovered in 1876 by a Frenchman who gave his name to the mine. It has paid very well, making for thirty-two months from two thousand to three thousand seven hundred and fifty dollars per month with a mill of ten stamps. The vein is narrow, varying from six inches to two feet, with walls well defined. It was run by James Meehan, Sanguinetti, and Muldoon, until March, 1880, when it was sold to Lloyd Tevis, of San Francisco, for twenty thousand dollars. The new owner put in ten more stamps, making a twenty-stamp mill. The vein pinched out soon after and the mine is suspended. It is generally thought Tevis got the worst of the bargain.

THE KENNEDY MINE,

So named from its discoverer, was developed by John Fullen, James Fleming, and James Bergon, working the rock at the Oneida mill. In 1871 it was taken by a joint-stock company, the Richlings being large owners. The mine has hardly been a success, and in 1880 it was closed down. The vein is close to the foot-wall and has pitched rapidly to the east, following a pitch of nearly forty-five degrees, which is considered very flat. It is believed that it will eventually join a vein about six hundred feet to the east, called the "Volunteer." The lode does not follow the rift of the slate and consequently is not a true fissure vein.

THE TUBB'S MINE

Was on the eastern part of the lode near the Gate. It did not pay and was shut down. Stephen Kendal was the manager of the works. There seems to have been no substantial wall rock and consequently no permanent vein.

THE ONEIDA.

This location was made in 1851, by a number of men from the central part of New York. Like all the companies engaged at that time in quartz mining, the Oneida had extravagant expectations. When a run had been made, the interested parties gathered around to see the batteries cleaned up. The sand, quicksilver, and amalgam were gathered, and the operator commenced the panning process, turning off the quicksilver as it ran together. As the sand was washed out the amalgam grew less and less as did the prospects of the miners. The whole proceeds of several days' crushing finally shrunk to a handful containing a few ounces of gold, not half enough to pay expenses, to say nothing about a fortune. The mill and mine were leased, in 1854, to Dr. E. B. Harris for a nominal rent, for the purpose of having it developed. He was endowed with great physical strength and indomitable energy, as well as good judgment, and by selecting good rock, and acting as fireman, engineer, amalgamator, machinist, miner, and superintendent, by turns, making about a dozen men of one and that one himself, he made the mine pay, for that year, about twenty thousand dollars over expenses. At that time machinery was generally taken to Sacramento for repairs, necessitating long delays and much expense. One day a cam-seat, or groove, on the shaft which holds the key gave away, and the cam was dangling like a broken leg. To take out the shaft and send it to Sacramento was expensive, both in time and money, and it was resolved to drill a hole through both cam and shaft and put a large pin through them to hold the cam. By superhuman exertion this was done in about three hours, the order to "fire up" ringing simultaneously with the coming through of the point of the drill, and in half an hour the mill was pounding away. A year or two afterward the mine was rented to Swain of Ione, who in one year lost as much as Harris made.

The mine afterward fell into the hands of Fullen, Flemming, Bergon & Co., who worked it with but moderate success for some years. About 1865, it was purchased by William M. Stewart, then U. S. Senator for Nevada, James Morgan, and others, for one hundred thousand dollars, of which sum the shareholders received eighty thousand dollars, the other twenty thousand dollars going to the negotiators of the sale, Seaton and Farley. The mine was retimbered, the mill enlarged to sixty stamps, and new hoisting works erected, making the mine an investment to the stockholders of something over a quarter of a million. The vein was fifty feet thick, though of low grade, and with improved machinery it was expected to realize large dividends; but the mine was an expensive one to work, the walls being soft and apt to swell or crawl, and also full of water. Sometimes great masses of soft earth, mud, and *gouge* would break loose and run down the stopes and shafts, burying up or clogging the lower works. Sometimes a shaft would close up, timbers two feet in diameter being slowly crushed endwise into kindling-wood. Where there was so much movement underground, the surface must become unstable also, and the hoisting works required frequent rebuilding or adjustment. The mine proved a losing concern and became a grave for about four hundred thousand dollars.

It is now owned by a Boston company, and is under the superintendence of Robert Robinson. Water-power has been substituted for steam-power, making a saving of many thousand dollars in a year; the water is to some degree exhausted, and at a lower level the walls become harder and more easily timbered, so that the mine, almost for the first time in its history, has been, perhaps, put on a paying basis.*

The depth on the slope is eleven hundred and fifty feet, but at the lower level the vein is nearly flat, and the vertical depth is not much over six hundred feet. The eastern or lower workings are about in a line with the buddle house, perhaps four hundred feet east of the shaft. At this point the vein, which seems to have followed the rift of the slate, and is, therefore, the true fissure, is nearly pinched out, and a drift of six hundred feet lengthwise the vein, failed to discover any swell or deposit. A single boulder or bunch of quartz weighing a few hundred pounds, and very rich, was all that was found at this depth that was encouraging. How this was deposited, or perhaps *lost* there, is a question for geologists. As the lower level has been allowed to fill up with water, it is probable that no deeper explorations are contemplated.

There are some encouraging indications of a vein or body of ore in what is called the west wall. In working out bodies of ore left in the upper levels, a stringer, or thin vein of quartz, was found leading to the west, which experienced miners think indicates another ore body. If this should be realized the mine may have a brilliant future.

*Since writing the above, we learn that the mine has indefinitely suspended work.

North of the Oneida, the range is buried for some distance under a pliocene river, with perhaps two hundred feet of gravel, sand, and boulders. As this has not been found to be rich, no explorations under it have been made, and if the *lode* crops out it has not been seen. Farther north is the

SUMMIT MINE,

Or, more properly, a prospect hole, for no paying quartz was found, though the shaft was sunk several hundred feet deep, at a cost of some twenty or thirty thousand dollars. The experiment was made by Hall McAllister of San Francisco.

HAYWARD MINE.

The next mine north of the Summit mine is the Consolidated Amador, better known by the name of the man whose energy, with a good share of luck, developed it into, probably, the best-paying gold mine in the world. In 1853 three mines on the south side of Sutter creek—Wolverine, Eureka, and Badger—were struggling for existence, Alvinza Hayward owning the largest interest in the one last named. None of the quartz mines at that time were giants ready at the asking to bestow fortunes; on the contrary, they were always requiring enormous outlays for sinking shafts, running cross-cuts, timber, wood, and machinery—all making quartz mining a precarious employment. The Wolverine was among the first to fail. The Eureka was divided into about sixty shares, most of the holders being working men. The Badger was equipped with hoisting works and a mill on the creek below the town. The quartz was hauled on wagons to the mill. Whether because the rock was inferior or unskillfully handled, it hardly ever paid expenses, oftener less than more, to such an extent that the mine, though a promising one, had promised so much that its credit was utterly destroyed. Ninety thousand dollars or more hung over it, not like the sword of Damocles, suspended by a single hair, but due for wood, steel, provisions, and labor, besides borrowed money. Many times the proprietor was tempted to throw up the works and turn them over to the creditors; but they as often told him to go on; that he could make it pay if any one could. Often on a Sunday morning, when the laborers came for their pay, a dollar or two for tobacco money was all that could be spared. On one occasion, the proprietor was seen carrying wood on his back from the side-hill to keep the engine running. A Mr. Norton furnished wood on long time, and relieved that source of solicitude. Four or five years of such struggling had broken down, one after another, the most of those who had commenced quartz mining in 1851. In 1857 the struggle still continued. There was a change impending. The pay chimney was struck, and now the double eagles, instead of scant half dollars, were paid to the men. The pay streak was likely to run into the Eureka ground, and the owner quietly commenced buying up shares of that company's stock. Five hundred dollars a share, considering the mill which they had erected at an estimated expense of thirty thousand dollars, just the amount at which the shares were rated, was not too much. It was soon known that a majority of the stock had passed into his hands, and the balance hastened to part with their stock, selling as low as four hundred dollars per share; though assured that no *freezing out* was intended, the shares all passed into Mr. Hayward's control. It now became known that it had been placed on a permanent, paying basis, yielding from twenty-eight thousand to sixty-five thousand dollars per month.

GENERAL CHARACTER OF THE HAYWARD MINE.

As this was not only the best mine in the range, but the deepest, the explorations having reached the depth of two thousand two hundred and fifty feet, a particular description of its locality, wall rocks, and surface indications, will be interesting, as throwing light on the nature of quartz veins in general. Although there were large masses of rock in the vein, and covering the ground in the vicinity of this mine, the ravine below was only moderately rich. The surface rock that was within a few hundred feet of the top, paid from eight to twelve dollars a ton only. In the early days of quartz mining, when the means of closely saving the gold had not been discovered, this would hardly pay; though after the mine passed into other hands, the same rock, by means of improved machinery, being taken out and reduced for two dollars and seventy-five cents per ton, according to the report of the superintendent, J. C. Faul, paid one hundred and fifty thousand dollars in dividends. The wall rocks of the *range*, which here was only two or three hundred feet wide, were firm, metamorphic slate, called by the miners, granite, a term which often misleads persons seeking information. It scarcely ever has any of the appearance of true granite, and in most instances is similar in texture to the great reef of rock lying west of the quartz belt, or range of mining towns, which has already been spoken of as one of the axes of elevation, and the western boundary of the ancient valley. This wall rock, on the east side of the vein, went down, solid and firm, about one thousand seven hundred and fifty feet, after which it was much broken up, the quartz paying to this depth. There were two principal veins; perhaps deposits would be a better term, as but one of the deposits was in the shape of a vein, the other being called a boulder vein, from its being in detached masses, like boulders, through occupying a regular rift or fissure in the slate. The continuous vein was next to the hanging or eastern wall, and both veins had a pitch or slope to the east of about twenty feet to the hundred, so that a perpendicular shaft, to reach the vein at a depth of two thousand feet, must be started about four hundred feet east of the croppings. It may be as well to mention here that experienced miners never expect to find the true course of a vein until they have sunk from four to eight hundred feet on it. An ore-bearing vein or fissure, if an extensive one, is always more or less open, admitting water. A few calculations as to the power of displacement in a seam containing water may be interesting. "Water presses in proportion to its perpendicular height." At a depth of thirty-three feet the lateral pressure is two thousand one hundred and sixty pounds to the square foot, at sixty-six twice that, at one hundred three times, and so on as far as the water reaches, which is usually as far as any ore is found. Let us now estimate the thrust or lateral pressure on a hill one thousand feet high, and exposed to the action of the displacing force along a distance of another thousand feet, though hills containing ore are not often elevated above the surrounding country more than a few hundred feet; but the power of displacement acts in other instances as well as in mineral veins, as a powerful agent in the formation of valleys, and more especially, as we shall hereafter see, in the formation of the mineral veins themselves. Making the pressure at thirty-three feet a ton, (in round numbers, for the sake of convenience,) at one hundred feet it is three tons; at five hundred feet, fifteen tons, which will be the average of the one thousand feet in depth, or fifteen thousand tons for the column, one foot laterally, and one thousand times that for the whole thrust of the little seam of water of, say, an eighth of an inch in thickness, making *fifteen millions of tons.* What wonder then that we find the surfaces of quartz veins thrown hundreds of feet out of line, or in some instances doubled quite over. If those persons who are so ready to invoke the agencies of earthquakes for every displacement of rocks and mineral veins, would study the effect of agencies, silent and slow, yet irresistible as fate, now at work, they would not be obliged to conceive of mountains being tossed from place to place like foot-balls.

Both veins had a dip to the north, the boulder vein soon leaving the other, which only dipped slightly, so that it passed into the Eureka ground some hundred feet below. At a depth of six hundred feet, the hanging-wall or eastern vein pinched nearly out. As the pay was mostly in this vein, the other paying only in spots, the mine for a while appeared to have been worked out; but the same pluck which had developed it came in play, and the gouge, or soft clay in the fissure, was followed down two hundred feet further, and the vein opened better than ever. A vein of sulphurets, one inch in thickness, ran diagonally across the main lode, that was half gold. Immense quantities were surreptitiously taken by the workmen, who were compelled to strip themselves on coming out of the shaft, step across the room, put on other clothes, leaving the mining suit to be examined by the inspector, a person appointed for the purpose. All sorts of devices were employed to conceal the gold. One miner threw away a pair of old boots. The inspector examined them, and found several ounces of specimens, which the owner expected to get after nightfall should enable him to get the boots unobserved. Some concealed specimens in their hair; and even the *anus* was used for that purpose. A small quartz mill was set up in an abandoned tunnel, for reducing rich rock. Notwithstanding all possible vigilance on the part of the superintendents, a great deal was stolen. A kind of demoralization existed among many of the miners, especially those of foreign birth, which caused such abstractions to be considered as commendable, sharp tricks rather than crimes.

A great number of persons have lost their lives here, some by carelessness, and some by unavoidable accidents. Any one may see that familiarity with danger will breed contempt for it, by watching the miners going up or down the shaft. Three or four will get into the tub, and as many more on the outside, and go up or down as though they were riding along a smooth road instead of being suspended, where a fall would precipitate them a thousand feet, against timbers and rocks. An indiscreet movement of the head, when the bucket is in rapid motion, has resulted in shaving a man's head half away. Sometimes incorrect signals are made with the bell wire, and a bucket is raised when it should be lowered; at other times, a trap along a level will be left open, and a man walking along with a dim light will fall a hundred or two feet, to be killed or maimed for life. Sometimes a ladder will give away, and a man will fall from the carelessness or awkwardness of the carpenter who put up the ladders. Some sixty men had been lost in the first twenty years of its working.

Although the mine was called the Hayward mine, several other men have had interests at different times. When the mine was in debt, partial interests were disposed of to obtain necessary means to work it.

O. L. Chamberlain, Dan Fiddler, Charles McNemair, and A. H. Rose, have been at times part owners. The latter's interest was a result of a piece of questionable enterprise, not, however, unusual with that smart operator in quartz mining. In 1864 or 1865 a number of persons were willing to take the usually unprofitable position of Public Administrator. After the election it was learned that not only a share in the rich Hayward mine, but a hundred thousand dollars in dividends, were the unclaimed assets of Charles McNemair, who went to Frazer river in 1857, before the Hayward mine had become a paying institution, and was supposed to be lost. In due course of time Mr. Tynan, the Public Administrator, filed a petition for letters of administration, showing at the same time probable proof of the death of McNemair, who was last seen going up the river in a boat, which was reported to have foundered with all hands on board. A stay of proceedings was obtained by the introduction of an affidavit to the effect that McNemair had been seen in British Columbia subsequently to the alleged loss of the boat, and consequently might be still living. It is said that this affidavit was procured by A. H. Rose, to delay events until he could purchase the interests of the different heirs of the McNemair estate. At all events, he soon appeared as claimant, he having sent a trusty agent to Illinois, the former home of McNemair, who had purchased the whole estate, a share in the mine, as well as the accumulated dividends, for about three thousand dollars, a mere bagatelle compared to its real value. What representations were made to effect this transaction is not known; but several visits were made to California by lawyers in the interests of the heirs, and it was some years before the matter was hushed up. It is needless to say that no more information of the missing man was received after the purchase of the estate by Rose.

After the mine had been successfully worked for about fifteen years, it was sold to a joint-stock company for six hundred thousand dollars, and was listed on the mining market at the Stock Exchange as the Consolidated Amador. The mine was too well known to be used as a bait for the public, and was not called on the board a great while. The mine perhaps paid for itself but did not equal the expectation of the stockholders. It was twice burned out, the immense amount of timber in the mine and the great chambering, making it an impossibility to stay a conflagration after it had once got fairly started.

The first of these fires occurred in April, 1870. It was supposed that it originated from a lighted candle being left on a timber in the north shaft. The men below were hoisted out of the other shafts and the mine closed up. Some days after an examination was made; a number of men going down the shaft were rescued with the utmost difficulty on account of the noxious gasses engendered by the fire. As the lower levels were still burning, the shafts were covered up and the hoisting works removed. The mine was repaired at an enormous expense, as it was supposed that the rock would continue at an infinite depth, but though the sump, or advanced shaft, was carried down to two thousand two hundred and fifty feet, no ore body below the seventeen-hundred-foot level was worked. At that point the great lode had shrunken from forty to less than six feet in width, with a run from north to south of thirty feet, instead of four hundred and fifty, and very moderate in pay at that. The lower sinking failed to discover any new development of the vein; in fact, the fissure was all that was found, and when the last great fire occurred, it was deemed best to abandon the locality and open the mine in a new place, some six hundred feet towards the north, on the ground near the old Wolverine claim, which had been many years before consolidated with the Badger and Eureka. The rock now being taken out at a depth of four hundred and fifty feet, is not of the kind formerly found in the south end of the claim, but perhaps will pay for

FRUIT RANCH AND RESIDENCE OF JOHN NORTHUP.
JULIAN DISTRICT, AMADOR COUNTY, CAL.

RANCH AND RESIDENCE OF A. A. VAN SANDT.
TP N° 2 AMADOR COUNTY, CAL.

crushing. The superintendent does not expect to find good rock until the walls become well defined.

THE RAILROAD MINE

Is the name given to a vein of quartz some two or three hundred feet east of the Wolverine. It was worked down four or five hundred feet, and, though some rich rock was found (a thousand dollars once being taken out of a candle-box full of rock), the vein was neither rich nor permanent, and the work was suspended. The wall rocks were hard, with little gouge, a surface opening only being indicated.

THE WILDMAN MINE

Was on the north side of the creek. Some good rock was taken out of this ground, but, like the majority of quartz veins, has not made its owners rich. As this vein is located out of range with the other mines, many experienced miners believe that proper cross-cutting towards the west will be likely to strike a paying chimney.

THE MAHONEY.

This ground was formerly owned by Hayward, who thought he had found a thousand dollars when he sold it to the Mahoney brothers for that sum. Though not equal to the Consolidated Amador, it made very handsome dividends for a good many years. The vein, forty feet wide or more, was worked down nearly eight hundred feet when work was suspended on account of the death of the last of the four Mahoney brothers, by consumption, in the course of a few years. A few years since it fell into the hands of Senator Stewart of Nevada. Some sinking was done by James Morgan of the Oneida Mining Company, nothing new being developed. The company erected a mill near the hoisting works, the rock formerly having been crushed by a water-mill on the creek some distance away. At a depth of eight hundred and fifty feet the vein is not well defined, the walls being much broken. The rock is supposed to pay only moderately. Those who saw this place in an early day would be ready to say that the quartz veins here made a sharp turn to the east, into what is called Tucker hill. This hill is netted with quartz veins sometimes in slate and often in the hard hanging-wall of the main range. Some small fortunes have been made out of the occasionally rich veins, which, though promising on the top, soon pinch out. Nearly all the surface has a little gold in it, and the gulches in the vicinity were the best around Sutter creek.

The true direction of the main lode may be seen by the cavity made by the falling in of the upper portion of the mine worked twenty years ago.

THE UNION OR LINCOLN,

Or, as it is sometimes called, the Stanford mine, was the first discovery in Sutter creek. E. B. McIntyre, Samuel Hanford, Levi Hanford, R. C. Downs, N. Drew, and others of Amador, formed a company in 1851 to hunt a quartz mine. They first tried Quartz mountain near Lower Rancheria. This not proving satisfactory, they divided into smaller parties and tried other places. One of the parties came on the south side of the ridge, Sutter creek then having about a dozen inhabitants. Much money had, even then, been expended in sinking on barren veins, and the company had made it a condition that no shaft should be commenced until gold was found in the ledge or vein in place. Floating rock with gold in it was found on the flat west of the present Mahoney and Union locations. Some narrow veins were found on the hill-side near the sulphuret works, but these not proving satisfactory they ran an open cut a few feet in depth and struck the main lode, in which they found a speck of gold. As this satisfied the conditions of the incorporation, a shaft was commenced and good rock soon after discovered, from which, with modern machinery, fifty or seventy-five dollars to the ton could be extracted.

They found a company of men working quartz on the south side of the Tucker hill, who set up a claim to the discovery they had made. To quiet all disputes, the south side company, consisting of Malvaney, Sherwood, Armstrong, and others, were taken in, making the company which was thereafter called the "Union," numbering about sixteen men, E. B. McIntyre being president, and N. Drew, secretary. A water-mill was built, near the present residence of R. C. Downs, with five stamps. This was the first mill in Sutter Creek, the Hayward mill being next. David Armstrong, who afterwards built a saw-mill near Pine Grove, was the mill-wright. The power was a breast-wheel, with a wooden shaft and wooden cams, the latter being set into the shaft in mortises and curved at the end to match the tappits, which were also of wood, set into mortises in the square wooden stems of the stamps. Armstrong was a good mechanic, and the work was well done, though much power was lost in the unavoidable friction of the wooden machinery. It worked as well as could be expected, and something over expenses was made out of the quartz. The gold was saved on blankets laid along the sluices, which were washed every half-hour. Quicksilver was tried, but it would not unite with the gold. An amalgamator from the Nashville mine, on the Cosumnes, was hired to superintend the sluices. He discovered that the quicksilver was adulterated with lead; after this was gotten rid of there was no difficulty in amalgamation.

In 1852 the mine and mill were leased to a company that made five thousand dollars to each partner. After the expiration of the lease, the Union company again worked it, Frank Tibbetts being superintendent. It was a common report that two million dollars were taken out of the mine during the next eight years, but the company became bankrupt, and in October, 1859, the mine fell into the hands of Leland Stanford, who made R. C. Downs superintendent. Under his management the mine became highly remunerative. It was now called the "Lincoln," and was worked by Downs and Stanford until 1873, when it passed into the hands of some foreign capitalists, who put up a mill on the south side of the hill, and made other improvements. At present the mine is not worked, the shaft and pumping machinery being used to drain the Mahoney mine. In this mine the paying vein was next to the hanging-wall, which, as in the Mahoney, the adjoining mine, was the hard, metamorphic slate, called "blue granite" by the miners. A cross cut into it indicated no change or prospect of a parallel vein. The gouge was on the foot-wall, which at a depth of five or six hundred feet, gradually changed to a quartzose character. The pitch of the vein was sixty-seven to seventy degrees from horizontal, and was from two to twenty feet thick. It will be seen that this cluster of mines was practically exhausted at a depth of less than one thousand feet, though deep sinking may, as in the Hayward mine, reveal a stronger vein than the surface one; the well-defined foot and hanging-walls favoring the presumption.

The most startling and serious accident that ever occurred in the mines in this county, happened here, in 1875. The following account taken from the *Independent*, a daily paper published at Sutter Creek at the time, will be read with interest:—

"Now that the dead and alive are all out of the mine and properly cared for, we shall attempt to give a correct version of the affair. On Friday morning, at seven o'clock, the day shift were let down, consisting of fifteen men, part of whom went on the three-hundred-foot, and part on the five-hundred-foot level. Those on the first were working in the stope, and three running the tunnel toward the old south shaft, which had been deserted for upwards of eight years, and was filled with stagnant water and foul air. Hardly had the drifters worked an hour when they broke through, and, at first, a small volume of water rushed in and drove them out. The alarm was immediately given, and foreman Horn, with another man, went down. They found William Wadge and Antonio Robles almost dead from suffocation, and took them to the top. Wadge soon recovered and was taken home, while Robles suffered terribly for some hours, when he was removed, but died during the night. The most intense excitement now prevailed, and Superintendent Stewart, Foreman Horn, and others, commenced the work of getting to the remaining men below. The foul air had become so strong that no light would burn within thirty feet of the three-hundred-foot level. The workmen exerted every nerve to extricate the now supposed dead men. Finding that all chances were lost to pass the first level, the water buckets were put to use, and at night they had cleared the water out to within a few feet of the five-hundred-foot level, yet they could not descend. All night the work went on, and by morning four of the unfortunate men were found. Saturday afternoon the shaft was so cleared of the bad air, by the aid of the air pumps, that Mr. Horn managed to reach the top of the lower level.

"About eight o'clock, while the water bucket was down, the signal rope was pulled and the bell rung, which caused great excitement above. When the bucket arrived at the top, there sat upon it Joseph Bath, and alive. He sang out to the astonished crowd, 'I am all right, there are three more alive in the lower level.' Reader, imagine the scene. We cannot give it in words. The bucket was lowered, and up came the three other men. It is impossible for us to give a description of the feelings of the people at this time. Mr. Bath has given us a full account of the whole affair—at least what happened underground—and in all history nothing has ever come to our notice that can in the slightest compare with this. None of the men about the mine have a word of fault to find with the management from first to last. We hear nothing but praise to Superintendent Stewart and Foreman Horn for their untiring perseverance. For over two days and nights Mr. Horn never left his post, and not till the last man was found and taken out did the brave man have any rest.

"We here give the names of the dead and living in full. Dead—Patrick Frazier, leaves a wife and four children, Ireland; John Collier, wife and five children, Ireland; Dennis Lynch, Ireland, wife and two children; William Coombs, England, wife and two children; W. H. Rule, England, single; G. B. Bobbino and Bartolomeo Gazzolo, single, Italy; Antonio Robles, Mexico, single; Nicolas Balulich, Austria, wife and four children. Saved—Jos. Bath, wife and four children, England; Bart. Curotto, wife and four children, Italy; Stefano Poclepovich, wife and six children, Italy; William Wadge, wife and several children, England; John O'Neil, Ireland. Mr. Frazier had an insurance of one thousand dollars, and Mr. Collier a policy of two thousand dollars in the Phoenix Mutual of Hartford.

"Seven were buried on Sunday, and two on Monday. Never before has so much sadness and sorrow been mixed with so much joy and happiness as has been the case within the past three days."

The accident was evidently owing to a faulty survey, which failed to indicate the proximity of the old works. It is said that some of the victims had presentiments of the danger, and bid their families good-bye on leaving home the morning of the accident. The feelings of the parties inclosed in the drift must have been terrible. It was expected that all were dead, but the drift being ascending, the chamber of air prevented the water from filling it. Those who attempted to swim out through the submerged end of the level were lost. Can imagination conceive a more terrible situation?

THE MECHANICS' MINE

Was a vein a mile east of the Mother Lode in the vicinity of Sutter creek. The rock was good-looking, and for a time the mine was considered promising, but it proved a losing concern, and is not worked at present.

THE HERBERTVILLE MINE

Is some mile or more north of the Sutter creek cluster, the intervening ground not having any strong croppings indicating a large lode, though several shafts have been sunk on the thin veins which appear at the surface. The Herbertville is singular in having the foot-wall of the hard metamorphic slate. The direction of this vein hardly conforms to the general trend of the Mother Lode;

it is also somewhat out of range, being to the east of the other mines; from these circumstances it is considered, by many experienced miners, as an accidental deposit, not occupying a true fissure. It was first worked in 1854, by Jones & Davis. The vein was twenty feet wide in places, and had a run of nearly three hundred feet, pinching out at the depth of six hundred feet. The rock was very good, frequently paying forty dollars a ton. It was among the best mines twenty years ago, but is not worked at present. If this was an accidental vein, it was a happy accident—for the owners at least. A cross-cut to the west might discover the true vein. A boulder, weighing several tons and quite rich in gold, was found, some years since, in a situation which indicated it as a float from a vein farther west. E. B. McIntyre of Sutter Creek is the owner of this chance for a mine.

SPRING HILL.

Though promising at the beginning, these mines had ruined nearly all who had been connected with them. "Quartz-mine" debts were harder to collect than saw-mill debts, which is saying a great deal. Sharp practice was often necessary to get pay for hay, grain or timber furnished the mines. In 1857, Stone, of the Buena Vista ranch, sold the Spring Hill Company a quantity of hay, but when he called for his money he was put off on various pretexts. He was as shrewd as they and had a sheriff watch the mill, to attach the amalgam when it was taken up. It was hidden in the lower works out of his way. The sheriff went down after it. The mining company quit pumping and let the shaft fill up with water, not soon enough, however, to save their amalgam. Stone got his pay. It is not intended to convey the idea that quartz mining is necessarily demoralizing, more than any other business which happens to be unprofitable. The mill and mine (Spring Hill) was owned by P. M. Randal, B. F. Pendleton, and —— Palmer until 1858, when they finally broke up, the creditors taking the property and running it with success, paying off the debts, after which, about 1861, it fell into the hands of Isaac Porkins. He ran it for four years at a loss; then the Hoopers, father and son, tried it with no better success. In 1867, work was suspended until it was consolidated with the Keystone Company's property.

THE KEYSTONE.

This mine has the most eventful history of any of the Amador mines. Though never called on the stock-boards, it has almost a world-wide reputation. It was here that quartz mining in this county commenced, and here were made the first failures as well as successes. In the history of the beginning of quartz mining, we left the Spring Hill and Granite State making their first efforts in the work. We have seen that the Spring Hill was located by the minister company, consisting of Davidson, Herbert, Glover, and Cool. The Granite State was located by Wheeler; the Walnut Hill, named after Beecher's famous seminary near Cincinnati, by two brothers named Holt. The mill was in the house now used by the Keystone company, as an office and assaying room. After the mill and mine had been run for a while at a loss, the two brothers proposed to run it themselves for what they could make out of it. They found a bonanza, making twenty thousand dollars in a short time.

The Granite State was located near the present Keystone mill; the Spring Hill towards the creek. these mines had, at first, been worked with arastras which made selected rock yield one hundred dollars per ton, but the process was slow and was abandoned, though an attempt was made to run the arastras by water-power, which also was a failure. These three mines constitute the property now known as the Keystone.

CONSOLIDATION OF

The Granite State and Walnut Hill. About 1857 these two mines had some share-holders in common, one of whom, Samuel Mannon, made a proposition that they should consolidate, which was adopted, the new company being called the Keystone; but the move did not relieve the indebtedness which was overwhelming, everything being attached for much more than it was worth. A mortgage on it was foreclosed, but an older judgment, in the hands of A. H. Rose and Phil. Crusart, took the mine, Rose eventually becoming sole owner. It was not supposed to be a paying property, though it was worked more or less, the mill being used for custom work as well as for the mine. Once during the time it was sold to Frank Tibbetts, who run it at a serious loss, and the property reverted to Rose. In 1869 it was sold to J. M. McDonald, Michael Reese and others, of San Francisco, for one hundred and four thousand dollars, which was thought by outsiders to be an enormous price. It had previously been offered for fifteen thousand dollars, but the rich discoveries then being made along the range in the vicinity of the Seaton mine shot quartz up with alarming rapidity. It is currently reported also, that the Mint receipts for custom work, were used to enhance the apparent value of the mine. At all events the first workings were a total failure. The old proprietor was heard to say that that no child born would live to see the mine pay for itself!! This may all be legitimate among stock-dealers.

DISCOVERY OF THE BONANZA.

Old miners had suspected another vein to the east in what was considered the hanging-wall, though this opinion was not shared by the former proprietors. Occasionally a blast in the hanging-wall would show stringers of quartz which indicated another deposit. A cross-cut was started, but a beginning had hardly been made when rich quartz was uncovered. Quartz in the hanging-wall was a novelty, but there it was sparkling with gold. The first month's crushing paid forty thousand dollars, and the next—and ever since the same. By selecting the best rock it could be made to pay a million a year for an indefinite time, but all rock that will pay two dollars, which is considered about the cost of extracting and crushing, is worked. The vein is a boulder vein, that is, lying in bunches, kidney-shaped, and varying in size from a few tons to forty thousand tons. The bunches are connected by stringers. It will be recollected that the boulder vein in the Hayward mine was next the foot-wall, and was not uniformly rich. There seems to be no rule governing in such deposits. The pitch of the mine is about forty-five degrees. The following figures from the actual survey will give an idea of pitch.

Distances.	On the slope.	Horizontal.	Vertical.
1st Level	475 ft.	294.77 ft.	394.23 ft.
2d "	556 "	358.63 "	424.88 "
3d "	681 "	439.25 "	520.40 "
4th "	812 "	523.75 "	620.51 "
5th "	950 "	612.76 "	725.96 "
6th "	1080 "	696.61 "	825.30 "

The run north and south is seven hundred and sixty-five feet between the pinches. The best deposits are found on the flat portion of the foot-wall, these places acting like a riffle in retaining the quartz. Within the last two years new and substantial works have been erected. From the hoisting works to the mill, everything is arranged for convenience. The ore falls into substantial ore houses, that will hold a month's crushing, so that a repair of the shaft or mine will cause no delay of work.

One hundred and thirty men find constant employment here. The rates of labor have not varied much for twenty years, and are

For Under-ground Miners, per day,		$3 00
Laborers above ground,	" "	2 50
Blacksmiths	" "	3 50
Carpenters	" "	4 00
Engineers	" "	3 00

The lumber used in one year is enormous:—

5,000 round timbers with sawed lumber	$25,000 00
25,000 pieces of lagging, @ $95 00 per M.	2,375 00
2,000 cords of wood @ $6 00 per cord	12,000 00

It will be seen that nearly two hundred thousand dollars is distributed annually by this mine in the matter of expenses.

The Assessor furnishes the following report of the proceeds for 1879, which may approximate the facts.

Amount of rock crushed, in tons	39,000
Total yield	$451,000 00
Expenses claimed by mine	273,000 00
" allowed by Assessor	195,000 00

BIG GRAB.

The history of these mines would be incomplete without an account of the daring attempt, under cover of an agricultural claim, to obtain possession of all these mines. In August, 1869, that portion of the county was surveyed and sectionized by J. G. Mather, and the plot of the section and mines, and other improvements thereon, reported to the general office at San Francisco.

A. H. Rose had a vineyard and farm east of the town of Amador; so it was supposed that it would be on the east half-section, section thirty-six. As sections sixteen and thirty-six in each township had been donated to the State for school purposes, no alarm was raised or objections interposed when a patent for the east half-section was applied for, and obtained from the State; though the fact that Henry Casey, instead of A. H. Rose, the actual owner of the vineyard, applied for and obtained the deed to the land, Rose acting as his business agent, would naturally cause inquiry and suspicion of fraud.

The plot, as subsequently corrected, and now on file in the State Surveyor General's office at San Francisco, is as follows:—

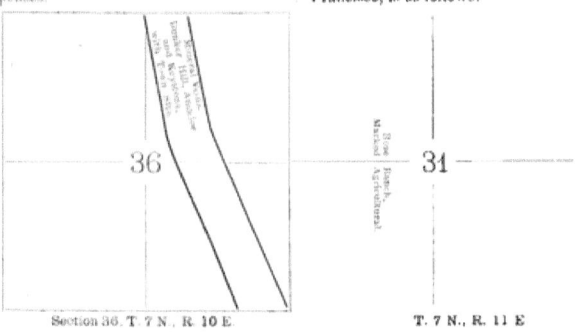

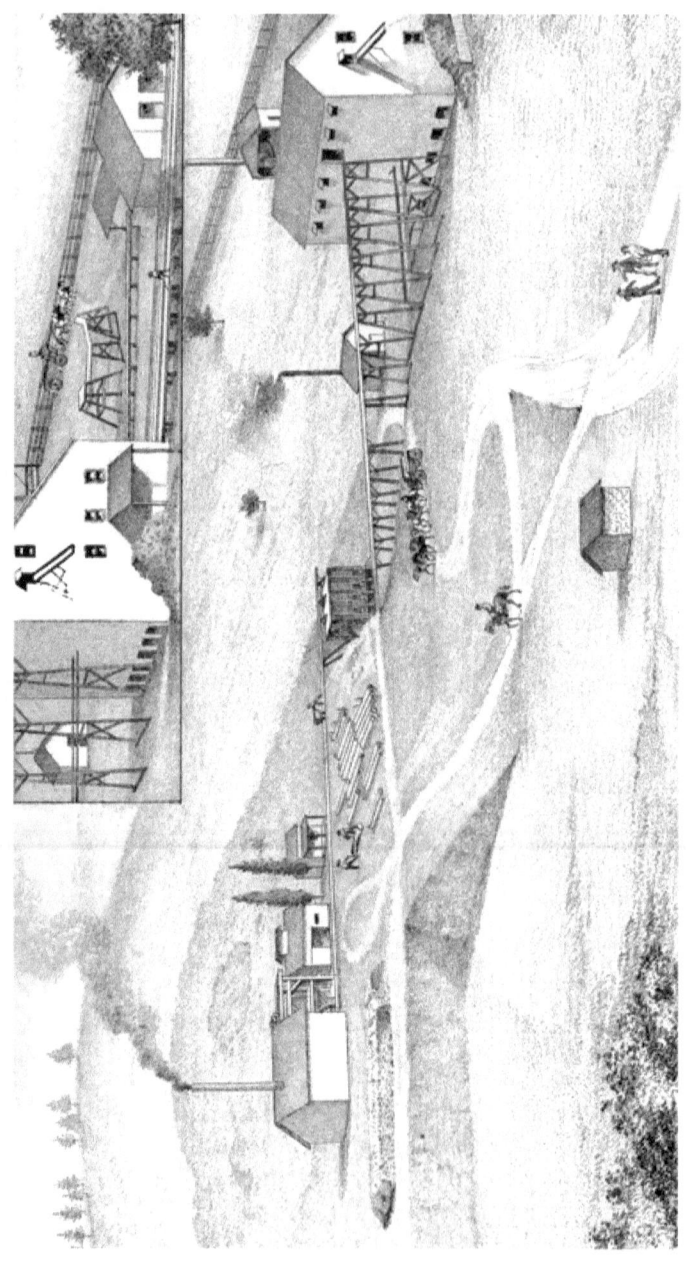

When the plot had been consummated Henry Casey disappeared, and A. H. Rose appeared, armed with a deed from the State, as the claimant for millions worth of property. It is not necessary to follow the matter through the courts. It is sufficient to say that it was finally carried up to the Secretary of the Interior. The following, from the Washington correspondent of the *Sacramento Union*, will give a clear idea of the dangers the Amadorians have surmounted:

"WASHINGTON, April 9, 1873.

"Extraordinary professional and lobby interests are being organized and concentrated here by A. H. Rose, to bear upon the Secretary of the Interior in the important case of the Keystone Consolidated Mining Company, the Original Amador Mining Company, Bunker Hill Quartz Company, and the town site of Amador, against the State of California. The purpose is to secure a reversal of the decision of the General Land Office, whereby to turn over to Rose and his associates property worth millions of dollars, for which the nominal sum of four hundred dollars was partly paid by Henry Casey, the alleged grantee from the State. The case involves extraordinary features, apparent frauds, as well as a principle of the utmost importance to thousands of mine-owners and mines in controversy, situated on the Mother Lode of California, which have been worked since 1850. Rose sold, for one hundred and thirty thousand dollars, the Keystone mine, and he now seeks to recover it in the name of Casey. The town of Amador was founded in 1850, its site, and all the mines situated upon the east half-section of section thirty-six, township seven north, range ten east, Mt. Diablo meridian. In 1870 certain parties procured a United States survey of that township, and, it is alleged, induced the Deputy Surveyor, by fraudulent field notes, to represent the mines and town as located upon the west half of the section. This was to deceive occupants, so as to induce them to apply for the wrong tract, while the speculators could, without opposition, purchase from the State for four hundred dollars, and receive a patent for the tract on which these properties were actually located. The fraud was discovered and exposed by abundant proofs, demonstrating unquestionably the surveyor's infidelity, in returning as agricultural land the richest half-section of mineral land ever discovered. The patent not having been issued, the *bona fide* mining claimants and town authorities immediately applied to the Land Department for patents under the mineral and town land laws, but the would-be purchasers from the State then boldly claimed that the School Land Act of March 3, 1853, was a grant *en presente* of both surveyed and unsurveyed, and both mineral and agricultural, lands comprised in the sixteenth and thirty-sixth sections of every township, and consequently that the mineral lands in controversy situated in the thirty-sixth section, passed to the State immediately on the passage of the Act of 1853. To this it is replied that mineral lands were excluded from the grants to the State; that the State title did not vest in any lands until surveyed, there being prior thereto no sections sixteen and thirty-six; the Act of 1853 provided that as to mineral lands only township lines should be run, which provision was not repealed until July 9, 1870; that it was competent for Congress, before vested rights attached, to make a different appropriation of the lands; that before the survey Congress did, by the Act of July 26, 1866, make a different appropriation of the mineral lands; that if this were not so, yet the particular tract in controversy was expressly excepted from the State grant by the seventh section of the Act of 1853, by reason of its settlement and the erection of dwelling-houses thereon prior to the survey. The local land officers and the Commission-General of the Land Office decided against the pretentions of the private claimants who use the State's name, and the case is now pending on appeal before the Secretary of the Interior. The danger grows out of the fact that the Supreme Court of the State of California, in the case of Sherman against Buck, decided that the Act of 1853 did vest title to all sixteenth and thirty-sixth sections in the State prior to the survey. And although it is believed the court will grant a rehearing and reverse that decision, its action, nevertheless, lends color of support to the attempt now making to obtain possession of the Amador mines and establishes a principle fraught with immense danger to thousands of other interests. Rose is here personally pressing the case, in addition to Wm. H. Patterson and other well-known California lawyers and lobbyists to assist in its prosecution. It is probable dilatory tactics will be employed to postpone the decision of this tainted claim until the Benjamin Snelling case from the Marysville district can be presented to the Secretary for a decision of the naked question of the right of the State to the sixteenth and thirty-sixth sections of mineral lands; so that if the right of the State is affirmed, it will be comparatively easy to find a pretext for deciding Rose's case in his favor. The question has a vital importance to all mineral occupants on the sixteenth and thirty-sixth sections. If the mineral claimants in either the Keystone or Snelling cases are defeated, then all mines upon similarly numbered subdivisions, or which upon future survey may prove to be so numbered, are at the mercy of the first applicant to purchase from the State at one dollar and twenty-five cents an acre. It is represented here that the parties who are initiated in this speculation have already taken the requisite steps to file the first applications for all similar sections throughout the State. The same dangers threaten mineral occupants in every other mineral State."

"WASHINGTON, April 28, 1873.

"The Secretary of the Interior to-day decided the very important and much contested cases of the Keystone Mining Company *et. al., vs.* State of California, and of Benjamin Snelling *vs.* the State of California, both of which involved the question whether the grant to said State of sections sixteen and thirty-six for school purposes by the Act of March 3, 1853, included said sections when they were on mineral lands. The Secretary held, first, that the title to said sections sixteen and thirty-six does not vest in the State until survey has been made, which brings into existence and locates said section, and that said mining companies, having appropriated said lands under the Act of July 26, 1866, prior to such survey, they had the better right. Second, that the seventh section of the Act of 1853 excepts from the grant all of sections sixteen and thirty-six, on which there had been, prior to the survey, a settlement by the erection of a dwelling-house or the cultivation of any portion of the land, and that the settlement referred to was technically known as pre-emption settlement. Third, that the grant was not intended to include, and does not include, said sections when they are on mineral lands. The decision was given against the State in both cases."

Extraordinary reports are current as to the means by which this fraudulent survey was accomplished. J. G. Mather was not in the field at the time, though his name was attached to the plot returned to the office. His deputies were Uri Nurse and Marcellus Nurse, father and son, the latter doing the work. Some say the survey was made by moonlight, others that a lantern was used, and some go so far as to name the persons who acted as chain and torch bearers in these midnight surveys. Young Nurse is reported as saying that he made fifteen thousand dollars during the season. Mather is made to bear the responsibility, and has not since been employed by the Government in any work, nor is he likely to be.

The contest was finally terminated November 22, 1880.

"In the case Ivanhoe Mining Company vs. Keystone Consolidated Company, the Supreme Court held that in the grant of the sixteenth and thirty-sixth sections of the public lands to the State of California for school purposes, the title to the mineral lands did not pass, for the reason that it was the established policy of the Government to withhold the mineral lands from sale, and that in this case the land in question, having been improved before the survey, it was exempt from sale by reason of section seven of such law."

The owners of mines and houses on the famous thirty-sixth section may now rest, secure in the results of their industry.

THE ORIGINAL AMADOR,

Sometimes called the Little Amador, is the mine on the north side of the creek, which was taken up by Thomas Rickey and son in February, 1851. This mine was about the first to pay dividends, J. T. Burke, still living in Amador, being the superintendent. In 1854, it passed into the hands of some Germans, who ran it until 1857, when it gradually failed, work being totally suspended in 1858. In the meantime it was sold to Haverstick and Leninger of Ione, the latter soon becoming the sole owner, the mine at this time being valued at only two hundred and fifty dollars. J. T. Burke, the first superintendent, leased the mine from Leninger, giving him half the profits. His knowledge of the mine enabled him to pay Leninger the sum of eight thousand dollars for his share of the profits. After the expiration of the lease, work was suspended until 1862, when J. T. Burke bought it for three thousand dollars, one-third down, balance in installments. The mine paid for a short time, but the rock failing, it went back to Leninger, who sold it to John C. Faul for a nominal price. The mine was developed under his management, the hoisting works and mill being rebuilt. The reputation of the mine was such that it was sold to an English company in 1870, for six hundred thousand dollars. It is not considered a paying property. Work is nearly suspended at present. Old miners think that a cross-cut to the west might strike a paying vein. The present works are near the hanging-wall. A shaft is now being sunk on the summit, near the Bunker Hill ground. The hoisting is done with a wire cable from the old hoisting works nearly a thousand feet away.

THE BUNKER HILL.

This is one of the mines included in the famous thirty-sixth section, a portion of the ground being on the doubtful tract. Superintendent Palmer furnishes the following information about the mine: It was worked in 1851, by Snediker, Briggs, and others, making the quartz pay twenty dollars per ton, until the works were carried down some depth. It is now four hundred and fifty feet deep, with two veins of paying rock. The vein next to the hanging-wall is about five feet thick. The second one varies from one foot to thirty feet in thickness, and is what is called a chimney, dipping to the north about forty-five degrees. The hanging-wall is well defined and regular; the foot-wall being somewhat broken. The general pitch is about twenty-eight degrees from a perpendicular. The two veins are about sixty feet apart, no gold being found in the slates between the veins. The sulphurets, constituting about three per cent. of the entire rock, are worth about eighty dollars per ton, this being about one-tenth of the entire product, which at these figures would be about twenty-five dollars per ton. The rock shows an improvement as a greater depth is reached.

New hoisting works, mill and chlorination works are being erected, and a new shaft is being sunk. The mill is to have forty stamps run by water-power, and everything is to be substantial and first-class. The property is owned by a joint-stock company and bids fair to be highly remunerative.

There are no mines of note for some distance north of the Bunker Hill; though several shafts have been sunk no valuable lodes were opened.

THE PENNSYLVANIA.

This mine was worked by J. W. Pierson, of Oakland. Either bad management or other causes have given it an unenviable reputation. About a year since, fortunately while there was no one in the works, it caved in, the whole works collapsing. As the mine is being dismantled it is likely that it was not found profitable.

THE GOVER.

This is an old mine with a varied experience, the balance generally being on the wrong side of the ledger. It has been worked to a depth of one thousand and thirty feet; has two veins, the one next the hanging-wall about seven feet thick containing the pay. The pitch is about forty-five degrees. The vein one hundred and thirty feet west is about four feet thick and does not contain much gold. A cross-cut at seven hundred feet showed no improvement in the west vein, at this depth the eastern or hanging-wall vein was good, averaging twelve dollars and a half per ton, but gradually became poorer as a greater depth was reached. The west vein was not tested below the seven-hundred-foot level.

There is no appearance of a chimney in this mine, the vein maintaining about the same width on a run of seven hundred feet. This is a solitary case, every other paying vein being in the shape of a channel, chute, or chimney. The hoisting works and water-power mill (twenty stamp) are substantial and well arranged. The town, called New Chicago, built up on the strength of this and the adjoining mines, is distressingly quiet. There is a prospect (January 1, 1881) of the Gover resuming work.

THE BLACK HILLS.

This is, to some extent, a repetition of Murphy's ridge in the southern part of the county, the veins being irregular in location and very much so in their value. Immense sums have been taken out by the Italians, Austrians and Mexicans, who have been working this section for twenty years or more. There is a strong hanging-wall but no foot-wall except the ordinary slate. Sometimes the quartz shows in large chimneys of barren rock a hundred feet thick; at other times it ramifies into a thousand seams all containing gold. The hills have been sluiced, hydrauliced, coyoted, and tunnelled and worked in every way conceivable, and still a great number of men make a living for their families, most of whom live in the hollows below the mine in a primitive style, with goats and children swarming over the hills. Efforts have been made to mine this scientifically, and long tunnels have been run under or down the hanging-wall, which has a slope of about forty-five degrees, but the Mexican with his crow-bar and batuya still holds the country. The gulches heading against this quartz reef were all rich, clear to the summit, and it was by following up these that the rich threads of quartz interlacing the hill were found.

THE SEATON MINE.

Twenty years ago this was a power in the land. It was immensely rich in places. It adjoins the Black hills on the north. The same rule as at the other mines in this cluster holds good, i.e., a strong hanging-wall. A mill and hoisting works were erected, and the results were such as to make a boom in quartz; a million of dollars seeking investment in the county in a short time. Some of these ventures have proved failures, others exceeded the most sanguine expectations of the investors. The mine is owned by an English company, and at present is not paying dividends, but perseverance may uncover another bonanza which will repay them for all their toil.

THE POTOSI.

This mine was developed by the Hinksons of Drytown, and for many years was a source of profit, if not of fortunes. The wall rock on the east is here broken off, and for two miles, or until Plymouth is reached, the veins are scattered, spreading in some instances to two thousand feet in width. Some mills have been erected, and though occasional runs have been made which were profitable, the mines in general proved a poor investment. Most of the veins are held by persons too poor to sink on them, the prospects not being good enough to induce capitalists to invest. Some of the veins, with economical management, may pay for working at the top, and thus pay for testing them.

QUARTZ MOUNTAIN.

Although this is not usually considered on the range, or Mother Lode, it is most convenient to consider it here. It is an immense body of quartz covering twenty acres or more of ground. It seems to be a vein, perhaps one hundred feet thick, and perhaps a thousand feet long, which, from its original inclination, has fallen over to the eastward, as much as twenty acres lying nearly flat, forming a prominent object for miles around. It early attracted the attention of quartz miners, and was examined and claimed in 1851, at the time of the first quartz excitement. The ravines in the immediate vicinity were not rich, although a three-hundred-dollar lump is said to have been found in the long gulch running from it towards the creek. It is rock of a peculiar character, being much purer, and more compact than the quartz of the Mother Lode. The bullion from it is of low value, being worth only ten or twelve dollars to the ounce, and very light, forty per cent. of it being silver, on which account it is hard to save. The quartz, notwithstanding its favorable appearance, has not yet milled above two dollars per ton, and has proved a losing business to all persons engaged in it. The ore has been treated in every possible method, but the successful reduction of it has not yet been accomplished. The sulphurets are extremely rich, being worth five or six hundred dollars a ton. South of the Quartz mountain the country has been very rich in coarse gold. Some quartz veins crop out on the heads of Deep and Indian gulches, which have the same pitch to the west that characterizes the Quartz mountain, and are probably a part of the same formation. As Rancheria creek above the town contains little gold, and there is little indication of an ancient river bed in this vicinity, it is highly probable that Deep and Indian gulches, as well as the flats around, were enriched by the system of quartz veins, to which Quartz mountain belongs. Mack Culbert and sons are working a vein on the hill above Indian gulch, with fair prospects of making it pay. It is likely that a thorough search will discover workable veins. Reference was made to this mountain in the article on quartz veins.

PLYMOUTH GROUP OF MINES.

It is more convenient to consider them under one heading, although there are several incorporations, the management being by one set of men. The situation of the mines will be understood by a diagram:—

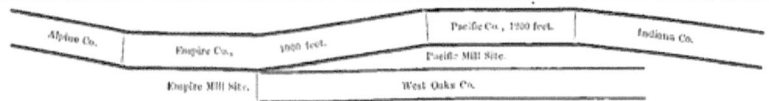

The Plymouth mine was discovered by Green Aden in 1853 or 1854. The mine, then called the Phœnix, was developed by the Hoopers, and was worked by them until 1871, when it passed into the hands of Hayward, D. O. Mills and Company. It was then worked under the superintendence of Charles Green, who developed it into its present profitable condition. The mine is singular in the fact that it is the site of a glacier erosion, which smoothed down every rock, however hard or soft, leaving none of the hard reefs so prominent in connection with other paying quartz veins. A reef of rocks across the lower end of the valley, west of Puckerville, formed the *moraine* or terminal line of the erosion.

The ordinary hanging-wall is thought to be some six hundred feet to the east of the vein, but as a drift has been run only eighty feet in that direction, the hanging-wall may be much nearer than is supposed. The vein, which averages fifty-two feet in thickness, had a moderate slope towards the east, until it reached a depth of one thousand feet, when it suddenly became much flatter, having a slope of about forty-five degrees. The richest quartz was found on this slope, there being a sudden increase in quality as well as quantity at this bend. Another peculiarity of the mine is that the pay chimney runs towards the south. In this connection it may be well to speak of the lawsuit now pending for trespass and damage. Though Alvinza Hayward is a principal owner in both the Empire and Pacific, other stockholders have interests in but one, and in working down on the chimney, which runs into the Pacific, the Empire men received profits which accrued from the Pacific ground; hence a suit for two hundred and fifty thousand dollars damage. The Empire acknowledged a demand for eighty thousand dollars, but this did not satisfy the Pacifics. To complicate matters still more, the Merchants' Exchange Bank of San Francisco, through some business complications with Hayward, stepped in as an intervener, and the suit became a triangular duel. An army of lawyers and short-hand reporters was brought up from San Francisco and quartered around Jackson. Two thousand pages of testimony were taken to be used in the higher courts, for this was but the beginning or skirmishing line in the war. Those who have never read the account of the "triangular duel" in Captain Maryatt's "Midshipman Easy," may get an idea of this suit by imagining a three-handed game of *euchre*, all parties playing against Hayward, who was bound to be *euchred* in any event, having the most of the cost to pay. An award of seventy-one thousand dollars damage was made by Judge Moore,

before whom the case was tried, and the matter is still running through the courts.

The chimney at the depth of twelve hundred feet has gone five hundred and ninety-two feet to the south, at which point hoisting works of the most substantial kind are being constructed, the shaft being square, with four compartments. The tall tower stands over the shaft, a prominent feature in the landscape. This elevation is to give room for waste rock that often accumulates to an inconvenient degree around mining works. The *eighty-stamp* mill, the largest in the county, is run by water-power, the canal being a portion of the company's works. A large portion of the timber and lagging used, comes down the canal, which receives its supply of water from the Cosumnes river. About four thousand tons of rock are crushed each month, yielding forty thousand dollars or upwards.

Like other large mines, this consumes a great amount of material, the yearly demand being—

3,500 cords of wood valued at............. $21,000
7,000 pieces of round timber............... 21,000
35,000 pieces of lagging................... 3,500

In addition to this, half as much may be reckoned for dimension timbers for new works on the surface. The names of some one hundred and fifty men are on the pay-roll.

ENTERPRISE.

North of the Plymouth group the mines have not been developed, though there are indications of extensive quartz deposits. Indian creek, which follows nearly the course of the quartz lodes, was quite rich, as were the side gulches putting into it. A few years since a town was started on the prospects of the Enterprise mine, which flourished for a time, but when the work was suspended the place shrunk away. The mines along this range seem full of water, the west or foot-wall (the west bank of Indian creek) having numerous springs, which *may* come from extensive mineral deposits on that side. A mineral lode has once been a water channel though subsequent erosions and cleavages may have changed its course.

NASHVILLE.

On the north side of the Cosumnes is the place called Nashville, formerly Quartzburg, which, though in El Dorado county, may be mentioned in connection with the Amador mines as being the extension and probable termination on the north, as the Gwin mine is on the south, of that remarkable deposit which we have endeavored to describe, called the Mother Lode in Amador county, as north of the Nashville group, and south of the Gwin mine, the quartz deposits are irregular and cannot compare, in pro-

ductiveness or regularity, with the mines between the two named points. This mine was worked at an earlier day than any of the Amador mines, as the mill was a model for some of them. The mine was developed by Dr. Harris of Nashville, Tennessee, who sunk for his company some forty thousand dollars. The first power used was steam, but afterwards a dam was thrown across the river at a cost of thirty thousand dollars, which was a needless expense, as a small canal a mile or two in length, has since been equal to the power gained by the dam. During the Summer of 1851 a man by the name of Eustice, from Missouri, discovered a rich vein near Nashville, which he allowed the Mexicans to work for a royalty, which was an arrangement that they should purchase their supplies of him, which condition they generally observed. The Mexicans worked the rock with *arastras*, with which they are experts, and made it pay much better than did the mill men who came after them. As many as thirty or forty of these might be seen grinding at a time. Perhaps two hundred men, women, and children were congregated around the mine, which pinched out at a depth of about a hundred feet. The arrangement was mutually satisfactory and profitable, and Eustice carried away about sixteen thousand dollars for his share. The mines are not worked at present, and seem never to have been as rich and as extensive as the mines in Amador county. This closes the account of the great Mother Lode as it exists in Amador county. In the chapter on the formation of mineral veins, reference to the mines is occasionally made.

CHAPTER XXIX.

QUARTZ MINING EAST OF THE MOTHER LODE.

Downs Mine—Marklee—Tellurium—Thayer—Clinton Mines—Mace Ranch of Miners Pignons and Golden Gate Mines—Quartz Veins West of the Mother Lode—Kirkendall—Soap-Stone or Steatite Mine—Quartz Mining in the Future—Put Money in Thy Purse—School Cabinets—Copper Mining—General Craze—Country Formed into Districts—Funny Notices—New Towns—Result of the General Search—Chrome Iron—Failure of Meader—Remarkable Discovery—Present Condition of Copper Mining.—Newton Mine.

No man who has made gold mining a subject for thought, ever doubted that the gold found in our gulches and rivers originally came from the quartz veins. When the news of the discovery of gold in the quartz at Sutter Creek and other places was learned, the belief that the quartz veins on the upper range of placers, which were not inferior in richness to the lower ones, became general. Soldiers' gulch had several veins crossing it, and so had numerous other rich placers. Quartz boulders, with gold riveted through and through them, were sometimes found, as well as rough quartz, which did not appear to have been moved any great distance from the vein. Small veins were found with considerable gold in them, and in 1867 there were not less than one hundred stamps in operation within a few miles

of Volcano, and nearly two hundred on the upper range. The following table will show that the upper veins were being fully tried:—

Location in Amador county	Name of Mill	Ft. Stamps	No. Stamps	Amalgam	Power	Cost.	Present Occupants.
Amador City	Amador	1856			steam	10,000	Middleton & Co.
"	Bunker Hill	1855	8		s & w	12,000	William A. Palmer.
"	Flecharts	1856	10		steam	10,000	Gardner & Flechart.
"	Hazard	185?	5		water	6,000	Gardner & Flechart.
"	Keystone	1856	40		steam	40,000	Gashwiler & Co.
"	Spring Hill	1856	40		s & w	40,000	Hooper & Co.
Clinton	Rocky Falls.	185?	10		steam	10,000	W. J. Paugh.
"	Tacob	1858	10				E. T. Steen.
Drytown	Plymouth	1859	20		s & w	20,000	Hooper & Co.
"	Potosi	1855	16		water	10,000	Creed & Wood.
"	Seaton	1865	30		s & w	100,000	Seaton M. Co.
Fiddletown	Richmond	1865	10			10,000	Eagon & Co.
Jackson	Omega	1854	16		steam	16,000	C. T. Meader.
"	Hubbards	1860	10		water	8,000	S. C. Fogus.
"	Searsings	186?	10		"	5,000	C. T. Meader.
"	Tubbs	1866	10		steam	10,000	Tubbs & Co
"	Oneida	1854	40			40,000	James Morgan
Lower Randlecia	Italian	1854	4		"	7,500	Bruno & Co.
Pine Grove	Tellurium	1864	10			10,000	Cushing, Ryder & Co.
Rancheria	Loyal League	18 8	2?		water	15,000	Hend. & Co.
Sutter Creek	Badger	1856	12			10,000	A. Hayward.
"	Downs	185?	10			10,000	B. C. Downs.
"	Eureka	1858	40		s & w	40,000	A. Hayward.
"	Lincoln Q M Co		20		water	10,000	B. C. Downs, Supt.
"	Mahoney	1868	10			13,000	Mahoney Brothers.
"	Meader	1856	20			19,000	C. T. Meader.
"	Wildyeans	1850	12			10,000	C. T. Wheeler.
Volcano	Bobbing	1864	10		s & w	12,000	California Furnace Co
"	Eagle	1856	10			8,000	Pico, Supt.
"	Fogus	1856	10		water	10,000	J. T. Farley.
"	Golden Gate.	185?	10		s & w	20,000	Hurd & Co.
"	Italian	1863	10		water	8,000	Rose & Co.
"	Moseby	185?	6			4,000	Fogus & Co.
"	Mitchells	1856	6		steam	20,000	Larkin & Co.
"	Pioneer	1855	10		s & w	15,000	C. T. Meader.
"	Scorco	1859	5		"	20,000	J. T. Farley.
"	Sulphuret	186?	2			9,000	W. M. Thom.
"	Tulloch	1856	15		steam	10,000	Lawton & Co.
"	Tulloch	1866	1		water	1,000	Tulloch & Co.
"	Tynan	186?	12		steam	8,000	M. Tynan.

It took twenty years of costly experience to learn quartz mining and the nature of quartz veins. There were these differences in the veins on the Mother Lode and in the other parts of the county; on the Mother Lode the veins generally had a north and south direction; on the others they ran in all directions, conforming in directions to the rifts of the slate, they turned apparently at every little obstruction and had no uniformity of direction, dip, or strike. There was a gouge or selvage beside the Mother Lode; scarcely any at all on the upper veins, many of the largest of the veins being encased in solid walls, in fact, as the miners use to say, melted into it. Along the Mother Lode was a solid wall (frequently on both sides) which was continuous, and could readily be traced through the county; on the upper ranges the wall rock, or rock adjoining the quartz, would change its character every few feet, sometimes being a hard metamorphosed flinty rock, at other places turning to steatite, or soft, earthy slate. Those of our readers who studied the Mother Lode, in its entirety, will remember the functions of a firm wall rock and the importance of a gouge, one as holding the quartz deposit to its place, the other showing a deep fissure or a greater length of deposit. There is a probability that the aggregate amount of gold in the West Point system of veins, which also crosses Amador county, is greater than in the Mother Lode of the same length, and so of the other veins that traverse the eastern part of the county within a few miles of Volcano. The great sea that deposited the rocks, did not leave the material for a firm overlying bed. The corals, building up reefs, and modifying the influence of the ocean currents, perhaps, interfered with the deposit of a stratum as uniform in its character as was done a few miles farther west. At any rate, when the mountains were lifted out of the sea the mass of rock overlying the gold-bearing strata opened in various directions, besides at the axis of elevation; hence the water holding gold and other minerals in solution found its way to the surface, sometimes through limestone, sometimes through granite or syenite, and sometimes through soft slate, the fissures following no direction long, nor extending to great depths, as at the Mother Lode, though the conditions admit of exceptions.

With these few general remarks the subject of their formation may be dismissed and a few of the mines noticed.

THE DOWNS MINE

Apparently conforms more nearly to a true fissure vein than any in the upper series yet found, though differing in its direction from veins on the Mother Lode. It has a gouge, a large amount of vein matter or distinctly characterized rock, and firm walls, all of which conditions are favorable to permanence and depth. This mine was located as early as 1857 by Phil. Seibenthaler, Geo. Felmath, and others. The rock on the surface was worked by arastras and paid from forty to one hundred dollars per ton. They then enlarged the works and put up a twenty-stamp mill. There was not rock enough available to keep the mill running, and the company failed, work being suspended until 1866, when the whole property was bought by James M. Hanford for one hundred dollars. Work was resumed, the quartz being hauled to the Fogus mill, two and a half miles below Volcano, for reduction. The milling was badly done, saving only eight dollars and twenty-five cents per ton. A year later the shaft was sunk forty feet deeper. Two tons ground in an arastra paid twenty-six dollars per ton. This so encouraged the proprietor that sinking was continued still further. A swell was struck in the vein which now became four feet in thickness, though the body of the vein had no greater amount of gold than before, now paying only twenty dollars per ton; but this was good rock. Fifteen feet deeper the vein contracted to its original width of two feet. The next crushing of rock, taken from below the swell at a depth of ninety feet, paid sixty-eight dollars per ton by the arastra process. It was also discovered that there were two continuous parallel veins within the two wall rocks, which were about thirty feet apart, though one of the veins was of much less value than the other. The narrow vein (the first one worked) is now paying, by mill process, twenty-five to forty dollars per ton. The mill is run by water-power and all the appliances are calculated to work economically. All the circumstances point towards a permanent and profitable mine. The vein has an easterly and westerly direction and can be distinctly traced some distance towards the west, showing good rock all the way. J. N. Peck & Co. own one extension under the name of the Golden Star, and Benjamin Ross another.

THE MARKLEE MINE.

This mine is north of Volcano and not far from Dry Creek. It was worked with profit for about two years. Many good runs were made on it. May 11, 1872, sixteen days' run with twelve stamps netted thirteen thousand dollars. It was sold to an English company, who put some one in charge who was either unacquainted with quartz mining, or had a job on hand, as he drifted away from the pay chute, at least in the opinion of the workmen who seemed to be better acquainted with the nature of the quartz than the foreman. The mill and hoisting works were removed and the mine and improvements left to ruin. In the opinion of many the mine is still good.

THE TELLURIUM

Is a few hundred feet east of Pine Grove. The quartz in this vein is in considerable quantity, forming a regular vein. It appears rather white and pure to contain much mineral, but is said to pay thirty or forty dollars per ton, which, however, is very doubtful. The name Tellurium seems to have been given rather as a fanciful title than because any of that mineral exists in the rock. As usual with mines owned in cities or out of the State, the management has been given to incompetent men, the working of the mine being experimental rather than practical.

THE THAYER MINE

Was on the north side of Grass Valley creek, and in 1859-60 was a promising vein. A man by the name of Thayer (from the city, of course) gave his name to it, and also demonstrated the inutility of new quartz machines, like many before and since, and probably many yet to come. His plan was an enlargement of the Chile wheel, which, in this instance, was made ten or twelve feet in diameter, shod with iron castings, and traveling in a circular gutter fifty or sixty feet in circumference, also lined with iron. The principle was correct enough, and has since been used with good effect with heavy cast-iron balls rolling in a cast-iron basin four or five feet in diameter; but in his case the castings worked loose, both in the track and on the circumference of the wheel, making a total wreck in the coarse of a few days. The machinery was sold for old iron, and work suspended for some years. Some miners jumped the claim and opened a paying vein, at least for a time. The surface of the vein, or a sheet of it, perhaps twenty feet wide, was found flat on the ground, having apparently fallen over. A hundred tons of this rock, crushed at the Fogus Mill, paid about thirty-four dollars per ton. An attachment was laid on the money by three lawyers from Mokelumne Hill, all of whom were dignified as Judges. An expensive lawsuit followed. Surveyors were sent to map the ground, experts to theorize on the probabilities of the existence of a vein, and, in fact, the whole legal mining machinery which had been introduced into Comstock mining litigation, was brought into play on the real discoverers of the paying vein. They had to yield. The mine is now nearly forgotten.

THE CLINTON MINES

Were once considered good, but are not worked at present. These belong to the Pine Grove range, and, like them, have a short run in length as well as depth.

THE MACE RANGE

Has the north and south trend following the rifts of the slate. Though rich on the surface, they pinch out at a short depth, and are not true fissure veins. It would seem possible that these veins are produced by surface action, that is, by the precipitation of minerals held in solution, by water flowing over the surface, as the veins seem to have no connection with a gold-bearing strata, like the veins on the Mother Lode.

A good vein of ore in this vicinity may yield three or four thousand dollars before it pinches out. The milling is done by a custom mill at five dollars per ton, owned by F. Mace.

Though these veins have a family resemblance, they differ much in character in the course of a few miles, sometimes being clear, hard, and blue in texture and color, and then shading into syenite sandstone or hornblende. In some, the gold, though paying well for milling, is so fine as to be almost impalpable. In this case, the breaking down of a vein by glacial or other erosion would not make rich placers.

It may be observed of the country generally, that quartz boulders of any size usually indicate the proximity of a quartz vein of similar character, proving that the streams or rivers forming the beds of gravel, were small. This, however, does not apply to the great east and west river, which had its channel on the divide between Dry creek and Sutter creek, which escaped the great glacial erosion. A river which could sweep millions of tons of volcanic boulders down the slope of the mountains, could and did, sweep along boulders of quartz three feet in diameter. Such a boulder was found in 1857, on Union flat, above any bed rock. It was of clear, blue quartz, without any admixture of iron, and had several hundred dollars in pure gold in a kind of stratum on one side, the other side being barren. The rock bore a great resemblance to that of the Sheep Ranch mine in Calaveras county, said to be one of the best paying mines in the State.

PIONEER AND GOLDEN GATE MINES.

Between the Mace, or West Point range, and Volcano, are veins of a very distinct character. They are narrow but well defined, going straight down, neither widening or pinching out. Of this character are the veins named at the head of this paragraph. The veins do not follow the trend of the country rock, but seem to be rather in a transverse fissure. They are from sixteen inches to two feet in width, paying from twenty to forty dollars a ton. The mine owned by W. Q. Mason, is of this group. The vein varies from three to nine inches in width, averaging about thirty-five dollars per ton, though in places the rock is quite rich, paying several dollars to the pound. This range of mines has not been sufficiently explored to determine the value of them.

QUARTZ VEINS WEST OF THE MOTHER LODE.

These are numerous, and some of them quite large, being in some instances thirty or forty feet thick, as at Dr. Randall's ranch near Ione, and at Mrs. Nichol's ranch, in Jackson valley. The lower range is quite as extensive as the Mother Lode, and in the rich gulches and placers adjoining, bears evidence of having considerable gold. In the vicinity of French Camp, some of the small veins are said to have gold enough to pay for crushing, but as they do not hold their size, but ramify into numerous branches, they are not likely to be extensively worked. The Kirkendall range near Irish hill, was thought to be rich, but work on it is generally suspended.

In the vicinity of Stony creek the quartz seems to be auriferous, but here, as at French Camp, the veins are neither permanent nor well defined. It would seem that in all this western range of quartz veins, copper, not gold seems to be the predominating mineral.

SOAP-STONE, OR STEATITE GOLD MINES.

These mines are some miles east of the lower range of quartz veins, and seem to be connected rather with the serpentine or green ledge formation. There is considerable doubt in the minds of many who have not examined the locality, as to the presence of gold in steatite; but the fact that all the gulches running from the locality were rich, ought to set all doubts to rest. Attention was called to these places twenty years since, by specimens of the steatite with gold, like bronze, well-distributed through it. There was some coarse gold found occasionally. Major Barting, who did the most to test these veins, found a piece in this vein thirty feet from the surface, which weighed some sixty grains or more.

It is claimed that the rock contains twenty or thirty dollars to the ton; but all attempts to save it have been failures, the gold being so fine as to float off on the top of the water.

QUARTZ MINING IN THE FUTURE.

Much money has been expended in quartz that has not been returned. A few have become wealthy, others have made a living, and many have worn themselves out in the unsuccessful search for gold. The fact that gold, which made the placers, was originally derived from quartz, and that many of the veins are still rich, will induce the examination of the last one where there is any probability, or even possibility, of finding it. GOLD! what a magic in the word! What a spell it will work. For gold, man will dare the depths of the earth, the heights of the mountains, the heat of the tropics, and the ice regions of the pole, the solitude of the plains and the crowds in cities.

Those who preach moderation in seeking it are the first to sniff a *strike*, and the fiercest to strive for its possession. Until human nature is changed, the gold hunt will continue.

"'PUT MONEY IN THY PURSE.'

"Make it thy soul's delight to gather coin. Suffer not thy thoughts to stray from this purpose. Make corners in bread, so that the poor shall go hungry. What is it to thee that hundreds suffer? Make corners in water, though the great Father poured it out without stint for all his children. Fence it up, gather it into reservoirs and make the thirst as well the hunger of the people fill thy purse. What were hunger and thirst made for but to help thee put money in thy purse? Watch the progress of industry, and buy up the land that lies in its course. Hold it for high prices; hold it until the homeless and landless must have it at any price. What is it to thee that industries are paralyzed? Put money in thy purse.

"Thy brother may be fainting by the wayside, crushed by misfortune and sickness. Heed not his cry of agony. Shut all avenues of the heart to the cries of suffering humanity. What is the world to thee? Put *money* in thy purse.

"The world is full of beauty. Every little flower that opens its petals to drink in the sunshine, is full of marvelous, self-acting machinery. Heed it not. Turn not aside from thy great work. The rocks of the earth, all the elements, tell a wondrous story of the creation, extending through myriads of ages, of changes from chaos to order; from darkness to light and life; of alternating ages of torrid heat and icy solitude. The stars spangling the infinite blue deep, tell a marvelous tale of the extent of God's works, and suggest the possibility of a future greatness of the soul; of a wandering at will through endless beauty—wondering, admiring, and learning. Leave such things to fools; they are nothing to thee. Put money in thy purse.

"Work for money with all thy might, mind, and soul, and it shall flow to thee, as the water floweth to the sea, in streams ever widening and deepening, gathering strength as it comes. Thou shalt own broad acres in the hearts of cities, and principalities in the country. Thy flocks shall cover a thousand hills, and thy bank accounts increase by day and by night. Though in the pursuit of wealth thy features become the incarnation of all that is vile, a record of years of sin, at thy approach with the golden key the doors of palatial residences will fly open; obsequious servants will conduct thee to the innermost shrine; melodious voices will sing for thee the sweetest songs; gray-haired wisdom will lend thee its aid, and youth and beauty will come to thy arms. Thou mayest ride rough-shod over the people, for hast thou not the wherewith?

"But know, O mortal! that thy millions cannot purchase one atom of love or respect; that the poorest sewing girl in the city, or the dirtiest dustman, is richer than thou art, for some one may have for them a tender thought; but thou shalt be abhorred of all. When sorrow cometh to thee, no heart will beat in sympathy, no tears will mingle with thine. Every man's hand will be against thee, as thine has been against mankind. Every dollar of thy millions will be a demon to gnaw thy withered, shrunken soul. Thy heart shall be like a desert land, without green thing, fountain, or shade. The harpies of the law shall quarrel over thy ill-gotten wealth, as the wild dogs and wolves over the fallen bison of the plains, and thou shalt have lived in vain, for what doth thy wealth profit?"

Gold mining and the pursuit of wealth will go on nevertheless, and may be regulated, but not prohibited.

SCHOOL CABINETS.

Cabinets of elegant curiosities abound everywhere, but, notwithstanding, there is a great deal of confusion regarding the names of the commonest rocks. The metamorphic slates, constituting the wall rocks of the quartz veins, are generally called granite, than which nothing is more different. A collection of a hundred common rocks, properly labelled and cased, at the school-houses, would cost but little and would soon have a perceptible effect in remedying the confusion.

COPPER MINING.

Copper, in quantity, was first discovered in Calaveras county, at the place afterwards called Copperopolis, by W. K. Reed, July 4, 1861. The outcrop, along where the Union and Keystone mines were located, was very marked, and large quantities of oxidized ores were taken out near the surface, as well as fine specimens of native copper, some of which were arborescent or crystallized in form. There were also large quantities of impure oxide of copper (copper smut) mixed more or less with red oxide. These ores were all shipped to Swansea, England, for reduction, and the profits were such that fortunes of half a million were made in a little time. It is said that the Union mine opened the largest body of ore ever discovered in the world, the shipments from it being made on an immense scale. The run of ore was three hundred and fifty feet long, and from four to nine thick at the upper level; twenty-one feet at the depth of two hundred, and thirty-one feet at the depth of two hundred and fifty feet, all of No. 1 and No. 2 ores. Other mines in the vicinity were also rich. The shipments from Stockton of the Copperopolis ores, netted in 1863 six hundred thousand dollars; in 1864 over one million dollars. For the first year or two little attention was paid to copper in other places, but the rapid development of the mines, and shipment of ores with profitable returns, soon set hundreds to tracing out the copper formation. The gossan or calico rock, so named from the spotted appearance caused by patches of iron rust, was found in a thousand places, and on uncovering

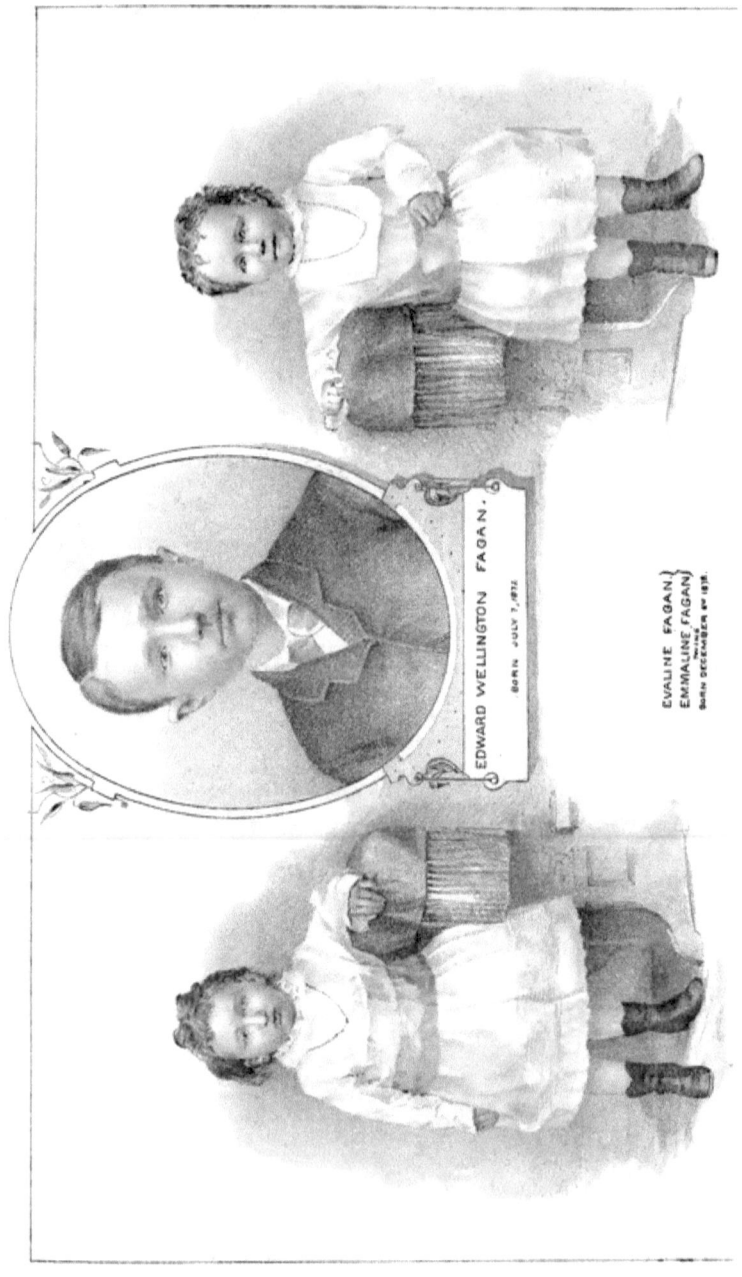

RESIDENCE AND LIVERY STABLE OF PETER FAGAN, SUTTER CREEK, AMADOR CO. CAL.

the rock, mundic or sulphuret of iron was generally found a few feet from the surface with a little copper also. Considerable veins were found at Lancha Plana and Campo Seco, especially at the latter place. Several companies were organized and the shipping of ore commenced. In 1862 Dr. Newton, near Ione, commenced sinking for copper on general principles rather than any practical knowledge of the ores or croppings; but the following Summer, 1863, he struck a vein of shipping ore, and the excitement in Amador county commenced. It was found that the calico, or gossan rock, was common over a tract of country eight or ten miles wide, east and west, and extending from the Mokelumne to the Cosumnes rivers.

GENERAL CRAZE.

Within four months, or by the first of October, at least one thousand men were at work sinking on every discoloration of rock that could be found. At first some attention was paid to the range, but soon the veins were found everywhere, though not in sufficient quantity to be of any commercial value. A vein of four inches of black oxide of copper was discovered on the top of Bald hill, near Buena Vista, and shares were soon selling at the rate of two hundred thousand dollars for the prospect. This claim or mine was known by the name of Bull Run. The Star of the West, not far away, also went up to a fabulous price. Quite a town, Copper Centre, sprang up in the vicinity and many more sites were staked out. The Ione City company struck a vein of a few inches in thickness near Stony creek, and shares were immediately held at two thousand five hundred dollars per hundred feet. Shares in an adjoining claim without the color of copper were worth two hundred dollars. Copper could be melted out of the ores of many of the veins with a common blacksmith's forge. This was the case with a vein an inch or two in thickness near Sutter creek (name of the mine forgotten), and forthwith each hundred of the two thousand feet was worth one thousand dollars. Many of the companies incorporated with a capital stock of one hundred thousand to one million dollars, and opened offices, hired secretaries at salaries from fifty to one hundred dollars per month, issued handsomely printed certificates of stock, and did everything that Washoe companies did. Large handsome signs such as, Office Ione City Copper Mining Company; Office Chaparral Copper Mining Company, indicated the "Copper on the brain" which was afflicting almost every one.

COUNTRY FORMED INTO DISTRICTS.

The country was all districted off, recorders elected, and laws passed, which were recognized in the courts as valid and binding. The fees for recording a location were usually one dollar, with an additional twenty-five cents for each name attached to the notice. Some of the recorders would make one hundred dollars a month at this alone. Placer mining was nearly suspended in the hunt for copper. Not less than three hundred companies were doing constant work between the northern and southern boundaries of the county, besides others who were doing enough to hold the ground. Tunnels hundreds of feet long were run in the hard metamorphic slates, *just to strike the supposed range*. The serpentine range had a green color, and was thought by many to be copper ore. "Uncle Thomas Rickey" formed a company of two hundred or more, to run a tunnel into this, near Poo's ranch. "It would only cost a dollar to get in, and if they struck anything there would be enough for all." This tunnel was run something over two hundred feet. Fifty companies were sinking near Horse creek, one hundred near Forest home, fifty or more in the vicinity of Ione, as many more near Jackson and Stony creeks; in fact, it was hard to find a hill which was not claimed, with a little work done to hold the ground. Some of the notices were amusing enough.

FUNNY NOTICES.

Hon. W. A. Ludlow, now of Oakland, is authority for the following:—

"tack Notes thee unter singd clant two Huntent foot Sought on thes Loat from thee muns Noten bushes
Febuary 12 1863
Clamte sought ter Pint three"

"Nota Bean Is here By given notes ter unter signed clame too cooben clames of too Hunter feet square sought Nort too 200 Hunter feet
Thounship
No 5
AmTore country feb 12 63 "

"Take Notes the untersiGent chlames North 400 foot to a mains noeten Bush for Preubens of Mining Coper
Febuary 12 one thousand 800 63 "

Lest people should think this style was owing to the absence of the school-master, the following notice for the sale of property in Berkeley, in the shadow of the University, is apponded:—

"Fern Sall Tur Mes Eli."

Selling claims or shares was a profitable business, and stock gambling came near being established. Almost every person had his pockets full of *rocks*, and wanted to sell shares.

The finest and best arranged collection of ores and croppings was collected by Judge Carter, of Ione. Some twenty or thirty of the leading mines were fully represented, cropping and ores being arranged in the natural order from the top down. It should have been preserved for the use of schools.

NEW TOWNS.

Forest Home, Mineral City, and several other towns sprang up in the northern part of the county, where the excitement was greater, if possible, than in any other part. The *One Hundred and One*, or

Cosumnes Company, shipped considerable ore, as did several other companies. The McNealy Company (Arroyo Seco Copper Company), near Muletown, also shipped several hundred tons of ore. C. T. Meader, of Stockton, became the copper king of the State, buying into many promising locations, the Newton mine among others. This was extensively operated, and numbers of teams loaded every day for the water-front.

RESULT OF THE GENERAL SEARCH.

A thousand shafts were sunk, many of them striking copper in small quantities. The serpentine range, spoken of in the chapter on geology as an axis of elevation, seemed to be the center of the copper belt. The deposits on the eastern side were generally in bunches of a few tons, capped with iron ore. At one point, between Stony and Jackson creeks, twenty-three of these chimneys could be seen within a space of half a mile square. Around the Mountain Spring House the "*mineral caps*" were equally noticeable before they were removed for grading the turnpiked road. This section of the country is well worth the attention of mineralogists for its indications of other minerals than copper. Some of the shafts near the serpentine struck *asbestos* in considerable quantities, which is likely to be valuable.

CHROME IRON

Was also found in quantity in several places, one vein, now claimed by the Westfall brothers, being nearly three feet thick. Twenty years since, this ore was worth sixty dollars per ton, but since the discovery of large quantities of it in Sonoma and other places, it is worth only the cost of mining it.

In the Autumn of 1863, some five or six companies were shipping ore, and a hundred more were expecting to do so soon, but the whole thing collapsed in a few months, leaving the million of dollars or more, which had been expended in the search, a total loss.

FAILURE OF MEADER.

The first intimation of the coming panic was the failure of C. T. Meader, the copper king. He had not only bought into copper mines, but into quartz mines as well. The Coney mine had passed into his possession, and he had engaged extensively in shipping under the name of "Meader, Loler & Co."

When his failure came, it involved the mines in which he was engaged in litigation, which had the effect of tying them up for several years. Among the causes mentioned was the depreciation of copper, which went down, in the course of two years, from twenty-eight to fourteen cents a pound. It was said at the time that this depreciation was the result of a conspiracy on the part of the Swansea Companies, to break down the mining of copper in California; but the reports of the discoveries, not only in Amador and Calaveras, but all over the State as well, would be likely to affect the market. In Nevada county the Well claim was said to be inexhaustible, having a body of ore two hundred feet in width.

In Arizona there were, as it was said, miles of dykes of ore standing in sight on the top of the ground. The mines of Lake Superior were also pouring into the trade a marvelous quantity of copper, so that it was hardly necessary to suppose a conspiracy.

Four years afterwards, Meader, in accounting for his failure, said that his copper stocks had depreciated in value two million two hundred and forty thousand dollars, and that his total indebtedness was one million two hundred and ninety thousand dollars. The extreme depreciation continued for several years, totally suspending copper mining, many of the claims being abandoned, and *all* being allowed to fill up with water. From this latter circumstance came the discovery of a cheaper method of reducing the ores.

At the time work was suspended many of the tools were left in the mines. When the water was pumped out three or four years afterwards, a

REMARKABLE DISCOVERY

Was made. Every piece of iron or steel left in the ground had been decomposed, and around it was an oxide of copper, with a brown luster, which would assay ninety-five per cent. copper. Shovels, hammers, drills, iron bars, car wheels, and spikes used in fastening timber, were solid copper, bearing some resemblance to the original articles. The steel drills were irregular tubes, the hollow part retaining the shape of the iron. This was a discovery. Instead of having to ship the ores to Swansea at an enormous expense, they could be leached; that is, after the exposure of the ores to the air they decomposed, and became converted into sulphate of copper (blue stone of commerce) which was soluble in water. The water, being run into large vats, was brought into contact with scrap-iron, which could be bought for a trifle; the iron had a stronger affinity for the sulphur, and the copper was precipitated in the form of a brown powder, which was nearly pure copper. By this method very poor ores can be worked with a profit. It must be said, however, that not all the copper ores can be worked in this manner. The number of veins containing workable ore, is, perhaps, hundreds, possibly thousands. Though no colossal fortunes will be made, yet they are likely in the future to give profitable employment to a great number of men.

PRESENT CONDITION OF COPPER MINING.

The Newton lead, owned by a Boston company, is the only one that is extensively worked. This was the first to make use of the process of leaching and precipitation. Under the able management of Edward Johnson, the mine has not only been put on a paying basis, but the way shown to utilize the small bodies of copper ores which abound on the east side of the serpentine ledge, as well as the larger ones on the west side. The works now cover several acres of ground. The vats, piles of scrap-iron— which now come near to the mine by rail—the piles of ore, through which the water is slowly soaking, and the hoisting works, all serve to make a business appearance.

The main shaft is four hundred and thirty feet deep, from which four levels have been run each way about two hundred feet, exposing large bodies of double sulphurets of copper and iron. These levels are all connected by winzes with the air shaft. Some of the higher grades of ore are sent to Swansea for reduction, but the larger part are reduced on the ground. About forty men are employed about the works.

Reduction by leaching is also in use, to some extent, in the mines near Forest Home. Copper mining is a promising element in the prospects of the county.

CHAPTER XXX.
JACKSON.

Capture of the County Seat—Killing of Colonel Collyer—Loss of the County Seat—Bull Fight and Election—Mines—First School—Improvements in 1854—Hanging Tree—Griswold Murder—Great Freshet 1861—Great Fire 1862—Flood and Loss of Life 1878—Big Frolic—Celebration of Admission Day—Mokelumne River—Murphy's Gulch—Hunt's Gulch—Tunnel Hill—Butte Basin—Butte Mountain—Butte City—Marriage in High Life—The Gate—Ohio Hill—Slab City—Clinton—Spaulding's Invention.

DURING the Summer of 1848 this was a stopping place for persons traveling between Drytown and Mokelumne river, though some mining was done with *batayas* by the Mexicans, at the spring near the National Hotel. The number of bottles left around the spring by travelers, gave it the name of Bottilleas, until it was changed to Jackson, in honor of Colonel Jackson, who afterwards settled there. It does not appear that any number of men wintered here in 1848, though some of Stevenson's soldiers wintered at Mokelumne Hill. The first permanent white resident of which any account can be found is Louis Tellier, who still resides on the first location. When Jim Martin and his company of eight passed through Jackson, or rather where it was not, there was a Mexican cart standing near the spring. Louis Tellier's first house was a log cabin covered with rawhides; he also had a large army tent which had been used in Mexico. In early days freight to Sacramento was as high as one thousand dollars per ton. In 1850 it was reduced to two hundred dollars per ton. To Volcano from Sacramento it was two hundred and fifty dollars. There were no bridges, and, even in Summer-time, both men and animals were sometimes drowned. Lumber was worth three dollars per foot, the floor of a small room costing six hundred to one thousand dollars. The roads were mere Indian trails, which were, in many instances, too narrow to let wagons through.

There were two roads to Sacramento; one by way of Rancheria and Drytown, the other by way of Buena Vista. Louis Tellier caused the latter trail to be cut wide enough for a wagon, at his own expense. The trail nearly followed the road towards Lancha Plana to Stony creek, thence to the right over the Blue ridge. During the Summer, Mr. Hough, Mrs. Hough and her sister, came to the town, these two being the first white women in the town. Mrs. Hough is now living in Diamond Springs, the second is living in Jackson, the widow of McDowell, the first Justice of the Peace in Jackson. The union of Miss Hough and McDowell, was the first wedding. Mrs. Silas Penry is the daughter by that marriage. Charles Boynton built the "Astor House," and also a bowling saloon. History does not give us many particulars regarding the architectural merits of the "Astor House," nor as to the architect who planned it. It was equal to any building in the city, however, though it was built of logs, and daubed with mud. There was a cabin near where R. W. Palmer's house now stands; also one on the site of his stable, occupied by John Papac, a Chileno. Towards the Gate was a cabin, with the sign, "brandy and sugar," hence called the Brandy and Sugar Hotel, kept by a man by the name of Kelley. He also sold bread and butter; a slice off a loaf baked in a Dutch oven, was sold for one dollar; if buttered, two dollars. He charged one dollar per night for room to spread the blankets on the ground floor.

A Dr. Elliot had a tent near the site of the Central House where he sold goods. During the Autumn an emigrant sold his tent for six dollars; the rains coming on soon after, he paid one dollar a night for the privilege of sleeping under it. Evans came in March, 1850, with some beef, slaughtered on the Cosumnes, packed on some animals. He hung his meat on a pole resting on two forked posts, and soon sold out and went after more. His business flourishing, he soon after opened a store at Secreto (near Clinton) another at Butte, and a larger one at Jackson, near the site of the National Hotel. His store was of logs, and, not being well chinked, he filled up the holes with hams, the shank bones sticking out all around. He soon associated with him D. C. White (who afterwards put up the soda works), and A. Askey, the latter having remained with him since.

Duncan & Gage (who afterwards kept a Chinese Bazar at San Francisco), Levinsky, Sloan, Stevens, Steckler, Captain Dunham, and others, came soon after Evans. Levinsky had a large store for many years, as also did Steckler. Stevens run the Young America saloon; Sloan afterwards lighted Jackson with Aubin gas. Captain Dunham kept a meat market near the hanging tree. There were also the two Doctor Shields (called the big doctor and the little doctor), one, it is not certain which, having a wife.

In August, 1850, there were but seven buildings in the town, some of which were empty. These were Louis Tellier's, White & Evans', Henry and Frederick Reeves' (on the hill near Butterfield's), one where Kent now lives, occupied by Mr. Hough and family, one at Palmer's house, and also one near his stable and the Brandy and Sugar Hotel. Dan Worley, now living near Drytown, visiting Jackson one day, thought to get a clean square meal cooked by a woman, but except for the name of the thing would as soon have eaten in his own cabin. Bill of fare: Fried steak, bread, and black coffee, $1.00, with, "If you don't like it stay away."

FIRST GREAT EVENT IN JACKSON.

This was no less than the capture of the county seat. This brilliant exploit seemed to have had its origin in the fertile brain of Charles Boynton. When Calaveras county was organized, Double Springs somehow obtained the county seat. It had but one house, which answered for Court House, saloon, store, and hotel. The place had not grown as was expected. The county seat, metaphorically speaking, was reaching out its arms for a more suitable home; and Jackson, with its less than a dozen houses, was willing to receive it, and nurse it to greater strength. Elections and Acts of the Legislature, means usually invoked in such matters, were set aside as involving too much time, altogether too slow for the lively town of Jackson. One morning, while Double Springs was resting quietly on its dignity as a shire town, the enemy appeared, smiling as usual. They (Charles Boynton and Theo. Mudge) walked up to the county seat's bar, and throwing down the coin, according to the custom of the country, invited all hands to imbibe. The population of the town, or at least the larger part, responded with alacrity, the larger part being Colonel Collyer, a rather pompous, portly Virginia gentleman, fond of telling good stories, and fonder still of good liquor, never refusing the opportunity for either. While one detachment of the enemy artfully engaged the attention of Colonel Collyer, who was county clerk, and in that capacity custodian of the archives, another detachment at the other end of the room gathered the archives under his arm, tumbled them into a buggy, and ran away with them to Jackson. When the Colonel found the county seat had vanished, he raised his portly form an inch or two higher, swung his cane furiously around his head, and swore that the army should be called out to vindicate the dignity of the court.

A shake shanty, at the foot of Court street, had been prepared for the bantling, and, on the arrival of Boynton and Mudge at Jackson, the archives were desposited with the proper ceremonies, the liquors being remarkably fine; and Jackson became the center of government for the great territory of Calaveras, which extended from Sacramento to the Rocky Mountains. Judge Smith, the County Judge, seemed to be on hand, ready to administer justice; in fact, he was suspected of having connived at the abduction, which act, it is said, was in part the cause of the tragedy occurring soon after. The County Clerk was induced to take his place, and issue the proper papers, dated at Jackson, for the convening of a court.

TRAGEDY—KILLING OF COLONEL COLLYER.

At the election for county officers, held soon after the removal of the county seat, Joe Douglass, candidate for the clerkship against Colonel Collyer received the larger number of votes. The Colonel locked up the returns in his desk, in order to hold the office until his successor was qualified, which could not well be done without the counting of the votes, with his official signature to the result. Judge Smith broke open the desk in the absence of the Colonel, counted the returns, and issued the certificates of election to the successful candidates, Joe Douglass among the rest. This put a new face on the affair. The feud, occasioned by the removal of the county records, now grew into an open war. Threats to shoot Judge Smith on sight induced him to arm himself, and when they met, near the foot of the present Court street, Smith commenced firing, hitting Collyer, who does not seem to have been armed, two or three times. The shots were fatal, and Collyer fell at the foot of a large oak tree growing there, and shortly after expired. Smith was not tried for the homicide, but public indignation was so strong that he resigned. It is said, however, that as Smith was a Northern man and Collyer a Southern man, the people took sides accordingly in approving or condemning, and thus foreshadowed the great contest of ten years later.

The few residents of Jackson got up a celebration of the Fourth. McDonnell was the orator, and compared the Constitution to a "crystal palace with its pedestal towering to the skies."

EIGHTEEN HUNDRED AND FIFTY.

In the Fall a great immigration came in, and by the 1st of December, Jackson had in the neighborhood of a hundred houses. Harnett, who afterwards lived in lone valley, built and kept a restaurant near the Astor House. Henry Mann and John Burke also had a restaurant, near the tree afterwards famous as the "hanging tree." It was in this house that the Indian, Coyote Joe, was tried for killing the blacksmith near the Gate. The wife of Helmer Turner, present Deputy County Clerk, is a daughter of Henry Mann; a son is junior partner of the firm, Hutchinson, Mann & Co., engaged in insurance in San Francisco. Mr. Mann lost his life in a singular manner. A tame bear was kept tied to the famous tree near Mann's restaurant. One day he had been moved to a lot where some shoats were kept, which his bearship commenced killing. Mr. Mann, in trying to return the animal to the tree, angered the bear, which gave him a hug that proved fatal in two or three days. Mrs. Mann afterwards married W. L. McKimm, the wedding taking place on the top of Butte mountain.

Streeter and family, who afterwards lived on Dry creek, resided here during the Winter of 1850-51. Sheldon Streeter was the first white child born in Jackson.

Residence and Lumber Yard of E.S. Potter, Plymouth, Amador Co. Cal.

Medical attendance was expensive in those days, physicians charging enormous fees. The following fee bill was posted up in a doctor's office:—

For one visit with medicine..........................$ 16 00
Reducing a fractured limb..............$50 00 to 100 00
Parturition 100 00

The following story on medical charges is on the *said so* of Tom Springer of the *Ledger*:—

"Doctor Marsh, who was murdered in Contra Costa county about 1856, was formerly owner of a ranch in this county. Being called upon in a professional capacity to visit a sick child, he got the mother to wash a shirt for him.

"On leaving he made out a bill for services amounting to fifty cows—the exact number of the woman's herd of cattle. She acknowledged the debt, but at the same time made out a bill to the same amount for washing his shirt. The doctor went off grumbling at the high rate for washing in California."

SECOND REMOVAL OF THE COUNTY SEAT.

Mokelumne Hill having outgrown Jackson, was hankering for the distribution of the public moneys among her own people. According to the law passed by the Legislature in 1849–50, the county seat might be moved every year if a majority petitioned for an election and two-thirds voted for the change. It was little trouble to get names on a petition of any kind, and, as events subsequently proved, not very much trouble to get votes in those days. An election being ordered, Jackson would make an effort to keep it. Though Mokelumne Hill had the votes, Jackson had the talent and daring, which, once before, had captured the county seat.

It was determined to gather a great multitude by means of a free bull-fight, hoping to out-vote Mokelumne Hill. Accordingly a corral was prepared, bulls engaged, and great inducements offered, or, as the play bills said, unparalleled attraction.

The bulls, some seven or eight in number, were brought in some day or two before, and fierce looking fellows they were, with their long slender horns and sleek hides, and the excitement was immense. It looked as if Jackson had got the bulge on the Mokelumne "Hellyons." Lest the cattle might be surreptitiously turned loose, a guard of three or four men with rifles, was stationed at the gate to insure the safe keeping of the animals. But the Mok-Hillians were not asleep. They began to gather in horses; they were not going to be beaten with a bull-fight. They announced that the bull-fight was not coming off. A delegation of trusty men was sent to Jackson to watch the enemy. During the night they plied the guards so well with whisky that they slept at their posts, during which time the Mok-Hillians quietly undid the fastenings without disturbing the sentinels. Getting on the opposite side of the corral they raised a great hullabalo, hearing which the guards sprang to their feet only to be tossed and trampled by the infuriated beasts, which charged at a run through the open gate and were gone in a moment.

22

The Spanish bulls having gone, an attempt was made to get up an entertainment with American cattle, but they would not entertain worth a cent, and the crowd programme was a failure. It was now learned what the horses at Mokelumne Hill were for. Bands of men were riding furiously all over the country voting at every precinct, but the horses of Jackson were few, and when the sun went down Jackson was beaten, because the other side had the most horses. An enormous vote was cast, out of all proportion to the population.

MINES.

The gulches around Jackson were generally good, though no such strikes were made as in Mokelumne river. The north fork of Jackson creek was good to its head; the south and middle forks were also good. The best spots were near the junction of the creeks, not far from the National House. A few men made as high as five hundred dollars per day at times. Thomas Jones had one of the best claims. Nuggets worth two hundred and fifty dollars were taken out near Dick Palmer's house. Hough also had a good claim near the same place. One day some immigrants inquired where they could find diggings, and a place was pointed out. In a few days they took out fourteen pounds each, and went home. The flats in the vicinity of Tunnel hill were also good. Jackson owed its prosperity more to being a convenient center than to any mines about the town. The different forks of the creeks came together at Jackson. The roads to Volcano, Mokelumne Hill, and the southern mines, passed through here, and all helped to make it a center for a large extent of country.

FIRST PREACHING.

The meeting was held in Mann's saloon in 1850. The preacher (Southern Methodist), took a drink before commencing service. His preaching was profitable to himself at least, his receipts at the close of the sermon being over a hundred dollars, of which sum Harnet gave twenty dollars, and Laura Stubbs, afterwards Harnet's wife, giving ten dollars. This was about all the preaching that Winter. Davidson and his three partners (of what was called the Minister Quartz Company, working at Amador), preached occasionally the following Summer. I. B. Fish was the first established preacher. He belonged to the Methodist Episcopal Church. He was a fearless man, of good mind and great force of character, and did not hesitate to denounce the popular vices of the age. At Ione, especially, he won the enmity of saloon-keepers and gamblers. The first church was built in 1853 by subscriptions, costing two thousand dollars.

THE FIRST SCHOOL

Was taught by Mrs. Trowbridge, using the Methodist church for a school-house. She was one of the few pioneer women who felt the responsibility of living where female influence was so great, and will be remembered as using it for the advancement of society. Several children, around Jackson at the time, were going to ruin for the want of a mother's care. Mrs. Trowbridge obtained clothes for them, induced them to go to school and otherwise cared for them. Geo. O. Ash, now a leading member of the Methodist Episcopal Church in this State, owes his early training and subsequent success to Mrs. Trowbridge's care when he was a motherless waif.

IN 1854

The advent of the county seat gave Jackson a great lift. Several brick buildings were put up about this time, among which was the building at the bridge used as a Court House after the big fire, the house used by Ingalls as a drug store at the corner of Main and Water streets, and some others not recollected.

With the increase of population came also all kinds of mercantile institutions, where beauty and frailty had a market value. The sounds of music, the clinking of glasses, the chink of money as the gambler paid out his losses or raked in his winnings, were in time and tune with the other towns of California, neither better nor worse. The town was organized, and a Board of Trustees and Mayor elected. When the first term of court under the new organization was in session, the Grand Jury recommended that some attempt be made to suppress the disorderly houses—meaning the houses of ill-fame. No attention was paid to it, but at the next session the Grand Jury acted more vigorously. Several men were indicted for keeping disorderly houses. The Grand Jury, visiting some of the houses, were shown licenses for doing business, which the parties construed into doing their kind of business; so they, the Grand Jury, indicted the town authorities for issuing the licenses, though the charge was "for obtaining money under false pretenses." A. C. Brown, acting as attorney for himself and other members of the Board, acknowledged the service of the papers, and gave security for appearance.

The affair caused quite an excitement, but ended in nothing, as District Attorney Axtell appeared in court the next morning and entered a *nolle prosequi* in the cases, and Judge Gordon dismissed them.

The indictments against the parties keeping the disorderly houses were continued until the next term, and then dismissed for *want of evidence*. Although these matters did not result in suppressing these institutions, they showed that public opinion was getting intolerant of the display of such places, and from this time they rather evaded than courted publicity.

GAS WORKS.

About this time, Sloan and some others established gas works. Pipes were laid along the streets and in all the public places. The works were on the ground occupied by the rear of R. W. Palmer's stable. There was a bench of three retorts, and a tank or gasometer holding perhaps five thousand feet. Pitch wood was used for making the gas which was called *Aubin* gas. Great hopes were entertained of the project, but the quality of the gas, owing to the defective machinery for purifying it, was uncertain. Sometimes the light from it was brilliant, then going entirely out; and the experiment was abandoned. The pipes were afterwards utilized as water-pipes.

THE GREAT FRESHET.

Eighteen hundred and sixty-one found Broadway built quite across the creek, the houses resting on posts, which were set in the ground but a little ways. It was nine years since the flood of fifty-two and three, and the people either had forgotten, or would not believe that the forks of Jackson creek would sometimes float a steamboat, and so they rested in security. The American Hotel, Young America Saloon, and other good houses, were built over the channel on Broadway. On the continuation of Main street, beyond the Louisiana Hotel (now National Hotel), was a row of barber-shops and saloons. The rains commenced about the first of December, and continued without much intermission for some weeks, until the ground was so full it could hold no more, each shower sending the streams, already full, over the banks. When the main rise occurred, bringing down trees, timber, fences, and mining machinery, the channel soon choked. The flood now turned into Water street, running along in front of the Louisiana Hotel, carrying off the wagon-shop to the west of the hotel, with its contents, and endangering the safety of all the buildings along the street. At this point the buildings began to give way. The American Hotel actually floated up stream a little, which caused the remark that it always was a contrary concern and would not go like other buildings, referring to its having been an unprofitable investment. Slowly the mass of buildings, with the bridge, gave way and started, grinding along and tearing away the outbuildings which had been built from both sides into the creek. The row of barber-shops and saloons on the next crossing hardly checked the movement, and the mass went grinding and crashing into the cañon below, and the channel was cleared and the danger passed. Some twenty buildings went off in this burst, involving a loss of perhaps fifty thousand dollars. The quantity of lumber of all kinds that went down the creek through Jackson was enormous. It was fished out at all points. Several thousand feet could be gathered in a few hours, so much broken, however, as to be useless except for wood. Much of it went into the bay and thence to sea.

INCIDENTS OF THE FRESHET.

The buildings taken away from the foot of Broadway and Main streets, with their contents, went tearing and crashing down the cañon, and for some weeks, broken doors, windows, counters, and all kinds of goods, were thrown ashore or fished out of the creek below. One day, Dr. Crawford and Sam Folger, the latter now in business in Jackson, were engaged with others in wrecking in Jackson valley. Now a door, which they recognized as coming from the Young America saloon, would come to land; then a window from the American Hotel; then a part of the outhouse of the Louisiana, the parties extracting a good deal of fun out of the work. A bottle of some kind of liquor, miraculously preserved from breaking, during its journey through the Devil's Mill, as the cañon was called, came rolling and bobbing along, and was fished out. Now the Young America had the reputation of keeping the best liquors in the county. If it should be some of Bristow's whisky, as Mrs. Toodles says, "it would come so handy;" but there were barbers' and doctors' shops carried away also, and it might be hair oil, or hair dye, or some other horrible stuff, and it naturally fell to the Doctor to try it. He smelled and tasted, and smelled and tasted again, and ominously shook his head. "Better not touch it, Folger, it may be poison. Let me try it again;" taking a liberal sample, again shaking his head, but the indescribable look of satisfaction over-spreading his countenance, induced Folger to test it also. It was some of Bristow's best, and a very acceptable find to the wet fishermen.

THE HANGING-TREE.

This tree which has become noted wherever the name of California is known, formerly stood near Louis Tellier's saloon, and was a live-oak, with several branching trunks. It was never very beautiful, but was a source of so much pride to the citizens, on account of its history, that its likeness was engraved on the county seal, so that its appearance is not likely to be forgotten.

Its use at first as a hanging-tree, was quite accidental; but in the course of time the tree was a terrible hint for the quick solution of a criminal case, and when the tree was injured by the great fire of August, 1862, so as to necessitate the cutting of it down, the feeling regarding its fate was not altogether sorrowful.

The first case was "Coyote Joe," an Indian, charged with killing a blacksmith at the Gate, for the purpose of getting his money. He was tried by a jury of miners, Dr. Pitt acting as foreman, and found guilty, as some of the specimens the blacksmith was known to have, were found on the Indian's person. The trial was in a restaurant, not far from the tree, and he was soon hanging.

The second case was that of a Chileno, who stabbed a woman who was his cousin; he was tried by a jury of citizens, found guilty, and shortly hung.

In 1851, two Frenchmen were murdered in Squaw gulch near the Gate. One was stabbed with a long bowie-knife thirteen times, dying immediately; the other, though cut five or six times, lived for several days. Suspicions were fixed upon a young Mexican, who was afterwards arrested by Waterman H. Nelson, Sheriff of Calaveras county (this being before the organization of Amador) at Sacramento, and brought to Jackson handcuffed to another young Mexican who had been arrested for horse-stealing. The examination was before Bruce Husband, Justice of the Peace. The testimony was so positive that there was no doubt of the guilt of the accused, and as the atrocious details of the murder came out the French portion of the population became excited beyond all control, and they determined to hang the Mexican at all hazards, and so told the Sheriff, who determined that the prisoner should be taken to Mokelumne Hill for trial. The French armed themselves with shot-guns, and the Americans with pistols, the latter with the intention of defending Nelson if he was assaulted. The murderer was still handcuffed to the other Mexican who was arrested for horse-stealing. How to get them apart was the question, and at one time it seemed as if both would be hanged together, but Martell, the blacksmith, finally cut the chain in two, releasing the horse-thief. Now commenced the exciting part of the affair. The Frenchmen had assured Nelson that they would not hurt him. The Americans looked on, admiring the pluck of the officer, caring little what became of the "greaser." It was remarked that if one shot-gun went off there would be fifty dead men in five minutes. Twice the rope was placed around the fellow's neck, and twice it was cut by the Sheriff. Sompayrac, a French merchant, was asked to say something to allay the excitement, but he only shouted, "Hang him! hang him!" Nelson was finally overpowered and the Mexican was hanged. It may be a matter of doubt whether Nelson's apparent struggle to maintain the dignity of the law was not half, at least, in the interest of the mob, as no arms were used or exhibited by him.

The other prisoner got out of the crowd and went to the Union Hotel. The proprietor, Colonel Allen, remarked that the crowd would hang him also. "Did you steal a horse?" asked Allen of him. "Yes, I took a horse and rode him." (Allen.) "*You sabe este camino?*" pointing to a trail that led down the creek. "*Si Señor.*" (Allen.) "*Vamos,*" giving the Mexican a shove. He left, making excellent time as long as he was in sight, and thus escaped, for that day at least, a hanging.

Some accounts state that the two Mexicans were hanged, but the above statement seems to be the most authentic.

In 1853, a party of Mexicans, said to have been Joaquin's band, robbed some Chinamen, killing two of them and tying the others on the creek below the town. Joe Lake, a butcher, in his rounds to sell his meat, rode up to the camp at the time the robbery was going on, and was killed by the Mexicans. One Chinaman escaping, came to the town and gave information of the tragedy. A party was made up and the Mexicans were pursued and overtaken; in the running fight which ensued one was severely wounded and was afterwards arrested in Lancha Plana, taken to Jackson and hanged.

In 1854, in March or April, a Chileno living in Jackson, attempted to rob a China camp on Cook's gulch, west of Jackson. The Chinamen got the better of him, tied him and brought him to town, where he paid the penalty of his crime by hanging.

March 23, 1854, a Swede, name unknown, was hung at Jackson, for the stealing of a horse from Evans and Askey. As there has been much talk of this matter, a short account of the stealing of the horse and its subsequent recovery, and the capture of the man, may not be out of place: The horse, a valuable and noticeable one, was taken from the stable on the night of the 17th. Suspicion immediately fixed itself on the person afterwards arrested, who had been camping in the vicinity, with no ostensible occupation. The camp was visited, but the man was gone. A blanket stolen at the same time, was found there, however, which served to confirm the suspicion with regard to the author of the theft. He was traced out of town towards the south; thence he turned north, making a wide circuit, and got on the Drytown road. At the Cosumnes ferry, the man and horse crossed early in the morning, both man and horse being identified, as they were subsequently at Mud Springs (El Dorado). Here they lost the trail for one day, but recovered it again on the Auburn road, both horse and man being in company. Here he offered to sell the horse, saying that he had sold the mate for three hundred dollars. He was eventually captured near Bridgeport, in Nevada county. The chain of evidence establishing his possession of the horse from the time of the stealing to his capture, seemed perfect. From these circumstances, no value whatever was attached to the bill of sale which he produced, which read as follows,—

"Sac. City, March 16, 154.
"Mr. C. Bennet Bot of C. Cuper, for one gray horse, Three Hundred & Forty Dollars. Title guaranteed.
"W. Holman, *Auctioneer*. C. CUPER."

Nor of the story which he told of having purchased the horse from a traveler on the road, with the transfer of the bill of sale.

On the way back, hundreds recognized both man and horse, so there seems no possible doubt of the guilt of the man, whatever may be thought of the hanging. He had a trial of only a few minutes, on the steps of the Louisiana House, at sunrise, soon after coming to the town. A rope was put around his neck, and he was hurried to the tree, only a few people being present. He tried to explain away the charge against him, saying that he bought the horse of a traveler, who transferred the bill of sale with the horse. He could not speak English, and Levinsky, whose store was near, interpreted for him. His body hung until noon before it was cut down.

There was a valuable ring on one of his fingers. A man, now living in Jackson, whose name does not deserve mention in this book, not being able to pull the ring off the swollen finger, cut it off; some say on a butcher's block, which was near by. It is also current that the several claimants to the ring played a game of cards, to see who should have it.

Public opinion was very much against the lynchers in this affair, and the next Grand Jury found bills for a high crime against several prominent citizens, who took an active part in the matter, and they found it convenient to be absent from the town, at several subsequent courts, to give color to the legal fiction that the parties named in the indictments could not be found.

In 1855, two Mexicans tried to rob a China camp, about four miles below Jackson. They met with unexpected resistance; one being stunned with a blow from a hatchet, the other making his escape. The Chinamen wound their prisoner with ropes from head to foot, so tightly that he could not bend, and then guyed him up liked a smoke-stack to a steam saw-mill, and sent to town for help to arrest him. When the whites got there they found him standing in the middle of the camp with ropes reaching out from him, all around, holding him to his place. He was brought to town and hung.

August 10, 1855, Manuel Garcia, one of the Rancheria banditti, was wounded in the running fight on the Calaveras river, taken and carried to Campo Seco, from which place he was taken to Jackson by Perry and Eichelberger. He was immediately hung by the people.

Soon after this, or about the 15th of August, two Mexicans were hung for complicity in the Rancheria murders. Manuel Escobar, of the same party was the tenth and last. The tree was injured in the great fire of 1862, and was cut down.

GRISWOLD MURDER.

On November 7, 1857, Martin Van Buren Griswold was murdered under circumstances that attracted the attention of the people, not only of the county, but also throughout the State. Griswold was a daring, self-possessed, and powerful man, who crossed the plains to Oregon in 1848. On his arrival in Oregon he learned of the discovery of gold in California, and, with his usual decision of character, he immediately turned toward that place. He arrived in San Francisco in April, '49, and went to Placerville, where he mined with rather indifferent success, but afterward struck it rich at Oregon Bar, "making his pile." After traveling about California awhile, he started for New York by way of the city of Mexico. While there he got out of coin and went to the mint to get his dust exchanged for gold, which they agreed to do, but afterward insisted upon his taking silver. He brought the mint officers to a sense of right by drawing his revolver upon them, and departed with the gold coin. He reached New

York without farther mishap, New Year's day, 1850. After spending a few weeks with his family, he started again for the Golden State, this time by way of Milwaukee and the great North-West, the then *terra incognita*, but now the great wheat-field of the world. Passing down the Red River of the North to the Selkirk settlements, he swung away toward the McKenzie and Copper Mine rivers to the outposts of the fur companies, and from thence made his way to Oregon, which place he reached Christmas day, 1850, having been nearly a year in making the trip, passing through the territory of twenty different tribes of Indians without a mishap. For some years he oscillated between San Diego and Siskiyou, San Francisco and the Sandwich Islands; was a prisoner among the Klamath Indians, from whom he escaped after two years of imprisonment, during which time he experienced many desperate adventures. He finally settled down with Horace Kilham, an extensive mine and ditch owner near Jackson. Large quantities of gold-dust were bought and sold at this place, the safe having at times fifty thousand dollars or more in it, a great temptation to Chinamen (several of whom worked about the place) who were in the habit of working for a mere pittance. One day he was missing; on examination the gold in the safe was also gone. For a moment suspicion fell on Griswold, but his friends scouted the idea of Griswold playing the scoundrel. Foul play was certain. With a man of his active temperament it was difficult to tell where he might not have been waylaid.

Hundreds of men from the adjoining mines were soon there; every possible contingency was canvassed. It was discovered that the China cook was also gone, and had been seen some miles away in company with other Chinamen. A thorough search of the premises was now made, but not until the next day was any clue to the mystery found, when the body of Griswold was found under the Chinaman's bed. Death was produced by two fractures of the skull, apparently by a blow from the rear, by a blunt instrument, though it was apparent that after the infliction of these wounds he had been struck in the front by some sharp instrument, again breaking the skull. To make assurance doubly sure, the murderers had drawn a chord tightly around the neck; but this was needless, the work was thoroughly done. In the room was found a heavy club, also a slung-shot, which had been seen in the possession of the Chinaman some weeks before the murder. Large rewards were offered for the apprehension of the China cook and his friends, who had been seen with him, the Chinese residents of Jackson contributing largely. The whole State was on the watch. The parties were arrested in Marysville through the assistance of the Chinese residents there. The key of the safe, some jewelry, and other articles known to have been in the safe, were found on their persons. They received a fair trial, had the benefit of able counsel, and were found guilty. Three were sentenced to be hung, and were executed on the sixteenth day of April, 1858. The fourth one indicted was given the benefit of a doubt, and his trial postponed; but he anticipated justice by committing suicide in his cell. Fou Seen, the cook who is supposed to have planned the murder, and called in the other parties to assist in the matter, was none of the simple "Heathen Chinee," but had been an extensive traveler, and was, in China, a desperado.

GREAT FIRE AUGUST 23, 1862.

So far fires at Jackson had been comparatively insignificant. Drytown had been swept as if by a whirlwind. The citizens of Jackson had looked across the river and seen Mokelumne Hill, their ancient rival, blackened with the charred remains of their town. Jackson had, to some extent, provided for a fire, having two fire-engines and a hook-and-ladder company. Shortly after one o'clock the alarm of fire was raised, and smoke was seen issuing from an out-building in the rear of the assay office. The firemen were quickly at their posts, and for a few minutes it seemed that the firemen had the better of it. There are different accounts as to the cause of the failure to control it; some say that the water in the tank or cistern failed; others that the assistant engineer ordered another stream from the main engine to be turned on without increasing the supply hose, which so weakened the force of the streams that they would not reach the fire. Whatever may have been the fault, the fire spread, and in a few minutes was beyond all control. The houses, mostly of pine, shriveling in the hot sun, caught like powder and flashed the fire from one to another, until the only question was to save life—property was not to be thought of. The Court House being some distance from the fire, permitted the saving of the records; but the house itself went like a pile of brush. In some instances people had to make their escape from besieged houses with wet blankets over their heads. Iron bars, one inch by three, used for the support of balconies, though on the outside of the buildings, were seen to melt and fall from their own weight. A phenomenon occurred here that is much disputed: the smoke, rolling along the ground in the narrow alleys, would become so intensely heated by the flames above as to take fire and explode like powder. The Union Hotel was built around three sides of a quadrangle, which was filled with bedding that the occupants had thrown out of the windows in hopes of saving it, but the flames lapped over the place, and in an instant the whole mass added new strength to the hungry element. Colonel Allen, the proprietor, left with his music-box under his arm, that being the only thing saved. Stoves, hardware, church-bells, and glass, were melted into one conglomeration. The fire swept everything on the road towards Sacramento, till it reached the wagon-shop near Trenchel's brewery, where it was stayed with the aid of a hose used in that establishment. On the south side it was met by the fire department from Mokelumne Hill. At night the town was a smoking ruin, the tall, ghostly chimneys keeping watch over the seething embers, while the inhabitants were camped on the surrounding hills, houseless and supperless. Children, for the first time in their lives, went supperless to bed, and that bed the earth, and the sky for the coverlet. There was no despair, however; no wringing of hands and shedding of tears. Before darkness came, lumber was engaged to rebuild some of the houses, and in the morning was actually awaiting the cooling of the hot ashes and cinders. Provisions came pouring in from the surrounding towns, and there was no suffering. As the people sat around the smouldering ruins of the town, many incidents were related, which, if recorded, would be interesting reading now. Hairbreadth escapes of children and women snatched from burning buildings which fell a moment after, were common enough. In some instances, women seemed to have been helpless from fright; in others, the love for home seemed to be stronger than the love for life, and they had to be carried out by force.

The fire department came in for its share of the heroic. Some cynical man had predicted that in case of a general fire, the *boys* would lose their engine. When the engines failed, and the flames were flashing from street to street, most of the men ran to save their families, leaving but a few to see to the *machine*, and for a time it looked as if the prediction was to be verified. Two or three men, however, commenced tugging at it, when the cloud of smoke which enveloped them, flashed like an explosion of gas, compelling the men to get under the truck for protection; in a moment the smoke and flame cleared away, and the boys rolled it out.

After the fire was over many a deed of heroism and devotion came to light; for misfortunes have the good effect to bring to light the jewels of character that otherwise might have never shone through the incrustations of selfishness. The savings of years of industry were gone, but the indomitable energy and perseverance that had built up the town were not destroyed, and the people went to work. A hundred new buildings were erected before the rainy season set in, and in one year all marks of the fire were effaced.

It has been impossible to collect anything like a full list of the losses; a few may be mentioned:—

Levinsky, $20,000; H. W. Allen, $15,000; W. L. McKimm, $7,000; J. Samuels, $15,000; Tellier, $1,000; Harris, $3,000; Evans & Askey $5,000; A. C. Brown, $10,000; Steckler & Co., $10,000; M. Bruml, $5,000; H. Kress, $3,500; Moses Medina, $7,000.

The following, from the *California Spirit of the Times*, edited by Marcus D. Boruck, will give a lively idea of the fire:—

"LETTER FROM MOKELUMNE HILL.

"MOKELUMNE HILL, August 25, 1862.

"You are probably aware, by this time, of the total destruction of the beautiful and flourishing city of Jackson, Amador county. On Friday last I passed through it at four o'clock, and everything betokened peace and security; but it is now no more, the lines of the city being scarcely perceptible. I visited the place yesterday morning, and a more desolate and melancholy looking place I never saw; and seeing it a short time before in all its beauty, I could more keenly appreciate the destruction which surrounded me on all sides. But the people, with that wonderful elasticity which so far forcibly characterizes all Californians, were smiling and passing jokes on each other with scarcely a thought of what had passed. With the exception of three or four brick buildings on Main street, and a few private residences to the right as you enter the town from this place, the city has been totally destroyed. All the principal buildings, including the Court House, theater, *Amador Ledger*, and *Amador Dispatch* printing offices, the post-office, Colonel Allen's Union Hotel, and the Louisiana Hotel of Evans & Askey being in the wreck and ruin.

"The smoke of the fire was seen at this place at fifteen minutes of two o'clock (five minutes after it broke out) and there could not have been less than a dozen opinions as to its locality; every other place but the right one having entered into its discussion. At last, Mr. Moses, the telegraph operator, said he could not get the operator at Jackson, as the circuit was broken; and then all became satisfied that it was Jackson. The fire, in the meantime, had materially decreased; but all of a sudden the flame and smoke could be seen ascending from the hill-tops, and the conflagration increased with alarming rapidity. A large number of people from this place started for the scene (many of them on foot), a distance of six miles, over the roughest kind of a mountain road, and the thermometer ——, as high as you please. They arrived at the scene, however, in time to save the houses of Mr. Coney and Mr. Axtell, situated on either side of the road this side of the gulch, and thus prevented the further spread of the fire in that direction; all they could do in the town itself, was to save the Masonic building. The fire broke out at twenty minutes of two o'clock, and at five o'clock the destruction of the town was complete. When the alarm was first sounded, there was not the remotest idea entertained that the place was doomed, the city being provided with an effective fire department, and full cisterns of water. The fire broke out on the right hand side of Main street, as you leave the town for Sacramento, a few doors from Court street, an avenue which led direct to the Court House, and in the rear of the *Ledger* office. When the fire was first discovered, it was about as big as a man's hat. The apparatus was promptly brought out, and taken to the cistern on High street, a few doors from the Court House; the firemen, under the direction of Chief Engineer Wells, working admirably. There was a fatal mistake in getting to work, which consisted in not placing one of the engines on Main street, where there was an abundance of water (the cisterns being full to the brim when I saw them yesterday morning), thus preventing the fire from bursting through on to the front, it having commenced in the rear from hot ashes having been thrown into a barrel which stood against a frame building. Both engines being at the same cistern, and that a small one, it soon became exhausted, and in a short time the firemen were horror-stricken to find they were drawing nothing but air. It was at this point that the people of this place saw the fire decrease, and then as suddenly increase, for at one time the firemen had the fire entirely under their control, when the Chief Engineer was compelled to give the order to change position; and, in carrying it out, before it could be accomplished, the fire gained such headway on them that they could not master it, and spread three different ways, barely giving them time to save their apparatus, with a loss of four hundred and fifty feet of Button's patent coupling hose. It was then that no further reliance could be placed in the fire department, and the apparatus was abandoned, except by a few who removed it to a place of safety. The fire now spread with fearful strides, which, combined with the intense heat of the weather, added to the terror of the scene. The safety of women and children was looked to, and an effort made to save property, but it was useless. The fire swallowed up everything in its capacious maw, and when the sun went down on the disaster, the town, including all the provision in it, was turned to ashes.

"As I have before stated, the fire broke out at a quarter before two o'clock, and ended its course at five. At that hour definite information was received at this place of the great disaster. In fifteen minutes a meeting was held in front of H. Atwood's Union Hotel, presided over by Jeff. Gatewood, Esq. The circumstances were narrated, and a committee consisting of Dr. Hœrchner, W. S. Moses, and Dr. Sober appointed to collect subscriptions. At six o'clock a four-horse team, belonging to Mr. Taft, started laden with provisions and blankets, under charge of Mr. Chas. Spiers, which reached Jackson about half-past eight o'clock, much to the joy of the inhabitants of the desolate place. At eight o'clock an adjourned meeting was held at the Court House, where reports were made that at least fifteen hundred dollars in provisions and money had been collected, and seven or eight teams forwarded to Jackson with provisions. Judge Badgely spoke at this meeting, and gave a detailed account of all the circumstances, he having gone through the fire. I never can touch good feeling manifested by any people as those of this place, and more promptitude shown in acting in such a matter; without their aid, the people of Jackson would have been in a terrible condition. They acted in a manner which will always cause Mokelumne Hill to be remembered with pride and pleasure.

"On this morning sixty dollars' worth of fresh bread, innumerable provisions and blankets were sent. When I arrived at Jackson this morning, thirteen hours after the fire, there were at least a dozen loads of joist, lumber, and planking, in different localities, waiting for the burning embers to cool, preparatory to rebuilding. The town will be rebuilt long before the rainy season, although the losses are severe, at least seven hundred and fifty thousand dollars, upon which there is said to be an insurance of one hundred and fifty thousand dollars, which I hope is the fact. The fire-proof buildings were about as much fire-proof as a sheet of paper. The Chief Engineer ordered the walls of Steckler & Newbauer's building, at the corner of Main and Court streets, to be pulled down, and also that of Levinsky Brothers, on Main street, on account of their tottering condition. I should judge that in the construction of the former, at least two barrels of cement were used, and, in the latter, not less than a barrel and a half—perfect counterfeits on the name of fire-proof.

"The Amador Ledger will be issued from the Chronicle building this week. I have not learned what disposition the Amador Dispatch people have made in regard to a re-issue. Springer saved his two inside forms, but not a letter of type besides. In regard to the fire department of Jackson (every member of which is a sufferer by the fire), too much praise cannot be awarded for their efforts. They were unfortunate, it is true, in their choice of position, and, like McLellan, were forced to change their base of operations, and in doing so the enemy attacked their right, left, and center; but notwithstanding all that, they made a gallant fight. Disastrous fires have befallen other departments much more experienced than they. In rebuilding the town, I would suggest to the department of Jackson to locate one of their engines in the neighborhood of where the Louisiana and Union Hotels stood, near where the new hall was to have been built, and the truck, on Court street, above where it stood before.

"It will never do in the world to mass the apparatus as was the intention before the fire; and above all, more cisterns and larger ones; they are the real dependence for a prompt supply of water in the event of a fire. To say that we sympathize with Jackson in this great disaster is unnecessary. The Spirit gives prompt assurance of that. To condole with Californians is not to be thought of, but that there may never be a repetition of the event of Saturday last is our fervent wish. B."

JACKSON FLOOD, FEBRUARY 17, 1878.

A remarkable flood occurred in Jackson and vicinity, on the 17th of February, 1878. For some weeks the streams had been bank full; but, as sailors say, everything was made snug and tight, and no one anticipated any particular trouble, and were unprepared for a flood which had no precedent in the history of the State. Since the denudation of the hills of their wood, the country has become subject to extraordinary showers, the rain coming down in torrents, or, as the people usually call them, cloud bursts, which seem to be a condensing point, or meeting, of two opposing currents of wind which remain stationary for some considerable time over a tract of country. The strip of land ten or twelve miles wide near the foot-hills, seems to be particularly subject to these rains. Several of these showers have passed over the bare hills in the vicinity of Lancha Plana, and more particularly along the ridge west of Jackson and Sutter creek. Fifteen, or even ten minutes' rain, was enough to raise a stream three feet deep, in a gully two or three hundred yards long; and streams that have a mile or two in length, come roaring along with a breast or wall of water, generally held back to some extent, by trash or timber, of five or six feet, running a stream deep enough for a steamboat to float, where ten minutes before there was scarcely a drink for an ox. Usually, these showers extend over but a small space; otherwise, general destruction would occur. Those who were watching the weather on that Sunday morning, noticed a dense bank of clouds to the south-east, with a line something like the colors seen in tempering steel, dividing this bank from a similar one in the north-west, both banks of clouds charged with water; both seemingly determined to "fight it on that line," the ominous line of precipitation being drawn just over Jackson. The wind which for some time had been quite a gale, ceased, like a breathing spell before two opposing armies lock themselves in the embrace of death. The fall of a leaf could be heard on the ground, but, high up in the air could be heard the roaring of the fierce, surcharged currents, as they met each other. Down came the rain, great drops as large as bullets, some feet apart at first, but soon nearer together, until one could not see ten steps away; in five minutes the hill-sides were a sheet of running water, the little gulches were creeks, and the creeks, rivers; still the rain continued for some time. When its force seemed exhausted, and silence had come, a great roar of rushing waters, mingled with shouts and shrieks, was heard; the waters from the head of the north fork, and the other forks heading near the New York ranch, had come rolling in a wall or breast, variously estimated at five to ten feet high, carrying before it houses, barns, logs, fences, and uprooted trees.

It struck Chinatown (the north end of Jackson). carrying everything in its way. A few were able to take out some articles, but in five minutes the stream was full—struggling Chinamen, houses, shops, goods, all in a rolling mass. Most of the Chinamen escaped before the stream entered the cañon. Six of them went down the stream in the wreck, the bodies being afterwards found all the way from Jackson to Buena Vista. Some white men, assisting the Chinamen, were carried down the stream, but saved themselves before they entered the cañon. In half an hour or more after the flood had swept Chinatown away, the middle fork, which is longer than the north fork, came booming the same way, with a bulk-head of timber, fences, and trees. It struck the bridge across the creek near Genochio's store, forming a dam, and for a few minutes the stream turned through Jackson, in front of the National House; and at one time it seemed as if all that end of the town would be swept away in one wreck. Several persons narrowly escaped drowning in the streets. A foot-bridge, belonging to Mushet, lodged in the street in front of the National. The bridge finally gave way, and the channel cleared, carrying with it all the out houses and lumber in its course. The flood was over, and people could then estimate their losses.

The Amador Canal Company were damaged to the sum of thirty thousand dollars by the breaking of reservoirs and ditches.

The French garden above Jackson lost about two thousand dollars; Geo. Clark, four miles above Jackson, one thousand dollars.

Some considerable damage was done to ranches in the valley also.

The following is a partial list of the losses:—

ON WATER STREET.		ON MAIN STREET.	
J. B. Phelps........	$ 500 00	A. S. Kelly.........	$ 100 00
H. I. Stribley.......	200 00	National Hotel.....	250 00
Mrs. Westfall.......	100 00	Benjamin & Lelon..	1,000 00
N. Draper..........	100 00	Thos. Jones.......	500 00
R. S. Sanborn......	300 00	R. W. Palmer......	600 00
R. M. Briggs.......	100 00	R. F. Richtmyer....	100 00
Henry Barton......	500 00	Bridges	7,500 00
Mrs. S. Bradley...	1,000 00		
E. G. Freeman.....	100 00	Frank Guerra......	100 00
Mat. Ryan.........	100 00	Madam Betrou.....	200 00
W. Little...........	100 00	B. Sanguenetti.....	400 00
A. C. Brown.......	100 00	Benjamin & Carreau	1,500 00
C. Weller..........	100 00	Eight China stores	
E. Hall............	50 00	and contents.....	15,000 00
J. Williams........	100 00	P. Kelly...........	700 00
E. Genochio........	300 00	Geo. White.........	300 00
F. Rocco...........	2,000 00	Antone Silva.......	250 00
J. A. Butterfield....	700 00	John Bellenondai...	200 00

INCIDENTS.

As one Chinaman sat astride of his house, which was whirling in the cañon, some one asked him:—

"Where you go, John?"

"No sabe," says the Chinaman, in an impatient, savage manner. It was supposed that he was drowned in the cañon, but two or three days after the flood, he came to life, or rather he came walking into town, being probably the only man who ever successfully navigated Jackson creek through the cañon.

BIG FROLIC.

Thanksgiving day, 185-, was the witness of the most extraordinary frolic that ever occurred in the county. No one could tell how, or exactly when, it commenced, but as the sun went down it was evident that there were sounds of revelry in the air; but this was no gathering of beauty and chivalry. As the whistling of the wind through the rigging sends the sailor aloft to make all snug, or the moaning of wind around the chimney portending a storm sends the thrifty housewife out to gather in her wash from the clothes-line, so at the ominous signs the careful mother sends after her son, and the prudent wife seeks her husband, for the Bacchanalian press gang were out.

Some were drinking who never drank before;
Those who always drank now drank the more.

As usually sober men found themselves getting more than was good for them, they determined that their friends should share the pleasure or disgrace. An eminent lawyer once asked, how do men, who never get drunk, know each other? Did not Byron say of a man, "He is a splendid fellow and I long to get drunk with him"? and of another that he had "tried him drunk and tried him sober, there's nothing in him"! All who had held office, or had run for it, or were known to want it, as well as those who drank, were sought out and pressed into service. When the hunt commenced some retreated to their homes, but the warrant for arrest reached them even there, and men were torn from their wives' arms. O. D. Araline's wife, firmly locking her arms around her husband, declared that if they took her husband

Residence and Ranch of Mrs MARY M. KIDD, Jackson Valley, Amador Co. Cal.

Residence and Ranch of 320 Acres, INGLEFIELD B. GREGORY, Jackson Valley, Amador Co. Cal.

they should take her also, and looked as if she meant it too, and the party had to leave him.

They took possession of the Young America saloon and appointed a door-keeper who locked the door on the outside, opening only for the admittance of new victims, no egress being permitted. A press gang waylaid the Judge, who was expecting to hold court the next day. He resisted their importunities a long time on the grounds of public duty, but he had been known to take a spree and no excuse would answer now. "Good-bye, boys," said he; "it can't be helped." What took place on the inside can only be guessed. Some in their wild excitement were tossed like foot-balls over the tables. Speeches and songs, and shouts mingled in confusion dire. Fourteen dozen of champagne had their necks broken. Some were soon helpless on the floor; one or two escaped from an upper window, and some were able to keep up the orgies till midnight. When morning came those who were able had left. The Judge's pants were found on the steps of the Court House, other garments in other places. He, with a sense of public duty still uppermost, was delivering a charge to an imaginary jury. The officers of course took care of him until he was sufficiently sober to attend to business, which was not for some days. The Grand Jury found a Bill against him for misdemeanor and conduct unbecoming a magistrate. The Judge complimented the jury on having fearlessly done their duty, acknowledged the delinquency and promised that they should never have occasion to do so again, and with his silver tongue, which so often had charmed away opposition, turned aside the righteous indignation of his constituents.

CELEBRATION OF ADMISSION DAY.

[Taken from *Amador Dispatch*.]

"The celebration of the 30th anniversary of the admission of California into the Union by the Amador Pioneer Association, in this place last Thursday, was one of the most pleasing, unique, and successful affairs of the kind ever witnessed in the county, and reflected great credit upon the Association, owing to the excellent manner in which the programme was carried out from beginning to end. The procession was formed about ten o'clock, and was quite an extensive and imposing affair, extending nearly the whole length of Main street, and consisting of pioneers and others on foot to the number of about one hundred and fifty, many of whom were armed with guns of various kinds, axes, and other implements generally used in frontier life, also, pioneers and others on horseback, followed by a large number of vehicles of various kinds, including a regular emigrant ox-team, driven by our pioneer friend, William Cook of Buena Vista, who was rigged up for the occasion in regular '49 style, including a huge leather belt to which was attached the inevitable pistol, bowie-knife, tin cup, etc. This and the dilapidated looking emigrant wagon which followed, loaded with women, children, frying-pans, pots, kettles, tin pans, and other cooking utensils, formed one of the most familiar and noticeable features of the grand procession, and created much merriment among the hundreds of spectators who thronged our streets. After marching through the principal streets of the town, under the command of the handsome and energetic Marshal of the day, R. W. Palmer, who was closely followed by Kay's Ione Cornet Band, the procession wended its way to the picnic ground in Walker's ranch, where the literary and musical exercises were gone through with, consisting of an oration by Hon. J. A. Eagon, poems by C. B. Swift and J. F. Gould, an impromptu address by Hon. J. T. Farley, singing, music by the band, etc. Our room will not permit us to speak in detail of these exercises, but suffice it to say that they all did well, and the audience were well satisfied therewith. At the conclusion of these exercises, all hands were invited to partake of a sumptuous lunch, consisting of pork and beans, and other substantial edibles, and the invitation was accepted with a vim seldom surpassed in this or any other country. After dinner, horse-racing, foot-racing, and other amusements were indulged in until near sundown, when the procession and many of the spectators returned to town to prepare for the grand ball in the evening.

"The ball, like everything else connected with the celebration, was a grand success, Love's hall being well filled with gay and festive pleasure-seekers of both sexes, who enjoyed themselves in a manner well calculated to create envy in the heart of a king or prince—or even a country editor. In short, nothing transpired during the day or night to mar the pleasures of the occasion, and the affair will hereafter constitute one of the most pleasing pages in the history of Amador county."

MOKELUMNE RIVER.

It is uncertain whether gold was first mined on the Mokelumne river or at Ione valley, though the discovery, according to Weber's account, was on the Mokelumne. In the Summer of 1848 James P. Martin passed through Ione valley, on his way to Mokelumne river, Hicks' rawhide house being the only improvement there. A man was mining at Ione. A Spanish cart was doing duty as a house near where the National Hotel now stands, there being no houses at the time, or even mining, at Jackson. At first, Martin's company of eight men were the only ones on the river, though quite a number came in shortly afterward. They did very well, making several thousand dollars each in the course of two months. They had some fears of Indians, who, however, did not trouble them. Nearly the whole party were taken sick with diarrhea, and compelled to leave. Colonel Stevenson, with about one hundred of his men, who had previously been mustered out of service, mined here and at Mokelumne Hill in the Autumn of the year. The Colonel drew up the first code of mining laws, perhaps, ever written in the State, for the use of his men. A party of his was the first to turn the river, the place being near the crossing. A cabin was built on the ground, afterwards proving very rich, though his party did not discover it. He returned to Sutter's Fort in December, at the beginning of the rainy season, a few inches of snow having fallen at Mokelumne Hill. With regard to the report that a deep snow fell all over the State in that year, and that he had to send a party of relief to his men, the Colonel says he knows nothing of it; that the men were well supplied with provisions, and could have stood any siege of snow. Colonel Stevenson, from whom these facts were gathered, though nearly eighty years old, is still hale and hearty, his memory having a full retention of the early incidents in his California life.

SPRING OF '49.

Very many came the following Spring. A company, consisting of J. S. Smythe; Michael and John O'Neal; Peter Jacobs, a German; Captain Rogers, from the Sandwich Islands; Godey and Perry Lake, the two latter of Stevenson's regiment, dammed the river near the mouth of Rich gulch. The claim did not equal their expectations; that is to say, it did not yield a bucketful of gold a day, and they abandoned it.

Colonel James gave his name to the bar. His partners were two brothers, Vanderslice, one a doctor, the other a gambler. Judge Smith, who afterwards killed Colonel Collyer at Jackson, and a man by the name of Haskell, kept a store there. Soon after the immigration got in it was estimated that a thousand men were mining on the river within a distance of two or three miles, mostly with pans and rockers. A large meeting of miners was called to drive away foreigners, which project however, did not carry. McKimm mined here in '49, as also did Donnelly (who is now driving a wood team), J. D. Davis and Dr. Elliott. McKimm had at one time seventy-five pounds of gold-dust; Donnelly had, also, about the same quantity. N. W. Spaulding and Company whipsawed out thirteen thousand feet of lumber one season, to flume the Mokelumne river. The project was determined upon by getting a few cents' worth of gold in a shovel of dirt out of a deep hole in the river. When, after immense labor, the river had been dammed and flumed, and the channel exposed, all the gold of consequence found in the claim, was in that immediate spot, and amounted to about one hundred and sixty dollars. As many thousands would not have been considered anything great.

The river in the vicinity of Rich gulch and Murphy's was very rich, men taking out with a rocker several thousand dollars in a day. In some places the gravel would be "lousy" with gold. It must not be supposed that all fared this way, however. As many men then were wandering around "broke" as now. When Winter came on most of the men left, some going up the gulches and others to Jackson and Mokelumne Hill, which now began to be permanent camps. At the present writing, one walking along the banks of the Mokelumne river, can hardly realize that the stillness, broken only by the murmur of the water, was ever otherwise. A few old cabins rotting away on the side-hills, or the relic of some chimney, where thirty years since the miner fried his slapjacks or dried his wet clothing, are all that remain to tell the story of the thousands that toiled under a broiling sun, in the ice-cold water.

The following poem by Charles Boynton, written in 1853, will give an idea of the river in its best days:

TO THE MOKELUMNE RIVER.

To thee, Mokelumne, the bard
His humble tribute pays,
And should he work but half as hard
In chronicling thy praise,
As he has labored on thy bars,
His daily grub to gain,
The reader would pronounce his verse
A very labored strain.

Of thee, Mokelumne, I sing,
For I have known thee long;
And, from that knowledge, I can bring
Some truth into my song.
Four long and tedious years have passed
Since first I reached thy shore,
And near thy stream my lot is cast,
I fear, forevermore.

For now my pile is quite as small
As when I saw thee first;
Thy early freshets in the Fall
My bubble fortune burst.
The rise of water and of flour,
And every drink a scad,
Together with the monte-bank,
Soon took what dimes I had.

Time was—I mean in '49—
When in each wild ravine
And tributary gulch of thine,
A jolly crew was found.
Who dug up chispas by the pound,
And spent them fast and free,
Thinking that gold would still abound,
As late as—'53.

But ah! a change came o'er their dream,
Ere yet a year had sped;
For '50 brought a living stream
Of miners to thy bed.
Old Pike with hail his stalwart sons,
And Hoosierdom was thar,
While all the Suckers in the world
Camped on each gulch and bar.

They turned thy waters from their course,
Through many a rude canal;
They dammed thee, from thy very source,
Down to the lowest fall.
Ingratitude personified!
Without the slightest shamming,
Each company was occupied
In the hardest kind of damming.

But those who dammed thee, were the men,
Who never made a dime;
Thy waters raised indignant then
Long ere the usual time;
They burst all dams and carried off
Toms, rockers, pans, and kettles,
And left each claim not worth a dam,
And raised the price of vittles.

Mokelumne, thy source is in
Nevada's hills of snow,
And, when thine icy torrents reach
The burning plains below,
A draught from thee is better far,
The miners' thirst to slake,
Than choicest cobblers at the bar,
That ever Howe can make.

And though thy waves have ever been
As free and uncontrolled,
As when the New York Volunteers,
First sought thy banks for gold;
Soon will the Anglo-Saxon race,
With science, labor, skill,
Throw over thee their mighty chain,
And make thee work their mill.

Thy waters will be made to come
 And go at their command,
Led around to wash their ore,
 Or fertilize the land.
And even here in Jackson town
 We are expecting soon
To see Cap Ham* and all his men
 Come sailing down the flume.

Reader, if Logan † had the time
 He would extend the song,
But, like his liquor bills up street,
 'Tis even now too long.
Beneath Mokelumne's dark waves
 Lies many a precious nugget,
And there the poet's fortune is
 If some one has n't dug it.

Soher & Parrish's Big Bar bridge was quite a history. The first ferry, a dug-out, was run by a Scotchman, the price of passage being one dollar. Getting tired of the business, he donated it to Dr. Soher, who in turn gave it to John Hasley, who sold it in 1850 to Pope & Burns for fifty dollars. They bought some lumber and built a small ferry-boat, charging the same for crossing as formerly. Horses were made to swim by leading them beside the boat. Travel increasing, they began to make money rapidly, seeing which, Dr. Soher thought to buy it back; but the stock had now gone up, the parties asking twelve thousand dollars for it. The Goodwins, Soher, A. J. Houghtaling, and Kenny bought it, the latter selling his share for six thousand dollars. The bridge was built in 1853, costing twelve thousand dollars—the road on the Amador side, twelve thousand dollars, and on the other, three thousand dollars.

MURPHY'S GULCH

Was naturally traced up from the Mokelumne river, into which it empties. It lies parallel to the great quartz lode, crossing it once, and derives its gold from the breaking down of that auriferous reef of slate. It has been the source of many fortunes, having been worked and re-worked for years. It is threaded by many veins of rich quartz, not extensive enough, however, to justify large mining. Murphy's gulch starts on the west side of the lode, keeping its course along the base for a mile or so; then crosses the lode, emptying into the river on the north side.

BLACK GULCH

Is the continuation of Murphy's gulch on the same side, and, though shorter, has the same characteristics as that gulch.

HUNT'S GULCH

Was also enriched by the breaking down of the Mother Lode along its course, and also by the stream of gravel which left its deposits on Tunnel hill and Ohio bill. This gulch was perhaps richer than Murphy's, though somewhat harder to work in consequence of the great deposit of gravel on it. The Tunnel hill gravel has been run into it, prolonging its thorough working. If the Dewitt hill should be worked off as it is now being worked, the gulch will sometime pay for working again.

TUNNEL HILL.

This was the largest deposit of the drift, belonging to the north and south rivers of the county. Here it seemed to have spread out into a large body, most of which was swept away by the subsequent glacier erosion. The remains of the ancient plain may be easily see around the base of Butte mountain, also on all the hills around. The great wealth of the gulches around Tunnel hill, soon taught the miners to look for the source of the gravel; and we find that, as early as 1850, some of the miners had ascended the slope of the hill, until they had struck it sinking bed rock.

Daniel Haskell and Martin Love have the credit of being the first to work the dead river bed of gravel. They hauled the dirt to the south fork of Jackson creek about half a mile away. The dirt was rather hard to drift, but paid from one to two ounces to the cart-load. Madame Pantaloon, a woman dressed in man's clothing, and doing a man's work, made a large sum of money out of this hill; she drove a team and did light work at first, and for some time was supposed to be a boy.

The hill was first tunnelled in 1852, by Braxton Davenport, R. M. Johnston, and William McLeod, who, after one year's labor of drifting, sold their interest to Peter A. Martin, who in the Spring of 1853, erected a trestle work, with a car track and chute, extending to the survey of the Cunningham ditch, which was soon after constructed along the western and southern side of the hill. The second tunnel was run by A. C. Loveridge, in the Spring of 1854, which year inaugurated a thorough prospecting of the hill, which was all claimed, and worked by the usual drifting system, until water was brought on the hill in 1858, when piping and sluicing succeeded the former slow process of removing the dirt. By this method the whole surface was made to pay, as well as the rich gravel at the bed rock. It is impossible to tell how much gold was taken out, as many lucky miners judiciously kept the results to themselves.

BUTTE BASIN

Is, and always was, a mystery. Butte mountain looks down upon it from the north, Tunnel hill from the west, and rich gravel hills on the south. On the west is the high, rocky wall of the Mokelumne river, broken through in a narrow gorge, so as to form an outlet to the basin. The west and south sides have been very rich, and the whole surface of the basin was rich enough to pay for piping. On the west and south sides the gravel followed the slopes of the hills down under the volcanic matter with

---

*Cap Ham was the projector of the Jackson flume, which being four or five feet wide was expected to be navigable for boats both ways. A model propeller, with a stern-wheel, which should rest on a track on each side of the flume, and thus force a boat upstream against the current, was constructed, but, like many other brilliant ideas, was wrecked soon after being launched.

† Boynton's nom de plume.

which the basin is filled. Efforts have been made to follow this down and work it out, but so far without success, on account of immense quantities of water the miners meet in sinking. Not long since a company, under the superintendence of C. W. Tozier, an experienced miner, sunk one hundred and forty feet. At this point there was no appearance of bottom, and the water was so strong that two pumps, eight and twelve inch respectively, driven by a powerful engine, were not sufficient to control it. After expending about twenty thousand dollars, the company was obliged to abandon the enterprise. The material with which the basin is filled, though of volcanic origin, bears the marks of having been deposited by water. The descending lines of deposit on the sides indicate a former lake, the gravel, following down the slopes of the basin, being left at, or near, the edge of the water, while the lighter matter was carried further on—a phenomenon any one may see where a set of sluices dump into a river or body of water, and which may be seen in a thousand places along the foot-hills.

Formerly the surface of the basin was much higher, but the wearing away of the outlet has lowered it, perhaps several hundred feet.

A project has been started to run a tunnel into the basin from Mokelumne river, tapping it three hundred feet below the outlet. The length of the proposed tunnel is one thousand seven hundred feet, and the estimated cost is twenty thousand dollars. James Morgan is the owner of the east side of the basin, C. D. Horn of the west side; the latter owning some two hundred acres of land, a large portion of which was formerly an orchard and vineyard, bearing the best of fruit, which he sluiced away.

BUTTE CITY.

This was a camp on the south side of the basin and for a while bid fair to rival Jackson. Only a few houses now mark the site of the former city. An orange tree bearing regular crops, on the place of H. L. Loveridge, shows the fertility of the soil and the mildness of the climate.

BUTTE MOUNTAIN.

Is a landmark for twenty miles away. It is a puzzle for geologists, many believing it to be of volcanic origin. The rock has the appearance of being trachyte, but as a pretty thorough examination fails to bring to light anything like a crater; the solution may be left to the coming geologist.

WEDDING IN HIGH LIFE.

W. L. McKimn and Mrs. Mann were married one fine morning, many years ago, on the top of the mountain. It is not recorded whether the reporters were invited or whether, if they were, they had the energy to make the ascent. The height of the mountain (two thousand five hundred feet) and its isolation, caused it to be selected for one of the stations of the United States Geodetical Survey. Whether from its grand appearance, or from the clear atmosphere around its summit, or other causes, this mountain has caused the outflow of an immense amount of wit and wisdom. Some years ago when the periodic epidemic for the removal of the capital was raging, R. M. Briggs, then Assemblyman from Amador, introduced a Bill for the removal of the capital to Butte mountain. The Bill provided for a sufficient number of balloons to be attached to the capitol to float and hold it suspended, so that in case of high water or other danger, it might be removed without expense. A petition for the change accompanied the Bill, signed by every voter of the county, or at least the great register itself was attached to the petition. The Bill did not move the capitol, but it moved the members to laughter, and helped to throw ridicule on capitol movers.

Once, when the project for building a bridge across the Mokelumne river was being considered, a wag proposed to construct one of rawhide from Butte mountain to Mokelumne Hill. It should be made of rawhide cables, laid along the ground and covered with planking in the ordinary way. He thought, when the hot weather came, and the bridge shrank, it would come up taut!

THE GATE.

This place is on the north fork of Jackson creek, about one mile from Jackson. It takes its name from a fissure in a reef of rock, which crosses the creek, about twenty feet wide with nearly perpendicular walls on each side, through which the creek flows. The place was discovered in 1849 by a boy who ran away from Sacramento. It was not as rich as many other places, but uniformly good, paying eight to sixteen dollars a day to the man.

In 1850 as many as five hundred miners settled around the Gate. Diarrhea prevailed here as elsewhere at the time. The miners were shocked one day by seeing two boys carrying away, to bury, the corpse of their father, who, unknown to the miners, had died of the prevailing epidemic a day or two before. The boys were induced to suspend the interment, and in a short time several hundred men were collected together, to give him as decent a burial as the circumstances would permit.

Claims were fifteen feet square. This was the usual size of claims all over the country, until the Spring of 1851. Several of the Johnston family who came from Pennsylvania, were settled here. One of them being sick, a man called "Grizzly," jumped his claim. A meeting of the miners was called and it was decided that a sick man had no right to a claim. The decision was thought to have been brought about by the fear of "Grizzly's" ill-will, and an appeal from the decision was made by a friend getting on the claim with a drawn revolver, and promising a quick passage to the happy hunting-grounds to any one who should attempt to work it. The decision was reversed and the claim respected until the owner was able to work. The largest lump of gold ever

found at the Gate came out of this piece of ground. It weighed four ounces and was shaped like a bull's head.

During the dry part of the season dirt was carried in sacks to the spring near Kennedy flat for washing. The ditch still visible on the north side of the creek, said to have been the first ditch in Amador county, was dug by the Johnstons. It was but a mile or two in length, but the water sold for one dollar per inch. One evening one of the **Johnstons** being out late, called at a Mexican camp for a drink of water. The Mexican drew an immense knife and putting himself in a position of defense, said in Spanish, "Speak louder, sir; I am hard of hearing." The Mexicans, as well as the Americans, were on the alert for danger.

OHIO HILL

And Squaw gulch were rich places in the vicinity. From the former place one man by the name of Bodkin carried away some forty or fifty thousand dollars as the result of a Winter's work. Madame Pantaloon took out one hundred thousand dollars and then sold the claim for twenty-five thousand dollars more. This hill was of the same formation as Tunnel hill, with the same polished, but not rounded, boulders, indicating a river of moderate size as the source of the wash. It is highly probable that the gravel was never moved any great distance, and that the veins of quartz near by are the ones from which the boulders were formed.

SLAB CITY.

This place took its name from the cabins being built of slabs from Huffaker's mill in the early fifties. It had in 1855 to 1860 some fifty or sixty miners. The shallow gulches were soon worked out and the place is now converted to farming ground. The same may be said of Irishtown, once a lively camp.

CLINTON.

This place, which is north-east from Jackson some six miles, was first worked by Mexicans, who drifted under the red hills around the town, making moderate pay. After the introduction of water, by means of canals, quite a number of miners settled here. Judge Hugh Robinson, J. **W. Paugh**, Sheriff of Amador county for several terms, and now a resident of San Francisco, L. N. Ketchum, afterwards State Senator, N. W. Spaulding, since Mayor of Oakland, D. B. Spagnoli, and many others of note, were first heard of in Clinton. Some small quartz veins traverse this part of the country, which probably have supplied part of the gold found in the gulches; but the hills indicate an ancient river system, probably the same that left deposits of gravel at Pine Grove and Aqueduct City. The mines, at the best, were but moderately rich, and to this fact, perhaps, is due the political careers of many of its citizens. This town was the occasion of some talk a few years ago, in connection with an election, one man acting as both Judge and Clerk. A good deal of eloquence was displayed before the Board of Supervisors when this vote was canvassed, which is lost to the world for want of short-hand reporters.

N. W. Spaulding is the inventor of the famous circular shank saw tooth. He was a mill-wright by profession, and after mining a few years, returned to his trade, which became profitable in utilizing the vast forests of the Sierras. Movable teeth had been used before, but under such conditions as to cause them to be set aside. The improvement consisted in using a circular instead of a square shank. The continued vibration of the saw, incident to a high speed, caused a crystallization of the plate to take place, it being most intense at the corners of the cavity, causing a cracking and ultimate ruin of the plate; by distributing the crystallization evenly around the cavity, the plate would endure an indefinite amount of work. This little improvement became of so much value that it revolutionized the methods of sawing lumber, the circular saw being everywhere adopted, the improvement being appropriated by saw-mill men without leave or license. Four different lawsuits concerning this tooth were carried to the United States Supreme Court, one of which involved costs to the amount of twenty thousand dollars. An attempt was made to prove that this form of tooth had been in general use for years, and particularly in a mill owned by Tupper and others, in a certain town in Vermont, a man by the name of Percival, who was said to have been dead for some years, being the mill-wright who had made and used them. Mr. Spaulding, with his accustomed energy, set inquiries on foot, and found that Percival, though somewhat advanced in years, was still living, and among the pineries in Wisconsin; notwithstanding the distance, he was brought into court at San Francisco, before the close of the case. Every attempt to prove a previous use of the circular shank had failed, except in the case of the Tupper mill; and, when Percival's name was called, a look of astonishment ran over the countenances of the opposing lawyers, one of them audibly remarking, "Rather a lively looking corpse," referring to the oft-repeated statement that Percival was dead. He had a vivid remembrance of the kind of tooth used in the Tupper mill, and, what was of much importance, had a veritable sample of the teeth then used, which he had kept in his tool chest for nearly a quarter of a century. When these were produced in court, behold, they had the square shank. This settled the matter, the defendants' lawyer remarking, "Well, Spaulding, you've beaten us." The saws now go to every quarter of the globe.

CHAPTER XXXI.
IONE VALLEY AND VICINITY.

First White Men in Ione Valley—First House—First Ranches—Judge Lynch—Starkey's Case—First Mill—Fun with Grizzlies—Origin of Name Ione—First School—First Flour Mill—First Brick Store—Methodist Church—Centennial—President's Address—Extracts from Poem—Extracts from Oration—Ione in 1876—Railroad—Stockton, Narrow-Gauge-Galt Road—Overflows—Fires—Buena Vista—First Settlement—Mining—Arroyo Seco Grant—Dispossession of Settlers—Present Appearance—Buckeye Valley—Irish Hill—Quincy—Muletown—Miners' Court—The Funny Man—Faithful Wife.

IONE VALLEY is situated about twelve miles west of the county seat, and is formed by the junction of Dry creek, Sutter creek, and Jackson creek, soon after they leave the mountains.

Who has not heard of Ione valley. Whether one rides over the dusty plains from Sacramento, or descends from the pine-clad hills of the Sierras, Ione comes on his view like the realization of a dream. None ever saw but to admire. When the plains are sweltering in heat, when the scanty herbage is withering under a scorching sun, Ione is green and delightful. The tall oaks send their long, flexible limbs to the ground, reminding one of tropical scenes. The wild grape-vine climbs to the topmost boughs, and, trailing into natural arbors, invites to repose and rest. The natural grasses, taller than horses or men, attest the unexampled fertility of the soil. Rumors of this paradise occasionally reached the far-off miners; of oats nine feet in height; of six tons of hay to the acre, but the melons, forty or fifty pounds in weight, wild oats half an inch in diameter and long enough for a fish pole, onions weighing four pounds, potatoes seven or eight, and squashes two hundred and fifty pounds, were witnesses whose testimony could not be impeached. It is not known that any white man visited this valley previous to 1848. The Indians relate that, at the time Sutter settled in Sacramento, numbers of them went to see the man with a white skin; that afterwards they were captured (*corralled* would be a proper term), and driven to Sacramento and made to work for Sutter, though they soon after went voluntarily.

It is extremely doubtful whether Teodosio Yorba, or any other Mexican, ever saw the valley even from a distance, the name Arroyo Seco being given the Drytown branch of the creek by the miners who went there soon after the discovery of gold. Some of the Weber party in prospecting from the Stanislaus, might have passed through the valley, as it is recorded that they found gold on the Mokelumne river first, and at every place until they reached Weber Creek, in El Dorado county. Sutter, in an early day, 1846, got out timbers for a ferry-boat on the divide between Sutter and Amador, about three miles above the towns, but it is said that his wagons

---
* This chapter is largely made up from the Centennial address of the Hon. C. B. Swift. When practicable, his own words are used.

---

passed up on the north side of Dry creek, this route being the one over which wagons passed to and fro in the earliest days, Lower Rancheria being one of the way places. The pit where the sawing was done is still visible. J. T. Wheeler of Pine Grove, saw this in 1849, some of the partly-finished timbers being still on the blocks. J. P. Martin passed through Ione on his way to Big Bar, on the Mokelumne river, in 1848. At that time a man was mining on a gulch emptying into the creek on the north side of the town, this being soon after Hicks opened his store near Judge Carter's residence. It is said that the man made seven thousand dollars with a rocker in a short time. There was but one house in Jackson, a Spanish cart doing duty as a house near where the National Hotel now stands. The first mining of which any knowledge can be obtained, was by a Mexican early in 1848, before Hicks had pastured cattle here. The Mexican told Indian Tom that the ore (gold) would buy beef and sugar, which induced the Indians to go to work.

FIRST WHITE MEN IN IONE VALLEY.

About the last of August, 1848, two men then mining at Mormon Island, at the head of the American river, imbued with that restless spirit which characterized all early Californians, started out on a prospecting tour, and headed directly for this valley, reports having already reached them of its existence and its great fertility. They entered the valley where Dosh's store now stands. Those two men were William Hicks and Moses Childers, who crossed the plains in 1843 in company with J. P. Martin. There were then living here (1848) in an adobe house, on the ranch now owned by the Winters brothers, the Patterson family, and a man named Edward Robinson. Soon after the arrival of Hicks and Childers, General Sutter, who was then living at Sutter's Fort in Sacramento, came through here with a retinue of Indians on an excursion to the mountains, and camped on the spot where Sutter Creek now stands, which event gave that town its name, and also the creek on which it is situated. Andreas Pico, with a large crowd of Mexicans, also visited this section the same season.

FIRST HOUSE.

Hicks built his first house, with poles covered with hides, on the knoll where Judge Carter's house now stands. He and Martin engaged in the stock business, buying cattle in southern California and driving them here to fatten for market, the valley being then covered with a luxuriant growth of grass, "high as a man's head." The business proved to be lucrative. In the Spring of '49 Hicks converted his house on the knoll into a store, the first in the valley, with Childers as manager. His first goods were hauled from Sacramento in a cart. They sold all sorts of trinkets to the Indians, such as beads, jewsharps, calicoes, and—whisky. They received gold-dust in exchange. Extravagant prices ruled. A bottle of whisky would often bring its "weight in gold-dust." It was estimated that there were five thousand Indians within a radius of ten miles around the valley at that time. Previous to its settlement by the whites, they disposed of their dead by raising them into the tops of the trees and fastening them with withes. Robert Ludgate, who came to the valley in 1851, relates that as he was walking one day down the lower side of the valley, he saw something in the crotch of a tree which attracted his curiosity, and climbing up to look at it, was startled to see the grim skeleton of an Indian.

FIRST RANCHES.

The Q ranch was taken up in 1850, by James Alvord, Buck Tarrier and one or two others. Henry Gibbons, who was a member of Company Q of the Ohio Volunteers, gave the ranch its name, which it will probably retain until the next centennial celebration. A D ranch was taken up by Harry Hensner and —— Merchant. They branded their stock with the letters "A D," which gave that ranch its name. The 2 L ranch, taken up by the Luther brothers, was named in the same manner, their brand being a figure 2 and the letter L. The Q ranch was bought in 1853 by Charles Green, who, in company with John Vogan, established a line of stages between Sacramento and Sonora, via the Q ranch, Jackson and Mokelumne Hill; and the Q became quite a noted place, having a post-office, blacksmith shop, and race track.

JUDGE LYNCH.

Two Mexicans were hung on a tree a few rods south of the Q dwelling-house, for stealing stock. Another was hung on a tree by the roadside, about half-way between Dosh's store and the Alabama House, by the side of a little stream called the Wolverine. A negro was tied up and whipped for stealing a horse. He stoutly objected to that mode of punishment on the ground that it would injure his character. These transactions took place after a trial and conviction of the parties before Judge Lynch. The first wedding ceremony occurred in a house which stood near J. P. Martin's present residence, where William Hicks was married to a Mrs. Wilson, a widow lady. The first child born in the valley only lived two or three months, and was named Ione Harnett by its parents, who then resided on the place now owned by the Winters brothers. The second child born was named William Burris, who is still living. The first sermon was preached in Andes Courtright's house, which stood a short distance west of Mr. Dawson's present residence, and is now torn down. No one recollects this preacher's name. But he is represented as having preached a most excellent discourse, and under its influence quite a large collection was taken up. He immediately went to Drytown and opened a monte-bank, where he was followed, the next day, by Courtright, who won back the entire proceeds of the collection.

It may be proper to state that the present representatives of the cloth in Ione do not accept that example as a standard of ministerial dignity and propriety.

STARKEY'S CASE.

In the fall of '50, it became known to the valley that the two Starkey brothers and a man named Haines, who lived at the lower end of Jackson valley, were engaged in stealing stock. They also had a rendezvous at the forks of the Cosumnes. One of the Starkeys, and a hired man by the name of Reed, were arrested and brought to Hicks' ranch, where forty or fifty men were awaiting their arrival. Starkey was immediately put on trial. Williams, Mays, Robinson, Clark (afterward Judge in Fresno county, and connected with a cutting affray at the same place), Dr. Jabez Newton (discoverer of the Newton copper mine), and others, acting as jurymen. It was proved beyond a doubt that he had been in the habit of slaughtering cattle and selling the meat, though he put in a plea that the cattle seemed to be abandoned property and without owners. The crime of grand larceny had so far been considered greater than murder, the penalty prescribed by the statutes being death, although it is doubtful whether any court in California, other than Judge Lynch's, ever passed such a sentence, or if so, that it was executed, so early had the people begun to revolt against the code.

A motion was made that he should receive one hundred and fifty lashes on his bare back, have his head shaved, and the letter R branded on his cheek, with the understanding that he might be hung if he preferred. On taking the vote, all but one present voted aye! One person, Robert Reed, voted no. The crowd turned fiercely upon him, demanding his reasons for voting against the sentence, and for awhile it seemed as if he also might be lynched. He said that no man could live through such a punishment, and urged a mitigation. It was finally agreed that Dr. Newton should stand by and stop the whipping when it should be necessary to do so, to save his life. Upon Starkey being asked his choice of punishments, he replied that he would take the chance for his life. He was tied to a log with his face down, and his back stripped. A Spaniard, or Mexican, then doubled a rawhide riata, and commenced the work. The first blow, made with a long sweep of the arm, left two blue stripes across his back. The flesh quivered, but no groan escaped him. Blow after blow followed with the same cruel deliberation, for the greaser had feelings of his own to satisfy.

Starkey was a powerful man, and bore it until the flesh was cut into shreds, and the blood was dripping to the ground. At every swing of the riata the blood would fly off in the air and fall among the crowd. At the one hundred and twenty-fifth blow the doctor made a sign to suspend the whipping. He was untied and his shirt put on. He was able to step up to the bar and take a drink of whisky, after which he laid down on a mattress in the corner of the room. A branding iron in the shape of the letter R, about two inches each way, was made from a piece of hoop iron. Hicks applied it to the man's face. It did not make a very distinct letter, as the victim turned his face during the operation. Perhaps Hicks had mercy on the man and purposely made it indistinct. Starkey's wife, who was present, wanted to share the punishment. After it was over, he was mounted on a horse behind his wife, and they left for their cabin, near the mouth of Jackson creek, where Frank McMurray's house now stands.

The hired man, Reed, received the twenty-five lashes, which came near proving fatal, as he did not have the iron nerves of Starkey.

Many cattle had been stolen during the year, and Starkey's conviction had fixed the whole loss on him, though in after years it became a current opinion, in the mountains, that stealing cattle was a common practice on the ranches. It is quite certain that teamsters and others would, at the close of Summer, drive their cattle and horses to the valleys to trespass on the farmers, who might sometimes have taken that way to get even. At any rate, a great crowd, mostly from the mines, came to Starkey's the next day to hunt their missing cattle. Not finding them, they burned his house and voted to hang him, which they were in the act of doing when Hicks, Reed, and other parties, who witnessed the punishment of the day before, coming up, persuaded the crowd to remit it on condition of his leaving the country. He recovered, and was seen afterwards driving a team in some of the Territories.

FIRST MILLS.

In 1851 Wooster and the Reed brothers built a saw-mill where J. Farnsworth's barn now stands. Reed was then living on the place now owned by D. Younglove.

FUN WITH GRIZZLIES.

In going to their daily work of hewing timber for the mill, they discovered bear tracks in the road, and the provisions, which they hung up in the trees over night, were stolen by the grizzlies. Wooster and Baker, the latter of whom was a blacksmith, made steel traps, and succeeded in catching three of these monsters. The difficult and dangerous task of tying them was accomplished by R. Reed, with one assistant. They sold one to Hicks, who advertised for a bull and bear fight. A great crowd came from all directions to see so novel a spectacle. Among those who came from Winters' Bar, on the Mokelumne river, was Dr. Brusie, who was then a Justice of the Peace there. The bear, however, died before the day fixed for the fight, and the day was turned into horse-racing. They also sold one to the Q ranch folks for the same purpose, and with the same result. The other one was caged up in a pen on

the ground where Woolsey's lumber yard now stands, but finally broke out and ran away. A California lion, or panther, was caught in a ravine north of Ione. An attempt was made to take him away alive, but the animal struggled fiercely, and died on the way, the day being very hot. Dr. E. B. Harris, who built and was then keeping the afterwards "Newton Copper Mine House," stuffed the panther's skin and made it look natural as life, and twice as fierce. It was placed at the head of the chamber stairs. Many a stranger, who was induced to precede the landlord, has been frightened out of half a night's sleep by the glaring eyes and open mouth with the frightful fangs, of the well fixed up skin.

One Indian, trying to get the meat with which the trap was baited, got caught and had to stay until help could be got from Ione, the Indians not knowing how to free him from the trap.

J. M. Wooster built the first house of hewed logs. It still stands where it was built, and is used as the sitting room of the Arcade Hotel. The house in which Judge Carter resides was the first frame built in the county. It was brought around the Horn in 1850 and is still a very good house. A man by the name of Baker did the first blacksmithing at a forge under a tree below the steam flour-mill. Abraham Sells built the first blacksmith shop on the corner west of the livery stable. He was bought out by A. Sheakley, who run it until he was burnt out in the fire of 1865. In the Spring of 1851, A. G. Lane opened the first store, on the corner now occupied by J. P. Ferner's saloon. Reed, Wooster and Lane built the brick grist-mill in 1855, which runs by water-power and is now owned by Dr. Cumming. Daniel Stewart built the first brick store in 1855. Dr. E. B. Harris was the first practicing physician who located here.

ORIGIN OF THE NAME IONE.

The valley was named Ione before a town was started here, by Thomas Brown, who was a great reader. He was reading a historical romance of Bulwer, entitled "Herculaneum; or the last days of Pompeii," one of whose heroines was a very beautiful young girl named "Ione." By one of those happy thoughts which sometimes come to us like a revelation, it occurred to him that "Ione" was a most appropriate name for this valley and he accordingly gave it that name. But the town itself did not escape the fate of most California towns, without being christened evil names. It was named first, Bedbug, then Freezeout. Finally a meeting was called to decide on a name, a few were in favor of Wooster, but a majority were in favor of naming it after the valley, so it was christened Ione City. Thus it remained for Bulwer, the great English scholar, novelist and poet, to furnish a name for this beautiful town and valley. Wooster, after whom it was proposed to name the town, was the discoverer of the big trees in 1850, having followed some miners in that direction who were supposed to be going to

Gold Lake. He cut his name on one of the trees with a hatchet. Andes Courtright was the first Justice of the Peace. W. C. Pratt was the first Assemblyman elected from this town. Mr. Pratt was a man who went for everything with his whole might and strength. While in the Legislature he either knew or thought he knew of immense sums of money being expended in the Senatorial election then pending, Broderick and Gwin being the candidates. He made a very enthusiastic speech without throwing much light on the subject however, but he told the members that he knew something of it. In those days people had a habit of mixing Spanish words into their talk. "I sabe moucha," said he. He was known ever after as "sabe moucha." Amador was then included in Calaveras county, of which Henry A. Carter was the first District Attorney.

FIRST SCHOOL.

The first school was taught by a man by the name of Meade in 1853, in a house owned by Reed. The Methodist church was organized in 1853, Thomas Rickey being the most active person in promoting the organization. He also kept the Irene Hotel, and a store at the same time. George B. Taylor was the first minister stationed here. He was a man of considerable talent, though some of his subsequent actions would hardly square with the notions of church people. The church building, used at that time, was converted into a paint shop some years since. About this time several families began to exert a moderating influence on the manners of the people. There were then living here the families of Thomas Rickey, Robert Reed, R. D. Style, A. Pecater, John T. Poe, I. B. Gregory, Judge Turner, Phillips, the McMurrays, Spencer, and others. There were several marriageable girls, who unconsciously exerted a good influence in elevating the morals of the young men, who would visit the town to get a glimpse of them. Dr. E. B. Harris, the first practicing physician to locate here, taught a singing-school which drew a crowd of well-behaved people.

FIRST FLOUR MILL.

The first flour mill was built in 1855 by Reed, Wooster, and Lane. At first it was intended for a feed mill but was soon afterwards improved so as to make flour. The steam mill was built in 1856 by Thomas Rickey, though, at the time of the erection, it was but a small affair compared to what it afterwards became under the ownership of Hall & Son.

Daniel Stuart built the first brick store in 1855, John Edwards putting up the next, now occupied by George Woolsey. The school-house was built in 1858, the upper story being occupied by the Masonic fraternity. A town hall was also built in 1858, which was afterwards used by the Presbyterian denomination as a church. The Baptist church was built in '59.

THE METHODIST CHURCH

Was built in 1862, Bishop Simpson laying the cornerstone July 4th. Dr. Peck, Dr. Owens and several other prominent men of the Methodist church assisting. Some effective solicitation was done and a large amount of money was raised, not enough to complete the church however, which, owing to reverses which will be mentioned hereafter, remains, nearly twenty years afterwards, hopelessly in debt. A man by the name of Mandel was the architect. The estimated cost of the edifice was eight thousand dollars, but whether from incorrect estimates of labor and material, or other causes, the church cost twice as much, which, with interest paid on mortgages, and other debts pertaining to it, will make the total not far short of twenty-five thousand dollars.

A celebration was held the same day, Thomas Fitch, the celebrated orator, being the speaker. A car of young ladies representing the galaxy of States was a noticeable feature of the occasion. A circus, and afterwards expensive fire-works, concluded the day. So many notable events are not often crowded into one occasion.

The centennial celebration was an event in the history of Ione. It was notable in many respects; for the unanimity and good feeling with which it was conducted; the general and almost universal attendance of the people, and the marked difference of the assemblage, in character and sex, from all former gatherings. In early days a few seats of honor near the Chair would have accommodated all the females and children who would be present. What a difference a quarter of a century had made. As the hour for the exercises approached, wagon after wagon unloaded children of all ages, and before long they took the town. They swarmed through every street and lane, and out of every door. The old '49ers who had danced in glee around a woman's cast-off bonnet, or taken a walk of miles to catch a glimpse of a sunbonnet flitting around a house, now stood aghast with the change. The tide had turned. Men were now emigrating to the mines, leaving a redundant female population. If the quails in '49 or '50 had donned female gear and come tripping around the miners' cabins, the pioneers would not have been more astonished than in 1876, to see the turn affairs had taken. Scores of attractive, blushing damsels thronged the grounds as if a natural product of the valley. The miner, with a red shirt, and revolver slung to his side, must now be sought in our Territories.

A procession was formed under the charge of J. Brannan. An immense carriage had been improvised for the occasion in shape of a pyramid, with the goddess of liberty seated on the apex, and young ladies seated around to represent the galaxy of States. Then followed a troop of boys dressed in continental uniform, with military companies, citizens, and carriages containing the officers of the day. The exercises were held in a grove of shade trees at the foot of Church street, near Hall's mills. Two thousand people were estimated to be present.

PRESIDENT'S ADDRESS.

"J. D. Mason, president of the day, opened the meeting with the following remarks:—

"FELLOW-CITIZENS: It is unnecessary to announce the object of this gathering. The old and the young alike know why we celebrate this day. The centennial of our nation's birth is a festal day in every civilized land. From an inauspicious beginning—a birth in pain and sorrow, and surrounded by adverse circumstances—our country has grown to marvelous dimensions, reaching from ocean to ocean, including in its boundaries the longest rivers, the largest lakes, mountain ranges rich in all valuable minerals, fertile valleys and plains, producing all the heart of man can desire, where the humblest laborer can rest in the bosom of his family, secure in the protection of just laws. Unlike nations of the Old World, no millions toil in sorrow that a pampered few shall rest in wealth and power.

"While other nations have marched to greatness through blood and carnage, crushing out other governments and civilizations, ours has achieved its victories over the silence of the desert, the loneliness of the forest, and the rock-guarded treasures of the mountains. Her victories are the triumphs of peaceful industry, filling the land with churches, schools, and comfortable, happy homes.

"The earth is filled with the wrecks of nations that have flourished a time, only to be submerged in the surrounding barbarism; but the student of history will discover in the upheaval of thought which produced our free institutions, the germ of a greater, better, and more permanent civilization than the world has ever seen, surpassing the wildest dreams of the ancients. With the aid of the telegraph, the steam engine, and the printing press, remote nations now share their wealth and wants, their joys and sorrows. All our surroundings are conducive to prosperity.

"We begin the second century of our existence with these substantial achievements and brilliant prospects. It is well to commemorate this day that our children may learn the value of the estate we transmit to them. It is proper to usher in the second century of our existence with bonfires, illuminations and hymns of joy."

The Declaration of Independence was read by F. C. Hall, after which the Rev. A. K. Crawford, formerly Professor of *Belles-Lettres*, at the Santa Clara College, delivered the poem, portions of which are given here:—

* * * * * * *

Honor, all honor to-day to those men,
And their labors and triumphs—
Labors that shaped a new world,
And triumphs that crown them immortal.
Rude was the wild they traversed,
A continent, virgin and pathless.

An unformed chaos of men,
From the ends of the earth flung together,
Mingled as quartz and feldspar
And hornblende are mingled in granite;
Mingled by fiery fusion,
To make the bedrock of the nation.

Fierce were the forces that fought
In the furnace where freedom was molded,
"Tyranny kindled the flame,
But Liberty fanned it and fed it,"
Till the crude mass, refractory, stubborn, chaotic,
Blended at last in a union of hearts
And of States in firm compact,
Welded in blood and fire, established for ages of ages.

* * * * * * *

The Declaration made that day
Was no mere mass of glittering words;
It set the nation in array
Against far more than British swords.
'Twas the proposal we still make
That all mankind shall here be free.
Jehovah smiled and said, "Go take
The right to nationality."
That smile, sent for our pledges' sake,
Is now the ground on which we stake
Our hope of perpetuity.

Each nation of antiquity,
When first its life began,
Gave promise to co-operate
With God in his great plan
To elevate humanity.
And each was made invincible
While faithful to her trust;
But when she failed to do her work,
Her heroes bit the dust.

* * * * * * *

We have passed through some terrible conflicts,
Our banner still kissing the sky,
While star after star has been added
Before the world's envious eye.

Shall that banner, hereafter, by traitors
Be trampled in dust and decay?
Or shall it float on, over liberty's sons,
Till the dawn of unending day?

Say, friends, shall it wave
O'er the free and the brave,
Till the stars and blue sky
It resembles on high,
Into ruin shall roll,
Like a shriveling scroll?

The oration which was delivered by the Rev. J. T. White, was somewhat lengthy, and was a historical review of the circumstances out of which grew the modern Republics and the spirit of freedom, moving governments to ameliorate the conditions of the people.

* * * * * * *

"And here the question arises, Was the Revolution, taking all the circumstances of the case into review, right? Was it right? This is a very proper question to ask, and this is the proper time to ask it. I say, then, was it right? Every American will answer with an emphatic 'Yes.' Every true patriot, no matter in what land born or reared, will answer, Yes. Every lover of liberty, in whatever country his destiny may have been cast, will answer, Yes. The truest men in old England at the time said it was right, and protested in indignant terms (still to be read) against the cruelty and oppression that rendered such a step necessary on the part of the colonists. The splendid eloquence of Pitt, and the brilliant oratory of Burke, were heard in denunciation of such flagrant wrong-doing. The long halls of the British House of Parliament rang again with the echoes of the clear voice of the great Earl of Chatham, as in bold and uncompromising language he declared, 'Were I an American as I am an Englishman, while a foreign troop was landed in my country I never would lay down my arms—never, never, never!' And the circumstance that I stand here to-day to voice my voice in this matter is a proof—a solemn assurance in fact—that I think it was right. Were it otherwise, I should not be found on this platform to-day. Money couldn't buy me, and threats couldn't intimidate me, and flattery couldn't induce me to get up here and let sentiments escape my lips, either on the subject of liberty, or any other topic that didn't find an echo in my heart.

You will consider it no breach of etiquette for me to remind you that the spirit of liberty is neither native to the American soil, nor exclusively confined to the American people. Wherever on the face of God's wide earth there is a true man with a true heart in his bosom, the spirit of liberty is there—is there inspiring him with a noble love for everything that is beautiful, and pure, and good, and filling him with a lofty scorn for everything that is low, and base, and mercenary. My position, therefore, and the post assigned me in connection with this centennial celebration to-day, although one from which I naturally did shrink on the ground of conscious incompetency for many reasons, is yet one from which I do not shrink, and have no reason to shrink, on the score of want of sympathy with this day's proceedings, or with the grand object which we are assembled here this day to commemorate. I yield to no man in my love of liberty. I yield to no man in my sympathies with the enslaved. My mission from week to week is to proclaim 'liberty to the captives, and the opening of the prison to those that are bound.' Why should I shrink from the performance of a duty so nearly allied to that to-day?"

"And now before quitting this part of our subject, let us consider what is the grand lesson taught us by the history of the Revolution. What do you think it is? As I read that event, I take it to be this: that man was made to be free. God ordained every man to be a free man. Liberty is the inherent, inalienable birthright of every son and daughter of God. The American Revolution, and similar revolutions in other lands and other times, have been nothing more nor less than asserting his claim to this God-given heritage. All down the ages, ever since the primal curse rested upon the race, men have been saying here and there, and yonder: 'We want you to be subject to us—bow down and serve us;' and over the reply has been hurled back: 'We shall not do it—we were born free as you—we shall not do it—we shall die first.' And hence on this very point have arisen all the battles that were ever fought on the theater of this world, between despotism on the one hand, with its chains for the vanquished, and freedom on the other, with its glorious charter of equal rights for every man, and unfettered liberty for all. It was to conserve and preserve intact this grand principle, this legacy of God to his children here below—that marshaled that little band of Grecian warriors on the plain of Marathon; that filled their hearts with a courage almost superhuman, and nerved their arms with almost more than mortal strength, and sent a thunderbolt of God scattering confusion, and dismay, and disaster, throughout the length and breadth of the mighty hosts of Persia, making Marathon the grandest name in the military history of our world—a synonym for Liberty herself. It was in behalf of this great principle that that tiny handful of three hundred heroic men disputed the narrow pass of Thermopylæ, against the combined hosts of Asia, and on gory death-beds, under the open firmament of heaven, testified their allegiance to the spirit of liberty, and practically said, writing it in their hearts' blood in the soil of their native Greece, 'We shall not wear your chains; we shall not do it; we shall die first.' And they did die, every man of them, every man of the three hundred. Died, did I say? Such men never die! The world will not let them die. They shall live, embalmed in the memories of the nations, as long as the world itself has an existence. It was over the settlement of this great question that the continent of Europe during the early part of this century was turned into an immense battlefield, where despotism and liberty were pitted against each other in mortal conflict, the victory at one time inclining toward despotism, and then again alternating on the side of liberty, until on that memorable 18th of June, there was drawn up to settle the contest the grandest and most imposing military spectacle that the world has ever witnessed—the grandest because of the mighty issues at stake, the most imposing because of the unrivaled and wonderful combination of power, skill, discipline, zeal, courage, and extraordinary military genius of the opposing forces—and there and then, on that memorable Sunday in June, on the plains of Belgium, amid smoke, and slaughter, and carnage, and ten thousand deaths, and confused noise, and garments rolled in blood, the great battle of liberty was won, and the name of Waterloo crowned for all time with imperishable and deathless glory! Such cases as these teach us (what your own Revolution teaches with equal force and clearness) that man was made to be free. This, I take it, is the grand lesson to be learned from the important events we have had under review."

After the oration the Hon. C. B. Swift, in accordance with the recommendation of the President of the United States, gave a brief history of Ione valley, the most of which has been incorporated into this work; as it will be of interest hereafter, the condition of Ione, as given by him at that time, will be added.

IONE IN 1876.

Ione City contains a population of about six hundred. Of this number one hundred and thirty-eight are between the ages of five and seventeen; two hundred and twenty-nine are under seventeen. Nine women and eleven men are over seventy. The Chinese population numbers about one hundred. It has four churches, two Sunday-schools, one public school, one division of the S. of T., with sixty members, one Masonic lodge, one Legion of the K. of A. C. Pastor of the M. E. church, Rev. A. K. Crawford; pastor of the Presbyterian church, Rev. James White; pastor of the Catholic church, Rev. Father Welch. The Baptists have no minister here at present. Teachers of the public schools, Miss Augusta Withington and Mrs. T. Stewart. It has four stores, two hotels, one meat market, one brewery, one restaurant, one millinery establishment, one art gallery, six saloons, one drug store, one barber shop, two paint shops, two blacksmith shops, one harness shop, one tin shop, three shoe shops, one variety store, one jewelry store, one cabinet shop, one powder house, one livery stable, two flouring mills—one running by steam, the other by water-power. The water mill has not been running the past year. The steam mill grinds a yearly average of over two thousand tons of barley, one thousand or twelve hundred tons of wheat, and one hundred and fifty tons of corn.

Ione will close the centennial year with a railroad completed to her town limits. The project of a road from Galt to Ione, was first broached to the directors of the Central Pacific by F. C. Hall, about the time of the "miners' strike," in Sutter. The company then agreed to lay the track and put on the rolling stock, whenever the road-bed should be graded. The general depression in business which followed the "strike," postponed the enterprise. Finally, Messrs. Hart, Goodman & Co., seeing that their coal interests demanded a road, entered into a contract with the Central Pacific to build the grade from Galt to Buckeye. While this work was in progress, the citizens of Ione called a meeting to take measures to continue the grade from Buckeye to Ione, a distance of six miles. A committee was appointed to raise the necessary funds, and to let the contract. Nine thousand nine hundred and forty dollars was raised by subscription, one thousand of which was appropriated to buy the right of way.

At the close of the meeting the president cordially invited all to be present at the next centennial. Perhaps a few may be able to accept the invitation.

RAILROAD.

Previous to 1876, Ione was connected with the outside world with only the poorest kinds of wagon roads. Many persons had advocated and others had opposed a railroad. Those who favored it pointed to the fact that, with few exceptions, cheap transportation aided to build up a country; that, though a few local interests suffered, a railroad made markets and also made more things marketable. Others said that we had a market for all that we could raise now; that a railroad from the plains would put down the price of grain to the extent, that it would lower the price of transportation from the great valleys with which the farmers were now competing. This was evidently true for the producer, also for the consumer. But the desire for a railroad yearly grew stronger. A ride over the abominated stage route between Ione and Galt was sure to convert one to the railroad system. About 1872 things began to shape themselves in this direction. The discovery of extensive beds of lignite, which made a very good substitute for coal, which had not then been found in quantities that it since has, turned attention to the valley. Occasional articles in the county papers which were copied into the city papers also called attention to the projects.

STOCKTON NARROW-GAUGE.

This was projected by Dr. E. S. Holden, who was instrumental in building the Stockton and Sacramento road afterwards incorporated into the Central Pacific Railroad, and also the Stockton and Copperopolis, which was also absorbed by the Central Pacific Railroad. It was advocated by the Stockton Independent and the other city papers. J. K. Doak, Mayor of Stockton, H. E. Hall, N. M. Orr, J. H. O'Brien, John Willson, Dr. A. Clark, Geo. Gray, E. Lyon, all prominent citizens, became the officers of a joint-stock company. The design at that time was to build a branch road from Linden to Ione, but the embarrassment of the company caused by the failure of the copper mines and the inability to complete or maintain possession of the road, induced them to re-organize and attempt the building of a narrow-guage direct from Ione to tide-water at Stockton. Some of the coal was taken to Stockton and tried. It was thought that it could be delivered in Stockton for three or four dollars per ton, which was less than half the ordinary price of fuel. Subscriptions to the amount of one hundred thousand dollars were made by the citizens of Stockton. A survey was made under Schuyler, and the project fairly inaugurated. A favorable contract for coal and the necessary land for depot grounds was entered into and the building of the road let to W. H. Platt, of San Francisco, for the sum of four hundred thousand dollars, payable in installments as the road progressed. The route of the road was to have been by way of Waterloo, Lockford, Poland House, Zimmerman's creek, Jackson valley, to Ione, a route involving but few heavy grades or expensive bridges. A few miles were graded and a few rails laid down; a passenger and two or three box cars were partly built. Two narrow-guage engines were shipped from the East and brought to Stockton, and, at one time, it looked as if the road might be built. Considerable money was paid in on the subscriptions, which seemed to be wasted in mere show, and finally the project fell through. The engines were soon removed and put upon the Nevada Narrow-Guage, and the half finished cars upon which a hundred or two dollars were expended is all to show for the fifty thousand dollars or more paid in by the citizens of Stockton.

GALT ROAD.

This was projected by F. C. Hall, who never had much confidence in the Stockton enterprise. In 1876 the Central Pacific Company having finished some of their main lines, were induced to turn their attention to some of the side lines. A survey was made and the route found to be inexpensive. It was intended to run the road up Dry creek, but some of the farmers evincing hostility to having the road pass over their lands, it was deflected up Buckeye creek, running directly to the coal mines, at what is now Carbondale. The road was intended mostly to carry away coal, and it seemed that the company were in no hurry to extend it to Ione. This did not look favorable for the prosperity of the town, as the travel from the upper towns might be diverted from Ione. A donation of some twelve thousand dollars, nearly or quite enough to pay the right of way and grade the line from Buckeye, was made by the citizens, and the cars came into the town about December 1, 1876. Much difference of opinion exists as to the benefit of the road. Freight on goods is somewhat cheaper, though not enough to prevent wagons from doing some of the work. A greater number of teams get

RESIDENCE AND RANCH OF ISAAC W. WHITACRE, NEAR PLYMOUTH, AMADOR CO. CAL.

employment into the mountains than were engaged before its completion. Considerable wholesale trading is now done at Ione. The amount of goods received by rail is constantly increasing, necessitating a recent increase of storage at the depot. Those who believe that freshets, drought, pestilence, famine, and failures of mines follow in the march of railroads, will undoubtedly think that Ione and the other portions of the county have been damaged by it. When the farmers adapt their crops to the changed circumstances, and raise such things as the fine soil and climate ripens to perfection, such as grapes, peaches and apricots, they will probably discover that the railroad is beneficial.

OVERFLOWS.

The same agency which has deposited the fertile soil of the valley, occasionally becomes a means of destruction. A large water-shed is at the head of Dry and Sutter creeks. In early days when no *tailings* or *slickens* burdened the water, the overflows were comparatively harmless, but not so when the streams are taxed to their utmost capacity to precipitate on the valleys the mud, sand, and rocks, from a thousand mining claims. The most disastrous overflow occurred in 1861-62. The piles of tailings—the accumulations of years—were forced through the cañon, and, though pulverized by the constant attrition, lodged soon after reaching the valley, filling the channel, nearly to the surface; consequently the great mass of water either eroded new channels, or carried great quantities of sterile sand over the farms, destroying orchards, vineyards, and gardens—the work of years of industry—leaving only a waste producing willows and malaria. Some of the finest farms were hopelessly buried up in this way. A stream of water several hundred foot wide left Sutter creek near Ione; portions of it going through the town swept across the ranch formerly owned by Thomas Rickey, in some places carrying away several feet of soil, in others leaving as much sand. Houses, bridges, fences, and all improvements were swept away. At the lower part of the valley, the waters from Mule creek had already buried some of the land with tailings. This freshet piled on new horrors, adding several feet more of *slickens*, and covering a still larger area. At Dry creek a new channel was eroded through, perhaps, the finest corn field in the State, leaving, as on Sutter creek, a great waste of useless sand. Mr. Scott, an elderly and much esteemed man, was swept away at Ione, and drowned, his body being found some miles below, after several days' search.

A great destruction also occurred on Sunday, February 16, 1878. This overflow was not the product of a long-continued rain, but of a *cloud burst*, which was only of a few hours' duration and limited in extent, the rain-fall being the greatest nearly on the line of the Mother Lode or along the towns of Jackson, Sutter Creek, and Amador. The *shower* has been more particularly described in the history of Jackson. Only one inch of rain fell at Ione; probably ten times that fell at other points. The nature of a cloud burst limits it in its operations, or we might have a repetition of Noah's flood. In this instance, the torrents from the neighborhood of Sutter and Amador filled the channel full, and overflowed the surrounding country, Ione being for a time another Venice. Doctor Cummings' costly improvements were swept away, and many farms were damaged.

These overflows produce malaria, as well as destroy land and property. The *debris* question is the most serious danger the valleys have to confront, and will be treated more extensively in the chapter on gravel mining.

FIRES.

Ione has been particularly fortunate in not having shared the usual fate of California towns—a general conflagration. Occasionally, a small fire would arouse the population to greater watchfulness. On the night of October 8, 1865, occurred the largest fire that Ione has experienced. The block bounded by Main, Buena Vista, Jackson, and Church streets, was entirely consumed. The night was perfectly calm, and the blaze went straight up in one tall column; otherwise the whole town would have been destroyed. The losses were: Farnsworth's blacksmith shop; Stevens' paint shop; Bona Beiter's bakery; Ringer's saloon; Miller's saloon; Ludgate & Surface's livery stable, and a barber shop. The block was soon rebuilt, much better than before, many of the new buildings being of brick.

In this fire the old Ione Valley Hotel, one of the first buildings erected, was destroyed.

BUENA VISTA.

This is the center of a farming region, and, as its name implies, is perhaps one of the most beautiful places in the State. Jackson creek here comes out of the mountains, and the valley spreads out from one to two miles in width, maintaining this character until Dry creek comes into it, some five or six miles below. The long sweep of hills around the valley have the effect of a fine setting, and the Buena Vista mountain, with bold castellated peaks, varying their outlines with every change of view, bring to mind some of the ruins of the older world, and make one feel that he is on the ground of ancient civilization. The rich, black soil, covered with grass as high as a man's head, early attracted the attention of settlers, though it is impossible to learn who first visited it. It forms part of the tract of land granted to Teodosia Yerba* in 1840, by Governor Juan B. Alvarado; though it is doubtful whether Yerba, or any Mexican, or other citizen of California, ever set foot on the land at that early date, as it was inhabited by the Nesheans, Lucklumlas, Mokelkos, and other Indians, who had taught

---

*The name is spelled Yerba and Yorba. It is probable that the family did not know how it was spelled, as they signed their names with a cross.

the native population to respect the San Joaquin river as the boundary line.

Cattle were grazed here as early as 1848, whether by some of Hick's and Martin's vaqueros, is not known; but the land was claimed by a man by the name of Diggs, who kept a trading post, ranched cattle and sold beef, in 1849. In 1850, it was purchased by Charles Stone, Warren Nimms, and Fletcher Baker, all from the eastern part of New York. Stone seemed to have been the business man of the firm, and, under his management, the valley had quite a princely look. They ran a log fence around a thousand acres or more of land, put up buildings, costing, with the then high price of lumber and labor, several thousand dollars. They purchased large herds of cattle in southern California at low figures, kept them on the place until the condition of the market or the cattle was favorable, and sold them at a great advance. They also went into farming, and raised large quantities of barley, when it readily brought from one hundred and fifty to two hundred and fifty dollars per ton, hay being sold on the place for fifty dollars per ton. It is said that the yield of barley was sometimes one hundred and twenty bushels to the acre, and seven tons of weighed hay were sold from an acre at fifty dollars per ton, though, says the narrator, it was not quite cured. They were not suffered to enjoy such abundance in peace, however. The Johnston family, as well as others, laid hold of a quarter section, here and there, and expensive lawsuits resulted. An attempt was made to get a bill through Congress, donating the land to them in consideration of their improvements, which were estimated at forty thousand dollars, but Congress failed to give them any relief. In 1852, Congress donated to California five hundred thousand acres of land for school purposes, and the State issued warrants for the same to settlers who wished to purchase land. Attempts were made to locate under these warrants, but the land was unsurveyed, and no land offices had been created; and all that could be done was to record in the county archives, the intention of locating them. These disturbances produced a dissolution of the copartnership, Baker selling out to Stone, and going East. A division of property then took place between Stone and Nimms, the latter taking the western half of the tract. He put up fine buildings (fine for that day), and maintained the suits against the jumpers with increased vigor, which soon reduced his purse to such a low ebb, that he was compelled to dispose of the land, although he had succeeded in holding it on the ground of *priority of possession*, Judge Murry, before whom the case was tried, holding that the log fence, being sufficient to turn cattle and save the crops, was an inchoate title, which was good until a better one was known. Nimms went to preaching the gospel, and is now (1880) engaged in the same profession somewhere in Nevada.

Stone, more prudent and, perhaps, wiser, suffered Nimms to carry on the suits, and awaited results. It is said that he kept the squatters off his portion of the ground with his lariat, with which he was an expert. He would ride up to a beginning of a house, throw his riata around it, and in a few minutes the residence, that was to be, would be scattered in fragments a mile away, fences being served the same way. He could not always scare men away, however. Jim Johnston, one of the Johnston family, commenced building a house somewhere on Jonathan Ringer's present ranch, which, Stone discovering, he rode up and commenced swinging his riata in preparation for an immediate move on the works. Johnston quietly drew a revolver, and warned Stone that he had better not make any such demonstrations with him. Stone seemed to be of about the same opinion, and let the house building go on. After the termination of the Nimms suits, the squatters, who were on the portion claimed by him, bought or left, and this ended the land suits for the time.

About 1856 to 1860 the ranches were generally sold to the present size, Alexander Thompson, William Spray, Samuel Williams (on the farm now occupied by Lyman Tubbs), Moses Hill, John P. Hoffman, P. Y. Cool, William Joiner, Joseph Fithian, Mathew Leary, William C. Thompson, J. D. Mason, Azariah Sollers, and others, settling in the valley. Calvin Dillon, John Kite, Patrick and William Sculley, Samuel Deardorff, George Martin, J. C. Hamrick, and Thomas Jones, came in a year or two earlier. In 1857 a school-house was built, which was also used for church purposes. Religious meetings had been previously held in Stone's house. The first school was taught by Cyrus James in 1858. From this time forward the place had much of the style prevailing in eastern rural communities.

MINING.

On the north side of the valley considerable mining was carried on in the early days. The pay was generally on the top of the ground, and the working inexpensive. Some of the gulches were rich, in some instances as much as eight dollars to the pan being obtained. When the Turner ditch was brought in, quite a town sprang up in the neighborhood of Dillon's ranch. George Walker established the first store. William C. Richey afterwards engaged in merchandising, and moved his store to the corner near his present residence, where he traded for a year or two, selling out to John Fitzsimmons about 1860. Fitzsimmons had formerly traded at Poverty Bar, but on the failure of the mines there, he chose a surer if not more profitable trade, in a farming community. He remained in trade until about 1874, and was succeeded by William Cook, from Lancha Plana.

EFFECT OF THE ARROYO SECO GRANT.

This grant included a larger part of this valley, which, like Ione valley, was a great sufferer, though not to the same extent as much of the land had been purchased of the first claimants, in 1857. Some of the principal sufferers were Calvin Cole, Patrick and Wm. Sculley, Chas. Black,— Strobridge, and Samuel Deardorff. When the ejection took place the soldiers were quartered on the premises of Cole, his goods being piled rather roughly out on the common. They made free use of his property, killing his sheep and appropriating whatever was needed by them. It is believed Captain Starr tried to preserve the property from harm, but soldiers are not apt to starve in the midst of plenty, and the old man had plenty, for he was as saving as he was thrifty. It is said that one of the soldiers, while dressing a stolen sheep, received a bullet in his leg, inflicting a severe though not dangerous wound. No inquiry was made for the author.

Charley Black's house was opened in the absence of the family, and the goods, a valuable organ among the other things, thrust out into the storm to be ruined. At other places the same rudeness was displayed. It must be remembered that the soldiers were not in reality acting under the commands of their own officers, but under the command of Herman Wohler, one of the grant proprietors. The soldiers disliked the business and did not hesitate to avow it. After a representation of the matter to the authorities they were relieved from handling hot stoves, and other household goods. When they came to Joe Fithians he had the United States flag hoisted, for Joe was an out and out Union man, and the soldiers disliked more than ever to tumble his family of little children into the street, but the orders were peremptory, and they were loaded into an army wagon and hauled out to the boundaries of the grant with the flag flying over the wagon, so that it had the appearance of a triumphal march. At Deardorff's they found the door locked (which they broke open), and the cooking stove red hot, which was Mrs. Deardorff's system of war. They found means to carry it away however. When they were about locking the door of Bill Sculley's house, after having taken possession, Bill shook his fist in the agent's face (the agent's name was Clark), observing, "I would like to lock the gates of hell on you," and looked as though he might make short work of the job then and there. Clark called for protection, but Sculley was not arrested. The following night Sculley's house was burned, no attempt being made to save it. It may be remarked that Sculley obtained very easy terms when he purchased his property, perhaps, for the reason that the grant owners did not care to have him for an enemy, for capital is quite as cowardly as it is unscrupulous and selfish.

In a few years the excitement abated and industry was resumed, although men rested uneasy, not knowing when the torch should fire the dry grain fields and the fire sweep away the accumulations of years of industry, but the law was suffered to take its course; indeed, the people of this valley have ever been remarkable for their law-abiding character, not a single homicide ever having been committed in the valley.

The valley suffered considerably from the overflow of 1861-62, getting a foretaste of what *slickens* can do in ruining land. For nine years mining had been carried on above, but most of the *debris* had lodged in the small gulches, and up to this date no overflow had left any serious amount of sand or gravel. The unusual quantity of water in that season sent it down all at once. The channels were filled with moving sand to the depth of several feet. After the water went down, boulders weighing several pounds were found in the cañon above, nine feet above the bed of the stream, showing that the moving gravel had been that high. The most of the gravel had been ground to sand when it had reached the valley, but the streams were so full even when the water was down, as to make crossing dangerous. The stage generally managed to get through, but frequently eight or ten horses hitched to the wagon with a long rope, would be required to pull it out. When the wheels commenced sinking, the only alternative was to get the horses loose from the carriage and pull them ashore, as they were utterly helpless in the quicksand. Early in the storm the creek broke over its banks a mile or two below the foot of the cañon, and carried a great quantity of coarse sand on the ranches of John Kite, Samuel Williams & Son, William Spray, and others below, burying the fertile soil from one to three feet deep with the *debris*. Some of these lands have been partially reclaimed; others still produce nothing but worthless weeds.

Recently the *debris* has begun to dam up below and seems inclined to bury the lower part of the valley first, though every year the point of deposit is advancing up the valley. Since 1861-62 the overflows have not seriously injured the land in consequence of the almost entire suspension of hydraulic mining on the different branches of Jackson creek. Some years since, when what is called the Isaacs claim, on the east side of Jackson valley, was opened, it was feared that the valley would be inundated with tailings, but fortunately, for the farmers at least, the claim did not prove remunerative, and work was suspended and the danger averted.

The "cloud burst" which played such havoc in Jackson in February, 1878, dumped the broken buildings and dead Chinamen on the ranches near the foot of the cañon, the bodies of several of the drowned being found on Mr. Tubbs' farm.

At the present writing (1881) it is by far the most beautiful spot in Amador county. The finest fruit as well as the abundant crops attest the capacity of the soil. Artesian water enables the people to have green crops through the year (although all the fruits and cereals flourish without irrigation) and have perpetual, blooming flowers around their generally elegant residences, and altogether the people may feel proud of their homes as well as their history.

BUCKEYE VALLEY.

This valley, beautifully situated with low rolling hills for a setting, was inferior to Ione for cultivated crops, but furnished an abundance of the finest quality of hay. It was occupied mostly by stockmen. Samuel Hill, Captain Good, I. N. Kay (now of Alameda), Wayburn, Mugford, Barrett, and others, being the first settlers. The Ione & Galt R. R. Co. have a station here called Carbondale, from which is taken annually a great quantity of the soft coal, or lignite, which is said to underlie the whole valley. Miss Wilbur, the poetess, better known under the nom de plume of "Gordon Bracket" resides in this valley. She has written some very good lines. Perhaps her poem on the death of J. W. Coffroth is an average of her work.

The soil of the valley having been farmed and cropped many years with no return, has ceased to be productive. In the northern part of the valley Addington & Son have, for many years, made a good article of fire brick, also of pottery, out of the clays overlying the coal. He was the first to utilize the clays for this purpose, his works having been in operation some twenty-three or four years. Until the opening of the C. P. R. R., which crossed the same formation at Lincoln, quite a trade existed in this clay, the return freight-wagons loading with it and supplying several potteries at Sacramento.

IRISH HILL.

This hill, situated on the north side of Dry creek, where it leaves the cañon, was a mixture of river and beach diggings, unlike Muletown, having boulders from river-wash mingled with the beach-wash. It was also very rich in an early day. Four men, Hawley, Nelson, Millner, and —— (name unknown), made nine thousand dollars each in seven months. Nelson is still working in the vicinity—poor. Hawley went East, and by a fortunate venture converted his dollars into thousands. He came back recently to see the place where he had made his start. Millner was killed by the caving of a bank in his claim. He was buried in the graveyard in Ione. A hundred or more men, dressed in black pants and gray shirts, walked in procession from Irish hill, taking turns in carrying the bier.

The place is still worked, the ground being owned by Alvinza Hayward and Stanford & Co., the latter being owners of the grant of which this hill forms a part. The water used comes from the Plymouth ditch, after being used at the Empire mills.

This town also had its fun with the enrolling officer in 1863. When he put in an appearance, some one blew a tremendous horn which gave notice to all the able-bodied to decamp, which was done to an extent sufficient to make the enrolling rather difficult.

QUINCY.

Scarce one man in ten who lives in Ione valley has ever heard of Quincy, though they can scarcely look up from their plowing without seeing the former site of this town, which is as much a thing of the past as Babylon or Nineveh. But for a newspaper published there in an early day, its very existence would remain unknown. According to this paper (the *Quincy Prospector*), edited and published by Alexander Badlam, now Assessor of San Francisco, the town was quite large, having a Broadway with houses numbered; stores, with stocks of general merchandise; saloons; doctors', lawyers', and even real estate offices. From the paper it might be inferred that it was quite a city, rivaling Sacramento or even Muletown in its best days. The locality of the town is uncertain, but it is known to have been somewhere between Muletown and the Boston store. Some of our antiquarian societies will confer a great favor on the world, and advance the cause of science, by sending out an exploring party to dig up its valuable relics before the tooth of time shall have obliterated them.

MULETOWN.

This place was about two miles north of Ione, and in the fifties was a very lively camp. It belonged to the foot-hill diggings, the gold in the gulches and hills having been liberated from the quartz veins by a wash of the sea, all the gravel having a peculiar, polished appearance without the rounded form usually seen in river deposits. The ravines were very rich. Yancy, a native of the Argentine Republic, often made a hundred dollars a day with a pan alone. Others made nearly as much. A Chinaman picked up a piece weighing thirty-six ounces. He was so elated that he immediately left for home. The first store was kept by Charles Simmons; others were started soon after by the Dillards, and also by a man of peculiar character, named Cunningham. These insignificant places, with not a tenth as large stocks as the present stores at Ione, would sell thousands of dollars' worth of merchandise a day. Water was brought in in 1854 by the Johnston brothers. After the ravines were worked, the hills were attacked with hydraulic power, and paid better than the ravines had ever done. The first hydraulic was put up by Wm. H. Fox & Co., consisting of penstock, flume and hose. The next was by Willson, Miller, & Bagley, with iron pipe, then but recently introduced. Some of the claims paid as high as one thousand dollars per week to the man. In its best days, Muletown had several hundred inhabitants, mostly Irish, though other nationalities were well represented. The peculiarities of the Irish had full sweep. Most of those who could afford to, purchased horses, and on Sunday would ride out in quest of fun and adventure. They were not skillful or graceful horsemen at first, and a Muletown crowd could be distinguished at a long distance by the flopping limbs and furious riding. The pranks and funny affairs of Muletown would fill a book. A few only will be related.

Residence & Stock Ranch of **JAMES ROBERTSON**, near Mountain Springs, Tp. 1. Amador Co. Cal.

Residence of **MATTHEW MURRAY**, Lancha Plana, Amador Co. Cal.

MINERS' COURT.

In 1850 the miners had got tired of being taken from their work to testify in cases of disputed mining titles, and a public meeting was called to consider the situation. It was finally resolved that all such cases should be settled by arbitration; that no appeal should be taken; that any party that should feel aggrieved should fight his opponent a fist fight, according to the rules of the ring, the best man taking the ground. It was also agreed, that in case of a great disparity in size or strength, the weaker person might substitute a friend to do his fighting. In order not to interfere with the work, the fights were to come off on the first Sunday after the dispute. It happened that the first trial of this kind fell on a Sunday on which there was to be a Catholic service. How to proceed so as to keep the priest in ignorance of the matter, so that he might not interfere, was the question. At a meeting held the evening before to make arrangements, it was determined to commence the fight at daylight at a spot a little distance from the town. It was thought that by conducting the matter quietly the Father might not hear of it. There were several parties to the affair, involving several fights, but it was hoped that they might be finished before the women and children should awake, as the custom was to sleep late on Sunday.

The morning came and nearly all the male population were present. The ring was marked out, the bottle-holders and seconds appointed, and the fight commenced. The contest proved longer than was expected. The litigants were both plucky. Round after round was fought, still no sign of yielding. The sun was getting well up and the women and children would soon be moving. So far there had been no cheering. The blows had fallen thick and fast, taken and given. It is not strange then that the friends of each party began to cheer the combatants, until the noise aroused the women and the priest, who came rushing to the ground, about the time each side thought the other side was about whipped. "How dare you desecrate the Sabbath this way?" says the priest, addressing one of the seconds, whose shirt, from sponging his principal's face, was quite bloody. The second, answering for the meeting, replied that it was much better to settle a difficulty by a fist fight than with knives and pistols, as had been recently done at Volcano, where the priest lived; that it was sometimes necessary to choose the least of two evils. The priest turned away, mounted his horse and left the place, without saying a word. There was no service that day. It was expected that he would give them a fearful admonition the next time, but the subject was never mentioned. This method of settling disputes involved so many inconveniences that it was not tried again.

THE FUNNY MAN.

Muletown had a philanthropist by the name of Cunningham, who had very original ways of benefiting mankind. He had been very successful in trade, also in mining, and wanted to use his money for the benefit of the community. "He was rough, but generous and brave," as the poet would have it, a good deal addicted to drink, fully conscious of his importance, and inclined to be dictatorial when in his cups. He built a hall which was free to all churches, public meetings, and respectable parties, which was dedicated with a dancing party, with the following schedule for tickets:—

Tickets to gentlemen without ladies......$6.00
   "   "   with one lady...... 3.00
   "   "   two ladies...... free.

The entertainment was magnificent, and gave satisfaction to his numerous guests. The hall was used also as a school-house, the old man contributing liberally to the support of the school.

While the camp was still flourishing, his wife died. She was buried without the usual funeral ceremonies, which were postponed to a more convenient season, that he might get them up in a style becoming his wealth. Sometime after, he stipulated with Elder Sharp, the Methodist preacher at Ione, to preach two sermons at twenty dollars each. He gave notice of a free dinner to all who would attend, and as the style of his entertainments was well known, the attendance was numerous. As the old man was somewhat wanting in reverence for the cloth, and apt to make disparaging remarks, the Elder thought it best to take along Father Rickey, and some of the elder members of his church, to overawe the old man, which did not succeed, however, as he was quite ready to applaud or condemn, when anything pleased or displeased him. "That's good," said he, "that's bully, that's first rate," looking around in triumph. "The next sermon will be better than this." The Elder continued his remarks without being disturbed by the applause. During the sermon, Mr. Cunningham felt a call from nature, and asked Elder Sharp to wait a few minutes till he could go out; but the preacher, not being used to such interruptions, continued his sermon. Cunningham commenced raising his bulky form, some of Sharp's friends trying to hold him down in his seat. He shook them off, however, for his strength was immense, and balanced himself in front of the preacher, wrath oozing out of every inch of his bloated face, his bulky form and baggy cheeks quivering with rage. "By G—, sir, I would like to know who is running this funeral!" The Elder heaved a sigh and subsided, waiting for the old man to come back. Cunningham died, and was buried near his wife, nearly a score of years since, and the sheep and goats feed where once stood his hall and the surrounding town, but the memory of his many benevolent deeds will last until the pioneers have gone to their final rest.

A FAITHFUL WIFE.

In the early fifties, two Mexicans getting into a difficulty, agreed to settle the matter in dispute with an exchange of pistol shots, the contest to be continued with knives, in case both parties survived the shooting, until one was slain, which was done. The wife of the party slain wished to continue the fight, but was not allowed. She remained faithful to his memory, and once every month, for years afterward, lighted twelve candles on his grave, and, alone, watched the whole night.

When copper was discovered in the McNealy claim, Muletown took a little start upwards, but soon resumed its decay, one house after another being removed, or falling to ruins. The removal of the inhabitants was accelerated by the prevalence of chills and fever, supposed to be generated by the immense pile of tailings, which cover the low lands in the vicinity. The house owned by the Johnstons, the proprietors of the ditch, was consumed by fire a few years since, and now, naught but the scarred hill-sides remain to show that twenty years ago the place was alive with a striving humanity. Woodburn, Member of Congress from Nevada, mined in Muletown in 1860.

CHAPTER XXXII.
LANCHA PLANA' AND VICINITY.

Its Early Settlers — Cholera and Diarrhea — Judge Palmer's Bridge — Fires — First School — Notable Homicide — Bluff Mining — Open Sea — Chaparral Hill — Growth of the Town — Bonita Affair — Indian War — Butler Claim — Decline of the Town — Put's Bar and the Fruit Interest — Overflows — Townsville — Camp Opera — French Camp — Copper Centre.

This town, situated in the south-western part of the county, where the Mokelumne river leaves the mountains, was settled soon after the discovery of gold. Though the foot-hills were not as rich as at the main gold belt, the gold was finer, more evenly distributed, and over a great surface of country, enabling a great number of persons to make remunerative wages. Like nearly all such places, it was first worked by the native Californians, or Mexicans. It did not amount to much as a town until 1850, and then the population was scattered along the river at Poverty Bar, Winters' Bar, and other places, Winters' Bar, perhaps, having the largest number. As these towns were in the same county, and intimately associated together in early times, a history of Lancha Plana will involve, to some extent, a history of the other towns, although not included in the county of Amador.

In 1850, we find the towns in a flood-tide of prosperity. Many men, since noted in the history of our country, settled here about this time. The Dudleys, Al. and Bill, and others who had a love for intellectual strife, but none for hard work, and were, consequently, generally flat broke, gave name to Poverty Bar. A man by the name of Luffton, formerly a lieutenant in the regular army, who was cashiered in Jackson's time for some irregularity in money matters, was also in the vicinity, living with a squaw

* Flat boat.

for a wife. He was a braggart, pompous, and consequential, professing to hold his honor in high estimation, and ready to avenge an insult with his sword, which was always ready for emergencies. His professions of valor were taken for what they were worth, and were finally squelched in a difficulty by a shower of flour upon his person, which caused a great laugh but no bloodshed. General Stedman, afterward a noted soldier in the Union army, mined on the Oregon bar. He had been an engineer on the Ohio canal, was used to the control of men, and was employed by the Oregon Bar Company to construct a dam to turn the river, all previous efforts to make a dam stick having failed. He constructed log pens, eight or ten feet square, floated them to the desired place, and sunk them by filling them with rock. Timbers and brush against these, and then gravel, made a good dam, enabling the company to work the river, which, however, proved worthless. The operation bursted the company. Some of the cribs could be seen as late as 1860. Gen. Stedman would take off his wet clothes when he came out of the river, don a pair of overalls, and walk around on the hot sand barefooted, like the rest of the boys. He was very fond of whist, being a skillful player. The Oregon Bar Company was composed mostly of Southern men, who brought their negroes with them. The miners generally looked upon the introduction of negro labor with disfavor, and to this antipathy, more than to any moral principle, we owe the prohibitive clause in our Constitution. When the company had determined on removal, the negroes were sent out to gather up the horses, but they failed to find their way back to the camp, though the party remained several weeks to give them a chance to return. Koon, one of the principal owners, tried to enlist the miners in a search for the missing slaves, but they did not respond to his efforts.

Charles T. Meader, afterwards merchant at Stockton, and the great copper miner, also commenced life in California at this place, besides many more of note whose names appear in the course of our history. The criminal element was well represented. Sam Brown, who, perhaps, committed more murders on this coast than any other person, also resided in Lancha Plana, though at a later date, as also did Sam Marshall, the murderer of Dan Childs, and Ritter, of Willow Springs. A company of men from Steubenville, Ohio, also made their influence felt. They were roughs, shoulder strikers, much like the New York firemen, and were the cause of many disturbances, generally being in the lead whenever a mob was gathered. Most of them perished by violence, for the forbearance of men would not last forever.

In 1850 an effort was made to expel the Mexican population. A mass-meeting was called, violent harangues were made, and resolutions calling for the immediate expulsion of the Mexicans offered. General Stedman opposed the measure as an unfair and unreasonable act, and contrary to our solemn treaties, and probably to his influence was due the failure of the movement. Soon after this, his trusted servant, a Mexican boy, robbed Stedman's camp of the money and other valuables, and left, and was not seen afterwards, though a thorough search was made. Some persons who were angry at Stedman for the part he took in opposing the expulsion of the Mexicans, openly rejoiced at his loss.

CHOLERA AND DIARRHEA.

Cholera and diarrhea prevailed in this vicinity in 1850, as in nearly all the towns of California. Poor living, the great change of the thermometer, (as many as sixty degrees between midnight and midday,) the working in the cold water of the river, and the blazing sun overhead, with the reduced condition of the system after a long voyage at sea, or trip across the plains, predisposed the system to disease, and made an easy harvest for the epidemic; a few days of diarrhea and the cholera finished the work in an hour or two. There were no homes, no medicines, no nurses, and but few physicians, though some quacks, pretenders, seeing a chance to make money, put out their M. D., and for a fee of an ounce, gave bad medicine and worse advice, which accelerated the fatal journey. Hundreds died whose names were never known, and whose families, perhaps, are living in hopes to this day, to hear from them. Dr. Brusie, then living here, was active in relieving suffering, and won the esteem of all by his disinterested efforts, and is remembered with kindness by numbers who have not kept trace of him since. He is still living, hale and hearty, at Ione, and can relate many thrilling incidents in his long career in California and in the army for the suppression of the Rebellion.

The first ferry was established in 1850, by Kaiser and Winter, the boat being a kind of raft made of casks lashed together; it carried over passengers only, the fare being fifty cents. A French Canadian by the name of Frank, opened the first store.

Lumber was worth one dollar per foot; tacks, one dollar and a quarter per paper; inch screws, one dollar per dozen; a sheet of iron large enough for a rocker, three dollars.

Tom Love was the first to introduce the long tom, which soon took the place of the rocker. At first the water was conducted to the tom through hose and short ditches, but the elevating wheel was shortly introduced; this resembled the flutter wheel, and was ten to fifteen feet in diameter. It was placed in a strong current in the river, and elevated the water in buckets (sometimes oyster cans were used), nailed to the rim of the wheel, which went up partly filled with water, and were emptied, by the turn of the wheel, into a trough which carried the water to the tom. As many as twenty or thirty wheels were sometimes running near a camp.

JUDGE PALMER'S BRIDGE.

This bridge was built in 1852, and seems to have been a slender affair, set on bents or posts in the river, with timbers reaching from one bent to another, much like the bridges which Cæsar built two thousand years ago, when he made his famous campaign among the German tribes. The Judge, being a Latin scholar, probably got his plan from Cæsar's Commentaries. Accounts differ as to how long the bridge stood. The Judge says until the rains came; others say that it fell the next day after it was completed; that only one man, a Dutchman with a horse and cart, crossed on it. As it was completed in the Fall, just before the big rise of '52, all the stories may be correct. All parties agree that it was raining very hard; that he was engaged in a game of pedro, or something like it; that a great outcry among the Chinamen caused him to get up from the table and look out of the door. The bridge was taking its departure for the bay without as much as *by your leave*. Not a muscle of his face stirred. With his usual serenity he reseated himself at the table, inquiring "Whose deal?" That, and nothing more.

After the departure of the bridge, Westmoreland's ferry continued to be the only way of crossing, though a bridge some distance up the river was built by Delaney, now a resident of San Francisco, which, having been put up of green lumber, fell when the hot Summer shrank the timbers. About 1856 the present bridge was built. It has witnessed the quarter-century which marked the rise and decay of the mining towns of the river, and is likely to do service much longer.

FIRES.

The first and only fire in Lancha Plana was in 1853, burning the entire town, which, at that time, was a cluster of tents and brush shanties. It is needless to say that the loss was inconsiderable, and did not much retard its prosperity.

THE FIRST SCHOOL

Was taught by James Gould, who came from Volcano and set up a private school in 1853. At this time there were but few families in the place, and perhaps not more than ten or twelve children.

The church was built by subscription in 1855, and was used by all denominations for religious purposes, and also by the citizens generally as a town hall.

NOTABLE HOMICIDE.

This occurred in 1855, and from the respectable standing of the parties, was an event in the history of the town. A stream of water used for running a wheel was turned away, causing a dispute in which some high words were passed. A man by the name of Norton, who was not interested in the affair, came up to quiet the dispute, when Dr. Beck, a man of generous though hasty feelings, threw a rock, breaking Norton's skull. A general row ensued, in which knives and pistols were freely used, without any further serious casualties, however. Dr. Beck gave himself up, and seemed to be extremely penitent in regard to the matter, even giving directions for dressing Norton's wound, and would, doubtless, have done everything in his power to prevent a fatal result. He was acquitted of the charge of murder, and afterwards went to Santa Fé to settle the estate of a brother, who had been engaged in trade, and who had been shot in a difficulty. A hasty temper provoked another shooting affair, in which he was the victim this time: thus ends the tragedy with three victims.

BLUFF MINING

Commenced in 1856. It is not known who made the first discovery, probably several about the same time. A bed of gravel, several feet thick, extended over the flat and through the bluff, richer than the river ever was; it was, in fact, the former bed of the river in *pliocene* times, though, when the river ran long enough to deposit such a mass of auriferous gravel a hundred times greater than was found in the river-bed proper, when the stream buried it as deep or deeper than the bluff; when it eroded the valley where Winters' Bar, Poverty Bar, and the flat on which Lancha Plana rests—are questions involving many doubtful points. The history of Buena Vista mountain, is the history of the bluffs around Lancha Plana, and a short digression from the *recent* to the *ancient*, may be interesting to those who either have, or will hereafter, mine in this vicinity. Lancha Plana furnishes, perhaps, the best point in the county to study the effect of erosions and deposits. The bluffs and deposits of gravel around Campo Seco, must also be considered in this history. The story shall be short, though marvelous, and the proofs such that any thinking man can see them for himself in an hour's walk.

THE OPEN SEA.

First, suppose that around Lancha Plana all of the sandstones are away, only the slate, and rocks of that character, stand in the shallow bay, or water of the sea, which extends west from the foot of the mountains, which are not yet cut and eroded into channels as deep as now by hundreds of feet. A stream is flowing in here, but, though it has force enough to bring in moderate sized gravel, it does not bring sediment faster than the tides, which daily sweep past the boulder-like slate rocks scattered up and down the present river, can carry it away. Then was deposited the gravel along the foot-hills, forming the beds now lying under the pay-streak under consideration, and separated from it in many places by a hard floor of sand. It may be seen under the claim of Mat Murray, on the bedrock north of the town, and *wherever gravel lies under the coal formation* all the way to Jackson creek, the position fixing its age. The coal formation may be seen under what is called Alum peak. A liberal allowance of time may be made here. Above the coal formation allow time for a deposit of clay, say an eighth of an inch a year; this is during the glacier period, when little gravel is being brought down, all being ground into fine clay. This being done, let the sandstones, the fine building stones of Lancha Plana, appear; after that, gravel in moderate quantities. Some of the hills north of Lancha have this gravel, notably around China gulch. In some instances, the gold is in paying quantities.

Lancha Plana by this time was several hundred feet under ground. Now the streams begin to run with greater force. The ocean line is crowded out miles and miles. The progress of the filling is now much faster. Gravel, sand, clay, and lava, alternate with each other, until the first deposits are buried a thousand feet deep, and the whole country to the east is a plain higher than Buena Vista mountain. In Calaveras county is a mountain of peculiar structure, that may be a part of a plain a thousand feet higher than the Buena Vista mountain. If it should prove to be so, then we may provide for the lapse of a still greater number of years, not only in the filling, but in the erosion which is to follow. Then the present system of rivers was formed. They begin to gnaw away the great masses of matter which had taken so many millions of years to heap up. Little by little, as now, the earth is carried out on the plains to fill up the San Joaquin valley which heretofore has been an open sea. The great masses of gravel deposited in the mountains, like that at Mokelumne Hill and Jackson, in fact, covering the greater part of the country, is now being moved and re-adjusted. The gravel hills around Campo Seco and Camanche are now one after another deposited, the streams eroding, in all instances, more than they deposit, wearing away and concentrating the gravel and the gold. Now the rivers are beginning to find their present channels, as they wear deeper and deeper into the sandstones and rocks, for they have again struck the slate rocks. They have now worn down far below the glacier erosions, and now flow in saw-like channels, instead of the long, smooth valleys of the time when such vast masses of gravel were on the move. The volcanoes have now been quiet for ages. The whole country is comparatively in a state of repose. The bluff banks by Lockford and the Poland House may begin to show, as the stream is not pressed with sand and gravel from the mountains. Having no serious work on hand, the river may commence eroding a valley in the former deposits, making room for the present bottom-lands. When this condition has arrived, we may look for the river to reach the level of the big gravel deposits forming the base of the bluffs. How many years the river was wearing into the sandstones, into the hard clays, carrying them off ounce by ounce, perhaps only as muddy water, none can tell. It had to make room for the gravel; then had to have uninterrupted ages to bring the gravel down from the deposits in the mountains. Running in a nearly straight course towards the plains, it slowly piled up acres of gravel, perhaps a hundred, and for some unexplained reason buried it up in sand again, until a flat appears, of which the bluff where Maroon's house, Judge Palmer's, and others are situated, is a relic. This piling up of fine quicksand, must also have been the work of ages. It will be obvious to any one, that a slight difference either in the obstruction in carrying off of the *debris* from the mountains above, or an increase in the erosive and carrying power of the mountain streams, would produce a change in the lines of deposit in the valley.

It might have occurred by a change of channel, as there is much to show that the Mokelumne river has occupied various channels; for instance, it once ran through Story's chain south of the bluff through which he tunneled; also, at the Metzer ranch, it ran in a channel north of the present one. The next change was the erosion of the present channel and the wearing away of a large portion of the bluff, leaving the flat where the town was standing in 1860, now covered with alfalfa patches, vineyards and orchards. What a period of time to contemplate! Yet all these changes are recorded in rocky bluffs around the town, in such characters that all may read who wish to. One step will lead to another until the whole will be like an open book.

After this somewhat lengthy digression, the bluffs may claim attention. The claims were very rich. In many instances the proceeds of a week's drifting would pay the whole expense of opening. The first to go down met with a great amount of water. It was feared for some time that the water could not be controlled, but when several companies began to work, the water was so reduced that it gave but little trouble. William Cook had a claim which paid a hundred dollars a week to the man. Kidd, Porter & Lyman had a claim near where Judge Palmer's residence now is, which paid even better than that. Krail, Perkins & Barnett also had a good claim in the same vicinity. The Murray brothers, Waddell brothers, Phil. Kennedy, McCarty & Hinkley, Christie, English & McIntyre, Walters, John Cook, Calvin Cole, also mined on the bluff with success, as did many others. The mines on the hill north-east of the town were also discovered about this time and many moderate fortunes were made. This place was called

CHAPARRAL HILL.

Miner Frink, afterwards member of the Assembly, Joseph Cochran, Mat. Leary, Patrick O'Keefe, Ned and Jerry McGraw, Geo. Wagner, who was Associate Judge and member of the Assembly, etc., Joe Hall, Geo. Sitzer and brother (the latter being killed in his mine), Tom Love and Joe Clark (fighting Joe), all had good claims here. The town began to grow. Restaurants, saloons, breweries, stores, hotels, and other institutions common to California mining towns, also came and flourished as long as the mines lasted. Several substantial buildings, made of fine sandstone resembling granite, with fire-proof shutters and doors, still attest the prosperity of the years of the bluff diggings. Main street, running towards the river, had the best buildings and largest stores, some of which would do credit to a city. Among these were those of J. W. D. Palmer & Co., John Cook, William Cook, Holman & Co., Nye & Co. The building of the Cooks was removed to Buena Vista some five or six years ago and the place mined out by Chinamen. Palmer & Co. were at the foot of the street nearest the river. Chinatown, also a large settlement, was between Main street and the river. From Palmer's present store to the bluff was a solid line of buildings. The bluff was also laid off into streets and was considerably built up, as was the hill north of the town. In its best days Lancha Plana had perhaps a thousand inhabitants. During this period many shafts were sunk in the hills around Lancha Plana. A line of holes were sunk northward towards the Boston ranch to connect with the French Camp lead. In some places considerable gold was found, and the blue clay above the gravel led the miners to think they had discovered the Blue Lead. The blue clay was eventually found to indicate coal. Many of the prospectors sunk through the half-charred, half-decayed piles of drift-wood and encountered noxious gases, destructive to life. In one of these shafts near the big reservoir, a man, on going down, was overcome and fell insensible to the bottom of the shaft. Men had been crushed by falling banks of earth and had met death in various ways, but the fire-damp was a new fiend, and when it was known that a man was killed with it, and that his body could not be recovered, the whole population left their work for the scene of the accident.

The shaft was about one hundred feet deep, and the pile of dirty, black, decayed vegetable material, with a disagreeable smell, indicated too well the nature of the gas which had destroyed the man's life. Dr. Tillson, a druggist, asserted that he could saturate a handkerchief with a liquid that would murder the gas innocuous. Thus assured, a man volunteered to go down slung in a rope, so that in case of being overcome, he could be hauled out before fatal results should happen. He succeeded in fastening a rope to the body, and it was hoisted to the surface. Life was of course extinct, as the body had been in the shaft some hours.

A tunnel was run under Alum peak all the way in a coal formation. A man by the name of Packard ran a tunnel into the hill in which the Waddell brothers afterwards developed a coal mine. The nature of this deposit is fully treated in the chapter on coal. Suffice it to say here that probably Lancha Plana has the largest and best deposit in the county.

Lancha Plana had its largest population about 1860. At this time the *Dispatch*, now of Jackson, was running here under the charge of Heckendorn & Payne, and was quite a lively paper. From 1865 the town gradually decayed. The population left after the working out of the bluffs; the houses fell to ruins or were removed, and for many years the voting population has been less than one hundred.

The vines and trees make a nearly successful effort to cover up the scars caused by mining.

Among the first to develop the fruit business, were A. F. Northrup and Captain Kid. The former had an orchard on the flat, where Mat Murray's claim now is, early as 1859. In 1861, it became quite a place of resort, and was the source of much profit. The extraordinary productiveness of the land, as well as the excellent quality of the fruit raised, induced a great many to embark in that business. For some miles down the river as well as at Lancha Plana, fruit has for many years formed a heavy item in the production. Kientz, Lucas, Foster, De-Bolt, Northrup, Goodings, Van Zant, Bamert and others, have places noted for fine fruit.

PUT'S BAR.

This was discovered in 1853 by Putnam, now residing at Ione. It was a "wage-claim," never having been very rich, though in 1855 to 1860 it had several hundred miners, mostly Chinamen. In an early day it was found to be good for raising watermelons, in fact, a "bonanza." Old Man Borden, as he was called, would bring them into market on the Fourth of July and get a great price for them. This was weeks earlier than Ione valley could do it, and eventually the river melons monopolized the market. A large vineyard was planted by Palmer and Woolsey below Put's Bar, but owing to the depression in the wine business, it was mostly dug up some years since. Table grapes have been found to be the most profitable. The quantity of ground suited either to the wine or table grape, is unlimited.

OVERFLOWS.

Lancha Plana and vicinity have suffered some from overflows. In 1861-62 the Mokelumne river rose nearly thirty feet, sweeping off the bridge between Lancha Plana and Poverty Bar and burying up the fine peach orchard owned by A. F. Northrup. The river took a "shear" against Poverty Bar, on the opposite side, and wore away nearly all the ground on which the town stood. Stores, dwellings, and barns, one after another, would be undermined and tumble into the stream, taking passage for the tules around Stockton. The town never recovered from the blow. Lancha being on higher ground, escaped.

THE BONITA AFFAIR.

This occurrence was on the south side of the river, and, consequently, in Calaveras county; but, as the people engaged in it were from both sides, it is properly a matter of record in this book. In 1852, during the flush times in the vicinity of Lancha Plana, the miners received notice that a greaser was to be hung; and a large number of men, perhaps a thousand, soon came together. The crime of which the Mexican boy was said to be guilty was of unmitigated atrocity. A Portuguese family in the vicinity had a beautiful little girl, four or five years of age, named Bonita, who was a general favorite with the miners.

Every one had a kind word for her, which she repaid with loving smiles. One day it was announced that she was lost. A general search was instituted, and the hills, ravines, thickets, and old shafts, in the neighborhood, were thoroughly searched. The worst fears with regard to her were realized. After some hours' search she was found in a thicket, insensible, with every appearance of having been outraged. Some way, suspicion was fastened on a Mexican boy of twenty or such a matter, who had formerly been in the employ of the father of the child. He had been seen fondling the child but a short time before her disappearance. Suspicion soon turned to accusation, and that to conviction, for the crime was of such a character that few men could remain cool enough to listen to reason. There was sense of justice enough to give the form of a trial, and a jury of twelve men was selected, ostensibly to try the accused, but really to confirm the popular verdict of *guilty*. Only a portion of the names can be recollected: A. Norton and Jefferson Tarr, of Amador county; Alfred Small, Captain Allen, and Captain Knowlton, residences unknown; and B. S. E. Williams, now in the employ of the Central Pacific Railroad at Oakland. A man by the name of Beaty volunteered to act as counsel for the accused. The jury sat around a miner's table, under a large tree, the spectators crowding around and interfering very much with the comfort and deliberations of the jury. The "Steubenville boys" were anxious to commence the hanging, and impatiently waited the taking of the testimony, and the deliberations of the jury. The voluntary attorney, Beaty, proceeded to cross-question the witnesses after the usual manner of lawyers. One of the "Steubenville boys" backed up and took what they call the rump lock on him, *i. e.*, took him by the seat of his broadcloth pants and dragged him, squirming and kicking, out of the court, leaving a vacancy in the covering of his rear part which compelled a hauling off to repair damages. This rough though comical treatment of the lawyer was not unacceptable to the jury, who were perfectly competent to question the witnesses for themselves, and had been rather annoyed by his officious conduct.

As the trial proceeded, it appeared that there was no evidence to prove the connection of the boy with the outrage; that he was asleep on a porch during the time of the absence of Bonita, though he joined in the hunt after the alarm was raised, and they brought in a verdict of "not guilty." This was not what the crowd had come for. They had come to see a hanging and meant to see it too, especially the Steubenville boys. One of their number had been killed by a Mexican, not long before, in an affray in a dance house, and they were ready to hang all greasers on the slightest excuse. The crowd soon began to boil. The larger part had been partaking freely of whisky, and were in no mood to listen to reason or be thwarted. Some of the jurors (who, by the way, had early become alarmed at the quantities of whisky which had been drunk, and resolved to drink nothing and were consequently sober), were roughly handled. Captain Knowlton was knocked down for asserting the innocence of the boy. It was now evident that a first-class riot was impending. It was hundreds maddened with whisky against dozens only of sober men. The sober men stood around the intended victim, and protested against the hanging. A proposition was made to give him a new examination before Dr. Brusie, the Justice at Winters' Bar. The doctor was a man high in the esteem of the community. This brought a few more men to the side of the jurymen. Taking advantage of an opening in the crowd, the boy was hustled into a wagon and hurried away to Winters' Bar, and an examination commenced; but the crowd soon came up, more violent than before. Though the evidence against the boy amounted to nothing, it was evident to the Justice that the only chance to save his life was to send him to jail. A powerful man by the name of Cunningham was deputized to take charge of him. It was now getting nearly night, and the rioters feared they were about to lose their prey. Some dozen or more, among whom was Tom Love, resolved to drag him out and shoot him, and with drawn pistols rushed into the crowd. The boy retreated behind the burly form of Dr. Brusie, who was thus placed in an interesting situation. He was thoroughly aroused by this time. Shaking his fist in the faces of the rioters, he shouted: "I will have you all arrested for this." Though so many pistols were pointed towards him in the effort to cover the boy, the mob had no intention of killing him. They rather admired his pluck, knowing him to be in the line of his duty, and furthermore, to have injured him would have arrayed the whole country against them. Two of the mob succeeded in getting the boy, and were leading him out—a man on each side, when the drawn pistols pointing towards them caused one of the men to let go the boy, who immediately swung to the rear of the other man who was holding him, crying to Manuel, the father of the girl: "Shoot him! shoot him!" At this point of the affair, Williams, who had from the first to the last used every effort to save the boy's life, shoved him into the crowd, so that to shoot would endanger the life of the rioters, as well as others. Cunningham now tried to get the boy away. A scuffle ensued and Cunningham was thrown to the ground. While the attention of the crowd was engaged, two men, Williams being one, rushed the boy over the bank of the river, which here was ten or twelve feet high, got him out of sight, and conducted him to a store owned by a man by the name of Waters, who concealed him in a back room. When the row over Cunningham had subsided, and the would-be executioners had time to look around, the intended victim was gone. It was now moonlight and a search was made. Dr. Brusie had deputized Waters to take the boy away to Mokelumne Hill, which he intended to do the next morning; but a party of the rioters getting on his trail, and shortly afterward entering his store, he took the boy out through a rear entrance and safely made his way with him to Mokelumne Hill, where he was detained until the session of a Grand Jury, when, no evidence appearing against him, he was set at liberty.

INDIAN WAR.

This affair occurred in the Summer of 1859. A large number of Indians, variously estimated at from three to six hundred, had been holding a fandango or war dance, on the hill north of the town. Some were from the northern part of the county, some from Calaveras, and quite a large number from Tuolumne. The festivities were mostly over, and many of the Indians had gone. An American, not much above an Indian in appearance, and, probably, far below one in character, claimed a horse which one of the Indians had in his possession. The Indian declined giving it up, alleging that he had bought it of the white man, which, on inquiry, afterwards proved to be true, or, at least, had won it in a game of cards. The white man employed Miles Huntsman, the Constable, to get the horse for him. It does not seem that the Constable had any writ to replevy the horse, or that he even made a demand for it, but went as an individual, took the horse and was leading him off, when the Indians commenced shooting arrows at him, and the claimant of the horse. Huntsman returned the fire with his revolver, which he emptied of the six shots, and then retreated; by this time all the Indians were after him in full cry, the arrows flying in clouds. He fell, pierced by several arrows, not far from the junction of the Winters and Lancha Plana road. When it was learned in the town that Miles was killed, every one that could raise a fire-arm started in the pursuit of the Indians, who commenced dispersing with all possible rapidity. The Jackson valley Indians, who had always been peaceably inclined, claimed protection at the houses of some who had employed them for washing, and other purposes, and would not join in the stampede, and probably saved their lives by so doing. Some of the Indians remaining near the camp were pursued, and one was shot near Waddell's ranch; he died game, shooting his arrows after he was shot through and through, and unable to stand on his feet. Great numbers had forded the river, and others had crossed by the bridge. These were also pursued, and as a great many shots were heard, it was supposed that numbers had been killed.

Exaggerated stories prevailed that day and evening, with regard to the number slain, but careful inquiry limits the casualties to two Indians slain—one at Waddell's ranch, and one near Campo Seco, who was shot by a sailor who was pursuing him, and who got shot in turn by the Indian—and one Indian's leg broken by a ball from the revolver of Huntsman in the beginning of the fight, and the two white men mentioned, though many valiant (?) men boasted of having slain scores. One Wallace, a Canadian (we hope he was no descendant of Sir William), was found shooting at a squaw and some little children, who, when overtaken in the pursuit, sat down and buried their faces in their laps, the Indian token of submission, which, however, did not prevent the valorous man from emptying his revolver on them. Their escape was due to his nervous feelings, or their being in a hollow below him, which caused him to over shoot. He was stopped in his shooting by Tom Love, who, though on the war-path against the Indians, had no heart for shooting squaws. The wounded Indian was taken to the office of Drs. Boarman and Schoneman, and his leg amputated, some squaws acting as nurses. He recovered, and has become a famous beggar, in fact a nuisance, thrusting his wooden leg forward everywhere as a reason for charity. It has been to him quite a fortune.

MIDNIGHT SCARE.

While the extravagant reports of numbers slain were still believed, a report got into circulation that three hundred Tuolumne Indians were nearing Lancha Plana with a determination to avenge the slaughter of the Indians; the place was to be wiped out. It was impossible to learn the origin of the rumor, but it was believed, and runners were sent to all the houses on the outskirts of the town, and the people all brought in. The stone stores were considered as the best for a defense, and as many as could be were quartered in these buildings. All the arms were collected, and put in the best condition. A military company was formed, and R. W. Palmer, who claimed some knowledge of military affairs, was put in command, Dr. Tillson being second officer. The men were drilled to charge and retreat, to act as skirmishers or advanced pickets, and were marched and countermarched until it was thought they would do to trust as soldiers. Their arms were then inspected, and the amount and quality of the ammunition ascertained. Some of the arms were woefully deficient. Tim Conway had a little pistol, but it had no lock.

"What do you expect to do with that?" says Captain Palmer.

"Oh, be jabers! won't I make it hot for the Indians when I touch it off with a match?"

He thought he was "good for one Indian, any how." Guards were stationed at the different crossings of the river, and at all points where there was a probability of being attacked. Instructions were given to the women and children to put out the lights and lie flat on the floor, when the shooting commenced—a proposition that some of the more nervous were in favor of putting into practice at once. Mrs. Boarman, who seemed to have some of her husband's coolness, or which is better some of her own, remarked that, "We might as well sit up until the Indians come." Dr. Tillson, who was but recently married, made his wife a very affecting good-bye. "My dear wife, my country calls, and I must obey. I trust that we may meet again. Good-bye, my dear." It is said that she urged him to take a frying-pan to hold before his face when the arrows began to fly. She was very proud of the Doctor's handsome face, and did not want it disfigured. The population did not all muster at the drum-beat to defend the town. John Sprague, who owned a livery stable, got out a buggy and team, took his wife and children, and started as fast as horse flesh could go, and did not stop until he reached Stockton, alarming the whole country on the way. At Poverty Bar, as Milton said of Satan after he awoke from his sleepy drench,

"He called so loud that all the hollow depths of Hell resounded."

"Turn out! Turn out, for God's sake! The Indians are murdering everybody at Lancha Plana."

Bill Morrow got out his team and buggy, and went after the Wheeler girls, and ran away with them, hardly giving them time to dress. At Comanche, Sprague gave the alarm also, and for a while confusion reigned there. Morning came at last, but no Indians, though during the day the Tuolumne chief, a venerable and dignified Indian, came back to inquire into the shooting, which had taken place after he had left the fandango. He said that if any of his young men were guilty, they should be surrendered for punishment, and two or three days afterwards, a couple of young Indians were sent up, securely tied, for the Lancha folks to do with as they thought best. The panic was over, and the two Indians were sent to Jackson for trial; but no evidence against them appearing, they were set at liberty, and thus ended the Indian war. At this day it is impossible to form any correct conclusion as to the cause of the alarm, or whether there was any cause at all. It seems so much like a burlesque that we are sometimes ready to conclude that it was a huge Irish joke, the Irish element being in the ascendency in the town at that time. If any race of people could have a bit of fun out of such a matter, it would be the Irish. Captain Palmer, who lives at Jackson, upon being questioned as to the three hundred Indians marching upon Lancha Plana, says, "Certainly; they would have attacked the town if we had not prepared to defend it." But who saw them?

ORIGIN OF PANICS.

Lest some of our friends might undervalue themselves while remembering these events, it may be well enough to make an extract from Washington Irving's "Life of Washington," page 196, volume I:—

"In the meantime the panic and confusion increased. On Sunday an express hurried into town breathless with haste and terror. The Indians, he said, were but twelve miles off; they had attacked the house of Isaac Julian; the inhabitants were flying for their lives. Washington immediately ordered the town guards to be strengthened; armed some recruits who had just arrived, and sent out two

RESIDENCE OF J. D. STOLCKEN.
VOLCANO AMADOR CO. CAL.

RESIDENCE AND RANCH OF J. E. PETTITT.
PLYMOUTH, AMADOR CO. CAL.

scouts to reconnoiter the enemy. It was a sleepless night at Winchester. Horror increased with the dawn; before the men could be paraded, a second express arrived, ten times more terrified than the former. The Indians were within four miles of town, killing and destroying all before them. He had heard the constant firing of the savages, and the shrieks of the victims. The terror of Winchester now passed all bounds. Washington put himself at the head of about forty men, militia and recruits, and pushed for the scene of carnage.

"The result is almost too ludicrous for record. The whole cause of the alarm proved to be three drunken troopers, carousing, hallooing, uttering the most unheard-of imprecations, and ever and anon firing off their pistols. Washington interrupted them in the midst of their revel and blasphemy, and conducted them prisoners to town."

This was in Virginia, and among the countrymen and neighbors of Washington.

THE BUTLER CLAIM

Was situated at the foot of the deep gorge which came out of the mountains, and was first owned by a party of negroes, hence was called the "Nigger Claim." The river was dammed and turned as usual in river claims. The channel was straight and smooth and offered no holding-place for the gold, and all of the party except Butler left the claim. The following year Butler borrowed five or six hundred dollars of Uncle Pompey, another colored man, and opened the claim a little lower down in a bend. It proved the richest piece of ground ever found in the vicinity, or even in the two counties, being a mass of gravel six or eight feet deep, literally lousy with gold. A day's work with a rocker would produce ten, twenty, thirty, and even fifty thousand dollars. Fred Westmoreland, a cool and sensible person, not liable to be excited, says he frequently saw a milk pan, the ordinary gold pan, heaping full for a day's work, so full that it could not be lifted by the rim without tearing in pieces. Some of the dirt, not so rich, was washed in a long tom. According to Tom Love a hundred dollars' worth of dust could be seen following the dirt along the sluice-box, the hands who were tending it stealing the dust by the handful. A face or breast was worked on the bed of gravel, and the gold showed from the top to the bottom, a distance of six or eight feet. At the bottom the pure dust could be gathered with a spoon. When it was known how immensely rich it was, a number of men were anxious to have a share. The former partners of Butler were hunted up and induced to sell interests in the claim. A number of suits were commenced against Butler, and some half-dozen or more lawyers engaged to share the proceeds if successful. A receiver was appointed to take charge of the claim pending the suits. Robert Bennet, known as Bob Bennet, a well-known citizen of Lancha Plana, was once appointed custodian for a day. In a few panfuls of dirt he obtained dust to the amount of two thousand two hundred dollars, which, "Damned fool that I was, I turned over to the court.

Everybody was taking and keeping all they could get." It was too much for the old man. He was taken sick with fever and shortly died. It was known by his friends that he had some eighty thousand dollars on deposit at Mokelumne Hill, as much more at Sacramento, and also immense sums buried in unknown spots. The Public Administrator took possession of the property and there was not enough found to pay a few small outstanding debts.

TOWNERVILLE,

Or "Hotel de Twelve," as it was sometimes called, was the place of operations of a man by the name of Towner, who was sent up by the San Francisco Philharmonic Society, during the copper excitement, to make a fortune for each member of the society. He did not manifest much knowledge of mineral veins, but showed uncommon skill in manipulating stocks and mines for his own pocket, the vouchers, when examined, always showing a margin for his benefit. This camp was composed largely of the Irish element, and true to their reputation, fun was the general order. When the officer, appointed in 1863 to enroll the able-bodied men in the county, made his appearance in the camp, a general scampering to the chaparral thickets took place. Scarce a man was to be seen. Several families of children were running about, but they were so well instructed that they did not know their names. The officer questioned a woman who had six little bright-eyed rascals running around, as to her husband's name. "I have naw husband." The officer ventured to remark that the circumstances of such a large family without a husband was rather unusual. "Oi, there's meny a woman has childer without a husband." A demand was then made of the superintendent for the pay-roll, which, after quite an elaborate argument, was shown, which afforded part of the requisite data. When this had been given up most of the men came back to their work. A general jollification took place, the men seeming to be well satisfied with having bothered the officer for an hour or two. After taking dinner with them, every luxury the camp afforded being put upon the table, he left with mutual good feeling. Soon after he was gone the last of the absconding men came in. Now was their time for fun. He had evaded the draft; he was to be fined five hundred dollars and sent to Alcatraz to carry sand bags for a year. A reward was to be offered for his apprehension. A file of soldiers was to be sent after him and much more to the same effect. He might yet overtake the officer and get his name put on. Pat started like a shot out of a gun; he scaled the side of the mountain like a deer, and two miles away from the camp overtook the officer, only to be informed that he had been hoaxed; that his name was already on the roll. Another person in the vicinity, a first-class wag, bothered the officer considerably by putting on a new face every time they met, invariably getting the laugh on him.

CAMP OPERA.

This was a small town or camp at the foot-hills in the south-western part of the county, and had at first a population of only twenty-five or thirty, mostly Mexicans, who worked with *batayas*, there being but little water. When the Lancaster ditch was brought in in 1853, the population swelled to several hundred. Camp Opera was known as a rough place, being a resort for desperate whites as well as Mexicans. It is said that Joaquin made it a stopping place in his frequent excursions. The first trading post was kept by a white man from Mexico, by the name of Kemp, and Ike Mansfield. Kemp was charged with stealing some specimens of gold, and was hung up by the miners, who, however, let him down before life was extinct, and let him go on condition that he should leave the country, which he did. Patrick Sculley had a trading post afterwards, and trusted out nearly his whole stock of provisions to the men, who were throwing up dirt for Winter washing. The rains not coming according to expectation, he was compelled to take the piles of dirt for pay, and realized very little for his goods. Near Camp Opera is a small graveyard, said to have been peopled with victims to whisky. Several cabins were said to have sent their whole number of occupants to this settlement. In 1857, the place maintained several stores, a dozen or more saloons, and two dance houses, and was considered a lively place. It gradually went down, and now only a few men make a living, where hundreds formerly took out the means for riot and extravagance. The ground in places was quite rich with coarse gold, which was found in gravel underlying the coal formation, though it had, in many places, been swept out towards the valley by an over-wash.

FRENCH CAMP.

This place is a mile or two south of Camp Opera, and is much like it in character. It has had rather more extensive gravel claims, however, which are probably a relic of the wash of Mokelumne river in pre-glacial times. It was occupied by a party of Frenchmen in an early day, hence the name, though afterwards mined mostly by Mexicans and Chilenos. Some coarse gold was found here. The country is threaded by small quartz veins, which are supposed to have helped to enrich the ravines and flats. In 1854, a band of Yaqui Indians, numbering forty or more, mined here. They were wild, savage looking fellows, but lived peaceably with the other miners. They were fond of whisky and cards. In 1854, an old man named Finley, who drove an ox-team to Sacramento, and frequently carried considerable gold-dust, was set upon by a Mexican, who drew a long knife and rushed upon him. Finley having no arms, ran away, taking to the brush. The Mexican came near enough to strike at him, slitting his coat and shirt open, without hurting him, however. He made his way into Ione after dark, and recovered his team the following day. About the year 1856, Joe Septen, an Italian, traced the gravel range under the hills, finding a rich deposit, taking out, sometimes, several thousand dollars a week. Many theories were advanced as to the source of the gold. Some maintained that a great river formerly ran along the foot-hills, that it could be found by sinking deep holes in the hills in the vicinity. A hundred deep shafts and numerous tunnels attest the enterprise of the miners. Some of the holes were four hundred feet deep. One company struck boldly to the west with a tunnel in the descending strata, and struck a vein of coal, without knowing what it was, however. The only paying place fell into the hands of James Moore and Thomas Barnet, who mined it successfully for nearly twenty years. It is now generally considered that these gravel deposits are the relics of a sea-shore line, which may be traced the entire length of Amador county. Scarcely a sign of the camp remains, and the country is mostly used for grazing.

COPPER CENTER.

This was quite a lively camp during the copper excitement in 1863, having several stores, saloons, and hotels, and any amount of prospective *millionaires*. The "Star of the West," a company in which Chas. Meader had an interest, was made the basis of considerable stock speculation. It never proved to be good, although drifting on the vein might have revealed paying ore. The "Bull Run," a claim on the high hill east of the town, had a narrow vein of black oxides of copper from the top down, but it was never a source of profit. A windmill on this hill was a conspicuous object for miles around. The hill is interesting to the geologist, having on its summit a bed of volcanic boulders, a relic of the vast plain existing previous to the glacial erosion. The site of Copper Center is now part of the ranch of J. Q. Horton, two or three miles east of Jackson valley.

CHAPTER XXXIII.
VOLCANO AND VICINITY.

As it Looked in '49—Georgia Claim—Sharp Mining Broker—Prof. Stowell—Agriculture—Society—A Philosopher—Hydraulic Mining—Nature of the Gravel Deposits—China Gulch—Volcano Tunnel—Former Project of Lowering the Outlet—Fires—Largest Fire—Fire of 1865—Year of Fires—Burning of Hanford's Store—Miners' Joke—Nocturnal Visitor—Murder of Beekman—Lynch Law—Stage Robberies—Miners' Library Association—Dramatic Societies—Russel's Hill—Fort John—Upper Rancheria—Aqueduct City—Centreras—Ashland—Grizzly Hill—Wheeler Diggings—Plattsburg—How Named—Hunt's Gulch—Spanish Gulch—Whisky Slide—Large Crystal Caves.

Volcano is situated on Sutter creek, twelve miles above the town of Sutter Creek, and about twelve miles north-east from the county seat. This place seems to have been discovered in 1848, as a party of Stevenson's soldiers were here about the time that another party was mining on the Mokelumne river. They built two huts on Soldiers' gulch, so named on that account, near the place afterward occupied by Hale's sash factory. The party of Mexicans, who were first in the camp in the Spring of '49, found two dead bodies in the huts, and buried them on what was afterward called graveyard hill. How these came to their death, or what became of the balance of the party, is not known. Colonel Stevenson, who resides at San Francisco, full of memories of that day, though at the advanced age of eighty-one, has no knowledge of any of his men ever having mined there. The huts, two in number, formed by setting poles endwise in the ground in the shape of an A, the whole being covered with dirt, were standing during the Summer of '49, but were torn down as the immigration came in. It is difficult to ascertain who came first in '49. The first wagon was driven in by William Wiley, now living on a ranch six miles north-east from Jackson, at the foot of tanyard hill. He was of a party of eight, from Dayton near Ottawa, Illinois, consisting of John Green and his sons, Joseph and Jesse, Erick Erickson, Torkle Erickson, Charles Ewebanks, and Jackson Beam. They had been camping on Sutter creek near the present town, and represent that place at that time as entirely vacant; not a man, not a hole even sunk there, though the works of General Sutter and his party, who mined there in 1848, might have escaped their attention or have been forgotten.

At that time, there were no houses in Volcano, except the huts built by the soldiers. Soon after the arrival of the Green party, Jacob Cook and party also came in with a wagon, and the numbers augmented until by Winter there were about one hundred persons. Some of Green's party had preceded the main body, and staked off claims where the Cross & Gordon claim and Georgia claim were afterward located.

A VIEW OF VOLCANO

As it then was, would make a great contrast with the present appearance. Standing on the point at the junction of Soldiers' gulch with Sutter creek, toward the east was a flat, terminating near the Griesbach ranch, covered with tall grass, as high as the backs of the animals feeding on it. Large white oaks, with branches drooping nearly to the ground, were scattered over the grassy plain, giving it the appearance of a cultivated and well cared for park. The clear water of the creek meandered along the meadow, rippling over the quartz gravel, warming in the sun on a sandy beach, or cooling itself in a deep hole under a shady bank, where the mountain trout of pounds in weight lurked for the coming of the unwary insect. The gray limestone formed a pleasing contrast to the dark green of the pines, which waved from all the hills around. A spring of the purest and coldest of water, large enough to turn a mill, well remembered by all the residents down to 1856, bubbled out of the rock, on which the Masonic Hall was built, near the junction of Sutter creek with the south branch. For untold ages the Indian had gathered acorns and pine-nuts, or captured the deer and other game with which the hills abounded. But there was gold in the hills, gold in the flat, in the gulches, everywhere; gold that opens the roads to influence, power, and happiness. The grassy plains have been torn up, the rich soil sluiced through the cañon, and are but unsightly piles of rock, holes of mud and stagnant water. The hills, robbed of their graceful pines, are furrowed into deep gullies, while the clear, limpid waters of the creek, turned from the channel and carried into the surrounding hills, are laden with mud, sand, and gravel, carrying destruction to the farms in the valley below. Such was and such is Volcano. It is not intended to find fault with the work done—it is probably well; for until the great balance sheet is made out, who shall say that the activity, the commercial life, the enlarging of man's powers by these operations, may not more than compensate the apparent destruction.

The Illinois party, Green & Co., went to work on the ground staked off. The surface was a reddish clay, evidently a wash from the hill to the west. About eight feet from the surface they came to the gravel, which was so rich that they could pick out gold with the fingers. They carried the dirt to the creek, some two hundred yards away, in buckets, and washed it in a rocker. They made about a hundred dollars a day to the man, some of which was coarse gold, one piece being worth over nine hundred dollars. At a depth of fifteen feet they struck a yellow clay, so tough that they could not wash it and abandoned the claim as *worked out*. The same place was worked continually for thirty years. Probably a million of dollars in all was taken out of it, or in the immediate vicinity. Some years after it was known as the Cross and Gordon claim. They had a pump, worked by several horses to keep the water out. It is said that they divided thirty thousand dollars profits at the end of a year. It was afterwards known as the

GEORGIA CLAIM.

There were sixteen shares in this company, and the stock was rated as high as three thousand dollars per share. It is said that some of the men carried away as high as thirty thousand dollars each. Various devices were used to get rid of the water. One engineer, of *questionable* ability, induced them to put in a pendulum pump, with which one man could do as much as several by the ordinary method. A gallows fifty feet high was erected, and a pine log hung in it as a pendulum. Two stout men could scarcely keep the thing swinging with no machinery or pump attached to it, and the machine was consigned to the tomb of all attempts to manufacture power out of nothing. A stout fellow was hired, for four dollars, to keep the water down during the night, which he did and had time to spare to dance away his wages at fifty cents a round, at a dance house in the vicinity. He afterwards found his way to the State prison for the theft of a watch, valued at fifty dollars, at a time that stealing fifty dollars was a capital offense. It may be also mentioned that this same fellow belonged to an organization that had agreed to *lick* any man that would work for less than four dollars a day. The claim was afterwards kept dry by a steam engine and pump. Once, in a storm, the water got the better of the engine, and rose several feet above all the works, leaving only the smoke-stack above the water. John Goodwin, a waggish fellow, proposed that a man should take some kindling and wood and dive with it down to the furnace, and start a fire. The plan was not adopted.

To return to '49. About the first of October two houses were built, one near the Odd Fellows' Hall, there being a spring in that vicinity, and also a brush and pole shanty, covered with dirt, not far away. Besides the Green company, there were Dr. Kelsey, afterwards President of the First National Bank, Stockton, also Treasurer of San Joaquin county, who was afterwards found dead in a boat on the slough; Bunnel, from Ohio; Ballard, of Illinois; Kelley, from Ohio; Jacob Cook, now living at Pine Grove; Henry Hester; Jim Gould, now at Jackson; Philip Kyle, now of San Joaquin county; Mills, P. Fellinsbee, McDowell, Rod. Stowell, and other names not remembered, making a population of about fifty. Most of the mining was in Soldiers' gulch, the dirt being carried to the creek for washing. A number of men made hand-barrows, on which they carried the dirt. Finally a cart was rigged up, and, with a yoke of cattle to draw it, readily rented for eight dollars per day.

Cook & Co., got a barrel of syrup, one of whisky, and one of vinegar, from Sacramento, and started the first store. Syrup was worth five dollars per gallon, vinegar the same, and whisky was fifty cents a drink. They also kept a few boarders, at twenty-one dollars per week.

The Indians worked in Indian gulch, hence its name. A Missourian *jumped* an Indian's hole, throwing out his tools. The Indians came around and ordered him out. Upon his refusing to leave, they drew their bows, and prepared to enforce the command. He ran away, going to Soldiers' gulch, where a party was raised to pursue and chastise the Indians. When the party came in sight, the Indians ran, and the whites fired at them, Rod. Stowell, a Texas ranger, killing one. They followed them towards Russel hill, occasionally getting sight of them and firing, though no more were killed. The following day, one of a party of three or four men, traveling from Jackson to Volcano, stopped to let his horse eat grass at the flat where Armstrong afterwards built a saw-mill. When the others of the party had got out of sight, the Indians fell upon him and killed him; stripping off his clothes, they partially concealed the body by laying it by the side of a log, and burying it with brush. Being missed, search was made, and his body discovered, the Indians having left one foot sticking out. He was buried at the graveyard hill. This murder was supposed to have been in retaliation for the killing of the Indian by Stowell.

On the approach of Winter, Green's party, with others, numbering about twenty in all, built a log cabin containing several compartments, making it compact to avoid attacks of the Indians, who were evincing some signs of hostility, stealing all the stock they could. They got it all except a mule, which was saved by locking a chain, fastened to a log by a staple and ring, around its neck. There was only one house between Volcano and Jackson, and that was on the top of tanyard hill. Two of the men in the big cabin died of scurvy during the Winter Captain Updegraff had a cabin near the Consolation or present Union House.

The rains commenced in the latter part of October. Green's party sunk a hole in Clapboard gulch at the beginning of the rainy season, and got two ounces to the pan, but were obliged to abandon the place on account of water. They afterwards mined in the heads of the gulches, and by the first of January had accumulated about seventy-five pounds of dust, worth about sixteen thousand dollars, when they abandoned the camp as *worked out*. It may be here remarked that that was the saying when the writer came in 1850. It was said in 1848 that the middle of a few little ravines paid a spade wide and no more In 1853, when the writer came to Volcano, Fred Wallace, one of the lucky miners, said the camp was worked out, and Jacob Cook, now of Pine Grove, says that in '49 they would have abandoned Volcano if their cattle had not been too poor to draw their wagon up the hill.

During the Winter, Rod. Stowell, a Texas ranger, killed Sheldon, a Missourian, by stabbing him with a long knife. The statements concerning this transaction are very conflicting. Stowell claimed that on entering the cabin, which was a kind of public house, Sheldon shut and locked the doors, making him (Stowell) a prisoner, and then drew a knife to kill him, and that he acted in pure self-defense. Jim Gould, an eye-witness, states the house was not closed; that Sheldon drew a small knife and jocularly told Stowell he was going to kill him; that the killing of Sheldon was uncalled for and wanton. It may be observed that the habit of retributive justice was gradually adopted by early miners as a kind of necessity, and had not grown into a practice at this time, or Stowell might have fared hard at the hands of the miners, who were much shocked at the affair.

In the Spring and Summer many additions were made to the population. Mann, afterwards of Jackson, opened a restaurant—meals one dollar. The Hanfords opened a store, with W. I. Morgan as manager, which stock was afterwards increased until it was the largest in the county The Fourth of July was celebrated by the reading of the Declaration by

ROBERT STEWART.

MRS. C.A. STEWART.

McDowell, who afterwards resided at Jackson. Mann got up the dinner for five dollars a head. A family camped near Grass Valley about this time, and many of the miners walked out, a distance of three or four miles, to catch a glimpse of a woman.

In the Summer of 1850, Billy Rogers, Sheriff of El Dorado, passed through Volcano with his party of men with whom he had been hunting Indians in the mountains. They purchased some beef, somewhere in the vicinity, of a man by the name of Rhodes, who, dissatisfied with the payment, followed Rogers' party into Volcano. Meeting Skaggs, one of the party, in a saloon kept by Ingalls, a dispute ensued, during which Rhodes shot Skaggs in the wrist, but while cocking his pistol for another shot, Skaggs fired, killing Rhodes. As the matter was evidently in self-defense, nothing was done about it. F. M. Whitmore, still resident in Volcano, and James L. Halsted, afterwards member of the Legislature from Santa Cruz county, came early in 1850.

The graveyard was fenced in during the Summer with shakes taken from the roof of the Green cabin, which, it seems, had been abandoned by the owners when they left the camp in January. Volcano had a kind of sleepy existence during the Summer of 1850. It was evidently waiting for an infusion of more active blood into the population. There was some carting to the creek, and Captain Graham and Biggs were enterprising enough to rig up a water-power to run rockers. It was a wheel, of the simplest construction, turned by water carried to it in spouts or troughs chopped out of logs. It would keep five or six rockers on the move, the charge being sixteen dollars per day, each. This was thought to be a great stride in mining improvements.

In the Autumn of 1850, many persons came in by the plains, and Volcano began to assume the appearance of a permanent settlement. The Jeromes, three in number, one of whom is still in Volcano came this season. Jerome, Hansen & Smith opened a store with a respectable stock of goods. The first religious service in the town was in a building of theirs, by Mr. Davidson of the ministers' company at Amador, being the same Davidson who afterwards built the church now going to ruins on the hill. Henry Jones' family was the first to settle here. He was a shrewd, sharp man, with one eye half shut; this half-closed eye, in the opinion of the people, being gifted with the remarkable quality of seeing "clean through everything." Two little children (girls) always looked neat as dolls. When they got a speck of dust on their clothes, she would wash and spank them, and put on clean dresses. Mrs. Jones had a mania for neatness, and her *puncheon* floor would not soil a lavender kid. She met a man calling to see Mr. Jones, with: "Don't come in here with your dirty feet." The red dust certainly was very annoying to a neat housekeeper. At the opening of a saloon in 1851, the good-natured, but rough miners cut a hole in the lining of the roof, chucked the owner up through, and kept him there until he came to terms.

At the election this year, when Joe Douglass and Colonel Collyer were the candidates, the friends of the former voted a rancheria of Indians.

During the Winter, portions of the graveyard were found to be rich, and the gulches were worked much deeper. It now began to be suspected, or rather learned, that the deposits of gold were enormously large, and that they extended to great depths. Henry Jones, L. McLaine, Fred Wallace, Dr. M. K. Boucher, Doctor Yeager, Ike West, —— Thomas, Ellec Hayes, and others, had claims in Soldiers' gulch that were enormously rich. A cart-load of dirt would have two hundred and fifty dollars in it. Sometimes a pan of dirt would contain five hundred dollars. Men who never in their lives had a hundred dollars, would make a thousand dollars a day. A company of Texans would make a hundred dollars each in a day, and gamble it away every night, and come to their claim in the morning *broke*. This was their way of having a good time, and gambling saloons came in for a large share of the profits. Clapboard gulch also paid good wages; though not so rich as Soldiers' gulch, the pay-dirt was easier washed and near the surface. Indian gulch was also found to be rich, especially at the head. The Welch claim had a mound of dirt a few feet across that had more than a hundred thousand dollars in it. Some of the gold was found in a tough clay that defied washing by any ordinary method. Boiling was found to disintegrate the clay, and boilers were erected in many places to steam it so that it would come to pieces. It was observed that when left in the sun to dry hard, the clay would fall to pieces, and drying yards were established where the rich dirt was dried and pounded.

A SHARP MINING BROKER.

A sharp trade was driven in claims, a thousand dollars being frequently paid for a piece of ground thirty feet square. Moore Lerty was particularly successful in selling claims. His operations were bold, and perhaps original. He would open a claim in a good vicinity, down to good-looking dirt, and then would load an old musket with gold-dust, and shoot the ground full of gold. It is said that he has been known to punish a claim with two or three hundred dollars in this way. If he did not sell the claim, he could wash the dirt, and recover the dust. He sold a claim for one thousand dollars in this way to Henry Jones, notably the sharpest man in Volcano. Jones tried the claim for a day or two before purchasing, it is said, even going into the hole at night to get the dirt, so as to be sure that he was not imposed on. The dirt was all rich, so he bought it. The fun of the matter was in the fact that the place proved to be really rich, one of the best in the camp. Another salted claim, in China gulch, also proved good, but several of his swindles coming to light, he fled before the wrath that began to manifest itself, and left the country. A number of houses of respectable appearance were built in 1851, among which were the Volcano Hotel, by G. W. Gemmil; the National, by Dr. Flint, of Flint, Bixby & Co.; the Philadelphia House, by Downs, and some others. The last two were standing until a few years since, a relic of pioneer days.

STOWELL TO THE FRONT AGAIN.

Dr. Flint, since an extensive stock raiser in some of the southern counties, under the name of Flint, Bixby & Co., went into the mountains on the line of the emigrant road, and purchased stock. In driving it down to Volcano some of it escaped, and was taken up by some miners at Fort Ann, who advertised the cattle as well as they were able at that time, as *estrays*. They refused to give them up to Flint on the proof of ownership which he presented, and a lawyer advised him to avoid the preliminary costs of a suit, a hundred dollars or more, by taking the cattle by force, so as to compel them to initiate the lawsuit if they wanted one. Flint took Rod. Stowell along as the force element; but force was something that both sides could appeal to, and a row ensued, Rod. getting a ball which made a cripple of him for life; and the two miners, wounds which were thought by the physician to be mortal. Stowell was arrested, and found guilty of murder by a jury of miners, and a resolution was passed to hang him when either of the victims should die, and a guard was set to watch him. Unexpectedly, the two miners recovered, and Stowell escaped hanging, more on account of the pleadings of his mother than any good-will the people bore him, for his name had become offensive. Clark, then Sheriff of Calaveras county, was present, but did not attempt to rescue the prisoner.

AGRICULTURE.

It could not be expected that such a piece of ground as the Volcano flat should remain idle. In 1851, it was taken up for ranches by several parties. James L. Halstead and Thomas Bryant took up the lower part next to the town, and Van Metre, and another man, the upper part. Halstead and Bryant raised potatoes in 1851, both on the main stream and on the south branch. In 1852, Henry Jones became the owner of the upper ranch, and several acres of potatoes were planted. The soil produced enormously. According to Jones, who testified to it under oath, in a suit for the restitution of water which the miners had directed from his ranch, the yield was seven hundred and fifty bushels to the acre. He had ten thousand hills which would average ten pounds to the hill, worth ten cents per pound. Tomatoes, and all kinds of vegetables, flourished with unknown luxuriance, the produce selling at enormous prices. Halstead would make twenty dollars per day carrying vegetables around in a sack. Wash. Lewis at this time was a partner in the ranch. In 1853, an enormous crop of potatoes was raised, in fact, twice the amount required for the consumption of the place. Jones succeeded in quietly disposing of his while holding out that he would not sell for less than a certain rate. Most of the others, stored in some cabins, were ruined by a hard frost, and potatoes were a white elephant. Prices for vegetables in the early years were, for green corn, one dollar per dozen; cucumbers, fifty cents; tomatoes, ten cents per pound, as also were beans (green), carrots, beets, turnips, parsnips, and cabbage; watermelons, fifty cents to one dollar each; figs, peaches, and pears, twenty-five cents each, the last being imported from Lower California. An Oregon apple, in the Winter, was worth one dollar as late as 1857.

SOCIETY.

In 1852, Colonel Madeira, John Turner, Captain Richards, Story, Else, Oaf, Addison, Shultis, Wash. Lewis, Joe Lewis, Downs, Hartram, and Stevenson, settled in the place, and there began to be society. It was now possible to get up a respectable dance by pressing into service all—mothers as well as children. Mrs. Henly, a woman who cooked at the Volcano Hotel, and Mr. Hunt were married in 1851, this being the first wedding in the town. The next was Halstead and a sister of the Lewis brothers, soon after crossing the plains; the next, John James and a daughter of Else.

Perhaps few towns could boast of as much talent *lying around loose* as Volcano. On the flat, back of the town, was a number of cabins where a cluster of intellectual lights daily discussed and solved all the abstruse questions since modestly treated upon by Spencer, Huxley, Tyndal and others. Tom Boucher had edited a magazine in Cincinnati, and disliked to come to shoveling the tough mud in which gold was found in Volcano. Some half a dozen more of the same kind felt and thought the same way. The days were too hot for work, but the cool evenings were conducive to profound thoughts, so they wore their old broadcloth into dirty gloss, read all the books and newspapers that could be found, and trusted to heaven, or the generosity of the boys, for a square meal. This constellation of stars of the first magnitude finally became scattered. The country was not advanced enough in 1853, to sustain such a society.

This does not finish the subject, however. There were others who adapted themselves to the circumstances. Ellee Hayes, who worked on the graveyard hill, was a West Pointer, and afterward a brigadier-general, and was killed in the battles of the Wilderness. Sempronius Boyd was afterward a Union general, and also member of Congress. Rufus Boyd also became a member of Congress. James T. Farley commenced his career in this place, his first cases being before Justice Stevens. Halstead, who carried vegetables on his back over the town, is now a distinguished lawyer in Santa Cruz, having filled many positions of honor and profit. S. J. K Handy,

Judge Black, Moses Tebbs, Judge Reynolds, all men of note, were residents of Volcano in early days, and have made their mark in the world. J. W. Porter, now a lawyer at Jackson, sunk the deepest hole for gravel ever seen about Volcano, and perhaps, in the county. He was as fond of going to the bottom of things while mining as when searching out his law points, and started a shaft on the clay between the limestone and slate at the head of Soldiers' gulch. He went down one hundred and fifty feet, striking the limestone at the bottom, finding gold all the way. Morris M. Estee, one of the foremost lawyers in San Francisco, was a boy here in 1855, just commencing the study of law. M. W. Gordon, since member of the Legislature, and several times County Judge, and always, from the necessity of things, a foremost man, could be seen thirty years since swinging the pick as lustily as any of the miners.

There were some prominent physicians, also Dr. Ayer, now of San Francisco, mined in Humbug gulch in an early day. Dr. Morgan, afterward of Sacramento, mined in the Soldiers' gulch, and also on the south branch. He was a wag of the first water, and generally kept some good thing in the way of fun traveling about the camp. He gave "Shirt-tail Bend" its felicitous name. It is related of him that he once sold a good claim for a very insignificant sum. When it proved a *big thing*, he was so mortified that he took himself out one side and chastised himself with a big hickory, exclaiming, between the blows, "Take that you d—n fool; sell a good claim for nothing, will you?" M. K. Boucher, a brother to Tom, the magazine writer, was a man of thorough knowledge in his profession, and of varied reading in general science. Dr. Ives, an eminent physician, helped for years to make the waters of Sutter creek a stream of mud and sand. In the chaos of social elements these men threw away the university gown and donned the hickory shirt and canvas pants of the miner. Some, discouraged by the apparent worthlessness of their scientific training in the hurly burly of this kind of life, sunk and never recovered, dying in poverty and obscurity; others, gathering wisdom from the rough experience, arose mightier than before, and pushed their way to eminence. With such elements, it is not strange that the old-time laws of ethics and religion should be swept away like cobwebs, as unsuitable for the new circumstances, and new ones established, or at least tried. We, who look at the comparatively orderly days of 1881, can scarcely form an idea of the chaos of thirty years since.

A PHILOSOPHER.

Volcano was famous, in some places at least, for other things than its gold. In 1855 a resident wrote and published a work on natural philosophy, which was sent over all the world, copies of it going to the sovereigns of Europe, the Pope of Rome, and also to the principal scientific and literary men of both continents. The work was entitled, "An Examiner into the Laws of Nature," and was written "principally for those who had not examined much into the laws of Nature, and who had not made a variety of galvanic and other experiments, and more especially for the benefit of children." It was so clear and pellucid in argument, so simple and grand in expression, that children, undoubtedly, could appreciate it as well as older persons. A few extracts from the work will give an idea of the majestic sweep of thought which characterized the work from the beginning to the end.

"From examining into the external organization surrounding the surface of the earth, we find there are fixed laws created within the physical organization to bring on periods of changes. Said changes appear approaching towards perfection. By tracking some of said changes to the present period, we learn that all animated nature has undergone changes. From said changes said cause, so existing in and among men, has been so changed from time to time that it is difficult for one to become acquainted with said cause. Man can only become acquainted with said existing poisonous cause in and among men, in all its branches, from tracing said effects from causes up to the present period, as before said. * * * I believe a general knowledge of said cause, so existing in and among men, that man will greatly diminish said cause, so existing in and among men, and the effects that must follow and from so diminishing said poison, must be beneficial results flowing therefrom. * * * So of the growth of wheat; When said grains become composed in said heads and perfected, said two statutes, male and female, remained in said grains until the next planting time, if said grains did not become decomposed from some cause. When said wheat stalks and head were perfected, the affinity which composed said stalks and head, through said liquid formation, and holds said stalks together in forms and shapes, and said stalks were strong and tough, the power of affinity existed in said stalks and heads. What effect followed said wheat stalks, heads, and grains? When said liquid circulation within said stalks and heads ceased circulating, the power of affinity commenced decreasing, and said stalks commenced losing their power and strength gradually, as said power continued diminishing within; and by the time said power had ceased holding said stalks together in form and shape, said parcels within had composed said stalks, and occupied the same position in parcels as they did when said formation commenced. Said grains, when perfected and become hard and somewhat solid, said power of affinity existed the greatest in some grains, and if left subject to said law, undergoes the same process as said stalks did."

The author in this lucid way, described the formation of the earth, seas, and mineral lodes; the decomposition of the "said water into said seas into the fine parcels they occupied previous to the formation of said seas," thus forestalling this book by more than a quarter of a century! His biography written by himself is:—

"The author of this work is in and about five feet and five inches tall; possessed of dark brownish hair and eyes; a projecting forehead over his eyes; rather flat on the top of his head; and has been subject to a crook in one of his fingers on his right hand, the second finger from the thumb, at the first joint from the nail, crooking towards the thumb; and weighs in and about one hundred and twenty pounds.

"My mother did inform me that I was born in Northampton county, and State of Pennsylvania, February 18, 1807. And it was my parents' lot to be poor, and to become a subject to the support of a large family, and I being the youngest of the family, and through said cause I did not receive a proper education in my youthful days. All the schooling I did receive at different periods, did not receive one year. Notwithstanding, in the construction, form, and shape of my physical organization, was constructed organs possessed of power to create natural impressions in my mind; although said organs was merely excited into action in my youthful days owing to said cause. * * * *

"I had a little money left. I did deposit said money into a banking house, and took a check from said banking house; and I put said check into a letter, and I put said letter into the post-office to be sent home to my friends. The next day it was reported through the city that said banking house had failed. From said report, I became aware that said money could not reach the Atlantic States. I was grieved for a few days with sorrows, but on meditating I became at once aware, if I did continue fretting and grieving for said disappointments, that I should soon destroy my mind, and I must remain hopeless of doing anything for myself or my friends. I at once came to a conclusion, as I thought that I was born so unlucky; and if I was born so unlucky there must be a sure cause for it. But why was it so, or what cause existed in me that made me so unlucky? but said cause thereof I could not tell."

He labored in the mines three years with poor success.

"In December, 1854, I became so reduced in means that I had but one suit of clothes, which I had on my body. My clothes became subject to lice, and I had to suffer the torments of said lice for five days, before I could possibly raise means to buy clean clothes; and became hungry and did go into a house and ask for something to eat, and told them that I had no money to pay for it."

FORMATION AND COMPOSITION OF THE EARTH.

"In describing the organization of the earth I shall first commence on her surface, and then penetrate into her internal parts. First, the earth has an outside crust or shell, extending from her surface towards her center, from five hundred to a thousand miles, more or less, which forms a roundish arch within her. Said outside crust or shell is of a nature like the bark of trees, and like oyster shells, and like rocks found on her surface. Said crust or shell is the hardest and most porous on and near her surface, like trees are the most solid on and in their center. Oyster shells possess the same nature. * * It is often difficult by looking small children in the face, to tell whether they are males or females; the greatest distinction only develops itself in and about the time they mature. The moon is possessed of the same organization as the earth. The moon has a current of air round his or her body, but said air does not as yet carry vapor, for this reason: The moon is not as yet matured to his or her full size; and if the moon is a female her surface cannot produce vegetation as yet. The sea is the stomach of the moon the same as the sea is the stomach of the earth, and in its organization collects matter of space in parcels possessed of all the different qualities and properties required to compose every separate and different internal and external organ of the moon, in the same order that animals and men receive into their stomachs liquid and all the vegetable ingredients for their entire organization. The different organs in said organization separate the different properties required to compose the different parts of the body, although all are mixed up at once in the stomach."

The Professor, by means of electricity, was able to detect all the phases of character.

"I happened to be at a hotel where a number of men had collected, and, by looking at said men in their faces, I soon saw that said men were possessed of different temperaments; and I looked at one man, and thought, owing to his organization, that his body must contain too much electricity, and not enough of caloric, and that his head must contain too much caloric, and not enough electricity. I asked said man if he was not a subject of exciting uneasiness at spells, and if he did not become a subject of blues or horrors during said exciting days? He said, yes. I asked him if said blues did not come on him, and he did not know how. He said, yes. Knowing the days of said periods, I referred him back to said days, and asked him if he was subject of said blues during said days? He said, yes. Knowing the days of said negative period which followed, I asked him how he felt bad in said days. He said he had in a manner become relieved of said blues."

The *Knickerbocker Magazine*, replied: "Fervently appealed to as an organ of Eastern scientific opinion (?) to make known the views of Professor Horn, we have yielded to the request. Our own views are respectfully requested. We give them freely. We do not believe there is at this moment on the globe a really scientific philosopher who can, in any respect, compare with Professor Horn." What the Pope, Queen Victoria, and the other dignitaries of Europe thought of it, is not known.

EIGHTEEN HUNDRED AND FIFTY-THREE.

This season witnessed the infusion of new energy into mining operations. It was found that many of the hills and flats, like Union flat, Mahala flat and the hills along the junction of the limestone and slate, had gold in paying quantities. Extensive canals were surveyed, and mining was put on a new basis. The Jackson Ditch Company was organized by J. C. Ham, Alonzo Platt, and, soon after, the Volcano Canal Company, by J. C. Shipman, B. F. Wheeler, M. W. Gordon, William Roberts, J. T. Farley, W. A. Eliason, and others. The waters of the different forks of Sutter creek were carried on to the hills and flats adjoining, and ground-sluicing inaugurated. Large masses of earth were now moved in a very short time. *Slickens* was born in the Winter of 1853-54, though few persons had at that time any serious idea of the future growth of the monster, else he had been strangled then and there. On the south branch, near the foot of Humbug gulch, was a nice little garden of an acre or two

FOREST LIVERY STABLE.
THOMPSON DAVIS & MERWIN LEACH, PROPS., PLYMOUTH, A

FOREST HOUSE.
T. W. EASTON, OWNER & PROP^R. PLYMOUTH, AMADOR C^O

only in extent; but the soil was rich, and produced an abundance of vegetables. An immigrant, by the name of Payne, gave all he had, about eight hundred dollars, for this little place. The miners carried a stream of water into the head of the gulch, which was but a mile in length, with a fall of three or four hundred feet, and moved a hundred thousand cubic yards of earth down the gulch, which ran a stream of mud, which, in a short time, buried the ranch several feet deep with the *slickens*, leaving only the roofs of the buildings above the ground. The mining law, the only one in force then, gave him no remedy, and he was obliged to submit to the destruction. The impetus given to mining gave a corresponding growth to the town; and brick, stone and *grout* (cement), buildings went up in a short time.

INTRODUCTION OF HYDRAULIC MINING.

Some attempts were made in the Winter of 1853-54, but the *idea* was not fully developed. The invention or use of hydraulic pressure in mining, is generally accredited to Matthewson, of Mokelumne Hill. It is uncertain who first used it in Amador county. Some persons claim it for N. W. Spaulding, near Clinton. In the Winter of 1853-54, tin pipes were used as nozzles, with a pressure of twenty to thirty feet. It was thought impossible to use a hundred feet pressure, but experiments quickly taught the miners that no practical limit was probable; and we soon find the fall increased to seventy-five, one hundred, and even one hundred and fifty feet. The hose began to be made of the heaviest canvas, with two or three thicknesses. With a pressure of one hundred and twenty-five feet, the toughest clays around the camp would melt away like snow before a driving wind, and more gold was saved than before. Experience suggested improvements, and the way was pointed out which led to the Monitor, through which five hundred inches are hurled with force sufficient to move rocks tons in weight.

At first it was customary to build pen-stocks on high and costly frames, which, not only encumbered the ground, but were liable to blow down, or fall, by the moving or sliding of the ground, near large excavations. It was learned that all the pressure was utilized by laying the hose on the ground, along the slope of the hill. Mason & Foster were the first to use iron pipe for hydraulic purposes. This was five and a quarter inches in diameter, and something over two hundred feet long, which, with canvas hose at the head, gave a pressure of nearly one hundred and fifty feet. This was sufficient to burst copper-riveted, four-inch, leather hose, and force twenty inches of water, miners' measurement, through an inch nozzle. Some difficulty was experienced in providing for the expansion and contraction of the pipe. In a hot day the pipe would expand several inches; a stream of cold water turned in would suddenly contract it, and, of course, cause a break. This was remedied by making flexible joints, and in a few weeks the "new notion," as it was termed, became a starting-point for other improvements. The pipe, constructed in March, 1856, is still in use.

THE NATURE OF THE GRAVEL DEPOSITS

Began to be studied. The fact that gulches crossing limestone ranges were generally rich below such junction, was observed, though the reasons were then, and are even now, little understood; a subsequent conclusion, that the hills adjoining must be rich, caused many good claims to be opened. The Mason & Foster claim was of this character. The point of rocks near the foot of the Boardman hill, was as unlikely a place to find gold, except for the theory referred to, as one could well find; yet the ground payed in places from the top down forty or fifty feet. There appeared to have been several channels worn through the rocks by a former river, a subsequent flow diagonally across the first channels supplying the gold, which was much rounded. As no quartz veins are found in the vicinity, the gravel containing the gold must have been moved from a considerable distance. The same deposit was traced for some miles along the limestone towards the Mokelumne river. It is now believed by many intelligent miners that these deposits are lateral *moraines* of the glacier period, the location being, to some extent, the consequence of the usual friable nature of the slates along the junction of the limestones, which favored the cutting of a channel on that line.

IN CHINA GULCH.

The Chapline boys, Story & Co., A. J. Holmes, now owner of the Northern Belle mine in Nevada, had good claims in China gulch, on the same range. The south branch, which ran parallel with this range and touching it occasionally, was also immensely rich, though the gold was distributed through gravel in places sixty or seventy feet deep. Some places, like the Green claim in Soldiers' gulch, seemed to have no bottom, but kept on paying, though no gold was found on the bed-rock—soft mud "and nothing more." S. B. Boardman worked a channel up through the South Branch flat, striking many rich pockets. This was a potato field in 1853.

The main branch of Sutter creek where Halsted, Bryant, and Henry W. Jones had their ranches, was also immensely rich in places. The Italians mostly worked this, some of whom carried away twenty-five thousand dollars each. Bed gulch, formerly called Hines gulch, along the eastern side of the limestone, has also been rich. Recently large machinery was fitted up on this place to run dirt up an inclined plane to a dump box, but the great expense of raising the dirt, and the amount of water to contend with, induced the proprietors, Moyle & Co., to change their plan of working.

VOLCANO TUNNEL.

A joint-stock company was formed, nearly all the ground on the flat on the south branch as well as on the main creek purchased, and a tunnel started.

This was a bold project; its length is two thousand three hundred and fifty feet and strikes the flat forty-two feet lower than the present outlet. The opening or dimensions are eight feet square, with a grade of two inches to the rod. In other days this would have been impracticable, but with the aid of modern machinery it has been comparatively easy. The compressor drill will strike two hundred and fifty times a minute, and requires but one man to manage it. It takes but little room, makes no mistakes, and though apparently spiteful, is more subject to control than horse, mule or man power. The tunnel was commenced four years since, working from both ends; the workmen met about the first of January, 1881. The work is estimated to have cost nearly two hundred thousand dollars. Like all projects of this kind it has its prophets of good and evil. It will take a year or more to carry the works up to Red gulch, where the heaviest pay is expected. It is to be hoped that the investment may pay.

FORMER PROJECTS FOR LOWERING THE OUTLET.

In 1854 J. W. Bicknell, William Grubb, Odell, Davis, and Harmon, ran a bed-rock flume up the Volcano cañon. The intention was to make only a straight channel for a flume and make the pay out of the waste from the claims above. This did not pay, and in 1857 Thomas and John Goodwin, Captain Richards, McGrath, and others, commenced blasting up through with the intention of lowering the outlet fifteen feet. The work was more expensive than was calculated, on account of the hardness of the rock, which would require a fresh drill every inch; and the work was abandoned by the company, and was finished by Gonan for the Amador Canal Company, to aid the sale of water. The channel was narrow and rough, and did not have the carrying capacity to convey the water in a rise, and it was found impracticable to keep it open, and was abandoned.

About the same time that the last project was started, Judge Black, a lawyer of Volcano, organized a company to tunnel through the cañon, much like the present tunnel project, making a shorter tunnel with less depth for outlet. A few hundred dollars exhausted the resources of the projectors, who, not being practical miners, could not obtain the confidence of capitalists, and the project was soon abandoned.

The largest population was in 1855, the place casting nearly one thousand two hundred votes in that season. The population was by no means permanent, having been attracted to the place by the reports of rich mines that would pay down an indefinite depth. It remained at about that figure until the Table Mountain excitement in Tuolumne county, in 1856. That drew away a great many, and the Frazer River boom a year or two later, drew off a still greater number. Notwithstanding some discoveries in quartz and many good claims which continued to pay, the place showed a steady decrease in population until about 1876, when, in consequence of some important discoveries in quartz, notably the Hanford and Downs mine, the Golden Gate and the Pioneer, a reaction set in. Volcano may now be reckoned as a promising town again. Some new buildings are being erected and old ones repaired and enlarged.

FIRES.

Volcano has had rather a large share of destruction in this way. The first large fire occurred in August, 1853, commencing in the Eureka Hotel, kept by Myers. This occurred near midnight. The house had just been built, was a two-story building, costing perhaps five or six thousand dollars. There was no bell or other means of arousing the people, and the first alarm was the shooting of revolvers like fire-crackers, the progress of the fire being so rapid that the boarders had not time to remove their personal property. The building being of a light and combustible material, was soon consumed. The flames spread north towards the National Hotel, and south towards the creek, consuming several buildings, Myers and Duke (the latter owning the store at the junction of the old streets, near the present St. George, which is on the site of the old Eureka,) being the principal losers. But for the fact that there was a deep hole of water in the vicinity, the whole town would have burned. A line of buckets was quickly formed and a stream of water poured upon the adjacent buildings, and the fire stayed.

THE LARGEST FIRE

Occurred in November, 1859. This commenced in a bakery on the corner of Consolation and Main streets, about seven o'clock in the morning. The buildings were very dry, no rain having yet fallen. The hook and ladder company, the only organized fire company, attempted to arrest it by pulling down buildings, but without success, as the ruins could not be dragged out of the way in time to keep them from taking fire, and the buildings down the street as far as Thurston's store were all consumed. During the early part of the fire it progressed towards the lower end of town against a gentle breeze from the south-east; but the wind soon freshened and drove it back on its first course, burning the buildings on the back streets that had been saved in its first movement. The Mahoney Hall and the buildings north of Consolation street were saved by covering them with wet blankets. There is no recorded list of losses obtainable, but the following are among some of the larger ones, the aggregate being about sixty thousand dollars:—

Henry Fredericks	$ 3,000
J. Goldsworthy	2,000
Elso Estate	1,000
Ballard's National House (built in 1851)	2,000
Gerhard Spohn & Co.	3,000
Fredenburg's Saloon and Bakery	4,000
B. F. George's Empire Hotel (formerly Eureka)	10,000

The losses numbered about twenty-five, the buildings being partially insured. It was late in the season, but by the first of January most of the burned district was rebuilt. The goods saved were stored in Clute's and Handford's stores until new ones were built. The town quickly recovered from this fire.

FIRE OF 1862.

This occurred in October, and commenced in the St. George Hotel (formerly Empire, Eureka), in the kitchen roof, burning the whole block on which it stood. The fire was arrested by tearing down Jerome's livery stable.

Partial list of losses:—

B. F. George	$10,000
Fridenburg's Saloon	4,000
G. Spohn & Co.	3,000

FIRE OF 1865.

This commenced in a building north of Handford's store, burning all on that side as far as Whiting's shop; all the wooden buildings across the street, including the old Volcano Hotel, built by Gemmil in 1851, several residences, also several China stores. This part of the town was the first built, and contained many old landmarks, such as Mahoney Hall, Philadelphia House,* etc. Aggregate losses, twenty-five thousand dollars.

LOYAL FLAG.

Mahony Hall had been used as an armory by the Volcano Blues, an intensely loyal company. The flag was flying when the building took fire, and in the hurry and confusion was overlooked when they were compelled to leave the building, much to the regret of the Blues. The old flag refused to burn or to fall, and waved in triumph until the tall flagstaff burned off, when it fell beyond the fire, and was saved by the boys, who made a rush for it.

YEAR OF FIRES.

The year 1868 was called the year of fires, no less than five having occurred. Most of the buildings burned had been insured when property was high, and the town prosperous. When the town began to decline, and property depreciate, the amount for which the buildings were insured was often greater than any sum for which they could be sold; hence a suspicion that the fires were not altogether accidental. The locality of the next fire was a matter of speculation based on the notoriously high insurance. The first fire was in Fabian's store, near the post-office, burning all on that side of the street to Handford's store, six or eight buildings being destroyed. By extraordinary efforts of Robert Stewart, Q. Mason, Pettis Williams, and Isaac Whitney, who stood on Goldsmith's saloon and kept it wet, the fire was prevented from crossing the street. Some of these men fought the fire so closely that their clothes were charred on them. The losses were about fifteen thousand dollars. Two or three weeks after, eleven o'clock at night, the fire broke out in a saloon and bakery, on the corner of Consolation and Main streets, owned by George Schaffer, burning all on that side down to Burleson's store. The flames reached over the store, setting fire to the next building, but by courageous efforts the fire was stayed at that point. Losses, about six thousand dollars. The next fire was in the bend south of the creek, burning Sorrocco's store, with the contents. Loss, about twelve thousand dollars. The next, two weeks after, at eleven o'clock at night, commenced in the stable belonging to Nicolas & Wendal, butchers, communicating to Fridenburg's saloon and bakery, and Mrs. Hemlin's dwelling-house. Losses, about eight thousand dollars, all insured. Fulton's dwelling-house was burned the same season. The fire commenced in the night, and was quelled, as it was thought, but soon after the house was found to be again in flames, and was soon destroyed.

HANFORD'S STORE.

One of the oldest and most expensive structures in town was burned in 1872. A kerosene lamp fell into the hatchway of the cellar, about nine o'clock in the evening, breaking in pieces and setting fire to the goods in the vicinity. The flames were extinguished and no further trouble was apprehended, but the fire had unexpectedly communicated to the extensive stock of liquors, and flames were soon bursting out all over the cellar. A few minutes' attempt to put out the flames showed the doom of the building, and the hatchway was closed down, and as many goods removed as was possible, about four thousand dollars being saved. The removal of the goods, by as many as could work, was kept up until the floor commenced sinking, when all hands were ordered out and the doors closed. Soon after this the liquors, being raised to a boiling point by the great heat in the cellar, exploded, blowing out the rear of the store and raising the floors and roof a few feet, which fell in as they settled back, and the work of destruction was completed in a few minutes.

As there are some reports in circulation to the effect that this fire was contemplated to get the insurance, the author has taken some trouble in getting the true history of the matter. The stories that the goods had been secretly removed and empty boxes substituted; that the cords on which the lamps were suspended had been arranged so as to burn off; that a train of combustibles had been laid so as to connect with the inflammable liquors, may be true, but considered in connection with the known facts, that ten thousand dollars had recently been added to the stock; that Hanford seriously risked his life in saving the goods, being almost dragged out of the building after the floor had commenced sinking; that he left his watch and many valuable relics in his desk, which were destroyed, they seemed so improb-

---

*The writer had a residence for some time in one of these hotels in 1853, and begs leave to say if they were as densely populated as in that day, the destruction of life was inevitably enormous.

able that the insurance companies did not consider them worth notice.

The careful reader will notice that the site of the present St. George, owned by A. Petty, has been burned over three times, as well as the ground adjoining on the north. The first hotel, the Eureka, was burned in August, 1853; the second, by the same name, B. F. George proprietor, in 1859; it was next called the Empire, with the same proprietor, and was burned in 1862. B. F. George seemed to rise with the necessities of the occasion and twice raised it over the ashes, each time better than before. It *still lives*, perhaps the best hotel in the county.

MINER'S JOKE.

In an early day, Major Shipman, a favorite of the public and several times a County Clerk and otherwise honored with office, was mining in a tunnel in Volcano. One day he was rather unfortunate, a piece of steel from his pick breaking off and cutting him severely over the eye. The wound was more frightful than dangerous, and it occurred to him to *sell* some of his friends. He first called on the Goodwin boys. They were alarmed at his appearance, the blood running freely over his face, and inquired how he got hurt. He told them he had a difficulty with a man by the name of Steel, whom he found in his tunnel; further inquiry elicited the fact that the man was still in the tunnel, and was likely to stay there until he was brought out. They thought it a matter of prudence to take the body out of the tunnel, for if found there it might make trouble when the miners found it out, and actually started off to remove the body, but returned when they found they were sold. They went to Jim Farley, known to be a warm friend of the Major's, and told him that Shipman had got into a serious difficulty. Farley immediately responded, and advised Shipman to leave the country, as the miners might lynch him if they got enraged, " if, as you say, every miner in the camp is a friend of Steel's." " Have you any money ?" says Farley. " None to speak of," replies Shipman. " Well," says Farley, " I have but little. I can get you two hundred dollars and a horse, and the sooner you are off the better." The Major's heart began to relent at the part he was playing, as Jim seemed to be quite alarmed, and the Major was obliged to explain. " Few and short were the prayers" Farley said, as he turned on his heel. " Oh, h——ll!"—nothing more.

PLEASANT NOCTURNAL VISITOR.

Some time in the fifties, a showman, traveling with a tame bear, gave an exhibition at Mahoney Hall. During the following night, the bear escaped from its keepers, and started out in search of adventures. The rear part of the hall opened on the roofs and balconies of several buildings, and the bear made his way into a chamber occupied by a shoemaker, by the name of Poole, an odd, irascible character, who had been made the butt of many practical jokes.

When he felt the bed-clothing being dragged off, he thought the boys were at their old tricks again. He made a grab for the intruder, and was lucky enough to catch him by the scalp. The supposed boy making no resistance, Poole's courage rose to the occasion, and he determined to light a match, and see who had so often disturbed his slumbers. Now, Poole was considered the ugliest man in all those parts, his face, according to judges of physiognomy, indicating a decided progression, or divergence, towards the catfish type of animals. When the German match flashed into a bright flame, revealing the parties to each other, their astonishment was mutual. If Poole was terrified, so was the bear, which gave a horrible howl, and tumbled out of the window with all possible dispatch.

MURDER OF BECKMAN IN 1853.

This was attended with such unmitigated atrocities that the community was thoroughly aroused. Beckman, a German, kept a store nearly in front of Mahoney Hall, and by his straightforward character had won the good opinion of all his acquaintances. One morning he did not open the store as usual. On examining the premises the rear door was found partly open, though not broken, and Beckman in his bunk alive, but speechless and insensible from a terrible cut with an ax, which had cleft his skull; the bloody ax, the broken safe or chest, in which he was known to keep his money, and other circumstances, revealing the details and motives of the murder. It was ascertained that Chris, a German, mining on Mokelumne river in company with Harry Fox, an Englishman, had been in the habit of sleeping in the store on his occasional visits to the town; that he had been there at a late hour the previous evening. Other circumstances also pointed towards Chris and Harry as the criminals.

After a fruitless search for several days it was learned that they had left the State by the emigrant road. They were afterwards recognized on a Nicaragua steamer by an eastern bound passenger, who had them apprehended and sent to California by a return vessel. On their way up, Chris threw himself overboard and was drowned. Fox was carried to Mokelumne Hill, and placed in jail to await his trial. He soon after escaped, the ten thousand dollars of which Beckman was robbed, being, possibly, a factor in the matter. The fugitives had made their way towards the East as far as Salt Lake, where, fancying they were pursued, they turned towards Mexico, and made their way towards where they were arrested.

LYNCH LAW.

The only execution in Volcano under this code occurred in November, 1854. A young man from Arkansas, by the name of Messer, had, during the Summer, evinced a very bloodthirsty spirit, evidently desirous of " getting away with his man" as soon as convenient. He wore a knife in a conspicu-

RESIDENCE & RANCH OF **J. H. HOLMAN**, NEAR PLYMOUTH, AMADOR CO. CAL.

RESIDENCE AND RANCH OF **S. C. WHEELER**, NEAR PLYMOUTH, AMADOR CO. CAL.

ous manner, and often boasted of his ability to cut his way with it. He had already crippled for life a young man by the name of Byrne, in a trifling dispute over a game of cards, and, when the final offense was committed, there was no sympathy for him.

In the Autumn of that year a family by the name of McAllister had located in the town. The father and mother were ignorant, uncultivated people, and felt rather flattered than otherwise with the numerous visits to their house, the chief attraction being a girl of perhaps fourteen years. One evening, Messer and his three or four companions were refused admission. By listening at the door they had ascertained that several men were already in the house, and Messer's companions urged him to clean them out, promising to "back him up." The door was fastened on the inside with a pin inserted in the doorpost, a usual method of securing doors in new countries. Messer, familiar with this kind of lock, succeeded in prying the pin out with the point of his knife, and, opening the door, entered with his companions. The old man expostulated with him, begged that he would make no disturbance, and it seemed, put his hand on Messer's shoulder, though without using any force, or trying to eject him. Messer drew his ever-ready knife, and, with a back-handed thrust, plunged it into the old man's bowels, completely severing the liver from the body. The wound was of course fatal, the pallor of death coming over his features in an instant. This seemed to have satisfied Messer and his companions, who left immediately. Several young men in the house witnessed the affair, which was so sudden and unexpected that they could offer no resistance. They were, apparently, too astonished to raise an alarm, and could hardly give a coherent account of the murder. Mrs. McAllister raised the neighbors by yelling at the top of her voice: "——, ——, jiminy, send for a doctor!" with a persistency that under less serious circumstances would have been quite laughable.

A general pursuit of the parties commenced, and Messer was apprehended in a short time and taken past the scene of the murder. He was now bellowing like a baby, his courage having failed at the sight of danger. The crowd passed over the bridge toward the town. At the Miners' restaurant they halted a moment. In answer to the question—"What shall we do with him?" the cry was "Hang him! hang him!" A proposition was made to do something for the widow, but no response was made. Up through the main street, every house helping to swell the stream, no voices, no sound but the dull tramp, tramp of hundreds of feet, the crowd made their way. At Consolation street they turned toward the Methodist church. Up that street, no one knew whither, to the foot of the hill, thence to the left, halting in a ravine to the north of the church where there was a leaning oak tree, the top of which was broken off twenty or thirty feet from the ground.

There was no consultation, no form of a trial; everything seemed to be done by common consent. Here an unsuccessful attempt was made, by Constable Scott, to arrest the lynching. Messer seemed to have partially recovered his self-command, gave some directions as to the disposal of his property, and the payment of a few dollars he was owing in the town. His last words were to this effect: "If I was right in killing him, God will forgive me; if I am wrong, I hope God will punish him," evidently referring to himself. There was so little noise that persons sleeping in houses a little way off heard nothing of the affair, and were much astonished, when they awoke in the morning, at seeing a dead man hanging so near them. There was no frantic excitement or rage, usually manifested on such occasions. The hanging seemed a foregone conclusion from the start.

Had this murder been committed by an influential man a quarter of a century later, a plea of hereditary insanity would probably have saved him from execution or any other serious punishment. Messer was not insane; he was simply acting his ideal of manhood. He had been educated in that way; was taught that a gentleman must "get away with his man." Though the murder was of the most atrocious character, without the motive of anger, revenge or lust, purely wanton, some might say thoughtless, he placed himself on trial before his God. "If I was right in killing him God will forgive me. If I was wrong I hope he will punish me."

Men ought not to be punished for acting up to their instincts or convictions. Crime is the result of moral and physical infirmities, modified by education and circumstances, and to a great extent, is inevitable. Punishment is an absurdity, an impossibility. It does not restore the victim to his family or to society. The right to take the life of a criminal must rest on the broader ground of self-protection: that whether from choice or necessity, his further existence is not consistent with the security of life and property, and must cease. The present insecurity of life does not result so much from the want of law as from its refinements. The upper, not the lower classes, are now setting law at defiance.

Substantial justice had been done without the forms or delays of the law. No friends claiming the body for burial, it was taken by the doctors and *skeletonized*, some of the attending circumstances being revolting. Portions of the body were said to have been devoured by hogs, which had discovered the pool of water into which the remains were placed to disintegrate the flesh from the bones. The skeleton was used to illustrate public lectures on anatomy and physiology. All the circumstances were such as to strike those criminally inclined with terror, if such a thing were possible. Mark the result. Among the most prominent of the volunteer executioners were Dr. Goodwin, who was shot in a row at Snelling's ranch, Si Maynard, who was hanged by a mob for stealing cattle, and Johnson, who was hanged in Sierra county for murder. Mansur, who assisted, died shortly afterwards of consumption. These results are not related as retributive justice, but to show the frequent inutility of lynch law as a means of reform, or deterring others from committing crime. It often happens that in new countries like California crime precedes the organization of courts, compelling the community to fall back on the first principles of government, by organizing in self-defense; but when it is necessary to anticipate courts, or supplement their inefficient authority by "Judge Lynch's" code, it should be done by those whose motives in undertaking it are unquestionable; who look upon the proceeding as a deplorable necessity, rather than as an act of vengeance.

STAGE ROBBERIES.

This place has become noted for the stage robberies occurring in the vicinity. The hill was usually selected for the operation, the early morning hour at which the stage started for Sacramento also favoring the robbers. The largest robbery occurred May 1, 1872. A suspicion that an attack was contemplated caused the agent of the express company to send through a corresponding weight of rocks for several days, which went without disturbance. One morning the bullion, worth about ten thousand dollars, was started. It was thought that no one had a knowledge of the affair, but when near the top of the hill the driver, Dick Hipkins, was confronted by two masked men with revolvers, who ordered him to dismount, which he did. One of the men mounted the box, took the lines and drove the team a short distance into the timber where the horses were unhitched from the coach. The men then proceeded to detach the treasure box from the wagon, after which it was broken open with an ax. After having taken out the treasure, the robbers told Hipkins to proceed on his way, the robbers taking the road to Volcano. John N. Boardman was arrested for the robbery, tried and acquitted. Several prominent men were suspected, but no other arrests were made. The express agency was disestablished and the shippers of dust have experienced much inconvenience in consequence.

MINERS' LIBRARY ASSOCIATION.

Such a gathering of professional and literary men was sure to ripen into action. Some attempts were made by Robert Beth as early as 1850 to bring about a public library. Some of the merchants bought a stock of novels and light reading, which was loaned at ten cents a volume. The first organized effort to get reading matter was in the Autumn of 1854, when the "Miners' Library Association" was formed, with admission fees of one dollar, and monthly dues of twenty-five cents. Weekly meetings were held to discuss social, political, and scientific questions. Such talent as was obtainable was engaged for occasional lectures. The Baptist church, the building now going to ruin, was frequently filled with attentive and interested hearers. When a hundred dollars had been accumulated a list of books was ordered, and a respectable nucleus of a library formed. The institution ran smoothly for three or four months, when a series of revival meetings, held at the Methodist church, drew away the audience. The society made the mistake of neglecting to incorporate, and when the weekly meetings began to lose their interest, a rumor got into circulation that the society was broken up, whereupon a *grab* was made for the books, and the Library Association dissolved in a day or two, never to recover, as there was no power to compel restitution of books. Among the founders of this society, were John King, R. C. Jacobs, I. W. Whitney, Robert Stewart, Henry C. Foster, Charles, William, and Bartholomew Chapline, James Whitesides, J. D. Mason and others.

DRAMATIC SOCIETIES.

The Volcano Thespian Society was formed in the Winter of 1854-55. Many of the promoters of the defunct Library Association, threw their energies into this institution, and for a few months gave occasional exhibitions. "The Golden Farmer" was played, with James Whitesides for the farmer; R. C. Jacobs, for Elizabeth; Dr. Gibson, now of Stockton, for Jimmy Twitcher; other parts forgotten. James Rile was scene-painter. He was mining in Humbug gulch, and gave the society the benefit of his skill as a scenic painter, which was considerable, whenever a man was put in his place in the mine. Two young boys, by the name of Geo. Y. and Louis Miller, now stalwart, bearded men in San Francisco, made two handsome actresses. This institution gave the school a benefit or two, ran a few months until the evenings got too short for work, and collapsed. A wandering theatrical party afterwards borrowed the small property, and left without remembering to return it.

About the time this society started, another put in appearance. The second one embraced some musical talent, and played for a few times; once for the benefit of the Baptist church. For the "benefit of the Baptist church," became a by-word; the gamblers opened their games for the "benefit of the Baptist church."

RUSSELL'S HILL.

This is a gravel deposit on the line of the Volcano ridge, and probably belongs to the same range as Upper Rancheria. It was left in the great glacial erosion which cut out the valleys north of Volcano. It was good for an ounce a day in early time.

FORT JOHN

Is a limestone deposit similar to Volcano, which place it bid fair to rival in 1850. Two or three men (names forgotten) who first mined here in '49, were killed by the Indians. P. Y. Cool, Thomas Rickey, and James, his son, mined here in 1850, previous to working quartz in Amador. They were instrumental in building a church and school-house, perhaps the first in the county. The deposits were neither extensive nor rich, and the place soon fell in the rear. In 1856 it contained a little one-horse store, with a dozen or more miners, who were said by those who visited the place, to be always waiting for water to come or go down, amusing themselves in the meantime with bean-poker.

In 1850 several hundred miners made good pay on the flat; now one man, who has been there all these long years, is the sole inhabitant. He seems to have staid to point out the site of the former town, and relate to occasional visitors the glories of the ancient days. He remembers where and when every event of note transpired.

UPPER RANCHERIA.

This is a continuation of the Russell's hill lead, some of the gravel running under the deep lava bed in the vicinity. In 1856 to 1860 there were fifty or sixty miners here. Some fine structures, built of the indurated lava, from the adjoining hills, are still standing, relics of the former glory of the town. The place is famous as the former residence of Jacob Emminger, a Justice of the Peace, who sentenced a Chinaman to *jail for life* for stealing chickens. Upon being questioned about the matter, Jake denied the impeachment, but finally justified the matter by saying, "If I had not done so the crowd would have hung the poor fellow." Sam Lorce now keeps a lonely watch over the site of the ancient town.

AQUEDUCT CITY

Is at the head of Grass valley, which was taken up in 1850 by James Dolan, as a ranch. It was afterwards sold to Thompson and Perrin, who fenced it and cut the grass for hay, which was worth sixty-five to one hundred dollars per ton. Mines were discovered near the head of the valley in 1850. It was first worked by a party of four or five, Braden & Co., who made a secret of the discovery, but not long, for one morning James Henry and party appeared and staked off claims. The new comers had not yet built cabins, and when the rain came, in September, they were sleeping in blankets on the ground. They got up and sat out the night astride of a log, with the blankets over their heads. There was no more rain of any account until Spring. The Huet claim was the richest in the camp. French gulch, coming into the valley near Ham's Hotel, was very rich. One man carried away fifty thousand dollars from it. Sleeper, Lucas, and Bisbee (Bob, now of Sutter Creek), had claims that would pay an ounce each for two or three hours' work. When they had made this, the day's work was finished, and they put on white shirts and mounted their horses for a ride to Jackson, or some other town.

The water by the Ham ditch passed the Mokelumne divide at this place. An aqueduct one hundred and thirty feet high, carrying the water to the next ridge, gave name to the place, which, about the time of the coming of the water, had several hundred inhabitants, three hotels, two livery stables, three stores for general merchandise, one drug store, besides numerous saloons. The first store was kept by Henry, Graham & Biggs.

The old residents of the place remember the sensation created by the two tall Bell sisters, who rode like centaurs, whenever they appeared on horseback. The livery stables had several *pairs* of fine saddle horses, which were much in quest at that time. Dr. Crawford and the Johnston brothers had a saw-mill there, with quite a history. It was formerly located in El Dorado county; some kind of attachment being laid on it, or expected, it was determined to move it into Amador county. The removal had to be done between Saturday night and Sunday morning, to prevent a legal process for injunction. The engineer, Underwood, afterwards of Amador, ran the mill as usual, but had loosened every bolt and nut possible, and, when twelve o'clock came, the mill was shut down, dismembered and loaded on a wagon, within an hour, the boilers hot, and the furnace fires still glowing. Sunday morning found the place deserted, which caused the remark that Dr. Crawford, who planned the elopement, carried off a saw-mill while it was running. Before midnight it was in Amador county, beyond the reach of attachment.

The gulches were soon worked out, and the hill diggings did not prove rich or permanent. The place now has a few families, one store, and one hotel. Captain Ham, the engineer and financier of the Ham ditch, resides here. Forty years of active life has not dulled his capacity for gigantic projects, one of his especial favorites being a canal which would transport the entire amount of wood and lumber in the Sierras to San Francisco.

POTATO DIET.

In the Winter of 1852–53, Major Shipman, Albert and Carter Land, had been prospecting a quartz vein near Grass Valley, boarding at Thompson & Perrin's, at twenty-one dollars per week. When the roads got so bad that they could not get provisions at all, Thompson & Perrin were obliged to close their house. The Major had cultivated a small patch in potatoes the Summer before, and the party now started in on roast potatoes. Jim Henry, Ike Eastman, Jake Cook, and other boys at Grass Valley, being out of provisions also, were invited in, and they all lived like kings on roast potatoes until the storm was over, and the roads got so that better food could be obtained.

CONTRERAS.

Twenty-five years ago a party of Mexicans, led by Pablo Contreras, who seems to have been a man of much education and influence, was mining at this place, which was a few miles east from Volcano. There were numerous small veins of quartz, from three inches to eighteen inches in width. They were pocket veins, a thousand dollars being often found in a small space. A large number of *arastras* were running, three of them by water-power. There were several veins in the vicinity which were worked by larger companies. The Belding vein, worked by C. C. Belding of Sutter Creek, changed owners several times, at twenty thousand dollars. The Thierkauf vein was also rich, some good crushings being made. The wall rocks were mostly granite, and the veins were soon exhausted. The system belongs to the West Point range, the Mace veins being a continuation of the same. The gold in some of these veins is so fine as to be unappreciable by the ordinary processes of working. Careful panning of the decayed quartz will sometimes show a thousand microscopic specks of gold, as fine as bronze, which will float off on the water. Tavernier, the noted caricaturist and painter, operated here for a while. Contreras had a family of very pretty and virtuous girls, who fascinated a score of young Americans, some of whom followed the family back to Mexico. The place had three or four hundred inhabitants at one time, and was worked for some years. Very little work is being done at present.

ASHLAND, GRIZZLY HILL, AND WHEELER'S DIGGINGS.

These are names of once flourishing mining camps, to the northward of the quartz veins last mentioned, on the different branches of Sutter creek. Ashland was worked by Colonel Bicknell and party. It sometimes paid as high as two ounces per day. Wheeler's diggings, on the north fork, were not quite so rich, but furnished remunerative employment some years for quite a number of men. In 1869, Mr. H. Parlin, James Hall, and —— Halsey, experienced miners, traced the pay into the hills or ridges between the hills, and in 1876, succeeded in carrying a stream of water on to the hill, developing probably the best paying gravel mines in the county at the present time. James Hall, the present owner, has a tract of twenty acres, which will probably put him in easy circumstances for life. A ditch from the middle fork of Sutter creek, which runs nearly the whole season, supplies him with water; the elevation above the hill gives plenty of fall for tailings, and the quantity of ground, twenty acres, ensures a life-long and profitable job.

The deposit seems of an alluvial character, the stream running transversely to the present streams. The pebbles are little rounded, the boulders of curious looking quartz, seen in many places lying near the veins of which they were once a part, showing that the stream or river was insignificant, running at a small depression.

PLATSBURG.

Or Prospect hill, one of the places that *was*, the former site being overgrown with pine trees, so thick as to deter even a rabbit from attempting to explore it, was in the vicinity of Foster's ranch, Hunt's gulch, Spanish gulch, and Whisky flat or Karney's diggings, belonging to the same cluster of gold deposits.

Plattsburg has strong indications of being the bed of a river, the boulders being large and well rounded. When discovered it was a flat of a few acres in extent, having four or five feet of gravel under two or three feet of red soil. In 1854 and '55, it had forty or fifty miners, but was soon worked out and deserted. When the place was discovered, Colonel Platt and Judge Gale, two lawyers, intent on immortalizing their names, played a game of euchre to see whether it should be called Plattsburg or Galesburg; the former winning, and giving it his name.

HUNT'S GULCH

Heads on the Plattsburg hill, a man by the name of Hunt working it at an early day. One day when Hunt was in Jackson he was informed by Evans, the gentlemanly proprietor of the Louisiana House, that a lady in the parlor wished to see him. As he was young and rather good looking, the request was not surprising, and he responded with alacrity. The lady had arrived that morning from the East, on her way to her husband, whose name was Steven Hunt, of Volcano. On inquiring for him she was much pleased to learn that he was in the house at the time. Evans was not aware that Hunt had no wife, and thought to give him an agreeable surprise. She clasped her arms around Hunt's neck, kissed him, and sunk her face, bathed with tears of joy, into his bosom, as any faithful wife would naturally do after a separation of years. After reposing there a moment she took a second and better look at his face and starting back with a look of about equal parts of alarm and indignation, exclaimed, "You are not my husband!" "No," says he, "unfortunately for me, I am not." A little inquiry elicited the fact that the true Steven Hunt was in Volcano, unconscious of the proximity of his wife. As the interested parties were sensible persons, there was no shooting or other display of foolishness.

Spanish gulch emptied into the south branch near Hunt's gulch. It was worked in 1850 by James L. Halstead, who has been referred to before. It was said to be good at first but was abandoned in a year or two.

Whisky Slide, where Andy Karney and Charlie Ackerly made a *raise*, was a flat near Spanish gulch, and probably was once the channel. It was good for an ounce a day. It was discovered about 1855 by a rather ludicrous accident. The lucky discoverers were in the habit of returning to their cabin late at night and in an inebriated condition. On one of these trips one of the party tumbled into a prospect hole. It was not deep enough to seriously injure him, but too deep for him to climb out without aid. While the others were gone for ropes and a light, he took a notion to try some dirt from the bottom, and refused to come out until they gave him the means of getting a pan of dirt. When it was washed the next morning it proved to be rich, and was the starting point for several fortunes.

RESIDENCE, HOTEL AND RANCH OF MRS. MARGARET FOSTER,
AMADOR WAGON ROAD, 6 MILES FROM VOLCANO, AMADOR, CO. CAL.

RANCH AND RESIDENCE OF CHARLES BAMERT,
NEAR MOKELUMNE RIVER, TP. No. 2, AMADOR, CO. CAL.

CRYSTALS.

Fine specimens of crystallized quartz, of a smoky color by transmitted light, and black by reflected light, are found near Volcano. Mr. Williams, near Peter Dentzler's house, has some fine specimens five or six inches in diameter. Some of these show the lines of deposit and are valuable for illustrating the processes of crystallization.

CAVES.

There are many caves around Volcano. Several of the smaller ones were discovered at an early day, but the large one was not explored until 1854. This is supposed to underlie the hill south of Stony Point. E. Samanis, with a party, is believed to have been the first to enter it. The opening, about eighteen inches across, is near the top of the hill, and descends rather precipitously to the water level, one hundred and fifty feet below, the distance on the slope being about two hundred. The first thorough exploration was made in the Summer of 1854 by a party of which the writer was one, the previous explorers having gone down but a short distance. The long rope was fastened to the rock at the surface, and the coil thrown forward and downward into the darkness. Several pounds of candles were taken along and placed in the soft clay, which formed the sloping floor of the cavern. The advanced man of the party, not having a realizing sense of the abyss yawning below him, stood without fear on the steep slope, where a slip of the foot would have sent him sliding to the bottom. As the descent progressed and the cave became lighted up, a vaulted chamber, large enough to contain the largest trees, came to view. Stalactites, or rather crystals of rhomboidal spar, sparkled like diamonds all over the roof. As the size of the cavern, and the depth and almost perpendicular descent, became apparent by the lighted candles a hundred feet below all except the advanced portion of the party beat a retreat, the descent looking too dangerous. The courage of the first to descend was rather a matter of unconsciousness of danger, than a knowledge of the situation and a willingness to face it, as, when coming up, the at first fearless persons clung with a nervous feeling to the rope, nor dared to take a full breath until they were well on their feet on the ground above. About one hundred feet from the surface a small space was found which was comparatively level, affording a resting-place. From this place the cavern seemed to branch off in several directions; towards the north was a narrow fissure, or nearly vertical opening, corresponding in pitch and direction to the lines of cleavage of the country rock, and might have been, under other and more favorable circumstances, the location of a quartz vein; in fact, the capping or roof of this fissure is a kind of jasper or ferruginous quartz. On the south side there was a perpendicular descent of perhaps twenty feet, and then another comparatively level place. So far the bottom or floor was soft clay, which,

apparently, had been washed in from the surface of the ground through the opening; but they now found the true floor, which seemed of infinitely small stalagmites, fine as snow, which crunched under the foot like frost. This formation was all destroyed in a short time by the tramping over it of numerous visitors. Some thirty or forty feet below this second flat or floor was the lake, a pool of clear water, sixty or eighty feet across, which is, probably, the source of supply for the numerous cool springs in the vicinity. This last floor seemed to rest on numerous pillars of rhomboidal spar, which were originally stalactites, or pendant formations from the roof, which had grown by continual precipitation of calcareous matter, until they united with the floor. Some of these columns were round, some thin and slab-like, the latter being the prevailing type. When struck they would give forth a peculiar bell-like, musical sound, each column having a different note, which reverberated through the cave like the sounds of an organ in a cathedral. One of these columns, a thin slab, perhaps three feet wide, one-fourth as thick, and fifteen feet high, had a peculiarly rich tone. In trying to see how loud it could be made to sound it was cracked, and its voice forever silenced. This act of vandalism has been, and always will be, a source of regret, though the other columns, in consequence of repeated hammerings by subsequent visitors, were soon silenced and have given forth no song for a quarter of a century. The side caves were full of the beveled crystallizations, which, when broken off, fell to the bottom of the cave with a tinkling, jingling sound, as of a hundred tiny silver bells. The last-mentioned crystals, though formed of rhomboid spar, stood out from the walls in every conceivable direction, turning and bending into many shapes, according to the law of obtuse angles, prevailing with that variety of crystals. It is thought by some naturalists that they result from vapor containing lime, as it is impossible for them to have been formed from dripping water, like stalactites or stalagmites.

Soon after the discovery of the cave the entrance was enlarged, for the purpose of putting a stairway down, and making it a place of public resort. The project was abandoned, and in a short time the numerous visitors despoiled the cave of all the spar; and visitors of the present day can form no idea of its splendor twenty-five years ago. The other smaller caves had no curiosities like the large one. It is believed that the hill north of Volcano also contains a large cavern, as in many places water runs down that does not again make its appearance at the surface. The name of Volcano was given to the place, under the impression that the masses of chalcedony, carnelian, cacholong, onyx, and jasper, were of volcanic origin. Many beautiful specimens have been carried away, some of which were cut into jewelry. The composition is of silicia, lime, red oxide of iron, and perhaps other minerals in minute quantities, the color varying from translucent to milky white, or flesh color, as the minerals named, predominate in the mixture. They have no value except as curiosities. The same formations on a smaller scale, may be found in many other places, especially in the serpentine range in the western portion of the county. Pebbles of various kinds of agate, cut away from these ranges during the glacial era, may be found on the plains west of the county line. They have the same character and origin as the famous Pescadero pebbles found on the sea-beach near Santa Cruz.

CHAPTER XXXIV.
NORTH-WESTERN PART OF THE COUNTY.

Sutter Creek—First Foundry—Knight's Foundry and Machine Shop—Planing Mill—Society at Sutter Creek—Schools and School-Houses—Shipment of Gold—Fires—Incorporation—Future Prospects—Amador—Ministers—Placer Mines—Gold of Lower Rancheria—Oleta—Execution by Lynch Law—Killing of Carter by Doctor Unkles—Home Rule—Fatal Explosion—Bad Case of Erysipelas—Lynch Law Vetoed—The Famous Safe Robbery—First School—Churches—Present Mining Prospect—Sewell's Addition—Cosumnes River—Amusing account of Mining Machinery—Famous Lynching Affair at Jamison's Ranch.

Though General Sutter and his party mined here in 1848, there was little done until the discovery of quartz in 1851. In October, 1849, persons passing through could see no evidence of any mining. There was a small, cloth tent at the crossing of the creek, owned by a man by the name of Jackson, from Oregon, where meat, whisky, and some provisions, were sold. A few miners gathered here on Sundays when the weather did not permit them to go to Drytown or Jackson. After the discovery of the quartz mines on the north side of the creek, the gulches and flats began to be worked. The placers were only moderately rich. Perhaps the streams making off of Tucker hill were as good as any. A report is current that a twenty-five pound lump was found in the ravine below the Lincoln & Mahoney mills, but it cannot be traced to any reliable source. The gulch below the Hayward mine was only moderately rich. Indeed, it seems quite certain that a vein which has enriched many gulches has nothing left for milling purposes. Gopher flat, above the town, was worked mostly by Spaniards, by drifting from one hole to another, only a few feet below the surface. Sometimes the dirt was carted to Sutter creek to be washed. The hills east of the town are gravel deposits of the *pliocene* period. Though worked in many places, they were only moderately rich. They are interesting as showing the course of the streams in past ages. One may still trace the directions by the bodies of gravel left in many places. The divide between Amador and Sutter is full of interesting points, showing a river running towards the west before the close of the volcanic period. Four or five miles west of Sutter this stream seems to have terminated in a precipitous fall, boulders of many tons in weight, some of granite and others of volcanic matter, being piled in a confused mass. Some few places along this line have been mined out, but, as in nearly all the rivers of the volcanic period, the irruptions of lava kept the stream from wearing away the beds of auriferous slates, the sources of the river gold. On the south side of Sutter creek is the largest stream of volcanic gravel in the county, which may be traced from Prospect Rock twenty-five miles east of Volcano, to some miles west of Ione, where it spread out into the ocean. This channel is remarkable as having at one time in the volcanic period a body of hot lava running from the summit to the sea. What a sight for the primeval man, which, according to Whitney, must have lived here at that time.

The mining here at first was of a primitive order, the rocker being the main reliance for separating the gold. In the Spring of 1850, a great improvement was introduced. Jim Wheeler, Boz. Goodrich, and Dick Moulton, brought a long tom, which was first used in the northern mines, from Sacramento. It was a daring innovation, and, like most new things, was unmercifully ridiculed by the conservative portion of the miners. It was only seven feet long, and sixteen inches wide. Small as it was, it effected a great saving of labor, and was soon brought into general use, though a year later it was displaced by the string of sluices, which enabled men to make wages out of still poorer dirt. After the discovery of the quartz mines, the energy of the best men of the camp was turned in that direction, and placer mining became a minor interest. The development of quartz mining, which built up the most flourishing town in Amador county, that annually sent a million or more of dollars into the general circulation, is described in another chapter.

The first families in the place were those of McIntyre, Stewart, Jones, Tucker, Rice, and Hanford. E. B. McIntyre's family, as well as Levi Hanford's, came in 1852. Some of these families were from the frontier, and others from the East, and the Yankees, and the extreme southerners and westerners, met here for the first time. Thirty years after, when these streams are flowing in the same channel, marriage and intermarriage having obliterated nearly every distinction, the aversion which they entertained towards each other has become the subject of much merriment.

Mrs. McIntyre tried to start a Sunday-school, but could get only three or four children to attend. Mr. Barlow, from Drytown, acted as Superintendent, Mr. Davidson and Mr. Glover, of the Amador quartz mines, preached occasionally, as did I. B. Fish, who was stationed at Mokelumne Hill. The preaching was usually in the school-room; sometimes in an unfinished room in Harding's Hotel. Money was raised to buy a Sunday-school library. Robert McLellan is remembered as having donated five dollars. "Dick's Works" were among the books bought.

NORTH-WESTERN PART OF THE COUNTY.   219

The first church was built in 1860, and dedicated in 1863 by Doctor Thomas, who was slain by the Modocs. This church has been occupied by the Methodists since that time.

Mrs. Rice, now living here, is remembered as the first person who wore a *store bonnet* to meeting. This, with blue silk gloves and some other finery recently imported from the East, was quite enough to distract the less fortunate sisters, and turn their thoughts away from holy things.

The first school was taught by N. Harding, who received seventy-five dollars per month. This was raised mostly by subscription. Judge Carter, now of Ione, who happened to be present, generously donated ten dollars toward it. Mr. Harding sent one child, McIntyre one, Stewart two, Mrs. Jones one, others to the number of twelve in all. Sutter Creek since has been noted for its interest in educational matters. E. B. McIntyre was the first County Superintendent. He remembers that it was extremely difficult to get the trustees to report to him, the law permitting no appropriation of money without an annual report from the districts.

The first wedding was in the boarding-house of the quartz mine (afterwards the Lincoln mine). The bridegroom was named —— Dick; the bride was a girl living with the family that did the cooking. The town boys honored them with a serenade and *charivari*. Soon afterwards Allen Tibbetts was married to Letitia Tucker; and Dwight Crandall, afterwards State Senator, to Mary Jones.

FIRST FOUNDRY.

Soon after the commencement of quartz mining, the want of a machine shop and foundry induced a small beginning in this way at the lower end of the town near the water-mill of the Lincoln mine. As it was a small affair and did not answer the purpose, it was removed to the present site, and enlarged so that the smaller parts of the quartz mills, such as dies, stamps, etc., could be cast, utilizing the worn-out castings. Frank Tibbetts was the proprietor for many years. The machine shops and melting capacity have been enlarged until now almost any required machinery can be put up, the cupola having a capacity of four tons. They have several large lathes, some of which have a swing of fourteen feet. The works are run by water-power. Water-wheels are a specialty with them. The one used by the Empire mill, at Plymouth, made by them, runs eighty stamps, with a head of six hundred inches at a pressure of sixty feet. Dan. Donnelly & Co. own the works. Several of the best mills in Amador and the adjoining counties, have been constructed by them. About one million pounds of castings are turned out annually.

KNIGHT'S FOUNDRY AND MACHINE SHOP.

This was established in 1873 to construct water-wheels of a peculiar character, calculated to utilize small heads of water at a high pressure. Though no new principle was discovered, the adaptation of old ones to new conditions has all the merit of a discovery. A small wheel, seven or eight feet in diameter, looking much like a cart-wheel with a rim of tea-cups, drives a quartz mill of eighty stamps, with all the necessary shaking tables and amalgamators. The opening through which the water strikes the wheel, contains only two and a quarter square inches, and the gate to this is so arranged that it may be reduced to any desired size, running half or a quarter of the stamps, keeping the tube or pipe from which the power is derived, full, thus utilizing the whole pressure. The Amador mill is driven by a wheel of this kind, utilizing the five hundred feet full from the Amador canal to the mill. The wheels are in use throughout this State, Nevada, Arizona, and Utah. The works have been enlarged until any sized machinery needed in mining can be constructed. Seven to ten tons a week is the usual amount of melting. They have about thirty thousand dollars invested in the foundry and machine shops.

PLANING MILL.

The Walkmeister brothers have started a planing mill near Sutter Creek, where all kinds of fine work is done equal to the best of city work. The machinery is driven by water-power, the water being used again by the miners at Amador.

SOCIETY AT SUTTER CREEK.

Though a large portion of the population is made up of a class that is not noted for refinement or culture, there has always been a nucleus of highly cultivated and refined people, as any one would perceive who took the pains to stroll around the town. Among the many families who have in times past contributed to this result may be mentioned the families Dunlap, Wildman, Belding, Hanford, Downs, Sewart, McIntyre, Keyes and Corliss.

There has always been a choir of good singers, which lead the public taste in the county, principally through the industry and devotion of E. F. Hughes, Mrs. Dudley, Mrs. Keyes, and others.

SCHOOLS AND SCHOOL-HOUSES.

This place has always been noted for the educational interest manifested; not always harmonious in its operation, but resulting, as it is believed, in substantial success. The first school-house built, some twenty-five years since, was burned, as it is thought, by the act of an incendiary. After a proper agitation of the matter an election was ordered to determine whether a sum to build a school-house should be raised by a property tax. The result was a school-house costing perhaps ten thousand dollars, the best one in the county, if not in the mountains.

THE SHIPMENT OF GOLD

Through Wells, Fargo and Co.'s, express will show the relatively prosperous years. No account was kept previous to 1870, though the annual amounts often reached one million dollars. Since then the amounts have been,—

1871	$412,853	1875	$517,569
1872	645,135	1876	516,615
1873	530,112	1877	517,548
1874	463,590	1878	449,675
	1879	$185,194	

FIRES.

Sutter Creek has had its share of the destructive element. The largest fire happened September 9, 1865. The following is a list of the losses:—

Antonio Garbini	$500
Bishop & Kelly	600
McHenry & Tibbits	4,000
C. E. Armstrong	4,000
Nickerson & Joy	1,200
J. Steinmetz	2,000
E. W. Rice	1,000
J. C. McDonald	1,000
W. B. Hubble	600
Odd Fellows	500
W. E. Fifield	3,500
J. D. Dennis	1,800
Hayward & Chamberlain	1,000
Joseph King	4,000
John B. Keyes	500
Bright & Hatch	700
M. Shields	500
J. Caneo	500
J. Devoto	300
Italian	200
J. Mahoney	200
Mrs. Amcandes	250
C. Weller	100
W. T. Wildman	250
Thomas Grady	600
W. Schauffer	600
D. Myers	800
I. N. Randolph	3,000
Brinn & Newman	1,750
V. Latusky	500
M. Silver	500
P. Fagan	1,000
Randolph & Watkins	1,500

This included all the business portion of the town. It was soon rebuilt better than before, and enjoyed a greater prosperity, in consequence of mining development, than ever. A smaller fire had occurred about the first of September, 1862, shortly after the big fire at Jackson, burning nearly all the buildings on Humbug hill, including Wildman's store, Birdsall's store, Rice's blacksmith shop and dwelling. This fire was at last stayed at the butcher shop at the foot of the hill.

INCORPORATION.

Sutter Creek incorporated as **early as 1856**, under the general law for incorporation. The organization was found to be defective in many respects, and in 1873, it was re-incorporated by a special Act of the Legislature, an election **for township officers** being ordered, February 12th. The government was invested in a Board of Trustees (five in number). Town Marshal and Clerk, to be elected annually. **The Trustees** were authorized to purchase the necessary real estate on which to erect a jail, and other necessary buildings; to assess taxes not exceeding one per cent. on the whole taxable property, no assessments, however, to be made on mines except the improvements which were above ground; to assess a poll-tax of not more than two dollars; to determine and abate nuisances; to prevent animals from running at large; to prevent and punish disorderly conduct; to license shows, theaters, hawkers, and peddlers; and to make all necessary regulations not inconsistent with the general law. The Marshal was to receive seventy-five dollars per year for collecting taxes, and to have a salary not exceeding one hundred dollars per month. The Town Recorder was to have the jurisdiction of a **Justice** of the Peace, and to pay all fines over to **the Treasurer**, who was to receive one-half of one per cent. for receiving and disbursing money. The Clerk was to receive no salary.

The effect of the organization was found to be salutary. A number of hoodlums, who had rendered night hideous and the streets disagreeable, dangerous even, to females especially, found themselves confronted with a lodging in a calaboose for any disorderly conduct. Nuisances were now removed at **the expense of** the authors. Boys were required to be at home at eight o'clock, and there was a marked **improvement in the** appearance of the town, especially after night-fall.

FUTURE PROSPECTS.

At this writing (1881), the town is in a depressed condition, owing to the suspension of mining operations. It is by no means certain that Sutter creek **is** "worked out," on the contrary, but little of the ground is even prospected, a few hundred feet of many thousands, only, having been explored. No one knows what chimneys of rich ore are slumbering "just below," waiting for the miner to lay bare its wealth.

AMADOR.

Situated on the Mother Lode, where it is intersected by Amador creek, about seven miles north of Jackson, was mined soon after the discovery of gold. Some Oregon men built two cabins and stayed during the Winter. James T. Wheeler and two others built a large double cabin in the Fall of 1849, near where the Spring Hill mill was afterwards built. Some men from Virginia also built a cabin and kept a stock of goods, mining at the same time. W. H. Mitchell, William Leaue, J. A. Tucker, Joseph Wright, Silas Reed, —— Ashley, and Wilson, are names remembered of the company who wintered here in 1849. Silas Reed was a famous hunter, and kept the camp supplied with game.

RESIDENCE OF FR. HERMAN, SUTTER CREEK, AMADOR CO. CAL.

RESIDENCE OF FATHER P. BERMINGHAM, SUTTER CREEK, AMADOR CO. CAL.

NORTH-WESTERN PART OF THE COUNTY.   221

MINISTERS.

Mr. Ashley was a minister of striking appearance, wearing green spectacles for weak eyes, slender in form, helpless in appearance, of soft and humble address, being one of those who prefer laboring where there is a well-furnished parsonage, with a membership of weak sisters who are satisfied with milk and water sermons. Finding the preaching of the gospel an up hill business among the rough miners, he turned to mining for a living, but according to the testimony of his neighbors, "He did not have energy enough to dig a hole in a day big enough to bury a cat," and failed as a miner. Several persons died of cholera during the Fall. On one occasion he was requested by some miners to attend the burial of a man, putting a man and neighbor into the ground without some marks of respect not having become common. Ashley refused to go, saying he was not in that line of business. His friends raised money and sent him back East as a flower too frail for a new settlement.

This man was not one of the firm of ministers, Davidson, Glover, Herbert, & Cool, who in 1851 settled in Amador and commenced quartz mining. These were all working men as well as preachers, ready to bear their part in any labor or hardships necessary to develop a new country. Willson had a family, the first who resided in Amador. He kept a store, the same which was afterwards occupied by Hanford & Downs, in the Spring of 1850. When Hanford's family came out, he located in Sutter Creek, moving to Volcano in the Spring of 1853.

PLACER MINES.

The mines were never as rich as at Drytown and other places, the gold being rather fine. Twelve to twenty dollars per day was considered good work in the best days. When the water failed in the Spring, the largest portion of the population left. Drytown was better than Sutter Creek, and had much the largest population previous to the discovery of the quartz mines. Like Sutter Creek, its history is mostly in connection with quartz mining, which has received an exhaustive notice in a special chapter.

LOWER RANCHERIA

Is about two miles east from Drytown, and is about one mile east of the Mother Lode. Quartz mountain and the other veins of the same formation, are supposed to have enriched the flats and gulches around this place, which were worked in 1848, and some years after, with great success. From all accounts, Deep gulch and Slate gulch were as rich as any places in Amador county, as much as ten thousand dollars being taken from a claim fifteen feet square and three feet deep. Lumps were found at the foot of Deep gulch weighing twelve pounds. John Eagon, who mined here in an early day, picked up a piece which was worth about one thousand dollars. The mines were first worked by Major Redding and his party in 1848. One of his men had a dozen bottles full of gold-dust. Quite a number of Americans mined here in 1849 and '50; during the latter year, several persons, who preached in the eastern States, settled here, but abandoned the profession as inconvenient and unprofitable.

The population was much mixed, the **Mexican and Chilean** predominating. The camp at one time had five or six hundred people, gambling with its usual accompaniments being the usual recreation. Sombreros, scrapes, knives, horses, and jingling spurs were the striking features in every gathering. In September, 1852, a Mexican stabbed a Dutchman, for which he was whipped. The Dutchman dying sometime after the stabbing, the people reconsidered the whipping and hung the Mexican.

The character of the population remained much the same until 1855. After the occurrence of the dreadful tragedy, an account of which has been given in the County History, the place has been avoided by the Mexican population.

Lower Rancheria is remarkable in the history of mining as being on a break of the hanging-wall of the great Mother Lode, being enriched by a system of veins perhaps three thousand feet to the east. The pitch of the lode on the west of this is as much as forty-five degrees, so that if the veins were followed three or four thousand feet, a position nearly perpendicular to Quartz mountain would be reached. The fact that one such break in the overlying rock hanging-wall has been found, may be an inducement to look for others.

The valley, which is evidently a glacier erosion, is now the site of a beautiful farm owned by R. D. Ford. The graves of the parties murdered are carefully fenced in, and form about the only reminder of the terrible tragedy of August 6, 1855. The old broken safe of Dinan's store, forms the support of one corner of a barn. There are but few persons to be found who have any memory of the transaction; and rosy-cheeked, innocent children romp and play, where a quarter of a century since the very ground seemed accursed, for the crimes it had witnessed. Some two miles above the site of the old town, is the ranch formerly owned by Burt and Perkins. In 1851-52, this furnished a large quantity of vegetables for the miners; and with its green patches of cultivated land, was like a gem set in the brown hills. Perkins, one of the owners, had sold his share of the place, and with his savings, about six thousand dollars, started for Sacramento, on his way home. While he was passing through a point of chaparral, he was shot and robbed by some concealed party. Though his body was discovered before it was quite cold, no clue to the murder was obtained for many years. It is now said that a big, one-eyed Indian, who formerly lived around Volcano, confessed to the murder of Perkins, and several other white men, some years since. Burt afterwards lived on this ranch, planted a large orchard, built a saw-mill, and otherwise improved the place. The orchard is still one of the best in the county.

OLETA—FORMERLY FIDDLETOWN.

It may be well to give the origin of the first, as well as the last name. The place was settled in 1849 by a party from Missouri. The early records of the settlement, if kept, are lost, and only tradition is left to account for the musical name. It became necessary to name the young town. "They are always fiddling," says an old Missouri patriarch, "call it Fiddletown;" and Fiddletown it was, not only when it was a hamlet of three or four wagons and a tent, but when it was a town of large streets and a hundred houses, some of brick and stone. Judge Purinton is said to have started the movement for the change of name, which was done by Act of the Legislature, in 1878. In his annual trips to the capital, or San Francisco, he saw his name among the arrivals as C. A. Purinton, *Fiddletown*. Merchants on the lookout for a customer would come across the man from *Fiddletown*. The hotel clerks would grow a trifle more dignified as the ominous *Fiddletown* was attached to his name. The best of hats, faultless coat, gloves and boots, were of no avail as long as the name was anchored to *Fiddletown*. The first settlers certainly manifested little taste in the selection of names. *Poompoomatee* they metamorphosed into *Suckertown*. Every Spring where the Indians camped had a name, generally sonorous and sweet, with a meaning sometimes full of poetry. What possessed men to baptize places Hogtown, Helltown, Shirt-tail, to say nothing of names which cannot be repeated, is a phenomenon to be explained. Oleta was settled in 1849, and had but a small growth until after the discovery of American flat, French flat, and American hill, in 1852. Previous to that the houses could be counted on one's fingers. Captain Stowers, in company with Carter and Curtis, kept the hotel which had the eminent distinction of having a real glass window. The bar-room was also sitting-room, dining-room and bed-room, the beds being potatoe sacks stretched across poles, furnished with blankets, but no pillows, a man's boots being expected to serve that purpose. The floor was the original red soil, sprinkled, swept, and tramped every day. There were two stores, one kept by Jesse Hendricks, long since passed away, and another kept by —— Gilbert. Saloons outnumbored, as usual, all other places of business. Dr. Unkles, a little, old man, perhaps five feet four inches in height, kept a drug store in a house about six feet by eight, made of shakes stuck endwise in the ground. A few rows of bottles on a shelf or two contained the entire stock of drugs. A Frenchman, name forgotten, was blacksmith, gunsmith, machinist, and *gasconader*, for, according to his account of himself, he was a most terrible man. The country was quite good in places, but as there were no permanent streams of water, there was an abundance of waiting and little work. Oleta early developed a spirit of self-government. The inhabitants soon staked off all known auriferous ground, and held it against all suspicious new-comers. Captain Stowers was usually the spokesman of this committee of safety. When strangers with their frying-pan, coffee-pot, pick, pan, shovels and blankets, came into town and evinced any intention of tarrying, the old gentleman generally managed to find out what State they were from, how long they had been in the State, and where they had been mining. If the answer was considered favorable, a committee would show him where he could locate ground. The writer of this article, then one of the interviewed, could find no resting-place nearer than the south fork of Dry creek, three miles away. Mrs. Gilbert, afterwards wife of W. T. Gist, was then the only white woman in the town.

The Summer of '52 witnessed a large accession to the population. In that year several families of the highest respectability located in and around the town, among whom were those of R. M. Briggs, the distinguished lawyer, LaGrave, afterwards Treasurer of the county, McKenzie, Stribling, Bain, Votaw, and others whose names cannot be recalled. The first wedding was that of E. R. Yates to Miss Scott, member of the numerous and respectable family of that name. A large party was made to welcome the bride to the town.

In that year many respectable buildings were put up, among which was the United States Hotel, then kept by McDevitt & Cope, the latter person having since been a Judge of the Supreme Court and now an eminent lawyer in San Francisco. The discovery of American flat and hill was made by Jerry Ruth, George Shoemaker and Samuel Nase; Charles McLain, Samuel Parker, J. W. Croff and William Dunn also had claims there. This discovery was made on the south-west side of the hill, about the same time that a French party of five men, who were working the place called French flat on the east side, traced the deposit into the hill on that side. The channel was from three hundred to five hundred feet wide, the pay gravel being from five to seven feet thick. The Frenchmen are said to have carried away two hundred and fifty thousand dollars, though this may have been too high an estimate. The deposit was one of the ancient streams, and probably derived its gold from a pocket-vein of quartz in the immediate vicinity. A slab from a big boulder dumped out the mouth of a tunnel, was found years after, when the tunnel had fallen in, to be very rich. The ancient river deposits in the vicinity are very extensive, though in no instance as rich as the American Hill. Loafer flat and hill seem to be a continuation of the channel towards Dry creek, but the gravel as far as explored is smaller, having but little resemblance to the American hill gravel. The same may be said of Lone hill, also the ridge between Suckertown and Slate creek, all having gravel in paying quantities. At the time the French flat was being worked a vein of quartz was discovered which seemed riveted through with gold, but it did not prove to be permanent, or as the miners term it, a *true fissure vein.*

Oleta occupied an anomalous position with respect to county governments. El Dorado was bounded on the south by Dry creek and Calaveras, on the north by Dry creek. There were two forks of about equal size, Fiddletown being between the two. For voting purposes the strip of intervening territory on which stood Fiddletown, or rather Oleta, was, in El Dorado county, but when taxes were called for it was neutral territory! as was Vermont in the Revolutionary war, belonging neither to New Hampshire nor New York. Fiddletown did not prove a harbor for thieves, but rather the reverse, setting up courts of its own to administer justice.

The first court under *home rule* was held in 1851. There had been, as was believed, an organized band of horse thieves operating in the present territory of Amador, with head-quarters at Ione. The matter had gone so far as to be brought before the Grand Jury of Calaveras, without, however, convicting any one. A man by the name of West was arrested in Fiddletown for stealing a horse. Major Shipman, then residing there, was appointed Judge. He was familiar with law forms, having been a Magistrate, also County Clerk, in some of the older States. Witnesses were sworn, and the whole proceedings conducted in accordance with the form and spirit of the law, without its technicalities. The jury found him guilty and fixed his punishment at *one hundred stripes.* His fortitude gave way at this severe sentence, and he agreed if they would mitigate the punishment to thirty stripes he would make such statements as would expose the whole gang, enabling the people to convict them all. The thirty stripes were first administered by Abe De Haven, a powerful man, after which he made a statement in private to E. Walker and Major Shipman, it being deemed best not to have the statement made in public, as being likely to interfere with the arrest of the gang.

A man by the name of Mills, a New Yorker of good family and education, was brought to trial. He had many friends, and was furnished with money and a lawyer to defend him. Judge Carter of Ione undertook his defense. He brought logic and pathos to bear, and finally induced the jury to bring in a verdict of *not guilty,* on condition that he would leave the country immediately. He went back to Ione, which, as Oleta was an independent community, he considered complying with the sentence. He soon left the county, however, and was afterward shot, as was said, while engaged in unlawful act.

A tax gatherer from Coloma, the county seat of El Dorado, put in an appearance one day and expressed the determination to collect poll-tax from every one in the place. He stopped long enough to take a drink or two, and was sped on his way by numerous threats, backed by revolvers, with his purse no heavier for poll-taxes.

EXECUTION BY LYNCH LAW.

In the Autumn of 1852, a man passing by the name of "one-armed Smith" turned out an old and worn-out horse, supposed to be worth about five dollars, to graze. A Mexican, seeing it apparently without an owner, put a saddle on it and rode a short distance, without attempting to take it out of the country, however. He was apprehended, and hung on a tree north-west of the town. While the trial was in progress, E. R. Yates, the Magistrate, ordered Walker, the Constable, to quell the riot. The result was, to use the words of Abe De Haven, "*Rast. come out and ordered us to stop. I was about to slay him right and left, when he jumped back and says, don't you understand!*" from which it was inferred that no very serious opposition to the execution was intended.

KILLING OF CARTER BY DR. UNKLES.

Some ill-feeling existed on the part of Captain Stowers, Carter, and Curtis, towards Unkles, in consequence of a misunderstanding in some commercial transaction. Captain Stowers went into the old man's drug-shop, gave the bottles a sweep with his cane, exclaiming, "This settles my account." Carter had his to settle also, and went, with some others, to the door of the cabin, and commenced abusing the Doctor. There was scarcely room for more than two or three men in the little box, and as they (Carter and his party) commenced crowding in, he met them and civilly requested them to stay out; that he wanted no trouble with them; that they evidently intended no good. This remonstrance not being heeded, he drew a small pocket-knife, and began thrusting and making passes at Carter, the foremost man in the crowd. Little attention was paid to his words or his thrusts, but the old man was in earnest. With an instinct born of his knowledge of anatomy to direct his hand, the little knife was a most deadly weapon. The first stroke laid bare the jugular vein; another, directed towards the chest, was stopped by folds of Carter's shirt; another penetrated his side, producing a sickening sensation, which compelled him to lie down, producing death in a few minutes. Carter's friends picked up a tree upon which to hang the Doctor; but when the circumstances that Unkles was physically insignificant, and that the parties pressing him were intent on serious mischief, became known, few were found willing to assist in his execution, and he was not molested.

FATAL EXPLOSION.

In the early part of 1853, H. C. Farnum and James McLeod built a steam saw-mill at Oleta, to utilize the fine timber which covered all the hills around. Some two or three months afterward, in the early part of April, the boiler collapsed a flue. The force of the steam, reacting against the bed in which the boiler was placed, threw it out of position, propelling it through the side of a building, also through the office or **counting-room.** McLeod, standing in the line of the movement was caught **on** the end of the boiler, and **forced along until the** boiler stopped. **Both** legs and **one arm were broken,** and he was in addition thereto **much burned,** lacerated, and internally injured, yet when the clouds **of** steam cleared away, he was soon dragging himself by his remaining arm to the water. **He survived** but a day or two, suffering intensely, and begging his friends to kill him. Farnum and another party were sitting on the opposite sides of a table in the counting room, when the boiler, with McLeod on the end, came crashing through the building, passing between the two. Farnum had one arm broken, and **was otherwise** bruised and burned; the man sitting **opposite,** **inhaled the hot** steam, **which** resulted **fatally in** a year or two. McLeod was a native **of Canada West,** and was universally esteemed.

STRONG CASE OF ERYSIPELAS.

Captain Stowers and his friend Slater, **who lived in one of** the shanties called by courtesy **"hotels,"** came out one day, **bandaged and bundled, terribly sick.** Swellings all **over them, angry swellings and indolent** ulcers that **would not heal, were symptoms of very bad cases of erysipelas!** **They were going to die,** nothing would save them. **Squire Yates was** consulted **as to settling their affairs. His good sense,** or, perhaps, **experience, solved the difficulty. "You dirty dogs,"** said he, after an examination, **"you** ought **to be hung! You are rotten with** *lice,* graybacks"—**which was the case. The lice were three** deep, **all** gnawing away **at the** portly Captain, sucking the delicious juices **out** of his body. His feelings experienced **a** sudden **revulsion,** not exactly **from** mourning **to joy,** but wrath rather. Some few "cuss words" like scattering drops of rain before a shower, **fell** from his lips, and then **the** storm burst. —— Better ring down the curtain.

LYNCH LAW VETOED.

In 1854, a Mexican and a Frenchman, journeying **together** towards Oleta, **drank each other's** health **so frequently** as to produce confused perceptions **of passing** events. On arriving at Oleta, **the** Frenchman missed his watch, and accused **the** Mexican of *stealing* it. The dispute coming to the knowledge of **some** of the "home-rulers," they proposed to have a **'49 trial.** As they were ravenous for blood, they **soon** found the Mexican guilty, condemning him **to be hung** immediately, and set about executing the **sentence.** Henry Kutchenthall, **R. M.** Briggs, [ ] **and Jonathan** Patmer, expostulated with them and **told them** they were not there; that **'49ers** acted in such an infamous **manner, and much** more of the same effect, to no purpose, however, until, led by Katchenthall, they rushed in **with** drawn revolvers, and liberated the Mexican.

Three or four courageous men, backed by revolvers and a sense of right, **were** often able to subdue a cowardly mob of scores.

THE FAMOUS SAFE ROBBERY.

Wells, Fargo and Company had **their agency** at the United **States Hotel,** kept then by the Kendall brothers. **One morning** the safe was **found robbed** of the **contents, some ten** thousand dollars. **A liberal** reward was **offered for** the recovery of the **money** and the apprehension of the thief. Many persons were anxious **to get the** reward, and set about the matter with **more** zeal than discretion. **Charles** Ackerly, **a** dissipated **man,** stated that being **out late** the night before and **looking** through the window of the office, he saw one of **the** Kendalls tampering **with** the safe. This rather un[likely] story was not credited, especially as he refused to testify at all in court, though kept at jail some time for contempt. **Three** strangers who happened to come into the town **about** the time of the occurrence, were suspected, arrested, and brought before the Magistrate for examination. While this was in progress, three marked **men** stealthily took Supperfield, one of the strangers, out of the custody of the officers, conducted him **to the** outskirts of the town, and commenced trying to extract in a manner not laid down in modern works on evidence, but one in vogue a few centuries since, and occasionally resorted to in California at an early **day.** They told him **that** his **partners,** meaning the other two strangers, had confessed the crime and had been hung, and that they were going to serve him the same way unless he told them where he had hidden the money. He asserted his innocence of the charge; said he was a respectable man; **had never committed any** crime unless it **was gambling a little, and** expressed the fear that **if** he **was hung it would kill** his mother and sister. He asked some one to take the address of his mother and sister, **and write to** them his last words, that he died innocent of any crime. Some one volunteering to gratify him, was thrust rudely aside, with the unfeeling remark that "The man had better be praying, for his time is mighty **short."** The noose was fixed around his neck and **he** was drawn up and held suspended until he ceased struggling, when he was let **down until** he recovered. Denying any knowledge **of the** transaction, he was again strung up, and again let down. Though unable to speak, he was drawn up a third time by the baffled reward hunters, who were getting enraged at the man who would not "own up." At this stage of the affair Dr. Phelps, who came up, interfered to save the man any further torture, or rather to save his life, for he had now become insensible. He reached over the heads of the **executioners,** and with a Bowie knife cut the rope **and the man fell to the** ground. Deputy-Sheriff Gist coming up **about** the same time, the crowd dispersed. The **man** was with difficulty resuscitated, but, aside from being paralyzed for some time in consequence of injury to his spinal cord from the repeated hangings. It turned out that Supperfield as well as the other **two strangers** arrested, were in Forest House.

RESIDENCE OF R. W. PALMER.
JACKSON, AMADOR CO. CAL.

RESIDENCE OF MRS. ROSA FROELICH.
JACKSON, AMADOR CO. CAL.

the night of the robbery. Public opinion has fixed the robbery on one of the parties engaged in this hanging. As the men were masked, it is unsafe to attempt to name them, though many persons have no doubt about their identity. It is better that posterity should remain ignorant of the names of the parties, than have the doubtful honor fixed on the wrong person.

There are many conflicting statements about the matter, some saying that Stupperfield was taken away from the presence of the Magistrate, others that the maskers took him from a deputy, after the preliminary examination, before a decision was rendered, the latter hypothesis having the weight of evidence.

The affair did not terminate with one prosecution. Lee Warden, the Constable, acting on the testimony of Ackerly, watched the house closely, and from some movements therein, concluded that the money was concealed not far away, a suspicion that proved correct, as it was found in an old oven not far from the house. The storm of persecution was now turned on him. He was arrested and thrown into jail, and as Job says, "escaped by the skin of his teeth," though public opinion has exonerated him of any connection with the robbery.

FIRST SCHOOL.

Dennis Townsend, afterwards county Superintendent of Schools for many years, taught the first school, Mrs. Bain sending one child, Rolands two, Gilpin three, Lagrave one, and Burt one. Lizzie Scott, now Mrs. Button, at Ione, was also a pupil. Few men were more devoted to their profession than Dennis Townsend. Coming to California when gold-hunting was the sole object with most men, his educational feelings were aroused to action by the sight of the children growing up untaught. Leaving the making of a fortune out of the question, he adopted the profession of a teacher, at a time that it meant inevitable poverty, and sacrifice, which profession he followed during his life, or, until the arduous duties ruined his health and mind. If we measure men's wealth by the accumulation of gold, he died poor; if by the love of thousands of human beings, who have modeled their lives after his instruction, and hold his memory in veneration, he died one of the wealthiest men in the country. He was the inventor of the folding globe, by which the study of geography has been greatly simplified.

CHURCHES.

The first church was built in the Winter of 1852–53, it being a small room, perhaps twelve by twenty, fitted up with desks and seats. Elder Blain, of the Methodist Episcopal church, held service occasionally with a few miners, and the wives of Briggs, Lagrave, and occasionally the Scott girls from Amador, sisters to the first-named woman. A new church was erected in 1855, which was elegant and commodious.

The town continued to grow until about 1863.

At one time, four stage-lines concentrated here, taking passengers to Indian Diggings, and other mining towns, also for the cities. The hill diggings, though not rich, furnished remunerative employment to a great many men. Soon after the discovery of the Nevada mines, the population began to decline in common with the other placer mining tows of Amador county. As the placers were worked out, the Chinese, who are willing to work for the smallest pittance, began to occupy the country. They now own nearly all the older part of the town. The buildings, water-worn and sunburned, would burn up in a moment if a fire were once kindled, and the old landmarks would be gone. The Chinese portion of the town shows gradual and certain decay. Though manifested in different ways, prosperity and adversity make their own record. Pomposity, obesity, contentment, and fine raiment, indicate easy circumstances; modesty, leanness, irritability, and shabbiness, belong to adversity. The latter conditions prevail in the Chinese quarters in Oleta to an alarming degree.

MINING PROSPECTS.

There is more placer mining around Oleta than in any other of the mining camps. The gulches were soon worked out, but the low-grade gravel hills remained unworked until smaller wages were satisfactory, or until improved methods of mining were adopted. The reduced price of water also has had much to do with the working of low-grade gravel mines. Loafer hill, as well as other hills in the vicinity, has many years of drifting. The ridge between Slate creek and Sucker creek is also paying ground. At the Brown claim, on Sucker hill, may be seen the most advanced methods of gravel mining. There is a large area of cemented gravel of low grade. The ordinary process of sluice-washing failed to make it remunerative. A stamp mill was tried, but the cost of crushing absorbed all the returns, leaving no margin for dividends. The crushing process, however, was supposed to get the most of the gold that was in the gravel; so a point was gained for further experiments. The Duham "Gold and Water Saving Machine" seems to have solved the problem for this kind of mining.

Fancy an old-fashioned churn about twelve or fourteen feet long, with staves of bar-iron half an inch thick and three inches wide, riveted to stout hoops instead of being banded or held together, the spaces between the staves being, say, one-twelfth of an inch. This is hung nearly horizontal on pivots, like a flour bolting machine, and partly immersed in a bath of water. The gravel is poured into one end of the *churn*, the rotary motion, which may be obtained by the same water which is used for the bath, or by steam-power, tumbles the gravel from one side to the other, all the time passing it through the water until it is washed comparatively clean, rolling out at the lower end, out of the way. The gold is caught on amalgamating plates under the cylinder. The arrangement of these are such as to be with difficulty understood without drawings.

The results are as follows:—

Cost of mining out the gravel per ton	.50c.
" " crushing in cement mill	.50c.
	$1 00
Total yield	$1 00
Profit, nothing.	
Cost of mining being the same	50c.
" " reducing by Duham's process	10c.
	60c.
Total yield by same	90c.
Margin for profit	30c.
	90c. 90c.

The capacity of the machine is ten tons per hour. The machine weighs about three tons, and may be taken in pieces of less than fifty pounds each. About two inches of water will run it.

SEAWELL ADDITION.

The tract between Dry creek and the Cosumnes, originally belonging to the El Dorado Company, was set off to Amador by Act of the Legislature in the Winter of 1856-57, through the instrumentality of Seawell, member from the Amador side. Indian creek, emptying into the Cosumnes at the forks, heads not far from Oleta. Pigeon creek is a short stream between Indian creek and the Cosumnes. These streams were never rich in gold, though mined even to the present time. This country was a part of the ancient river system, and much of it was buried up in lava or lava wash. The glaciers swept out wide valleys, which are now the sites of fine farms. The volcanic *debris* forms a fine, warm soil, suitable for the vine and stone fruits. Ulinger's ranch has perhaps twenty thousand vines of different varieties flourishing finely. The wine is said to be of fine quality. Other farms in the vicinity are also promising. The farming interests in this portion of the county will, no doubt, soon be the predominating element in the prosperity of the people. The soil is deep, generally free from boulders, and, having a granitic base, strong and enduring. The shallow mines have in many instances materially assisted the owners to tide over the unproductive time of "opening up a farm." Fruits and grain flourish without irrigation, though it is generally believed that apples and pears, and more especially small berries, would be much improved by it. At present the want of a market prevents the development of the cultivation of fruits. When canneries and dryers are established the resources of this portion of the county will be appreciated and developed.

COSUMNES RIVER.

This, by Act of the Legislature, 1856-57, constitutes the northern boundary of the county. The south fork was probably the poorest in gold of all the rivers in the mines, though around Fairplay, Cedarville, and Indian Diggings, a range corresponding with Volcano and Murphy's, there were some very rich placers. Near the lower end of the flat, above the falls, were some deposits of fine gold, where the miners made from two to six ounces a day. This flat, like many places both north and south of the river, is a glacial erosion, one peculiarity of which is to pile up irregularly rounded gravel, clay and other *debris*, peculiar to such agencies, against the dam or terminal wall, called by geologists a *moraine*. If the track of the glacier is over auriferous slates or through gravel containing gold, rich deposits will be found at the lower end of a valley, or, as the miners say, at the wrong end, reversing the usual methods of deposit. Two or three rich riffles of small extent were discovered and worked in 1851, and subsequently in 1852. The following rather amusing account of an attempt to introduce improved mining will not only explain itself, but give an idea of the mistaken notions prevailing among miners with regard to the nature of gold deposits. The article was originally published in the *Oakland Times:*—

The south fork of the Cosumnes heads among some very good placer mines, or rather what were good mines, for the once busy places are indicated by the scarred hills, and the chimneys of the long since deserted cabins. The main channel was rather poor, though some of the riffles or bars were rich in the scale gold, which was characteristic of this river, some small deposits paying as much as one hundred dollars per day to the man, which was enough to justify, in the then uncertain knowledge of the nature of river deposits, a belief in the unbounded richness of the inaccessible deep holes with which the river abounded. Early in 1852 some sailors, who had been on a slaver on the coast of Africa, obtained possession of a long, deep hole, just below one of these rich bars, which had paid for a few days astonishingly, every bucketful of dirt having a dollar in it. The hole was supposed to contain at least a bushel of gold, which opinion was strengthened by finding several dollars' worth of dust on the naked granite rock which crossed the channel, forming the dam which retained the water. This appeared to have been swashed out of the hole by the freshet which occurred in March of that year. The sailors, knowing little or nothing of mining, had taken in as partners two experienced miners to engineer the working of the claim. A race, or canal, was cut around the hole, a dam thrown across the river, and about the first of July the water was all turned into the canal, the seepage through the dam being but trifling. Still there was five or six feet of water over the supposed treasure; how to get rid of it was the question. In the latter days of mining a steam engine and pump would have made short work of it, but in those days such a thing was not thought of, and the proposal to blast down the channel was rejected on account of the expense. At this stage of the affair one of the men who had been taken in as engineer proposed to construct a syphon to drain off the water, and made a model to show its workings, bringing forward Comstock's Philosophy as authority The sailors had no faith in " book larnin," and came very near rejecting the proposal, but finally gave a reluctant consent, and the construction of a syphon out of inch pine lumber, with no tools but a jack-plane, saw, and auger, was commenced. The lumber, all the way from Maine, cost twenty-eight cents a foot, and was carried over the mountains from Yeomet, the nearest town. The syphon was made eight inches square in the clear, the edges of the lumber being put together with white lead. The ends of the several sections were joined by wrapping them with several folds of tarred canvas. To prevent leakage through the small worm-holes and pores of the wood, several coats of hot tar were applied to the outside. When finished the "simon," as it was universally called, was near a hundred feet long, looking much like "the great sea serpent we have read of." The project had excited much derisive comment among the several hundred miners in the vicinity, and when the day came for putting it in, all work was suspended, a great crowd gathering to see it work, or rather fail to work, for not one had an encouraging word for the projector; even the sailors had lost what little confidence in it they had at first, and were threatening personal violence to the originator. Those who have ever undertaken anything contrary to the universal opinion have some idea of the soreness a hundred wagging tongues will produce. From this point it may be as well to let the narrator use his own words: "I now floated one end of the tube out into deep water and sunk it to the bottom, putting a large rock on it to hold it down; the other end was bent over the rock so as to obtain a fall of perhaps eight feet. I had gates at the ends and a valve opening outward at the highest part of the bend to aid in filling it with water. Everything being arranged I stationed a man at each end to tend the gates, taking charge of the valve at the top myself. When the syphon was full I let it stand a moment to see that all was tight, and then closed the valve, wedging it down tight, and gave directions for the gates to be withdrawn. The syphon ran a few barrels of water, gave a kind of snort, and was apparently dead! The crowd gave a derisive shout, using such expressions as 'Yer! do ter travel, won't yer? Gonter take out a patent! Reckon yer! have ter study yer book a while longer, my friend. Yer've been ter college, have yer?'

Though these expressions were made more in fun than anger, I was exceedingly mortified. Science had gone back on me. Comstock was a cheat! To add to my discomfort, my partner, who had contended for my knowledge of such matters and who, when the growling had assumed ominous proportions, had taken his little pile of three hundred dollars and told the sailors they had abused his partner long enough, and offered to bet his whole pile on the "simon" and thereby silenced their clamors, for a while at least, gave me a reproachful look I shall always remember, and went off to the cabin. The crowd of spectators, after venting their opinions, went to a saloon near by to finish the day at cards and whisky. After the first shock of disappointment was over I commenced a critical examination to see where the failure was. I half expected that some one had thrust a bowie-knife through the flexible joints, or that some crack had admitted the air, but all seemed as perfect as when I laid it down. At the lower end I made a discovery. When the water started through the syphon it raised the light pine box out of its bed so as to let the air in. I now dug away so as to let it down a little deeper and put a heavy rock on it to hold it to its place, and put in the gates without assistance, not wishing to have any spectators at the next trial. A second time I filled it and carefully closed the valve. I then waded out into the deep water and pulled out the upper gate and floundered back as soon as possible to take out the lower one, being apprehensive of failure on account of the difference in time. The reader will bear in mind that the water in the pond was up to the top and running over the rock, consequently the syphon would discharge the water as at a pressure of eight feet, or the difference between the water-level and the lower leg of the syphon. When I pulled out the gate the water poured through the syphon like a young flood. In two minutes the claim below was flooded, sluice-boxes, pumps, and everything made of wood being afloat, which I was not sorry for, as the owners had laughed the loudest at my failure. A whirl-pool over the mouth of the upper end of the syphon showed the force with which the water was being drawn through. I gave a shout or screech of delight which brought every one within hearing to the spot. A man came to the door of the saloon and shouted, "I'll be dogoned if the simon ain't jest a bilin." The cards were thrown down, and a rush made for the syphon. Since then I have "struck it rich" and made my "pile." I have mingled in politics and won the race, and have received a blissful answer from the woman I loved; but I doubt if anything brought the happiness of that moment. Science was victorious.

Various were the speculations about the "simon." One suggested that the moving power was suction. "Suction be d——d," said the other, with a look of pitiful contempt, "Where's yer suck?" It may be explained that the plunger of a pump is called a suck by many Far West people. The theory most in vogue was: "Yer see, this end er the simon's a heap the lowest, and the water is gonter run out heah any how; nothin' can't git inter it 'cept at the eends, and the water has ter come; somethin' has ter come, you bet."

In a few days the wonder ceased. I was known as the "simon man," which afterwards was shortened to Simon. There was no fortune in the hole, the bottom being as smooth as your hand.

A visit to the river after an absence of nearly thirty years shows little change. No deep bank diggings, such as characterize the other rivers, are seen; no canals, blasted through the rocky sides, show where the river was turned. The slickens from the mines around the head of the river, have given a smoothness to the channel that it did not formerly have. The cañon, as it was termed, where a pile of boulders ten to a hundred feet in diameter, which filled the whole river-bed in 1851 so that no water was seen or even heard, except during floods, is now so filled with tailings that the water runs over the tops of the rocks. A few timber slides and wood roads show the occasional presence of lumbermen, but otherwise the deer might wander undisturbed.

FARMS.

Above the falls are several good farms. This ground was taken up for farming purposes in 1851, by John M. Jamison and son. They were from St. Louis, where the former had held many positions of trust and honor. They afterwards removed to Pigeon creek, where they erected a saw-mill, put up good buildings, and made a home for the family, which soon joined them. The original location was good land, but rather frosty, owing to the conformation of the outlet of the valley, which was a glacial *moraine*.

LYNCHING AFFAIR.

Jamison's ranch was the scene of an affair in 1852 that occupied the attention of the people and authorities of El Dorado for some time, involving the Jamisons, both father and son, in a vexatious and costly lawsuit.

John Crouch, then living on a place now occupied by Mrs. Williams, found the hide of one of his missing cattle in a Mexican camp, at the forks of the Cosumnes. With the help of some friends, he gathered up five or six of the Mexicans, and took them to Jamison's ranch for a trial. Knowing the hasty manner of such trials, and the summary justice meted out, Beebee and other respectable persons at the Forks (Yeomet) sent an express to Coloma for the Sheriff, Buchanan, to be present at the meeting the next day. While the gathering was in progress, the Sheriff and deputies, two or three in number, with some friends and acquaintances of the Mexicans, came also. Some high words ensued, the Sheriff urging the citizens to give up the Mexicans for trial, the citizens insisting upon trying them then and there, as the courts were unreliable. While the angry colloquy was going on, several Mexicans, with arms in their hands, were discovered hanging around on the outskirts of the place. Whether they came with peaceful intent and were afraid to come in, is not known. Several persons went with guns and pistols and drove them away. Among this number was the elder Jamison. There is no mistake about his being of the party, and it is particularly noticed here, as being important in connection with the charge subsequently made against him of resisting the officers. Several shots were fired at the Mexicans, and perhaps some were returned. They retired however without much delay. The shots on the outside of the camp seemed to inflame the crowd, many of whom drew their revolvers and told the Sheriff to leave. One person struck his horse with the barrel of a rifle. Perhaps a dozen pistols and guns were exhibited with the intention of overawing him. The Sheriff was obliged to go, as it would have been madness to have drawn a weapon in his own defense in the presence of so many weapons ready to be used. He turned his horse, and rode slowly away, evidently angry, but holding himself in good order, followed by the friends of the Mexicans. Perhaps the presence of the hide might have been explained if the folks at the Forks had been heard. Beebee, of the firm of Beebee & Simpson, claims that the Mexicans were not guilty of any crime; that the parties punished were hard-working, honest men. After the Sheriff and his party had retired, the citizens proceeded to try the accused. A jury of twelve was called out. The evidence left no doubt of the stealing of the cattle by some one or more in the camp to which the Mexicans belonged. The accused one of whom could speak English, told the jury that there were some bad men in the settlement to which he belonged; that neither he nor his friends ought to be held responsible for their deeds, for they were desperadoes, as ready to rob their own countrymen as the Americans. The statement looked reasonable, but the accused were found *guilty* by the jury, mostly on the ground of not having prevented the stealing by other parties, and were sentenced to some thirty lashes each, on the general principle that a *greaser* was always guilty. One after another was taken out to a tree and whipped. One of them, a fine-looking man—the one spoken of before—bowed to the people with a smile, saying in good English :— "Gentlemen, I am as innocent of this stealing as any of you," and held his hands up to be tied to the tree.

The executioner, whose name will be omitted, said: "G——d you, I'll take that smile off your face."

John McCauley, one of the participators in the affair, protested against his receiving any severer punishment than the others. It is said that the last-mentioned person was Joaquin Murietta. There are so many conflicting reports concerning him that it is difficult to believe anything. The report that he was unjustly whipped somewhere, is probably true. Persons acquainted with him say that it was in El Dorado county; others say that it was in Sonora. Whether it was Joaquin or somebody else, is not material. The sting of the lash may be borne with indifference, but the disgrace, the insults, connected with it, who will forgive? One enemy at least was made who probably wiped out the disgrace, according to his code, in blood. The fact that Joaquin commenced his murderous career in Fiddletown; that the participants in the "Jamison affair," as it was called, were apparently hunted, gives an appearance of probability to the theory.

The Sheriff left with no pleasant feelings. The firmly set jaw and steady eye, indicated another chapter in the play. In a day or two after, he returned with a *posse comitatus* of three or four hundred men, to arrest the rioters.

"Then there was hurrying to and fro,
And cheeks all pale which but an hour ago,"

———Well—the rioters ran now. Runners were sent up and down the river, also to Fiddletown, warning them to flee from the wrath to come. Some visited with the Indians for a while; others found a hunting trip on the upper waters of the rivers, to be the best thing at hand. Jamison and his son were both arrested, and taken to Coloma. The *posse comitatus* helped themselves freely to hay, grain, and provisions, wasting what they did not consume, and doing damage to the amount of several hundred dollars. At the preliminary examination before a magistrate, the Sheriff found it difficult to fix any participation in resisting him, on either Jamison or the son, for the reason, as before stated, that they were of the party that were out at the time to drive away the Mexicans who were hanging around the place. The principle of law, that *he who is present when an unlawful act is committed, without using his influence to prevent it, becomes "particeps criminis,"* was cited with the proof of influence, which, if it had been used, might have averted the resistance. Mr. Jamison's house, or place, had been used on account of the convenience of meeting there, not because he took an active part in the matter. The offense, if any had been committed, was purely technical, and by a general understanding the Jamisons plead guilty, paid a nominal fine, and were dismissed; but the active lynchers did not rest quite easy, until after several months had elapsed.

CHAPTER XXXV.

NORTH-WESTERN PART OF THE COUNTY.

Drytown—Details of Settlement—First Justice of the Peace—Arrival of Families—Scurvy—Great Fire—Farming—Dry Creek — Rattlesnake Gulch — Mile Gulch — Murderers' Gulch—Forest Home—Arkansas Creek—Yankee Hill—Big Nugget — Willow Springs—Central House — Plymouth—Puckerville—Mineral Springs—Fires—Enterprise—Yeomet.

DRYTOWN is on Dry creek, in the northern part of the county, about twelve miles from Jackson. Dry creek, from which the town takes its name, runs through the place. It is the oldest town of any size in the county. As early as May in 1848, some fifty or more persons were working here, the most of whom were Mexicans from Monterey and vicinity. Isaac E. Eastman, now mining in the vicinity of Volcano, was here a few days at that time. Two ounces a day was the ordinary day's work, though occasionally, when a rich crevice was found, the ounces would become pounds. During the Summer, the number was still greater. In the following Spring, more white men came, among whom were G. L. Thomas, who had resided in Thomas O. Larkin's family at Monterey, also some of Stevenson's regiment, names unknown, though one of them went by the name of Leather-stocking. All accounts agree in the statement that the ravines and gulches were very rich, the gold being on the bed-rock near the surface. A hundred dollars to the pan was not an unusual occurrence. The tussocks, or bunches of grass along the ravines, would often have five or six dollars adhering to the roots. Mr. Thomas, who still lives in Drytown, thinks that in the Spring and Summer of '49, men averaged one hundred dollars per day. The town was very quiet, the Indians, Mexicans, and white population generally getting along without much trouble. The four or five white men began to think they were not having a fair show, considering they were *the owners of the country*, and posted up a notice ordering all foreigners to leave within a certain time, which, however, was not noticed. An Englishman by the name of Pilkinton, who had formerly lived in Mexico, and understood the Spanish language, kept a store in a brush shanty and got most of the Mexican trade. A man by the name of Williams, who had a store on Chile hill, got the Indian trade, his stock being mostly shirts and other cotton goods of gay colors, with which the Indians loved to decorate themselves. At this time there were but three or four log-cabins.

Pilkinton was the first Justice of the Peace, or the first elected rather, but as the election was carried by the residents of the town, who were mostly gamblers, it did not give satisfaction to the miners, who called a meeting in the evening to reconsider the matter. There was no town hall, but a big fire was built against a log, and the meeting was organized by the election of a man by the name of Beiterman as chairman—the *chair* being a portion of the log at a little distance from the fire. Mr. Beiterman was a portly, good-looking man, and had the only stovepipe hat in the country, and had the further distinction of having married a runaway wife of Brigham Young, hence was considered a suitable person for chairman. The fact that Pilkinton was an Englishman, and was chosen by the gamblers, was duly set forth, and the election was annulled.

During the Summer, when the "around the Horn men" began to arrive, there was a large accession to the white population. All the passengers, numbering thirty or forty, from the barks *Strafford* and *Anna Welch*, from New York, came in a body to the town, and a new impetus was given to affairs. An election for Justice of the Peace was called, and two candidates were set up. The old citizens nominated and supported a man by the name of Mulford, from Pennsylvania. The Straffords nominated a man by the name of Coffin, who was elected after a very spirited contest. He left, however, in the course of a week. A love for a political contest, more than the want of a magistrate, was the source of the interest manifested in the election.

In the Autumn a great many families came to Drytown, among whom were the Hinkstons, Boone, 'lineal descendants of Daniel Boone,' Weston, and Richmond families; a family also settled in Mile gulch. Miss Mollie Boone, now Mrs. Frank Henderson, living at Drytown, was born December 2d, 1849, on the north side of the creek, then in El Dorado county, Dry creek being the county line. *She was the first white child born in the present limits of the county.*

The first attempts to have anything like permanent residences, commenced about this time. So far, the people had camped under trees or brush shanties, or in tents. The boots and hat often served for a pillow. Coyotes prowled around the camps at night, gathering up all that was eatable, or had the smell of human hands on it. One morning, a miner missed one of his boots. He remembered that he put it under his head; why any one should steal one boot, he could not imagine. It was found some distance away, gnawed by a coyote, that had managed to pull it from under his head, without disturbing his slumbers. In another instance, a man, distrusting his companions, put his purse, containing several pounds of dust, under a flat rock some ways from the camp. In the morning it was gone. He was loud in his complaints of having been robbed by some one of the company. Instead of getting up a row, they were cool enough to inquire into the circumstances, and went with the loser to the defaulting *bank*. The depositor showed the line between two trees, where the gold was buried under the rock, which appeared to have been moved. A closer examination showed marks of a paw that had scratched around the stone. The purse, gnawed in holes and empty, was found not far away, the dust being scattered over considerable ground. It was mostly recovered, and good feelings in the family restored, though coyotes fared badly in the vicinity after that, all on account of "*that thar blamed crittur that stole his puss.*"

ROCKERS.

The Beitermans made rockers out of "split stuff," and sold them for seventy-five dollars each. A year afterwards they were sold for twenty-five dollars. The Americans used rockers, packing the dirt in sacks to water, sometimes half a mile away. The Mexicans dry-washed, with their *batayas*, with much the same movement that is used in cleaning sand out of gold dust. When less than an ounce a day was made, new diggings were sought.

CABINS.

When the rains commenced there were few or no cabins; those who had been prudent enough to build them gave a place on the ground for a *spread* to those who were out of doors. It was found that the western man, either from having crossed the plains or from being accustomed to a rough life, was readiest to adapt himself to circumstances. He soon "knocked up" a log cabin, while the eastern man cursed the country and lamented his hard fate. The first rains were of short duration and before the heavy rains set in all were sheltered. Shakes were worth sixteen dollars per hundred, and a man with a cross-cut saw and *froe* could make two ounces a day.

SCURVY.

Nearly everybody was afflicted with what was called scurvy, which seemed to be a disease similar to what afflicted the people the following year, though accompanied with other symptoms. The limbs and body would swell, the tongue crack and bleed, and the gums get so sore and ulcerated that the teeth would become loose, sometimes falling out. It was usually accompanied with diarrhea and flux, which became to a great extent epidemic. It is supposed to have been caused by the hardships of the long journey, both by sea and land, and the scarcity of vegetable food. About thirty persons, one-fifth of the white population, died during the Winter, of this disease. Doctors charged eight dollars for a visit in town, and sixteen to fifty dollars per visit to the country. Dan Worley, who suffered from this disease for some time, employed a physician, who salivated and otherwise demoralized him, without doing him any good, for which he charged one thousand one hundred dollars. Dan thinks he could have got his teeth knocked out for a much less sum than that if he had set about it.

Potatoes were worth two dollars a pound; a bottle of sauerkraut, four dollars; vinegar, when it could be had, was dealt out as medicine at twenty-five cents a spoonful. The scarcity of good water might have had something to do with the violence of disease, as there was but one place (near the present slaughter house) where drinking water could be obtained. Men would go there before daylight and await their turn for a chance at the small seepage which came out there. Five years afterwards no such awaiting would have occurred, for the sinking of a shaft deep enough to reach the abundance of cool water everywhere found in that vicinity, would not have caused ten minutes conference.

Until 1853, Drytown was a collection of log cabins and shake shanties, without much attempt at architectural display or even comfort, but the people caught the prevailing spirit of improvement, and commenced improving. A hall for general purposes was built. It was also used as a church and schoolhouse. In 1854 several brick buildings, supposed to be fire-proof, were erected. In 1856-57 the town was at its best as far as numbers were concerned, though it was even then considered a "worked-out" place, the shallow gulches having been easily exhausted and no hill diggings taking their places.

GREAT FIRE.

In the Autumn of 1857 a fire broke out near the creek, and, aided by the wind, situation of the town, and combustible nature of the buildings, in an hour it laid the whole place in ashes. Three buildings, Williams' and Louis & Richtmyer's, and the present store of William O. Clark, were the only ones saved. Those who have never seen a California town burn, have no idea of the progress of the flames after a start is made. The shakes and pine boards, rendered spongy by long exposure to the Winter rains without protection from paint, and then made dry as tinder by a six months' exposure to a heat of one hundred and forty degrees in the sun, flash like shavings, the flame leaping from house to house as on the dry prairie grass, rendering useless any attempts to stay its progress or save property.

Drytown never recovered from this misfortune. The Mexicans and Chilenos, who had constituted the larger part of the population in times past, left, no white people taking their places.

Some of the brick buildings and most of the dwellings of the white residents were rebuilt, but some of the brick stores were soon after without tenants, and served to shelter the weary pigs and goats from the noon-day sun. When the Gover, Seaton, Pennsylvania, and other mines along the lode were developed, the town showed some signs of revival, but New Chicago soon appropriated that source of prosperity, and the old routine was resumed. The travel between the different mining towns still goes through Drytown, and the stages from Ione and Latrobe connect with stages for the upper towns twice a day, bringing some trade to the stores.

There is some farming in the vicinity, the soil being well adapted to cereals and fruits. Wine of a fine quality is manufactured in considerable quantities, the capacity of the soil for grapes being unsurpassed. William O. Clark, the famous temperance orator, recuperates his exhausted energies by ploughing the hill sides and harvesting the tall oats, as a recreation. Robert Cosner, a successful politician, several times elected to the office of Sheriff, and now a prominent man in San Francisco, commenced his career here as a clerk for J. C. Williams. Doctor Fox, a stock broker in the city, also resided here in early days, as did W. F. Curtis, a lawyer, afterwards a noted man in the Union army. D. W. Seaton, successful as a lawyer, politician, and miner, was also resident here from his first coming to California to the day of his death (soon after his election to the State Senate) by the explosion of the steamer Yo Semite. He gave his name to the Seaton mine.

DRY CREEK.

From the crossing of the Mother Lode, down, this creek was probably the best in the county. It was the first to be extensively worked, having several hundred miners while there was yet but a house or two at Amador and Sutter Creek. The source of the gold which enriched all the gulches in the vicinity is a mystery. No rich quartz veins traverse the hills which are nearly a mile west of the Mother Lode, and no place on the Mother Lode in the county was as rich as at Drytown, excepting, perhaps, Murphy's and Hunt's gulches. If there were ever any ancient river beds, they are gone, only a trace in two or three places being left; but as Drytown is two or three hundred feet lower than any mining town in the county, the ancient rivers may have been swept away. Some traces of one are found on the high hill south of the town, also on a hill near the quartz lode, also at Rattlesnake flat, east of the quartz lode. The clayey bed on which the gravel rested at the latter-named place indicates a bed of a glacier, and Drytown may have been the outlet for a vast floe of ice, the flats at the Central House and Plymouth forming a part of the same. The fact that the wall-rock of the ancient valley is broken down here lower than any point between the boundaries of the county favors this theory. Some indications of benches or shores of an ancient lake may be seen on the hill-sides south of Drytown.

The creek was rich several miles below town. At Campbell's store, five miles below town, the creek was as good as at any other point, and at Irish Hill, the ancient outlet of the glacial stream, it was no unusual thing for men to make fortunes of ten to twenty thousand dollars. Whoever has time and inclination to study the connections between the ancient river beds of Fiddletown (Oleta) and the glacial marks at points farther west, will find a rich field for study and discovery.

RATTLESNAKE GULCH

Was one of the richest gulches around Drytown. Its several branches start from the crest of the Black hills, (the rich quartz deposit heretofore described,) and empty into Dry creek, not far above the town.

MURDERER'S GULCH,

An ominous name, was so called from its being the scene of several murders in 1849-50. It lies along the reef of jurassic gravel, from which it probably derives most of its gold. Blood gulch also was the scene of a murder in the same year. Some men seeing blood mingled with the water, went up the stream a few yards, and found a man who had been shot and robbed, hence the name.

MILE GULCH

Heads near Lower Rancheria, and runs north-westerly towards Dry creek. This was also the scene of a tragedy during the excitement of 1855. The gold was from a pliocene river, which enriched Rattlesnake flat, this being one of the very few places remaining of the great gravel deposits. A family (name forgotten) settled here in '49. Rattlesnake flat was mined in 1859 or '60, by a party who brought water to it by means of a ditch and flume, from Rancheria creek.

FOREST HOME.

This was the center of a mining district in the north-western part of the county, which was, perhaps, the poorest in gold of any portion that was extensively worked. The serpentine range here reached its largest development, some of the peaks forming landmarks for many miles around. This development, or rather extraordinary elevation of the metamorphic series of rocks, perhaps had some influence in preventing streams or channels from being formed which could be enriched by the Mother Lode, as the country further south was. The Cosumnes river along this tract was not rich, the paying claims being farther down, in the vicinity of Michigan bar, in Sacramento and El Dorado counties.

ARKANSAS CREEK,

So called because no "Arkansaw traveler" ever came that way, has its source near Forest Home, runs westerly several miles, and empties into the Cosumnes, near the county line. At the head of this creek were some deep diggings, called the "Yankee claim" and Wind hill. These places seem to have been the remains of a pliocene river, perhaps of the same age as the hills around Stony creek, in the southern part of the county, Arkansas creek receiving its wealth from these hills.

YANKEE HILL

Was worked in 1850 by Griswold, Emerson, Purtham, Alexander, and others. Griswold is now an eminent composer of music in Boston. The lower part of the creek only paid moderately, three to five dollars being the usual result of a day's work. William B. Ludlow, afterwards member of the Legislature, now a resident of Oakland, Edmond Tanner, Wallace Wallace, and Charles Bennett, the latter since a resident of Sutter Creek, are remembered as mining there in 1850, and since. Potter, now of Plymouth, and also Gideon Babb, kept stores there. Some coarse gold was taken out occasionally. The hills were generally composed of sand and gravel, the gold being found in a kind of ferruginous, cemented gravel, on the bottom.

BIG NUGGET.

One day a Mexican, named Antone, struck a nugget with his crow-bar, which refused to give way. He enlarged the drift, and approached it two or three inches farther back, and struck his bar, as he thought, behind it. To his astonishment, the nugget still continued into the hill. A second enlargement produced a like result, and not until he enlarged and extended the drift a third time, did he get behind it. He began to be rather excited by this time, and when it came out, he thought he had about all the money he should ever want. He rushed to the nearest saloon, and treated all hands, depositing the *chispa* as security for payment. He continued to treat so many times, that the margin vanished, the nugget eventually falling into the hands of J. Elkins. The piece was seven and a half inches long, and worth three hundred dollars. The gold in this vicinity was mixed with silver, and was worth only thirteen dollars per ounce, forming a great contrast in appearance with the gold from Drytown, which was worth seventeen dollars and seventy-five cents per ounce.

In 1860, the sluices were often robbed. Some person would cut small creases in the bottoms of the boxes, and with a sharp, conical scraper, would clean several sets of sluices in a night. The act becoming common, Edward Evans, one of the miners, kept watch, and when the robber went at his work, gave him a load of shot. The culprit proved to be a Chinaman. The Chinese in the vicinity were compelled to bury him. Evans received no punishment. In 1850, John Ballou and Nehemiah Barnes, got into a difficulty about a right to a mining claim, which resulted in the fatal shooting of the former. Barnes soon after left the country. In an early day, a Frenchman named Raymond, mining on the river, shot a Chinaman with very little provocation. The miners gathered, and giving the Frenchman a trial, hung him. At that time there was no especial prejudice towards the Chinese race. The Arkansas House, not far from the county line, was kept by a man by the name of Haynes, who died some twenty years ago, of consumption. He was the first Justice of the Peace in that section of the county.

WILLOW SPRINGS.

This is the site of a glacial erosion, like Plymouth and other places. It was settled by —— Richardson and William Jennings, who put up a first-class hotel, the place being on the line of the travel from Drytown, Fiddletown and other places to Sacramento. Travelers a quarter of a century since recollect well the good fare of those days. The place was afterwards sold to Mathews. W. D. Castle, now of San Jose, owned the place for many years. The mining was never of much importance around this place.

THE CENTRAL HOUSE,

Two miles north of Drytown, is another place similar to Willow Springs in location and character. As before stated, the gold mining never attracted many persons to this vicinity. Soon after the breaking out of the copper excitement, several veins of copper were discovered, and for some years this "North-West Territory" bid fair to become a second El Dorado, or Copperopolis. This epoch of the history will receive more particular attention in the history of copper mining, which will form a chapter by itself.

PLYMOUTH

Is on the Mother Lode, near the northern boundary of the county, fifteen miles from the county seat. It has very little history separate from the history of its quartz veins. At the lower end of the flat, on which the town is built, there was formerly a small hamlet called Puckerville, or Pokerville. It might have had twenty or thirty miners in its best days, which were nearly a quarter of a century since. At the present time, a solitary house marks the site of the ancient town. Ruined chimneys, the usual relics of a "dug-out" town, are totally wanting, and at this day the history of the town is irrevocably lost. If the name was Pokerville, we may imagine the citizens playing poker, with beans for stakes, while waiting through the long Summer for water to come, or, through the Winter for the water to go down, so their claims could be worked, a practice quite common in early days in many a mining camp which has since made a town. As for Puckerville, there is no accounting for that name. There were no persimmons to contract the beef and potato gates; no old maids to put on Sunday rig, and draw the mouth together like a rose-bud to look sweet and tempting; in fact, there were no females at all, save occasionally a wandering *mahala*, with a basket on her broad back, gathering acorns and bugs. The Indian belle never pressed her mouth to look sweet; that were impossible, but delighted rather in an immense spread, which showed a set of ivories like a quartz breaker. The wildest imagination fails to find a probable reason, and the question "Wherefore Puckerville?" must be left to the wisdom of some of the numerous debating societies of the mountains. Perhaps the orator of the "sand-lot," when he has

A. K. DUDLEY.

decided all the questions of theology, political and social economy, whether moral or financial, to the satisfaction of the people, will give this question the benefit of his profound erudition.

Plymouth proper was settled upon in an early day by Green Aden and others in search of quartz, but the commencement of its growth as a town, dates to the working of the mines by the Hoopers, father and son. About 1873 the town took a sudden start, occasioned by the purchase of the mines by Hayward, D. O. Mills and company. In the same year the precinct cast one hundred and seventy-five votes; in 1877, two hundred and seventy-five; in 1880, something over three hundred, showing a steady growth which is likely to be permanent.

The town is identified with the prosperity of the mines, though there is considerable farming land in the vicinity, which partially supplies the demand for hay and barley. Shenandoah valley is one of the rural places in this vicinity. It has many fine farms and orchards, that of Oliver Balls being among the best.

MINERAL SPRINGS.

The White Sulphur Springs, about two miles north of Plymouth, possess relaxing qualities useful in cases of constipation and inflammatory diseases. No improvements have been made yet. The property is owned by Albert Stevens. There is also an extensive marble quarry in the vicinity, furnishing an abundance of rock for ornamental purposes, as well as lime for building.

FIRES.

The following letter from Plymouth to the *Dispatch* will explain itself:—

About three o'clock on Monday, the tenth of June, 1877, occurred the largest fire over experienced in this town (Plymouth). The fire commenced in the rear of J. C. Williams' stable and spread over the upper part of the town in an incredible short space of time, reducing twenty or more buildings with their contents to ashes. The following is a partial list of the losses: Easton's hotel, McMullen's boarding and lodging house, James Davis' store, John Davis' dwelling house, Baer & Coblentz's store, Odd Fellows' hall, P. Quin's saloon and dwelling house, dwellings of Williams, Thomas, and Richardson, Wentworth's blacksmith shop and dwelling, Jacob Smith's shoemaker shop and dwelling, Potter's barn and outhouses, J. C. Williams' stable, five horses, lumber yard, wagons, hay, grain, etc., the residences of the Misses Snyder, and a number of other houses and buildings, about twenty-two in all.

The fire was said to have been started by some children who were playing with matches in some straw in the rear of the stable. The total loss is estimated at fifty thousand dollars, only a small portion being covered by insurance.

ENTERPRISE

Is the name of a town that was started up about the time that Plymouth commenced growing, and had at one time a hundred or more men busily prospecting quartz, which was thought to be very good. Whether from too much water, as some

allege, or from other causes, capitalists failed to take hold of the work, and explorations ceased, the town with the fine name being relegated to obscurity. A house or two keeps guard over what was once a lively camp.

YEOMET

Is an Indian name signifying rocky falls, and was given to the forks of the Cosumnes river. Indian creek, north fork, middle fork, which received the south fork a mile or two above, all coming together here. Indian creek rises east of Oleta, runs west until it strikes the quartz range; thence along the course of the vein three miles to the Cosumnes. The north fork also runs for some miles parallel to the Mother Lode; hence, as might be expected, the river was rich, a large number not only mining here, but drawing their supplies from this base. Up to 1853, it had the appearance of becoming a town. Simpson, Beebee & Co., Bowman & Co., and others, had large stores, the latter persons also having a bridge across the river, and a hotel of considerable pretensions. Many of the settlers were from Pittsburg, Penn., perhaps induced to remain here by a fancied resemblance to the forks of the Ohio at that town. Some were steamboat captains, some merchants and clerks, some workmen from the great machine shops, that even then had learned to rival Birmingham and the Clyde in making ponderous machinery. Captain John King, who had steamed up and down the Mississippi a hundred times, told his stories, how he had entrapped a load of passengers once at New Orleans, by pretending that he had a famous French general on board, having arranged for a smart Frenchmen to play the part, which worked to a charm, his boat being crowded, while the boat having the real general was a few hours behind—empty! Some of these men made fortunes and went home; others told their stories, all the better for a drink, which at last got the better of them, leaving them in a nameless grave.

Beebee & Simpson were favorites among the miners for their thorough honesty in trade. "Have you some good coffee, sugar, flour, or bacon?" generally elicited, "only a moderately good article," which, however, was found to be as good as the market afforded; but the miners knew their men, and that answer was sufficient. Old man Simpson (E. M.), as the miners used to call him, was subsequently elected to the Legislature, and won the esteem of all he met, by his unswerving honesty and good sense. H. E. Hall, afterwards County Clerk, and Sam Loree, the latter now resident at Upper Rancheria, built saw-mills near the forks in the Summer of 1852. The former was swept away by the high water of the following Winter. The miners gradually encroached upon the town, one building after another giving away, and now a solitary house holds all the population, he watching for a quarter from an occasional footman across the bridge. The river now is not vexed with dam or wing-dam, but follows its own sweet will to the sea.

A general air of lost, forgotten, or dead pervades this section of the country, north as well as south of the river. Many springs pour cooling streams out of the hill-sides, but no little homes, decorated with vines and trees as at other places, relieve the eyes wearied of the everlasting brown of the hills. Some of the cabins built in 1850 maintain a tottering standing, with the aid of props and braces. Inside you may see the gold-pan and pick as of yore, but the men, weary and worn with a quarter of a century of unsuccessful search for gold, seem waiting for the last act of the play, though still hoping to *strike it*.

CHAPTER XXXVI.

EASTERN PART OF AMADOR COUNTY.

Elevation Above Tide-water—Ione, Jackson, Volcano—Pine Grove—Dentzler's Flume House—Claiborne Foster's—Antelope Springs—Hipkins & Wiley's Station—Ham's Station—Mud Springs—Stevens' Lumber Yard—Emigrant's Pass—Amount of Timber Remaining—Climatic Effect of the Loss of Timber—Summer Pasture—As a Summer Resort—Practical Jokes—Salt Springs—Mammoth Quartz Vein—Trout Fishing—Silver Mines—Sunset from the Sierras—Climate—Droughts—Freshets—Rain Table for Amador County, as Compiled by Frank Howard—Rain Table for Sacramento, corrected for Sutter Creek.

This county is shaped much like the famous Pan-Handle of Virginia. As the force of the name may not be apparent to our younger readers, an explanation may be in order. A half century ago, before the invention of the cooking stove, telephone, high-heeled shoes, *creme de lis*, and other modern improvements, the universal frying-pan had a handle some five feet long, to enable a woman to cook by the roaring fires that our ancestors found necessary to have in Winter, without roasting her face to more than a cherry red. In time every long strip of territory became a *pan-handle*. Amador county in the Sierras, has much the same attachment. The south fork of the Cosumnes was established as the northern boundary, the north fork of the Mokelumne as the southern boundary; but as the Cosumnes was a short river, not reaching the summit, leaving the eastern boundary in doubt, Amador took the benefit of the doubt and set up a claim reaching to the State of Nevada. When Alpine county was created the dividing line between that county and Amador was fixed at Kirkwood's house in Hope valley, leaving his house on the Amador side. This threw the line of the Amador wagon road, Silver lake and considerable of a tract of Alpine character, into Amador county. Though no towns or even hamlets abound in these mountain regions, they are in many respects the most interesting part of Amador, and no one should feel themselves acquainted with the whole county until they have breathed the pure attenuated air, seen the tall pines, or fished in the streams of the upper Sierras.

A statement of the different elevations, with some of the characteristic productions, will be a good starting point for a general description.

THE ELEVATION ABOVE TIDE-WATER.

Ione 270 feet. Prevailing timber, oak and scrubby pine, nut pine predominating; no sugar pine; natural grasses, wild oats, etc.; all annuals (except along water courses) in perfection; soil and climate adapted to all fruits; apples, however, lack the flavor of the colder altitudes.

Jackson 1,300 feet. Timber, oak and pine, pitch pine predominating; sugar pine makes its appearance; natural grasses inferior to the valley; fruits of all kinds flourish, including the orange, in favored localities; grapes are in perfection.

Volcano 2,162 feet. Prevailing timber, oak and pine, pitch pine in perfection; sugar pine improving; fir makes its appearance, also the cedar, laurel, pepper, nutmeg pine, etc.; apples improving; grapes at this point (owing to the situation of the town in a basin) are liable to frosts; the wild plum, gooseberry and other berries, make their appearance.

Pine Grove 2,675 feet. Prevailing timber, oak and pine, pitch pine predominating; pitch pine in perfection; sugar pine improving and now towers above all the trees; cedar and fir becoming frequent; grapes good but require sheltered situations; apples have a sharp flavor; peaches late but good in flavor. Snow sometimes falls a foot in depth, remaining on the ground a week or two.

Dentzler's Flume House 2,980 feet. Timber, oak and pine; nut pine ceases; pitch pine in perfection; sugar pine still improving; the fir and spruce now stately trees; new varieties of the cedar make their appearance; natural grasses scarce, varieties of ferns taking their place; grapes uncertain and lack sugar; apples improving; peaches good; wild plum and gooseberry plentiful, forming thickets; best potatoes in the county raised at this elevation. This includes the altitude of J. A. Foster's ranch, also F. Mace's and B. F. Whitmore's. Snow falls occasionally two or three feet deep, and may remain on a month or more.

Claiborne Foster's 3,100 feet. Timber principally pine, all kinds in perfection; immense quantities in favorable localities, and so thick that the surveyors cannot run a hundred feet in a straight line; sugar pines may now be found six feet in diameter a hundred feet from the ground; best apples raised at this height; peaches sure in favorable localities, though the later varieties will not ripen; potatoes in perfection; wild plums, gooseberries, chinquepins (a kind of dwarf chestnut) in abundance. Snow in considerable quantities.

Antelope Springs 4,250 feet. Pines, firs and cedars now a solid forest; oak thinning out, only found on exposed points and dwarfed in stature; potatoes still good; no attempts made to cultivate fruits above this point.

Hipkin's & Wiley's Station (on the Amador wagon road) 5,000 feet. Best pine lumber; the oak becomes insignificant.

Ham's Station 5,425 feet.

Mud Springs 5,975 feet.

Steven's Lumber Yard 6,422 feet. Potatoes and alfalfa raised here; the best pine ceases, tamarack taking its place. Snow falls eight or ten feet deep.

Emigrant Pass (second summit) 8,300 feet. Above seven thousand feet the timber is found only in sheltered depressions. The snow falls anywhere from ten to twenty feet in depth, which may all melt and go away in the course of three days, if a warm rain prevails. The most striking features in all this upper region are the bare volcanic or granitic peaks, the heavy rains and floods denuding them of every particle of earth. This region is the source of the freshets which occasionally pour down and inundate the lower valleys.

East of Volcano but little farming is done. A few men cultivate small farms to supply the lumbermen with a portion of their needs. Hay and grain are hauled up, and exchanged for lumber. Hay, worth ten dollars in the valleys, becomes twenty dollars at the saw-mill, and lumber which is worth ten dollars at the mill, brings twenty dollars in the valleys. Though the cash values have constantly decreased for twenty years or more the relative values of each have remained about the same. Nearly all the mountain land will raise grain or hay by ploughing and sowing it every year. It is a question of cost alone. If any means should be inaugurated whereby the lumber could be floated to market by water so that teams would not be required to haul the lumber down, and consequently have no inducement to haul hay and grain into the mountains, farming would be put on a remunerative basis.

AMOUNT OF TIMBER STILL REMAINING.

Formerly the pine timber covered the entire country from the foot-hills up to the bald peaks of the Sierras. Below the altitude of one thousand feet, the timber was dwarfed and inferior. The trees looked body. A few of the pitch pines may still be seen in the valleys, towering among oaks, but very much inferior to their tall, stately brothers of the mountains. A cluster of fair-sized pines once stood on the south side of Jackson creek, where it runs through the green ledge. These were all cut down and hauled to Laucha Plana some twenty years since for bridge timbers. Between Ione and Jackson scarcely a pine can be seen, and around the latter place they are by no means plenty. A few, far up the side of Butte mountain, have escaped the slaughtering axe of the lumbermen. One sugar pine, too crabbed and crooked for shakes, still holds its long arms to the breeze, the only specimen to be seen for miles around. At Pine Grove enough are left to give a plausible reason for the name of the town. Practically, the timber is cut away for a distance of thirty-five miles from the foot-hills, the little that is left within that distance being in inaccessible places. The sawed lumber is only a small portion of the amount annually used. Hundreds of teams are hauling lagging and timbers for the underground works which daily swallow up loads of each. The introduction of water as a motive power for driving the machinery saves a consumption of wood amounting to thousands of cords a year; but no substitute can be found for the underground timbers. The Plymouth cluster of mines have used up nearly all the available lumber along the line of the ditch, and now have to rely on the supplies farther up in the mountains. The side-hills along the Cosumnes and Mokelumne, as well as Dry creek and Sutter creek, are now being denuded of everything that will burn, to be floated down in the high waters of Winter. Bryant and others put an immense amount of lumber, consisting of logs, cord-wood, cuts and bolts of sugar pine, into the Mokelumne, far up in the mountains, to be floated down and taken out near Woodbridge, for a match and sash factory. Thousands of cords, floating out on the bottoms of the Mokelumne, or caught in the rocks of the cañons above, were left to rot. In some instances heavy damages were collected of them for the piles of timber left on the overflowed ranches.

Feeble efforts have been made by the United States inspectors to prevent the waste of timber, but our liberal land laws enable any one to make a claim on the land, strip off the timber and then abandon it, without much expense or trouble.

Benjamin Ross, of Volcano, a deputy United States Surveyor, thinks the lumber belt is hardly reached; that the portion already cut over, though thirty miles or more in width, is only the ragged edge of the true belt. Others have also expressed the same opinion; while others, whose opportunities for observation are good, feel much alarm over the destruction that is going on. A thorough survey of each section will be required to set the matter at rest.

In all ages the destruction of the growing timber of a country has been considered a most disastrous proceeding. The old Greeks bestowed the most opprobrious epithet on those who would wantonly kill trees. Trees were religiously preserved as necessary to the regular fall of rain. Perhaps it was for this that the priest and oracles taught, that every tree was the abode of a spirit who would certainly avenge the destruction of its home. If any tree could make a fitting residence for a god, the sugar pine with its straight shaft, as beautiful as a Grecian column, a hundred feet high, without a limb or knot to mar its magnificent proportions, would be the one. Yet a *shake-splitter* will ruthlessly cut one of these monarchs down, use a few feet to make shakes, or, if it does not quite suit him, abandon it, and move on to another, which he will serve in like manner. Far in advance of the regular lumberman may be seen the shake-splitter selecting the best trees, which he will destroy to get means to purchase a bottle of whisky and sack of flour, or get enough to indulge in a day or two of debauchery in the nearest town.

The only estimate of the quantity of lumber remaining in the mountains, that the writer is aware of, is that of Capt. J. C. Ham, who built the canal known by his name. His estimate is as follows:—

Common lumber (feet)		1,200,000,000
Sugar pine	"	72,000,000
Cords of wood		800,000,000
Mining timbers (sticks)		2,000,000

He proposes to carry this all to San Francisco by means of a canal and railroad. It is likely that the general government would interfere if this project was undertaken.

CLIMATIC EFFECT OF THE LOSS OF THE TIMBER.

Whether the destruction of timber has already affected any change in the climate, is an open question. The thirty years during which a rain-gauge has been kept, is not a sufficient length of time to determine the average amount of rain, as one or two exceptional seasons would make the amount greater or less than the general average, and lead to a wrong conclusion. After a series of dry seasons it seems easy to prove a serious change, and after a rain like the one occurring in February, 1878, no change at all. The old Spaniards speak of seasons of drouth. The year 1825 was said to be so destitute of rain that even large rivers dried up, the San Joaquin being so low that cattle could ford it at Stockton; but as no cattle were ever seen at that point prior to 1843 (except when stolen by the Indians), when Gulnac, in the interest of Weber, established a cattle rancho there, the tradition is not worth much. The tremendous bursts of rain or cloud breaks, seem to be a phenomenon peculiar to treeless countries.

There is one condition that may mitigate to some extent the cutting away of the timber. Everywhere there is springing up an immense number of small pines, hundreds for every one that was cut away. For miles around Volcano they have started up so thick, that a hundred to the square rod is a low estimate. In some places these second-growth pines are a foot or more in diameter, though where there are a hundred to the rod, they may be only a few inches in thickness. The writer of this article assisted, in 1856, in building a small reservoir in Boardman's gulch, near Volcano. A small pine, about an inch in diameter, was left in the embankment, as likely to do no harm. Twenty-four years afterward it had grown to be considerably over two feet in diameter. This may be considered exceptional, but hundreds in the immediate vicinity, which have sprung up since, are a foot or more through. If these young pines could be protected, it is not likely that a serious change of climate need be apprehended. As a commercial speculation, an investment in young pine trees is quite as promising as stocks in Arizona or Colorado, or even better than cutting them down and sowing the ground to grain.

SUMMER PASTURE.

Near the head-waters of the American, Cosumnes, and Mokelumne rivers, are many valleys which produce an abundance of clover, and other grasses. Thither, in the Summer, many herds of cattle and sheep are driven, to remain until the falling snows or cold weather remind them of the return of Winter. Butter, of a quality equal to that made at Point Reyes, is manufactured in considerable quantities. The cattle, fattened on these green pastures, bring an extra price. The work of tending these herds, though lonely, is not without enjoyment. The clear, cold water; the pure, exhilarating air; the glorious prospects from the hills; trout fishing in the streams; and an occasional deer, or perhaps the advent of a grizzly, serve to keep the mind employed, and build up a wasted nervous system. Almost every valley is thus claimed as Summer pasture by laws, or rather common usage. Cattle pastured here in the Summer retain a lively memory of the green grass, and every Spring, on the approach of warm weather, manifest an intense uneasiness, and, if possible, break away and make their way by themselves. The instinct of the buffalo in emigrating from Texas to Montana, is perhaps of the same origin.

AS A SUMMER RESORT.

The upper valleys are unsurpassed. It is true there are no such tremendous gorges as the Yo Semite, or groves of the *Sequoia Gigantea*, but there are numberless sources of amusement and health. Silver lake is one of the most beautiful sheets of water in the world, and a sojourn on its banks in the Summer is one of the pleasantest enjoyments possible. The lake is full of small trout, that despise all the patent flies and other deceitful contrivances for their destruction, and bite eagerly at, as Izaak Walton would say, a hook baited with a grasshopper or a vile worm. While they do not bite so as to load down a man or a boat in a few hours, the angler is sure of enough to make him a hearty supper, and also the necessary appetite to relish, as well as a tone of stomach to safely and profitably, for the body at least, dispose of them. Nothing can be better to restore a worn out nervous system, or repair debility induced by overwork of any kind, than a residence of a few weeks in the Sierras. A delicate, feeble woman, who had to be lifted into a carriage at the beginning of the journey, has been known to improve so rapidly in a few weeks as to get up in the morning and, from very exuberance of feeling give half a dozen Indian yells that could be heard a mile, or catch up a pair of oars and row a half-mile out into the lake, singing and shouting in a way that would bring the police down on her or cause an examination for lunacy if done in a city.

The peaks around about are excellent hills to climb to give one wind and muscle, and try them, too. The months of July, August and September are best for these visits, and a tent with plenty of bedding the best outfit. Hotels are rather scarce and not of extravagant size when found, and a dozen or two visitors would tax the lodging capacity, as well as the larder, to the utmost. Fresh beef and milk can

RESIDENCE, RANCH AND BUSINESS PLACE OF **A.C. HAM**
AQUEDUCT CITY, AMADOR COUNTY, CAL.

generally be found at the Summer ranches in the vicinity, and bacon, coffee and bread will always relish when nothing better is at hand. Camp on the shores of the lake, for a mile or two away there is frost every night; but the lake, absorbing the sun's rays during the day, parts with the heat at night, making a delightful temperature for sleep and rest. Thunder peak, south of Silver lake, is said to exhibit at times some very curious electrical phenomena. It will be remembered by some of our readers that a scientist has recently discovered that zones of different electrical conditions are found at different heights; perhaps some of our young scientists may work out this problem on Thunder mountain. Several persons report curious things, such as quite perceptible shocks, as if from a Leyden vial, flashes of flame from the points of knives. sparks from metallic buttons, etc.

PRACTICAL JOKES.

The following letters, from Ed. Briggs of Plymouth to the *Dispatch*, will give one a vivid idea of the rollicksome feelings a party is likely to have, and the consequent character of their amusements:—

PLYMOUTH, August 26, 1880.

EDITOR DISPATCH: I promised several sports in different parts of the county that I would, on my return from a hunting and fishing excursion to the head-waters of the north fork of the American river, write a brief description of the same, and send it to you for publication.

Our company consisted of the following well-known gentlemen: James Dohman, captain; J. E. Brown, guide; L. G. Noris, assistant; G. K. Goble, camp guard; Frank Potter, teamster; E. B. Muggy, commissary; J. J. Dohman, and C. W. Wild, cooks. With a four-horse team loaded with a month's supply of provisions, ammunition, etc., we set out upon the third of August, calculating to spend a month in the Sierras, on the head-waters of the north American river.

Nothing of interest occurred on the journey until we reached a line is called Silver creek. Here we found quite an encampment of excursionists from Sacramento and other localities, all in fine health and good spirits. The fishing here is excellent. The waters of this beautiful stream come pouring and dashing down from the snow-capped mountains, foaming and sparkling in the beautiful sunlight, in its native purity, cool from the snowy mountains, and clear as crystal; and oh, what a treat, after leaving the brackish and mineral water of the valleys and foot-hills, to sit beside this beautiful stream beneath the shadows of those towering firs and pines, and drink from this pure fountain. Here we struck camp for the remainder of the day, our fishing tackle was unpacked, and soon our entire company was busy trying their luck among the finny tribe which inhabits this stream in great abundance. The creeping shadows of evening now warn us that it is time to repair to camp for supper, and as the boys began to drop in, each with a long string of regular beauties, their countenances radiant with smiles, tell but too well how delighted they all felt with their success. All hands now busy preparing the fish for the cooks, who, with their pans and corn meal, begin their work, and in a few moments we have all surrounded our frugal table, when the conversation goes back to the boys left behind, with such remarks as, "now if old George Durham was here, wouldn't he enjoy this." I then told the story about George and "Pat," coming into a wood camp once up in the mountains; that the cook had prepared a whole sheep for the wood-choppers, but George being very hungry, could not wait for the boys to come in, and persuaded the cook to let him eat; that to the astonishment of the cook, and the disappointment of the hungry wood-choppers, and in spite of the remonstrances of the cook, he ate the entire sheep at one meal. Cook, Breese, and other fellow sportsmen were not forgotten, and the demijohn was brought forth, and a health drank to all the sports left behind. Then the big fish-eat commenced in earnest. Supper over, and pipes well filled, amongst other topics it was discussed what we should name our first camp, when one very enthusiastic Democrat proposed to call it Camp Hancock, in honor of the distinguished gentleman who heads the Democratic ticket, whilst an equally sanguine Republican proposed Garfield as an appropriate name. The arguments on both sides were put forth in a very forcible manner, and for a while it seemed that the camp would be left without a name, as neither side was willing to yield, when luckily, a very conservative member of the party proposed a compromise name, which seemed to satisfy the entire party, and the name of "Garcock" was unanimously adopted, and the new name, with the names of the entire party, was the next morning neatly carved on a beautiful tamarack tree. The fishing being so good, and the feed for our animals so plentiful, we concluded to enjoy another day at Camp Garcock, in which we were equally successful, catching all the fish we wanted, and at every recurring meal the flask and camp jokes went round. The deer hunt of Dry cañon, in which our mutual friend W. T. Jones participated, was related in a most interesting manner by L. G. Norris and others of the party; and after spending a very happy day and night, we again packed up and started for the head-waters of the Rubicon river, one of the finest deer parks in California, and after two days of hard travel over one of the roughest countries there is in the mountains, we camped for the night, within six miles of the park. The next morning we packed the horses—leaving the wagon behind—and after considerable difficulty, reached our camping place about five o'clock P. M. Away up among the lofty peaks of the Sierras, and the shadows of evening again began to creep over the towering rocks that have stood sentinel over this lonely spot for centuries gone by, and as we listen to the mournful music of the wind as it comes sighing through her cragged heights, we became conscious of that sublime power and greatness which awes and uplifts like God himself.

This park is located where the Rubicon comes dashing down from the summits of the mountains in all the grandeur that nature could invest it with—the mountains on each side of the stream, rising in regular amphitheatrical style, that is, in a succession of benches one above the other, for miles on either side, these benches or tables varying in width—sometimes the ascent from one bench to another being very steep and rocky. Among these rocks on the benches are the homes of the fleet-footed and keen-sighted deer; and from the vast numbers found here, it would seem that this is to them a favorite resort. We found them here in countless numbers, from the tiny fawn in all the beauty of his spotted dress, to the largest buck, with horns like a young forest. This splendid park has never, as yet, been disturbed by the shepherd, and in all probability never will, as it is almost inaccessible for man or beast, and I do think there should be some steps taken by the proper authorities to secure this as a public park to the exclusion of all shepherds, for it is an established fact among hunters that sheep and deer will not range together.

I am admonished by counting my pages that I am trespassing upon your valuable space, and will hasten to a close for this time. Suffice it to say that we spent ten days in this secluded place, with more excitement and pleasure than was ever enjoyed by us before; we killed twenty-one deer, and caught three little spotted fawns which we very reluctantly had to turn loose again, as it was impossible for us to obtain milk for their subsistance; but we have them all marked, and we may at some future day have the pleasure of reclaiming them with the trusty rifle. We could fill two or three columns with incidents of the hunt, which we know would interest the sporting boys, but we cannot crowd it into this letter. Probably at some future time we will write a letter of incidents connected with this remarkable hunt.

We were gone three weeks, and all returned in excellent health, thinking that no party that has gone to the mountains this summer has had a better time than we have.   NIMROD.

PLYMOUTH, Sept. 9, 1880.

EDITOR DISPATCH: Having been strongly urged by a goodly number of your readers for another letter descriptive of some of the incidents connected with our late extraordinary hunt in the mountains, I hope will suffice as a sufficient apology for our appearance again in your columns with another sporting letter. Then, to commence with, we wish to state, that before our departure, we all had a mutual agreement that nothing that we should say or do should, in any way, mar or disturb the friendly feeling that existed one for the other—in other words, jokes should all be free. It was a good time we were out for, and a good time we would have. Almost the first thing that attracted our special attention in our new camp, was a fight with a large rattlesnake, which infests this part in untold numbers. Almost every rock has its rattlesnake, sometimes two or three, and some of our boys were terribly afraid of snakes, particularly our young friend Wilds. He could see more snakes than all the rest of the boys put together. I think it was the second day that Mr. Norris and Mr. Muzzy killed a large deer close to camp, and in dressing the deer, a happy idea struck Muzzy for a good practical joke on Wilds. So he carefully rolled up the small entrails of the deer, and packed them into camp in his pocket, and then posted all the boys, except Wilds. After supper we made a big camp-fire, all hands lying around, smoking and recounting the exciting scenes of the day. Among other topics the number of snakes seen and killed; the habits of the snake, and particularly his venom and great antipathy to the whole human race. During this time Muzzy had found a place alongside of Wilds, and taking out his deer guts, without Wilds' knowledge, carefully pinned one end to the seat of Wilds' pants, while the rest of it, about ten feet, lay in a heap by his side, all hands awaiting the discovery with suppressed mirth. Pretty soon he rolled over on his side, and his hand came in contact with the gut. With one wild yell he sprang to his feet, clearing the fire at one bound, and as he went over the gut wrapped around a small brand of fire. Away goes Wilds around the camp shouting:—

"Snake! help! shoot!" and "Oh, my God, boys, don't let it eat me alive!"

Three or four of the boys fired off their guns, and by this time the whole party had become so convulsed that they were rolling and tumbling on the ground. The snake caught around a bush and pulled loose, and Wilds fell breathless in among where the boys were rolling and laughing. He now began to take in the situation, and raising himself up he says:—

"Now look here, you d——d fools, I don't see anything funny about this, and if it wasn't for breaking our pledge, I would lick every d——d scoundrel of you. You all think you have played smart, don't you?" By this time the demijohn was produced, and I tell you there was justice done her this time. The next morning Wilds and Brown were out early, and killed a fine large buck, the biggest I ever saw in my life. Wilds had it now, for he had found out that it was Muzzy that had perpetrated the joke on him; so he takes the head off the buck with a long neck, then carefully arranging it on a stick, he placed it so it looked like a deer lying beside a rock, with nothing visible of him but his head. Next morning he invites Muzzy to accompany him on a hunt. He takes him up on the right side of the rock, then he whispers to him to keep a sharp lookout. Just then, bang goes Muzzy's gun, Wilds pulls up, but Muzzy says, "hold, Claib, I want this one," (up to this time he had not killed any) bang, again, with the same result; d——n you, he says, I will fetch you, and this time he missed the head and struck the stick, and the head fell to the ground; he dropped his rifle in the excitement, and rushed up; imagine his surprise to find a deer head without a body. It was now Wilds' time, who sings out, "look out for snakes." He describes Muzzy as looking more like an idiot than anything else he could compare him to. Muzzy now tries to bribe Claib to say nothing about it when they return to camp, but he was uncompromising, and that night the jug and the joke went high. It was about this time that Mr. Norris placed the deer head, which was literally working with deer "ticks," under Captain Dohman's blankets; he had not lain there very long until he sprang up exclaiming "Lightning has struck the traveler, or the traveler has struck lightning, one or the other." The Captain did not sleep much that night, but he affirms that there was not less than a bushel of ticks on him at once.

A hunter from Virginia City, named J. N. Robinson, joined our party while we were up there, whom we found to be a very genial, social gentleman, and a remarkably successful hunter, and devotedly attached to this hunting-ground. He informed us that he had spent two months each year for the past four years, at this place, and always succeeded in killing all the deer he wanted, and in honor of him we call the place "Robinson's Park."

This will now finish this hunt, but as our quail season soon commences, we expect to have rare sport in this end of the county, and will, from time to time try and make your sporting column interesting to at least the sports of the gun.   NIMROD.

SALT SPRINGS.

These are about six miles south of Silver lake, on the south side of the Mokelumne river, and consequently in Calaveras county; but properly belong to the Silver lake region, and merit the notice of all who visit that vicinity. They are on an elevated bench of rock a few yards from the river, and, unless special search for them is made, might be passed unnoticed by persons fishing along the river. The salt water is found in holes of various sizes, from a few inches to three feet in depth, in the solid granite rock which characterizes the whole region. These are so regular in their shape as to induce a belief that they are hollowed out by human agency, in the manner that the holes where the Indian women grind or pound their acorns and pine nuts are, which they resemble. Reports differ as to their number. Captain J. C. Ham, estimates them at nine hundred. Eli Smith, of Volcano, who has visited them several times, thinks there may be one hundred and fifty. The holes are always found filled with water. At the bottom is a mixture of dirt and salt, which, being washed, leaves a residuum of remarkably pure table salt. The water with which the holes are filled appears to have trickled over the rocks from above, and seems to come from a small shallow lake or pool, a hundred or two feet in diameter, which is surrounded by tall reeds and grass, so that one might pass quite near without seeing the water. There is no apparent trail leading to these salt wells, but as the surrounding rock is the indestructable and *trackless* granite, no conclusion as to their origin or use can be formed from that circumstance, as thousands might visit the place, and leave no trail. In the early days of silver mining on the Comstock ledge, the Indians brought in considerable quantities of salt, which was thought to have been found out on the plains beyond Carson river. It seems likely that the whole Washoe tribe may have for centuries annually visited this place for salt; that the wells were gradually hollowed out, and constantly enlarged by use. A thorough examination of the subject might reveal many interesting things in Indian history.

MAMMOTH QUARTZ VEIN.

In wandering over the rocks one will see innumerable quartz veins of all sizes and kinds, crossing each other with *faults* and other geological phenomena, highly suggestive of the disturbed condition of affairs when earth was young, ere the Sierras were lifted from the sea, or of the earth in our own time, thirty thousand feet below, where new Sierras are slowly being formed. Between Silver lake and the salt wells is a quartz vein, said to be the largest in the State. It appears to be barren of gold, which, however, may, in its own time, have been deposited near the surface, as in our present worked veins, twenty thousand feet above the present summits of the Sierras.

THE RUBY OR SCHORL MINE

Is in this vicinity, on what is called Burley's peak. This is a form of quartz crystallization of various colors—white, green, red, and black, some of the varieties bordering upon emerald. It is likely that a thorough search might reveal valuable stones in this vicinity. The mine is claimed by J. C. Ham, of Aqueduct City.

TROUT FISHING.

Mention has been made of the small trout in Silver lake. Whether they are of different species, or whether the climatic character of the lake prevents their growth, is uncertain, but no large fish are found in the lake, while in the streams around are trout of several pounds in weight, which have all the wariness and vigor, when hooked, characteristic of the trout family. The *unlucky* fisherman will see hundreds of "fine speckled beauties" lying at ease in a hole twenty feet deep, from which fly nor worm will draw them. Some persons in times past, in revenge no doubt, have blown them up with **dynamite, or strangled** them with pounded **soap-root**. The law makes these acts high misdemeanors, but who cares for law forty miles in the woods, when the trout refuse to bite at a reasonable bait?

The rocks in all this vicinity are *glacier*-polished, and none but an active, sure-footed man can clamber safely over them.

SILVER MINES.

Some twenty-five miles west of the summit argentiferous galena in considerable quantities has been found. The slates and other rocks in the vicinity of the junction of the old Placerville and Volcano emigrant roads have all the appearance of being metalliferous, and may yet prove the source of much wealth. Lyman and Silas Tubbs, and others, made the discovery, some years since, of such an outcrop; but they have never developed the prospect.

MAGNIFICENT VIEWS FROM THE SIERRAS.

Standing on one of the western spurs of the Sierras, the valleys of the San Joaquin and Sacramento, as well as the hills of the Coast Range, are in full view; Mount Shasta in the north, and the treeless plains of the south, the sharp outlines of the Mendocina peaks; **Diablo** in the middle, with the hazy atmosphere, now shading everything with the tint of autumnal ripeness, now drifting away towards the sea in crimson clouds, and leaving the air so clear that the streets of Sacramento, though fifty miles away, are distinctly visible, are evidences out of which the most splendid sunsets that imagination can conceive, will occasionally appear.

Sometimes the fog comes rolling in from the ocean like a sea of molten silver, spreading over the valleys, until only the tips of the highest mountains are visible above the feathery masses of vapor that lie at rest, or, slowing melting, blend and fuse into a thousand shapes, reminding one of an invading host taking the land, and, sometimes, of the spiritual world, where millions of departed souls re-enact the stories of their earthly careers. Sometimes, at the close of a storm, when the clouds, in dense, black masses, hang suspended around the summits of the Sierras and high over the plains, the setting sun, **blazing through the rifts**, will strike across the wide **plains, tinging the hills** with a rich orange hue, and the clouds with crimson and purple, giving one an idea of possible landscapes in the better land.

Again the thunder clouds gather in dark masses around the base of the mountains and over the wide valley, leaving all serene above; hill and cloud answering each other in lightning flashes and peal on peal of rolling thunder that dies away in deep mutterings a hundred miles distant, until we could almost believe that all the artillery of the world was parked in the great valley, engaged as an accompaniment in a grand anthem sung by the millions of all ages.

Bayard Taylor, the poet and traveler, expressed the opinion that the view from a point a few miles above the Mountain Spring House, was the most magnificent landscape to be seen in the world. How much the world has lost, that a man, with his soul to appreciate, his eyes to see, and his pen to describe, has not seen the landscape mentioned in one of its magnificent moods. If he had passed over it as many times as the writer of this article has, he could not have failed to see that which would have tasked his pen, facile as it was, to the utmost, to have described. Every season has its moods. The Winter with its storms sweeping the horizon with clouds, drenching everything in falling rain, alternating with clear days when every arm of the bay and rivers, every tree, every dwelling for fifty miles around is so distinct as to appear like a view through a telescope reversed; the Spring with its lights and shadows chasing each other with railroad speed, or resting for hours in lazy dalliance over wide portions of the plains; the Summer, with the haze blending with the brown hills and plains ripening into autumnal tints; the Autumn in dreamy obscurity, its deep golden veil occasionally lifted aside or piled in majestic folds on the Coast Range by the contending sea and land breezes, may well cause the painter to throw down his brushes in despair, or the writer to wish for a pen tipped with fire, so utterly above all human ability is the task of giving a representation of the constantly varying, beautiful, grand, or awful landscapes.

Let us stand on one of the foot-hills at the close of a day in October. If the gods of the air are favorable to our wishes, and grant us an exhibition of their powers, the deep haze, which all the day has hung around the mountains and over the plains, wrapping everything in a dreamy uncertainty, will gradually settle away towards the Coast Range of mountains, bringing trees, orchards, vineyards, and grain-fields into high relief. The oaks and pines in the mountains and plains will blend in the retreating haze until the one is lost in the other. The retreating veil will now form long wavy lines along the Coast Range, the tops of which are visible, and, by their presence, serve to aid in the illusion. The sinking sun, striking through the horizontal cloud-rifts, tinges all the openings with crimson and purple, like hills and mountains of a far-off land. The hills of gold and precious stones, the gates of pearl seem just in sight. These wide and glorious valleys must be peopled by millions on millions of happy spirits. We see the rivers and lakes, for they are but the continuation of that which we know to be water. We can almost hear the songs of the beautiful beings who float in fairy boats on those crystal lakes. The air seems filled with the soft murmur of music that comes in gentle echoes from the thousand harps played by angel hands. Lo! towards the south a breeze through the Golden Gate makes a riffle in the crimson clouds, rolling them into domes and amphitheaters. The horizontal lines of the cloud-strata are crossed by perpendicular divisions. A great city, vast in its proportions, with its streets and squares, lofty towers, temples, and palaces, comes into view. Yes, it is Rome. That huge circle of towering height is the Coliseum. That dome is the Pantheon. We hear the fierce debates in the forum. We hear Cicero denouncing Cataline. We see the triumphal processions with kings chained to the chariot-wheels of the conquerors. We hear the eighty thousand spectators in the Coliseum shout as the victims of the popular thirst for blood go down under the fierce blows of the successful gladiators. We see Cæsar, the Imperator, throw his robe over his head, and die like a god. We see the hordes of Attila rushing through the streets, slaughtering the miserable inhabitants, until the very swords are weary of blood. Rome of Augustus Cæsar! where art thou? As the shades of night deepen over the mimicry of thy palaces and amphitheaters, so did the barbarism bury the beautiful, the glorious, the good, and the infamous, in one common ruin.

The gorgeous pageant does not end here. Pericles summons the Athenians, and Mount Diablo becomes Mount Olympus, towering above the Acropolis. I see the Parthenon, with its unapproachable architecture. I see the hill crowned with palaces and works of art, and its six thousand statues, every fragment of which is now worth its weight of gold. I hear the finished periods of the Athenian orators. I hear the shouts of the people at the Olympic games. I see the approaching clouds, like the barbarism by which Athens was surrounded, gradually obliterate every line of the sunset scene.

Lo! another age appears. On the treeless plains of the San Joaquin the mimicry of cloudy fabric goes on. The pyramids, dark and sombre, now fast sinking into obscurity, rise to view, dim as if the vital energy that had first raised them had exhausted itself, and the very spirits had become faded spectres in a spectral world. The obscurity of four thousand years rests on these cloudy shapes of the toil of millions. Is there death and change in the spiritual world also? Have the millions, who cultivated the valley of the Nile, who built the cities of Memphis, with its temples that almost defy the tooth of time, ceased to re-enact, even in the spectral world, the actions of real life? Is a future existence dependent on the permanency of works?

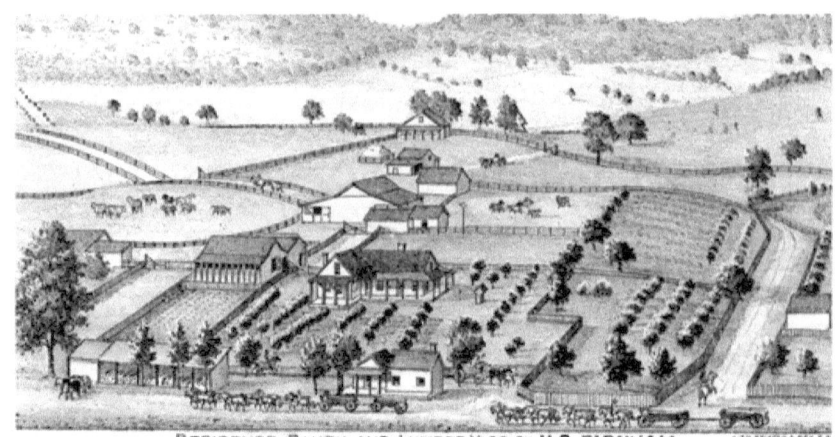

RESIDENCE, RANCH AND LUMBER YARD OF H.C. FARNHAM,
OLETA, AMADOR CO. CAL.

Gradually the crimson and purple deepened into night, and Cæsar, and Pharaoh, and Demosthenes, and the millions of spirits that had gathered to build the spectral towers, temples, and pyramids, vanished as the sun set behind the hills, and the dusty road, the cooling breeze from the mountains, and darkness, brought back real life, with its duties and vicissitudes. Is it all imagination? Is there no mind in the gorgeous landscapes that occasionally gild all the western horizon? Why should not the spirits of the departed, wandering in ether, pile together the half material substance of the air, and lead the world to a sense of beauty, and glory, and power?

CLIMATE.

So much has been written about the climate of California that it would seem useless to attempt any further description, especially for California readers. The temperature falls a little lower in Winter than in Sacramento, and rises a little higher in Summer. But once or twice during thirty years' observation did the temperature at Ione valley fall to 16° above zero. The coldest spell perhaps ever experienced was on 14th, 15th, 16th, and 17th of March, 1859, when the ground, in shady places, remained frozen all day. A dry north wind helped to reduce the temperature. The ground in some places was frozen two inches thick. The season was early, fruit trees being in full bloom, which was mostly destroyed. Grass and grain in many places was killed, so that as the sun came up it wilted and turned black. The temperature occasionally falls to the freezing point during a storm; an inch or two of snow may then fall, to remain on until the sun comes out, and then vanish in a few minutes. Occasionally there is a flurry of hail, which has been known to seriously injure young vines and fruit trees. The most dreaded, because most destructive, feature is the dry, north wind, that occasionally sweeps over the country. "Whence it cometh, or whither it goeth, no man can tell," but the moist ground becomes dry and hard; the promising crop droops after three or four days, and, if the season has been dry, the farmer hastens to cut his fields of grain for hay. So drying is this wind that the furniture in the house will warp and crack, wagons will fall down, and general shrinkage takes place. The atmosphere is charged with electricity, and combing one's head will produce a multitude of sparks. This wind is the bane of farming in California, but it does not prevail in the mountains as in the San Joaquin and Sacramento valleys. In Amador it sometimes injures, but scarcely ever ruins a crop.

DROUTHS.

Once only during the history of Amador county has there been an utter failure from drouth. In the winter of 1863–64, so little rain fell that scarce a fourth of a crop was raised, though, in the opinion of the best farmers, early sowing and deep, thorough ploughing would have doubled the yield. So short was the straw, both of hay and grain, that aprons were attached to the reapers and mowers to save a little handful which otherwise would be lost among the clods and stubble. Barns and granaries were empty, and cattle starved by the thousand. A few clouds would occasionally pass over, but they refused to part with their treasures, and the dry Summer completed the failure of the crops.

FRESHETS.

As might be expected the heavy rain-fall sometimes damages the farmer and miner. The snow will fall perhaps ten or twenty foot deep in the upper parts of the Sierras, and a warm rain will send it down in a three days run. Such a snow-fall, followed by a warm rain, occurred in December, 1861, inundating all the valleys, carrying off fences, and, in some instances, buildings. The overflow was much increased by the moving sand and gravel which obstructed the channels. But when the water went down the farmer went to ploughing, and bounteous crops rewarded his labor, and one year's work repaired all the losses. A few farms were injured with "slickens," and, in some places, as at the Q Ranch, the streams cut new channels, but the losses were trifling compared with the drouth two years after. Sometimes a "cloud burst," more particularly described in the history of Jackson, will create an overflow over a limited space, as did the one which swept Jackson and Sutter Creeks in February, 1878. But these are necessarily limited in territory, and though destructive enough when they prevail, do not bankrupt whole counties like the ice floods on the Missouri or Susquehanna rivers.

RAIN TABLE FOR AMADOR COUNTY.

Compiled by Frank Howard, of Sutter Creek, for the Years 1874-75-76-77-78-79-80.

MONTHS.	1874.	1875.	1876.	1877.	1878.	1879.	1880.
September	*				.11		
October	4.12	.66	3.61	.71	1.69	2.59	.36
November	7.50	14.04	.18	1.93	1.16	2.88	.35
December	.36	5.04		1.40	.35	6.84	11.42

MONTHS.	1875.	1876.	1877.	1878.	1879.	1880.	1881.
January	17.18	7.43	6.94	9.35	5.34	3.25	10.89
February	1.40	4.40	.94	12.96	5.74	3.93	5.22
March	2.14	6.46	2.68	6.20	8.07	3.81	2.49
April	.22	1.62	.46	1.94	5.08	15.85	3.00
May	.59	.75	1.74	.20	2.45	3.02	
June	1.26	.75	.18	.60	.29		
July		.36					
August		.29					
Total	34.77	39.80	16.73	35.29	29.68	42.17	33.73

Sacramento totals for same years: 23.64, 25.67, 9.32, 21.24, 16.77, 18.51.

* Sprinkle.

From these comparisons the average rain-fall appears to be nearly seventy-two per cent. greater at Sutter Creek than at Sacramento. Other places in Amador would show a still greater difference. It has been known to rain continuously for hours at Vogan's (Mountain Spring House) when no rain fell at Buena Vista, six miles below. During the Spring of 1864, when rain was so anxiously looked for, showers were frequent on the Mokelumne river when no rain fell a half mile away. The cooler temperature at the above places is supposed to have caused the clouds to part with their moisture.

CHAPTER XXXVII.
ARROYO SECO GRANT.

Claim Rejected—Claim Confirmed on Appeal—Character of Grant—Matters of Record—Letter from T. A. Hendricks, Attorney General—Final Survey—During Hancock Agency—Proposed Settlement—Sale to J. Mora Moss & Co.—Memorial to President Lincoln—Dispossession—Settlers' League—Shooting of Herman Wohler—Last Effort—Memorial to Congress.

THE policy of making homes for the people of easy attainment has been so long established in the United States that few living have any recollections to the contrary. In New York the Patroon estates, and in Louisiana the Spanish grants, had hung like a pall over the inhabitants, but the majority of the people knew nothing of the relics of feudalism, which made one man the owner of the rents at least, of thousands of acres. When the great immigration poured into California in 1849-50, they found the valleys and plains around the bay and larger rivers in the possession of a few men. General Sutter at New Helvetia, Charles Weber at Stockton, were near the mines first discovered, and first gave an idea of the scope of the princely estates, which afterwards, in the hands of professional land-grabbers, whose infernal resources seemed unfathomable, became such a source of oppression and robbery. The confusion in the early records of the California government; the loose manner in which the records were kept in the national archives in the city of Mexico; the difficulty of gaining access to them on account of the distance, all conspired to render the grant system a fruitful field for the operations of rascals. Grants were manufactured by the hundred after the treaty of peace with Mexico. In some instances the paper itself on which the grants were written, bore water-marks of a date subsequent to the treaty; these were of course rejected. Others as fraudulent, but more cautiously manipulated, were made to fit the lands made valuable by settlement. The uncertainty of titles to the agricultural lands around the bay were, to the earlier settler of Amador county, far away matters.

The first glimpse of the impending calamity came in 1853. Dr. E. B. Harris and H. A Carter of Ione were visiting the Legislature then in session at Benicia, to further the project of the organization of the new county of Amador. There they casually learned of a claim recently filed in the General Land Office with "IONE" marked in the center of a plot of the claim. The reader will remember that "Ione" was a name given to the valley almost by inspiration. Who had any business with that name? A visit to the Land Office was next in order. There was the title

EL ARROYO SECO,

Situado asi a los Cordilleras la Sierra Nevada tene endo for limites at Norte el vio de los Cosumnes al sur el do Moquelemes at *aiccenie*, el camino del Sacramento Y, al Este Las Sierras.

[Filed with Secretary of Land Comission, November 1, 1852.]

This purported to be a tract of land granted to Teodocio Yerba May 8, 1840, containing eleven leagues of land. Sierra Nevada mountains! Cosumnes river! Moqueleme river! Sacramento road! Which were the Sierras? Where was the Sacramento road? It may well be supposed that our friends had no heart for lobbying a bill through the Legislature for the division of the county of Calaveras. They returned home and called a public meeting, to announce the coming disaster. Charles Walker was made chairman. Judge Carter explained the situation. Some were for treating the claim with contempt. The uncertainty of the boundaries, the enormous area included in the description, were conclusive evidence of fraud. Others reasoned differently. If the grant had been fraudulent it would have been more carefully worded. Its uncertainty, the awkwardness of description, such as one might make who never had seen the country, or such as he might get from the Indians, was in favor of its realty. There was the Shaddon & Daylor ranch, the Pico ranch, and the Weber, only a little ways off.

A society or league was formed to contest the grant. It does not appear that any forcible or illegal means were thought of. Money was raised and legal talent engaged. A. C. Brown and H. A. Carter were employed to engage a competent man to watch the affair. O. P. Sutton, a clerk in the Land Office was first employed, Thorntorn & Williams, two eminent land lawyers, being afterwards associated with him.

CLAIM REJECTED.

February 27, 1855, the claim was rejected by the Commissioners appointed by the United States Government to try the validity of the Mexican claims. On the 12th of May, notice of appeal from the decision of the Commissioners was filed in the United States District Court, followed by a petition for review on the 11th of June. On the 21st of April, 1856, the decision of the Commissioners was reversed by Judge Hoffman.

CLAIM CONFIRMED.

By this decision, Andres Pico was entitled to eleven square leagues of land, somewhere in the boundaries set forth in his grant. On the 3d of October, 1856, an appeal to the United States Supreme Court was perfected, and the transcript sent up. It does not appear that the Court ever took the case into consideration. So far, in this matter, the people had a right to think the Government would watch their interests. The claims for land were against the Government, not against the people; but we can hardly consider the Courts and their officers as acting for the people, but for the speculators. It is now, after the lapse of a quarter of a century, difficult to ascertain the true facts in the case. Whether Williams & Thornton did their duty during this stage of the affair; whether any attorney for the people made an appearance when the case was called in the United States Court, is not known; but, at any rate, on the 4th of May, 1858, the case was, on motion of Attorney-General Black, dismissed, and the order for dismissal of suit filed in San Francisco.

CHARACTER OF THE GRANT.

As the claim to the land is now confirmed, a little knowledge as to the character of the men concerned may not be out of place. Yorba, or Yerba, for it seems that he could not write his name; and probably did not know how to spell it, was connected by marriage with some of the higher families. Juan B. Alvarado was an intriguer, first a Secretary in the department of Customs; then a revolutionist, who by means of an arrangement with Isaac Graham, a Tennesseean, wriggled himself into the position of Governor. It is said of him that he gave to all his followers whatever land they asked for. The date of the grant is May 8, 1840. Sutter did not settle at New Helvetia until the latter part of 1839. His grant was not completed until 1841; Weber's not until 1843.

In the Autumn of 1841, the Mokelkos, a tribe of Indians living on the Mokelumne, below Lockeford, stole some cattle from Sutter. He organized an expedition and attacked them, marching thirty miles in the night. This march would carry him across the Cosumnes, and in sight of the Jim Martin and Lyon range of hills, which are probably described in the grant as the "neighboring Sierras." But he did not obtain his grant from Alvarado until June, 1841. Pio Pico's grant covered the lower portion of the Mokelumne river. Charles Weber did not get his grant until some years after he had resided with Sutter, and not until after the termination of Sutter's war with the Mokelkos, and a treaty of peace with them. He obtained permission to settle on the slough at Stockton from the chief, by agreeing to defend them against the Mexicans, the mortal enemies of the Mokelkos. In the subsequent revolutions, while Alvarado was striving to mantain his position as Governor, it is said that Sutter assisted him materially with men, in return for which he not only gave Sutter a large tract of land, but granted to other persons, such as Sutter should recommend, in his capacity as Justice, other tracts. If the date of this had been but a year and a month later, it might have been genuine, but reason is against such a conelusion. It is absurd to suppose that the outside grant should have preceded the larger ones by a period of one to three years.

Yerba's grant was made May 8, 1840, by Juan B. Alvarado; Sutter's grant, June, 1841, by same person; Guillermo Gulnae's for Weber, July 13, 1843, by Manuel Micheltorena.

The Hudson's Bay Fur Company had a trading-post at French Camp (hence the name), south of Stockton, for many years, and left about the time that Weber obtained his grant, which induced him to locate temporarily on the Cosumnes, until he got on better terms with the Mokelkos.

Andres Pico, who bought of Yerba, was brother of the last Governor, Pio Pico, and is said to have been addicted to drink and gambling. De Zaldo was in 1850–51 a clerk in the Land Office. It seems more probable that the whole matter was *cooked up* in the Land Office after the discovery of *gold*, than that the grant should have preceded such settlements as Sutter's and Weber's. The fact that at the time of making the grant no Mexican dared show his head east of the San Joaquin or Sacramento rivers, serves to confirm the former hypothesis. Governor Downey, who is believed to have a good knowledge of the nature of Spanish claims, denounced the Arroyo Seco as a rank fraud.

For the purpose of keeping our history clear, it may be best to have a list of titles passed:—

Grant to Teodosio Yerba, May 8, 1840.

Sale to Andres Pico, October 4, 1852. Consideration five hundred head of cattle.

[COPY OF DEED.]

Know all men by these presents, That we, Teodocio Yerba and Maria Antonio Lugo his wife, for and in consideration of the sum of five hundred head of cattle, paid and delivered to us by Andres Pico, the receipt whereof is hereby acknowledged, have sold, bargained and transferred and by these presents sell, bargain and transfer to the said Andres Pico and his heirs and assigns, all that tract of land situate and lying in the county of Sacramento, bounded and described as follows: "Situado asi a las Cordilleras la Sierra Nevada tene endo for limetes at Norte el vio de los Cosumnes al sur el do Moquelemes at aiccente el camino del Sacramento Yal este Las Sierras inmuratus," and known by the name of "El Arroyo Seco," and being the same tract of land granted to the said Teodocio Yerba, by Governor Juan B. Alvarado, 8th May, 1840, and containing more or less, eleven leagues, together with all the improvements thereon, the rights, easements, and privileges appertaining thereto, to have and to hold for the use and benefit of the said Andres Pico, his heirs and assigns forever. And we for ourselves our heirs and administrators, hereby covenant with the said Pico, his heirs and assigns, that we will warrant and defend the said premises hereby conveyed against the claims and demands of any person or persons claiming by, through or from us.

Witness our hands and seals this fourth day of October, 1852.

(Signed)   TEODOCIO X YORBA.   [seal.]
                     his mark.

            MARIA ANTONIO X LUGO.   [seal.]
                     her mark.

Filed September 22, 1856, in Recorder's office, Amador County.

Andres Pico to Ramon De Zaldo. April 4, 1855. 2-11 Arroyo Seco. Consideration, $2,000. Filed in Amador County July 21, 1856.

Pico & De Zaldo to Green & Vogan, June 13, 1856. 317.69 acres (Q Ranch) Consideration, $3,176.90.

Same to Fixary & Sompayrac, July 23, 1856. Town lots in Jackson. Consideration, $600. Fixary Ranch, 240 acres. Consideration, $1,500.

Same to James Brown, December 2, 1856. 5,700 acres. Consideration, $9,516.

This was the famous sale of the mines, and included all of the quartz leads that were then known to be valuable, Spring Hill, Keystone, Herbertville, Amador, Union, Eureka, Badger, etc., also the town sites of Amador, Sutter and Jackson.

Pico & De Zaldo to Bruce Husband, December, 1856. Town lot in Jackson. Consideration, $1.

Same to Isaac Silver, January 9, 1857.
Same to Thomas Jones, January 13, 1857.
Same to William Pitt, January 12, 1857.
Same to Luther K. Hammer, February 9, 1857.
Same to John Williams, February 24, 1857.
Same to Geo. Durham, February 21, 1857.
Same to A. Sheakley, February 21, 1857.

The most of these were town lots in Jackson. Contracts for sale were also made in many places in the valley. In most instances the sales were made to influential persons upon favorable terms, the object being to detach them from the party of opposition. This was particularly true of the sales to Green & Vogan, John Edwards, Charles Stone, and James P. Martin.

Soon after the confirmation of the grant by the District Court, Pico employed Sherman Day to survey and sectionize the ranch in accordance with the United States survey, making Mount Diablo a base and meridian point. The lines were run to include all the valuable farms and mines possible. Many thousand dollars were obtained for the mines. After all had been got from them that was possible, the claim to the mines was abandoned, new lines being run to include other farms. For some years it was a floating grant. The lines were run so as to include a greater area on Dry creek. An improvement in any direction was sure to bring the grant line around it.

LOCATION OF THE TRACT.

This was next in order. During the location of the claim, high up on the mountains, the United States had sectionized and sold some of the valley lands on Dry creek. Parkey being among the purchasers. When the miners had been bled, the claim was again projected west on the lands recently sold by the Government, again making the United States a party to the affair.

For three or four years the people saw surveyor's lines run around their homes. Surveyor-General Mandeville being among those engaged. As he was supposed to be acting in his official capacity, a remonstrance against the crooked lines was forwarded to President Buchanan, but it seems that the article was not sufficiently explicit in describing the claim. Thomas A. Hendricks, Commissioner of the General Land Office, returned the following answer:—

LETTER FROM THOMAS A. HENDRICKS.

GENERAL LAND OFFICE,
August 18th, 1857.

SIR: There has been referred to this office a letter from you, dated 27th of June last, addressed to the President of the United States, complaining of a location of a private claim, under a Mexican grant called the "Arroyo Seco," so as to cover the settlements and improvements of yourself and others. The claim referred to is presumed to be that entered as No. 186, on the Docket of the Board of Land Commissioners, rejected by Board of Land Commissioners November 22d, 1853, but afterwards confirmed by the United States District Court, and the appeal dismissed in the United States Supreme Court, and therefore, stands finally confirmed.

The survey of this claim has not been returned to this office, and we have, therefore, no means of judging of the manner of its location. Though your letter presents a case of hardship, and the policy of the Government favors the protection of the settlers on public lands, we regret that you furnish no such specific information in the matter as would justify action by the Department. When, however, the final survey of the claim shall be returned, it will be carefully examined, particularly in respect to the "zigzag form" of its location, as represented by you.

Very respectfully,
Your obedient servant,
THOMAS A. HENDRICKS,
H. A. CARTER, ESQ., *Commissioner.*
Ione Valley P. O.,
California.

The Arroyo Seco was filed November 1, 1852, and was numbered 441; was rejected February 27, 1855, so that the claim referred to by Commissioner Hendricks could not have been the Arroyo Seco. Upon further inquiry it proved that Mandeville had been employed and paid by the grant party while ostensibly acting in an official capacity.

October 17, 1858, Mandeville wrote to the settlers that he should not make a final survey until after he returned from Washington, to which place he was then going. He assured them that all should be heard.

THE FINAL SURVEY

Was made in August, 1859. At the hearing of this, before Judge McAllister, a great many witnesses were examined as to the character of the country. The lagoon west of Ione, on Buckeye creek, according to some, was the valley intended to be covered by the grant. It was urged, with much reason, that the mountains between that lagoon and Ione valley were the "Sierras immaratus;" others ridiculed the idea of calling the hills of the *tertiary* formation a part of the mountains. Judge McAllister decided, April 26, 1860, that the grant of land was west of the Lyons and Martin Mountains. This, for a time, seemed to have removed the load of misery from the residents of Ione valley; from this time to December 10th was the golden opportunity, as we shall hereafter see. The survey was confirmed by Judge Hoffman, September, 1862. It is said that Hoffman examined the ground personally. This survey, and the new ownership which had occurred, fairly realized the worst fears of the settlers. In order to make a connected history, it will be necessary to retrace our steps and consider the condition of affairs.

DURING HANCOCK'S AGENCY.

For the purpose of acting as a partner and giving more authority to his deeds, Henry Hancock bought of Andres Pico one-fifth of the grant for sixty thousand dollars, deed dated April 20, 1859, and redeeded it for the same consideration the same day. The first deed was filed April 28, 1859, the second, June 9, 1860. Andres Pico also sold to De Zaldo a further interest of two leagues, for five thousand dollars. De Zaldo sold his entire interest in the grant to Pio Pico, commonly called Governor Pico, brother to Andres, December 10, 1861, for four thousand dollars. As at this time the principal contest was on the location of the grant; many efforts being made to compromise the matter, and end the contest. January 7th, Pico had written to the settlers assuring them of his good will, and asked them to consult with each other, so as to come to some amicable understanding. In May, Hancock commenced acting as agent for Pico and De Zaldo. May 27th, he wrote that a further contest would only waste their mutual substance, which would go to enrich strangers. A report becoming current that, in case the survey was confirmed, those who had been most active in opposing the grant, would have to pay a high price, Pico assured them that all should have their land at the same rate. During the time while the confirmation of the survey was pending in the United States Supreme Court for the Northern District of California, a number of the settlers, H. A. Carter, W. H. Harron, W. K. Johnston, assisted by O. P. Sutton, of their counsel, acting for the settlers, entered into an agreement with Pico to the following effect:—

AGREEMENT.

Pico should sell the land at the following rates:—

First class bottom-land in Ione valley, per acre		$ 10 00
" " " Jackson valley, per acre		9 00
" " red land, per acre		4 00
Second class red land, per acre		2 00
For town site of Ione, excepting such as had been heretofore sold or contracted		5,000 00

One-fourth at the time of completing the sale, and the balance to be paid within ninety days after a United States patent or its equivalent should be recorded at the county seat, without interest until the ninety days had expired. All indebtedness to be secured by mortgage. Pico to extinguish all liens and taxes outstanding on the land, so as to give the settlers a clear title. The settlers were to withdraw all opposition to the confirmation of the survey now pending in the Supreme Court of the United States for the Northern District of California. In case of disagreement as to the class of the lands in question, each party interested was to name one person, and these two a third, if necessary to effect a classification.

This was about one-fourth of the price at which the lands were valued, yet very few seemed to be willing to accept the terms. If the land was theirs, they wanted it without paying a *greaser* for it. Ten dollars an acre for a person who had already taxed himself twice that, to oppose the grant, was no easy matter to raise. It was hard to bring the men to concert of action. The moderate terms which Pico offered were considered as indicating a consciousness of a weak case, and so the matter remained undecided.

SALE TO J. MORA MOSS & CO.

Pico, as well as the settlers, had become exhausted with the long effort. Twenty-three hundred head of cattle had been driven into market and sold, to maintain the suit, and a mortgage for thirty-five thousand dollars was resting on the grant, as an evidence of further expenditure. Tired of the profitless contest, and, perhaps, disgusted with the dilatory action of the people, he sold on the 19th day of December, 1861, to J. Mora Moss, H. W. Carpentier, E. F. Beales, Herman Wohler, and others. This firm was composed of men who had become notorious in connection with land grants. They had even then acquired the reputation of hesitating at nothing which would forward their suits.

Bribery and perjury were openly talked of. The suits, or contests, whatever they may be called, still at this date, 1881, overshadow whole communities and paralyze the industries of cities and towns. Look at the cases of the Sobrante ranch, and the water front of Oakland. When the news of the sale came, and afterwards the confirmation of the survey by Judge Hoffman, September, 1862,

"Hope for a season bade the world farewell."

No astonishment was felt when, in 1863, Attorney-General Bates dismissed the appeal to the Supreme Court of the United States, and swept away the last ground for hope. If the Central Pacific Railroad Company can make the Sierras reach within five miles of Sacramento, perhaps Mora Moss & Co. may drive them back as far.

As a last resort, a memorial in a few words was addressed to President Lincoln and Attorney-General Bates, asking that the case might be again put on the calendar for a hearing. The paper was signed by several hundred persons, nearly all the residents of the county.

To Hon. Abraham Lincoln, President of the United States, and Hon. S. M. Bates, Attorney-General:—

We, the undersigned citizens of the United States, having failed everywhere, and under all circumstances, in our efforts to obtain justice in a matter of the deepest moment to ourselves and families, now, as a last resort, appeal to you. Failing in this, we will endeavor to reconcile ourselves to our hard fate, and at once quit our humble homes, and make room for those who, by means of their greater wealth, have been able to tire us out and obtain our little farms and poor homes, which have cost us long years of toil and privation.

Here are the facts and circumstances of our case, as briefly as it is possible to put them upon paper:—

Most of your petitioners emigrated to California at an early day, bringing with us our families and all we possessed, intending in the far-off land to make homes for ourselves and our children.

We located where we now reside, in Amador county, and upon lands then claimed by none but Indians, and as we honestly believed, owned by the general government.

Here at the foot of the mountains, under the laws of the State of California, we took up for ourselves homes in small parcels, varying from fifty to one hundred and sixty acres each. Being upon mineral land we have enjoyed our possessions uninterruptedly, save when the miners saw fit to prospect and mine within our enclosures.

Upon these lands we have planted trees, built fences, and erected houses. In our midst churches and school-houses have sprung up.

Years after our location, and when the eastern border of the tract was found valuable because of its mineral deposits, and when the whole face of our section had become a community of happy families, the rumor reached us that a Spanish grant covered our homes.

We consulted and employed lawyers; we have exhausted ourselves and been beaten. Now we think we are wrongfully defeated, and appeal to you for interposition in our behalf, so far as is consistent and proper.

The private claim which overwhelms us like a pall, and of which we complain, is the "Arroyo Seco Grant."

This claim was defeated before the Board of Land Commissioners.

The decree of the Board was reversed by the United States District Court.

The decision of the District Court was appealed from by the Government under the administration of Attorney-General Black.

The appeal was dismissed without a hearing.

Then came the location of the grant. Surveyor-General Mandeville located the grant, extending the eastern boundary into the foot-hills of the Sierra Nevada, to a point (improperly as we insist) which embraces our homes within the location.

The Government was heard in a review of Mandeville's proceedings before the Hon. —— McAllister, who, after deliberating upon the case, modified or changed the location made by Mandeville, and thereby relieved us from the scourge.

About this time the grant changed hands, passing from Andres Pico to the present proprietors, consisting of the following gentlemen: J. Mora Moss, H. W. Carpentier, Surveyor-General Beale, and Herman Wohler.

This party, men of great wealth, procured a rehearing of the case before the Hon. Ogden Hoffman, District Judge of the United States District Court.

Judge Hoffman upset the decree of Judge McAllister, and confirmed the location made by General Mandeville.

An appeal was taken by the Government to the United States Supreme Court.

We are just now informed that the appeal has been

dismissed, and we are therefore deprived of a fair hearing before the Tribunal of last resort, whither we supposed we were advancing according to the rules and practices of the Courts of our country, and from which Tribunal we were fondly hoping to receive the relief from litigation and oppression from which we have suffered so long.

Now all we ask from you, gentlemen, is that the case may be reinstated upon the calendar, treated as a new case, and passed upon by the Court. The decision of that high Tribunal, though adverse to us, will be cheerfully acquiesced in.

FIRST ATTEMPTS AT DISPOSSESSION.

Soon after the dismissal of the appeal a United States patent was obtained, and an attempt was made to dispossess the settlers. It was wisely resolved not to bring the people of the county into collision with their own officers, and a man by the name of Benjamin Bellock, said to be a Peruvian citizen, was put forward, so as to throw the case into the hands of a United States Marshal, though Bellock's interest must have been very remote, as his name does not appear on record as an owner of any part of the grant. The Marshal put in an appearance one day, and was in the act of evicting Thomas Rickey when quite a number of men (the Marshal estimated them at fifty), armed with rifles and pistols, went along to see how the thing was to be done. It is said that Turner, one of the settlers, used some threatening language, but no violence was used. The appearance of opposition was expected, and, perhaps, desired. The Marshal went back to San Francisco.

SETTLERS' LEAGUE.

This has been referred to before. Its organization was a secret one, and the proceedings were never published. Public notices were printed in an odd kind of type, and were signed with a numeral as Secretary. It was supposed that the members numbered three hundred or more. It was not known, of course, what measures were contemplated. Resistance to dispossession was openly talked of. It was thought that the grant company would have to pay the expense of keeping the soldiers in the field. Others said that we should be compelled to yield; that successful resistance to one company of soldiers would only bring a regiment, to oppose which would be an insurrection, another rebellion; but that we might murder the proprietors, and annoy those who should undertake the cultivation of the land, so as to make it worthless. The feeling was very bitter, and a little indiscretion might have brought on bloodshed.

THE SOLDIERS HAVE COME.

On the eleventh of February the sullen boom of the cannon, heard for miles around, announced the arrival of the soldiers. Why the cannon was fired does not appear, but every one knew the meaning. There was no gathering, no appearance of resistance. What might have happened if a smaller number had commenced the dispossession, can only be imagined. The seventy-five might—could have been beaten, but these were the "boys in blue," who had been battling so bravely for the *Union*, who had borne the flag aloft mid shot and shell in many a bloody field, who had saved our country. It is quite likely that grief as well as anger pervaded the league, and no resistance was offered. The people were determined to lose no point by vacating voluntarily, but quietly suffered their goods, household utensils, their wives and children, to be removed into the streets, in the storm, even, for the eviction took place in February, the month of rains. Some formed camps, others went to the houses of friends, and some went back to the houses from which they had been ejected. The fastenings were slight, and perhaps it was expected that they would return, though as trespassers. A man by the name of Clark, venerable, respectable and prudent, was made custodian and superintendent of the property. So far, the dispossession of the settlers had gone on without violence. The dispatches sent to the principals were congratulatory.

SHOOTING OF HERMAN WOHLER.

Wohler was perhaps the smallest owner in the grant, and, likely, the smallest capitalist in the company, and was probably put forward to manage the eviction on account of having no moral weakness or humane feelings which should prevent him turning a multitude of men, women and children out of their homes. If he had feelings to gratify, if he wished to avenge the long and persistent fight the settlers had made for their homes, his opportunity was ample. His pitiless face was seen everywhere directing the soldiers in their work—the only one in the whole crowd who did not show disgust with the business. Every man who had been driven out marked his overbearing and unfeeling demeanor. The dispossession was complete. The Arroyo Seco steal was a fixed fact. Any settler now who wished to have his rights would have to wade through an awful quagmire of law and technicalities. A big dinner was given, to celebrate the successful termination of the matter, which was attended by some of the county officers, among whom was the District Attorney, Briggs. Hare, stewed in wine, was said to be one of the extraordinary dishes set at this entertainment. The celebration was generally known, and was considered, in view of the distress of the people, heartless, and even insulting. It passed off, however, without disturbance, the guests leaving about ten o'clock P. M. Wohler was about retiring, and went to raise the window, to let out some of the cigar smoke which filled the room. While he stood for a moment looking into the darkness, the report of a rifle, in the direction of the blacksmith shop, was heard; he felt the sting of a ball in his chest and fell back seriously wounded. It was supposed to be mortal, but he so far recovered, in a few days, as to be removed to San Francisco.

The news that a man had been shot in Ione on account of land matters, soon found its way over the State, and throughout the East. The settlers were now put on the defense. Those who were unacquainted with the previous facts denounced it as an atrocious act. Those who knew something of the circumstances, which have been related in this history, will find some reasons for a mild sentence. "To forgive is divine," they say. Forgiveness may be an attribute of divinity, but, though the Ione Valley people are, perhaps, as moral and as well-behaved as any community in the State, they have never made any pretensions to a divine nature. Let no one pass judgment on the act until he has first put himself in the place of a settler, ejected, with his wife and children, from a home which he has wrested from a desert.

Wohler recovered from this wound, and died about two years since in Sonoma county. The agent, Clark, put in possession of the property was prudent and obliging, as far as his position would permit, renting the land to the former owners at a nominal figure. In a few years the ill-feeling seemed to abate, the new owners were permitted to occupy the lands in security, and peace and industry once more resumed their sway.

THE LAST EFFORT

To get justice was made at the session of the Legislature in 1865-66. Through the instrumentality, principally, of A. H. Rose, State Senator from Amador county, Congress was memorialized on the subject. On hearing it read, many members of Congress denounced the system of grants as a store-house of fraud, but nothing beneficial to the settlers ever came of it.

The memorial will conclude this chapter on the "Arroyo Seco Grant."

MEMORIAL TO CONGRESS.

The Memorial of the Legislature of the State of California to the Congress of the United States respectfully represents—

That at the time California was acquired by the United States, a tract of arable land, containing some fifty thousand acres, well watered and exceedingly fertile, had remained, from its secluded position and its distance from the sea-coast, if not undiscovered, entirely unoccupied by civilized man. The tract lies near to the Sierras, and is surrounded by low hills, and beyond them sterile plains, and it is quite probable that up to the time when gold was discovered it had never been visited by white man; it is entirely certain that no vestige of civilization was ever found on it. In 1848, when General Sutter prospected for gold two miles above in the foot-hills, the principal stream which irrigates and fertilizes this valley had not even a name to designate it. It has been known from that time as Sutter creek. The same is true of its second principal stream, named for an early miner, Jackson. Another, still, from a miner, Amador; and, curiously enough, the grant, which will be hereafter mentioned, takes its name from a stream christened by the Mexican miners, after *eighteen hundred and forty-eight,* Arroyo Seco, or Dry creek, and the village in which they lived is still known as Drytown. The valuable belt of mineral lands embracing the villages of Drytown, Amador, Sutter Creek and Jackson, lies ten miles to the above and to the east of this valley, and was prospected by Amador, Sutter, Jackson, and others, in the fall and winter of 1848-49, and at that time the valley was *entirely unoccupied.*

In 1849 it attracted the attention of enterprising men, who found it as nature had left it, unoccupied and unclaimed. They believed, and were justified by all appearances in this belief, that this was public land, belonging to the United States. They were principally Western men, who had from their youth been familiar with the beneficent system of land laws in the new and unoccupied Territories of the Union, and they settled at once in the beautiful valley, each making out, as near as he could, his hundred and sixty acres, and felt as certain of his right to do so, and as secure of his possession, as any heir could be to his ancient inheritance. They knew the country had been ceded to the United States; they knew the lands were public lands, for there was neither occupant nor claimant—not a vestige of a house, not a hoof of stock, nor a settlement nearer them than Sutters Fort, forty miles distant. These lands were exceedingly fertile, and convenient to the best market for farm produce in the world, the mines of California. As soon as the capacity of these lands to produce both grains and fruits had been tested by these hardy pioneers, they became at once exceedingly valuable. Improvements were commenced of the most permanent character; orchards and vineyards were planted; beautiful and expensive dwellings were erected; steam-power was introduced; large mills for converting their grain into flour were built; hotels, stores, and villages sprang up from the plain as if by magic; extensive ditches and costly aqueducts, both for the purpose of irrigation and working the mines upon the borders of the valley, were constructed, while churches and school-houses told plainer than words could convey, who were the settlers of Ione valley "and this waste land, where no man came or had come since the making of the world," blossomed as only California valleys can under the hand of experienced cultivation.

This picture is not overdrawn, and but feebly conveys an idea of the prosperity, progress, and refinement of the settlers in this valley, for the first ten years of their California life. The value of the improvements which they had placed upon the lands could not have been less than *eight hundred thousand dollars.* From that date words will fail to depict the calamities of these most unfortunate families. Their lands and improvements have been taken from them without any compensation whatever. A Mexican grant to the whole of the valley has been confirmed. The land has been patented to strangers by the United States, and pioneers, the early settlers, the men who bore the heat and burden of the day, have been stripped of their all, and many of them in the decline of life turned literally out of doors.

All right-thinking men naturally ask, "Is there any redress for this calamity? Can any compensation be made these families for their great loss?" In plain words, ought the general government to stretch forth its powerful arms for the relief of this distressed community? If it can be shown that they settled these lands under encouragement from the United States, all questions will be at an end. That many of them did so is a fact recorded in the archives of the government.

A. Caminetti.

ARROYO SECO GRANT.

To establish the right of this community to relief from the general government, it will be necessary to give a brief history of the Arroyo Seco Grant, upon which a patent to their lands has been issued.

It appears from the records that in the year 1852, on the 1st of November, Andreas Pico filed a petition before the Land Commissioners for eleven leagues of land, known as the Arroyo Seco Grant, and lying in whole or in part, as the petition states, in Sacramento county, but giving only certain external boundaries, which embraced a scope of country containing at least six times the required amount of land; and at this time it must be borne in mind Ione valley and the lands referred to in the memorial, lay not in Sacramento but in Calaveras county, which barely cornered on Sacramento. The question is now, not whether Pico had any valid grant, but did his claim for eleven leagues of land, *lying in whole or in part in Sacramento county*, impart any notice whatever to the settlers of Calaveras county? If they ever heard that such a petition had been filed before the Land Commissioners in San Francisco, they certainly never once thought it referred to their valley, for the boundaries claimed by Pico, as well as the county, seemed clearly to exclude them. Pico's eastern boundary came only to the foot-hills, *which rise, sharply defined, to the west of Ione*. It is confidently asserted that this claim was never at that time heard of in the valley; if it ever was, the next news heard from it was that it had been rejected by the Land Commission on the twenty-seventh day of February, 1855. Six years had now passed in undisturbed possession, with no adverse claims to the lands on which they resided; for Pico stated in his petition to the Land Commissioners, that there were no adverse claimants to the lands which he desired, and as there was at least fifty leagues of land vacant and unoccupied within the external boundaries which his petition set forth, it neither imparted notice nor gave a hint of danger to these bona fide and actual settlers. Pico said: "Somewhere in that space of country bounded on the north by the Cosumnes river, on the east by the foot-hills, on the south by the Mokelumne river, and on the west by the old Sacramento and Stockton trail, I claim eleven leagues of land, and the land I desire is *vacant*, unoccupied land—there is no other to claim it." And his claim would have been satisfied four times over and never have touched them. Ought they, as the most scrupulously prudent men, to have thought the shaft was aimed at their peace? They did not think it was, and they continued to build, and improve, and enter into the fruit of their labors. They had the most unbounded confidence that the general government would now, as she always had, protect her hardy pioneers.

On the 12th of May, 1855, notice of appeal from the Land Commission was filed, followed on the 11th of June by a petition for review; and on the 21st of April, 1856, the Court reversed the action of the Land Commission, and confirmed to Andreas Pico eleven leagues of land, somewhere within his said external boundaries. No survey had yet been made; the grant had been confirmed, but not *located*. And it must be steadily borne in mind that there was abundance of land to satisfy the grant, and leave the settlers alone. Would not the United States undoubtedly see that this was done? Before proceeding, however, to the history of the surveys, we will complete the legal history of this calamitous grant. On the third of October, 1856, an appeal to the United States Supreme Court was perfected, and the transcript sent up, and, without ever coming to a hearing, was, May 4, 1858, on motion of Attorney-General Black, dismissed, and the mandate of dismissal filed in San Francisco on the 3d of September, of the same year. This, of course, ended the litigation. It must steadily be borne in mind that the United States, during all this time, was the party in interest, and, by her highest officers, managed this important suit, involving, it is true, only the price of the land, some sixty thousand dollars; to her citizens—her children—the increased value of improvements and cultivation, amounting to nearly or quite a million. We have now reached the Autumn of 1858, ten years subsequent to the discovery of gold, and nine since the valley was first settled. Many of the farms were worth a hundred dollars an acre, and, in the character and value of their improvements, would not suffer by comparison with the most highly cultivated sections of the older States.

The United States had surveyed and laid off into townships and sections nearly the whole of the valley, and have actually sold, as the records of the Land Office at Stockton show, four thousand nine hundred and ninety-six and forty-nine one hundredths acres; the balance had been all, or nearly all, pre-empted. We now ask, in all candor and kindness, if the United States could have so located these eleven leagues of land belonging to Pico, so as not to disturb these settlers, and did not do it, ought she not to reimburse them for their losses? To determine this question, so vital to their hopes, let us proceed with the history of the surveys.

Sometime during the Summer of 1856, Andreas Pico himself came with surveyors into the district, and proceeded to select and mark out his eleven leagues. It would seem that if any person knew where the land was he, the grantee, was most likely to possess this information. He located his eastern boundary ten miles further east than the line of the present survey, and included within his boundaries all the rich belt of mineral lands heretofore spoken of, and with the invaluable mines, assumed ownership of the thriving villages of Amador, Sutter Creek, and Jackson, the county seat of the new county, which, in 1854, had been carved from Calaveras. He established his boundaries by permanent monuments, and proceeded to sell and deed lands, as the records of Amador county will show, to numerous purchasers, across all this range. The wealthiest and most intelligent quartz miners in this State bought his title.

It will be remembered that this survey of 1856 left out a large number of those persons who are now included in the present survey, and these facts are stated to render the position impregnable that these settlers believed, and were justified by the facts surrounding them in this belief, that they were upon the public lands of the United States.

In the meantime to render this belief a certainty, the United States surveyed all the valley lands to the west of Pico's location, and sold them to these very men who now are memorializing Congress for relief.

But time rolled on; the survey had not yet been confirmed; the mines were growing poorer and the valley richer, and Pico in his great anguish, when he discovered that he had not included within his lines all the valuable property between the Cosumnes and Mokelumne rivers, and the old Stockton trail and the foot-hills, proceed at once to change the lines of the survey.

32

In August, 1859, that grant was surveyed by the United States Surveyor-General for the State of California, J. W. Mandeville, Esq. The eastern line of Pico's first survey was carried ten miles west, and of necessity, included many of the settlers who had purchased these lands of the United States. It must constantly be borne in mind that this was a *floating grant*; that there was at least six times as much land contained within its exterior lines as the grant called for; that all the lands outside of this valley were vacant lands, and that this survey was persistently and openly made to include the most valuable farms, and was made by a United States Surveyor-General, and confirmed by a United States District Judge.

This survey was confirmed September, 1862. An appeal was taken from the order of confirmation, and this appeal, on motion of Attorney-General Bates, was dismissed February 3, 1863. Not until this date were the settlers left without hope.

Soon after this confirmation, a patent was issued and a company of United States dragoons ordered into the valley to assist the United States Marshal in ejecting the settlers. Let us quickly draw a veil over this sad picture, and state at once the plan we propose for redress.

We appeal to Congress, and respectfully pray that a commission of disinterested and qualified men be selected and authorized, at the expense of the general government, to visit the land in question; to inquire into and ascertain all the facts of the case; to take testimony in relation thereto, and to award to each settler such amount as may be deemed by said commission to be just and right. And Congress is further requested to make such appropriation as will be necessary to carry out the objects of said commission.

Such proceedings on the part of Congress your memorialists believe to be consonant with reason and justice, and to be sanctioned by precedent.

His Excellency, the Governor, is requested to forward a copy of the above memorial to each of our delegation in Congress.

CHAPTER XXXVIII.

FARNHAM'S HISTORY OF ALVARADO.

SINCE writing the foregoing chapter, the writer found in an old history of California, a further account of Juan B. Alvarado, which may be interesting as throwing some light on the character of those persons who were, as is now believed, instrumental in the manufacture of the fraudulent " Arroyo Seco Grant."

J. T. Farnham, a man who had been an extensive traveler, arrived in the Bay of Monterey on board the bark *Don Quixote* in 1840, at the time that Alvarado, acting as Governor of California, had imprisoned all the foreign population on the charge of conspiring against the government. They were confined in narrow quarters and treated with the utmost inhumanity, and our author's statements, in consequence of his sympathy for the unfortunate prisoners, may have been colored more than facts warrant. His history of the affair places Alvarado in no enviable light. It may be found, commencing page sixty, " Early Days of California," by J. T. Farnham.

In 1836, a Mexican general by the name of Echuandria was the commandant general of Upper California. Some years previous, as will be particularly shown in another place, he had come up from Mexico with a band of fellow myrmidons, and, having received the submission of the country to the authorities of that Republic, commenced robbing the government for which he acted, and the several interests which he had been sent to protect. Nothing escaped his mercenary clutches. The people, the missions, and the revenue were robbed indiscriminately as opportunity offered. A few of the white population participated in these acts. But generally the Californians were the sufferers, and, as is always the case with unhonored rogues, raised a perpetual storm of indignation about the dishonest deeds of those they desired to supplant for the purpose of enacting the same things. An occurrence of this kind was the cause of the revolution in 1836.

A vessel had cast anchor in the harbor of Monterey. General Echuandria, not having that honorable confidence in the integrity of the Custom House officers which thieves are accustomed to have in one another, placed a guard on board the craft to prevent them from receiving bribes for their own exclusive benefit. To this the officers demurred; and, in order to free their territory from the creatures of one whose conscience would compel him to receive bribes for his own pockets instead of theirs, they sent their own clerk, a young rascal of the country by the name of Juan Baptiste Alvarado, to inform the general that it was improper to suggest, by putting a guard on board, that the officers of the ship which lay under the fort, either attempted or dared to attempt the payment of duties!

The general, however, was too well acquainted with his inalienable rights to be wheedled out of them in this manner, and manifested his indignation towards the clerk for attempting to obtrude his plebeian presence on his golden dream, by ordering him to be put in irons. Alvarado, however, escaped.

On page two hundred and eighty-six he again refers to this transaction in the following terms:—

In the year 1836, a quarrel arose between the Mexican Governor at Monterey, and Custom House officer by the name of Juan Baptiste Alvarado, in regard to the division of certain bribes which had been paid to the officers by the supercargo of a foreign ship, as a remuneration for entering upon the Government books only half the cargo, and admitting the remainder for a certain sum in specie and goods, paid to themselves; and the first result of the difficulty was a revolutionary movement under Alvarado and Graham, as I have heretofore related.

To continue the narrative in Farnham's own words:—

He (Alvarado) fled into the country, rallied the farmers, who still loved the descendants of Philip the II. more than *El Presidente*, and formed a camp at the Mission of San Juan, thirty miles eastward from Monterey.

Near this mission lived an old Tennesseean by the name of Graham; a stout, sturdy backwoodsman, of a stamp which existed only on the frontiers of the American States— men with the blood of the ancient Normans and Saxons in their veins; with hearts as large as their bodies can hold, beating nothing but kindness till injustice showed its fangs, and then, lion like, striking for vengeance. This trait of natural character had been fostered in Graham by the life he had led. Early trained to the use of the rifle, he had learned to regard it as his friend and protector; and when the season of manhood had arrived, he threw it upon his shoulder and sought the wilderness, where he could enjoy its protection, and be fed by its faithful aim. He became a beaver hunter—a cavalier of the wilderness—that noble specimen of brave men, who have muscles for riding wild horses and warring with wild beasts, a steady brain and foot for climbing the icy precipice, a strong breast for the mountain torrent, an unrelenting trap for the beaver, a keen eye and deadly shot for a foe. A man, was this Graham, who stood boldly up before his kind, conscious of possessing physical and mental powers adequate to any emergency. He had a strong aversion to the elegant edifices, the furniture, wardrobe, and food of polished life, coupled with a vivid love of mountain sublimity, the beautiful herbage on uncultivated districts, the wild animals, and the streams of water roaring down the frozen heights. Even the gray deserts, with the hunger and thirst incident to traveling over them, had wild and exciting charms for him. On these his giant frame had obstacles to contend with worthy of its powers. A projecting rock, against which blazed his camp-fire, a crackling pine-knot his light, a roasting sirloin of elk or a buffalo hump for a supper, and a sleep in his blankets on the green sward in the open air after a day's exciting hunt, were the objects sought with the keenest zest, and enjoyed with the greatest pleasure.

He forced his way over the Rocky Mountains and located himself in Upper California. This country was suited to his tastes. Its climate allowed him to sleep in the open air most of the year; an abundance of native animals covered the hills, and nature was spread out luxuriantly in wild, untrodden freshness.

As I have said, this brave man resided near the Mission of San Juan. He had there erected a rude dwelling and a distillery. On the neighboring plains he herded large bands of horses, mules and cattle. To this fine old fellow Alvarado made known his peril and designs; whereupon the foreigners assembled at Graham's summons, elected him their captain, an Englishman by the name of Coppinger lieutenant, and repaired to San Juan. A council of war was held between the clerk and the foreigners. The former promised that if by the aid of the latter he should successfully defend himself against the acting Governor, and obtain possession of the country, it should be declared independent of Mexico, and that the law which prevented foreigners from holding real estate should be abrogated. The foreigners agreed, on these conditions, to aid Alvarado to the utmost of their power. The next morning the united forces, fifty foreigners and twenty-five Californians, marched against Monterey. They entered the town in the afternoon of the same day, and took up their position in the woods, one hundred rods in the rear of the castello or fort. No event of importance occurred till the night came on, when the awe with which darkness sometimes inspires even the bravest minds, fell with overwhelming power on the valorous garrison, that, notwithstanding they were supported by the open mouths of the guns, the barking of their dog, the roar of the surf, and the hooting of an owl on a neighboring tree-top, they were absolutely compelled to forsake the ramparts, for the more certain protection of unmolested flight.

Graham and his men perceiving the discomfiture of their enemies, availed themselves of their absence by taking possession of the evacuated fort. Alvarado, meantime, actuated, it is to be presumed, by a desire to save life, and philosophical conviction of the dangers incident to bullets rendered crazy by burning powder, restrained the fiery ardor of his twenty-five Californians, and held his own person beyond the reach of harm, in case some luckless horse or cow straying over hostile ground on that memorable night, should scare the fleeing garrison into an act of defense. The next morning he and his brave men were found peering from their hiding-places in a state of great anxiety and alarm! A battle had almost been begun in Monterey! The blood of their enemies had almost begun to fatten the soil of California! They themselves had nearly stepped in blood knee deep, among the carcasses of the hated Mexicans. The besom of destruction had shaken itself, and had barely missed commencing the havoc of bone and flesh, which would have crushed every mote of Mexican life within their borders! Thus they gloried among the bushes!

Old Graham stood at sunrise on the earth embankments of the castello. A hunting shirt of buckskin, and pants of the same material, covered his giant frame; a slouched broad-brimmed hat hung around his head and half covered his quiet, determined face! In his right hand he held his rifle, the tried companion of many fearful strifes among the savages! Four or five of his men sat on a dismounted thirty-two pounder, querying whether they could repair its wood-work so as to bring it to bear on the presidio or Government House. Others stood by a bucket of water swabbing out their rifle barrels and drying the locks. Others of them were cooking beef; others whittling, swearing and chewing tobacco.

About nine o'clock flags of truce began their onerous duties. Alvarado came from the woods and took part in the councils. The insurgents demanded the surrender of the government; whereat the cavaliers of the presidio considered themselves immeasurably insulted. Two days were passed in parleying, without advancing the interests of either party. They were days big with the fate of the future; and who could weary under the dreadful burthens? Not such men as Alvarado. He bore himself like the man he was, through all this trying period. He uniformly preferred delay to fighting! He was sustained in this preference by his right-hand villain, Captain Jose Castro. Indeed it was the unanimous choice of the whole California division of the insurgent forces, to wit, the twenty-five before mentioned, to massacre time instead of men. For not a single one of them manifested impatience or insubordination under the delay—a fact which, perhaps, demonstrates the perfection of military discipline in California! The foreigners seemed different from their illustrious allies. Graham thought "two days and nights awaiting on them bars was enough." Accordingly, taking the responsibility on himself, after the manner of his distinguished fellow statesman, he sent a flag to the presidio, with notice that two hours only would be given the Governor and his officers to surrender themselves prisoners of war. The demand of the old Tennesseean, however, was disregarded. The appointed time passed without a surrender. Forbearance was at an end. The lieutenant of Graham's rifle corps was ordered to level a four-pound brass piece at the presidio. A ball was sent through its tiled roof, immediately over the heads of the Mexican magnates.

It is wonderful how small a portion of necessity mingled with human affairs will quicken men's perception of duty. No sooner did the broken tiles rattle around the heads of these valiant warriors than they became suddenly convinced that it would be exceedingly hazardous to continue their resistance against such an overwhelming force; and that the central government at Mexico would not be so unreasonable as to expect four or five hundred troops to hold out against "*Los Rifleros Americanos.*" This view of the case, taken through the shattered roof of the presidio was conclusive. They surrendered at discretion! Alvarado marched into the citadel of government! The Mexicans laid down their arms! The emblems of office were transferred to the Custom House clerk! When these things had transpired, General Echuandra was pleased to say with the most exalted good sense, "had we known we were thrice as many as you, we would not have surrendered so soon;" thereby demonstrating to the future historian of Alta California that he and his friends would either have fought the seventy-five with the five hundred, or protracted the siege of bravado much longer, had they been able to count the seventy-five at the distance of seventy-five yards, during the lapse of two days! Difficulties in the use of optics often occur in the Californian warfare which are not treated of in the books.

The end of this revolution came. The schooner *Clarion*, of New Bedford, was purchased, and the Mexican officers shipped to San Blas. Juan Baptisto Alvarado, custom clerk, proclaimed El Alta California an independent republic, and himself its governor. But more of this on a subsequent page. It suffices my present purpose to have shown how far this Alvarado was indebted to the foreigners dying in his prisons for the station and power which he was using for their destruction. He could never have obtained possession of Monterey without them. And had they not slept on their arms for months after that event; a party in the south under his uncle, Don Carlos Carillo, or another in the north under his uncle, Guadalupe Viego (Vallejo), would have torn him from his ill-gotten elevation.

Thus California became an independent State, and Alvarado its governor. The central government at Mexico was, of course, much shocked at such unpolished, ungloved impudence; threatened much, and at last, in September, 1837, induced Alvarado to buy a ship, send dispatches to Mexico, and become *El Goubernador Constitutional del Alta California*, associated with his uncle Viego, as *commandante general*. After this adhesion to the Mexican government, Alvarado became suspicious of the foreigners who had aided him in the "revolution," and sought every means of annoying them. They might depose him as they had done Echuandra. And if vengeance were always a certain consequent of injustice, he reasoned well. The vagabond had promised, in his day of need, to bestow lands on those who had saved his neck and raised him to power. This he found convenient to forget. Like Spaniards of all ages and all countries, after having been well served by his friends, he rewarded them with the most heartless ingratitude.

Graham in particular was closely watched. A bold, open-handed man, never concealing for an instant either his love or hatred, but with the frankness and generosity of those great souls, rough hewn, but majestically honest, who belong to the valley States, he told the Governor his sins from time to time, and demanded, in the authoritative tone of an affectionate elder brother, that he redeem his pledges. * * * He asked for justice, and received what we shall presently see.

Graham loved a horse. He had taken a fine gelding with him when he emigrated to the country, and trained him for the turf. Every year he had challenged the whole country to the course, and as often won everything wagered against his noble steed. Jose Castro * * * and his *Excellentissimo* were among Graham's heaviest debtors. Behold the reasons of their enmity.

Another cause of the general feelings against the Americans and Britons in California was the fact that the señoritas, the dear ladies, in the plenitude of their taste and sympathy for foreigners, preferred them as husbands. Hence José Castro was heard to declare a little before the arrest of the Americans and Britons, that such indignities could not be borne by Castilian blood; "for a Californian cavaliero cannot woo a *senorita* if opposed in his suit by an American sailor, and these heretics must be cleared from the land." Such were the causes operating to arouse the wrath and ripen the patriotism of the Californians. The vengeance of baffled gallantry bit at the ear of Captain Jose Castro; the fear of being brought to justice by Graham tugged at the liver of Alvarado; and love, the keenest, and hate, the bitterest, in a soul the smallest that was ever entitled to the breath of life, burnished the little black eyes and inflamed the thin nose of one Corporal Pinto. These were the worthies who projected the onslaught on the foreigners. Their plan of operations was the shrewdest one ever concocted in California.

Since the "revolution" of 1836 the California Spaniards had been convinced that the Americans and Britons were vastly their superiors in courage and skill in war. From the beginning, therefore, it was apparent that if they were to get one or two hundred of these men into their power it must be done by strategem. Accordingly Graham's annual challenge for the Spring races, in 1840, was conveniently construed into a disguised attempt to gather his friends for the purpose of overthrowing Alvarado's government. This suggestion was made to the minor leading interests, civil and military, and a junta was formed for the safety of the State; or in plain truth, for the gratification of the several personal enmities and jealousies of half a dozen scoundrels who, disregarding the most sacred pledges to their friends, would rob them of their property and sacrifice their lives.

This junta, marshalling their forces at Monterey, adopted the following plan for accomplishing their fiendish designs: The soldiers were detailed into corps of two, three, and four in number, to which were attached several civilized Indians. These bands were secretly sent to the abodes of the foreigners, with instructions to convey them with dispatch to the Alcaldes of the neighboring missions. This they accomplished. The victims, on receiving information that the Alcaldes wished to see them, repaired to their presence willingly, and without suspicions of evil intentions against them. As soon, however, as they arrived they were loaded with irons and cast into the loathesome cells of these establishments, in which the padres formerly confined their disobedient converts.

Thus, one by one, they succeeded in arresting one hundred and sixty odd Americans and Britons—brave old trappers, mechanics, merchants, whalemen and tars—men who, if embodied under Graham, with rifles in their hands, could have marched from San

Francisco to St. Lucas, conquered nine hundred miles of coast, and held the government in spite of the dastards who were opposing them. But they were caught in a net, skillfully thrown over them, and were helpless. After each man was bolted safely in his dungeon, the harpies proceeded to his house, violated his family, plundered his premises, and drove away his live-stock as private booty—the reward of the brave!

Having in this manner collected these unhappy men in the prisons of the several missions, Alvarado and Castro marched their whole disposable force to one mission after another, and brought them in, a few at a time, to the Government dungeons at Monterey. The names of these men, with their places of residence, are given below.

Here follows a list of one hundred and sixty names, which will be omitted, as the object is more to show something of the character of Alvarado than to give a detailed account of the transaction.

Farnham afterwards got a full account of the method of arrest of forty-one of these prisoners. The statement of Isaac Graham will serve to sample the lot and show the atrocious character of Alvarado. It will be remembered that Graham was the one who assisted Alvarado to his position, so that in treating Graham as he did, he proved himself—well, no term sufficiently expressive occurs at this moment.

I, Isaac Graham, a citizen of the United States of America, came across the continent to California, with a passport from the Mexican authorities of Chihuahua, and obtained from the general commanding in Upper California a license to run a distillery in that country for the term of eight years; this business I have followed since that time.

On the 6th of April last (1840) there appeared to be mischief brewing. But what it would prove to be none of us could tell. The California Spaniards usually travel much about the country, and converse with foreigners rather shyly. They had threatened to drive us out of California several times, and we tried to guess whether, at last, they were preparing to accomplish it; but from what we saw, it was impossible to form a correct conclusion.

On the same day, however, Jose Castro, Bicenta Contrina, Ankel Castro, and a runaway Botany bay English convict by the name of Garner, a vile fellow, and an enemy of mine, because the foreigners would not elect him their captain, passed and re-passed my house several times, and conversed together in low tones of voice. I stopped Jose Castro and asked him what was the matter. He replied that he was going to march against the commandante general, Viego, at San Francisco, to depose him from the command of the forces. His two companions made the same assertion. I knew that Alvarado was afraid of Viego, and that Jose Castro was ambitious for the place; and for these reasons I partly concluded that they spoke the truth.

A little later in the day, however, the vagabond Garner called at my house, and, having drunk freely of whisky, became rather boisterous, and said significantly, that the time of some people would be short; that Jose Castro had received orders from the Governor to drive the foreigners out of California, or to dispose of them in some other way. He boasted that he himself would have a pleasant participation in the business. I could not persuade him to tell me in what manner, or when this business was to take place. I had heard the same threats made a number of times within the past year, but it resulted in nothing. Believing, therefore, that Garner's threats proceeded from the whisky he had drunk, rather than the truth, I left him in the yard, and in company with my partner, Mr. Niel, went to bed. Messrs. Morris and Barton, as usual, took to their couches in the still-house.

We slept quietly until about three o'clock in the morning, when I was awakened by the discharge of a pistol near my head, the ball of which passed through the handkerchief around my neck. I sprang to my feet and jumped in the direction of the villains, when they discharged six other pistols, so near that my shirt took fire in several places. Fortunately, the darkness and the trepidation of the cowards prevented their taking good aim, for only one of the shots took effect, and that one in my left arm.

After firing, they fell back a few paces and commenced reloading their pieces. I perceived by the light of their pistols that they were too numerous for a single man to contend with, and determined to escape. But I had scarcely got six paces from the door when I was overtaken and assailed with heavy blows from their swords. These I succeeded in parrying off to such an extent, that I was not much injured by them. Being incensed by my successful resistance, they grappled with me, and threw me down, when an ensign by the name of Joaquin Terres drew his dirk, and, saying with an oath that he would let out my life, made a thrust at my heart. God saved me again. The weapon, passing between my body and my left arm, sunk deep in the ground, and before he had an opportunity of repeating his blow, they dragged me up the hill in the rear of my house, where Jose Castro was standing. They called to him—"Here he is! here he is!" whereupon Castro rode up and struck me with the back of his sword so severely as to bring me to the ground, and then ordered four balls to be put through me. But this was prevented by a faithful Indian in my service, who threw himself upon me, declaring that he would receive the balls in his own heart.

Unwilling to be thwarted, however, in their designs to destroy me, they next fastened a rope to one of my arms, and passed it to a man on horseback, who wound it firmly around the horn of his saddle. Then the rest of them, taking hold of the other arm, endeavored to haul my shoulders out of joint; but the rope broke. Thinking the scoundrels bent on killing me in some way, I begged for liberty to commend my soul to God. To this they replied: "You shall never pray till you kneel over your grave." They then conducted me to my house, and permitted me to put on my pantaloons. While there, they asked where Mr. Morris was. I told them I did not know. They then put lances to my breast, and told me to call him or die. I answered that he had made his escape. While I was saying this, Mr. Niel came to the house, pale from the loss of blood, and vomiting terribly. He had a lance thrust through his thigh, and a wound in his leg, nearly separating the cord of the heel.

They next put Mr. Niel and myself in double irons, carrying us a half a mile into the plain, left me under guard, and returned to plunder the house. After having been absent a short time, they came and conducted me back to our rifled home. As soon as we arrived there, a man by the name of Manuel Larias approached me with a drawn sword, and commanded me to inform him where my money was buried. I told him I had none. He cursed me, and turned away. I had some buried in the ground, but I determined they should never enjoy it. After having robbed me of my books and papers, which were all the evidence I had that these very scoundrels, and others, were largely indebted to me, and having taken whatever was valuable on my premises, and distributed it among themselves, they proceeded to take an inventory of what was left, as if it were the whole of my property, and then put me on horseback, and sent me to this prison. You know the rest. I am chained like a dog, and suffer like one.

The testimony of the other prisoners shows that the same cowardly, cruel spirit prevailed everywhere in making the arrests. It was at this period in the revolution that the bark *Don Quixote* came into the harbor of Monterey, from Honolulu. Though usually there were plenty of white men at Monterey, none were to be seen now. Thomas O. Larkin, afterwards the American Consul, was the only man to be seen, and a Spanish *hombre* was detailed to listen to every word that should be said to or by him, even sitting down to tea with them. It was with the utmost difficulty that the strangers were informed that the country was in a state of revolution, that it was probable that all the foreigners arrested would be shot in the cells where they were confined. The question naturally arose, whether anything could be done for them? Can they be saved? though the numbers on the bark were few. It was resolved to make the attempt, though they might all be shot in an hour.

The first duty on setting foot in California is to report one's self to the Governor, and obtain from him a written permission to remain in the country. This I proceeded to do. Mr. Larkin was obliging enough to accompany me to the Governor's residence. We found before it a small number of men who were usually complimented with the cognomen of "guard." They consisted of five half-breed Indians, and what passed for a white corporal, lounging about the door in the manner of grog-shop *savans*. Their outer man is worth a description. They wore raw, bull's hide sandals on their feet, leathern breeches, blankets about their shoulders, and anything and everything about their heads. Of arms they had nothing which deserved the name. One made pretensions with an old musket without a lock; and his four comrades were equally heroic with kindred pieces so deeply rusted that the absence of locks would have been an unimportant item in estimating their value.

We passed this formidable body, ascended a flight of stairs, and entered the presence of the Governor, Juan Baptiste Alvarado, a well-formed, full-blooded Californian Spaniard, five feet eleven inches in height, with coal black curly hair, deep black eyes, fiercely black eyebrows, high cheek bones, an aquiline nose, fine white teeth, brown complexion, and the clearly marked mien of a pompous coward, clad in the broadcloth and whiskers of a gentleman.

When we entered he was sitting behind a kind of writing-desk in the farther corner of the room. He rose as we entered and received us with the characteristic urbanity of a Spanish body without a soul; waved us to chairs, when he would have seen us tumbling from the balcony; smiled graciously at us one corner of his mouth, while he cursed us with the other; seated himself, laid his hands and arms on the upper shelf of his abdomen, and asked if the ship had anchored.

It seems that he had urgent reasons for asking this. The coming of a merchant vessel had, when he was a Custom House clerk, and since he was Governor, been the means of filling his exhausted exchequer and paying his debts. When he was informed that the vessel was not laden with merchandise, and did not propose to make any long stay, his disappointment was evident. He threw some red-tape formalities in the way of giving Farnham a permit to reside on shore. Farnham was a six-footer, looked like a man of nerve and power. In the present delicate situation of affairs he did not court the presence of such men; neither did he dare to refuse him. The vessel was standing in and out of the harbor; might be one of a fleet outside. Farnham was referred to the Alcalde, whom he found after passing the guard, which was a big dog, asleep on a rawhide in the corner of an *adobe* shanty. A full hour was consumed in writing the permit, an instrument of four lines, which had to be countersigned by the Governor. When this was accomplished he took up his residence with Mr. Larkin, the Consul, whose house was not far from some of the prisons where the prisoners were confined.

The shouts of the prisoners for water, food and air were distinctly audible.

"Breathe fast, for God's sake. I must come to the grate soon, or I shall suffocate!"

"Give me water, you merciless devils! Give me water!"

"You infernal sons of the Inquisition, give me water or fire on me!"

"Give us something to eat! O God! we shall die here! We can't breathe! Half of us can't speak!" And so on the night through.

Four hundred troops, such as they were, constituted the army. Old Graham, with fifty of his riflemen, would have sent them flying like a herd of sheep, but the old fellow was double chained. Through the influence of Larkin, who stretched the facts about the vessel several points to make Alvarado believe it was a government explorer connected with a fleet, Farnham was permitted to interview the prisoners, when he took the statements before referred to. It was noticed that the vessel went out of the harbor every night and returned in the morning, as if communicating with a fleet; that Farnham was making signals of some kind when the vessel was in the harbor, though, in fact, the signals were a sham, as neither party understood the other. Mr. Larkin professed to be in ignorance with regard to the visitors, said they certainly appeared to be persons high in authority. By thus working on the fears of Alvarado, Larkin was permitted to feed the prisoners. Sixty were found confined in a pen twenty feet square, where there was not room to lie down, the floor being knee deep in mud and filth. During the time it was learned that the authorities were considering the proposition of shooting all the prisoners in the pens. Farnham wore a sword with the American eagle on the hilt, and, assuming some airs of importance, resented any restraint on his movements, even refusing to give audience to Alvarado when sent for. Farnham had managed to communicate some courage to the prisoners, who defiantly sung some of the patriotic songs of their land. Pinto, before referred to, was commander of the guard, and became alarmed when the shouts of defiance reached his ears. He was told from the jail that the government of California had better commit suicide than to bring the British Lion and the American Eagle to war with them. Alvarado was finally moved to give them a trial, or at least a form of one.

On the morning of the 22d of April, 1840, twenty-one of the prisoners were brought before the Governor, and, one after another, questioned about the supposed conspiracy. Among the others was Graham, who also denied any knowledge of the conspiracy. A miserable tool of the Governor, who understood so little English as to fail to make himself understood by the prisoners, was the interpreter. By his aid a case was made against them. Garner, a Botany Bay convict, instrumental in the arrest of Graham, testified as to the existence of a conspiracy which was to exterminate the whole Spanish people of the province! Under this kind of testimony and trial forty-six were found guilty of conspiracy and were sent to Tepic for the Mexican government to deal with. Graham and Morris were so heavily ironed that four Indians were required to carry their emaciated bodies aboard the vessel which was chartered to take them away. Many of these persons had native wives who clung to the departing prisoners with cries of despair. They followed the prisoners from the jails as far as they could, helping to bear up the chains. They were driven away with blows. They had no homes to return to, as the soldiers had plundered their houses when the arrests were made, and stood wailing on the shore as the ship left the harbor.

A general thanksgiving was ordered and mass was sung in the churches for the *great deliverance!* It is said that Alvarado was much disappointed that he did not shoot Graham, and thus cancel twenty-two hundred and thirty-five dollars owing to him in mercantile transactions. This, and other events connected therewith, occupied Alvarado the rest of the month. *On the 8th of the following month he made the famous Arroyo Seco Grant.*

Much that is bitter denunciation has been left out of this narrative. It must be remembered that when Farnham arrived one hundred and sixty persons were lying in jail for an imaginary offense; that these were the persons who had helped Alvarado to power; that they had been arrested without warrant, confined in filthy pens, their families maltreated, and their homes destroyed, and we can excuse some of the writer's indignation. That Alvarado was making land grants in the mountains at this time, where no Mexican dared set his foot, is improbable. That he was capable of fixing up the records, in connection with others, so as to show a grant at that time, may be possible.

CHAPTER XXXIX.
THE ABORIGINES.

Origin—Probable Antiquity—Indian Relics—Personal Character of California Indians—Division of Tribes—Indian Huts—Food—Indian Mills—Indian Cooking—Meal Time—Clothing—Legal Tender—Grizzlies—Arms—Principles of Government—Family Relations—Marriage—Small Hands and Feet—Religion—Funerals—Military Reviews—Numbers Assembled—Military Evolutions—Games—Sweat House—Fandango at Yeomet 1851—Diseases and Treatment—Scourge of 1832-33—Anecdotes of the Indians.

Many attempts have been made to identify the Aborigines with the people of the eastern hemisphere, or at least to prove their descent therefrom. A Japanese junk sunk on our coast is taken as evidence of a Mongolian immigration. The figure of a cross on one of the temples of Central America is taken as proof of a former Christian worship, though the temples themselves antedate Christianity by centuries. Learned linguists find a resemblance to some words of the Welsh and a tribe of Indians in New Mexico, and forthwith a treatise or volume appears to prove that in the year 731, Ap Gllyyss and a hundred other Welshmen, driven out by the tyranny of a despotic prince, sailed away and were never heard of more until they were found, one thousand years afterward, settled on the head-waters of the Colorado in New Mexico, living in stone houses such as are found in Wales. It would seem that common sense in regard to such matters might be called in without detriment to the results.

PROBABLE ANTIQUITY.

The facts are the populations of the New World show as much divergence of character as those of the Old World, and can lay about as good claim to antiquity. Portions of the American continent are older in geological formation than Asia, and may have been peopled as early. From the north to the south, from the east to the west, on both Americas, are the indisputable traces of ancient empire. The thousands of mounds in the valley of the Mississippi, the ruins of temples in Central America, which appear to be as ancient as the pyramids of Egypt, the ruins of buildings in Arizona, all prehistoric, speak of the rise and growth of nations; of the struggles of infancy, of the dominion of maturity; of nations exterminated and others taking their place. The colossal character of these ruins, and the extent of ground covered by them, are evidences of thousands of years of growth, which may have been cotemporary, previous or subsequent to the Asiatic or European civilization. Even in California, though no granite temples record the ancient power and cultivation of the tribes, there is evidence of their possession of the country for ages. The shell mounds along the sea shore are the accumulation of centuries. Indian implements are found buried beneath mounds of earth and debris of rivers, which prove their antiquity beyond all doubt.

INDIAN RELICS.

In 1853, while mining out a portion of Humbug gulch, near Volcano, in Amador county, the writer of this history found an Indian mortar similar to those in use, buried under ten or twelve feet of soil, on which timber of considerable size was growing. The place seemed to have been used as a spring, burnt sticks and other trash indicating a camp near by. The spot was quite rich, having a hundred dollars or more in a little spot a yard square. If the squaws who used this spring had ever cleaned it out, they could hardly help finding some of the gold which was mixed with the trash. Others have had a similar experience. Indian relics, consisting of mortars, pestles, etc., were taken out of the ground at a depth of eighteen feet, by J. F. M. Johnston, showing a great antiquity.

PERSONAL CHARACTER.

The Indians of California are rather shorter in stature and stouter built than the Indians east of the Rocky Mountains, though occasionally one might be found who was tall and slender, like some of the Sioux or Pawnees. The Indians of the Pacific coast were also of a more dusky hue, but the same long, straight, coarse, black hair, beardless faces, and dark, dreamy eyes, characterized all the North American races. The divergence from the general type was not greater than can be seen in any race of men, in fact, it appears to be true that the less the cultivation the more uniformity of character.

DIVISION OF TRIBES.

The Indians of the Sacramento and San Joaquin valleys were divided into several tribes, though there seemed to be a blending by intermarriage so that the lines were not rigidly drawn. It is probable that individuals could change their allegiance without much trouble. The Indians living in the vicinity of the upper Cosumnes, including the Dry Creek Indians, called themselves Neshenams. The Poosoones lived about the mouth of the American river; the Quotoas, around Placerville, the Colomas, around Sutter's old mill, the Wapumnes, near Latrobe. The Mokelkos occupied that portion of San Joaquin county, lying east and north of Stockton. From Staples' Ferry to Athearn's, they called themselves the La-las. The Indians of the Ione valley called themselves Lucklum-las. The —— Machacos occupied the Mokelumne river to Campo Seco. The La-las were absorbed by the Mokelkos, who were the most powerful of all the tribes, and had nearly a score of towns, with a total population of three or four thousand. They were continually at war, sometimes against the Machacos, sometimes against the Cosos (Cosumne Indians) and the Jackson Valley Indians combined. The Mokelkos claimed to be Christianized, and had for chiefs four brothers—Sanato, at Staples' ferry; Lowāno at Woodbridge; Antonio, on the Calaveras, and Maximo, still living near Terry's mill. A favorite battleground was near the old brick church not far from Staples' ferry. The Walla Wallas from Oregon sometimes came into the valley, in which case the tribes all combined to expel them. This is supposed to have happened about 1833, as the Walla Wallas are charged with having poisoned the waters and produced a general sickness.

HOUSES.

They had no houses worthy of the name, their camps being a collection of brush shanties, with pieces of bark, sticks, and perhaps skins, put on the exposed side to protect them from the wind and rain. They were generally on the move, pulling up camp whenever game, fish or acorns, became scarce.

FOOD.

They never cultivated the soil until taught to do so by the whites. Nearly everything was at times converted into food. In times of plenty they feasted and wasted; in times of scarcity starved, the weak and aged dying. The acorn, pine nut, and seeds from plants furnished them with substantial food in the season.

INDIAN MILLS.

The acorn was gathered by the squaws and reduced to a powder, by pounding in mortars or holes worn into the rocks by the stone pestles. The seeds of plants were also reduced to flour the same way, as also was corn, wheat and barley after the advent of the white man. The mortars were holes pounded or dug out with infinite labor in boulders, generally of volcanic rock. These seemed to have been selected as much for shape of the boulder which needed no dressing on the outside, as for the quality of the rock. These mortars were carried from camp to camp by the squaws, and were a necessity in the valleys and in other portions of the country where there was no hard rock. In the mountains, where granite or other hard rocks were found, the custom was to pound the acorns in holes in the rocks, which by constant use had become worn to a depth of several inches, large enough to hold a gallon or more. Sometimes a dozen or more of these holes can be found in a space of a square rod, showing the sociable habits of the women, who, while pounding their acorns would chat, tell stories, and laugh with the greatest glee. These mill-sites may be found in the vicinity of every oak or nut pine grove.

INDIAN COOKING.

When the acorns or seeds were reduced to powder, the mass was mixed with water and boiled in baskets made of reeds. These were the only kettles and culinary vessels, though this boiling was sometimes done in a hole in the ground, which was lined with clay and patted down until it would hold water, the clay

P. N. PECK.

soon becoming tight by the soaking into it of the pulp or mush to be cooked. The boiling in either case was effected by dropping in the mass smooth stones, previously heated to a proper point in a fire. Stones were selected which, by experience, were found to stand the effect of the fire. When the mass was sufficiently boiled it was put away to cool, for the Indian never spoils his teeth or stomach with hot food, both being kept in the best condition to old age.

MEAL TIME.

When the meal time arrived the setting of the table was but a short affair. No dishes to wash, no table-cloth to spread or shake out. The family gathered around the basket and the open hand served for a spoon, and the open mouth (an Indian's mouth has a tremendous expansion) received the load and disposed of it without trouble. The acorn season was a time for rejoicing. When the harvest was over the different tribes visited each other and feasted until the acorns were gone. When this occurred they hunted rabbits, quail and deer, and when game was scarce would live on bugs, snails, lizards and gophers. Rats and mice came in with the white man, and probably were never used as food by them. Occasionally a daring raid would be made on the cattle ranches, and a supply of beef obtained. Grasshoppers and young wasps or yellow jackets were esteemed an especial delicacy, and no boy of the Northern States ever dug out and fought a swarm of "bumble bees" with more zeal than a young digger would a hornet's nest. The squirming innocents (innocent of stings) would vanish in a hurry, the Indian's face always asking for more. The young Indians were turned out early to hunt for themselves. During the latter part of the winter, especially if the winter was cold, they suffered greatly, and many would perish. Whenever any of them were hired on the ranches and ate the food of the white people, they usually suffered sickness of some kind.

CLOTHING.

It has been asserted that, previous to the advent of the whites, they went naked. I think this is a mistake. The young ones from childhood to near maturity wore no clothing except for ornament, and many of the males went naked or without any attempt to conceal their persons. The women wore a covering over the loins made of buckskin, or perhaps bark plaited. Considerable taste was displayed in ornamenting the very short breeches, for such they were, with pieces of quills or shells. The limbs and body were usually fully exposed. The young squaws soon learned to conceal their well-developed bosoms from the admiring gaze of a white man by donning a shirt, and, soon, a skirt, for modesty is to woman born, and is aroused by the first glance of passion, whether in a gilded saloon or in a pine forest. Both sexes wore shell ornaments, wrought out with much labor, in fact, pieces of abalone shells, strung on sinews, was the

LEGAL TENDER.

An Indian possessing three or four coils, long enough to hang on his arm, was rich. Soon after the coming of the whites, beads took the place of shells, but the supply becoming too abundant they soon ceased to circulate as money, and were used chiefly as ornaments. A very successful hunter was able to wear a necklace of bears' claws. This would give him a right to the highest seat in the council.

GRIZZLIES.

A grizzly was a full match for a band of Indians, and the latter generally let the grizzly alone. When an attack was made, the result was somewhat uncertain. An old Indian said, "Sometimes Indians eat bear, sometimes bear eat Indians; don't know." Bears abounded in all the valleys of the foot-hills. According to Powell, the Jackson valley chief, six or seven would come into the valley at a time, to eat the young clover. Three or four years before the discovery of gold, a big one was killed by a strong bowman in Jackson valley, and a great feast was made, a hundred warriors toning up their courage by helping to eat him.

ARMS.

The bow of the California Indian is a marvel of strength and efficiency. Although so small and light, it will, when well constructed, stand a pull of two hundred pounds. I have seen strong men place them under their feet, and lift with all their strength, and still fail to break them. They are made of wood, generally yew, sometimes cedar, and derive most of their elasticity from a covering on the back made of sinew, nicely laid on with glue. The string is made of the bark of the wild hemp, and is superior in strength to the best linen or silk. The arrows are made of wood, or reeds, a small bush growing along the creeks furnishing favorite sticks for this purpose. The points were formerly made of obsidian, and were about three inches long, flat, ovoid in shape, with a notch on either edge for a piece of sinew to hold it to the shaft; the feather, or thumb end, had some half feathers tied to it, to give it a rotary motion, like a rifle ball. This was the style of the best arrows, which were used only for war or large game. The arrows used for birds and rabbits were destitute of the obsidian point and feathers. An Indian brave will carry his arrows in an otter or beaver skin, and, with a quiver full, is a match for a white man with a navy revolver. After the advent of the whites, the points were often made of glass. If you want to try your patience and skill, make—or attempt to—an arrow-head out of an old junk bottle; yet an expert Indian will have no trouble in doing it. The light arrows of the Indians have only a short flight, and the natives soon obtained rifles and shot guns.

PRINCIPLES OF GOVERNMENT.

Personal prowess was the foundation of authority. Though the government was hereditary, the heir must prove himself before he could rule. He had to chastise the refractory and disorderly, and in some instances take the life of a subject, direct the tribe to new hunting grounds, arrange the hunting parties, and take the lead in all things. If a rival warrior or hunter disputes his authority, a duel is imperative, the survivor taking his place. Powell, of Jackson valley, won his position in this way. He is, or was, a person of immense strength, and, when not full of whisky, had much self-respect and dignity, and with the advantages of education and training, would have made himself respected in any community.

FAMILY RELATIONS.

The family relations were quite binding. The Indian considered his children as a species of property. They did not hesitate to commit infanticide when the means of living was scarce, believing with the Chinese, that an infant had better die than to grow up to starvation. There seems to be no want of affection, however, for when the child is permitted to live, it never perishes from neglect. It is wrapped in soft grass, tied to a kind of frame, which keeps it straight. Over the child's head is placed a hoop, as a sort of protection from accidental thumps, also to furnish a resting place or support for a shade, to protect the babe's eyes when traveling. The squaw will place a strap or band over her head and around their conical baskets, and carry a whole family, or, if necessary, pack a hundred pounds of flour, apparently with all ease, on a journey, while the buck leads the way, with his bow strung and arrow in place, for game or an enemy. The labor falls on the women. They gather acorns, though the buck will sometimes climb the tree to shake them off, pound and cook them, transport the baggage from one camp to another, fix up the hut, and do all the work except hunting and fighting.

MARRIAGE.

When old enough to marry, the daughter is sold to some agreeable bidder, for a sum perhaps equivalent to the price of a pony. The sale is generally agreeable to all parties, and the purchase money is regarded much in the light of a dower. The marriage ceremony is very slight. If with a neighboring tribe, the bridegroom usually resides, for a time, with her tribe. A chief may have several wives, each in a different camp. Infidelity is, or was, comparatively unknown among them, the penalty being death to both parties. A squaw was stoned to death in Sacramento county in 1839, for yielding to a white man. It is incumbent on the injured party to inflict the penalty.

SMALL HANDS AND FEET.

When young, the squaws have good shaped limbs, small hands and feet, which are the envy of white women. As they get older they take on fat, have Durham backs, large, flabby faces, and get terribly coarse. As they get old they loose their fat, become wrinkled and attenuated, and are no more lovely. They never get bald, and, as the hair turns white and learns to stand on end, they become absolutely hideous. Their voices are generally soft and sweet. Such a thing as scolding is never heard among them.

RELIGION.

Their religious notions are very dim. An old Indian says: "White man die, he go up; don't know where Indian go to." On the death of an Indian, the news is communicated from one camp to another by a peculiar, dismal howl by the squaws. It is heard for miles around, traveling from camp to camp. Soon the Indians begin to pour in to assist in the burial. Every trail brings a howling party. A grave is dug near, in fact, in the camp, four or five feet deep; the corpse is wrapped in a blanket, in as small compass as possible, the bones being often broken to effect the purpose. The body is placed in the hole in a sitting position, and the soil pressed thoroughly around it, a small mound raised, and a few trinkets placed thereon. The mourners (women) keep up the while the noise, which bears a great resemblance to the laments of the wild Irish over their dead. The lament, sung or howled within a compass of two or three notes with minor intervals, was translated: "Where is our brave man? who now will hunt for us and kill meat? who will lead us to catch the fish? who will now kindle his fire? who will make his bed? who will comfort him? who will make him happy? he was a brave man; he was a good man; we will perish without you; we all love you; come back to your wife, your children." The elderly women performed the part of chief mourners or howlers; and though it was evident that much of the grief was a formality, perhaps paid for, the ceremonies were rather impressive. After the funeral services were completed, the whole tribe left that place, not coming back for months. Occasional visits were made, however, and a few mournful words chanted over the grave. Sometimes the body was burned on a large pile of wood, in which case the mourning was kept up during the whole time of the cremation. The widow is said to anoint her face with a black paint made of the charred remains of the husband, and it is also said that it is never washed off, but is left to wear off, after which she is ready to marry again. The children are put up in a tree, on something like a crow's nest, to waste away. James and John Surface of Ione, when boys, found such a grave, and with boyish curiosity climbed the tree and peeped in the nest, but the staring face of a half-decayed child made them hurry down.

MILITARY REVIEWS.

The war dance was the great event in Indian life, though the name is about as appropriate for the exercise as it would be for the evolutions of cavalry or artillery. The war dance is of a gymnastic character, and is performed wholly by the most vigorous males in the tribe, and is about as well calculated to develop muscular power and endurance as any gymnastic exercise taught at our schools. When it was determined to hold a *military review*, invitations were sent to such tribes as it was deemed proper to invite, to come prepared at a certain day. The cards of invitation, or, perhaps proclamation would be a better word, was a string with knots in it, each knot representing a night and day, the announcement being made some fifteen or twenty days before the time of meeting. Every morning a knot was cut off, and thus the coming of the day recorded. On the eventful morning the camp was deserted by all except three or four of the aged and infirm. The warrior put on his necklace of bear claws or his belts of wampum (strings of shells); his arrows were burnished and straightened anew; his bow put in the best condition; a plume of eagle feathers adorned his head, and his fur cloak, made from the animals he had slaughtered, was thrown over his shoulders. If he was rich enough to own a horse, he mounted his steed and led the way to the rendezvous, followed by his braves, on foot or mounted, with drawn bows. The squaws and children followed with the supplies of acorn mush, rabbits, deer or other meat, and manzanita berries for making their *cider*. All the wealth of the tribe was displayed. The squaws wore their best ornaments, and everything was done to enter the camp in a superior style.

NUMBER ASSEMBLED.

As many as a thousand Indians would gather at these reviews. Eating, drinking and gambling were of course prominent events. The Indian is a good feeder when he has opportunity, though he can go without or subsist on a minimum when necessary. His capacious mouth, perfect, white teeth, and enormous chest, attest his eating capacity, and his sleek, plump look, the power of digestion. Before the introduction of whisky and the vices of civilization, he was a splendid animal. After a general interchange of civilities and current news, preparations for the *fête* were made. A space of ground sixty feet or more across was made smooth and hard. A hollow log was brought to be used as a drum for regulating the movements.

MILITARY EVOLUTIONS.

From ten to twenty of the warriors desirous of the honors would step into the ring and form a circle around the precentor, and, at a sign from him, commenced jumping, with lungs inflated and muscles contracted, jumping stiff-legged—as we say of a bucking horse—at each jump expelling a portion of the air from the lungs, with a sort of *ugh! ugh!* moving slowly around the circle, occasionally reversing their circular movement with loud shout and a flourish of the bows which they hold in their hands. The movements, moderate at first, each moment become more vigorous; the contracted muscles stand out in knots; the perspiration rolls off the bodies, and the air is redolent of the perfume of Indian, accumulated dirt and smoke.

It is now evident that this is no capering to the soft tinklings of a lute. It is work, the hardest kind of work. The multitude gather around, and encourage the performers. They redouble their exertions; they bound upwards with the mere spring of the toes without bending a limb, leaping a foot or more from the ground. When human nature is about exhausted, a signal is made, a few grand jumps are given, the performance ends with a shout, and the braves are taken away and rubbed down by the admiring squaws. After an hour's intermission, another band will repeat the performance, and, if possible, surpass it. This continues for several days, or until the provisions are exhausted, when the homeward march is made, and the ordinary life resumed.

GAMES.

The Indians had games involving feats of strength and activity, which were played one camp against another, one of which was much like foot-ball, which, however, was said to have been learned from the San Diego Indians, about 1850, so that it might have been introduced by the whites. The ball was made of skins, tied into a compact form, and was about as large as a child's head. It was rather hard on the naked toes of the Indians, occasionally breaking them. The Indians made as much noise while playing this as would a crowd of school-boys playing base ball.

THE SWEAT-HOUSE.

Every central camp had a council house, or fort, or sweat-house as the whites called it. It was probably used for many purposes; as a shelter in bad weather; as council room when important business called the braves together, and as a fort when attacked. It was from thirty to fifty feet across, circular, sunk three feet or more into the ground, was covered with branches and afterwards with dirt, so that at a distance it had the appearance of a mound of earth. There was an opening in the top for the escape of smoke, and had one entrance, long, low and narrow.

The middle portion of the room might be eight or nine feet high, sloping to four or five feet at the sides. The roof was sustained on forked posts upon which rested the cross-timbers. In a storm, or when attacked, a large number could take refuge in this house. It would be almost impossible to dislodge a body of Indians from one of these houses without large guns to shell them out. They are, in fact, a sort of bomb-proof. It is doubtful whether any of them remain in the county at this time.

FANDANGO AT YEOMET.

At the time of the opening of the mines, the relations of the white man and Indian was somewhat doubtful. The Indian mostly kept out of the way of the rifle of the far-west man, who would as soon draw on him as a deer. The Indian soon found that he was safer in the town than in the woods, and soon learned to pan out and exchange his dust for sugar or meat. It was the policy of the government, for a while at least, to gather them on reservations, as the easiest way of maintaining the peace. Many of the natives had retreated to the mountains, and occasionally a white man was murdered in retaliation for the slaying of an Indian by some thoughtless miner. Expeditions were undertaken to bring them in. Some were found far up among the snows, starving and freezing. When assured of safety they were not unwilling to surrender and be fed. On one occasion an old chief of gigantic size, being entirely naked, was induced to put on clothing. He was given a coat too small and short to cover much of his person. He observed that the commander of the party of white men who came after him wore a pair of spectacles and a plug hat, and manifested a desire to do the same himself, supposing these things to be marks of authority. He was gratified, and took great pleasure in strutting around in his uniform of small coat, plug hat and brass-bowed spectacles. A party of several hundred Indians were collected at the forks of the Cosumnes in 1851, by a government agent by the name of Belcher, who fed them for some weeks on beef. This was about the first opportunity of the miners of that vicinity to study the Indian in his peaceful relations, and a great many took advantage of it. Even at this time most of the Indians had put on clothing, and the men as well as the squaws had some sense of modesty.

When a beef was killed it was quickly skinned and cut to pieces by the Indians, and the gorging commenced. The bucks got most of the meat; the squaws, whether from choice or necessity, probably the latter, got the intestines. Those persons who desire to remember the Indian maiden as a model of beauty, purity and neatness, had better skip this article. The women would carry the intestines to the fire, rip them open, empty them of the undigested contents, and then proceed to cut them into long strips, holding on to the intestines with their toes for this purpose. They laid these strips, without washing or other preparation, on the fire, and when warmed through, would eat them with much gusto. I have witnessed the same thing at other times. Those who think that an artificial style of life begets a love for stimulants will have to find some other reason with the Indian, for he takes to whisky as a babe does to milk. A drunken Indian is not less foolish, noisy and brutal, than his white brother. In spite of all laws to the contrary, the sale of whisky to the Indian goes on and is doing as much as anything else to thin out the race.

PREVAILING DISEASES AND TREATMENT.

Like all tribes of uncivilized people, the Indians treated disease with a mixture of herbs and sorcery. Starvation, gluttony and exposure were the sources of most of their ailings. The survival of the fittest was a thing of course. There were few lame or deformed. The squaw about to become a mother would retire from the camp for a day or two and live in a hut prepared for the occasion in some secluded place. A "lying-in hospital" of this kind, for the Buena Vista Indians, was a nest under the brow of a rock on the south side of the mountain, so hidden by the bushes that no indication of it appeared to a person casually passing.

Some Indian in the tribe usually administered herbs and incantations when too much clover in the Spring, or too much meat after a successful hunt overtasked the powers of the stomach. Occasionally epidemics would sweep away half the population.

GREAT SCOURGE, 1832-33.

Colonel J. J. Warner, now of Los Angeles, a member of the Ewing trapping expedition, which passed north through these valleys in 1832, and back again in 1833, says:—

In the Fall of 1832, there were a number of Indian villages on Kings river, between its mouth and the mountains; also on the San Joaquin river, from the base of the mountains down to and some distance below the great slough. On the Merced river, from the mountains to its junction with the San Joaquin there were no Indian villages; but from about this point on the San Joaquin, as well as on its principal tributaries, the Indian villages were numerous, many of them containing from fifty to one hundred dwellings, built with poles and thatched with rushes. With some few exceptions, the Indians were peaceably disposed. On the Tuolumne, Stanislaus, and Calaveras rivers there were Indian villages above the mouths, as also at or near their junction with the San Joaquin. The most hostile were on the Calaveras river. The banks of the Sacramento river, in its whole course through the valley, was studded with Indian villages, the houses of which, in the Spring, during the day-time, were red with the salmon the aborigines were curing.

At this time there were not, on the San Joaquin or Sacramento rivers, or any of their tributaries, nor within the valleys of the two rivers, any inhabitants but Indians. On no part of the continent over which I had then or have since traveled was so numerous an Indian population, subsisting upon the natural products of the soil and waters, as in the valleys of the San Joaquin and Sacramento. There was no cultivation of the soil by them; game, fish, nuts of the forest, and seeds of the field constituted their entire food. They were experts in catching fish in many ways, and in snaring game in divers modes.

On our return, late in the Summer of 1833, we found the valleys depopulated. From the head of the Sacramento to the great bend and slough of the San Joaquin we did not see more than six or eight live Indians, while large numbers of their skulls and dead bodies were to be seen under almost every shade tree near water, where the uninhabited and deserted villages had been converted into graveyards; and on the San Joaquin river, in the immediate neighborhood of the larger class of villages, which the preceding year were the abodes of large numbers of these Indians, we found not only many graves, but the vestiges of a funeral pyre. At the mouth of Kings river we encountered the first and only village of the stricken race that we had seen after entering the great valley; this village contained a large number of Indians temporarily stopping at that place.

We were encamped near the village one night only, and during that time, the death angel passing over the camping ground of the plague-stricken fugitives, waved his wand, summoning from a little remnant of a once numerous people a score of victims to master in the land of the *Manitou*; and the cries of the dying, mingling with the wails of the bereaved, made the night hideous in that veritable valley of death.

ANECDOTES OF THE INDIANS.

Captain Charlie was quite a character in his way. He had seen the foreign mining tax collector going about among the Chinamen collecting $4 a month from them, and he concluded to try it himself. Knowing the value of an impressive appearance, he put on, in addition to his rather short hickory shirt which constituted his usual dress, a naval coat much too small for his well-rounded body, which had the effect of hauling his arms back and giving a peculiar strut to his walk. He also put on a pair of brass bowed spectacles. He managed to get a large book, a Bible as it was said, and with some pencils and paper he started out, backed by some half a dozen of his braves, to enforce the collection. His usual salutation was, "This my dirt, my countlee, my gold; you pay me folin miners tax," which they usually did without much dispute. He gave them, in exchange for their money, a paper full of pictures of arrows, bows, knives, and other warlike implements. This continued for some days, when the officers of the county interfered and told Jack that he must not do it any more. Jack was not to be thwarted so easily, however.

One morning, when Bill Gist, Deputy Sheriff, collector of the foreign miners tax, was on his daily round, he visited a camp where he had every reason to think a large number of Chinamen were at work, but none were in sight. Captain Charlie was perched on a rock, singing in his happiest mood some of his triumphs over the Indians, or perhaps a love ditty to some fascinating squaw. "No-wa-ha-bar Neshean, No-wa-ha-bar Mokelke," etc.

Gist—"Good morning, Charlie."

Charlie—"Good day. No-wa-ha-bar Neshean"— (in a most indifferent manner).

Gist—"Charlie, where are the Chinamen?"

Charlie—"Do no; me no see. No-wa-ha-bar, No-wa-ha-bar Neshean."

Gist suspected something wrong, and told Charley that he knew where the Chinamen were, but he denied knowing anything about it, and kept his song going in a provokingly cool way. He thought he would leave and come some other time, but Captain Charlie was on the watch.

"Bill Gist, how much you give me show you twenty Chinamen?"

"Five dollars," says Bill.

"You think Indian d——n fool, you catchlee eighty dollars; give five dollars? no-wa-ha-bar, Neshean."

"Ten," says Gist.

"No-wa-ha-bar, Neshean."

Gist offered fifteen, but Charlie was unmoved. Gist was about to leave, but Charley had not played all his trumps.

"You give me twenty dollars, make sixty dollars easy."

Gist offered the twenty, and had to pay the money down, for Charley had learned to distrust a white man's promise.

After Jack got his money he told Gist "to go into chapial," meaning the brush near by, "and go sleep; bime-by Chinaman he come."

Gist hid himself in the bushes, and soon the Chinaman came to work, when he pounced them, and exacted the eighty dollars in full. Soon afterwards, meeting Charlie, he learned that the rascal had hidden the Chinamen in a tunnel for twenty dollars, and after getting twenty out of him, had told the Chinamen to come out, saying to them,

"Folin miner tax-klector, he gone; no more come back."

The last seen of him he was showing his twenties with the remark that, "Chinamen heap good men. Catchee twenty dollars hide um; catchee twenty dollars find um; heap good Chinamen."

At another time, he undertook to run a boarding-house, at so much per week. He got a cabin, some flour and meat, table utensils, and a bell, and opened in style, ringing the bell three times a day; "all the same as white men." His institution flourished until the following Sunday (pay-day), when it stopped for the reason, as Charley said,

"D——n Indian no 'count, no pay."

He also engaged in mining. He found some good ground up on a side-hill, and undertook to carry water in a ditch to the place, but he failed to make the water run to it.

"White men make water run up hill, Indian no can do. White man heap *sabe*."

CHAPTER XL.

CANALS.

Killson Ditches—Ham Ditch—Amador and Sutter Ditch—Willow Spring Ditch—Floating Lumber—Novel Passenger Boat—Empire Ditch—Amador Ditch—Buena Vista Ditch—Lancha Plana Ditch—The Nigger Ditch—Poverty Bar Ditch—Volcano Ditch—Consumnes Water Company—The Amador Canal.

Soon after the coming of the miners, the want of water and the means to supply it were often the subjects of consideration. From turning the water out of a river or gulch to mine out the bed, to carrying it a mile or two to wash rich dirt, was but a small step. The season of 1850-51, was dry, little or no rain falling until April. During the Winter many short ditches were cut, and many more contemplated. The Johnston family, who settled around the Gate, cut a ditch about one mile long in the Spring of 1851, from the north fork of Jackson to the gulch below the Kennedy mill. This is said to have been, at the time, the longest ditch in the county. The most important system of ditches in the vicinity of Jackson was inaugurated by Horace Kilham and his associates. The following able account of them is furnished by Mr. H. L. Loveridge, who has been connected with them from their inception to the present time:—

KILHAM DITCHES.

The first ditch constructed in the neighborhood of Jackson was for the conveyance of water to the placer mines in the vicinity of Hunt's gulch, Murphy's gulch and ridge, and Butte City, and was surveyed by two brothers by the name of Watkins, in the Fall of 1851, the head of the ditch beginning at a point some three and a half miles above the town of Jackson, on the south fork of Jackson creek. After the filing of a claim to the right of way, and the completion of the survey of the ditch, the construction work was deferred till the Spring of 1852, at which time Horace Kilham, William Lewis, Thomas Campbell, and —— Merrill, purchased the interests of the Watkins brothers to the right of way for the ditch, as well as the right to diversion of the waters of the creek for its supply; and they at once commenced the work of construction, doing the principal portion of the labor themselves, completing the ditch to the immediate vicinity of Scottsville, about the 20th of November of that year, which, by the ditch line, was seven miles in length, with an outlay, besides their own labor, of two thousand dollars, the most of the money being expended in the construction of flumes.

During the Winter and Spring of 1852, Kilham, Lewis and Merrill appropriated the most of their share of the water supply to mining in Kentuck and Rich gulches, located north and west of Gold hill, while Campbell sold his portion of the water to the miners about Scottsville and Butte City, the ditch being completed to the latter-mentioned locality in January, 1853. During the Spring of the same year a branch ditch was constructed to Murphy's gulch and ridge, where the owners of good paying claims were anxiously awaiting the coming of the much-needed water. The price charged for water during the first season of its introduction, was one dollar per inch per day.

Late in the Spring of 1853 Campbell and Lewis sold their interests in the ditch to Kilham and Merrill, and returned to their homes in the East, while Kilham and Merrill remained to reap a rich harvest of gold in their sales of water, which averaged, during the full water supply of eight months each season, for two years, five thousand dollars per month. In the Spring of 1855 Merrill returned to his old home in Wisconsin, in company with Braxton Davenport, a prominent miner of Scottsville, to whom Merrill sold his interest in the ditch property. Davenport soon returned, and after a brief period disposed of his one-half interest in the ditch to Kilham.

One ditch being inadequate to supply the extensive mining region covered by its construction, a second ditch from Jackson creek, covering the same territory of mineral wealth, with an additional altitude of thirty feet, was soon considered to be a remunerative investment, and early in the Spring of 1853 Major Cunningham, W. V. Clark, and —— Munson, commenced the construction of a ditch, with its head on the south fork of Jackson creek, about a mile and a half above the Kilham ditch, and on the middle fork, six miles above the town of Jackson; and pushing their work ahead with all possible speed, their ditch reached completion in May of that year. East of Tunnel hill, in the Alpi ranch, a spacious distributing reservoir was built, which has ever proved a most valuable water depository in connection with the water supply of Butte basin and its surrounding country. From this reservoir to the point where the ditch heads on the south fork, the distance is seven miles, and from the head of the middle fork branch, fifteen miles; the cost of construction, not including the labor of its proprietors, was six thousand dollars. After the completion of this enterprise, water was sold at seventy-five cents per inch.

In the Fall of 1855 Mr. Kilham bought the Cunningham (so called) ditch property, and its retiring owners entered into the pursuit of mining—Cunningham and Munson remaining in the vicinity of Butte City for a couple of years, following their avocation successfully, while Mr. Clark became a mining proprietor in a wealthy mineral district of West Point, Calaveras county, where, we believe, he still resides. Cunningham and Munson left Butte City in the Spring of 1857, and became interested soon thereafter in some extensive mining projects in Placer county.

Soon after Mr. Kilham assumed the sole proprietorship of both of the Jackson creek ditches, he became involved in a lawsuit with a party on both the middle and south forks, in consequence of the attempt of some miners to divert the waters from the creeks above the head of his ditches to neighboring mining localities, from which places the water would flow into the streams below where he could utilize it; and after a protracted siege of litigation, Kilham beat his water contestants, since which time no trouble of a similar character that is worthy of note has occurred.

And now, in order to make an intelligible connection with all these ditch interests, it becomes necessary to digress a little for the moment and chronicle the addition of a new ditch enterprise—the Butte ditch—stretching its lengthy and rugged line twenty miles above Tunnel hill, where it was fed by the cold, crystal waters of the north fork of the Mokelumne river. This work was commenced in the Spring of 1856, and finished late in the Fall of the same year, at a cost of one hundred thousand dollars. The main trunk of the ditch was capable of conveying seven hundred inches of water, while its lateral branches were constructed to carry a sufficient quantity to accommodate the demands of the several mining sections which they supplied. Slabtown and Iowa Flat, hitherto without water facilities for mining purposes, were, by this ditch, favored with an ample supply, and during the few years that these placers lasted, the water sales were a handsome income to the ditch company. The uniform price established for water was fifty cents per inch.

In the Spring of 1858, after six years of almost uninterrupted prosperity in the sales of water, Mr. Kilham sold all his ditch interests to the Butte Ditch Company for twenty-two thousand dollars, the sale including an orchard and vineyard belonging to the property, which was soon thereafter sold by its late purchasers to Dr. Samuel Page and Peter A. Martin for two thousand dollars. The price of water from the creek ditches was at this time dropped from seventy-five to forty cents per inch.

During the Summer of 1858, a suspension flume was constructed from a point half a mile west of C. J. Ruffner's residence to the north end of Tunnel hill, a distance of thirty-three hundred feet, and which was, at its highest point from the surface of the ground, one hundred and eighty feet. The flume was built by Conrad & Holt for fifteen thousand dollars, and was not entirely a success to its contractors, for they warranted the structure to stand for one year from the date of completion, and a portion of it broke down before the expiration of the year, and the burden of rebuilding fell upon its contractors. The flume was repaired in the Spring of 1860, and stood till November, 1862, when it was entirely thrown down by a heavy wind-storm then prevailing. In consequence of the heavy expense incurred in bringing the water on Tunnel hill, the price established was fifty cents per inch—ten cents more than for other sections. In the year of 1861, water for diggings other than Tunnel hill, was reduced to thirty cents per inch, and two years thereafter to twenty-five cents per inch. About this time the company became financially embarrassed, and the two mortgages hanging over the property had to be paid, when three members of the company, Isaac Tripp, William Stickle, and A. M. Harris, who held the second mortgage, paid the first one and took the property. In the Fall of 1864, C. D. Horne purchased a fourth interest in the property, and at once became its active manager. In the Spring of 1866, water was again conducted to Tunnel hill by an eleven-inch iron pipe, but the sales of water there did not justify the expense incurred in conducting the water where the paying portion of the hill had before become so nearly exhausted.

In February, 1870, the river ditch was sold to the Amador Canal Company for twenty thousand dollars —the creek ditches not being included in the sale. The purchase of the Butte ditch by the canal company was no doubt for the object of securing the water-right of the former, as no portion of the old river ditch has ever been used by the canal company.

In a financial point of view, the Butte ditch was a failure, for it never paid one-fourth the cost of its construction, for its water market was too limited to warrant the expensive outlay of its building. But the Kilham ditches always proved a source of remunerative profit to their owners. For several years past the lower creek ditch has not been in use, as the upper ditch is of sufficient capacity (five hundred inches) to furnish the needed water supply along its entire line—the water being used for mining and irrigating purposes. The price of water for several years past has been for the irrigation of alfalfa, twelve and a half cents, and for trees and vegetables, twenty cents per inch, while for mining the price varies from four to ten cents per inch, according to the quantity used.

The ownership of the entire ditch interests have, within the past few years, passed into the hands of Mr. C. D. Horne, under whose superintendence the property has been managed since his first connection with the ditch.

THE HAM DITCH.

This canal, so called from the name of the constructor, the most costly and extensive, as well as unprofitable, of all the water projects inaugurated in Amador county, was surveyed in 1852 by Alonzo Platt and —— Hubbard. The intention was to supply all the middle and western portion of the county with water, at all seasons of the year, and lumber as well, for it was to be a flume, four feet wide at the bottom and five at the top, and three feet deep, with gradients and curves that should permit the floating of lumber of any dimensions likely to be required in the mines. The project involved the building of several mills at the different branches of the north fork of the Mokelumne river. The first mill was put up on Mill creek, and the work inaugurated in 1854. The mill, a water-power, was a splendid piece of mechanism, running a sash saw, two hundred and fifty strokes a minute, cutting twenty-three thousand feet a day. In 1853 J. C. Ham took the contract to build eleven and a half miles of flume, at the following rates: Earth grading, fifty cents per yard; hard-pan, two dollars per yard; rock, five dollars per yard; lumber, eighty dollars per thousand; nails, twenty-five dollars per hundred weight.

The mill was constructed with edger and mortising saws, so that the entire work, except laying the flume, was done by the machinery. By these appliances eleven thousand feet could be put into the flume every day, a quarter of a mile being laid on a wager in five hours and a half. This mill was burned up in 1856, by a fire set to burn the slabs and other trash which had accumulated around the mill. Water was carried to Aqueduct City, across the divide, in 1856. Much of the grading had been paid for in scrip, which entitled the holder to a preferred right to water when the flume should be finished. When the work was finished, the cost was estimated at three hundred and forty-four thousand dollars. Mill creek proving insufficient to supply the flume, the water failing in the Summer, an extension was determined on. To complete this extension the property was mortgaged to James Birch, for twenty-five thousand dollars. Being unable to pay this, the property was mortgaged to J. Mora Moss & Co., for fifty thousand dollars, the payment of the Birch lien with the accrued interest being effected in this way. The interest of the last named mortgage was fixed at one and one-half per cent. per month. The property eventually fell into the hands of Pioche, Bayurque & Co., who were said to be handling the money of Louis Napoleon. The project was disastrous to every one investing in it. The water scrip, or certificates for work done, payable in water on the completion of the ditch, were not recognized by the last owners. The flume was not capable of carrying lumber to any extent, and damages and breaks by storms, failure of the mines, cost of necessary lateral branches, with expensive, perhaps extravagant management, soon bankrupted the company, and a few years since the property was purchased by Chas. McLaughlin of San Francisco, for a few thousand dollars, or less than five per cent. of the original cost, which must have been near five hundred thousand dollars. The country at large derived some benefit from the distribution of water, which, however, was sold at high rates, being fifty cents an inch outlet, under six inches pressure. None of the originators made anything out of the affair. J. C. Ham, now an old man, who put such a portion of his active life as well as twenty-five thousand dollars in cash into the project, is comparatively poor, though still full of gigantic plans for utilizing the lumber forest of the Sierras.

THE AMADOR AND SUTTER DITCH

Was surveyed in the Spring of 1853, by Emanuel Wise and the Howard brothers, Lyman, Jerry, and Martin. The water was taken out of Sutter creek about four miles below Volcano, and carried to the towns of Sutter and Amador. The cost was about twenty-two thousand dollars. It did not prove a profitable investment, and was afterwards sold to a company of Italians for six thousand dollars, who got their money back in the first run of six months. The Keystone mining company now own it.

THE WILLOW SPRING DITCH.

Surveying commenced in 1851. The ground was broken the following year. The original proprietors were A. Wood, J. Riddle, John Cursner, Joe Jackson, Fitzgeral and others, twenty in all, most of the proprietors being engaged in the work. The cost was estimated at forty thousand dollars, but it swelled to eighty thousand dollars before completion. It took the water from the south fork of the Cosumnes and distributed it through the north-western part of the county, including the camps of Plymouth, Forest Home, Puckerville, Arkansas diggings, etc. Porter, who was afterwards murdered and robbed while engaged in his duties, was made superintendent.

Though managed economically the property did not pay according to expectations, and in 1854 it was sold to William Ritter and John O'Brien, for about twenty thousand dollars, who enlarged the channel and extended it to the middle fork of the Cosumnes, at a cost of twenty-four thousand dollars more. In June, 1872, the property was purchased by Alvinza Hayward & Co., for eighteen thousand dollars. The channel was enlarged to three feet on the bottom, five at the top, with a depth of three feet. Grades and curves were arranged with reference to floating lumber and mining timbers, for which purpose it proved well adapted, millions of feet having been successfully sent through to the works at Plymouth.

FLOATING LUMBER.

Thus after twenty years of experiment a part of the hopes of ditch projectors of carrying lumber was realized.

As this was the first successful operation of the kind in the county a few words as to the former expectations and failures may be permissible. The carrying of freight in artificial rivers is as old as the age of man. It is most successful in moderately level countries. The first great project of the kind in the United States was the Clinton ditch (as it was called by Thomas Jefferson, who was unsparing in his ridicule of it), which was projected three-quarters of a century since by the New York settlers from Holland, where they had been accustomed to see artificial rivers made the channels of a national commerce. But Holland is a flat country. New York, though not flat, is by no means a Sierra Nevada. The canal meanders through valleys and occasionally along a gentle slope, and when an aqueduct, as at Little Falls, Rochester, or Lockport is required, it is constructed of granite in a substantial manner, and even then a break will sometimes occur which necessitates costly repairs. Let one, who has seen the successful artificial water channels, pass along the line of a ditch in the Sierras, and compare the scarcely-flowing stream with only three or four inches grade to the mile, through a comparatively level country, with a stream in the Sierra Nevadas, diverted from its channel and carried around sharp ledges of rock, across ravines a hundred feet deep on a slender trestle work, winding its way until a dizzy height of hundreds of feet is attained, and the absurdity of trying to make it a channel for transportation will be apparent. The canal, to be successful as a supply of water, must have as much fall as is possible without washing the banks. A stick of timber turned crosswise in the ditch would, in

JAMES LESSLEY.

five minutes, cause an overflow that might wash away a quarter of a mile of ditch, where digging a new channel on the grade was nearly impossible. The slight manner in which many of the ditches were constructed was the cause of many failures. It is even now no unusual thing to see a flume of a capacity of several hundred inches, standing on one leg away up on the side of a mountain, in such a precarious situation that a man with a family depending on him for support would have no right to walk over the shaky concern. The utility of ditches as a means of transportation is undoubted, and success will result from numberless trials and failures. Engineering will overcome the difficulties, and the Sierras will be induced to give up their treasures of sugar and other pines without the weary dragging through the dusty roads, now incident to the lumber trade.

NOVEL PASSENGER BOAT.

While the Ham flume was building it was proposed to carry passengers up as well as down by means of the stream. The passengers could, of course, float comfortably down in a boat. To get up stream was provided for. A car, running on a track, which was to be laid on the sides of the flume, was to have paddle wheels at each end, which, turned by the water, would turn the car wheels, attached to the same axle, and thus propel the carriage up the stream. The model was tried, but no reporters being permitted to witness the experiment, the result can only be conjectured.

To return to the Plymouth or Willow Spring ditch. It was extended to Irish hill in the western part of the county, to work some gravel beds on the Arroyo Seco grant.

THE EMPIRE DITCH

Was constructed by George and Richard Withington, Charles Hutz, Samuel Ewing, Perrin and Crowell, taking water out of Sutter creek, about one mile below the town of Sutter Creek, distributing it around the country between Dry creek and Sutter creek, including the diggings around Muletown and vicinity. This eventually became consolidated with the Amanor canal, owned by the Johnstons.

THE AMADOR DITCH,

Said to be the first ditch of any length constructed in the county, was made to take water from Sutter creek to the placers in the vicinity of Ione. It was thirteen miles in length, and cost about twenty thousand dollars.

THE BUENA VISTA DITCH

Also was supplied by water taken out of Sutter creek. This was surveyed by —— Munger, and built by J. Foot Turner, about 1856, at a cost of eighteen thousand dollars. The main ditch was fifteen miles in length, and carried the water to the rich placers discovered between Buena Bista and Ione, about 1854 and 1855. Extensions were made to Chaney hill, also to Lincoln gulch, at a cost of several thousand dollars, which, however, did not prove remunerative. Water at first was sold for twenty-five cents an inch, but as the better claims were worked out, it was reduced to ten cents. The property was generally remunerative.

A few years since it passed into the hands of some Italians, at a valuation of some fifteen hundred dollars.

THE LANCHA PLANA DITCH

Took water from Jackson creek, carrying it across the dividing ridge near Waters' ranch. It supplied Camp Opera, French Camp, Steven's gulch and China gulch, and was also extended to the hills in the vicinity of Putt's bar. The entire length was about thirty miles, costing about thirty thousand dollars. Walker, Proctor and Lancaster were the builders. When it was built water was sold at fifty cents per inch. This was one of the few ditches which proved remunerative.

THE NIGGER DITCH

Was built by a colored man, who had made several thousand dollars as a rag picker. It took water from Stony creek to the Buena Vista placers. It was about eight miles in length, and has long been abandoned.

POVERTY-BAR DITCH

Was mostly on the south side of the Mokelumne river, in Calaveras county. A branch, by means of a suspension flume ninety feet high, was carried across the river into Amador county near the famous Butler claim. The whole work cost ninety thousand dollars, and was built by McNeely, Davis, Morrow and McCarty, in 1857. The branch into Amador county came into competition with the Proctor and Walker ditch, and caused a reduction of the price of water.

THE VOLCANO DITCH

Was projected in 1855, by George Monkton, B. F. Wheeler, James T. Farley, J. C. Shipman, M. W. Gordon, William Roberts, and W. A. Eliason, the latter person acting as the engineer. It connected Volcano with the head-waters of Panther and Tiger creeks and Mokelumne river, and had the greatest altitude of any of the canals in the county. The work was commenced in 1855, and completed the following year. The cost was estimated at one hundred thousand dollars, the length being thirty-six miles. It was proposed to pay for the construction one-third cash, one-third notes, and one-third water scrip, or paid-up certificates, calling for water when the work was completed. The ditch ran over loose gravel a great deal of the way; the water supply was not equal to the expectation, and the company got involved. They borrowed ten thousand dollars of Charles D. Horne at ten per cent. per month, expecting to be able to pay it in a short time, but the mortgage took the ditch. Dr. E. B. Harris also loaned the company some ten thousand dollars, but it was not so well secured, to him at least, and the money stayed loaned. Four or five years after it passed into the possession of Bayerque & Pioche, and within the last few years was transferred to Charles McLaughlin, with the Ham ditch and other property, for a consideration of twenty-five thousand dollars. The first cost of the property so conveyed is estimated as follows: Jackson ditch, four hundred thousand dollars; Open Cut flume, ninety thousand dollars; Volcano ditch, one hundred and forty thousand dollars; total, six hundred and thirty thousand dollars.

The water scrip was not recognized by the subsequent owners of the ditch, and the notes given by the company were worthless after the property had passed out of their hands, and the whole matter of building and running it was the source of much dissatisfaction. The water-rights conveyed by the sale of these ditches to McLaughlin are immense and may seriously affect, perhaps jeopardize, the prosperity of the community.

COSUMNES WATER COMPANY.

The ditch belonging to this company was commenced in 1852, by Samuel Lorce and twenty others. They brought water into Fiddletown from the south fork of the Cosumnes in 1853, the length of the ditch being about forty-five miles, costing forty-five thousand dollars. The ground over which the ditch ran was very favorable for the construction, but some bad management involved the company in debt. The lumber for the flumes was sawed at the forks of the Cosumnes, so far away from the work that the hauling cost two hundred dollars per thousand feet. The company borrowed money at ten per cent. per month, which soon took the property. The ditch passed into the hands of C. A. Purinton, who still owns it. A branch from Dry creek, called the Eagle ditch, running to Quartz mountain and the Gover mines, costing about seven thousand dollars, was added after Purinton's purchase of the property. Water, formerly sold for thirty cents, is now sold at eight cents per inch, with a probability of further reduction. This ditch, running through an agricultural country, is being used to irrigate orchards and vineyards, and offers great inducements for improvements in that locality.

THE AMADOR CANAL.

The enterprise of the present Amador Canal and Mining Company was inaugurated by —— Bowman and others about the year 1870, under the name of the Sutter Canal and Mining Company, by the purchase of the water-right of the old Butte Ditch Company, which right controlled a large proportion of the waters of the north or main fork of the Mokelumne river.

These parties nearly completed the construction of the canal from its lower terminus near the town of Sutter Creek to the vicinity of Bald Rock—a distance of over thirty miles—when, on account of financial embarrassment, the work was suspended.

The property subsequently went into the hands of a receiver, and was purchased by the present company in the year 1873.

The construction of the unfinished portion of the works was commenced in October of the same year; and being to a considerable extent through solid rock, although pushed vigorously, it required nearly a year for its completion. In the Fall of 1874 the water through it was first applied as a motive power for the mills and mines of the county; from that date it has formed a very important feature in quartz mining. Owing to its cheapness and its superiority as a motive power, much low-grade ore has been worked, which, under the expensive method of working by steam-power, would have still remained in the earth.

The surveyor under whose direction the work was laid out, was the late W. L. McKimm, of Jackson. The length of the main ditch is forty-five miles; size, six and a half feet on the bottom, nine on the top, and three feet deep; grade about eight feet to the mile. The velocity of the water is about two miles per hour. The distributing ditches aggregate about one hundred miles.

The ditch and its branches reach nearly every portion of the county where water is likely to be needed for mining or agricultural purposes, including in their course Clinton, Irishtown, Sutter Creek, Amador City, Jackson, Butte City, Rancheria, New Chicago, Drytown, and Ione. The towns of Sutter Creek, Jackson and Amador are supplied with the water for domestic and other purposes. The elevation of the canal at the head is about nineteen hundred feet above the sea level, which leaves it with an elevation sufficient to drive the heaviest machinery at all the towns along the lines of extension. The storage capacity is about six billion of gallons. The capital invested is about six hundred thousand dollars. The present price of water is twenty cents per miners' inch.

The project has been managed with the wisdom of thirty years' experience. It was built with labor at reasonable rates; has no extraordinary expenses, and the proprietors have no expectation of extraordinary profits. It may be considered as the inauguration of a new epoch in Amador county, which will witness an increased production in mineral, mechanical and agricultural industries.

The present officers are J. S. Emery, president; B. N. Van Brunt, secretary; H. H. Towns, general superintendent.

In reading this account of the ditches of Amador county, one will be struck with their generally unprofitable character as a financial investment. A few short ditches were extremely profitable, making their owners comfortable fortunes in a few years. This was especially true of the Kilham ditches, which from the start were managed with discretion. The small ditch running into Fiddletown (Oleta) paid its owners, in early days, one thousand dollars per month during the mining season; so of other short ditches in many places. Expensive flumes, which rotted down in two or three years; slides and washouts, and constantly decreasing market for the water, caused some of the ditches to be abandoned soon after their construction. The hope that was entertained, that they would be serviceable for agriculture, has not been realized. The long trestle-work on which they were built, which is now superceded by iron pipes; the high grades, sometimes twenty feet to the mile, causing a rapid flow and great wearing of the banks; and the location of ditches in other agricultural sections, has prevented those first constructed from being utilized by the farmers.

The following list of ditches, published in 1861, when placer mining was in its zenith, will be interesting as mentioning many ditches then in active use but now abandoned and forgotten:—

AMADOR COUNTY.

NAME OF DITCH.	SOURCE OF WATER.		COST.	NAME OF OWNER.
Amador	Sutter Creek	13	$50,000	J. Johnston & Bros.
Amador County Canal	Mokelumne River	66	400,000	Proctor & Bayerque.
Boyle		3	3,500	James Mehan.
Buckeye	Sutter Creek	3	3,000	White & Co.
Buena Vista	Sutter Creek	15	18,000	J. Foote Turner.
Butte Canal	Mokelumne River	50	125,000	Butte Canal Co.
Consumnes Water Co.	Consumnes River	22	40,000	C. A. Purinton.
Dry Creek	Dry Creek	1	8,000	Davis & Co.
Indian Gulch	Jackson Creek	10	10,000	W. L. McKlinns.
Indian Gulch	Rancheria Creek	2	2,000	Doull & Co.
Kellum Ditches (3)	Jackson Creek	5	22,000	Butte Canal Co.
Lancha Plana	Jackson Creek	30	30,000	Proctor & Bowden.
Loree's	Rancheria Creek	2	2,000	Samuel Loree.
Meeks	Jackson Creek	1	1,500	Meeks & Sons.
Miss Gulch	Rancheria Creek	2	2,400	N. Parsons.
Open Cut Flume	Sutter Creek	11	30,000	Phebe & Bayerque.
Parker's	Jackson Creek	1		
Purinton's	Sutter Creek	25	15,000	Reuben Fry, Agent.
Phelps & Co.	Dry Creek	6		Phelps & Co.
Pigeon Creek	Consumnes River	7	8,000	Simpson & Co.
Potosi	Dry Creek		2,500	Hinkston & Glover.
Proctor, Walker & Co.	Jackson Creek	11	10,000	Walker & Lancaster.
Reloading & Alt (2)	Sutter Creek	8	10,000	Redding & Alt.
Richtmyer	Dry Creek	15	10,000	B. F. Richtmyer.
Rich & Co.	Big Bar Canon	5	4,000	Rich & Co.
Ritter	Consumnes River	25	155,000	Est. of Wm. Ritter.
Sutter Creek and Volcano.	Sutter Creek	7	18,000	J. E. Warner.
Volcano	Mokelumne R. trib	42	40,000	Phebe & Bayerque.

The water-rights are likely to be a source of litigation in the future. It is an open question whether the old *riparian* customs should not be restored, and the right to divert a stream from its course be relegated to the *eminent domain* from which it has been wrenched by the temporary necessities born of mining interests. A water monopoly is not less detrimental to a country than a land monopoly, especially in a rainless climate requiring artificial irrigation to insure the maturity of fruits and grains.

CHAPTER XLI.
PUBLIC SCHOOLS.

First School in the State—School System—First School Report—First County Superintendent—School-book War—School Census in 1865 by Districts—School Statistics—Condition of Schools in 1871—Tribute to School-teachers.

PROVISIONS for public schools were made at the first session of the Legislature, in 1849. Five hundred thousand acres of land, which had been donated by Congress for this purpose, was to be used so as to make a perpetual fund, with a proviso, however, that it might be used for other purposes "*if the public exigencies required.*" This produced an animated debate, it being justly considered that "public exigencies" was rather an indefinite term, and would be found to endanger the existence of a school fund. The proviso was striken out by a majority of one vote. It was made essential to have a three months' school in each year, in order to have a portion of the public fund. Mr. Semple of Sonoma seems to have had the clearest ideas of the necessary details. The effort to organize a general fund sacred to public schools was opposed by William M. Gwin and General H. W. Halleck, and conditions were actually imposed on the formation of a fund which resulted in the sale and loss of fifty thousand acres of the school lands before the matter was placed on a secure basis. It was thought by many that these school lands, some of which were located in the mines, would furnish a revenue sufficiently large to run the whole State government.

THE FIRST FREE SCHOOL IN THE STATE

Was organized in San Francisco, April 2, 1850. Small schools were established in the mining towns in many places. The writer recollects of seeing in Placerville, in 1851, a class of half a dozen being taught by a carpenter in his shop, in the intervals of nailing together rockers and long-toms. The school lands seemed to benefit the State very little during the first years, the system of surveys being so bungling and impracticable that it was difficult to organize the fund out of the sales.

THE FIRST SCHOOL REPORT.

Was published in 1852, by John G. Marvin. He recommended several important changes in the school law, among others, that a tax of five cents should be levied on each hundred dollars; that the office of County Superintendent should be created; that provision should be made for school libraries, and that the proceeds of the swamp and overflowed lands be applied to the school fund. He estimated the value of the sixteenth and thirty-sixth sections, and the five hundred thousand acres, (special grant,) to be worth eight million dollars. In his report is the first intimation of the condition and number of the children in Calaveras county. He estimates the number of children at one hundred, and no school, El Dorado county being in the same condition.

In the second annual report, 1852, the number of public schools in the whole State was said to be only twenty; that the sales of land had produced a fund of three hundred thousand dollars; that the number of children in the State, between four and eighteen years, was seventeen thousand eight hundred and twenty-one, three thousand three hundred and fourteen attending school. He recommended that the county Assessors be made, *ex officio*, County Superintendents; that no Catholic schools be allowed any portion of the public fund. In 1852, the sales of land belonging to the school fund amounted to three hundred thousand dollars.

In 1853, the Legislature enacted that the school fund should not be used for any other purpose whatever; that religious and sectarian schools should not have a *pro rata* of the school fund. The County Superintendent was authorized to appoint three school commissioners for each school district. Paul K. Hubbs, State Superintendent, recommended that the school fund should be apportioned according to the number of children attending school, instead of the census returns.

In 1854, the Legislature provided that fifteen per cent. of the poll-tax should be paid into the school fund. An attempt was made this session to repeal the Article prohibiting the granting of money to sectarian schools, but the proposed law did not reach a vote. The Superintendent reported the number of children attending school as having increased from two thousand in 1853, to five thousand seven hundred and fifty-one, in 1854; this being the first attempt made to get a tabulated statement of school matters.

In 1855, D. R. Ashley introduced about the same measures that had been defeated the previous session. This, among other things, provided that no sectarian doctrines should be taught in schools receiving public money. It also provided that no money should be apportioned to any school not taught by a regularly examined and licensed teacher. It is likely that these stringent provisions forever settled the question of maintaining sectarian schools out of the public funds.

In 1856, Paul K. Hubbs recommended that a uniform series of text books be used. This was one great step in advance, as previous to this every school, in fact every pupil, had his own text books, creating much confusion in all the schools.

In 1857, Andrew J. Moulder became State Superintendent. The number of schools had now increased to four hundred and eighty-six; the number of children, from eleven thousand two hundred and forty-two to thirty-five thousand seven hundred and twenty-two. He was devoted in his attention to the prosperity of the schools, and did much to create an interest in the public mind. He strongly recommended the establishment of a polytechnic school, which should be able to turn out practical metallurgists and miners; predicted the immense mining interests to be developed. At this time no surveys had been made, and the sixteenth and thirty-sixth sections of land were practically useless.

Schools had been established in 1853 in Volcano, Jackson, Sutter Creek and Ione. Mention has been made in the township histories of schools in each of these places. In the records of the first Court of Sessions held in Amador county may be found a minute that J. K. Payne was excused from jury duty because he was engaged in building a school-house at Volcano. The sight of a child in early days would almost draw out a donation for a school. The first School Superintendent of Amador county was Dr. J. W. Goodin, who was appointed in 1855. Previous to this the duties of apportionment had been performed by Henry Eichelberger, the County Assessor. There were many persons who interested themselves in schools. In Volcano were Levi Hanford and wife, John Turner, W. H. Jones, and others. Mrs. Hanford taught a school in the old Methodist church in 1853, as did also Sempronius (Pony) Boyd in 1855. S. T. Tackerberry and M. M. Estee, two young men then studying law, are also remembered as having taught at Volcano in early days. The latter is now a prominent lawyer in San Francisco; the former has drifted out of sight. W. T. A. Gibson, now of Stockton, was also a teacher there.

Many dunces as well as able men found their way into the school-houses. The Trustees of the districts were appointed by the County Superintendent on the recommendation of the patrons, the process being a virtual election. Sometimes the Trustees were educated men, in which case competent teachers would be employed. They were also the examiners, and were compelled to go through the form of an examination, whether the candidate for teacher was a graduate of Dartmouth or Yale, or some one whose muscles were not adapted to achieving success in the mines, and whose moral and mental fibre was still weaker.

A college graduate was required to know the multiplication table, also how many pints make one quart, or how many inches make one foot, how many feet one rod, etc. If he was able to perform these mathematical feats he was permitted to teach in the public schools for one year, and so also of any one who could perform them, whether a collegian or not. The utmost latitude was allowed in books, any kind or none at all being equally permitted. Some were brought across the plains, some "around the Horn," and if any preference was shown it was for the voice of the majority of pupils, or rather the book that was in the possession of the majority. Sanders' readers were, perhaps, the most numerous, while grammars and arithmetics were unlimited in number. The incompetency of a majority of the teachers, the diversity of school-books and the irregular attendance of pupils, and rate-bills, all tended to render the schools, to a great extent, failures. They merely served as a starting-point for the system, which, under the management of such men as Geo. W. Minns, Crawford, Swett, Denman, Campbell, present State Superintendent, and others, has developed into a wonderful power for good.

In 1856, the

FIRST COUNTY SUPERINTENDENT

Was elected. E. B. McIntyre was an old school-master in the Eastern States, and brought with him the notion that the perpetuity of republican institutions rests on the general intelligence of the people. He labored hard to work the system up to a useful point, but the indifference of the public, as well as the organic defects of the system, were in the way. Successful schools are growths of civilization, not the results of legal enactments. Not until officers, teachers, parents and pupils have, to some extent, been gradually prepared for it, will a complex, though finally useful system, be successfully put into operation. Mr. McIntyre reported that he experienced great difficulty in getting the Trustees of the schools to report to him, although the failure to do so compelled him to withhold their *pro rata* of the public money.

In 1857, Paul K. Hubbs, State Superintendent, reported that no such thing as a public school existed in the State; that the rate bills and other expenses practically excluded many from the schools, and urged a greater appropriation, which was done by the Legislature of 1858, which not only increased the school fund, but authorized the separate districts to raise a special school tax on all the property. The bill was so carelessly drawn, however, as to render it, in many instances, inoperative.

Andrew J. Moulder was elected State Superintendent in 1858. He was a hard-working, conscientious man, and did much to arouse the attention of the public to the condition of the schools.

He made the first able report of the condition of the schools. The number of children had now reached 29,347. He reported that the cost of controlling and punishing the criminals had amounted to $754,193.80 in the past five years, while but $284,183.69 had been expended for school purposes; in other words, that the 400 criminals cost three times as much to the State as the 30,000 children, each criminal costing $1,885, each child, $9. He recommended that each district be required to have six months school in the year.

The total number of children in Amador county under eighteen was 2,114
Between four and eighteen 1,377
Boys 763
Girls 614
Under four 737
Daily average attendance 383

State funds for the year $2,336 00
Raised by county taxes 2,550 83
"   "   bills and district taxes 5,315 84

Total expenditure for schools ... $10,202 67
Estimated value of school property ... $12,825 00

This is the first account of the schools in the county which can be found in print. H. H. Rhees was County Superintendent.

The following list of School Trustees and Teachers by Districts, in 1858, will be interesting:—

JACKSON—Trustees, A. C. Brown, John Mushett, W. L. McKimm. Teachers, A. W. Kerr, Mrs. A. W. Kerr.

IONE—Trustees, J. F. Turner, J. H. Stevens, S. Love. Teacher, J. A. Peters.

PINE GROVE—J. D. Luttrell, A. Leonard, A. P. Clough. Teacher, Miss Dane.

DRYTOWN—Trustees, D. W. Seaton, R. K. Wick, C. W. Fox. Teacher, H. P. Hinkson.

SUTTER CREEK—Trustees, N. A. Green, W. T. Wildman, A. Hayward. Teacher, E. B. McIntyre.

VOLCANO—Trustees, A. N. Ballard, John Turner, S. B. Boardman. Teacher, M. M. Estee.

FIDDLETOWN (OLETA)—Trustees, John D. Williams, D. M. Goff, J. F. Ostrum. Teacher, W. J. Cooper.

AMADOR—Trustees, W. S. Porter, D. Barry, P. Kusart.

BUENA VISTA—Trustees, P. Y. Cool, J. T. Joiner, John Kite.

JACKSON VALLEY—Trustees, Simon Prouty, Joseph Lewis, W. H. Amick.

UNION CHURCH—Trustees, R. K. Sexton, A. F. Potter.

CLINTON—Trustees, Linus Morgan, Hugh Robinson, M. Tynan.

The school system met with many severe attacks, and had many battles to win before it could be firmly established in a working condition. The ablest opponent to the system in the State is now, and always has been, Zachary Montgomery, a lawyer, residence in Oakland. As a member of the Legislature, he fought the common school system and opposed its establishment with the same vigor which he has since shown.

In 1861 he introduced a bill providing "That every school numbering thirty pupils, established by the parents or guardians of such pupils, should have the right, on application, to be enrolled as a public school; that the common school branches should be taught five hours a day, with religious instruction and catechism as an extra at the will of the parents; that the parents or guardians should elect the Trustees of such school with full powers to control; and that the State fund should be apportioned according to the number of children attending school."

The bill was accompanied by a petition, numerously signed. The Honorable John Coness defended the common school system in a lengthy speech, reciting a portion of his own experience. The measure was defeated.

The new school laws of 1863 required the use of school registers for keeping a record of the daily attendance, deportment and progress of the scholars; made provisions and appropriations (one hundred and fifty dollars) for holding annual county teachers' institutes; provided for the annual election of a Trustee, who should hold office for three years; made new provisions for the collection of taxes for building school-houses and the maintenance of schools; and authorized the issuing of teachers' certificates for a term of years.

The most decided improvement in schools was made during the superintendence of John Swett. He was a graduate of the common schools, and had an abiding faith, not only of their utility in society, but as a necessity for a safe foundation for all the essentials of a republican form of government. In his first annual report, he recommended the raising of a sufficient sum by a property tax to support the schools free from all rate bills or local taxes, for at least five months in the year. He showed that but twenty-five per cent. of the children in the State attended school, and contended that, as the general voter had control of property in revenue matters, a portion of it should be taken to prepare him for that responsibility; that, considering the diversified character of our population, California needed the benefits of a free school more than any State in the Union. The Legislature of 1864 passed new school laws, laying an annual tax of five mills on each one hundred dollars of property in the State, and making it imperative on the counties to raise enough, in addition to the State appropriation, to maintain schools five months in the year.

The bill passed the Assembly without opposition, but the famous Zachary Montgomery was in the Senate, and there it came near being slaughtered. The vote stood:—

Ayes—Benton, Burnell, Crane, Cunningham, Foulke, Hall, Haswell, Kutz, Maddox, McMurtry, Moyle, Porter, Roberts, Shepherd, Tuttle, Wright—18.

Noes—Buckley, Dodge, Evans, Freeman, Gaskill, Hamilton, Hawes, Montgomery, Pearce, Redington, Bush, Shafter—12.

In 1863, the amount of money expended for schools in the whole State, was four hundred and eighty thousand dollars; in 1867 the amount of annual expenditure reached the sum of one million two hundred and eighty-seven thousand dollars. The direct tax on all property throughout the State was eight cents on the one hundred dollars, bringing in an income of one hundred and twenty thousand dollars.

Many of the Eastern States, Iowa and Illinois, had, about the same time as California, provided for the general education of the children. A well-to-do farmer, a bachelor of course, of the former State, became disgusted with the freedom with which the Legislature put their hands in his pockets and helped themselves to his cash for educational purposes, and sold out and left for California, where the people were supposed to retain some of the conservative, primitive virtues of old times. When he came to California and found that the same system of *robbery* was in practice here, he gave a terrible howl and turned the heads of his flocks and herds towards Oregon. The last heard of him he was making with all speed towards Alaska, where, it is confidently believed, he will not be disturbed by a general school-tax for at least ten years.

In 1872, the test oath requiring teachers to take the oath of allegiance, was repealed. This was, perhaps, a matter of unnecessary caution; doing very little good or harm, as no case is on record of any teachers leaving the profession on account of it.

In 1867, the State Superintendent reported that every school in the State had become FREE. The Legislature had added some new features to the school law. Formerly teachers were examined by incompetent men, and, as a consequence, men were sometimes admitted to the position of teachers who were unfit to have charge of dumb brutes, much less human beings. The law now required the County Superintendent and also the Board of Examiners to hold first-grade certificates. There is always much difficulty in executing a law that is much in advance of public opinion. There was no exception to the rule in this case. The County Superintendents bridged over the obstruction, and things went much as before, though there was a manifest improvement in the qualifications of teachers.

The system of free schools met with much opposition. There is a plausibility, at least, in the principles that every man has a right to accumulate and hold property; that he is under no obligation to educate or support his indolent neighbors' children; but in the other side of the scales is the fact that, if his neighbors' children are not educated to some useful purpose, they become criminals and paupers, and by their destructive habits endanger not only the existence of the property which was denied for educational purposes, but even life itself.

In 1872, Superintendent Bolander recommended compulsory education, and declared that illiteracy was incipient crime; and quoted Beecher, that, "*uneducated mind is educated vice.*" Bolander proposed five hundred dollars as the least sum that should be expended in any school district in one year.

THE SCHOOL-BOOK WAR.

The law requiring a uniformity of text-books was no exception to the average of laws, of which it has been said the unlooked for operations constitute the principal results. The value of school-books in use amounted to hundreds of thousands of dollars. A small profit on a book in general use, would make a fortune for the publishing house, or the firm holding the agency. Numerous advocates of each proposed work traversed the country proclaiming its merits, and even a lobbyist was thought necessary for the Legislature. Thousands of dollars were expended in getting the books introduced, all of which had to be paid for by the consumers or purchasers of the books in one way or another. The Sanders series of readers had been discarded, and Willson's generally adopted. They were well printed, finely illustrated, and were a great improvement on anything before in use. During the Superintendency of Fitzgerald they were cast aside, and the McGuffey series adopted. Now came the war. Willson was a northern man, and his books were the product of the northern system of education. McGuffey was President of the Virginia University, and his books were supposed to represent the style of southern education. McGuffey's series were said to belong to an ancient formation, a sort of pliocene stratum, containing only fossils of defunct ideas; the engravings were said to be old and inferior, having but one commendable quality; there were but few in the book. The change, which had cost the parents in the State something like two hundred thousand dollars, was brought about by the State Teachers' Institute. It was even said by the Willson advocates that money had been used to obtain the decision in favor of the southern reader. This insinuation was bruited about by the newspapers, and perhaps influenced some in their opinions, but the more candid part of the people scouted the idea, considering partisan feeling and the prejudice of birth amply sufficient to account for any apparent injustice or error of judgment, in producing the exchange.

The result was a defeat of Fitzgerald, who was much grieved about the matter. The Legislature at the next session took the control of text-books away from the State Board. The Willson readers were not reinstated. The change from Willson's to McGuffey's series received the condemnation of the people, yet having been introduced, it was considered better to retain it than to incur a new expense.

SCHOOL CENSUS IN 1863, BY DISTRICTS.

Amador	82	Lancha Plana	85
Butte City	49	Mountain Springs	41
Buena Vista	63	Pine Grove	75
Buckeye	56	Puckerville	52
Clinton	81	Rural	38
Drytown	66	Sutter Creek	133
Fiddletown	124	Union	101
Forest Home	64	Upper Rancheria	43
Franklin	59	Union Church	45
Ione City	162	Volcano	109
Jackson	205	Williams	30
Jackson Valley	51	Willow Springs	61
Total			1875

SCHOOL STATISTICS.

[illegible]	[illegible]	Year	[illegible]	Av'g [illegible]	No. [illegible]	[illegible]	Teachers Wages	
							Male.	Female.
John G. Marvin	....	1853	330	...	2	....	......	......
John G. Marvin	H. Eichelberger	1854	432	206	5	....	......	......
Paul K. Hubbs	Dr J W Gooding	1855	865	319	7	....	......	......
Paul K. Hubbs	E. B. McIntire	1856	898	426	8	....	......	......
A. J. Moulder	E. B. McIntire	1857	986	537	10	....	......	......
A. J. Moulder	H. H. Rhoese	1858	1160	5.6	12	$10,192.67	......	......
A. J. Moulder	H. H. Rhoese	1859	1577	625	16	....	......	......
A. J. Moulder	J. H. Bradley	1860	1580	734	[illegible]	....	......	......
A. J. Moulder	Samuel Page	1861	1675	807	23	....	......	......
A. J. Moulder	Samuel Page	1862	1738	975	26	....	......	......
John Swett	Samuel Page	1863	1875	906	27	....	......	......
John Swett	D. Townsend	1864	2962	1325	29	....	$65.96	$47.06
John Swett	D. Townsend	1865	2074	1315	29	14,591.05	73.96	52.00
John Swett	S. G. Briggs	1866	...	1779	..	9,816.49	70.00	62.00
John Swett	S. G. Briggs	1867	...	1860	..	16,278.68	70.00	56.00
O. P. Fitzgerald	S. G. Briggs	1868	1969	1327	..	13,869.86	74.33	50.25
O. P. Fitzgerald	S. G. Briggs	1869	1855	1322	..	15,140.33	81.13	51.35
O. P. Fitzgerald	S. G. Briggs	1870	1869	1461	..	12,446.46	31.66	56.00
O. P. Fitzgerald	S. G. Briggs	1871	1961	2148	..	17,742.51	81.06	59.00
H. N. Bolander	S. G. Briggs	1872	2097	...	28	15,376.97	......	......
H. N. Bolander	S. G. Briggs	1873	2134	...	28	18,493.10	......	......
H. N. Bolander	S. G. Briggs	1874	...	...	..	....	......	......
H. N. Bolander	W. H. Stowers	1875	...	...	..	....	......	......
E. S. Carr	W. H. Stowers	1876	...	...	..	....	......	......
E. S. Carr	A. Eisinger	1877	...	...	..	....	......	......
E. S. Carr	A. Eisinger	1878	2650	...	..	....	77.00	62.96
E. S. Carr	L. Miller	1879	2733	...	..	35,791.73	80.96	55.00
E. S. Carr	L. Miller	1880	...	...	..	....	......	......

*The total expenditures, from the organization of the county to 1867, inclusive, was $138,873.15.

CONDITION OF SCHOOLS IN 1871.

Amador City School.—This district has no recorded date of organization. Its progress has been rather slow; its present condition is rather flattering; its wants are numerous; no school furniture or apparatus, and a poor, dilapidated school-house.

Aqueduct City School.—This district was organized about 1865; has progressed finely as a rural district; has a neat little school-house, together with some apparatus; house poorly furnished. Its present prospects are hopeful.

Buckeye Valley School.—This district has been unfortunate. Its people were divided on their school interests, and the result of their troubles was the burning of their school-house, which loss they have not yet recovered from, and consequently are not in a very flourishing condition. They are in need of a house, furniture, and apparatus.

Buena Vista School.—This district was organized in 1857; has a very comfortable school-house, some apparatus, very poor furniture, but is in a very flourishing condition, notwithstanding.

Clinton School.—This district is poor. They have a neat little school-house, no furniture or apparatus, yet it is quite flourishing.

Drytown School.—This district was organized in 1853, and, for several years, only maintained a three month's school during the year; but the last few years they have been able to keep their school open seven months in the year. They have a nice school-house, costing some eight hundred dollars, some furniture, some apparatus, and the school is in a better condition than it has ever been.

Fiddletown School (Oleta).—This is an old district, without date of organization; has an excellent school-house, well furnished, with some apparatus, and is in a very flourishing condition, under the guidance of an efficient teacher.

Franklin School.—This district is small, situated in a very sparsely settled neighborhood; has a small school-house, some apparatus, but no furniture. It is in rather a state of progression.

Forest Home School.—This district, like many others, has no date of organization. They have a respectable school-house, but poorly furnished, yet in rather a flourishing condition.

Ione Valley School.—It is situated in a very rich and fertile valley which is covered by a Spanish grant, which has been very prejudicial to its interests. They have a comfortable school-house. The district was organized in 1853, is tolerably well supplied with apparatus and furniture and is quite flourishing.

Jackson School.—This district is also without date of organization; has a brick school-house, with two departments, and has progressed finely; has always been under the guidance of able teachers, and is well supplied with apparatus and furniture.

Jackson Valley School.—This district is a small one, and labors under the same difficulties as the Ione Valley, it being on the Spanish grant, also. They have a very commodious school-house, tolerably well supplied with furniture and apparatus, and is in quite a flourishing condition.

Lancha Plana School.—Situated in the south-west portion of the county, and at one time a very rich mining camp, but now in a dilapidated condition, and consequently the school has suffered. They have a shell of a house in which to impart instruction, poor furniture, some apparatus, and, notwithstanding the disadvantages under which it has labored, its prospects are quite flattering.

Mountain Echo School.—This district was organized in 1867, and has progressed slowly. They have a good wooden school-house, very little furniture and no apparatus. Notwithstanding the many difficulties with which they are surrounded, they have been able to maintain four or five months' school in the year. Their prospects are quite encouraging.

Milligan's School.—This district has no date of organization, and is also one of the rural districts. It has been able to maintain a four months' school some portion of the year. They have quite a comfortable little school-house, with very little furniture or apparatus.

Mountain Springs School.—This is a small district, and has a hard struggle to exist. By perseverance they have been able to keep open a school in accordance with the law. They have a school-house that answers the purpose, but need furniture and apparatus. Their prospects are anything but flattering.

New York Ranch School.—This district was organized about 1866. They have a very comfortable school-house, together with some furniture and apparatus. It has steadily advanced and its prospects for the future are quite flattering.

Oneida School.—This district was organized in 1865, with some twenty census children. It now numbers some eighty. They have progressed steadily; have a shell of a house, entirely destitute of furniture and apparatus.

Puckerville School.—This is an old district, without date of organization; has a very commodious school-house, well supplied with furniture and apparatus, and is progressing finely.

Pine Grove School.—This district is situated on the road leading from Volcano to Jackson. They have a neat and comfortable school-house, pretty well furnished with apparatus and furniture. This school has been conducted in the main by able teachers, and is in a prosperous condition.

Sutter Creek School.—This district like a number of others, is without date of organization; has had the misfortune of having its school-house burned up, but, nothing discouraged, its friends went to work and put up a magnificent two-story, brick building. The cost of the house was about six thousand dollars. It is well furnished with apparatus and furniture, has two hundred and twenty census children, and is situated in the richest mining district in the county. Its future is truly flattering.

Stony Creek School.—This is one of the rural districts of the county, and was organized in 1868, with small beginnings; but by perseverance they have a neat little school-house, with a moderate supply of furniture and apparatus. They have progressed beyond expectation. Their prospects are truly flattering.

Union Church and Muletown School.—These two districts have been merged into one, and will be known hereafter as the Union District, and is situated in one of the prettiest valleys in the county. Last Spring the friends of education went to work and put up a good school-house at a convenient center for both districts, and furnished the same tolerably well. They are getting along finely now.

Upper Rancheria School.—This district is also without date of organization; is an old school, but has not advanced as it should have done. But few felt interested in the education of the children, and consequently let both the school and the school-house run down. Now that it is necessary to have a new house, the people are divided, and cannot agree where to place it, and consequently their prospects are gloomy.

Volcano School.—This district was organized in 1855, and prospered finely until about 1861, when a state of confusion and strife sprang up, which resulted in a division of the district. Union district was formed out of a portion of its territory, and continued in that separate state until last year, when they united again and built a fine and commodious house that reflects credit upon the Trustees of both districts.

Williams School.—This district is among the oldest in the county. Its record shows no date of organization. They have a very pleasant school-house, with some furniture and a few articles of apparatus. They have progressed steadily. Its wants are considerable in the way of furniture.

Willow Springs School.—This district, like too many others, has been negligent of its records. Very little can be learned of its history, other than it has had an existence for several years. They have a tolerably comfortable school-house, some furniture, and need almost everything to conduct a school properly.

Washington School.—This district, like a great many others, has been quite negligent of duty, the record showing no date of organization. They have a very neat and comfortable school-house, tolerably well supplied with furniture and apparatus. They have progressed moderately well. Their prospects are encouraging.

The foregoing is from the report of the Rev. S. G. Briggs, County Superintendent from 1866 to 1875. Though a man of limited education, his integrity and devotion to the interests of schools enabled him to accomplish a great deal towards elevating them to their present high standard. It will be seen that the most of the statistics, in the table appended, were gathered during his incumbency. He died at the post of duty, beloved by all the teachers and pupils in the county. The same

RESIDENCE, STORE & RANCH OF CHARLES DOSCH.
IONE VALLEY, AMADOR COUNTY, CAL.

RANCH AND RESIDENCE OF J.C. BLYTHER.
TOWNSHIP 4, AMADOR COUNTY, CAL.

may be said also of W. H. Stowers, who succeeded him.

TRIBUTE TO SCHOOL-TEACHERS.

The limits of this work will only permit a brief reference to some of the devoted teachers, who have seen their sun of life rise and go far down the western slope in their devotion to the cause of education, and of some who have reposed in death for years after their work was well done. School-teaching, though holding so important a position in social economy, is a profession that is little honored. Day after day, weeks following weeks, until the youthful, vigorous form becomes old and feeble, the teacher coins his life into the coming generation, and finally sinks unknown and unsung to the grave. No plaudits of assembled thousands encourage him; no daily papers chronicle his coming in or going out, yet silently he fashions the future citizen, perhaps President, weaves his web of human affairs in poverty and obscurity, often in want, happy to see his former pupils performing an honored part in the world.

Many have lived their whole active life in Amador county. Among these we may reckon A. W. Kerr of Plymouth, who is now teaching the third generation; J. F. Gould of Jackson, who thirty years since commenced his work, and still holds on, Hiram Ford, of Buena Vista, also is well fixed in the groove. Some have gone down to premature graves, worn out by the terrible nervous exhaustion incident to watching and caring for a large school of children. Of this number we may reckon Dennis Townsend, whose mind gave way under the terrible strain; and also William H. Stowers, who gave all of life that was in him to children who are now taking places in active life. J. C. Gear, also a teacher for years, rests in the Ione cemetery, not quite forgotten by the children, now men and women, whom he led up the first low hills of science. Among the women we may reckon Mrs. Bartlett of Sutter Creek, Mrs. M. B. Church of Drytown, Mrs. Thomas Stewart of Ione, Miss Augusta Withington, Mrs. Trowbridge (deceased) of Jackson, and numerous others who have done, and still are doing, good work. All honor to them.

CHAPTER XLII.
NEWSPAPERS.

Charles Boynton—Amador Ledger—Dispatch—Union Record—Sutter Creek Independent—Ione News—Amador Sentinel.

The mining towns, with three or four hundred men hungry for news, were tempting fields for an ambitious man. The first institution after the hotel and saloon is a printing office. Who has not felt an idea in his—well, head, pressing and kicking to get out, aching for deliverance, that it might grow and overspread the world, revolutionize governments, and correct all things? Men will not try the law without study, or mercantile business without some practice, or a hotel without sitting around awhile to see how things might be run. But there is no measure for mental work; no rule of feet and inches, no measure of pints and quarts to gauge the product of the mind. Though a man may write over acres of paper, square measure will not apply; solid or leaded articles defy cubic measure and avoirdupois just as well; and, finally, though an article may be a drug, apothecaries weight will not weigh it, and, though it may be a golden thought, the jeweler's scales are equally powerless. If it is a living, active, vital thought, adapted to the wants of man, it will live and flourish; it is seed sown on good ground. If it is obsolete; if it is the effete matter of a morbid mind, though it is embalmed in print, or engraved in stone, naught shall save it from oblivion.

When lofty thoughts thy mind inspire,
Writ ; some slumbering soul that reads,
Touched by sparks of thy celestial fire,
Shall ripen into glorious deeds.

Charles Boynton was the father of the newspaper in Amador county. Though many recollect him, few can give an idea of his character, which seemed to be as changeable as a kaleidoscope, now foaming over with fun and good nature, now seriously discussing political economy; now poring over some old volume of forgotten history, and now going for the gold in the bed of the Mokelumne with all his might, mind and strength, with a woman's emotion and a man's power. He was in some way connected with the Mokelumne Hill *Chronicle;* at any rate he had sufficient access to the types and press to work off several numbers of the *Owl,* 1853 and '54, which set the whole country crazy with its fun, which, however, being of a local nature, is now understood only by those who remember the incidents referred to. It is said that he used to swim the river with the edition tied to the top of his head. It is also said that he never went over to the Hill without having a fight or two on account of the little paper. Soon after the organization of the county he started the *Sentinel,* an independent paper, devoted to no party or clique. It was printed for some months on the *Chronicle* press, the edition being so small that he carried it all under his arm to Jackson to be distributed. He soon after obtained a press of his own, and ran the paper successfully for some years. O. D Avaline, formerly of Fort Wayne, Indiana, became the proprietor of it about 1857 or '58, continuing the publication until the great fire of 1862, when he abandoned the newspaper business, raised a company of soldiers and joined the Union army. He died at Folsom of general debility, produced by exposure while in the service.

THE AMADOR LEDGER

Was started by Thomas H. Springer in Volcano in 1855, during the boom in that town. It was an independent sheet at first, but in 1856, during the Fremont, Fillmore and Buchanan campaign, it took

Democratic ground, which it maintained until the breaking out of the war of the Rebellion, when it became Union Democratic, and finally Republican. It was moved from Volcano to Jackson in 1857. In typographic appearance it was much better than the *Sentinel*, Springer being a first-rate printer. Though making no pretensions as a writer, he had a short, spicy way of dealing out the current news. He was, at different times, assisted in the editorial department by P. C. Johnson, John Bradly, E.Y. Hammand and others. When Springer was elected State Printer, the paper was managed by Grant Springer and Shearer, finally falling into the ownership of R. M. Briggs and J. A. Eagon, who made it a political organ. Both were able lawyers, politicians and writers. Some very able editorials appeared in it; but even a country newspaper requires the undivided attention of an able man to make it successful, and they soon tired of publishing it for the honor, and sold it in 1875 to Richard Webb, its present proprietor. Mr. Webb wields a sarcastic pen, and frequently gets into personal difficulties, and occasionally a libel suit, on account of his unsparing denunciations, but nothing can change his course; he returns to the attack with more *vim* than ever. He was formerly connected with a small semi-weekly publication at Sutter Creek, which, on his purchase of the *Ledger*, was discontinued.

THE AMADOR DISPATCH

Was originally started in Lancha Plana, by Heckendorn & Payne. It was a small and badly printed sheet, containing mostly local news. The old roller-press on which it was printed was, until a few years since, lying in a vacant lot near the town. It was enlarged into a sheet of better appearance and published for some months during the *boom* at that town. In 1859 it was purchased by — Mullen, and moved to Jackson, and started as a Democratic sheet. On the breaking out of the war, the proprietor sold it to Geo. M. Payne and Wm. M. Penry (the latter gentleman being still proprietor), raised a company of soldiers, and went to the aid of the Union. The *Dispatch* immediately took strong Democratic ground, attacking the administration at every assailable point, with arguments, sarcasm and ridicule, and made itself a power in politics. The famous L. P. Hall (Long Primer) was associated for some years with Penry in conducting the paper. At the time of the assassination of Lincoln it was suppressed for several months, and Penry and Hall immured in Fort Alcatraz, of which a particular account has been given in another portion of our history. Personally, Mr. Penry is "as mild a mannered man as ever" indicted an editorial, and his serene and kindly face gives no indication of the mental fires burning below; forming a parallel in this trait to the famous Brick Pomeroy, who wields the editorial tomahawk and scalping-knife with a fearful effect, without ruffling a line or curve in his well-fed face.

The paper has passed its twenty-first year, and bids fair to continue to a good old age.

UNION RECORD.

While Penry and Hall were incarcerated in Alcatraz, R. M. Briggs took the printing material of the *Dispatch* and published the paper bearing the above title. He let off the accumulated fire-works for a few months with considerable noise and effect. Some of his editorials on national questions had wide circulation in the East. On Mr. Penry's discharge from confinement, the publication of the *Union Record* ceased.

THE SUTTER CREEK INDEPENDENT

Was a small daily paper published about 1872 by R. V. Chadd, formerly of Stockton. It made quite a sensation for a while with its local hits and current news, but was discontinued for want of support. The material was finally purchased by Richard Webb, who published a semi-weekly for a short time, merging into the *Ledger* in 1875.

THE IONE NEWS

Was commenced in 1877 by Haley & Co. It was continued for about three years and discontinued. The make-up of the paper was good and the contents well edited, but the county could hardly support four papers, and some one must fail, and the publication was suspended about the end of November, 1880. In 1861 a weekly paper was published at Ione for a few months by Folger & Co., who afterwards moved the concern to Alpine county, where it flourished as a political paper for some years.

THE AMADOR SENTINEL.

This is probably a namesake of the *Sentinel* which was destroyed by the fire in 1862, though no descendant thereof. It was started in June, 1879, by Turner, McNeil & Briggs, but at present is owned by Turner & Sanborn, both young men but able writers. It is gaining an influence and circulation, having a subscription list of something over six hundred. It is Republican in politics though liberal in its opinions. It is the official paper, and seems to be on a paying basis, with a hopeful career before it.

CHAPTER XLIII.

SOCIETIES.

The Society of Free Masons—Modern Masonry—General Tendency of Masonry—Introduction into the United States—Volcano Lodge No. 56—Amador Lodge No. 65—Ione Lodge No. 80—Henry Clay Lodge No. 90—St. Marks Lodge No. 45—Drytown Lodge No. 174—Royal Arch Chapter No. 31—Origin of Odd Fellowship—Encampment—Degree of Rebekah—Volcano Lodge No. 25—Sutter Creek Lodge No. 31—Jackson Lodge No. 36—Ione Lodge No. 51—Telegraph Lodge No. 75—Lancha Plana Lodge No. 95—Plymouth Lodge No. 260—Grand Encampment No. 17—Marble Encampment No. 19—Temperance Societies—Subjects for Insane Asylums—Good Templars—Knights of the Red Cross—Blue Ribbon Society—General Tendency of Temperance Societies—Burlesque Societies—E Clampsus Vitus—Hautontimoroumenos—Knights of the Assyrian Cross—Pioneer Societies—Amador Society of California Pioneers—Sclavonic Illyric Mutual Benevolent Society—Grangers.

"UNITED we stand, divided we fall." Organization is the largest factor in modern civilization. In ancient times, in the rude beginnings of society, the family relation was the source of strength and prosperity. The mother who bore the most children was the most honored. Perhaps the best illustration of the enormous force of family relation may be seen in the ancient Israelites, who, holding to blood ties, became a great nation, with the full faith that they were destined to inherit the earth. But great as the Israelites were they were scattered by a host of innumerable families united under one government. Tribal and family organizations give way to combinations of still greater magnitude, which are made up of innumerable smaller parts, each being to some extent a body politic within itself. Individual valor, though a source of personal respect, can accomplish little compared to the united efforts of multitudes. An army is efficient in proportion to its discipline. A well-trained army of a few thousands, acting under the direction of one mind, will rout a mob of ten times their number. The principle holds good in all the relations of life, whether the object be to establish a nation, accumulate wealth, damage an enemy, or benefit mankind. The ability to combine conflicting or inert elements into a solid, active body will always hold the highest position in civilized society.

The so-called secret societies are the results of this instinct. Some of them, if not as ancient as any national or religious organization, have their origin in the ages of elementary government; have, what might be called an umbilical cord, running back to the origin of all government. All of them serve the important purpose in society of teaching authority and obedience, without which law and order is impossible. The most vicious member of a vicious society, by agreeing to sacrifice some of his privileges to better secure the others, becomes unconsciously better prepared to obey other laws, and eventually becomes a useful member of society; while as a member of a higher organization whose objects, in part at least, are beneficent towards society, he acquires the knowledge of parliamentary forms, and the habit of listening deferentially to opinions differing from his own.

Thus we have, as powerful auxiliaries in the maintenance of law and order, the numerous societies of the age, such as Masons, Odd Fellows, Good Templars, and Sons of Temperance, Knights of the Red Cross, etc. The former two of the list, especially, have become almost cosmopolitan in character and influence, modifying the rancors and cruelties of war, and carrying a benign influence into millions of places. The secrets, which are made of great account in all societies, are a means of attracting the public, and holding them together. The mystery of the Shekinah held the Israelites together. The Greeks had the Adelphos, and Elusinian mysteries. The Egyptians had mysteries, and, in later times, the Druids had a wonderful, valuable mystery in their possession. Men, as well as women, love a mystery, and are led away by it.

The society of Free Masons has, probably, the best claims to antiquity of any of the beneficiary societies of modern times. It is quite certain that at least one thousand years ago the builders of churches and palaces, who moved about over Europe as their services were wanted in the different towns, formed themselves into guilds, where each one's rank as a builder was fixed by his rank in the society. They were accustomed to camp in a body, under the direction of the officers. The society was not unlike the modern Typographical Union in its objects and organization. From the best accounts there were several of them in different parts of Europe, but a membership in one made it much easier to gain admission to another. In several instances the governments manifested considerable hostility to the organizations on account of their maintaining extortion rates for work. The terms, entered apprentice, fellow craft, free and accepted Masons, i. e., free to work at the trade, indicate beyond doubt the nature and object of the organization.

The signs and secret work enabled the members to recognize each other's standing as workmen without the trouble of testing the work, and also to assist each other in traveling about the country in those lawless times, in going from one job to another.

The changes in the system of building large cathedrals like those of the middle ages in sparsely settled countries, the denser populations and greater diffusion of knowledge, architectural as well as other kinds, obviated the necessity of societies for mutual protection, as every city of any note had an ample number of architects and stone-cutters to do all its work.

The churches or church had, in the first instances, rather encouraged the formation of the societies as tending to disseminate the knowledge of building. In the later years it discouraged the existence of the societies as setting up a secret which was superior to the confessional, an opposition which it still maintains with persistent action.

In the beginning of the seventeenth century the societies gradually ceased to be of a trade character, and began to take on a form of self-protection, admitting as members persons who had no knowledge of stone-cutting or other mechanical arts, the old emblems of the tools of the trade being retained as symbols of degrees and character.

MODERN MASONRY

Began in London, June 24, 1717, when the four London lodges united into one and named their grand master. From this time forward no practical knowledge of mechanical work was required for admission. The principal promoters of this union were, Desaguliers, a well-known popularizer of science, and James Anderson, a Presbyterian clergyman, who compiled the book of constitutions containing the charges, rites and traditions of the craft, reducing them to something like system and order. From this time no new lodge could be formed without a warrant from the grand lodge. The Duke of Montagu became grand master. Other noblemen also joined the order so that it lost somewhat of its democratic character. The principle of charity, as well as self-protection, became incorporated into it, and schools were organized at the time, some of which (Battersea and Tottenham) are continued to this day.

The latter part of the eighteenth century a kind of rebellion or assumption of authority took place by the old York lodge of masons, claiming the right to issue warrants for the organization of subordinate lodges. This lodge claimed to have existed from 926. They also had a new ritual, introducing the red color of the Royal Arch, which they declared of higher rank than the blue degree of St. John. It was claimed to be a degree used at the second building of the Temple. Another branch also introduced an order of the Templars. In 1813, the Dukes of Sussex, Kent and Athole, succeeded in uniting all these orders together under the name of "The United Grand Lodge of England." This patronage of the nobility gave the order an impetus which resulted in making it almost a national matter. About this time Jews were admitted to membership. They built a hall for the collection of material pertaining to the order, established several magazines such as the *Freemason's Magazine*, and the *Freemason*, and the *Freemason's Quarterly*, and built an asylum for indigent and unfortunate members of the order.

At present, England has sixty provincial lodges, twelve hundred minor lodges, grand chapter of the royal arch degree, grand lodge for the mark masters, grand conclave of the knights' templars, and a superior grand council of the ancient and accepted rite of the thirty-three degrees.

Masonry was introduced into Ireland in 1730. In Scotland the history of the order was much like that in England—except that at one time females, widows of members, were admitted as parties interested in building contracts. Desaguliers, the apostle of Masonry in England, appeared in Edinburg in 1721, and succeeded in modifying the character of the organization, and bringing about a union with the London societies. St. Andrew's day was substituted for that of St. John the Baptist, and on November 30, 1736, a grand lodge for Scotland was formed, acting in connection with the grand lodge of England.

It is said that in Scotland the growth of the order was rather towards conviviality than charity. Some of the ceremonies, such as drinking beer out of a human skull, had to be eliminated. The head of the St. Clair family resigned his hereditary office and became the first grand master. The supreme grand royal arch chapter was organized at Edinburg, but its authority is not recognized by other similar orders.

Masonry as a speculative order was introduced in France in 1725, and from the first was patronized largely by the nobility. An attempt to engraft on it the mysteries of Cagliostro, the most accomplished humbug the world ever saw, which were said to have been derived from the deciphered records of Egypt, and also the Rosicrucian mysteries, and still more, a pretension to holy inspiration, came near strangling the infant in its cradle. Some of the Bonapartes, and Marshals Kellerman and Massena, were members of the order. Napoleon the Great rather frowned on the order, as it contained too many of the nobility, who might come to a better understanding, and the members of the *familie* withdrew from the order. It does not flourish in France as in the more Protestant countries, the secrets of the order being out of reach of the confessional.

Germany claims the honor of organizing modern masonry, and have what is called the royal mother lodge of the world. Those best acquainted with its workings and history, or at least some of them, say that the masonic organization was older in England than in Germany; that it was carried to Germany, and flourished there while it was nearly forgotten in England; that it was brought back from Germany, getting its final movement in England.

GENERAL TENDENCY OF MASONRY.

It is impossible, even for members, to judge accurately what its general tendency is. It undoubtedly is to some extent a rival, for favor, with the religious societies of the world, in a manner satisfying the hunger for a religious belief by holding in its bosom a continued mystery, whose end cannot be reached. The claim to be a charitable institution, to do good to the whole world, has perhaps a tendency to make them brethren with those who cannot give the signs of fellowship. Others contend that there is a tendency to a degeneracy into a convivial club. It is likely that all these tendencies prevail in different places, depending upon the tone of the surrounding society.

The charge that was made against the order a half a century since of hatching treason to government, or the general plunder of society, has been forgotten and need not be defended here, though the Masonic lodges in some parts of Europe, especially in France, Italy and Austria, are said to be amenable to this charge, as also to the charge of entertaining irreligious opinions.

INTRODUCTION INTO THE UNITED STATES.

Masonry was introduced into Boston in 1733, which was followed by lodges in different colonies. After the war of Independence grand lodges were formed in the several States. It flourished until 1829, when an exposure was made by a man by the name of Morgan in Batavia, New York. He was spirited away, and never heard of more. The old Whig party, which had an existence of a quarter of a century, was formed out of discontents in regard to the tariff and opponents to Free Masonry. In the hurry and skurry of politics, Masonry was forgotten and allowed to outgrow the odium attached to it in Morgan's time. Ben. Franklin was a grand master of a lodge in Philadelphia. Washington was also a member. There are now forty-three grand lodges, and five thousand subordinate lodges in the United States, numbering four hundred thousand members, officers being elected each year by ballot.

The officers of an organized lodge are: Worshipful Master, Senior Warden, Junior Warden, Treasurer, Secretary, Senior Deacon, Junior Deacon, Tyler and Chaplain.

The Masonic library of books, written to explain its workings and claims to antiquity and support, numbers four thousand volumes.

VOLCANO LODGE, NO. 56,

Is the oldest in the county, having been in existence since 1855. The first officers were J. C. Shipman, W. M.; T. Stewart, S. W.; E. Sammis, J. W.; B. W. Payne, Treas.; W. Hudson, S.; J. H. Welch, T. Since then the position of W. M. was held by G. B. Walker, 1856; W. Ayer, 1857; J. W. Bicknel, 1858; R. Stewart, 1859-60-62-65; Charles Wilson, 1861; L. McLaine, 1863-64, 1869, 1878-79; A. Young. 1866-67-68; James Adams, 1870-71, 1873-74-75-76-77; Louis Miller, 1872. Many prominent men have been members of this lodge. Quite a volume might be written on the actions and adventures of the men who have at different times been associated in this institution.

AMADOR LODGE, NO. 65,

Was organized the same year, at Jackson, with W. W. Cope, as W. M.; W. M. Rogers, S. W.; C. Boynton, J. W.; P. Clark, Treas.; B. Hubbard, S.; J. J. Gibbons, T. Since then the chair of W. M. was filled by J. E. Graham, 1856-57; W. W. Cope, in 1858; M. J. Little, in 1859-60-62-63, 1865; M. Levinsky, 1861; J. Foote Turner, 1867; R. Aitken, in 1868-69-70-71-72-73; Wallace Kay, in 1874-75-76-77-78-79. This lodge also has had several distinguished names on its rolls, such as W. W. Cope, who was a Chief Justice, and also that of J. T. Farley, United States Senator for California. The institution is flourishing, having a hall of its own.

IONE LODGE, NO. 80,

Was also organized in 1855, with A. E. Callaway as W. M.; J. T. Poe, S. W.; E. Benedick, J. W.; I. B. Gregory, Treas.; J. C. Gear, S.; and W. S. Porter, T. Soon after the organization the lodge, in conjunction with the citizens, erected a two-story building, taking the upper portion for the Masonic Hall, while the lower was occupied as a school-house. About 1870, the Masons and Odd Fellows together purchased the Turner building, on extremely favorable terms, and converted the upper part into a convenient and commodious hall, which they have since occupied. The position of W. M. has been filled since the organization by A. E. Callaway, in 1856; J. C. Gear, in 1857; J. A. Eagon, in 1858; H. H. Rhees, in 1859; J. Foot Turner, in 1860; R. F. Stevens, in 1861, 1866; J. Farnsworth, in 1862; R. H. Withington, in 1863; George Haverstick, in 1864; A. K. Dudley, in 1865;

James Cumming, in 1867; M. C. Parkinson, in 1868-69; J. W. Surface, in 1870-71, 1874; B. Isaacs, in 1872-73; John Merchant, in 1875-76-77; W. A. Bennetts, in 1878-79. The members of this lodge are said to be worth, in the aggregate, near a million dollars, and the society is always in funds.

HENRY CLAY LODGE, NO. 90,

Was organized in 1856, at Sutter Creek, with S. F. Benjamin as W. M.; A. H. Rose, S. W.; O. P. Southwell, J. W.; James Murry, Treas.; A. Hayward, S.; and D. Crandall, T. The position of W. M. has been filled by O. P. Southwell, in 1857; A. Hayward, in 1858-59-60-61; H. Wood, in 1862; John Gaver, in 1863-64; Henry M. Fisk, in 1865-66-67-68; Thomas Dunlap, in 1869, 1871-72-73, 1875; A. C. Joy, in 1870; Henry Peck, in 1874; Morris Brinn, in 1876-77; J. E. Russel, in 1878; and John Lithgow, in 1879. This lodge is also in good financial circumstances, many of the rich mine-owners, as Hayward, Chamberlain and others, having been members.

ST. MARKS LODGE, NO. 115,

Was organized in 1857. at Oleta (Fiddletown), with T. L. Sullivan as W. M.; A. B. Rowland, S. W.; T. M. Horrell, J. W.; A. Eneas Quin, Treas.; Thomas Horan, S.; and H. A. Kutchenthall, T. This lodge, in consequence of the decrease of the population and failure of the mines, has had a struggle for existence. In 1875 it was consolidated with No. 85, at Indian Diggings, to which it was attached until 1879, when it was reorganized at Oleta. The position of W. M. was filled in 1858-59-60, by F. L. Sullivan; in 1861, by Thomas Horan; in 1862, by J. B. Hill; in 1863-64-65, by W. B. Norman; in 1866, by D. Coblentz; in 1867, 1872-73-74, by Charles Lee; in 1868, by A. P. Wood; in 1869, by J. W. McManus; in 1870, by C. A. Parinton; in 1871, by H. J. Dial; in 1879, by H. H. Bell.

DRYTOWN LODGE, NO. 174,

Was organized in 1865, with J. B. Hill as W. M.; J. M. Hinkson, S. W.; Daniel Worley, J. W; M. A. Hinkson, Treasurer; A. S. Richardson. S; and C. H. Misner, T. The first W. M. occupied the same position the two succeeding terms; the years 1868-69-70-71-72-74-75-76, by J. M. Hinkson; the year of 1873 by Henry Burchell, 1877, by J. A. Gessler, and 1879 by William Jennings. This lodge, the youngest in the county, has had its seasons of prosperity and adversity. When the mines along the lode employ a great many men the numbers on the roll increase.

ROYAL ARCH CHAPTER.

This is an advanced order of Masonry, and was derived from the York branch, having no connection with Scottish branch, which confers the thirty-three degrees. They date from the second building of Solomon's temple, which date is obtained by adding five hundred and thirty to the current year, 1881, becoming 2411 A. I., or *Anno Inventionem* (year of the discovery). The officers are High Priest, King, Scribe, Treasurer, Secretary, Captain of the Host,

Principal Sojourner, Royal Arch Captain, Masters of the third, second, and first vails, and Guard.

A Chapter, called the Volcano Chapter, No. 8, was organized at Volcano, May 3, 1856. At the session of the Grand Lodge in 1860, the name was changed to "Sutter Creek," retaining the same number. The present officers are John Lithgow, H. P.; T. Dunlap, K.; Robert Robinson, S.; V. Luten..:ky, Treas.; A. K. Dudley, Sec'y.; J. McDoug.., Post C. of H.; Wallace Kay, P. S.; M. Brinn, R. A. C.; R. Redpath, Mastr 3d V.; D. A. Patterson, Mastr 2d V.; John Oulds, Mastr 1st V.; John Jelmini, Guard; Past High Priests, Alvinza Hayward, R. Aitken, John Lithgow, J. W. Surface.

Members of the Royal Arch Chapter: James Adams, J. Q. Adams, G. Allen, W. A. Bennets, A. Berryman, J. M. Campbell, P. A. Clute, W .S. Coolidge, R. Cosner, D. T. Davis, P. Fagan, J. T. Farley, H. D. Ford, F. Frates, W. H. Gunsolus, H. F. Hall, J. W. Houston, B. Isaacs, John Marchant, L. McLaine, S. S. Manon, J. W. McMurry, J. Milliken, J. Miller, G. Newman, L. R. Poundstone, C. A. Purinton, J. Reardon, P. S. Robertson, J. E. Russel, S. G. Spagnoli, B. Spagnoli, J. A. Steinberger, J. F. Stewart, J. B. Stevens, W. Sutherland, J. P. Surface, F. K. Taber, W. H. S. Welch, D. H. Whitlatch, numbering fifty-six.

ORIGIN OF ODD FELLOWSHIP.

Unlike the Masons, the origin of this order was in a convivial club, existing in the latter part of the last century in London, called the "Ancient and Honorable Order of Odd Fellows." Attempts were made to change the character of the order to one of more sobriety and decorum, which not succeeding, a portion seceded, and called themselves the Union Order of Odd Fellows. The members in England now number about five hundred thousand. April 26, 1819, Thomas Wildey and four others organized the first lodge of Odd Fellows in the United States, acting under a charter from the Union Order of Odd Fellows. This day is frequently celebrated by the members. The order was established in Boston, March 26, 1820, and in Philadelphia, December 26, 1821, both lodges receiving their charter from the Baltimore lodge. A grand charter was then issued to the past grands of New York. Since then the order has been established in every State and Territory, and, perhaps, every county in the Union. There are forty-eight grand lodges, thirty six grand encampments, five thousand four hundred and eighty-six subordinate lodges, one thousand five hundred and twelve subordinate encampments, and five hundred and twelve Rebekah degree lodges. Candidates for admission must be free white males of good moral character, and twenty-one years old, who believe in a Supreme Being, the creator and preserver of the universe. Fidelity to the laws of the land and of the society, and the duties of good citizenship are strictly enjoined, though the order is moral and beneficiary, rather than religious. Its secrecy consists of an unwritten and unspoken language by means of signs, which serves for mutual recognition. Five or more members may constitute a subordinate lodge, whose functions are chiefly administrative. It provides means to relieve its sick and distressed members, to bury the dead, to relieve the widow, and to educate the orphan. The by-laws constitute the legal contract between the initiate and the lodge. The series of degrees with white, pink, blue, green, and scarlet, represent moral lessons. The officers of a subordinate lodge are Noble Grand, Vice-Grand, Secretary, and Treasurer, and are elected semi-annually. The degree of Rebekah was created in 1851, to be conferred upon the female members of the Odd Fellow families.

THE ENCAMPMENT

Is composed of members of the scarlet degree. The officers are Patriarch, High Priest, Senior and Junior Wardens, Secretary and Treasurer. They have the exclusive right to confer the patriarchal, golden rule and royal purple degrees, and are officered by a Chief Patriarch, High Priest, Senior Warden, Scribe, Treasurer and Junior Warden. All Past Patriarchs in good standing, are members of grand encampments. The grand encampment meets annually, and is officered by a Grand Patriarch, Grand High Priest, Grand Senior Warden, Grand Scribe, Grand Treasurer, and Grand Junior Warden, elected annually. The grand lodge and grand encampments derive their revenues from charter fees and per centage on lodge or encampment revenues, and a per capita tax. The Grand Lodge of the United States is composed of representatives elected biennially by the several grand lodges and encampments. Its elective officers are a Grand Sire, Grand Secretary and Grand Treasurer, elected biennially. The seat of government is Baltimore, where the order in the United States was first organized. Its revenue now amounts to over five million dollars annually. Since 1843 the order has had no official connection with or responsibility to the Union Order of Odd Fellows of England; hence the term Independent Order of Odd Fellows. The Independent Order of Odd Fellows has four supreme grand lodges—one in the United States; one in the German Empire; one in Australia, and one in New Zealand. In the United States it has 48 subordinate grand lodges, 30 grand encampments, 6,734 subordinate lodges, 1,318 subordinate encampments, and 870 Rebekah lodges, composed of members of the fifth degree and their wives. Total revenue for one year, $4,516,660.63. During the year 1877, there were 40,578 initiations. Since the organization to 1877, the initiations amounted to 1,064,928; members relieved, 816,882; widowed families relieved 108,385; members buried, 74,226. The whole amount of relief was $69,235,989.45. The membership is now (1881) nearly three-fourths of a million.

SOCIETIES.

VOLCANO LODGE, NO. 25,

Was the first in the county, and has held its way firmly ever since, the membership generally approximating to a hundred. The first officers were, N. Vipon, N. G.; J. W. Warner, V. G.; H. Hanford, R. S.; J. Fridenburg, T. Assets estimated at $3,000. The following persons have filled the position of first officer: H. Hanford, P. S. Wilkes, J. E. Warner, H. Lake, J. Halsey, T. A. Goodwin, A. Petty, E. Grant, D. S. Boydston, Chas. Wilson, A. Howerton, L. Miller, Geo. Collins, N. Ruddick, B. Ross. * * *

Members of the Rebekah Degree—Mesdames Hannah E. Warner, Elizabeth Phelps, Sarah Robinson, Christiana Weller, Catherine Burnhardt, Emma W. Halsey, Mary A. Mails, Lucy B. Hanford. Charlotte Barnum, Warren Tarr, Samuel Hale, Wm. Blakely, D. Lowery, — McKensie, Eva Walker, Sophia Babcock, Susan Boydston, Jane Largomarcino, Mary Cox, Julia E. McFadden, James Hall, A. Petty, C. B. Goodrich, R. D. Miller, J. Stainer.

SUTTER CREEK LODGE, NO. 31,

Was organized in 1860. First officers: C. B. Culver, N. G.; J. T. Skinner, V. G.; J. Davidson, R. S.; W. Gothie, T. Property estimated at $3,425.62. The position of first officer has been held by W. E. Fifield, Wm. Gothie, W. Palmer, E. F. Huse, J. S. Hill, D. M. Hardman, C. Weaver, W. E. Finn, J. Swift, H. B. Bishop, J. H. Hammond, B. F. Taylor, L. Fournier, A. Campbell, W. C. Harvey, James Bennet, J. R. Claxton, J. Higgins, Stephen Moyle. * * * The members of this lodge range from fifty-four to eighty. It is in a flourishing condition.

Members of Rebekah Degree—Mesdames C. E. Bishop, Lavinia Stowers, G. Shealor, J. Collins, R. Blake, G. King, J. Saunders, G. Allen, W. P. Jones, J. W. Allen, Alfred Howell, Jacob Turner, James Hammond, E. M. Corliss, C. D. Burleson, Daniel Donnelly, Richard Jones, A. E. Greenwell, Jane F. Ellis, Julia Tressider, M. E. Warkins, E. S. Bennett, Jane Smith, Jane Higgins, F. E. Dennis, Ellen Tucker, S. P. Taylor, F. S. Belding, Elizabeth Jacka, — Breedlove, — Bruce, — Keerfoot, — Gilmore, — Danell, — Payton, M. Brinn, — Fagan, — Scott, — Seaman, Stephen Moyle, John Laswell, Geo. Wrigglesworth, W. C. Harvey, Wm. H. Turner, J. R. Treglonn, Jane Trippit, D. T. Davis, Thomas Davis, J. R. Davis, F. Labin, Alfred Howell.

JACKSON LODGE, NO. 36,

Organized in 1860. First officers : H. Hoeber, N. G.; J. P. Alsover, V. G.; S. Page, R. S; A. Yoak, Treasurer. The value of property was estimated at three thousand one hundred and eighty dollars. The first officers since its organization were: E. G. Freeman, D. Cuppet, S. B. Bartlett, E. Agard, J. T. Shelborne, E. S. Hall, L. Brandt, E. B. Styles, D. B. Spagnoli, H. W. Allen, L. J. Dodge, J. A. Peters, J. Smith, J. Hollingsworth, J. C. McNamara. * * *

Members of Rebekah Degree—Mesdames B. B. Redhead, W. A. Rogers, E. G. Freeman, N. M. Bowman, T. D. Wells, Thomas Shelborne, Sarah S. Robinson, Nancy E. Miller, Elizabeth Keshler, Laura Brummel, Catherine A. Hall, E. Hesse, J. D. Mason, S. H. Bartlett, N. C. Briggs, Mary J. Perry, L. J. Littlefield, Susan Meek, Isabella R. Spagnoli, M. Lory, E. Warren, F. Brandt, L. J. Donyo, James Avis, Fred. Balls, H. L. Joy, O. Walther, T. A. Springer, I. Ideans, A. Gabrino.

IONE LODGE, NO. 51.

First officers: J. Bowen, N. G.; J. Bagley, V.G.; G. Haverstick, R. S.; D. Stewart, Treasurer. First officers since : Geo. Haverstick, T. P. Stewart, M. Zimmer, A. Preater, I. B. Fish, O. N. Morse, C. Burgen, G. W. Owens, C. B. Strong, H. Craner, R. Ludgate, J. W. Surface, A. B. McDonald, W. K. Johnston, Henry C. King, W. H. Prouty, James McCauley. * * * Value of property in 1860, fifteen hundred dollars. For many years this lodge was weak in numbers, though strong in purpose, the numbers varying from nineteen in 1861 to thirty as late as 1870. After that it took a start, and now numbers nearly a hundred, with an interest in a good hall, and is in a good working condition. Assets in 1872, twelve hundred dollars.

Members of the Rebekah Degree—Mesdames Margaret Bagley, Margaret Morse, Mary A. Dutschke, Elizabeth Baker, J. McCauley, Moses Myer, D. Stewart, R. Ludgate, John Hartman, Virginia Burgen, May Ann Brown, T. Richards, D. Fisher, L. H. Lang.

TELEGRAPH LODGE, NO. 79

Was instituted at Oleta (Fiddletown) in 1859. Charter members : James Burt, J. C. Chestnut, John Cumberland, John Cox, George Harridon, J. H. Howlett, J. F. Ostrom, Wilmer Palmer, F. P. Smith, C. O. Sloat, Leroy Worden, H. H. White. Third degree—W. R. Dean, J. W. Kendall, J. Keifer, B. F. Marble, Samuel Parker, E. A. Sloat, E. Wigal. Second degree, David Frazine. In a short time it had thirty-three members. Leroy Worden was the first representative to the Grand Lodge. N. G.'s since the organization : J. F. Ostrom, S. Parker, H. D. Ford, W. T. Ligget, J. E. Bates, F. A. Charleville, G. Coblentz, W. F. Knapp, C. Perry, A. F. Driver, E. A. Sloat, R. Brown, * * *

Members of the Degree of Rebekah—Mrs. E. S. Potter. * * *

LANCHA PLANA LODGE, NO. 95,

Organized in 1860. First officers : H. A. Messinger, N. G.; S. Kidd, V. G.; Wm. Cook, R. S.; J. P. McHenry, Treasurer. The assets were valued at eight hundred and eighty-one dollars and eighty-seven cents. The position of N. G. was afterwards filled by J. P. McHenry, H. Percival, * * * In 1864 the lodge ceased to report, the members uniting with other lodges.

PLYMOUTH LODGE, NO. 260,

Was instituted at Plymouth, June 15, 1879, by John Blower, D. D. G. M., assisted by I. N. Randolph, P. G. M., assisted by other P. G. Masters. Charter members: C. A. Cordell, W. Wright, J. A. Gessler, D. W. Walker, T. P. Bawden, S. G. Lewis, Charles Green, E. S. Potter, S. Ring, R. Summers, and John

Daviggio; D. W. Walker being the first N. G., and T. P. Bawden the next. This lodge, unlike some of the others, became numerous immediately. They have a fine hall, and have never felt the pinch of poverty. The prosperity of the Order has been largely due to the active exertions of Chas. Green, who was for many years the foreman of the Empire and Phœnix mines.

THE GRAND ENCAMPMENT, NO. 17,

Is composed of members of the scarlet or fifth degrees, these being, in their order, white, pink, blue, green, and scarlet. Two encampments have been formed in the county; the Amador, No. 17, at Sutter Creek, and the Marble, No. 19, at Volcano, the latter afterwards being removed to Ione, retaining the same name. The first was organized in 1859, with J. A. Brown as Chief Patriarch; J. T. Skinner, High Priest; J. M. Smith, Senior Warden, Charles Doveton, Scribe; D. Gardner, Treasurer; James Foster, Junior Warden. The officers are elected semi-annually; S. L. Sutton, Isaac Tripp, Wilmer Palmer, Morris Brinn, L. T. McLinn, J. H. Hammond, and G. A. Newton, having been Chief Patriarchs at different times since.

THE MARBLE ENCAMPMENT, NO. 19,

Was organized June 19, 1860, with E. A. Kingsley as C. P.; B. Ross, H. P.; G. Williams, S. W.; R. F. Logan, J. W.; Joseph Samuels, Treasurer. The following persons have since filled the position of Chief Patriarch: I. Butland, R. M. Bradshaw, George Collins, H. T. Barnum. This list is not complete, the official returns not being at hand, the object in this history being to give an idea of the workings of the order rather than a detailed history. As in the Masonic order the literature which one must read and become familiar with to be well up in the order, is immense.

The society is yet plastic in all its workings, readily adapting itself to the changing habits of mankind. The main object is relief to its members, but a great many other things are accomplished. The societies have numerous, well-stocked libraries, where the best of books are kept free of charge, for its members, though friends of the members are not rigidly excluded, but frequently admitted as a matter of courtesy. Much good is being accomplished in this way. The introduction of the Degree of Rebekah admitting females, was probably in response to the general demand for admitting women to greater privileges, which, in time, may be still farther extended. The friends of the order have ample cause to be satisfied, and are not wanting substantial reasons for claiming Odd Fellowship as the best fruit of modern civilization.

TEMPERANCE SOCIETIES.

These were organized in an early day. As early as 1853 a body organized after the manner of the Washingtonians held weekly meetings in the old Methodist church at Volcano. There was ample cause for work in this direction, for the habit of drinking was fearfully prevalent. All who ever drank, and many who never did before, were swept into the almost universal habit. The churches generally discouraged drinking, but the small voice was not heard amid the clinking of glasses and chinking of gold. Twelve or fifteen persons met and talked over the prevalence of the habit, and comforted each other in their loneliness. Occasionally they would capture for a few months some notorious drinker, sober him off and get a clean shirt on him, but the great mass kept on their course, and every barrel of flour brought into town was sandwiched with whisky, that kept company from the rising to the going down of the sun, until the mines were exhausted. In September and October of that year, the society grew until the roll numbered a hundred or more names. Many hard drinkers were sobered up for a time. The first division of the Sons of Temperance in the county was organized about the first of November of that year. — Davidson, of Amador, W. P.; — Daviss, P. W. P.; L. S. Scott, C.; R. Stewart, R. S.; Ned Lonegan, F. S.; D. Boydston, I. S.; Jacob Level, O. S. J. K. Stoughton and Sempronius Boyd were among the charter members. When this society was organized the old society was dissolved, most of the members joining the new order. In 1855 a new hall was built, which has been devoted to temperance work since, though occupied by different societies.

The Sons of Temperance have had organizations in nearly all the towns of the county at different times, flourishing notably in Ione in 1875-76, and in Sutter Creek, Amador and Drytown about the same time. These societies are maintained by small monthly dues. They have high-sounding titles, like Worthy Patriarch, Past and Grands of the same, with significant regalia to correspond. Persons of both sexes of fourteen years and upward are admitted. Though temperance is the professed object, the love of power inherent in human nature soon manifests itself, and a lodge or division soon becomes divided into factions, each striving for the mastery. Sometimes the younger members will combine against the elder, and make fun and merriment the main object. The societies have a preventive rather than a reformatory tendency, but undoubtedly exert a healthy influence in holding the evils of intemperance constantly in view, and in teaching habits of obedience and the responsibilities of authority.

THE GOOD TEMPLARS

Are of similar character, with perhaps a better system of organization, as the society holds together and accumulates property, having an asylum for orphans at Vallejo which would be a credit to any order. This society had a large prosperity in 1858-59-60 at Ione. C. B. Strong, J. B. Gregory, Mrs. George Withington, Wm. H. Scudder and wife being among the principal promoters of the organization.

RESIDENCE AND RANCH 320 ACRES OF JONATHAN SALLEE,
NEAR PLYMOUTH, AMADOR CO. CAL.

CENTRAL HOUSE RANCH.
RESIDENCE AND PROPERTY OF MRSS M.H. WELLS & J.H. CRAMBART,

THE KNIGHTS OF THE RED CROSS,

A beneficiary society, is flourishing of late years. This has engrafted some of the customs of the Masonic and Odd Fellows' organizations on the former temperance unions, and are consequently more self-sustaining. The order is flourishing in Ione at the present writing.

THE BLUE RIBBON SOCIETY

Is an order which requires its members to wear the badge of abstinence in the daily intercourse with mankind. The lodge at Volcano was organized by Doctor Haskell, an itinerant temperance reformer. It numbers about one hundred members. It has a President, Vice-President, Secretary and Treasurer. R. Stewart was the first President; James Jenkins, Vice-President. The present officers are: George Madeira, President; Miss Anna Whitehead, Vice-President; Miss Minnie McIntyre, Treasurer, and Miss Ellen Cottingham, Secretary. The *Blue Ribbon Bugle* is a manuscript paper read once or twice a month to the society and others interested.

THE GENERAL TENDENCY OF TEMPERANCE SOCIETIES

Is undoubtedly good, though a habit of indulgence which has prevailed for centuries cannot be eradicated in a generation. Inherited appetite, customs of society, and pecuniary interests are all conducive to the perpetuation of the vice of drinking. Sumptuary laws have ever been unpopular, and consequently laws regulating the manufacture, sale and consumption of alcoholic beverages have had much prejudice to contend with, much negative opposition; but when public opinion generally sanctions them they will be as effective as other laws.

SUBJECTS FOR INSANE ASYLUMS.

Whisky, and the excitement of mining, with its gains and losses, hopes and disappointments, sent a fearful number to the Insane Asylum, the average from Amador county, according to the reports, being one a month. As to whisky as a cause of insanity, the opinion of E. T. Wilkins, Commissioner in Lunacy for the State of California, as found in his report to Gov. H. H. Haight, December 2, 1871, may be to the point:

With regard to intemperance * * * It seems to be the bane of all countries, and claims its victims in every civilized nation and under every form of government. It is the common enemy of mankind, the destroyer of domestic happiness, the copartner of every crime from petit larceny to murder. It is the father of poverty, the creator of debauchery, and the principal working tool of the devil. No man is bold enough to defend it, and yet it is tolerated by all classes of society. It finds its way alike to the house of the rich and the home of the poor. It is the boon companion at the festive board of the aristocrat and the poorly provided table of the cottager. It has caused more heart-aches, produced more tears, engendered more sorrows, starved more *babies*, and led to more insanity than any other agent in existence—if not more than *all* other causes combined. We are strongly inclined to

the opinion that directly or remotely it is more potent in producing these results than *all* other causes. It is the sin of civilization that it has found out ways of extracting alcohol from natural substances, so that it is offered in tempting forms and accessible abundance to the weak and incautious who would not instinctively seek it, as well as those whose appetites demand it. If, then, civilization is responsible for the introduction of this destructive element among mankind, it is certainly its duty, and it should be compelled, to provide for its victims. How to arrest its progress, if, indeed, it be possible, we must leave to the wiser heads of the Legislature and the statesman; and he who can solve the problem will be the wisest of men, and a greater benefactor to his fellow-men than has ever yet appeared among them.

BURLESQUE SOCIETIES.

The essential object of these is *fun;* it matters little at whose expense. Ridicule is a chief element in all the ceremonies and exercises. All that admits of it is burlesqued. The members claim for the societies that in addition to affording amusement, which is a sanitary necessity, they take down the pretentious and pompous, prick the bubbles of egotism, and benefit society in many ways. If only the conceited, pompous and pretentious were made subjects of the initiation, there would be some claim for the respect of the community; but it often happens that the unsuspecting and honest are their victims.

THE ECLAMPSUS VITUS

Flourished in 1861-62, especially in Ione. The initiation was generally newly arranged for each subject. One ceremony was to make the initiate crawl through a portion of an old smoke stack and accelerate his movements by dashing buckets of cold water after him; another, to run him blindfolded over chains and other obstructions until his shins were well barked; another, to make him jump from a terrible height (?) into a tub of cold water, after which he was dressed up in some absurd way, brought before a mirror and the blind removed, that he might "see himself as the world saw him." Not all were admitted in this way; some were received for the purpose of assisting in the work.

Many sober, honest, middle-aged men were induced to join to become the possessors of the great secret.

THE HAUTONTIMOROUMENOS

Flourished in Amador, but had branches in Sutter, Jackson and other places. From the cuts with which their official papers were ornamented, the impression would be formed that the society was rather of the convivial order.

THE KNIGHTS OF THE ASSYRIAN CROSS,

Organized in 1873, have maintained a longer existence than any others of this class in the county. In Sutter Creek, where the first lodge was organized, they number one hundred members; fifty in Jackson, and about the same in Ione. The high, swelling names of the other societies are burlequesed in great style, the English dictionary being ransacked to find suitable superlatives. Grand Mogul, Great Grand Light of Ages, Grand Executioner, Bearer of the Great Seal, and everything else of a grandiose character are freely appropriated and bestowed. An antiquity of a half million of years is also claimed, antedating Masonic or all other societies. They claim to be benevolent, literary, scientific, philosophic and religious. They occasionally parade in costume, or rather in masks, representing all kinds of animals. They hold public meetings, at which characteristic poems, orations and other exercises are indulged in. Those who wish for further information may undoubtedly obtain it by applying to the proper persons.

PIONEER SOCIETIES.

Soon after the settlement, when it became apparent that California was destined to become a great and important State, associations began to be formed, some to preserve the records of the early events, some for mutual assistance, and some as claiming a kind of distinction for having been among the first to arrive in the country. Hence the Pioneer society, which required a residence as early as 1849 for membership, and the Territorial Pioneers that required a residence prior to September 9, 1850.

THE AMADOR SOCIETY OF CALIFORNIA PIONEERS

Was organized September 9, 1877, at Jackson, California. Its objects are to cultivate the social virtues of its members, alleviate their sufferings and sickness, secure them a decent burial, and, as far as possible, render assistance when needed to their widows and orphans, and also assist in perpetuating the memory of those whose love of enterprise and independence induced them to seek a home in the far West and become the germ of a new and great State. Members are required to have had a residence previous to December 1, 1852, to be citizens or desirous of becoming such. Male descendants of the above, twenty-one years of age, may become members. Admission fees must not be less than five dollars. Regular monthly dues are established by the society. Members, in case of sickness or bodily injury by which they are prevented from following their usual occupations, are entitled to such weekly benefits as may be fixed by law. Sixty dollars burial expenses are allowed. The regular meetings are on the first and third Mondays of each month.

Charter members—X. Benoist, Chas. Boarman, R. Caminetti, J. D. Davis, Peter David, George Durham, Ellis Evans, Thomas Greenhalgh, H. Goldner, M. W. Gordon, E. Gardner, J. Gross, J. F. Gould, Philip Gilbert, J. F. Harleman, J. C. Ham, Wm. Jennings, Thomas Jones, E. A. Kent, Thomas Love, John Martin, James Meehan, John Marlett, John B. Phelps, Wm. Pitt, R. W. Palmer, Chas. Peters, John B. Reeves, Chas. B. Swift, Joseph Smith, Louis Tellier, John Vogan.

REGULAR MEMBERS.

Allen, J. C.
Boarman, Chas.*
Billiard, J. B.*
Benoist, X.
Boxall, Wm.
Boyrie, Jacques
Burnhardt, P. K.
Boyer, Julian
Bales J. J.
Cook, Wm.
Durham, George
David, Peter
Davis, J. D.
Dwyer, P.
Desbro, Wm.
Evans, Ellis
Eagon, J. A.
Gilbert, Philip
Gould, J. F.
Gardner, E.
Greenhalgh, Thos.
Gross, Joseph
Goldner, Herman
Graham, Frank
Harleman, J. F.
Ham, J. C.
Howard, Frank
Hanley, Tim.
Hinkson, J. M.
Hinkson, R. S.
Hinkson, N. C.
Jennings, Wm.
Jones, Thos.
Jones, W. C.
Kent, E. A.
Koch, Albert

Kelly, Michael
Keshler, A.
Love, Thomas*
Latique, Vital
Laroussini, Jean
Marlett, John
Meehan, James
McKoy, R. K.
McKinney, A.
Peck, Henry*
Phelps, J. B.
Peters, Charles
Pitt, Wm.
Palmer, R. W.
Plasse, Raymond
Reeves, John B.
Swift, C. B.
Stevitch, J.
Straggozi, Paul
Schwartz, F.
Schwartz, E.
Steckler, Chas.*
Stewart, Robert
Silva, Thos.
Staats, F. K.
Sejers, Jas.
Styles, S. W.
Stewart, Danl.
Sullivan, Jeremiah
Stowers, W. A.
Tellier, Louis
Truel, H.
Tarwater, G. F.
Vogan, John
White, George
Weller, C.

LIST OF OFFICERS.

	1878-79.	1880-81.
President	James Meehan	James Meehan
Vice President	Thomas Jones	J. A. Eagon
Secretary	J. D. Davis	J. F. Gould
Treasurer	E. Evans	E. Evans
Trustees	Louis Tellier, J. F. Gould, P. Dwyer	E. A. Kent, P. Dwyer, John Vogan
Finance Com.	E. A. Kent, T. Greenhalgh, Charles Peters	Thos. Jones, H. Goldner, Thomas Love
Marshal	R. W. Palmer	R. W. Palmer

The society is making historical collections, and have some curious relics of early years, among which are copies of the *Owl* and *Quincy Prospector*, the first newspapers published in the county. The society is in a flourishing condition.

THE SCLAVONIC ILLYRIC MUTUAL BENEVOLENT SOCIETY

Is a branch of the San Francisco society of the same name. Monthly dues, one dollar; the members receiving in case of sickness, eight dollars per week. In case of death the funeral expenses are paid by the society. They own a hall, costing about three thousand five hundred dollars. The society was organized at Sutter Creek, 1874.

GRANGERS.

Some years since several of these societies were organized in the county. The first was in the vicin-

*Deceased.

ity of the Jackson valley school-house. The objects seemed to have been to protect themselves against the extortions of middle men, by combining to dispose of their produce directly to the consumers. The attempt was not quite successful, owing to the inexperience or incapacity of their agents. It was attempted to engraft them on the political parties, but the Grangers declined any alliance. It is likely, however, that both parties, seeking their votes, conceded legislation that would not have been given to unorganized sentiment. The influence of the grange is much less now than a few years since. There are still two or three societies in the county. It is probable that social enjoyment rather than financial benefits, is the motive power. The officers are divided between males and females, the latter being elected to offices such as Ceres, Pomona and Flora. A society of this kind meets once a month at Sutter Creek, occasionally holding a feast or day of general recreation. No statistics are at hand.

CHAPTER XLIII.
SKETCHES OF AMADOR COUNTY BAR.
BY J. G. SEVERANCE, SAN FRANCISCO.

At a very early period in the history of California, subsequent to its acquisition by the United States, the Bar of "Old Calaveras" was justly assigned a position in the front rank of the legal profession. It was, with few exceptions, composed of men of push and genius; of acknowledged worth, integrity, ability, and wit; men possessed of learning and culture, acquired in the best of Eastern schools, and of large experience, gained by near association and contact with the ablest lawyers, jurists, and scholars of the commercial and manufacturing cities, and populous agricultural and mineral districts of the Atlantic States. That air of rusticity, and the limited professional experience which usually characterize members of the profession in the interior of older settled sections, were wanting among these cosmopolitan argonauts. They were alike experienced in, and qualified to skillfully deal with, intricate questions of maritime, commercial, and international law, as settled and adjudicated by authority, and to cope with and adjust successfully such novel legal problems as the new industries, customs, and requirements of the newly acquired territory developed; they came prepared for city or country life, for metropolitan, bucolic or pioneer practice. They abandoned the homes of education and refinement in the East, for the rude life of the Western El Dorado, in search of the Golden Fleece, and, if funds ran low because of the too angelic visits of clients, instead of listlessly awaiting the coming of a brief in their offices, they sought and found lucrative employment on ranches, in work-shops, kitchens, mining claims, and other vocations, until a popular recognition of their talents gave abundant labor in their profession. Many a retainer of corpulent proportions has been dropped into hands made hard and horny by familiarity with rough labor, or softened by culinary employment, and the grease of the dish-pan; and the intricate details of many cases of great financial importance have been imparted to counsel while engaged with pick and shovel at the sluices and the long-tom.

Ably and well has the Bar of "Old Calaveras" been represented in both the Senate and House of Representatives of the national Congress, and in both Houses of the State Legislature, by not a few of its members; many, to its honor and credit, have worn the judicial ermine. It has furnished governors, and numerous faithful and competent officials for political positions, Federal, State, and municipal, and none have been found unworthy of the trust reposed in them. When, by the Act of the State Legislature of 1854, the little county of Amador was created out of a portion of Calaveras county, the former retained a fair and just proportion of the legal talent which had been embraced within the latter. A jealous, but friendly, rivalry was engendered between the denizens of the two sections lying on either side of the deep gorge through which flowed the Mokelumne river, and which seemed to have been designed by Nature for a political boundary line; and frequent contentions arose, in which the opposing clans acknowledged the leadership of the lawyers of their respective divisions. So equally matched were these generals in diplomacy and skill, that a segregation was acquiesced in, as the only method of adjustment, and Amador county was created, that each faction might have full scope for the exercise of its genius. A close intimacy and the kindliest feeling subsequently existed between the two Bars, which have at all times been so closely allied that great difficulty is experienced in recording the history of the one, without including that of the other.

The more important of the early litigation in Amador county was concerning matters affecting the respective and relative rights of the miner, the riparian claimant and the agriculturist, up to about the year 1866, when the Supreme Court decided that the interest of a miner in his claim was realty, hence questions affecting such interest were not within the jurisdiction of inferior courts. All cases involving the possession of mining claims, their boundaries and privileges were tried in Justices' Courts, irrespective of their values, subject to an appeal to the County Court. Consequently large fees were frequently paid to attorneys for conducting trials in these courts where the interests involved often amounted to thousands of dollars. The waters of the rivers and creeks were appropriated and conveyed in ditches and flumes to the mines by the construction of dams and tapping them at different points, and it frequently became a delicate matter to properly and equitably adjust the rights of adverse claimants. It often occurred that beneath the most productive soil, forming the surface of a flat or bar, the bed-rock was richest in its deposits of gold. Hence many questions arose without well-established precedents, and legislative as well as judicial skill was frequently invoked to settle them in such manner as the better to subserve the public welfare and the individual interests of each. Senator Norman, of Calaveras county, introduced a bill, which was known as the Norman Bill, in the Legislature, which became a law in the year 1857, and which, in a great measure, served to reconcile disputes concerning the relative rights of the miner and agriculturist, and the final adjudication of many other litigious propositions arising in the courts of Amador, of a novel character, have largely contributed to the settlement of vexed questions, and rendered certain what was before uncertain.

Following are the names of those who, as judges and lawyers, have taken an active part in the judicial affairs of the county since its organization: Marion W. Gordan, W. W. Cope, Robert M. Briggs, James F. Hubbard, S. J. K. Handy, James T. Farley, James W. Porter, A. C. Brown, Samuel B. Axtell, Thomas D. Grant, T. M. Pawling, H. A. Carter, John C. Gear, Charles Boynton, Judge Reynolds, J. G. Severance, George W. Seaton, John W. Armstrong, James H. Hardy, Alvinza Hayward, John Palmer, W. P. Buchanan, Alonzo Platt, W. T. Curtis, Claiborn Roarer, Henry L. Waldo, Nash C. Briggs, John A. Eagon, Wm. P. George, Fayette Mace, T. J. Phelps, A. Caminetti, Silas Penry, George Moore, P. C. Johnson, L. N. Ketchum, J. Foot Turner, J. A. Robinson, Henry Cook, Moses Tebbs, George L. Gale.

Amador county was first included within the fifth judicial district, of which Hon. Charles M. Creanor, now of Stockton, was the Judge. This district was comprised of the populous and important mining and agricultural counties of Amador, Calaveras, Tuolumne, Stanislaus and San Joaquin, and, to dispose of the enormous amount of litigation arising therein, required great energy, endurance, and dispatch. Court week at Jackson was an eventful season. Motions and demurrers for delay received but little consideration, and not to be ready when your case was called was to have it very summarily disposed of. Jurors, witnesses, and litigants, from all parts of the county, were largely in attendance, and one case followed another from nine in the morning until far into the night, when, not infrequently, rest and recreation were only found at the poker table until morning. Hon. Tod Robinson, of Sacramento, was so constant an attendant on the courts of Amador, that a history of its Bar would be incomplete without mention of his name; and time and again have the Court House walls at Jackson rung with the eloquent voices of Honorables E. D. Baker, N. Greene Curtis, Frank Hereford, and others whose oratory has won for them a national fame, and still oftener have they resounded with the blows of the Sheriff's knuckles upon his unoffending desk, in his efforts to bring order out of the chaos provoked by some sally of wit on the part of Col. A. P. Dudley, of Calaveras.

Judge Creanor possessed the exceptional power and ability requisite to discharge the onerous duties that devolved upon him as the judicial head of so large a district as his, and infused into those who practiced in his courts something of his executive zeal. So quick of comprehension was he that but few explanatory words were necessary to convey to his clear, grasping and judicial mind all the salient points in the facts of the most complicated and cumbersome cause; so impartial and just in his decisions and conclusions that no charge of personal favoritism, bribery, fraud or dishonesty was ever hinted at; so prompt in the dispatch of business pertaining to the courts that no attendant thereon complained of unnecessary detention; so firm and rigid in court *regime*, that it is said of him he imposed a fine upon himself for being ten minutes late at court one morning; so courteous to the elder and considerate to the younger members of the profession, that he possessed the highest esteem and fullest confidence of all; it was but a natural sequence that his example had much to do in moulding the character and habits of those who practiced before him. No judge ever retired from the bench with a fairer record than Hon. Charles M. Creanor; and if any errors of judgment are entered there, they are so obscured by the brilliancy of his sterling qualities that we pass them unnoticed.

As before stated, Amador was first in the fifth judicial district, with Hon. C. M. Creanor as Judge. In 1859, the district was divided, and Amador and Calaveras made to constitute the sixteenth judicial district, Hon. James H. Hardy being appointed the first Judge thereof. Hon. Wm. H. Badgley, of Calaveras county, succeeded Judge Hardy. Judge Badgley was a highly cultivated and polished gentleman from the State of New York, and is now engaged in practice in that city. Judge Silas W. Brockway, a native of New York, an earnest laborer in his profession, an able lawyer, and possessed of great force of character, succeeded Judge Badgley in 1864, Amador being then in the eleventh district, composed of Amador, El Dorado, and Calaveras. Hon. A. C. Adams, now of San Francisco, succeeded Judge Brockway, and Hon. George H. Williams, of El Dorado, succeeded Judge Adams.

That this sketch may not justly be compared to the great play of *Hamlet* with Hamlet omitted, the brief biographies of such prominent members of the Amador Bar as could be obtained, are appended.

J. W. ARMSTRONG was a blacksmith in early days in California, but took a notion that he could make a lawyer of himself, and commenced the study some twenty-two years since. He has been, and is, one of the most indefatigable students the world ever saw, exhibiting a most wonderful capacity for hard work. He commenced the practice in Amador county, some twenty years since, but, after some years, removed to Sacramento, where he has succeeded in building up a lucrative practice and a reputation for being one of the best informed men of the State. His acquirements are substantial and useful. Having little taste for the poetical adornments which ornamented the orations of Baker and other famous speakers, he deals in hard, incontrovertible facts, piling them up mountain high, leaving no possible escape for his adversary. He is still in the prime of life, and has promise of many years of usefulness.

HONORABLE SAMUEL B. AXTELL was one of those cold, reticent men whose *suaviter in modo* won the respect rather than the friendship of men. Indeed, he did not care for the friendship of many, and those such as could be of use to him. He was possessed of a high sense of honor, polished in manner, and uncompromising in his zeal when in pursuit of some purpose, and he always had a purpose in view. As an advocate, and especially in jury trials, he had few equals in method, terseness of expression, and clearness of style. Educated at Oberlin College, in his native State, Ohio, his earliest forensic efforts, were in behalf of abolitionism; he afterwards went South, and there became imbued with Southern ideas and proclivities; settled in Jackson as early as 1853, and was elected the first District Attorney in 1854, and was re-elected in 1856, making a most excellent officer, firm and unflinching in the performance of his duties, but never over zealous to the extent of persecution. He subsequently removed to San Francisco, and was there elected to Congress, where he was converted to Republicanism, having theretofore been a Democrat. He has never since returned to California, but was appointed Governor of Utah, and subsequently Governor of New Mexico, where his policy of Mormon conciliation became so obnoxious to the Government that he was recalled. His merits, however, seemed not to have been ignored, for recently the position of Receiver of Public Moneys in Idaho was tendered him, but whether he accepted has not transpired.

ROBERT M. BRIGGS. There has been no more active lawyer or politician in Amador than R. M. Briggs. His *petite* form seemed made up of a bundle of nerves, as unconscious of fatigue as the wires of an electric battery, which seemed to flash to his brain and concentrate there all the vast vitality which nature had so bound together, whenever occasion demanded. He was always ready for a speech, at the Bar or on the stump, and never failed to hold together and enthuse his audience. Unexpected bursts of eloquence were sandwiched between pertinent anecdotes in such profusion that his speeches were always received with unbounded applause. As an illustration of his oratorical power, the closing of a speech he made before the Fiddletown Scott and Graham Club, in 1852, is given. After expatiating upon the character of Scott, his services in the wars of 1812, and with Mexico, he electrified his hearers with these words:—

"When the end of all things shall have come; when the last great trump shall have sounded; when the angel of death shall be standing with one foot on the sea and the other on the land, swearing that time shall be no more; when the solid mountains of granite are rocking to their very foundations; the stars falling from their places in the heavens, and revolving worlds are wheeling into annihilation, then shall the names of Scott and Graham appear written all over the sky in letters of living *fire* !"

In 1861 a monster mass Union meeting was held in San Francisco, at which, it was announced, prominent speakers from every county in the State would be present. Briggs, who happened to be in the city at the time, was on the programme, from Amador. The meeting, which was a great success, was addressed by Colonel Baker and other noted orators, and immense enthusiasm was manifested by the enormous concourse of people present. The press of San Francisco concurred in the statement that by far the best and most soul-stirring speech of the evening was that of R. M. Briggs, of Amador. As no extended reports of the speeches were given, the friends of Briggs interviewed him to ascertain what he said that so eclipsed the orators of the Pacific. He declared that he could not recollect a word. He said that upon being informed by the committee that he would be called upon, he endeavored to arrange his ideas into some form suitable to the occasion, and, toward evening sought to ascertain at about what time in the evening he would be called upon, that he might be enabled to cut his fuse the right length; that the committee seemed to have entirely forgotten him, and he concluded he had been left out in the cold, which made him so d——d mad that he went to a neighboring saloon and imbibed brandy and water, one glassful upon another, to drown his disappointment, until he became—well—pretty well elevated.

Late in the evening some one came in and said, "Briggs, they are calling for you." He started up toward the place of meeting on the plaza, where the speakers' stand was a narrow balcony. He was conscious that in his condition he would not be able to stand there a moment, but would fall headlong into the crowd below. He, therefore, took a dry-goods box which was near at hand, and placing it on the sidewalk mounted it, remarking that he was one of the people, and did not desire to get above them—preferred to be with them and of them—and then commenced his speech. His remembrance of the occasion was confined to the vociferous applause and enthusiasm, the like of which, he says, he never heard. Sober persons present declared that the crowd had listened to Baker and others until they were fully charged, and only required to be touched off to cause it to burst forth into a terrific explosion; Briggs' union pyrotechnics, in which appeared the "glorious old flag," the "American eagle," "liberty and equality," "union now and forever," like the colors of a revolving kaleidoscope, was the torch. Briggs obtained the sobriquet of "Brother Crawford" by his forensic illustrations of his adieus, as well as those of others made to the Democratic party, by repeating a sermon of a divine named Crawford, in which was related the circumstances of his departure from the field of his former labors, and in which the preacher narrated how he visited each object with which long association had made him familiar and to which he had become endeared, and each in turn seemed to say to him, "Farewell, Brother Crawford!" that as he rode down the lane upon his horse, the trees and grain in the adjacent fields seemed to solemnly nod to him and say, "Farewell, Brother Crawford;" that the very stones of the wall that marked the lane seemed possessed of melancholy voices, which cried out, "Farewell, Brother Crawford!" that his horse took fright at a hog that rushed across the lane before him, reared and plunged, and throwing his rider in the ditch, speeded down the road with heels flying in the air, seeming to snort aloud, "Farewell, Brother Crawford!"

Briggs was by no means deficient in talent as a writer, and as the editor of the local papers, attained a well-earned reputation. He once wrote for his paper a lengthy article on Mexican affairs during the French invasion, which was re-published in pamphlet form, and widely distributed in the Eastern States, and, not improbably, had an influence upon the Administration in taking its decisive position against foreign occupation. He was a native of Illinois, developed his muscle in the lead mines, was a dry-goods clerk in Galena, afterwards moved to Grant county, Wisconsin, where he studied law, and was elected to the Legislature in 1851, and came to California in 1852. He was elected Assemblyman, and twice District Attorney, in Amador; was appointed Register of the General Land Office at Independence, and is now Superior Judge of Mono county, residing at Bodie.

Hon. A. C. Brown, born at St. Charles, Missouri, January 10, 1816, crossed the plains from Lancaster, Grant county, Wisconsin, when he was admitted to practice in March, 1849, and settled in Jackson in September, 1851, where he has ever since resided, and where he is now engaged in the practice of his profession, having been admitted to the District Court in 1851, and to the Supreme Court in 1879. For three several terms he served in the Territorial and State Legislature of Wisconsin, and three times represented Amador county in the Assembly; was County Judge from 1877 up to the time the new State Constitution went into effect in 1880. He has ever been an active politician, not a radical, but professed Democrat, and a staunch supporter of the Union cause during the Rebellion. The father of a large family, and possessed of considerable wealth, chiefly invested in improved town property, he has ever been regarded as one of the substantial citizens of Amador county. More than once the fire-fiend has swept away his possessions, but his energy planned more imposing structures before the ashes were cold.

Nash Corwith Briggs was one of the few young men raised in California who preferred study to such pastimes as the freedom of our early society tolerated. He was born in Hannibal, Missouri, February 1, 1838, removed to Grant county, Wisconsin, in 1849, and, in 1852, came to California with his father, Hon. R. M. Briggs, and resided in Jackson from 1854 to 1864, where he studied law, and, being admitted by the District Court, formed a law copartnership with his father, in 1860. In 1864 he removed to Alpine county, and upon its organization was elected District Attorney in that year, was re-elected in 1866, and again in 1868. In December of the latter year he removed to Hollister, and upon the organization of San Benito county, in 1874, was elected District Attorney, and re-elected in 1876. He married Miss Annie Barton, who was a native of Jackson, and has an interesting family at Hollister, where he is now associated in the practice of the law with N. A. Hawkins; was admitted to the Supreme Court in October, 1869.

Hon. R. Burnell, though a lawyer by education, was better known as a politician. He was a native of New York, was a stock-raiser in early days, having accumulated something like fifty thousand dollars in raising cattle on the Sacramento plains. His career as a politician is related in the body of this history, and need not be repeated here. After the termination of his political career he removed to Napa, where he formed a law partnership with his brother-in-law, Chancellor Harison, with whom he remained until his death, a year or two since.

A. Caminetti is a young man of Italian birth and California raising. He commenced the study of law under the tuition of Farley & Pawling, was admitted to practice in 1877, and two years later was elected Prosecuting Attorney, a position he has filled with marked ability. He is brilliant, thorough, and persevering, an easy and graceful speaker, with a good degree of that elasticity of temperament which enables him to adapt himself to circumstances. He has a promising future before him. He is Democratic in politics, and had his name on the ticket for electors at the last Presidential contest. He did good service for his party in the campaign of 1880.

Hon. H. A. Carter is a native of New York, where he studied and practiced law previous to coming to California, which was in 1849. He was the first District Attorney of Calaveras county, and has witnessed all the squabbles for the county seat since the time that Double Springs, with but one house, was the place of justice, and the jury-room the shade of a tree. His habit of advising litigants to settle without a lawsuit has militated against his success as a lawyer, but has made him a most valuable citizen and neighbor. He has generally rested content with being the Pericles of his county, the man in whom all had unbounded confidence. He is a man of extensive and general information, communicative in his character, with a keen sense of the ludicrous, and tells a splendid story. He has spent the larger portion of life in the cultivation of the soil, preferring the comforts of home and the companionship of his neighbors to the turmoils of politics or the law. He was seduced into running for the Assembly in 1875, traveled over the county, smoked and joked with his friends, told some of his best stories, and was triumphantly elected, fairly walking over the course. It will be perceived that his strength as a lawyer is in advising every one to keep out of lawsuits. According to lawyers themselves, Judge Carter, if he had turned the force of his character that way, would have excelled in the high courts as a judge in equity.

JUDGE COOK was a resident of Volcano for several years previous to the organization of Alpine county, and made quite a reputation as a safe and cautious counselor. He was well informed on general topics, dignified and courteous in his bearing, a gentleman of the old school. After the organization of Alpine he removed to that county, where he was quite prominent for several years. He has, in consequence of advancing age, mostly retired from the practice of the law.

HON. W. W. COPE. Amador has had but one representative upon the bench of the Supreme Court, and he, like all others of her citizens, when called upon to exercise official functions, was not found wanting either in ability or integrity. His professional experience in the semi-agricultural and semi-mineral regions of the foot-hills, fitted him well to consider and intelligently decide the many new and difficult questions affecting these two great interests of our State, and both the farmer and the miner are much indebted to his wisdom and foresight in establishing legal rules adjusting their respective rights.

Judge Cope was born in Kentucky on the 29th of January, 1824, where he studied law, and was admitted to practice, coming to California in 1850. Like most early pioneers he believed that fickle fortune's blandest smiles were easier won in other vocations than a profession, and he did not engage exclusively in the practice of the law until the organization of Amador county in 1854, when he opened his law office at Jackson, where alone and in partnership with James F. Hubbard, and with R. M. Briggs, he took a leading position at the Bar. In 1858, he was elected to the Assembly, and was made chairman of the judiciary committee. An appreciation of his services in that position was made manifest by his being elected Associate Justice of the Supreme Court the following year. After his election and previous to his entering upon the duties of his judicial position, Judge Terry, then Chief Justice, resigned, and Judge Cope was appointed to fill the vacancy. He remained upon the Supreme Bench until the 1st of January, 1864, having, as his associates during that time, Field, Baldwin, Norton, and Crocker. A short time after leaving the bench, he removed to San Francisco, where he is now associated with J. Thomas Boyd, and is enjoying a lucrative and high order of practice.

W. T. CURTIS came from Ohio in an early day, making his home at Drytown. He was a man of fine culture, gentlemanly in manner, and much more disposed to advise a peaceful settlement of a difficulty than costly litigation. He usually made himself prominent in allaying, rather than fomenting, the riotous spirit which so commonly existed in the mining towns in an early day. He was especially prominent in mitigating the not inexcusable anger of the population after the atrocious murders at Rancheria. He was a Republican in sentiment, and a candidate for District Attorney on the same ticket which was headed with the name of John C. Fremont, in 1856. He stumped the county for Fremont, speaking in every place of any size. His candor and gentlemanly qualities were appreciated by friends and opponents alike, and he was always respectfully listened to. On the breaking out of the Rebellion, he joined the Union army as aid to an officer in high rank. From the best information attainable, he was killed early in the contest.

HON. JOHN A. EAGON is a native of Virginia, and came to this State in 1851, and from the first made his home in Amador county. He mined for a time at Lower Rancheria with considerable success, having the good fortune to pick up a four-pound lump. He was engaged afterwards in mining near Ione. It was during his residence there that he began to be known for his conversational powers, which indicated his logical turn of mind, and led him to the adoption of the law as a profession. He has gradually worked up both professionally and politically, until he has become one of the leading men. As his name is connected with most of the prominent events in the county, related in another part of the history, it is unnecessary to repeat them here. He has a peculiarly earnest, nervous style of argument, replete with facts, but nearly destitute of humor, his speeches reminding one much of those of Silas Wright, in his best days. He is still young and vigorous, with no demoralizing habits, and is likely to go much higher before he pauses in his advancing career.

HON. JAMES T. FARLEY, one of the present United States Senators from California, is a native of Virginia. He was some time in the University of Virginia, but did not graduate, however. After spending some years in Missouri, he emigrated to California, arriving in 1850. He commenced the study of the law in Volcano, his first cases being in Justice Stephenson's court in 1854. He early entered into politics, and became famous for his success in attaching the voters to his interests. He was elected to the Assembly in 1854, re-elected in 1855, and made speaker. On the breaking up of the American party, he allied himself with the Democracy, where he has since remained. During the early years of the Rebellion, he was a Lecompton Democrat, and suffered defeat in company with other nominees of that party. After the union of the Republicans with the Douglas Democrats, his star began to rise, and he was twice elected to the State Senate by majorities far greater than the average of his ticket. His ability as a legislator is unquestioned; the same intuitive knowledge of human nature coming into use among the Solons of the capital as well as in a country town. Perhaps the best work, or at least the work involving the most comprehensive reasoning, was his report, as chairman of the Committee on Incorporations, on the bill regulating fares and freights. In 1878 he was elected to the United States Senate, and took his seat in 1879.

As a lawyer he is most efficient as a jury pleader. He has little of the overbearing character generally thought necessary in badgering a refractory or reticent witness; never arouses the antagonism of jury or witness by an abuse of his position; yet few witnesses can boast of carrying away any honors in a contest with him.

As a politician, he is strong in the ability to organize, uniting his friends and dividing his enemies. His private character is above reproach. He is genial in manner, sympathetic in feeling, making friends where possible. He is still on the sunny side of fifty, hale and hearty, having fortunately escaped the social perils which beset the paths of Californian politicians. Having apparently many years of hard work in him, it is quite possible that he may attain one of the two higher positions possible in his political career.

GEORGE L. GALE, though he did not often appear in court, generally having other business to attend to, *was was one of them*—i. e. the lawyers—in spirit and education. He was a native of Massachusetts, born, as he was wont to state, at the foot of Bunker Hill, and belonged to the true chivalry of the country, the "Bunker Hill chivalry," by which means he came to be known as Bunker Hill Gale. He was extremely original in his methods of reasoning, sharp, rapid and incisive in his language, prompt in decision, and quick in action. To contend with him on any subject was to meet a rattling fire of musketry, brilliant thrust of rapiers, and pyrotechnical flashes that dazzled and confused the ordinary mind. He made a splendid Justice of the Peace, and his decisions were hardly ever reversed in the higher courts, though he was too brilliant to become profound in the law, loving rather to deal with its puzzling technicalities. He would have filled the seat of paragraphist in a modern editorial room to perfection, his keen sense of the ludicrous and trenchant wit qualifying him for the position of critic. His sayings and doings would fill a good-sized book. He was once appointed sealer of weights and measures, and collected double fees by sealing them for the year past and then for the coming year on the same day. Upon being remonstrated with for exacting fees for two years, he told them, "either pay it or render yourselves liable to a fine for selling goods with unsealed weights and measures." The subjects, knowing Gales' strength in law technicalities, usually paid, though with much grumbling. He had no family, and died in obscurity a few years ago at Pine Grove.

JOHN C. GEAR was a young man who alternated the practice of law with mining and teaching school, in the vicinity of Ione. He was brilliant and enthusiastic, with many qualities that go to make up an orator. He died at Ione before he had the opportunity to make his mark in his profession.

HON. MARION W. GORDON is a native of Tennessee, of Irish descent. In early life he was a professor of elocution, and traveled extensively, lecturing on, and teaching the art. He was at different times connected with some of the leading papers in Missouri, and was associated with many of the prominent politicians, in shaping the policy of that State after the overthrow of the Benton *régime*. He came to California in 1850, and soon after located in Volcano, forming one of the *coterie* of philosophers heretofore referred to, who discussed questions of the lofty character which have employed such minds as Hegel, Descartes, Comte, Mills, and Spencer. In Judge Gordon's case, however, he mingled hard work with hard thinking, and in 1852-53 could be seen swinging the pick and shovel in the Volcano tail-race, which he, with others, cut through the deep flat. In 1853, in compliance with the wishes of many friends, he came before the county Convention for the nomination for member of the Assembly for Calaveras county, which he received. After a well-contested canvass he came out victorious, and took his seat in the Legislature one of the last of the old Calaveras delegation.* On the organization of Amador county he was elected to the position of County Judge, which he held for three consecutive terms.

Judge Gordon is a man of varied accomplishments and general information. Scarcely any topic can be introduced which has not been read up by him. Mesmerism, animal magnetism, clairvoyance, and all the modern occult sciences have been, at times,

---

*His name was omitted in the list of members of that year through a typographical error.

JAMES. MEEHAN.

assayed in his mental laboratory. His midnight lamp was often burning when all else was buried in deep slumber. As a politician he had few superiors. The habit of judging men and organizing them into solid parties was to him a matter of instinct, accomplished without serious effort. His ability to adapt his speech to the capacity of his hearers was remarkable. A scowling face was discerned, and the latent opposition neutralized by a happy allusion. Whether before a crowd of rough miners, a body of school-teachers, a convention of musicians, or an assembly of wary politicians, this faculty never failed him. As a lawyer, he dealt rather in the general principles than in the technicalities. His love for generalization, and a consequent knowledge of the laws of equity, enabled him to easily perform the duties of Judge. In Congress his general information and knowledge of the human heart would have enabled him to have taken high rank. That he never went to Congress is a matter of regret. That so many, vastly his inferiors, have found their way there, is, and will be, a mystery. Though his mental powers are still vigorous, he has retired from active practice, and is spending his old age in dignified leisure.

THOMAS D. GRANT was born, and educated for the law, in the State of New York. His early associations were with such legal luminaries as Judge Spencer and lawyers of his ilk, from whom he imbibed a true respect for, and due appreciation of, the honor and dignity of his profession, which he regarded above all others. This, coupled with his proverbial honesty and integrity, inspired a public confidence that secured to him a very desirable clientage. When the writer of this was first nominated for District Attorney, he was associated with Judge Grant in practice. The Judge was bitterly opposed to politics, and declared if the candidate persisted in running for office, he would dissolve their copartnership, and defeat him if possible. The young aspirant did persist, and a dissolution followed. When the votes were counted it was found that out of seventy-eight votes polled at a precinct down in the deep gorge of the Mokelumne river, six or eight miles from Jackson, where the Judge resided, the writer received more than seventy, although he was an entire stranger in the locality. Believing that this large vote was not wholly due to the fact that he was unknown, he instituted inquiries, and ascertained that the Judge,—being too heavy (some four hundred avoirdupois) to ride on horseback, and the roads being altogether too steep for a carriage,—had secretly walked down and back to the Bar, where he had formerly mined, and was loved and respected by all, and stuffed—not the ballot-box—but the voters, with the theory that the candidate was worthy of their suffrages. This is given as illustrative of the character of the man. Although he was rude and rough at times, in his words and deportment, his heart was in size proportionate to his Falstaffian physique—over-flowing with true sympathy and noble impulses—its beatings the power that moved his hands to the performance of generous deeds. When he died, in Jackson, 1859, the community lost one of God's noblest works—an honest man.

HON. JAMES H. HARDY had the brain of some fabled Lycurgus, and possessed the fecundity of a Jupiter's; the bare assertion that "Jim" Hardy sprang therefrom fully armed for the legal arena would require strong refutation. No one could tell when he applied himself to his books, and yet he was an animated encyclopædia of legal decisions, from the earliest to the latest. When he was upon the bench, attorneys become careless and would simply state that the Supreme Court had so decided, and wait for the Judge to tell them the title of the case, and in what volume it could be found. He possessed, in a marked degree, the two qualities, one at least of which is essential to success in the legal practice, but seldom found combined in one—eloquence and a clear knowledge and comprehension of the law. In the absence of a native talent for these, he could scarcely have reached the prominence at the Bar he attained, since he preferred the social companionship of his host of friends to the studious application most men find essential to a legal reputation. Judge Hardy was born in Hamilton county, Illinois, on the third day of April, 1832; first studied law with his father, and afterwards with Hon. S. S. Marshall; was admitted to practice in Illinois, where, notwithstanding his extreme youth, he acquired quite an extensive reputation as a lawyer, and came to California in 1852, locating at Sacramento; subsequently, he removed to Jackson, and, upon the creation of the Sixteenth Judicial District with the counties of Amador and Calaveras in 1859, was appointed Judge of the new district, to which position he was elected by a flattering majority, at the next following election. As a Democrat he always took prominent part in politics; was District Attorney of Sacramento county, and ran as a Breckinridge elector in 1856. In his numerous "stumping" excursions through the State, he always denied that he was out electioneering, but asserted that he was hunting for an ox which he lost while crossing the plains in '50. It is related of him that his first appearance in court at Sacramento was upon the recommendation of a friend who had known him in Illinois. "Jim" was found hard at work in a bakery, and at first declined to take the case, alleging his lack of recent practice, etc., but after much urging went into court without changing his garments, white with "miller's dust." The opposing counsel, who was somewhat overbearing and pompous in his manner, inquired who represented the other side. Young Hardy was pointed out to him, when he sneeringly asked, "And who is Mr. Hardy? I have not the pleasure of his acquaintance." Hardy immediately caught up a large volume lying upon the table, and hurling it at the interrogator, with great force exclaimed, "You will not require any further introduction the next time we meet!" Hardy was fined fifty dollars for contempt, but proceeded with his case, convincing his opponent, as well as others who listened, that "Jim" Hardy was not to be despised even in his baker's uniform.

SAMUEL J. K. HANDY was a native of Maryland, of the Virginia school of gentlemen, polished and accomplished, blending dignity and kindness together. He was prominent before the State Convention, in 1856, as a candidate for Congress; failing in which, he left the county. His present residence, if living, is unknown. As he was somewhat advanced in years at the time of his residence here, it is likely that he has accomplished his work.

ALVINZA HAYWARD probably had at one time some aspirations for a professional career, but rich quartz mines absorbed his attention, so that he had little time for thoughts of the law except as it concerned his own extensive business. He will be remembered as the man who developed the richest gold mine on the coast, and in that connection his history is related in another portion of this book.

JAMES F. HUBBARD was formerly a surveyor, but concluding that he could see to better advantage through the intricacies of the law than through the theodolite, he threw aside the chain and compass, and commenced Blackstone and Kent. His hopes and anticipations were fully realized, and, in due course of time, he took his seat at the Bar, and built up a most valuable practice. He was in company with several of the prominent lawyers at Jackson at different times. Though not considered a brilliant pleader, his opinion was highly valued. About the years 1862 or '63, he removed to San Francisco, where he practiced with fair success for a few years, finally returning to New York, his native State.

HON. P. C. JOHNSON.* Though Mr. Johnson occupied the attention of the county for some years, very little is known of his antecedents. He came into the county from El Dorado in 1855, in company with T. A. Springer, who established the Volcano *Ledger* that year. Though admitted to the Bar he scarcely ever appeared in court, giving most of his attention to literary matters. He was a brilliant writer, and was connected with the *Ledger* for many years as assistant or chief editor. He was elected to the Legislature in 1859, and died at the house of T. A. Springer in Jackson, in 1862. Though possessed of many excellent and brilliant qualities, they were impaired by a social weakness, which eventually terminated his life.

L. N. KETCHUM was brought into public notice in 1857, when he was elected to the State Senate, being then a resident of Clinton, where he had been mining. He made his mark as a legislator, and then

*His name does not appear in the continuous history as member of Legislature for that year. The accounts were made up from the Supervisor's records, which were very imperfect.—ED.

studied law. Possessed of great colloquial powers and an excellent education, it is not surprising that he met with success in his new vocation. He practiced, however, but little in Amador county, but removed to Siskiyou county, where he enjoyed a fine practice and was elected District Attorney. He died at Yreka several years ago.

FAYETTE MACE was admitted to the practice of law many years since, but owing to his extensive operations in saw-mills, quartz mills and farming, he has given the law little attention since, except as it was incidental in his business operations.

HON. GEORGE MOORE, the present Superior Judge of Amador county, was born in Davisville, Boyle county, Kentucky, February 14, 1850; graduated at Centre College in the class of 1870, and after pursuing the study of law for two years under the tuition of Hon. M. J. Durham, of Kentucky, attended the law school of Harvard University, Cambridge, Massachusetts, and was admitted to the Bar in 1874. In the political campaign of 1876 he was appointed one of the Tilden and Hendricks electors, and came to California in the Fall of 1877, settling in Amador county. He entered upon the discharge of his duties as the first Superior Judge of Amador county, under the New Constitution, on the first Monday of January, 1880. He married Mrs. V. B. Lackey, also a native of Kentucky, in 1879, and now resides in Jackson.

JONATHAN PALMER was admitted to practice on the organization of the county. His residence was in Oleta (then Fiddletown), and he divided his time about evenly between mining and the study of the law. He acted as Justice of the Peace as early as 1852. He was a man of solid rather than showy acquirements, and in the matter of oratory was eclipsed by R. M. Briggs, who was a resident there at the same time. He was one of the discoverers of the famous American hill, and to the fact of having a rich claim is probably due the little interest he took in legal matters. He has drifted out of sight in recent years.

HON. THOMAS M. PAWLING, a native of Philadelphia, whose lawyers have been traditionally the "hardest to puzzle" of any of their class, located at Volcano in 1855, where he was law partner of Hon. James T. Farley; was elected County Clerk in 1858, and upon the expiration of his official term resumed practice at Jackson, with J. G. Severance as his partner. Upon the discovery of the mines in Esmeralda county, he removed to Aurora, where he acquired considerable wealth, but returned to Jackson in 1865, and again formed a copartnership with Mr. Farley, and continued his practice until 1871, when he was appointed by Governor Haight to fill the position of County Judge, made vacant by the death of Hon. J. Foot Turner, to which office he was subsequently twice elected by the people. Judge Pawling made no great pretentions to oratory, but excelled as an "office lawyer," and had few superiors in the preparation of legal documents. He died at Jackson, January 21, 1877, while County Judge, at about fifty years of age.

T. J. PHELPS, is a native of Kentucky; came to California in 1849, and to Amador county, as since organized, in 1852; residing in Oleta until elected District Attorney in 1873, a position he filled with distinction for four years. Mr. Phelps has been identified with the material interests of the county since his residence here. He was one of the first to recognize the practicability of conveying water to the mines—the ditch from the north fork of Dry creek in which he was part owner being not only among the first, but among the most profitable of any that were ever constructed in the county. As a lawyer, Mr. Phelps is a counselor rather than an advocate, and much more disposed to heal dissentions than promote them. He has ever been distinguished as an upright and honorable man, modest and unassuming, but equal to any emergency that has ever called him to action.

SILAS PENRY is a native of Texas; coming to California at a very early age, he has made himself what he is in this State. He is still quite young, both in years and in his profession, but has the promise of being brilliant and useful. His life has been somewhat shadowed by the unfortunate affair resulting in the death of Elisha Turner, an intimate friend of his. On his trial the courts and public sentiment exonerated him of all malice, and it is quite certain that no other blame can attach to him than that of thoughtlessly using his weapon in a case of mutually angry words. It is believed that he will outgrow his self reproach, and attain the position to which his talents entitle him.

ALONZO PLATT was from the State of New York; was one of the original movers in the matter of the organization of Amador county, and one of the commissioners appointed by the Governor to establish the new county government and call an election for county officers. He was considerable of a politician of the old school, and came up for office several times; but as he did not have the plasticity of character necessary to succeed, he was distanced in the race by Messrs. Farley, Gordon, Cope, Briggs and Axtell, and withdrew from public notice.

J. W. PORTER is a native of Pennsylvania; came to California in an early day and engaged in mining, perhaps rather to obtain the means of gratifying his love of reading than with the expectation of making a fortune. It was observed of him, however, that much of his mining was experimental, rather to prove or disprove some theory regarding the deposits of gold, than as a means of acquiring immediate wealth. The hole which he sunk in the head of Soldier's gulch, one hundred and fifty feet deep, under the impression that gold would be found all the way to the bed-rock, was a case in point. The gold was found to that depth, proving his theory, but it was not in sufficient quantity to make his discovery valuable. His reading was largely ancient history, which caused the remark to be made, perhaps with some degree of truth, that he was more of a Roman than an American citizen; at any rate, he has many Roman virtues, such as sobriety, stern integrity, fortitude, and none of those weaknesses which endear some of our public men to the average voter, for no man could say that he had tried him drunk and tried him sober, for he was always sober. His aversion to the ordinary method of conducting a political campaign has prevented him from seeking office, for but once was he ever tempted to have his name placed on a ticket, when he ran for County Judge against M. W. Gordon, coming within a few votes of being elected. He refused to electioneer; some of his friends remarking that Porter would not solicit a vote if that one would elect him. His peculiar character of mind eminently fitted him for a judge, but did not fit him for getting the position which depended so much on personal popularity, though his utter contempt for human weakness might have made him a severe judge in criminal cases. Once while pleading before a Justice's Court, in the early fifties, in Volcano, he was interrupted by a half-drunken Irishman with threats of personal violence unless he ceased his offensive remarks. Porter bore the interruptions for a while, but as the court did not seem inclined to protect him he caught up a black-snake whip, which was near by, and lashed the Hibernian until he cried for mercy, after which he proceeded in his speech without apparently noticing the interruption. As might be expected, Mr. Porter remains a single man.

———— REYNOLDS was a Judge of the Court of First Instance, or as it was called, Alcalde, in some of the earlier settlements in 1850, and, in consequence, claimed a membership with the Bar, and was admitted to practice upon the organization of Amador county. His legal acquirements were rather limited, but in the chaotic condition of society twenty-five years since, he obtained some practice in the inferior courts. He was not remarkable for anything but pretension, and soon dropped out of sight.

J. A. ROBINSON is a native of Ohio, was born in 1838, removed to Illinois in 1858, enlisted April 23, 1861, in the Eighth Regiment of Infantry, Illinois Volunteers, and served under General Oglesby until discharged for disability incurred in the service. He came to California in 1863 and settled in Jackson; was at different times County Clerk, and Assistant United States Assessor, for Amador county. He completed his law studies, and was admitted to practice in 1866; removed to San Francisco in 1871, where, for several years, he was chief clerk in the United States Surveyor-General's office, under Hardenburg and his successors. He is now practicing law in San Francisco, making land cases a specialty, his long training in that business giving him great familiarity with the origin and perfection of land titles. He resides in Oakland, and has several times been before the public in connection with municipal offices. His training and natural temperament peculiarly fit him for investigations of complex land titles, and he is enjoying a remunerative and extensive practice.

HON. GEO. W. SEATON was a lawyer, politician, and quartz miner of considerable note in the early days of Amador. He, like many members of the old Whig party, joined the Know-Nothing, or American party, and afterwards both Democratic and Republican parties by turns. He was elected to the State Senate in 1865 by the Democratic party, but perished in the explosion of the steamer *Yosemite*, on the Sacramento, before taking his seat. He was a man of strong will and great energy, and when a move was decided upon it never failed for want of persistent action. His style of speech was, like the man, more forcible than elegant. He made no pretensions to learning or elegance, but appealed to the common sense of his auditors. He was better adapted to the forum than the Bar.

JOSIAH GOULD SEVERANCE is a native of Maine, born September 30, 1832. He prepared for college at Hampden Academy, and entered at Bowdoin in 1852, but, at the solicitations of friends, withdrew without graduating, and entered upon the study of the law in the office of Hon. Hannibal Hamlin, at Hampden, where he remained for about a year, when he entered the law office of Hon. John E. Godfrey, for years and now Probate Judge of Penobscot county, at Bangor; was admitted to the Supreme Judicial Court of that State in 1855, and arrived in San Francisco on the first day of January, 1856, and first located in the then flourishing mining town of Lancha Plana, Amador county. He was elected a member of the Board of Supervisors in the Fall of 1856, and in 1858, District Attorney by the Douglas Democracy, having as his opponents Hon. S. B. Axtell, Breckinridge candidate, and John C. Gear, the straight Republican nominee; was active in the organization of the Union party in the county, in 1862, and was made chairman of its first County Central Committee; ran for the Assembly, much against his will, that year, and, with the whole ticket, was defeated, coming, however, within twenty-nine votes of an election. In the Fall of 1862, he married Miss M. J. Tiel, of Jackson, and removed to Calaveras county, where he was elected District Attorney the following year, and re-elected in 1865. For some time he edited the Amador *Ledger*, and was the proprietor and editor of the San Andreas *Register*. He is now engaged in his professional practice in San Francisco, where he has taken but little part in politics, although he there served for a time as assistant District Attorney, under D. J. Murphy, Esq., and ran on and was defeated with, the straight Republican ticket, as Delegate at Large to the late Constitutional Convention.

MOSES TEBBS was a young man of rather promising abilities who came to Volcano in 1855. Remaining but a few years he went to Alpine upon the organization of that county, where he was heard from occasionally in connection with political matters. His present residence is unknown.

HENRY L. WALDO was a native of Missouri, and made his way to California by way of Oregon. He early chose the law as his profession, and alternated study with hard work whenever he had the opportunity, sometimes studying with his friends, sharing their hospitalities, and at other times becoming a habitant of a law office. His progress in his profession was rapid. In 1869 he was elected District Attorney, which position he held to the close of the term, performing the duties to the satisfaction of all concerned. He declined a re-election, justly concluding that he could find a more honorable and lucrative position elsewhere. He now holds a high judicial position in the Territory of New Mexico. As an officer he was courteous, firm and upright, swerved from the right course neither by blandishments nor fear. During the excitement attending the lawless action of the Miner's League at Sutter Creek, he was informed that he would prosecute the rioters at the risk of his life. He turned to the belligerent leaguer and invited him to commence operations then and there, for he should perform his duty.

[The biographies of the members of the Bar are somewhat limited, owing to the difficulty of obtaining reliable data. Some are too modest to narrate the prominent events in their lives; some, perhaps, are apprehensive of a too critical review of their careers, some are negligent, and others have gone to that region from which no correspondence is permitted. If some things important are omitted and others exalted to undue importance, we can only say that after awaiting letters and information some time, the demand for copy compelled us to close the sketches with what we had on hand.]

DROPS OF JUDICIAL WISDOM.

Mr. Axtell relates the following of ———, whilom Justice of the Peace at Rancheria: During the progress of a trial by jury in his court, the expression, *non compos mentis*, was used. One of the jurors, with a laudable desire to fully understand the case, asked the Court the meaning of the term used. "It is," said his honor, with becoming dignity, "the process by which the attendance of witnesses from another county is obtained." As witnesses were present from El Dorado county, the answer was satisfactory.

"Uncle Jake" Emminger was also Justice at Rancheria, and was very proud of his patriarchal beard, which he allowed to fall below his waist on Sundays and Court days, but carefully folded up on ordinary occasions. He was also proud of his political achievements in his township, where, by some *coup de main*, he obtained thirty-four votes out of a possible sixty-seven in the whole township, and was, therefore, elected. It is said that he once sentenced a Chinaman to jail for life for stealing chickens, but afterwards excused the error, as being of the heart and not of the head, by claiming that had a shorter term been imposed his constituency would have hanged the culprit. In a case before "Uncle Jake" the defendant presented and read an affidavit for change of venue. The Court listened patiently, stroked his long beard gravely and thoughtfully for a few minutes, then said: "The affidavit of the defendant is overruled, and judgment rendered for the plaintiff in the sum of ——" "Hold on," cried the defendant, "if I must have my case tried by this Court, I demand a jury!" "What in h—, sir, do you expect to prove by a jury?" demanded the Judge in his most severe manner.

"Judge" Hugh Robinson, an Irish gentleman of the old school, was for many years Justice of the Peace at Clinton, and mine host of the chief caravansary of the village. It was not a temperance tavern, and so great was the liberal hospitality of the "Judge," that even the Governor of North Carolina would have ceased his chronic complaint of "a long time between drinks," had he been his guest. S. B. Axtell and James F. Hubbard were once pitted against each other in a case before him. The testimony all in, the brief and terse argument of Mr. Axtell was listened to by the Court with marked attention, but the "linked sweetness" of Judge Hubbard's reply proved too much for the "Judge's" active temperament, and under the combined influence of somnolent logic and cordial hospitality, he fell asleep. Judge Hubbard had him aroused, and, in a somewhat indignant manner, remarked that if his case was not properly considered he would appeal it to a higher court. "Appeal to h—, and be damned to ye!" cried the "Judge;" "judgment for the plaintiff, and this court is adjourned!"

A marriage ceremony was once performed by one of the local Justices, so brilliant in its character that the name of the distinguished official, and the time and place, are omitted, that the honors may be equally divided. The candidates for matrimonial uncertainties presenting themselves before the magistrate, he ordered the bridegroom elect to hold up his right hand, and, in his most impressive manner, said: "You do most solemnly swear that you are twenty-one years of age; that you will support the Constitution of the United States, and of the State of California; that you will be a true, faithful, and obedient husband, and that you have not voted before this day, so help you God." What was said to the woman was not related.

The case of Owens *vs.* Shackles, *et al.*, was brought in Justice Palmer's court, at Lancha Plana, in January, 1856, to determine the right of possession to a mining claim. Henry Eno, who had been County Judge of Calaveras county, and was afterwards County Judge of Alpine county, was attorney for the plaintiff. The trial was had by jury, who rendered their verdict that the claim did not belong to either party. Without waiting for any action by the Court upon the verdict, there was a general rush of attorneys, clients, and witnesses for the disputed ground. It is said that Judge Eno, whose gray hairs were streaming in the wind, raised by his Iroquois pace, would have won the race and (boundary) stakes, had not Shackles caught him by the coat tail, and flung him aside, thus winning the race and suit, with Owens a very good second.

Apropos of Judge Eno, a story is told which may not be out of place here, since his practice was quite as extensive in Amador as in Calaveras. While he was County Judge of Calaveras, a young man was tried and convicted before him, of a felony. Judge Brockway defended the prisoner in his usual able manner, and upon the arraignment of his client for sentence made a most feeling appeal to the Court for leniency, moving his auditors to tears, and apparently producing a deep impression upon the Court. After waiting a short time for the excitement to subside, Judge Eno said: "Prisoner, stand up! You have been indicted by the Grand Jury of this county for the crime of burglary, to which indictment you pleaded 'not guilty.' You have been fairly tried by a jury of your own selection, who find you guilty of the charge contained in the indictment, having been ably and well defended during that trial by eminent counsel. Your counsel has made a most touching and eloquent appeal to the Court for its sympathy and indulgence, calling attention to the apparent fact that you are but a boy in years; averring that this is your first criminal offense; that you are the only son of one of our most respected and worthy citizens, and the idol of an almost brokenhearted mother; that the result of a long incarceration would be ruin to your future, which might be fair and even brilliant. The Court is deeply impressed with these facts, and its sentence, therefore, is, that you be taken by the Sheriff of this county to the State prison at San Quentin, and there be confined to hard labor for a term of fourteen years; and I only wish I could make it longer."

The prisoner was, however, pardoned a short time after, and, to the credit of Judge Eno, be it said, he signed the petition for the pardon and exerted himself in that behalf.

A DISGUSTED CREDITOR.

While Judge Gordon was County Judge and *ex officio* Judge of the Probate Court, and Jerry King was Public Administrator, two Swedes were drowned in the Mokelumne river, leaving, as was supposed, some property. King was duly appointed administrator of their estates. A few weeks after, an original specimen of humanity, with unkempt hair of an indescribable hue, crane neck and leathery features, his general appearance suggesting the idea of a dried-apple on the end of a ramrod, presented himself before Judge Gordon, and making an awkward bow of unusual vigor, and slinging his well-worn *sombrero* beneath his arm with the air and punctilio of a soldier presenting arms, his mental thermometer evidently at fighting point, said,

"Might Mister King be here?"

Judge Gordon ever ready to gratify his disposition for a quiet joke, and discovering rich croppings therefor, concluded to prospect, and answered,

"No. What do you want with Mr. King?"

Pat—"An' its meself that wants me money!"

Judge Gordon—"What money has Mr. King of yours?"

Pat—"Its me money that I arent like an honest man off them that died in the river beyant, bedad!"

Judge Gordon—"Did you earn it before or after they were drowned?"

Pat—"Do ye think they could hire me afther they were dead, bedad?"

Judge Gordon—"Mr. King cannot give you your money now. You must wait until the estate is administered."

Pat—"An' what's that?"

Judge Gordon—"Until it goes through the court."

Pat—"An' d'ye say that, now? Then it's Pat Rooney's son 'll give hisself no more trouble aboot it, at all, at all. Bedad, an' if it goes through the coort, it's meself that 'll niver see a cint. Ach, hone, I thought afther only one man's stalings, faith, there'd be some left—but if it's got to go through the coort, Holy Virgin, it's me own father's son that 'll niver get a cint. Good day ter yees, gintlemen; it's no more I'll bother me head aboot it, at all, at all!"

DEVOUT DEACONS.

About the year 1860, an Episcopal clergyman made an effort to establish a society of his form of worship at Jackson, and secured the court-room for the meeting. Of course it was popular, and it became the intellectual members of the community to identify themselves with the movement; hence, many members of the Bar who had been conspicuous by their absence from any church for years, were in attendance. It was necessary that deacons should be selected, and Counselor B—— and Judge H—— were among the elect. During service they were unable to find the places in the book for responses, and B—— asked of H—— in an audible whisper, "Jim, where in h—l is the place?" "Damfino," responded H—— earnestly turning the leaves of the one book with which he was not familiar.

A COLORED ADVOCATE.

J. W. D. Palmer, a most genial and intelligent gentleman, from Kentucky, and formerly connected with the press at Louisville, has been Justice of the Peace at Lancha Plana for years. In his court an action to recover the possession of a mining claim, situated in the basin of a hill, was brought by Hon. George Wagner, who had represented Amador in the Assembly, against a colored man named Smith, who had dug a "tail-race" through the rim rock of the hill into the basin, through which to run off the debris in sluices. Mr. Wagner was represented by Mr. Severance, and Smith appeared in *propria persona*. The testimony all in, Smith proceeded to sum up as follows: "Yer 'oner, I will please to state to dis Court dat I jist spent my bottom dollar on dat ar tail-race; an do statoots uv dis State says dat you can't steal away my prop'ty. My oppoleon has gone and payed a silver-tongued lawyer to come here and cheat me out ob dat tail-race, but I'll please to state to dis Court dat it can't be did. No sar! Now dar George Wagner, kase he's 'lected to de Legislater when people was scace down dis way, he thinks he can run ober de poor African!" In spite of his eloquence he lost his case.

A GAME OF WHIST.

One evening during court week, Tod Robinson and Judge Carter engaged in a game of whist, in the "Young America," upon opposite sides. After playing for some time, Judge Carter dextrously exchanged cards with Judge Robinson, and got a very good hand by that means. The act was witnessed by the spectators, but passed unnoticed by Judge Robinson. Trick after trick was taken by Carter, to the audible amusement of the lookers-on, when Robinson, irritated by the laughter exclaimed, in that clear, cut silver speech, for which he was noted, "Gentlemen, am *I* the butt of your merriment?" He soon discovered that Carter had played a trick on him, and, rising to his full height and assuming his most dignified and tragic style, said, "Judge Carter! [pause] Squire Carter! [pause—in a louder tone] Mister Carter! [contemptuously] Carter! [then in a tone of withering irony] Old Carter! You have played seven-up with Bill Hicks and Jim Martin on a rawhide until you are wholly unfit to play with a gentleman, and I'll leave you, sir!"

AN INDUSTRIOUS GRAND JURY.

A careful reader of our history will not need telling a second time, that gambling was alarmingly prevalent in early days. The Legislature passed laws making gambling a penal offense; but in the chaotic state of society, about the beginning of the sixties, the laws against it were considered more as moral maxims than as imperious rules, and gambling went on much as ever. It happened that a Grand Jury, more than usually conscientious was convened, and when they were sworn to bring to notice all known violations of the statutes, gambling was of course included. A few cases were brought in, and the persons indicted. This led to more, and the whole week was spent in obtaining evidence of the act, until the numbers amounted to over three hundred. The District Attorney urged the uselessness of the course, as no trial jury would convict a man of a State's prison offense merely for betting a quarter on *monte* or *faro*, but the Grand Jury thought otherwise. Blank indictments were printed so that the jurors themselves could fill up the blanks, and the work went on. One case was brought to trial, and a day spent in the vain effort to obtain a conviction. The District Attorney here told the jury that he was unable to obtain a conviction, and asked legal assistance. Fifty dollars was raised among the grand jurors, and the services of Tod Robinson obtained. He exerted himself to the utmost, still the verdict was "not guilty." Saturday noon had arrived, and the Grand Jury were still at work, increasing the list until it seemed as if half the county would be put on trial. The District Attorney communicated his dilemma to Judge Gordon. He said nothing, but gave that peculiar twist of the eyes and mouth which all his friends know forebodes —— well, something decisive. When some little business had been disposed of the Judge asked the usual question, "Mr. District Attorney, have you any farther business before this Court?" Upon being answered in the negative, he ordered the Court adjourned *sine die*. The Grand Jury met the following Monday morning to continue the business, but were informed that the adjournment of the Court had ended their life as a Grand Jury. Some were able to look at it as a good joke; others went home resolving that if they should again get on the Grand Jury, they would begin with the Judge first.

OFFICERS OF AMADOR COUNTY, CALIFORNIA,

FROM 1854 TO 1880.

YEAR	DISTRICT JUDGE	COUNTY JUDGE	DISTRICT ATTORNEY	COUNTY CLERK	CO. RECORDER.[2]	SHERIFF	CO. TREASURER	CO. SUPT EVO.	CO. ASSESSOR.[7]
1854	Charles Creaner	M. W. Gordon	S. B. Axtell	J. C. Shipman		W. A. Phoenix	W. L. McKim	David Armstrong	H. A. Eichelberger
1855	"	"	"	"		George Durham	"	"	"
1856	"	"	"	H. S. Hatch		W. J. Paugh	"	James Mastreson	"
1857	"	"	J. G. Severance	T. M. Pawling		"	Ellis Evans	John R. Hicks	"
1858	"	"	"	"		"	"	A. Moore	F. P. Smith
1859	"	"	"	"		"	"	"	"
1860	James H. Hardy	"	J. Foot Turner	Jas. W. Bicknell		R. Cosner	C. A. Lagrave	J. M. Griffith	F. McGrath
1861	"	"	"	"	A. Day	"	"	"	"
1862	W. H. Baldgely	J. Foot Turner	S. P. Axtell	E. S. Hull	H. Word	B. B. Redhead	F. McGrath	George Kress	"
1863	"	"	E. M. Briggs	"		"	Otto Walther	J. M. Griffith	"
1864	S. W. Brockway	"	"	J. C. Shipman	A. C. Hinkson	I. N. Randolph	"	T. C. Stowers	"
1865	"	"	"	"		R. Cosner	(5)	"	"
1866	"	"	H. L. Waldo	Add. C. Hinkson	P. Seilenthaler	George Durham	James Mehan	Arthur Spear	"
1867	"	"	"	"		"	"	"	"
1868	"	"	"	"		"	"	"	"
1869	A. C. Adams	T. W. Pawling	"	D. B. Spagnoli		"	"	H. C. Meek	J. W. Surface
1870	"	"	R. M. Briggs	B. F. Eichtmyr		H. B. Kelley	O. Batten	"	"
1871	"	"	"	"		"	"	D. D. Beaver	"
1872	"	"	T. J. Phelps	J. B. Stevens		"	J. A. Butterfield	W. L. McKim	"
1873	"	"	"	"		"	"	"	"
1874	"	"	"	Henry Peck		Peter Fagan	"	"	"
1875	G. E. Williams	A. C. Brown[1]	A. Caminetti	T. A. Chichizola		John Vogan	James Meehan	"	J. J. Jones
1876	"	"	"	"		"	"	"	"
1877	"	"	"	L. J. Fontenrose		"	"	"	"
1878	"	"	"	"		"	"	"	"
1879	"	George Moore[*]	"	"		"	"	J. A. Brown	A. Petty
1880	"	"	"	"		"	"	"	"

(1) Vice T. W. Pawling, deceased; appointed in February.

(2) Vice Henry Peck, deceased.

(3) The offices of County Clerk and Recorder combined, except in the years 1862-63-64-65-66-67.

(4) Appointed August, 1854, vice W. A. Phoenix, who was killed in the difficulty at Chinese Camp.

(5) Appointed November 25th, vice B. B. Redhead, deceased.

(6) In the election held September 6, 1865, L. Ridolit was elected Treasurer, but it being proved that he was not a citizen, Otto Walther, competitor, was appointed to fill the vacancy.

(7) Township Assessors during the years 1862-63-64-65-67-68.

(*) Superior Judge.

OFFICERS OF AMADOR COUNTY, CALIFORNIA,
FROM 1854 TO 1880—Continued.

YEAR	SUPT. SCHOOLS[a]	CORONER	PUB. ADMINISTRATOR[b]	BOARD OF SUPERVISORS[c]	STATE SENATOR	ASSEMBLYMEN
1854		L. G. Lyon	E. B. Harris	A. J. Houghtaling, Ellis Evans, Charles Barlow	D. Crandall	J. T. Farley, J. D. W. Palmer
1855	J. W. Gowlin		Wm. Jennings	C. Barlow, S. S. Bartram, A. B. Andrews		J. T. Farley, G. W. Wagner
1856	E. E. McIntyre	A. B. Kibbe	J. B. King	J. G. Severance, J. A. Brown, E. A. Kinealey	W. B. Norman	Wm. M. Seawell, James Livermore
1857				Thomas H. Locke, F. McBride, F. G. Hearst	L. N. Ketcham[?]	Homer King, R. M. Briggs
1858	H. H. Bloomer	John Vogan	E. Gallagher	Robert Stewart, R. D. Stiles, Jacob Lauter		W. Cope, John A. Eagon
1859		J. C. Shephard		G. Y. Hammond, R. Stewart, J. Kruse	J. A. Eagon	P. C. Johnson, J. B. Bowman
1860	Samuel Page	W. L. Fiskel		G. Y. Hammond, G. V. H. McWilliams, H. Allen		B. Burrell, T. M. Horrell
1861	"		Geo. W. Baers	C. Y. Hammond, Charles McWilliams[?] F. H. Allen	B. Burrell	G. W. Seaton, W. A. Waddell
1862	"	Louis Montzetti		I. B. Gregory, H. B. Bishop, James B. Allen	"	E. M. Simmons, A. B. Andrews
1863	D. Townsend	C. H. Kelly	H. Johnson	Jas. H. Allen, H. B. Bishop, E. A. Kinealey, I. B. Gregory	"	William R. Laidlaw, A. C. Brown
1864				E. B. Woolley		
1865	S. G. Briggs	J. Boarman	M. Tynan	H. B. Bishop, I. B. Gregory, E. A. Kinealey	A. H. Rose[?]	H. Lee[d], A. C. Brown[d]
1866		"	"	E. B. Woolley, Wm. Jennings, C. H. Ingalls		"
1867		"	W. A. Few	Wm. Jennings, C. H. Ingalls, L. McLaine		I. B. Gregory, George M. Payne[e]
1868				C. H. Ingalls, L. McLaine, D. M. Goff		"
1869		P. Cook	A. Yoak	James Carroll, L. McLaine, D. M. Goff		A. C. Brown, J. M. Johnson[f]
1870				L. McLaine, D. M. Goff, Henry Peck	James T. Farley	"
1871				Henry Peck, L. McLaine, L. E. Foundstone		H. L. Wakde, John A. Eagon
1872		Chas. Boarman		L. McLaine, L. E. Foundstone, J. A. Eagon, H. B. Ford		"
1873			B. Myers	John Eagon, H. D. Ford, R. Stewart		W. H. Stowers, L. Miller
1874			"	H. D. Ford, R. Stewart, John A. Phipps		"
1875			"	R. Stewart, J. A. Phipps, M. Murray		H. A. Carter, Thomas Dunlap
1876	W. H. Stowers		"	M. Philipp, Robert Stewart, J. O. Bartlett		"
1877				Robert Stewart, J. O. Bartlett, Robert Aitken	F. M. Brown[g]	B. Lodgate, T. Dunlap
1878	A. Edsinger			J. O. Bartlett, Robert Aitken, B. Ross		"
1879	L. Miller		B. H. Schacht	Robert Aitken, B. Ross, Dan Donnelly	B. F. Langford	L. Bruey, B. C. Downs
1880	"	"	"	B. Ross, D. Donnelly, R. Aitken		"

(a) County Assessor ex-officio. Superintendent in 1854.

(b) Offices of Coroner and Administrator combined in 1872.

(c) The time of taking the seat varied from September to January. When more than three are named, they all acted during the year. In 1863, Kingsley and Woolley, from District No. 1, both claimed seats, and voted at the same time. (See History.)

(d) From Alpine county. In 1865 Alpine and Amador were made one Legislative district, which continued until 1874.

(e) Miner Frink declared elected, but his seat was contested and obtained by A. C. Brown.

(f) In 1877 Amador was united to San Joaquin as a Senatorial District.

(g) W. T. Lewis, joint Senator with Calaveras.

(h) G. W. Seaton was elected, but killed by the explosion of the Ye Semite, previous to the session of the Legislature.

BIOGRAPHICAL AND DESCRIPTIVE SKETCHES.

GEORGE ALLEN

Is a native of the city of New York; born on the 11th of July, 1841. Being left an orphan at the early age of one year, he was taken to Rochester, where he lived about ten years. His education was obtained in different portions of the great "Empire" State, his occupation, after he was old enough to work, being farming. In 1860 he came to California, by way of the Isthmus of Panama, landing in the city of San Francisco on the first day of March. The second day of the same month found him at Sutter Creek, Amador county, which he has since made his home. He has been engaged in various kinds of business since arriving at this place, principally teaming, lumbering, and stock-raising.

For the first six years he followed the former business, and then engaged in the lumber trade, which business he still conducts, having the only lumber-yard in Sutter Creek. A good portion of the time he has several teams on the road, hauling lumber from his saw-mill, better known as Tarr's mill, situated about ten miles above Volcano.

He is largely interested in stock-raising, dealing in and raising horses, mules, and cattle, extensively. Mr. Allen has in the neighborhood of three thousand acres of land adjoining Sutter Creek, all under fence, and well supplied with the necessary arrangements for the prosecution of his business; has numerous barns for the shelter of his stock. He also has some fifteen hundred acres of mountain range, to which he drives his stock when the feed fails around his home ranch. Taking into consideration his being left an orphan when so young, Mr. Allen is a self-made man, and has accomplished what many others have failed to do. His honesty, integrity and punctuality have always been prominent features in his dealings with his fellow-men.

He was married July 11, 1870, in Amador City, to Miss Annie E. Bradbury, a native of the State of Maine. Their union has been blessed with five children, four of whom, two boys and two girls, are still living, their oldest child, a daughter, having died.

JEFFERSON BAIRD

Was born in Perry county, Pennsylvania, December 15, 1826, where he resided until the Spring of 1839, when, with his parents, he removed to Iowa. While there he learned the carpenter's trade, though principally engaged in farming. In 1850 he was swept off by the great California wave, which sent such a vast number of the best and most energetic across the plains to build up a new State. After resting and looking around awhile at Sacramento, he went to Rough and Ready, in Nevada county, where he remained one year, engaged in mining. From thence he moved to El Dorado county, making that his home until 1876, being engaged in mining ditches until 1856, when he bought into a saw-mill, which, in connection with the selling and transportation of lumber, he carried on until the year mentioned, when he finally located on the present farm, which he had previously purchased. It is situated three miles north-east of Plymouth, and contains three hundred and twenty acres of ground highly improved.

Mr. Baird was married September 14, 1868, to Miss Mary Ann Brown, who died May 1, 1877. The family consists of Mr. Baird and an only son, now twelve years of age. He is a man trusted by his neighbors, and is a member of the Board of School Trustees of his district.

CHARLES BAMERT

Was born at Baden, in Germany, April 2, 1830. The first five years of his life were passed in his native country; but coming to America at that early age, his first recollections are consequently located in this country. Upon his arrival in America, he went with his parents to Ontario, New York, where he remained until 1852. During that time he attended school and acquired a common school education.

In the year last named, he came to California, reaching San Francisco in the month of July. His first occupation was that of a miner, in Ophir district, in Placer county, where he experienced the trials and privations usually connected with that kind of life in those days. For eight years he followed that business, and in 1860 settled on the Mokelumne river, where he has since resided. Mr. Bamert has a fine ranch containing seven hundred acres, and is also largely interested in other tracts of land in connection with other parties. He has been extensively engaged in stock-raising, but more recently has turned his attention to the sheep business, in company with Pardeau & Borden. For thirteen years Mr. Bamert has been engaged in general merchandise, being first interested with Messrs. Woolsey & Palmer, afterward purchasing their interests in the stock of goods, and conducting the business himself. His natural ability for the trade has manifested itself throughout his years of experience and he ranks at the present time with the prosperous and successful business men of the county. He was married in 1876, to Miss Leah Shelburn, and their union has been blessed with two children, now aged three and one years respectively.

EDGAR BISHOP.

The subject of the following sketch is a native of New York State, having been born at Warrensburgh, Warren county, in 1839. Upon reaching his majority he left the familiar scenes of his childhood, and began the battle of life for himself, his objective point being California. His first location in this State was at Ione, Amador county, where he was engaged in trade from 1861 to 1866. In June of the last named year, he removed to the city of San Francisco, and for about fourteen years was widely known as a successful grocer of that thriving city. In the Spring of 1880, Mr. Bishop returned to Ione and purchased the stock and trade of Daniel Stewart, and is in possession of a large, thriving business.

He was married in San Francisco in October, 1873, to Mrs. Sophia C. Streeter, and their union is blessed with two children, both girls.

J. C. BLYTHER

Is a native of the State of Maine; was born in the town of Calais, Washington county, January 7, 1826. At the tender age of three years he removed with his parents to the city of New Orleans, Louisiana. In the "Crescent City" he received a liberal education, and resided there most of the time until 1850, at which time he came to California. Like nearly all the early pioneers of the "Golden State," his aspirations led him to seek his fortune in the mines, and his first occupation after reaching his destination was consequently that of delving in the earth in search of the precious nuggets. After a short time in his first location, he sought other places where it was believed dame fortune had deposited a larger supply of wealth for him; and, possessing a rambling nature, visited different parts of the State during the succeeding eleven years. In 1861 Mr. Blyther concluded to settle down, as he was a firm believer in the old adage that "a rolling stone gathers no moss," and in the last-named year located on the ranch, where he is very pleasantly situated at the present time, owning one of the best places on the Mokelumne river; though containing but two hundred acres, it is well cared for, and conducted on the true principle that land in order to be remunerative, must receive a certain amount of attention. He was married in 1866 to Mrs. Child, who had one child by a former marriage, that now lives with his parents, a bright, active young man of nineteen years. Mr. Blyther is a courteous gentleman, and in connection with his reputation as a good farmer, has the good-will and esteem of his neighbors, and is what might be called a self-made man.

JOHN A. BROWN

Was born in the town of Warsaw, State of Missouri, on the 25th of November, 1848. When he was a mere infant his parents came across the plains to California with ox-teams. The first recollections of which our subject is master, are of life in the golden State. His education was obtained in the schools of this State, and speaks volumes for the country that but a few years since, was known only to the hardy pioneers and the "dusky sons of the forest." The first location of the family after reaching the land of promise, was on Bear river, near Marysville. One year later they removed to Amador City, and soon after moved on to a farm near Sutter creek, where they remained fourteen years.

The subject of our sketch attended school until about twenty years of age, and at the early age of twenty-two years was elected as a Justice of the Peace, holding the office nearly two years. He was engaged in various kinds of business after leaving school, and put in some time prospecting; he also studied law for a couple of years, but during this time he had an ambition to become a civil engineer and surveyor, and accordingly fitted himself for that profession.

In 1878 he received the appointment of County Surveyor, to fill the vacancy caused by the death of that officer, and the same Summer received his papers appointing him a United States Deputy Surveyor. Since receiving his first appointment as County Surveyor, he has continued to fill that position to the present time, and has dispatched the duties of his office with entire satisfaction to his people and with credit to himself. In 1879 he made a survey of all the public roads of this county, and is at present engaged in making an elaborate county map. Mr. Brown is an accomplished and thorough gentleman in all the associations of life, and also fully appreciates the fact that his profession requires the attention, that he so readily gives to it.

He was married February 25, 1880, to Miss Virginia Hayden, one child having been born to them.

ANTHONY CAMINETTI

Was born at Jackson Gate, in Amador county, July 30, 1854, being one of the first children born in the county. His parents are natives of Italy. The first ten years of his life were passed in his native place, and at that age he went to the city of San Francisco, and attended school, for three years. In 1867, he returned to Jackson, and entered the employ of his Uncle, E. Caminetti, as clerk in his store. In this

GEORGE ALLEN.

MRS. GEO. ALLEN.

last position he remained about three years, and again went to San Francisco, and entered the law office of Quint & Hardy, as clerk, and remained in that capacity until the completion of the first trial of Laura D. Fair. He soon after entered the State University, at Oakland, where he pursued his studies until October 31, 1873, at which time he returned to Jackson, and commenced reading law in the office of J. T. Farley. In May, 1877, he was admitted to the Bar of California, and, during the same year, was elected as District Attorney. During the Legislative session of 1875-76, Mr. Caminetti filled the position of Assistant Journal Clerk of the Senate. He was at once recognized as a leader in politics, and in 1880 received the nomination as alternate elector on the Democratic Presidential ticket. In social life he is a genial gentleman, enjoying a large circle of friends, and though young in years, carries a well-balanced head; and we may expect to see him honored in a manner becoming his talents.

W. W. CARLILE

Was born in Carroll county, Ohio, December 3, 1839. He resided in that State until 1846, when he removed with his parents to Keokuk, Iowa, where he lived until 1862. When but little past his majority he discovered that it was not good for man to live alone, and took himself a wife, Miss Phebe Smith, who has blessed him with six children, four girls and two boys; all but one girl now living, who bid fair to inherit the virtues and industrious habits of both parents. May 7, 1862, himself and wife, packing their worldly estate into a wagon, started for California with an ox-team, full of hope and determination that if hard work would wrench good fortune out of the California chaos, they would have a share of the gold and other good things. The daily plodding through the sands and climbing of mountains terminated, and one evening they let their eyes feast on the green valleys of Ione, which formed such a contrast to the alkaline plains of the two thousand miles they had so wearily traversed. They rented a farm and orchard in the interior of the valley, and sunrise and sunset saw him either at work on his place or on the way to market. In those days all kinds of farm produce brought a good price, and in a few years he had accumulated several thousand dollars, enough, as he thought, to give him a good start in the *West*, for like most early comers to California he had not learned to consider California an inviting home. In 1872 he pulled up all his stakes and removed to Kansas, with the intention of making that State his home. But, alas! he had not calculated for the cold winters. He did not like the idea of having his heels freeze while his toes were toasting at a fierce fire; one winter of it was enough. The following Spring he was on his way to California, and reached it in due time a wiser, if not a wealthier, man, for this bit of experience had made quite a hole in his little capital. But the word fail had no place in his vocabulary. He was not long in getting under way, and soon bought the place on which he now resides, it being in the neighborhood of the noted Q ranch, containing some of the best land in the famous Ione valley. In addition to farming his own place he has been engaged in threshing for the many farmers in his vicinity. His love for machinery and knowledge of mechanics has enabled him to make many improvements in the steam power and separators, one of which is likely to become extensively adopted. This is an attachment to the engine to raise the grain to the separator without the aid of horses. As the machine is under the control of the engineer, it makes a saving of both horse and man power. It is needless to say that Mr. Carlile has secured a patent for the improvement, it being the first in this direction. Our readers will better understand the nature of the improvement by consulting the engraving in the body of the work. Coal in considerable quantity is found on his ranch, and the same stream of gravel that has made good *diggings* on the Coffin place, also traverses his.

JAMES CUMMING.

Few men have a more varied or extensive experience than Dr. Cumming. A volume of interesting incidents might be written without exhausting the subject. He is a native of Tennessee, first seeing the sunlight February 10, 1813, among the mountains of the eastern part of the State, which has produced so many extraordinary men, such as Andrew Johnson and Parson Brownlow, Grainger county being his birthplace. He received a liberal education, both classical and scientific, being a graduate of the University of Knoxville. He afterwards studied medicine, graduating in the Transylvania University of Kentucky. He spent some years in the practice of medicine in Decatur, Alabama, but, in consequence of ill-health, was forced to leave that section of country, removing in 1836 to Peoria, Illinois, where, in addition to the practice of medicine, he engaged extensively in real estate transactions. He rapidly accumulated property, soon becoming rich. January 17, 1842, he married Miss Mary Ann Dorsey, daughter of Captain Chas. S. Dorsey, of Kentucky. It was remarked that the richest man had married the handsomest woman in four counties, this seeming anomaly arising from the fact that the Dorsey residence stood on the corners of four counties. Miss Dorsey made him an inestimable companion, and still retains much of the beauty which forty years ago made her the queen of all the prairie flowers. They have had three children, none of whom are living to inherit the beauty of the mother, or the intellectual qualifications of the father.

His extensive business operations carried him to

different parts of the Union, his longest stay being made in New Mexico, near Santa Fé, where he engaged in trade, and also in government contracts. His knowledge of the Spanish language, and the character of the peons, enabled him to render the Government efficient service. His experiences among the ignorant and prejudiced, but not by any means bad, natives would make interesting and valuable reading matter, if the doctor could be induced to commit it to paper. In 1859, he so far closed his business in New Mexico as to permit his leaving the Territory and becoming a citizen of California. He was among the first to take passage by the line of overland stages established about that time. Soon after arriving in this State he purchased the property known as the brick flour mills, which he enlarged and otherwise improved, until he can do as good work as is done in the State. The mill has both water and steam-power, the water-power being obtained by a ditch which taps Sutter creek about two miles above the town, the steam-power being used when the water is low. Dr. Cumming is a noted inventor, he having constructed the first plow that would scour in the fat prairies of the West. He has patented two important improvements in the turbine wheel, one of which was to contract the openings so as to utilize the whole fall with a small head of water. He has also some thirty other patents, which have been generally adopted. He has occupied many positions of honor, such as army surgeon, member of the Illinois Legislature, magistrate, etc. Fort Cumming was named in his honor. He has not accepted any official position in California.

WILLIAM O. CLARK.

WILLIAM O. CLARK.

A personal acquaintance with the subject of this sketch enables the writer to give more of the history of this natural orator than he would be likely to communicate to any one for publication. He was born in Madison, Indiana, January 21, 1817, and consequently has seen most of the strides that Indiana, as well as other western States, has made in population and wealth. He came to California in an early day, and found ample material in the abundant dram-drinking of California to arouse into action all his powers of oratory, and he early sounded the tocsin of alarm, and proclaimed the evils of intemperance in every town, from Siskiyou to San Diego, organizing temperance societies in every possible place. He is possessed of a sanguine temperament that throws all power available into a contest when once a decision is made, and he made his influence felt wherever saloons existed. He is said to have spent several fortunes in the cause. He has been G. W. P. of the Sons of Temperance for many successive terms. In 1872 he made a trip around the world, visiting England, France, Sicily, Egypt, the Holy Land, India, China and Japan, carrying the temperance colors all the time, and lecturing upon it whenever practicable. He has resided in Drytown, except when traveling on his special mission, for twenty-six years. He suffered heavily in the great fire of 1857, but saved something from the general wreck. The brick store he claims to be the oldest brick structure in the county. Other brick buildings were erected before his, but went down in some of the numerous fires which visited every town. He was married in 1857, to Miss Julia Appleby of Ottawa, Illinois. She was noted as combining extraordinary beauty with a vigorous intellect, and in a suitable sphere would have taken high rank. There was little room in Drytown a quarter of a century since, however, for the exercise of those gifts which in the centers of population would have made her a queen of society. They have one child, a son, living. Mr. Clark amuses himself in his intervals of business, by cultivating the hills around Drytown in grain, and demonstrating their ability to produce something besides grapes.

THOMPSON DAVIS

Was born in the State of Missouri in 1833. At the age of twenty years he emigrated to California, settling at Placerville (Hangtown), in El Dorado county, where he lived for two years, when he came to Volcano, where he mined for one year; thence to Oleta where he lived for two years; thence to Upper Rancheria, where he also mined for two years. Placer mining becoming rather precarious, he tried farming in Buckeye valley, near Carbondale, for ten years. He then engaged in the mercantile business near Drytown for eight years. In 1879 he removed to Plymouth, where he erected a store and enlarged his business. He has since made this place his home. He was married in 1866 to Miss Maria A. Davies. They have four children.

R. C. DOWNS

Was born in Bristol, Hartford county, Connecticut, on the 19th of April, 1828, where he passed his early years. At the age of eighteen he went to New York City, where he was employed as a clerk in a dry goods establishment. On the 25th of January, 1849, he sailed from the latter city in the ship *Tahmaroo*, Captain Richardson, master; and on the first of the following July, landed in San Francisco. He at once left for the mines, his first location being on the north fork of the American river, where he remained until the Fall of that year. He then removed to Amador creek, and was engaged in the same business until the following Spring. From 1850 until 1859 he was engaged in merchandising at Amador, Rancheria, Sutter Creek and Volcano, in company with Levi Hanford, having establishments at each of those places. Mr. Hanford had charge of the stores, Mr. Downs generally remaining in the city purchasing and forwarding goods. They were eminently successful, the firm of Hanford & Downs becoming well known over the State. From 1860 to 1873 he was part owner and superintendent of the Lincoln quartz mine at Sutter Creek, Leland Stanford being a partner. He made the mine a paying institution. The succeeding four years he spent in traveling, making several trips to the Eastern States, as well as traveling extensively through California. In the Summer of 1877, in connection with J. M. Hanford, he opened a mine near Volcano, now bearing his name, which they have worked successfully ever since. Mr. Downs is also owner of the Golden Eagle mine, near Sutter Creek, which he is now prospecting. He was elected to the Assembly of the State Legislature in 1879–80, an office he filled to the entire satisfaction of his constituents. He has recently built a fine residence at Sutter Creek, where he intends making his permanent home. He was married in his native town, in October, 1856, and has three sons aged respectively eighteen, sixteen and thirteen years.

THOMAS W. EASTON

Is a native of England, though he came to America in company with his parents when he was but eight years of age. He was born September 1, 1823, in the county of Kent. The family settled in Otsego county, New York. Soon after reaching America, the boy, feeling strong enough to go alone, started out in life on his own account, going first to Cattaraugus county, where he engaged in farming for some years, or until he was twenty-one years old, when he went to Saginaw county, Michigan, where he followed teaching private school for two seasons. Following up the injunction to *go west*, he made another move, this time to Wisconsin, in which State he resided four years, engaged, most of the time, in farming. In 1848, being then twenty-five years of age, he married Miss Lucinda Jane Van Loan, who was a native of New York. In 1854 Mr. Easton, with his wife and two children—a daughter and son—crossed the plains to California, making their first halt in Sacramento county, going afterwards to Placerville for a few months, finally settling in El Dorado county, where he lived until October, 1873, his principal business being mining, though he united with this the business of keeping a hotel during seven years of the time. In 1873 he came to Plymouth, then rapidly growing up in consequence of the development of the mines under the management of Alvinza Hayward, and engaged in keeping a hotel. In June, 1877, he was completely ruined in financial matters by the great fire of that year; but the energy which had wrested success out of apparent defeat so many times was not exhausted, and another one was soon flourishing. His family consists of himself, wife and four children.

S. W. EMMONS

Was born January 31, 1829, at Chillicothe, Ross county, Ohio. When but three years of age he removed with his parents to the State of Michigan, where he lived on a farm until he reached the age of eighteen years. Having acquired a common school education from the meagre facilities of his neighborhood by attending school during the Winter terms, he left home and went to Detroit, and entered a machine shop for the purpose of learning the trade of a machinist, spending the next five years in so doing.

In 1853 he saw bright and golden prospects in California, and, to realize his hopes in that direction, sailed for the Pacific coast, which he reached in due time, by way of the Isthmus. He at once entered the mines in El Dorado county, but soon after went to Mokelumne Hill, in Calaveras county, where he followed mining until 1856, with varied success. In 1857 he accepted a position as engineer in Clinton, Amador county, where he remained one year. His next move was to accept a position at the New York branch saw-mill, and had charge of the engine from 1858 to 1864. In the last-named year, he took the management of the engine and machinery at the Oneida mine, which he retained two years. He was afterwards in a like position in Jackson, in the Kennedy mine. In all these responsible positions Mr. Emmons succeeded admirably in giving entire satisfaction to his employers, and became noted for his excellent management. Tiring of this occupation, and requiring out-door exercise, he engaged in farming at the New York ranch, which he followed about two years. He then bought the Pine Grove hotel, a place well and favorably known throughout the country, located on the Jackson and Volcano road, ten miles north-east of the former place, and has since catered to the wants of his guests in a creditable manner.

Mr. Emmons was married on New Year's day, 1873, to Miss Eliza Beem, a native of Illinois, and their union is blessed with one child, a son, about five years of age.

The hotel and surroundings of Mr. Emmons can best be appreciated by a glance at the view herein contained on another page.

PETER FAGAN

Is a native of Canada West, having been born at a place called Bytown, now known as Ottawa, in the year 1835. The first sixteen years of his life were passed on Canadian soil, and his early education was obtained in the schools of his native town.

In 1851 he emigrated with his parents to the State of Illinois, and located in Bureau county, and for about eight years devoted his time to the tilling of the soil, which experience was of service to him in later years. In 1858 he came to California, by way of New Orleans and Havana. He remained a short time in San Francisco, and then came to Amador county, locating at Sutter Creek, where he has since resided, engaged in various occupations. The first four years of his residence at this place, he was engineer at the Eureka mine, a position he filled with more than ordinary ability. He then turned his attention to teaming, and for two years followed that business.

Desiring something better suited to his tastes, he gave up teaming and opened a livery stable, and has the satisfaction of knowing that his is the only first-class establishment of the kind in the town, in fact, no better can be found in many large cities. He is also considerably interested in ranching, owning a fine farm, containing two hundred acres. He has a mill in which he grinds the feed for his livery stock, and also for the public. The mill was originally run by steam, but is now run by water-power.

Mr. Fagan is one of the live men, noted for energy and executive ability, and deserves, and does possess, the confidence of the community. He held the responsible position of Sheriff, in the years 1874-75, and performed the duties of the office to the satisfaction of all.

He was married in 1864, to Miss Maggie Duke, a native of New York. They have seven children living, six girls and one boy.

H. C. FARNHAM

Is a native of New York, having been born July 12, 1827, at Forestville, in Chester county. Here he acquired some education, and, what is of much more importance, the habits of industry and economy, which in every well regulated community are essential to success. At the age of eighteen, on foot and alone, with his whole estate in his hands, he started out on his life career. He was a splendid penman and felt confident of paying his way by teaching penmanship along the lines of travel, which he did, forming classes at many points, teaching the young ideas how to —— write. He brought up at Milwaukee after six months of this, his first experience, in the world. Seeing no opening for work with his pen, he turned to the plane and saw, and worked at the carpenter business until 1850, when he enlisted in the great column bound for California, and one hot, sunny day found himself wandering around the streets and mining holes of Hangtown, wondering *what next?* He mined around Placerville for a couple of years, and then, early in 1853, went to Fiddletown, now Oleta, and in company with James McLeod erected the first saw-mill in the vicinity. Through some faulty construction or setting, the boiler collapsed a flue and was thrown many feet out of its bed, fatally wounding two men (McLeod being one), and severely injuring Mr. Farnham, the flying boiler, with McLeod on the end, passing between Mr.

STEPHEN FINN.
(DECEASED)

Farnham and another man sitting at a table in the office. Notwithstanding the accident the mill was repaired, and has done good work ever since, though the cutting away of the timber has necessitated several removals of the mill farther into the mountains.

He has a fine ranch of two hundred and eighty acres, of the deep, productive granite soil, in the immediate vicinity of Oleta, with large barns and elegant house. Several large teams hauling lumber to the mills of Plymouth and Amador, make the place look like business. In fact, Mr. Farnham is a business man; every line in his face, every move of his feet and look of his eyes, together with the system of order displayed on his farm, in his barns and shops, and mill, indicate the ruling motive of the man. He has an unmitigated contempt for the whining, indolent men, who stand around with their hands in their pockets, saying "the country is played out, nothing more to do." He has full faith in California, and believes it the best State in the Union.

He was married April 1, 1854, to Miss Eunice Haynes, a native of New York, by whom he has had seven children, two daughters and five boys, now living.

STEPHEN FINN.

Few places in Amador county are better known than Finn's ranch. Like the Q ranch, Buena Vista, Buckeye, and other well-known places, it was not a town, but like them early became noted as among the first to establish the comforts of home and its refining influences, and reveal the possibilities of the new State. It was hardly possible to come into the county without hearing of Finn's ranch, or to converse about any matter without mentioning it. Every place was located as so many miles from Finn's ranch. Stephen Finn was born in County Wicklow, Ireland, December 26, 1829. Some nine years afterward his parents, following the great stream of emigration, went to Canada with their family of four children, Stephen being the youngest. They settled in the county of Kent, and commenced anew the struggle for a home. A rigorous climate, lands to be cleared of trees, and buildings to be erected, made this a laborious task, but young Finn did not flinch from the trial, but stayed by his parents until the coming of age, acquiring the habits of industry and self-reliance which proved so valuable in the State of his adoption.

On the sixteenth day of February, 1852, he married Miss Catherine Martin, a native of Canada, of French descent, who was born August 2, 1830. From this marriage came nine children, of whom six survive. In 1853 Mr. Finn, with his young wife, came to California, settling first in El Dorado, then known as Mud Springs. Their stay there was short, however, soon moving to this county, which he made a home for more than a quarter of a century, or until his death, which occurred on February 28, 1880.

He was a Roman Catholic in his religious opinions, but his charity and hospitality was not limited by church lines, all being welcomed to the comforts of his home, until the white house under the tree became famous for its good cheer. Easter, Christmas, New Years, and Thanksgiving, as well as birthdays, all found a large company of neighbors and friends at his table.

He was a good citizen, industrious in his business, true to his promises, and faithful in every position in life.

L. J. FONTENROSE.

This gentleman was born September 27, 1850, of Italian parents, coming with them to California seven years later. He received his education in the public school of Sutter Creek, carrying off a large share of the honors, being, in every sense of the word, but birth, a native Californian. His education has been supplemented by a liberal course of reading, encouraged by his father, who early perceived the advantages of education to a citizen of the Republic. At the age of fifteen he entered a mercantile house, which position he retained until he was twenty-one, when he abandoned that business and engaged in quartz mining, running an engine most of the time. At the death of his father, five years later, he returned to his home and took charge of the business until 1879, when he was appointed Deputy County Clerk, a position he was especially qualified to fill. At the county election held in 1880, he was chosen to the same position which he still retains. He is a trusty, patient, pains-taking man, and wins the confidence of all with whom he has business.

MARGARET FOSTER.

The lady referred to in the following sketch is a native of the State of Illinois, having been born in Madison county on the 15th of February, 1818. Her life was passed in her native State until the year 1852, at which time she, in company with her husband, crossed the plains to California and settled in Amador county. She was married February 14, 1842, to Claiborne Foster, who departed this life at the place where his widow still resides, September 6, 1876. Being left alone in the world with the exception of her two children, Mrs. Foster managed the business and ranch in a very creditable manner to herself. She has conducted a hotel for the weary traveler and teamster for some years, and it is a pleasure to become an inmate of her hospitable home. Her ranch is beautifully situated in the mountains six miles from Volcano, on the old emigrant road, and contains three hundred acres of choice land. Her union with Mr. Foster was blessed with two children, both girls, who are married, and each have families of their own.

JOHN H. GRAMBART

Was born July 22, 1830, near Bremerhaven, in the Kingdom of Hanover. He came to New York in October, 1845, and to California, via Panama, in 1853, arriving in San Francisco on the anniversary of Washington's birthday. He came to Drytown soon after, and engaged in the retail dry goods and grocery business with J. C. Williams. He was married August 15, 1860, to Miss E. D. Wells, daughter of Mr. H. Wells, of Amador Crossing. They have one child, a boy, thirteen years of age. He purchased the Central House in company with his father-in-law, Mr. H. Wells, February 4, 1863. This is one of the best known places in the county, occupying a central position on the lines of travel. It can hardly be surpassed for natural scenery and beauty of location, having an extended view of Sacramento valley and the western part of the State.

CHARLES GREEN

Is a native of Ohio, having been born in Licking county, December 5, 1830, in which State he resided until 1850, when he emigrated, coming to California. His first halt was made in Sacramento, when, attracted by the rich bottom-lands and beautiful crops, he went to farming, raising stock, hay and grain. He sold out in 1852, and moved to Yolo county, engaging in much the same business, where he again stayed about two years. Like almost every one, he had to try his luck in the mines, and mined two years at Salmon Falls, on the American river. In 1862 he went to Folsom and became interested in a large flouring mill, which he ran for three years. He then went out on the line of the Central Pacific railway, in the interest of T. H. Carroll & Co. He again turned to the mines, and in 1870 located in Amador county, looking for two and a half years after the property of the Sacramento and Amador Canal Company. In 1872 he went into the employment of the Phœnix Mill and Mining Company, then controlled by the Hoopers, as superintendent of the ditch, and was finally made foreman of the mill, and eventually superintendent. His incumbency was marked by a great development of all the works about the mine, until it became the most extensive in the county. He was married, June 23, 1878, to Miss E. M. Russell, a native of Illinois, having been born September 19, 1848, in the town of Fillmore, Cole county. Mr. Green has a beautiful residence with pleasant surroundings, situated on a gentle eminence overlooking the town of Plymouth, a large portion of the western part of the county, and part of the Sacramento valley. His family at this time, 1881, is himself, wife and one child.

I. B. GREGORY

Was born in Sumner county, Tennessee, April 5, 1819, and for the succeeding thirteen years remained a resident of that State. His advantages for obtaining an education were somewhat limited, but he managed, by energy and close attention to his studies, to acquire a knowledge of the common branches, to which he added, in after years, a large amount of practical knowledge, which places him on a firm basis in that direction. In 1832 he removed from Tennessee to the State of Missouri, where he remained until 1846, at which time he went to Texas, and for about three years was a resident of that State. In 1849 he again emigrated, this time to Iowa, and stayed there three years, and then returned to Missouri. One year later he started for California by way of the plains, and after experiencing the usual incidents connected with such a trip, reached his objective point and located at Ione City, Amador county, where he followed the occupation of contractor and builder. In 1862 Mr Gregory was elected a Supervisor of his district, serving in that position about three years. In 1867-68, he represented his people in the Assembly of the State Legislature, in a very creditable manner to himself and to the entire satisfaction of his constituents, and was solicited to again accept the nomination for the same office, but declined. Mr. Gregory possesses the enviable distinction of being almost the only man ever elected to office in the county who did not urge his canvass with whisky. Some years since he joined a temperance society, the secretary of which firmly pasted the two sheets containing his signature and pledge, together, in consequence of which he cannot erase his name, and still feels bound by the obligation. His honor and integrity are the brightest jewels in his character. About three years since he removed from Ione City to his present home in Jackson valley, a view of which is to be found in this volume. Mr. Gregory was married to Miss Martha Jane McMurry, March 2, 1843; nine children are living at the present time to bless their union, one being laid to rest to meet them no more on earth.

A. C. HAM

Was born on the Licking river in Kentucky in 1841. Soon after the family removed to Illinois, where they resided until 1855, when they came to California, joining the father, J. C. Ham, the extensive contractor and builder, who had preceded them some years. They made their residence at Aqueduct City, the headquarters of some of the largest enterprises of the senior member of the family. Young Ham soon "struck out" for himself, engaging in mining and other business. On the opening of the Amador wagon road our friend established a hotel, called Ham's Station, about twenty miles above Volcano, which he managed for some years, but which since the building of the larger hotel at Aqueduct City, he has left to the management of an agent. Mr. Ham has now become sole owner of the Modoc mine, in the Pioneer district. The mine bids fair to take its place among the bullion producers of the Pacific coast. Persons wishing for a few days' rural amusement in a romantic valley will do well to make Mr. Ham's place their headquarters, as he is familiar with all the resorts of the grizzlies and other game.

FRANKLIN HERMAN.

The subject of the following sketch is a native of Pennsylvania, having been born in Franklin county, February 27, 1830. When five years of age he removed with his parents to the wilds of Ohio, where he remained until he entered the army, and engaged in the war with Mexico. His education was received in the common schools, and leaving school and friends at such an early age, he was necessarily deprived of advantages in that line. He, however, obtained a thorough knowledge of the common branches, and with his one year's service in the army placed himself on a fair footing with many who received more advantageous schooling.

At the expiration of his term of service he returned to Ohio, where he remained about two years. He was married when quite young to Miss Mary G. Dreisbach, a native of Ohio, and soon after started with his bride for the Pacific coast, and located at Shasta in 1853, where he remained about four months. He is by trade a blacksmith, a business he has followed during all his life on this coast. Upon leaving Shasta he settled at Sutter Creek, Amador county, where he has since resided.

Mr. Herman is at the present time engaged by the Mahoney Mining Company, as a true son of Vulcan. He has very few superiors, and is withal a gentleman in whom repose the respect and confidence of all who know him. His family consists of himself, wife and two children, a son and daughter.

R. S. AND J. M. HINKSON

Are natives of Washington county, Missouri, where they resided until 1849, when they crossed the plains with the extensive family of that name, with their connections by marriage, the Boones. They located at Drytown, on the north side of the creek, in what was soon after El Dorado county, Dry creek being the dividing line. Few families have been better known than the Hinksons. They were the first to open and develop the Potosi mine. The elderly Hinkson did more, perhaps, to restrain and calm the anger of the people during the terrible affair of August, 1855, than any other man, his age and reputation being appreciated by the honest, though hasty miners. The two sons whose names are at the head of this article, came to Volcano in 1879, and engaged in the livery business, which they are still carrying on. They run a stage line to Jackson and also have a mail contract between Jackson and Volcano, and also carry the express for Wells, Fargo & Co., and do an express business on their own account. They both have families residing in Volcano. The Hinksons are reckoned among the solid, reliable men of the county.

FRANK HOFFMAN

Was born April 18, 1827, in Evarsdorf, in Germany, coming to America at the early age of sixteen, New Orleans being his first residence. After remaining here three months he went to St. Louis, in Missouri, where he remained seven years, engaged in the butchering business. In 1850 he fell into the big column of immigration and crossed the plains to California, reaching Mud Springs (El Dorado) among the earliest. Here he followed the same business as in St. Louis until the following Spring, in company with John P. Hoffman, now living near Ukiah City. In the Spring he went to Grass Valley and started business there, continuing in it for about six months, when he sold out and went to the Missouri House, near Auburn, where he remained about six months. Mokelumne river was his next location, settling on a ranch and remaining about four years. While engaged in ranching with a partner, they started a livery stable at Mokelumne Hill, but not being satisfied with it, they abandoned the project, but started in the following season the same business at Jackson, which venture proved profitable and permanent, for the business has been continued in the same place to the present day.

He was married in 1862 to Miss Christina Clem. They have no children.

He has a well-equipped stable, fine residence, and a highly cultivated farm of one hundred and sixty acres, adjoining the town of Jackson. He is one of the solid men of the county, who was willing to wrest wealth out of the chaos of early days, with hard work and close attention to business, and who did it too.

JAMES H. HOLMAN

Was born in the town of Versailles, Indiana, February 18, 1831, residing there until he was twenty-one years of age, acquiring the education and business habits which has served him to such good purpose in California. The great wave of gold fever, which swept over the country in 1852, took him from the parent home, and March 1st we find him among the crowd, driving an ox-team and plodding his weary way across the plains towards the sunset. The longest journey must have an end, and August 7th he looked down into the Hangtown (Placerville) basin, famous for murder, hanging and gambling, as well as its rich placers. What a contrast then with now; then Lucky Bill was coining money on the streets, a meal of bread, tough steak and black coffee was worth a dollar, and Coon Hollow was giving up its millions to those who would dig. The oldest *Yuba Dammer* would say that it was a "right peert place;" now——? He followed mining for two years and then went to teaming, a business which he has followed extensively to the present time, latterly for the Empire Mining and Mill Company at Plymouth. In 1856 he located at Fiddletown (Oleta) where he remained for five or six years. In 1870 he located on his present ranch one mile and a half west of the town of Plymouth, and commenced making a permanent home. His farm contains 160 acres of highly improved land. In connection with farming and teaming he has raised stock of all kinds. He enjoys the confidence of the community and has held several responsible offices. He was married August 4, 1856, to Miss Catherine Ashby, a native of Illinois, by whom he had one child, not now living. Mr. Holman's surroundings are pleasant and comfortable, a good place to anchor to, after the *hurry-skurry* of thirty years of excitement and labor.

JOHN HOSLEY.

"I knew him, Horatio; a fellow of infinite jest, of most excellent fancy." Who does not know John; "rough, but generous, brave and kind." He has played more jokes, said more pithy things, and spent and given away more money than any other man of his inches or avoirdupois in the county, if not in the State. The good jokes and sayings of his would fill a book, and make interesting reading, too. His love of fun is the strongest element in his character. Sample No. 1 of a lot: A number of San Francisco mining sharps had been to Washoe in an early day, and returning with sacks of ore from newly-discovered mines, stopped at his place. He listened to their speculations about the value of this and that package of ore, and after they had gone to bed, judiciously exchanged ores, putting in those he knew to be first-class. They continued their way to San Francisco, and hastened to put their specimens in the hands of the assayers. Their most extravagant hopes were realized. The ores assayed up into thousands. Companies were formed, the mines purchased, and the expectant millionaires started back in all haste to take possession and make their fortunes, but no ores of the same sort were found. When they related the circumstances, they had the comforting remark that they were sold by old John, whereat they went home wiser, but not wealthier men.

He was born in Yorkshire, England, July 14, 1825, emigrating when about ten years of age. He first lived in Canada, but afterwards in Vermont, coming to California in 1849 among the pioneers. He lived at Mokelumne Hill for some years, and ran the first ferry-boat that was established on the river, it being at first only a dug-out. He enlarged it to a plank-boat, capable of carrying three or four passengers, and finally sold out, having made all the money he wanted. Dr. Soher soon afterwards purchased the same institution for twelve thousand dollars, and expending some thirty thousand dollars more, inaugurated the Big Bar bridge. John was present at the birth of Mokelumne Hill, knew all its crooked habits; knew all the defaulting treasurers, sheriffs, and tax-collectors; can tell more yarns of their doings than they or their friends will like to have recorded. He has made many rich discoveries in quartz and placer, but money would never stick to his fingers long enough to stain them a bit. What he had belonged to all his friends, and their name was legion. As the country became settled up, and the free, flush times of '49 became impossible, he retreated into the mountains, and is now manager and proprietor of the toll-road leading over the mountains from Antelope Springs to Kirkwood's and Carson valleys. He has a nice place some nine miles east of Volcano, where we advise all to repair who wish to catch a whiff of pioneer times, or get materials for a book of fun.

JOHN W. HUTCHINS

Is a native of the State of Maine, and was born in Hermon, Penobscot county, June 24, 1828. His father was one of the principal farmers and lumber-dealers of that section of the country, and our subject was trained to those callings during his early life. He received a common school education, and in 1853 cut loose from the ties that bound him to his native town, and sought his fortune in the far West. During the last-named year he arrived in California, and for ten years was engaged in mining in Amador county. In 1863 he entered the United States Army as a member of the seventh regiment, California Volunteers, and served as a soldier for about eighteen months. His service was principally in Arizona, a country well calculated to destroy the ambition of the most valiant and patriotic of our boys in blue. After his discharge from the service he returned to Clinton, where he has since resided. Mr. Hutchins has held the office of Justice of the Peace, being elected in 1856 and '57, a position he creditably filled. The history of his successes and reverses in fortune would fill an ordinary volume. He is unmarried.

W. C. JONES

Was born in Lewis county, Missouri, April 1, 1834, where he spent his boyhood until he was eighteen years of age. Being of an energetic temperament, he broke away from the comforts of home and made his way to the land of gold, by way of the plains, arriving in Diamond Springs, El Dorado county, September 30, 1852, where he remained engaged in mining until 1857, when he removed to Amador county. He was married October 11, 1857, to Mrs. Elizabeth

ISAAC LEPLEY.

Kelley, by whom he has had six children, four of whom are now living. He takes naturally to keeping hotel, having been mostly engaged in that business since his residence in the county. All the travelers on the road in 1859-60 will remember the comforts of the Revere House under his management. He recently purchased a tract of one hundred and sixty acres among the romantic hills, two and one-half miles east of Ione, which he is fitting up as a pleasant stopping place, and as a resort for persons seeking rest and amusement. The character of his improvements will be best learned from the fine engraving of them which accompanies this volume.

THOMAS KERR

Was born in 1843 in Crawford county, Pennsylvania, where he remained until he was fourteen years of age, during which time he took advantage of such opportunities of informing his mind as the place afforded. He came to California in 1860, locating at once in the town of Amador which he has since made his home. For a few years he engaged in freighting, the immense quantities of timber and other supplies needed in the heavy mining around the town, making that a very extensive business. After four years of this kind of work he engaged in the livery business, which he has since followed. In 1871 he was married to Miss Augusta Fassett, a native of Illinois, who died February 25, 1880. Have three children, two boys and one girl. Mr. Kerr is a Californian in spirit and fact, his active years so far, having been given to the Golden State.

STEPHEN P. KIDD

Was born in Colne, Lancashire, England, in 1825, living there until he was twenty-three years of age, following the business of landscape gardener, seedsman and florist, callings for which he had been regularly educated. In 1848 he came to the United States, and four years afterwards to California in company with the Surface family, who settled on Dry creek. In the Summer after his arrival he engaged in mining at the old Winters Bar, opposite Lancha Plana, following his trade the following Summer on the rich lands of Dry creek. Being naturally of a scientific turn of mind he soon mastered all that was known of mines and mining, and his advice became valuable in connection with the mines afterwards discovered in Nevada, some of the most extensive and profitable ventures in that State being inaugurated by him. The fine, artistic plans on the Edwards place, now owned by Younglove, was the result of his skill as a landscape gardener. After spending some years in the Nevada mines he finally settled down on a beautiful place in Jackson valley to make a home for his young and interesting family, he having married Miss Mary M. Goodding December 13, 1870; but God disposes. In the midst of his projects he was taken sick, and on Sunday eve he breathed his last.

As a man Mr. Kidd was quiet and unassuming, always cheerful, with a kindly word for all. In his business relations he was exact and reliable, managing with justice and discretion. Nature forms but few such men.

MERWIN LEACH

Was born in Franklin county, Vermont, in 1837, and came across the plains in 1860, bringing up in Amador City, where he lived for ten years. In 1870 he went to Plymouth, residing there for one year; thence to Church Union mines in El Dorado county for two years; thence to Kelsey, where he remained until April 18, 1881, when he returned to Plymouth, and purchased a half-interest in the store of Thompson Davis, with whom he has since remained. He is not married at the time of this writing.

ISAAC LEPLEY.

It is to be regretted that we have no personal history of this distinguished inventor. We can only form an opinion of his early days by the fruits of his matured mind and judgment. Those who are familiar with mining will appreciate the value of the machine at sight. For the information of many of our readers who have never seen a mine, we may explain that thousands of framed timbers are put into the mines; some to secure the walls from coming together when the vein matter is extracted; some to secure the passages from one part of the mine to the other, in short, timber is wanted everywhere, with mortises and corresponding tenons or slots, as the case may be. In a building every stick is planned beforehand; a hundred men may work at the different parts, but in a mine no one knows what is wanted until the emergency comes. The bell rings; an order comes for a timber of certain dimensions with tenons and slots; the safety of the mine, perhaps of human lives, depends upon having it immediately. Sometimes dozens of carpenters are kept in waiting for such emergencies; when the order comes they jump on a log and work as if at a fire; but haste and want of space makes confusion, and liability of mistakes and accidents. The automatic timber-framing machine is equal to a dozen carpenters. The powerful cutting head, which, by means of hand screws, is easily handled, bends down to the log and rapidly chips a tenon or a slot, cutting a bevel or a circle at the will of the operator; makes a mortise, enlarges it to the required dimensions, and in a moment the piece goes whizzing down the shaft a thousand feet, ready to go in where the cracking timbers and crumbling rocks indicate a coming disaster, and the danger is averted. The following description, with accompanying engraving, from the *Scientific and Mining Press*, will be read with pleasure:—

Isaac Lepley, of Amador City, Amador county, has recently invented a novel piece of mechanism, which is intended for the framing of timbers of all kinds, which are to be joined together. One of the machines is now in operation at the Keystone Consolidated mine, Amador.

The invention consists in the employment of a cutter head or heads, which are caused to rotate upon a suitable frame, and this frame is moved both vertically and horizontally by means of slides and guides, so that the cutters may be carried across the timbers upon either one or all four sides to form a tenon, dovetail, or other cut; and if desired, a round tenon may be formed by the use of a link which has one end fixed to the frame, so that the slides will move in a manner to carry the tool around in a circle.

In the engraving, A represents the cutter head, which is caused to rotate upon its shaft by a belt to the pulley, B, so that the cutter acts as a planer. It may be of sufficient height for the tenon to be cut, or by moving the timber or carriage the length desired may be cut at two or more operations. Its shaft is journaled at the top of a frame, C. This frame is moved up and down in guides upon the frame, E, by means of friction rollers, F, which press against a vertical central bar, K, which extends parallel with the frame, C. These rollers, F, are driven by pinions upon their shafts, and a hand wheel or other device upon a main shaft at the end of the machine, as shown.

The frame, E, is also adapted to move horizontally upon the main frame, G, by means of similar gearing to that which moves the frame, C, and by these two motions, it will be seen that the cutters may be moved in any direction. The log is laid upon a carriage with its end near the frame, and its height is so adjusted, that when the frame, E, is moved across horizontally, the revolving cutters will be carried across, so as to make a cut to the depth desired.

The frame, C, is then moved downward, and the cutters will cut the vertical face upon one side. The frame, C, then remains stationary, while the frame, E, is moved horizontally backward upon the guides on the main frame, and the cutters will complete the lower part of the tenon. The frame, E, is then held stationary and the frame, C, is again moved upward, so that the cutters will be carried upward across the remaining side, and the tenon will be finished.

The cutters are blades secured to a head similar to those used upon planer-heads, but in order to make the vertical cut at the inner end of the tenon so that it will present a clean, square surface, sliding plates are fitted to move in grooves on the end of the planer-head. Their outer ends are toothed, or formed so as to make the proper cut, and they are held in place by set-screws.

In order to allow the cutter shaft and its driving pulley to move in the directions and to the distances as described, the belt which drives it is carried over tightening pulleys, suitably arranged in sliding frames with weights.

The tenons here described are those which are usually made upon the ends of timbers in timbering up mines. The timbers are united, and these tenons allow the timbers to be properly set together. It will be obvious, however, that this apparatus may be employed to make any kind of a cut on a timber, or to square up the ends of timber, as the cutter may be moved in any direction required. Upon the end of the cutter shaft, opposite the planer-head, is a peculiarly shaped boring and cutting tool, J, which is intended to form mortises either in the sides or ends of timbers. The end of this tool is nearly flat, but is provided with a cutting bit, which enables it to enter the timber as far as may be desired.

The sides of the tool (which is cylindrical in shape) are cut away so as to form an enclosed cutting edge, and after it has entered the timber far enough to give the required depth, the frame, E, may be moved upon the frame, G, where the side cutter will cut away the wood until the mortise is as long as desired. The same style of cutter may be employed to form what is termed the boxing, or the depression which is cut across the timber equal to the length of the mortise, to receive the foot of the timber which is tenoned to fit the mortise.

The tenon to fit the mortise is formed by the cutter, A, in the same manner as has been described, except that the ends must be rounded to fit the ends of the mortise, which may be left curved by the tool, J. In order to make these rounded ends to the tenon, it is necessary to produce a compound motion of the two frames, C and E, one of which, as before described, moves vertically, while the other moves horizontally.

This compound motion is produced by the aid of the arm, K, which has one end pivoted to the side of the vertically moving frame, C. The opposite end is adapted to slip into a slot in a block, L, which is pivoted to a slide, M, this slide moving in a slot in the bar, N, which extends from end to end of the frame, G, and inside the frames, E and C. Two stops, O, are fitted to be moved to or from each other by the long right and left screw, P, these stops having projections which enter the slot in the bar, N, and they serve to limit the motion of the slide, M, and block, L. When a tenon is to be made with rounded ends, the bar or arm, K, is slipped through the slot in the block, L, and is secured by a set screw. This arm is secured at a distance from the point about which the arm turns, equal to half the thickness of the proposed tenon, added to the whole diameter of the cutter-head, as the latter must pass all around the tenon.

The stops, O, are adjusted by turning the screw, P, until they are at a distance apart equal to the width of the tenon to be made, plus the diameter of the cutter-head.

The operation will thus be as follows: The frame, C, being set at a point which will allow the cutter to form the top of the tenon, the frame, E, is moved horizontally upon the main frame, G, until the slide, M, has moved the distance between the stops, O. This carries the cutter across the top of the tenon to the point where the curve of one side or edge commences. From this point the frame, C, is moved downward, and the frame, E, horizontally, the arm, K, acting as the radius or link to hold the frames in their relative positions and cutter to its work, until it has passed around the side, and formed the curve at that part of the tenon. The arm, K, having then passed around its pivot to form a half circle, the frame, C, is allowed to remain stationary, and the frame, E, is moved along to allow the cutter to form the bottom of the tenon, the slide, M, moving the distance between the stops, O. From this point the curve at the opposite side of the tenon is formed in the same manner as before described.

If it is desired to form a complete cylindrical tenon, the stops, O, are curved up close to the slide, M, the block, L, having been secured to the arm, K, at a distance from the centre pivot equal to half the diameter of the proposed tenon, plus the diameter of the cutter, and the frames, C and E, are then moved simultaneously, so as to produce a compound movement, the resultant of which will be to form a cylindrical tenon.

This machine is applicable to work upon any form of timber, and make any kind of a cut. The tool, J, may be made with cutters which can be detached to be sharpened or renewed. Mr. Lepley, who may be addressed for further information, at Amador City, has applied for a patent for his invention through the *Mining and Scientific Press* Patent Agency.

JAMES LESSLEY

Is one of our valuable men who go straight to work; satisfied with moderate prospects they turn neither to the right nor left, but keep on with slow and steady accumulations until they outstrip many who start in life with much more brilliant prospects. He was born in Putnam county, Missouri, February 16, 1849, and came to California with his parents in 1854, making his home since that time in Amador county. His education has been rather practical than otherwise, being acquired mostly in business operations. He was employed with a team soon after coming here, and in due time acquired a team of his own and engaged in the lumber trade until he became one of the principal dealers and manufacturers in the county. He was married, August 22, 1869, to Miss Mary McGhee. They have seven children, two boys and five girls.

M. J. LITTLE

Was born in Bristol, Lincoln county, Maine, January 14, 1821, where he resided until he was fifteen years of age, getting such education as the town afforded. Like most young men in a maritime town he had to try his fortunes on the sea, going abroad on his first voyage at the age of sixteen. Being faithful and efficient, he was promoted from one position to another. In 1844, we find him second mate; in 1846, first mate, and two years later in charge of the vessel *John F. Strout*. As might have been expected of one so ambitious and energetic, the gold excitement swept him off his feet, and a few months later found him on his way around the Horn on the brig *Hungarian*, arriving in San Francisco April 27, 1850. He remained in that Babel of nationalities but one month; then purchasing a small row-boat, made his way up the Sacramento and Feather rivers to Marysville, and from thence to the Butte creek mines. From here he soon returned to San Francisco, and made another start to the mines, this time to Stephens Bar, on the Tuolumne river, in Tuolumne county, where he engaged in mining, also in trading in general merchandise until 1853, when he sold out and traveled around the mines, visiting Mariposa and other places, finally settling down in Jackson in 1854, which place he has since made his home. He followed mining until 1863, when the unsurpassed fruit and other California productions led him to adopt agriculture as a calling, which he has followed since. He located at that time the farm of one hundred and twenty-eight acres of land adjoining the town of Jackson. It is pleasantly situated, has a fine orchard and vineyard, with good buildings, and has in itself enough charms to satisfy a reasonable mind, and induce one to forego voyages and explorations and live contentedly under his own vine and fig tree. He was married, March 18, 1861, to Miss Mary D. Pope, of Sherburne, Chenango county, New York. Mr. Little has the same straightforward, honest ways which induced the owners of vessels to entrust thousands of dollars worth of property to his care when he was young, and enjoys the fullest confidence of the community.

ROBERT LUDGATE

Was born in the city of Waterford, Waterford county, Ireland, September 22, 1833. He came to New Orleans while still a boy and from thence to California in 1850, settling a year later in Ione valley, which place he made his permanent residence. He was engaged most of the time in stock-raising and farming until 1863, when he became associated with J. W. Surface in the livery business, in which he continued until his death. In 1877 he was elected to represent the people of Amador county in the Legislature of California. He had been in feeble health for some years, and was illy qualified to perform the arduous duties of a Legislator, but with the conscientiousness and fidelity characteristic of his whole life, he gave his unremitting attention to the business until nature, overtasked, gave way, and he breathed his last February 15, 1878, at ten o'clock, having been present in his seat the same day. The next morning, after the calling of the Assembly to order, the following resolution was offered by Mr. Dunlap, his associate member from the county, and unanimously adopted by a rising vote:—

Resolved, By the Assembly, the Senate concurring, that a committee of five members of the Assembly be appointed by the Speaker, and five Senators be appointed by the President of the Senate to attend the obsequies of the Honorable Robert Ludgate, on Sunday, the 17th, at 3 o'clock, P. M., at the town of Ione City, in Amador county, and further that the Assembly attend the funeral in a body.

Upon this resolution being received in the Senate Chamber it was also adopted, the President appointing Brown of Amador, Craig of San Francisco, Rogers of San Francisco, Reed of El Dorado, and Nunan of San Francisco a committee to escort the remains to the late member's home. The committee from the Assembly was Dunlap of Amador, Wheat of Calaveras, Meyers of San Joaquin, Miller of El Dorado and Ames of San Mateo. A resolution was also passed to wear the usual badge of mourning for thirty days, and as a mark of respect both houses adjourned until the following Monday. In Sacramento, the Odd Fellows, of which body he was a distinguished member, assembled at their lodges and encampments and made arrangements to escort the remains of their late brother to the train which was to take them to the Amador branch of the road. On Sunday an immense cortege, consisting of the various branches of the Odd Fellows in regalia, members of the Legislature, delegation of citizens from Ione, and private citizens, accompanied the remains from the hotel to the depot. At Galt the escort was met by the members of the Ione Lodge No. 51 and the remains transferred to the cars running to Ione, where the cortege was received by the citizens of the county generally and accompanied to the home of the late member. The funeral services were observed the following day according to the established form of the society of Odd Fellows, the Rev. J. T. White acting as clergyman, assisted by the Rev. E. Jacka and J. W. Huston, N. G.

As a man Mr. Ludgate was upright in his character, warm in his feelings, strong in his convictions and outspoken in his opinions; a devoted husband and father, and a firm, unwavering friend. In business transactions his word was a bond, as sacred as though God were called to witness. He leaves a widow and three children, one boy and two girls, to sorrow for his untimely end, and inherit the honor of his untarnished name. Her maiden name was Mary O'Brien, and they were married November 8, 1869.

O. E. MARTIN

Was born in the town of Guilford, Maine, May 28, 1848. Mr. Martin had the misfortune to lose his parents at an early age, and has no recollection of the tender love and care of a mother. His grandparents made the loss less to him by watching over his young life, he living with them until he was eighteen years of age, at the town of Montville. From there he went to Boston, where he spent two years in the drug business. During the next four years he lived in Kansas, Missouri, and Maine, or at least such portions of the time as he was not traveling, for the desire to see the world was as strong in him as in most young men, and must be gratified ere the future business man can settle down to the work of life. In January, 1873, he left his native State for California, arriving in Sacramento in June, and immediately located in the county of Amador, at Sutter Creek, where he was engaged in the milk business for two or three years. In 1877 he was confidential clerk in the lumber establishment of

THOMAS KERR.

Tarr & Co., which resulted in the purchase of the business with J. O. Bartlett of Sutter Creek.

At the present time the firm name is O. E. Martin & Co., being the only extensive dealers in lumber in the town of Amador. The lumber is brought from Tarr's mill, which is in the mountains twenty-one miles distant.

Mr. Martin was married November 16, 1880, to Mrs. Sarah E. Price, a native of Illinois.

L. McLAINE

Was born in Charlottetown, Prince Edward's Island, March 22, 1830, where he remained until he reached manhood's estate. He received a liberal education, and in May, 1850, bade farewell to his early associations to seek his fortune in the much-talked-of California. In October of the same year he located in Volcano, Amador county, and for ten years followed the usual occupation of those days. He also served six years as Supervisor for District No. 2. In 1869 he commenced business as a banker and broker, which he has followed to the present time, his purchases of gold-dust and bullion often amounting to twenty thousand dollars per month. He has an assaying department connected with his establishment. He is at present also superintendent of the Consolidated Amador Hydraulic Gold Mining and Land Company.

He was married in 1872, to Miss Sarah E., daughter of Dr. Wm. Ives, of Volcano. Mrs. McLaine is a native of Moorefield, Hardy county, West Virginia, and was born in 1849. Their union has been blessed with five children.

JAMES MEEHAN

Is a native of county Monohan, Ireland, where he was born November 1, 1833. Coming to America at the age of thirteen and engaging in business, his education was somewhat limited, but by study and application during leisure hours he succeeded in fully remedying the want, and is remarkably well informed on all general topics. He came to New Orleans on the sailing vessel *George Washington*, arriving in July, 1847, in company with a brother, where he remained until 1849. On the breaking out of the gold excitement he embarked on the old sailing vessel *Ontario*, which carried him safely to California, though the vessel was nine months on the way, reaching San Francisco in 1850. After taking a look at the chaos of people of all nations and colors, he left for the mines, making his first efforts at mining in Chinese Camp, in Tuolumne county. The following two or three years he alternated from Downieville to the American river, and thence to Tuolumne again, finally reaching Volcano, where his wandering propensities were cured by meeting Miss Mary A. Rawle, who, in 1856, became his wife, since which time he has had a residence in Amador county.

During the year 1852 he made a flying visit to New Orleans, but he had seen too many of the advantages of California to remain in the older States, and soon returned to the State to make it a permanent home. At Volcano he engaged in mining, with varied success, until 1867, when he was elected to the position of County Treasurer, which place he held for four years, having been re-elected at the end of his first term. He then engaged in quartz mining for four years, when he was again elected to the position of Treasurer, which he holds to the present time. He has executed the duties of the office with marked ability. He was the author of the proposition to devote a portion of the county funds to the extinguishment of the county debt, which, under the operation of the law, has gradually been liquidated, and bids fair to soon take its place among the events of the past. He has operated quite extensively in quartz mining, having been a stockholder in the Kennedy, Monterichard, and other valuable mines; also owns a large tract of gravel-mining ground near Kennedy flat, and also a quartz vein called the Volunteer mine, east of the Kennedy.

He has had nine children, six of whom, four boys and two girls, are living.

HIRAM C. MEEK

Is the patriarch of Amador county, dating his birth as far back as 1792. He is a native of Virginia, a countryman and neighbor of Washington, whom he saw frequently, and remembers well. Since that time and this, eighty years apart, what a change. Then, Jefferson and Adams, Burr and Hamilton, were engaged in the political strife, which led to the death of one of the men, the political and social ruin of another, the destruction of the old Federal party, and the creation of a Democratic party, which, through a nearly unbroken line of sixty years, shaped the political character of the United States. Well may one say with Everett, "Venerable man, you have come down to us from a former generation." The last of the Revolutionary soldiers departed long since. Soon the last of that century, the last of those who were contemporaneous with the great men of that age, will have vanished; and the time is not far distant when to have seen a man who had seen Washington will be a matter of pride. Major Meek is perhaps the only man in California who has seen the father of his country; the only connecting link between this and the century just passed. The Major is a brother of the famous trapper, whose book has been read with such eagerness by all the youth of America, and accompanied him in nearly all his travels. He is now settled down in comfortable quarters, surrounded by members of his family, enjoying a serene old age. His portrait, an excellent likeness, indicates an amount of vitality that justifies the expectation of his reaching the beginning of his second century.

GEORGE MOORE,

Judge of the Superior Court of the county of Amador, was born in Danville, Boyle county, Kentucky, February 14, 1850, and is, therefore, at this time thirty-one years of age. His parents were W. I. and Elizabeth C. Moore, the former being a native of Pennsylvania, the latter a native of Kentucky. Judge Moore was educated for the profession of law, having graduated from Centre College, Kentucky, in the year 1870, whereupon, after pursuing his studies for two years in the law office of Durham & Jacobs, at Danville, he attended the law lectures at Harvard College, Cambridge, Massachusetts. When but twenty-five years old he was appointed one of the Tilden and Hendricks electors for the Eighth district of Kentucky. In the Winter of 1877 he emigrated to the State of California, and commenced the practice of law in Amador county soon afterwards. After the adoption of the New Constitution in 1879, which brought about such important and extreme changes in our judicial system, Judge Moore was nominated and elected as the presiding officer of the new Superior Court for the county of Amador, being at the time of his elevation to the bench one of the youngest judges of that court in the State. Judge Moore is of a turn of mind peculiarly adapting him to the position which he occupies; logic, and its natural sequence, law, being with him almost spontaneous growths. The writer recently had an opportunity of witnessing his ability in the great mining case involving the Empire and Pacific mines of Plymouth. Some of the most celebrated lawyers in the State, among whom were Belcher, Estee, and Boalt, well known in San Francisco, were present. His rulings and decisions won the respect of the entire Bar. It is hardly probable that Judge Moore will remain in the mountains when the cities offer such brilliant rewards for men of his ability. He is pleasantly situated, as the sketch of his house in another part of the book will show.

MATTHEW MURRAY,

The subject of the following sketch, is a native of Ireland, born in County Cavan, September 15, 1834, where he remained until, at the age of fourteen years, he emigrated with his parents to the United States, and settled in the city of St. Louis, Missouri, where for seven years he was engaged in the grocery business and in the cultivation of his mind, devoting his leisure moments to the study of such branches as are required in the interests of merchandising. Desiring a richer and more extensive field for the cultivation of his business talent, he decided upon California as the proper place, and landed in San Francisco on the second day of July, 1855. He soon after located near Michigan Bar, in Sacramento county, and was engaged in selling goods during the succeeding three years. His aspirations did not lead him into the mines in search of an immediate fortune, but his ambitions were centered in the business he adopted when he first arrived in America. In 1858 Mr. Murray removed to Lancha Plana, Amador county, and still continued the mercantile business until 1863, since which time he has been interested as owner and superintendent of water ditches used in working the mines. By strict application to business he has been successful in nearly all of his business ventures. He is well known throughout the county, and has held the position of Supervisor of the First district for several years, and still remains in that office, performing the duties acceptably to his fellow-men and creditably to himself.

Mr. Murray was married November 6, 1861, to Miss Celia E. Murray, and their union has proved fruitful, as the ten beautiful children, seven girls and three boys now living, can testify.

JOHN NORTHUP

Was born in the town of Hamburg, Erie county, New York, October 5, 1822, and remained there until he reached the age of fifteen years. During that time he attended school, and acquired a thorough knowledge of the common branches taught in the schools to which he had access. His next location was in Cass county, Michigan, where for fifteen years he was a tiller of the soil. The knowledge acquired during that time was of great advantage to him in the succeeding years of his life. In 1852 Mr. Northup came to California, and engaged in the usual occupation of those days, that of mining, in Amador county, and for about nine years followed that pursuit, experiencing the ups and downs of fortune peculiar to the early searchers for the golden nuggets. At length, after his long experience in that direction, he turned his attention to other pursuits, and engaged in farming, and for the past four years has been the "champion melon man" of the Pacific coast, often planting as high as one hundred to one hundred and fifty acres to that kind of fruit, and shipping the melons to San Francisco and Oakland, his sales sometimes running as high as two thousand melons per week. His "melon patch" is in San Joaquin county, and he was the first to ship fruit direct to the city from his locality for the wholesale trade, in which he has been successful.

His home place is almost a paradise, he having an abundance of fruit trees and vines, which are carefully cared for and "show their keeping." His house is beautifully situated near the Mokelumne river, and is one of the prettiest places in the county.

He was married in 1856, to Miss Ann M. Harmon, and they have six children, two girls and four boys.

Mr. Northup has the reputation of being fair and square in his dealings, and thoroughly wide awake when any business is on hand, not often being overreached.

R. W. PALMER

Is a native of Massachusetts; came around the Horn, or rather through the Straits of Magellan, in 1849, being among the first, and perhaps last of the Argonauts to make that interesting but perilous passage. The adventures of the passengers among the savages, as related by him, are among the marvelous things of a marvelous age. He was engaged in trade for many years at Sacramento, but in 1856 moved to Lancha Plana, engaging in merchandising in company with the Hon. J. W. D. Palmer, with whom he remained until the partial failure of that camp as a mining region. The amount of goods sold and exchanged for dust would astonish a merchant of the present day. At that time the river, bluffs, and hills, were all giving up their treasures, and thousands of dollars then were but as tens now; but all things must have an end. Lancha Plana followed the ordinary custom, and failed to pay. Upon removing to Jackson, about 1865, he engaged in the livery business, and still keeps first-class turnouts for those who wish to explore the country on business, or pleasure. He is married, and has an interesting family; is pleasantly situated, and if not acquiring riches, is in comfortable circumstances. He is a public spirited man, ready to leave his own business to benefit his neighbors; is generous and hospitable, ready to entertain his friends with the best in the house, or with the best of stories, of which he keeps an inexhaustible supply always on hand.

JAMES F. PARKS

Was born in Hooper county, Missouri, on the ninth of September, 1835, where he remained until he was six years of age, at which time he removed with his parents, to Benton county. His early life was passed in his native State, but as youth ripened into manhood, he was not content to remain quietly at home while other young men were exploring the much-talked-of gold fields of the Pacific, and he accordingly bade adieu to those he loved and started out to seek his fortune with the countless thousands that were flocking to the Golden State of California.

In 1855 he reached his objective point, and at once repaired to Kern river, during the great excitement upon the discovery of those "diggins." He did not find what he sought in that locality, and soon after engaged in mining in Mariposa county, and afterwards in Nevada county. In 1861 he crossed the Sierras to the Territory of Nevada, and for the succeeding eight years was engaged in mining at Virginia City. In 1869 he went to White Pine District, and from there to Plumas county, California, where he was appointed foreman of the Indian Valley mine. On the first day of April, 1873, he came to Amador county, to accept the responsible position of foreman of the Keystone mine, where he has since been employed. As a foreman he stands second to none in the State, always the same affable gentleman, much esteemed by his employers and the people generally.

His years of experience among the great mines of Nevada, place him in the front rank as a practical mining man, and, to add to his other accomplishments, he is a thorough practical surveyor and civil engineer, and does all the work in that line for his company.

Mr. Parks was married October 8, 1871, to Miss Mary Phebey, of Sacramento, and they have four children.

PALMER N. PECK,

The subject of the following sketch, is a native of New York State, having been born in Yates, Orleans county, December 23, 1831. During his youth he removed with his parents to the State of Michigan, where he remained until nineteen years of age. He had during these years acquired a good education, and after leaving school entered a plow factory at Peru, Illinois, where he was employed about one year. The western fever fastened itself upon him and like thousands of others he took up a line of march toward the setting sun, crossing the plains in 1852, and spending that Winter in Salt Lake City, Utah. The following Spring he continued his journey to California, arriving by the southern route in San Bernardino on the 15th of May, 1853.

After a stay of about three months in that town he removed to Stockton, San Joaquin county, where he had a step-brother. For the next three years he was engaged in business in that place, generally merchandising. He then became a trader in the southern mines, and for two years did an extensive business. Giving up this last enterprise he went to Tuolumne county and engaged in mining operations, which proved very unprofitable for him.

His next move was to Volcano, Amador county, where he has since resided, and generally engaged in mining, owning at the present time some thirty-one acres of "mining ground," from which he will undoubtedly realize a handsome fortune, as he fully understands manipulating such enterprises. He is also interested in flumes and mines in other places.

Mr. Peck is well and favorably known throughout the mines of California as a man of experience and worth, and is universally respected. He is still a single man and his elegant home is without a mistress.

A. PETTY

Was born at Circleville, Pickaway county, Ohio, August 6, 1820. At the age of eight years he, with his parents, emigrated to Missouri. In 1842 he removed to the State of Wisconsin, and worked in the lead mines of that State during the Winter and followed his trade, that of plasterer, during the Summer, for about seven years, In 1849 he located in the town of McGregor, Iowa, where he resided until December 28, 1852, at which time he started for California with ox-teams, accompanied by his wife and two children. They crossed the State of Iowa in winter, and arrived at Council Bluffs, March 14, 1853, where they encountered a terrible snow-storm. May 5th they crossed the Missouri river, and were fairly on their long and tedious journey, the incidents connected with which would fill a large volume. The Indians were very troublesome, and they had many thrilling adventures with members of "Mr. Lo's" band. Finally they reached California and settled at Volcano, Amador county, September 15, 1853, having, while en route, remained twenty-one days with the saints at Salt Lake, Utah.

Mr. Petty turned his attention to mining as soon as his affairs could be arranged, and for the succeeding sixteen months prospected the country without finding his expected bonanza. He then gave up the search for gold in the earth and looked in other channels for his supply, opening a hotel which he conducted but a short time. He then, in connection with Captain Richards, John James, and others, formed a company for the purpose of opening a bed-rock flume, or open cut, through the cañon below the town. They prosecuted this enterprise for about two years, expending some sixty-five thousand dollars, which was a dead loss. Mr. Petty has occasionally followed mining since that time, and also his trade, as circumstances required.

In January, 1880, he bought the St. George hotel at Volcano, and has since been the proprietor thereof. He fully understands catering to the wants of the traveling public, and is one of the few men who know how to keep a hotel. In 1879 Mr. Petty was elected County Assessor of Amador county, which position he fills at the present time.

He was married in 1844 to Miss Ophelia Cooper, and they have three children.

J. E. PETTITT

Was born in Licking county, Ohio, November 16, 1828, which place was his home until 1853; engaged mostly in farming and raising stock. In 1853 he came to California via Panama, and immediately located on Indian creek, in the northern part of the present county, or in what then was El Dorado county, making this county his home since that time. He followed mining for several years, but in 1869 turned to farming, locating on the place he now occupies. Though making farming his principal business, he has combined with it stock-raising and freighting, the immense amounts of lumber used making that business profitable.

He was married December 25, 1855, to Miss Christina Cox, a native of Indiana, and his family consists of himself, wife, three girls and two boys.

E. S. POTTER

Is a native of the famous Wooden Nutmeg State, which has sent such a vast number of keen business men into the commercial channels of the nation. He was born in the town of Litchfield, Connecticut, November 23, 1828, from which place he moved to Platteville, Wisconsin, in 1847, coming overland to Volcano, California, in 1852. After mining in that vicinity for about a year, he moved to Drytown, and spent about one year in mining on Poor Man's creek; thence to Arkansas diggings, near Michigan Bar, where he kept hotel in company with Geo. W. Harris. In 1860 he removed to Buckeye valley, where he raised stock until 1863, when he went to Pokerville, in the vicinity of Plymouth. When the mines failed at Pokerville he moved to Plymouth, then beginning to attract attention as a quartz mining region, where he has since remained engaged in various kinds of business, mostly teaming and lumbering. In 1873 he opened a lumber yard to supply the demand consequent upon the rapid building of the town. He was married, in 1858, to Miss Harriet Louisa Howard, of Forest Home. They have had fourteen children, six of whom are living.

HON. W. H. PROUTY.

The subject of this sketch is a native of the Buckeye State. He was born March 27, 1837, in Knox county, Ohio, his early years being spent on a farm. In 1846, in obedience to the general impulse to go west, the family removed to Jasper county, Iowa, being among the pioneers of that region. In 1852 they fell into the column of the California emigration and started across the plains. The emigration of that year was perhaps the largest that ever wended its way to the Golden State; and its march resembled the retreat of an army more than a triumphal march of settlers to a promised land. The grass was eaten off for miles away from the road, making long detours necessary to keep the stock in condition to travel. To add to these difficulties the father of the family sickened and died near the Devil's Gate. But the mother, picking up the reins of authority, with the aid of her elder sons, succeeded in reaching California, entering Volcano August 24th the same year, which, considering the circumstances, was a remarkably successful trip. After resting a few days, and watching the operation of extracting gold, the love for rural life asserted itself and the family continued their journey, settling in the beautiful valley which has since been their home. The younger child, W. H. Prouty, was early thrown on his own resources, and divided his time between farming and attending such schools as the county then afforded, spending considerable time in attending school at Volcano. By the time he was twenty-one he had mastered the common English branches and accumulated a small capital of two thousand six hundred dollars. It will be seen from this that he firmly set his face against the prevailing dissipations of those early days which swept so many young, and even middle-aged men into the vortex of destruction.

Having arrived at man's estate the desire to see more of the world before he settled down induced him to visit the home of his childhood, and other places in the West, or valley of the Mississippi, where he remained about five years, engaged in various kinds of business, mostly farming, however. While here he became acquainted with his future wife and companion, Miss Helen Charlesworth, whom he married July 26, 1859, by whom he has had seven children, six of whom are now living.

In 1863 the memory of the Golden State asserted itself and he turned his steps to California, making his way to the valley which had seen him while a boy assume the duties and labors of manhood. Four years later he purchased his present home, and set about improving it with the design of spending his remaining years here. His herds and flocks and well-filled granaries attest his judgment and devotion to his business. Like most successful business men he has little time or disposition to dabble in politics, but when a delegate to the Constitutional Convention who understood the wants of the farming community was wanted, the people instinctively turned to him as one whose judgment and integrity could be relied upon. His actions in the convention fully justified the opinions of his neighbors, and he returned to his home with unblemished honor. His farm and home is one of the pleasantest as well as most valuable places in the county, as will be seen by the view published in this work.

B. F. RICHTMYER.

Was born in Conesville, Schoharie county, New York, June 17, 1824, at which place he resided until he was twenty-two years of age, receiving such education as the place afforded. In 1844 he removed to Delevan, Wisconsin, where for some years he was employed in a flouring mill. In 1850, yielding to the prevailing California fever, he crossed the plains with the great emigration of that year, settling at Drytown the Autumn of the same season. Here he engaged in merchandising and mining, meeting with the usual gains and losses in those days; gains in large profits then customary, and losses by fires, bad debts, and ill-luck in mining, which, as many old Californians remember to their sorrow, were also common enough to be called customary. During his residence here, he was express agent for Wells, Fargo & Co., telegraph operator and agent, etc. He was associated with G. W. Seaton in the famous Seaton mine, which, in its day, had the richest quartz ever found in the county. It was a pocket mine, however, and did not continue dividends any great length of time. In 1871, Mr. Richtmyer was elected County Clerk, his personal popularity carrying him much beyond the average ticket in the election. He now removed to Jackson, the county seat, which place he has since made his home. After serving his term as County Clerk, he became the agent again of Wells, Fargo & Co., this time at Jackson, and soon after was made an agent for the

Western Union Telegraph Company, both of which positions he has since filled. In addition to his other duties, he has also filled the position of Notary Public; was seven years agent for the Home Mutual Insurance Company of California. He is also proprietor and manager of the Jackson water-works, and such is his methodical system of business that he can do all these things justice, and still have time to devote to society and domestic affairs. He was married September 10, 1855, to Miss Celina Vannetier.

As a man, Mr. Richtmyer is deservedly popular; unswerving integrity, *suaviter in modo*, capability and modesty, being united in a remarkable degree. He is unexceptionable in his habits, and if possessed of any faults at all, they are the amiable ones of being too generous and unsuspecting. He will be found equal to any trust the people of the county or State may choose to repose in him.

J. H. RINGER.

The gentleman to whom this sketch refers is a native of the State of Missouri, born in Ray county, on the 14th of June, 1843. He remained in his native State until he was eleven years of age, and then, at that tender age, endured the hardships, privations, and toil, consequent with a trip across the plains to California, where he arrived sound of limb, and located at Butte City, Amador county. He remained there until 1855, and removed to Aqueduct City, where he resided about two years. He then settled in Jackson valley, and has since been a resident thereof. As a farmer, Mr. Ringer is a decided success, and is the owner of one of the finest ranches in the valley, containing four hundred and thirty-one acres, nearly all of which is under a high state of cultivation, his improvements also being very fine. Mr. Ringer was married April 23, 1873, to Miss Emily E. Stamper, and is the proud father of three interesting girls. He is one of the most thorough and energetic business men in the county, and is rapidly making himself wealthy.

JAMES ROBERTSON

Was born in the town of Ottawa, Canada, November 26, 1828, where he resided until 1854, engaged in farming. Catching the prevailing California fever, and perhaps tiring of the long and tedious cold Winters, he turned his steps towards the land of sunny hills and mild Winters, reaching San Francisco by the Panama route, about the first of November. He located on his present place in 1856, and has pursued the even tenor of his way ever since, swerving neither to the right nor left. His place is a beautiful location, overlooking Sacramento, Stockton and the adjoining plains, which places often come into distinct view, as the atmosphere clears up after a storm. His business has been chiefly stock-raising and farming. He owns four hundred and eighty acres of land about midway between Jackson and Ione, at the junction of the old Sutter Creek and Jackson roads. Natural springs supply all the water necessary for domestic and stock purposes. For a view of the house and beauty of situation see engraving in the body of the book. Mr. Robertson never married, but has had all the care of a father in helping to raise the younger members of the family, and also to support a mother in her declining years, the mother being spared to him until the Autumn of 1880.

BENJAMIN ROSS

Was born in Portland, Maine, February 19, 1822, where he learned the trade of mounting pictures and mirrors; enlisted in Company E, Captain Charles B. Crowninshield, First Regiment, Massachusetts Mexican Volunteers; served under General Taylor on the Rio Grande until September; then under General Scott until the close of the war, being promoted during the time to the position of Sergeant Major. After the close of the war he returned to Boston, but started to California soon after by way of Fort Smith, Santa Fee and Salt Lake, arriving at Webertown, El Dorado county, in September, 1850. In 1852 moved to Volcano, which place he has since generally made his home except during a trip to Idaho in 1862-63. Has at different times been engaged in mining, merchandising, banking and surveying. In 1872 he was appointed United States Deputy Surveyor for mines by Surveyor General J. R. Hardenburgh, which position he still holds under Surveyor General Wagner. In 1878 he was elected Supervisor for District No. 2, and is now, by virtue of seniority, chairman of the Board. He was married December 6, 1865, to Miss McIntyre, and has a family of interesting children.

JONATHAN SALLEE

Was born in Lincoln county, Missouri, June 17, 1832, where he resided until he was nineteen years of age, when he crossed the plains with an ox-team, making the trip in four months. His first halt was at Mud Springs, now El Dorado, but he soon moved to Weber creek, where he engaged in mining until 1859, when he returned to Missouri, where he remained until 1871, when he returned to California with his family; for, however much we may think our State is played out, a few years' residence in the Eastern States is sure to make us long for the mild Winters and even hot Summers of this State. He located on his present ranch, about one mile and a quarter from Plymouth, on the road to Oleta, where he has since resided. His place contains three hundred and twenty acres of good land, favorably located for business and health, it being in the elevated part of the county, above the *malarial* region. He unites stock-raising with the cultivation of the farm, the country around being a fine range for cattle.

He was married April 25, 1861, while in Missouri, to Miss Mary E. Beach, who died in the Spring of 1865. By this marriage there were two children, a son and daughter. April 26, 1866, Mr. Salloe was married a second time, making Miss Sarah Jane Longfellow his wife. By this marriage they have had two children, but one of whom is living, the family now consisting of himself, wife, and three children.

ARTHUR B. SANBORN,

Of the firm of Turner & Sanborn, is a modest, industrious, and, consequently, promising young man. He was born in 1856, and received such education as could be obtained in the town of Jackson, until he was fifteen years old. He made the most of his opportunities, and, at the close of his school days, commenced a regular course of reading, political economy being a favorite study. He is steady and reliable, never having been given to the dissipations so common to the young men in California, or, in other words, he never took time to sow any wild oats, but went directly to work improving his mind. In 1879 he became connected with H. S. Turner in the management of the *Jackson Sentinel*, and is now part proprietor. He is a brilliant and forcible writer, and has a promising future.

JOHN SANDERSON

Is a native of Ireland, and was born in the month of June, 1830. He remained in the "Emerald Isle," until he reached his seventeenth year, at which time he came to America, and settled in the grand old State of New York, where he remained three and one-half years. He then removed to New Jersey, and was a resident of that State until he came to the Pacific coast in 1864. Having had experience on the "briny deep" in his trip from his native country to the United States, he naturally chose the steamer as his mode of conveyance, and arrived in California by way of the Isthmus of Panama in due time, sound of limb and buoyant in spirits, seeking like all others an easy fortune in the mines of this State. His first location was at Sutter Creek, in Amador county, where he followed the occupation of a miner for about six years. From his savings he purchased the beautiful ranch that is now his home, located about one and one-half miles west of Sutter Creek. This home place of Mr. Sanderson's is admirably situated and contains 320 acres of choice land, which he is cultivating in a manner that is bound to make it productive.

He was married on the 13th of February, 1863, to Miss Katy Hughes, a native of New York, and their union has been blessed with eight children, seven of whom are living. The only son born to them was called to the other world on Thanksgiving day, 1879.

BRUNO H. SCHACHT

Is a native of Germany, born about 1850. He is a young man of thorough business habits, and has the confidence of all with whom he associates. In 1879, shortly after being naturalized, he was elected to the position of Public Administrator, a situation more responsible than profitable, which he fills with eminent ability and integrity. He has a beautiful residence in the town of Jackson, and evidently intends making the place his permanent home.

ALEXANDER SHEAKLEY

Was born at Sheakleyville, Mercer county, Pennsylvania, May 1, 1827. In this town he spent his boyhood, and acquired the practical business education which has insured success in his many undertakings. In 1852 he followed the stream which set with so strong a current to the Golden State, arriving at Placerville, where he remained engaged in mining until September, 1853, when he came to Ione City, then growing into notice in consequence of the rich lands in the valley, and its being on the line of travel from the mines to Sacramento. This place he made his permanent home, and materially aided to develop into its present prosperous condition. He has been engaged in many kinds of business. For the first ten years he carried on blacksmithing. Close attention to his trade impaired his health, and disposing of the business, he engaged in hotel keeping, becoming proprietor of the Arcade, then one of the finest hotels in the State. Since then he has been engaged in many things, always, however, retaining the ownership of the fine tract of land containing one hundred and eighty-four acres, which is his residence. This place is beautifully located, twenty to fifty feet above the valley, which sweeps in a circle around the elevation on which his house is built. Sometimes twenty reapers can be seen cutting down the fields of golden grain, which alternate with orchard and vineyard. He has a fine residence, with all the modern improvements, which is a prominent object in whatever direction one may approach the valley. His place is underlaid by a vein of coal, which is likely to become valuable. Mr. Sheakley is one of the solid men of the county, always reliable. He was married, April 6, 1864, to Mrs. A. E. Montandon. No children have blessed the union, to inherit and improve the fine property, though judging from Mr. Sheakley's hearty appearance, he does not contemplate retiring from the care of it for many years to come.

JAMES W. SHEALOR.

The subject of the following sketch is a native of Virginia, having been born in Page county, August 24, 1830. At the tender age of six years he removed with his parents to the State of Missouri, locating at Springfield. The father of the present subject was a foundryman, and James followed that business, after leaving school, for some years. He also engaged in farming, and was a tiller of the soil when the western fever first laid hold of him. In 1853 he moved with his father and mother to California, coming by way of the plains, and experienced the trials usually attending such a trip in those early days.

His first location was at Volcano, Amador county. and his business for some years after reaching the Pacific coast was varied, he being engaged in mining, teaming, ranching, milling, and other branches of industry.

For the past seventeen years he has resided on his present ranch, situated six miles north-east from Volcano. He has three hundred and twenty acres of fine land, and thoroughly understands the cultivation thereof. On this ranch he has a saw-mill that was erected in 1860, and which Mr. Shealor runs about six months in the year, manufacturing pine lumber for the people in his vicinity.

He was married February 4, 1855, to Miss Melinda Simms, of Missouri. Their union has been blessed with five children, four boys and one girl.

The father of our subject is still living, but his mother died December 23, 1863.

D. B. SPAGNOLI

Is a native of Italy, having been born in the town of Roscgro, Province of Novara, November 30, 1840. He obtained his early education in the city of Pallanza. In 1852, he went to the French college at Vevey, remaining there until 1854, when, in company with his parents and one brother, he came to California. The names of the family were Deodato Spagnoli and Maria Antoinette, father and mother, and the two sons, Silvester and D. Benjamin. They reached San Francisco August 1, 1854, coming to Clinton, in Amador county, the following September. The elder Spagnoli mined near Clinton for several months and then bought a store and stock of goods, consisting of general merchandise. D. B., the subject of this sketch, at the breaking out of the Frazer river excitement, went north with the crowd, and had about as exciting experience of the dangers of navigating the Frazer river and of traveling among the Indians, as any man that ever returned alive. An interesting book might have been written on the subject, if book-making had been in his line of business. After his return in 1858, he followed stock-raising until the death of his father in 1863, when he took charge of his father's estate, consisting of store, mining interests and ditches, managing these until 1865, when he was appointed Deputy County Recorder, occupying the position two years. In 1867 he was appointed Deputy County Clerk. In 1869 the offices of Clerk and Recorder were merged in one, and he received the nomination for the double office at the hands of the Democrats, and in September was elected, serving two years. At the expiration of his term of office he formed a law partnership with R. M. Briggs, having studied law and been admitted to the bar while County Clerk. Mr. Spagnoli has had a liberal education, speaking some four or five languages with fluency. He belonged to a wealthy and refined family in Italy, and started in life with many advantages, which he has not failed to improve. He has had great influence among his countrymen, who would take his advice and trust their business to his care. He was married January 12, 1870, at Stockton, to Miss Rosa Isabella Bryant. In 1872 he returned to Italy on account of business, visiting London, Paris, Rome, Lyons, Milan, Turin and other cities of the Old World. After his return from Europe he became interested in the drug store at Jackson, finally becoming sole proprietor.

His mother died in Amador county in 1873. He lost his wife in 1874, who left two sons (now living), two and three years of age, named respectively, Sylvester Nelson D., and Urbono Giovani D.

SYLVESTER G. SPAGNOLI

Was born in the town of Roscgro, Italy; came to California in 1854 in company with his parents, Deodato and Maria Antoinette Spagnoli, and a brother, D. B. Spagnoli, now a resident of Jackson, and settled in Clinton, Amador county, in the month of September, 1854. In 1865 he went to Owyhee, in Idaho, on a mining excursion, returning the same year. On the location of his brother in Jackson in the Autumn of 1865, he took charge of the home business, consisting of merchandising, mining, and ditching, which he successfully managed. He was married November 23, 1868, to Miss Minnie V. Bryant, by whom he has had four children: Stella M. S., now eleven; Clotilde E. S., born in Clinton, and Minnie R. S., aged three years, born in Harmon, county of Penobscot, State of Maine.

Mr. Spagnoli enjoys the confidence and respect of the community, having held the position of Justice of the Peace three terms, once in 1876 by appointment, and twice since by election.

ROBERT STEWART

Was born December 17, 1826, in Donegall county, Ireland, and emigrated to the United States, after reaching his majority, by way of New York. He soon after went to Freeport, Stephenson county, Illinois, where he was engaged in farming operations for eleven years. He started for California in com-

BENJ^N ROSS.

pany with Young and Johnson, March 19, 1850, and reached Placerville the 4th of September following, visiting the city of the saints while on his way. He tried mining at Placerville (then bearing the ominous name of Hangtown) for two weeks, and removed to Rancheria creek, but in a few days went to Volcano, which place he has, since October 16, 1850, made his home. He early began to take part in politics, and, in 1859, was elected to the position of Supervisor from that district, serving two terms; was then appointed Deputy County Clerk, under T. M. Pawling, which position he held for two years. In 1873 he was again elected Supervisor, and re-elected again in 1876. When not engaged in his public duties he has been engaged in mining, placer and quartz, principally the latter, though during the years 1876–78–79, he connected banking and buying gold-dust with his mining operations. He is still engaged in quartz mining, owning a mine and mill on north fork of the Mokelumne river.

Ireland never gave birth to a more genuine, whole-souled man than the subject of this sketch. Whether in the mines or in the forum, as an officer administering the affairs of the county, or as a miner down in the earth hammering out quartz, his genuine Irish humor never left him. Though his education was rather limited, his native good sense and wit has always made him a fit companion for the highest as well as the unassuming. His solid and substantial qualities were appreciated by others than men, and July 2, 1876, Miss Celia Cottingham, the acknowledged belle of Volcano, consented to accompany him on the afternoon journey of his life, the silver threads contrasting finely with the gold. He has a well-stocked library of modern works, with which he employs himself in his leisure hours, and is, in consequence, in the front ranks of the thinking portion of the world.

J. D. STOLCKEN

Is a native of Germany, having been born at Hanover, September 7, 1838. He remained in his native country until he reached the age of about fifteen years, at which time he became interested in the "briny deep," and left the scenes of his childhood to become a sailor. His intelligence, and aptness for his new calling soon manifested themselves, and he was made an officer, and held the responsible position of mate on several ships during the fourteen years succeeding his first venture on the high seas. During that time he visited many parts of the world, and became familiar with the higher branches of the principles of navigation. In 1870 he came to California, desiring a change of occupation, and a more lucrative field for his labors. His first year in this State was passed in the mines of El Dorado county. He then came to Amador county, and located the Soto mine, at Pioneer creek, which he worked for nine years, finally selling the claim to an Eastern company. Desiring a change once more, he, with the proceeds of the sale of his mine, bought property at Volcano, and also a large stock of such goods as is generally to be found in a variety store, in which business he is at present engaged. His store is well appointed, and conducted on the "square" principle; and his stock is complete, consisting of fancy goods and notions, also "wet and dry" groceries. He is a single man as yet. A view of the residence of Mr. Stolcken will be found in this volume.

A. A. VAN SANDT,

The subject of the following sketch, is a native of the old "Buckeye" State, Ohio; was born in Hamilton county, April 22, 1832. His boyhood days were passed in that county until, in 1844, when he removed to Caldwell county, Missouri, where he acted in the capacity of plow-boy on the farm owned by his parents for some years. His facilities for obtaining an education were somewhat limited, but being a lad of more than ordinary ability he succeeded in obtaining a thorough knowledge of the branches taught in a district school. His next move was to Crawfordsville, Indiana, where he remained until the year 1852, when he came to the Pacific coast, and entered the mines of California, engaging in mining, which business in connection with ditching he followed with varied success until 1868, at which time he settled on his present ranch, where he has since resided. As a farmer Mr. Van Sandt has proved a success, and is to-day the possessor of a fine, large ranch, containing six hundred acres, and adapted to the cultivation of every kind of grain, hay, and fruits. The ranch is situated on the Mokelumne river, and commands a beautiful view of the surrounding country. He was married in 1875 to Miss McClosey, and their union has been blessed with two children, both boys, aged respectively four and one years.

In the possession of his interesting family, and beautiful home, Mr. Van Sandt stands second to none of the many farmers along the river, and being in the prime of life bids fair to enjoy the fruits of his labors for many years to come.

JAMES W. VIOLETT.

Was born in Logan county, Kentucky, July 1, 1828, residing there until 1849. He fell into the California column in 1850, making his way to Sacramento, where he followed the business of a carpenter until 1853, when he came to Ione valley, which place he has made his home, with some slight interruptions, ever since, engaged in farming, in some of its branches, in which he has generally been successful. In 1871 he purchased the famous Pardee orchard, one of the oldest as well as largest in the county. It contains one hundred and eight acres of, perhaps, as productive land as can be found in California. The fruit from this place has always borne a high character. The writer of this article has seen bunches of the Eschol or Palestine grape over two feet in length, growing on the place. Twenty-one acres are now planted in choice fruit trees numbering over two thousand.

Mr. Violett was married September 7, 1871, to Mrs. Martha Watkinson, formerly Miss Martha Gregory. They have six children. Mr. Violett is an honest, industrious, and intelligent man, having the confidence and respect of his neighbors, and is foremost in every work calculated to improve schools, churches or other beneficent projects.

JOHN VOGAN,

Whose name frequently appears in the body of our history, was born in Valley Forge, Pennsylvania, May 7, 1822. He early began to "go West," his first move being to Memphis, Tennessee. In 1849 he came to California, making his first halt at San Francisco, where he remained but a short time, his next destination being Sacramento. Here he engaged in staging, the business which afterwards developed into extensive proportions, having lines to Marysville, Auburn, Jackson, and Mokelumne Hill. In 1854 he moved to the Q ranch, and in company with Charles Green still further extended its lines, one of the longest being a daily from Sacramento to Sonora, via Jackson and Mokelumne Hill, a distance of one-hundred and twenty miles. These lines were all well stocked, the horses and coaches being first-class. The Forest line of stages were well known for comfort, speed and safety, through the State. Though the expenses were enormous, so were the profits, the fare from Sonora to Sacramento being twenty dollars; from Jackson ten dollars. The lines were afterward consolidated with the California Stage Company, which proved a losing concern. After the staging business had ceased to be profitable, Vogan commenced the construction of a graded wagon road from Ione to Jackson. An experience of ten or twelve years in staging over the rough roads, or rather over no roads at all, enabled him not only to appreciate the value of good roads, but also to plan the grades and curves that would make a good road. It was finished about the year 1863, and was, and still remains, a monument of skill and perseverance, being one of the best roads considering the circumstances, to be found in California.

He was elected Sheriff in 1876, and re-elected every term since.

He was married July 19, 1860, to Miss Lucy Green, at the Q ranch. They have six children, five girls and one boy. He has a beautiful home and twelve hundred acres of land at the well-known Mountain Springs.

Mr. Vogan is liberal in his sentiments, genial and pleasant in manner, with no disagreeable angles in his character, and is always reliable for a first-class anecdote of any and every prominent man of the country. In his business operations he is a square dealer, above reproach. As an executive officer he has exceeded the expectations of his friends, making one of the best detectives in the State, his quiet, undemonstrative manner enabling him to ferret out many transactions which would be successfully hidden from a noisy man.

RICHARD WEBB

Is a native of England, born about the year 1841; was naturalized in San Francisco in 1876, and made his appearance in Amador county the same year, as editor of a semi-weekly paper published at Sutter Creek, which was soon consolidated with the *Ledger* at Jackson, he becoming sole proprietor. Soon after removing to Jackson he married a daughter of Thomas Jones, Esquire, of the same place, thus completing his identification with American interests. His career as an editor has been more fully referred to in connection with the newspapers of Amador county. It may be added, however, that he has paid particular attention to the administration of county affairs, and has unearthed many irregularities (a severer term might be used), and has in many ways assisted in bringing about the present economical management of financial matters. No crooked official bears any good-will to Richard Webb.

CONRAD WELLER

Was born in the town of Helmstadt, in Germany, December 14, 1832, living there until he was sixteen years old, acquiring a good business education at the schools for which Germany is so famous. Following the tide of emigration, which was then beginning to set heavily towards America, in company with an elder brother, he landed in New Orleans in 1849, going directly to St. Louis, where he completed the trade of tinning and sheet-iron working, which he had partially learned in Germany. From thence he went to Belleville, Illinois, where his brother resided, remaining there until 1853, when he crossed the plains to California. He first located in Sacramento, working at his trade, but finally came to Jackson October 24, 1855, and three days afterwards opened the store which he has since occupied, except when interrupted by fires, the great fire of 1862 totally destroying his goods and store. In addition to the manufacture of tin and sheet-iron ware, he has always kept on hand the best stock of stoves and other hardware to be found in the county.

He was married in 1861, to Miss Katie Griesbach, of Volcano; have one child, a son, born August 3, 1862.

Mrs. Weller was born in Munich, March 3, 1845, of Jacob and Catherine Griesbach.

Mr. Weller and wife are good samples of the emigration from Germany, who, by honest, persistent industry which, satisfied with a fair prosperity, move straight along without grumbling to competence and wealth, and who have done so much to develop the resources of the country, and establish the habits of life so invaluable to a nation.

MATTHEW H. WELLS

Was born May 9, 1809, in Suffolk county, Long Island, and is, therefore, a New Yorker. He resided on the romantic island until he was seventeen, obtaining a practical business education while there. His next residence was in New York City, where he was engaged in an extensive grocery store for three years. The desire to see the world being strong, he enlisted in the service, going on the United States ship *Boston*, where he remained four and a half years. The next thirteen years were spent in New York City in various kinds of business. Upon the breaking out of the gold fever he took passage in the brig *Cordelia*, leaving New York January 30, 1849, reaching San Francisco July 15th, which, considering the character of the vessel and ignorance of the winds and currents in those days, was a remarkably quick trip. He followed mining for a short time, but soon engaged in butchering in Sacramento, which he followed for some months. Then he tried a boarding-house for awhile, and then a store, for in those days lawyers sold peanuts and blacked boots, and ministers occasionally dealt *monte*, no one following his own trade, or indeed any one, long. In 1852 he came to Amador creek, where he kept a store for eleven years, falling into the steady habits of the New England life. In 1863 he located on the ranch where he now lives, about forty miles east of Sacramento, on the road to Jackson, Plymouth and Oleta. He has large and commodious buildings, making a comfortable residence for both man and beast. His farm contains about seven hundred acres of land.

He was married in 1838 to Miss H. M. Watts, who lived with him, as companion and adviser, for forty-two years, dying in June, 1880. A married daughter, husband and family reside with him, sharing the ownership and labors of the farm.

ISAAC W. WHITACRE

Is a native of Pennsylvania, having been born April 16, 1823, in Lycoming county. At the age of nine years he removed with his parents to Logan county, Ohio, where he resided until he was fourteen years of age. In 1837 the family returned to Pennsylvania, where they remained two years, when they again made a move west, this time going to Washington county, Iowa, where the subject of this sketch resided until 1853, when he made his way to California with ox-teams, being *one hundred and seventy-five days* on the road. They doubtless wondered if a railway would ever be laid down over the interminable territory of sage-brush and alkali plains? He first located in Nevada county, remaining there one year, engaged in mining; from there to Fresno county, where he lived five years, engaged in teaming and freighting. In 1858 he removed from Fresno to Amador county, locating on his present ranch, about two and one-half miles from Plymouth, on the road to Oleta. The place contains two hundred acres of land, which is pleasantly situated and convenient for business. He was married in 1844 to Rachel Simmons, a native of Ohio. The family consists of Mr. Whitacre, wife and two children, a son and daughter, the latter being married, the son residing with the parents.

STEPHEN C. WHEELER

Is a native of Indiana, having been born November 14, 1828, at the town of Seymour, Jackson county, where he resided until 1852, when he migrated to California, traveling across the plains with an ox-team, reaching Amador county, September 30th, settling in that portion of it which at that time formed a part of El Dorado county. He followed mining some fifteen years with varied success, making, however, no big strikes. His experience in a gold-bearing lava bed was more interesting than profitable, interesting to mineralogists at least, as throwing some light on the method of the superficial deposit of gold. Most of his mining was done in Amador county, his family, during the time, living on the ranch which he is now cultivating, about two miles west of Plymouth. Since 1867 Mr. Wheeler has paid more attention to agriculture as more sure, if not so brilliant in its results, than mining.

He is also interested, with another party, in the introduction of the "Asbestine Sub-irrigation Pipe," which, it is thought, will be generally adopted, and work a great revolution in the method of irrigation, as agriculture, in many places, depends upon an economical use of water.

He was married February 21, 1850, to Miss Mary E. Thompson, a native of Indiana. His family consists of himself, wife and ten children, five sons and five daughters, two of the daughters being married.

F. M. WHITMORE.

Flint Monroe Whitmore was born at Ashburnham, Massachusetts, December 22, 1822. He remained in his native State until 1845, when he moved to Baltimore, which place he made his home until 1849, when he returned to Massachusetts, making his home in Boston. Following the current of emigration he embarked for California via the Isthmus, and arrived in San Francisco in June, 1850, reaching Volcano in November following, which latter place he has since made his home. Mr. Whitmore engaged in both placer and quartz mining with varied success, sometimes winning moderately, but not making himself a millionaire. In 1862, he engaged in farming a few miles above Volcano, planting out quite an extensive orchard; the climate, soil, and elevation, being peculiarly adapted to the production of fruit. Stock and grain farming also received a share of his attention. In 1862, he purchased a saw-mill and a tract of timber land on Antelope creek, which have since demanded the largest share of his attention. The region in which he is located is one possessing many attractions to the lovers of nature. The lofty pines, the magnificent prospect overlooking the great Sacramento valley, the pure atmosphere, and cool water, form a combination of pleasing objects which never tires the beholder. Though Mr. Whitmore has drawn around him many of the comforts and elegancies of life, he remains a single man, a niece, Mrs. C. E. Heath, doing the honors of his house. As a citizen, Mr. Whitmore is conscientious, firm, and independent, possessing the confidence and respect of the community, always maintaining the self-respect and honor, characteristic of his place of birth. A view of his mill and surroundings is given in another part of the work. No artist can do justice to the scenery, which must be seen to be appreciated. His ranch contains three hundred and twenty acres of land; his timber tract, one hundred and sixty.

N. C. WILLIAMS

Is a native of the State of Maine, having been born at Embden, Somerset county, January 20, 1834. His life was passed in the town where he first saw the light, until he reached the age of sixteen years. He had acquired a good education during these years, and in 1850 left home and obtained a situation in the city of Boston, Massachusetts, where he remained about three years as clerk in a ship yard.

As youth ripened into manhood, he aspired to something different from the old routine to which he was accustomed, and fired with enthusiasm from the reports of people on the Pacific coast, he determined to ascertain personally what Dame Fortune had in store for him in that region; accordingly with the thought came the action, and in 1855 he bade farewell to his eastern friends and sought new ones in California, arriving in San Francisco in due time, by way of the Isthmus of Panama.

His first permanent location was in Amador county, where he has since resided, with the exception of one year, during which he visited his old home in the States. His occupation for the first ten years of his California life, was in the usual vocation of mining; but upon his return from the States he engaged in various kinds of business.

In 1871 he settled on his present ranch, which is located on the Pine Grove and Antelope toll-road, fourteen miles east of Jackson. He is very pleasantly situated, and is a gentleman esteemed by all who have the honor of his acquaintance. He was married May 13, 1874, to Miss Rosella Worley.

JOSEPH WOOLFORD

Was born at Ramsbury, Wiltshire, in England, February 7, 1832, where he resided until 1858, when he went to Peru, in South America, by way of Cape Horn, where he resided for four years. After this he came to California and lived at the place then called "Puckerville," about a half mile to the west of the town of Plymouth.

Mr. Woolford is a blacksmith by trade, having followed it most of his life, being at present in the employ of the Pacific Mining Company, though he has at other times been employed by the Empire Mining Company. He is a first-class mechanic, and has suggested and perfected many improvements in tools and machinery. Among other things he has invented a ratchet wrench which works equally well on round as on square heads, for which he has obtained a patent.

He is a single man, living with his brother, who occupies his ranch. His experiences in the mines and in South America, make an interesting narrative when he can be induced to speak of them.

D. YOUNGLOVE

Was born July 13, 1833, at Great Barrington, Berkshire county, Massachusetts, where he spent his boyhood and acquired his education. In 1851, he removed to Waushara county, Wisconsin, where he engaged in farming until 1864, when he sought the Golden State. Here he engaged in freighting from Sacramento to the different mining towns of Amador, making his home at first north of Volcano. He followed this business until 1875, when he purchased the highly improved Edward's property, for about ten thousand dollars, which place he has since made his home. This place contains two hundred and thirty-three acres of Ione valley land, than which nothing better can be said. The orchards, buildings, and approaches, are laid out in European style, with drives and graveled walks, bordered with flowers and fragrant herbs. It was for many years, and probably is now, the most artistically improved place in the county. The coal vein underlies a large portion of the place. The Galt & Ione railroad passes through the southern side of the place, the depot being but a few hundred feet from his land, thus affording ample market facilities for coal, or the produce of the farm. The vein of coal is from three to fifteen feet in thickness, lying nearly on a level with the valley in the adjoining hills. The cost of mining is less than one dollar per ton. The coal burns freely, and is used for domestic purposes, and also as a steam coal, being worth per ton about the same as a cord of wood. The orchard contains about sixteen hundred trees, bearing choice fruit.

F PARKS

CHRONOLOGICAL.

1513.
Discovery of the Pacific ocean by Balboa.
1518.
Invasion of Mexico by Cortez.
1519.
First Navigation of the Pacific by Magellan.
1534.
Discovery of Lower California by Cortez.
1535.
Further Exploration of the California gulf.
1537.
Explorations on the Western coast by Ulloa.
1542.
Expedition of Cabrillo. Cape Mendocino discovered.
1554.
Death of Cortez.
1577.
Sir Francis Drake's discoveries.
1579.
California taken possession of by Sir Francis Drake in the name of Queen Elizabeth.
1596.
Viscaiño takes possession of Lower California.
1602.
San Diego harbor discovered by Viscaiño.
1683.
First attempt to colonize Lower California at La Paz by Admiral Otondo and Friar Kühn.
1697.
October 25. The first Jesuit Mission established at Loreto, in Lower California, by Father Salvatierra.
1700.
The second Jesuit Mission established at San Xavier, Lower California, by Father Ugarte.
First Expedition into the Interior by Father Kino.
1720.
Expedition of Father Ugarte to the river Colorado.
1766.
Expeditions of Father Wincestus Link.
1767.
The Jesuits expelled from Lower California, and the Franciscans installed.
1768.
Gaspar de Portala appointed Governor of Californias, and Francis Junipero Serra, Missionary President.
1769.
Expeditions dispatched by land and water into Upper California.
July 16. San Diego Mission founded.
1770.
June 3. Monterey Mission founded.
1771.
July 14. San Antonio Mission founded.

September 8. San Gabriel Mission founded.
Reinforcements and supplies arrive at San Diego.
1772.
September 1. San Luis Obispo Mission founded.
Father Serra returned from Mexico with reinforcements and supplies.
1775.
Expedition of Friar Garzes through the upper territory.
November 4. San Diego attacked by Indians.
1776.
June. San Diego Mission repaired.
October 9. San Francisco (Dolores) Mission founded.
November 1. San Juan Capistrano Mission founded.
1777.
January 18. Mission of Santa Clara founded.
1781.
September 4. Pueblo de Los Angeles established.
1782.
March 31. San Buena Ventura Mission founded.
1784.
Los Nietos tract granted to Manuel Nieto.
October 20. San Rafael tract granted to Jose Maria Verdugo.
1786.
December 4. Santa Barbara Mission founded.
1787
December 8. La Purissima Conception Mission founded.
1791.
August 28. Santa Cruz Mission founded.
October 9. La Soledad Mission founded.
1797.
June 11. San Jose Mission founded.
June 24. San Juan Bautista Mission founded.
July 25. San Miguel Mission founded.
September 8. San Fernando Mission founded.
1798.
June 13. Mission of San Luis Rey de Francia founded.
1802.
Humboldt visits California.
1804.
September 17. Mission of Santa Inez founded.
1810.
Santiago de Santa Ana tract granted Antonio Yorba
1812.
December 8. Mission of San Juan Capistrano destroyed by earthquake.
December 21. Church of La Purissima destroyed by earthquake.
1815.
W. Whittle claims to have arrived in Los Angeles, being the first English-speaking settler in California.

1818.
Bouchard's privateer attacked the coast towns. Joseph Chapman and Thomas Fisher captured and taken to Los Angeles.

1819.
December 14. San Rafael Mission founded.

1822.
Mexican independence established.
Captain John Hall, of the British Navy, examined and reported on the Pacific coast harbors.

1824.
Santiago McKinley settled in Los Angeles.
First Act of the Mexican Government toward secularization of the missions passed.

1825.
Jedediah S. Smith entered California overland.

1826.
Manumission of the Indians declared.

1827.
First Mexican school established.
Great drought.

1828.
Jesse Ferguson, Richard Laughlin, N. M. Pryor, Abel Stearns, and Louis Bouchette, settled in Los Angeles. Continued drought.

1829.
Michael White and John Domingo, settled in Los Angeles.

1831.
Manuel Victoria became Governor.
J. J. Warner, William Wolfskill, Luis Vignes, Joseph Bowman, John Rhea, and William Day, settled in Los Angeles.
The schooner *Refugio* built at San Pedro.

1833.
Death of Padre Sanchez.

1834.
August 9. Complete secularization of the missions decreed.
Hijar's expedition.
Destruction of the mission property.
Luis Vignes plants the first orange orchard in Los Angeles.
First soap factory established.

1835.
Hijar's insurrection. Death of Governor Figueroa.
R. H. Dana visits California.
Henry Mellus and Hugo Reid settle in Los Angeles.
The first lynching.

1836.
Census taken.
Graham's insurrection.
Los Angeles erected into a city.

1838.
Arrest of suspected persons.
Second Mexican school established in Los Angeles.

1840.
Isaac Graham and companions arrested and sent to Mexico.
May 18. Grant of Arroyo Seco made to Theodosia Yorba, by Juan B. Alvarado.

1841.
United States exploring expedition examined the California coast.

1842.
Micheltorena Governor.
October 19. Seizure of Monterey by United States Commodore Jones.
October 20. Its restoration.
Discovery of gold in Los Angeles county.

1843.
January 18. Commodore Jones visits Governor Micheltorena at Los Angeles.

1844.
Great drought.
Lancasterian school established in Los Angeles.

1845.
Continued drought.
February 21. Battle at Cahuenga between Micheltorena and Alvarado. A mule killed.

1846.
March. Arrival of Fremont and exploring party.
Sutter sawed lumber on the divide between Sutter and Amador.
April. The Donner party start for California.
May 11. War with Mexico declared by Congress.
June 11. First act of hostility by Fremont's party.
June 15. The Bear flag hoisted.
July 7. Monterey captured by Commodore Sloat.
July 8. Yerba Buena captured.
July 27. Fremont's battalion sent to San Diego.
July 28. Rev. Walter Colton appointed alcalde of Monterey.
July 29. Commodore Sloat sailed for the East.
August 1. Stockton sails for San Pedro.
August 4. Stockton captures Santa Barbara.
August 6. Stockton arrives at San Pedro.
August 15. Los Angeles City occupied by Stockton.
August 15. The *Californian* issued, by Semple and Colton, at Monterey.
September 4. First jury trial in California at Monterey.
September 23. Flores' insurrection against Gillespie.
Gillespie surrenders, and embarks at San Pedro.
B. D. Wilson's party captured by Varelas.
October 7. Captain Mervine landed at San Pedro, and was defeated.

1847.
January 8. Battle of the Rio San Gabriel.
" 9. Battle of the *Mesa*.
" 10. Los Angeles re-occupied by Commodore Stockton.
January 11. Proclamation by Stockton.
" 12. Treaty of peace agreed upon between General John C. Fremont and General Andres Pico at Cahuenga.
March 1. Stephen W. Kearney recognized as Governor.
April. Semi-monthly mails established between San Francisco and San Diego.
May 31. Richard B. Mason became Governor.

1848.

January 19. Discovery of gold at Coloma.
February 2. Treaty of peace signed at Guadalupe Hidalgo.

1849.

January 4. *Alta California* newspaper established in San Francisco.
February 7. First Pacific Railroad bill introduced in Congress.
February 28. Steamer *California* reached San Francisco.
April 13. General Bennett Riley became Governor.
June 3. Governor Riley issued proclamation for a Convention at Monterey.
October 13. Constitution signed.
November 13. Constitution ratified by the people.
December 15. First Legislature convened at San Jose.
December 20. Governor Peter H. Burnett inaugurated.

1850.

February 18. State divided into twenty-seven counties. Calaveras county organized.
County seat captured at Double Spring and moved to Jackson.
April 9. State Library founded.
May 4. Second great fire in San Francisco.
June 3. Third great fire in San Francisco.
Celebration of the Fourth at Jackson, McDowell delivering an oration.
Colonel Collyer shot by Judge Smith.
September 9. California admitted into the Union.
September 17. Fourth great fire in San Francisco.

1851.

Second Legislature convened at San Jose.
February 14. Act approved removing capital to Vallejo.
The Irving party massacred by the Cahuilla Indians.
Gregory's Atlantic and Pacific Express established.
November 12. Attempt to assassinate Benjamin Hayes.
September 9. Grand Division Sons of Temperance organized.

1852.

January 2. United States Land Commission met at San Francisco.
January 5. Third session of Legislature at Vallejo.
September. Riot at Jamison's ranch, four Mexicans being whipped. Arrest of Jamison and son by *posse comitatus* from El Dorado.
County seat removed to Mokelumne Hill.
August. Whitehead murdered near Butler's, on the road between Plymouth and Drytown.
August 4. Sacramento Valley Railroad Company organized.
November 1. Claim four hundred and forty-one, for Arroyo Seco, filed with Land Commissioners.

1853.

January 3. Fourth session of the Legislature met at Vallejo.

February 4. State Capital removed to Benicia.
Tejon Indian reservation established.
June. A man named Smith died from the effects of a rattlesnake bite near Fiddletown.
— Porter, superintendent of the Willow Spring ditch, murdered near the race-track, probably by Dutch Chris, and Harry Fox, who murdered Beckman at Volcano about the same time.
August. Eureka Hotel burned at Volcano.
November. A gambler, named Baldwin, shot and killed by another of the same profession, named Whitney.
Doctor Beck killed Norton at Lancha Plana.
Death of Joaquin Murietta.
December. H. A. Carter and E. B. Harris, citizens of Ione, learned the existence of the claim called the "Arroyo Seco," while at Benicia, the then capital.

1854.

January 1. California Stage Company began operations.
January 2. Legislature convened at Benecia.
February 25. State Capital removed to Sacramento.
March 1. California Steam Navigation Company organized.
March 23. Hanging of the Swede at Jackson.
April 4. Fire at Jackson, loss twenty-eight thousand five hundred dollars.
May 13. Act approved establishing a State Agricultural Society.
June 17. Election to determine whether the county of Amador should be formed out of a part of Calaveras.
July 3. Commissioners appointed by Legislature met to call election for county officers of the new county.
July 17. First county officers elected.
August 3. G. F. Elliot killed in a difficulty by C. Y. Hammond.
September 10. First Court of Sessions.
September 11. J. K. Payne allowed twelve dollars and fifty cents for services in building a school-house at Grass Valley.
E. P. Hunter killed at Lancha Plana by John Chapman.
October 4. First State Fair held at San Francisco.
October. Joseph H. Antonio, Francis Munioz, subjects of Coroner's investigations.
George Simmons on trial for manslaughter.
November 9. Sacramento Valley Railroad Company re-organized.
November. Messer hung by a mob at Volcano, for the murder of McAllister.

1855.

January 1. First financial report of Amador county. $10,532.50 in treasury, which on May 4th amounted to $16,649.59; outstanding orders, $7,972.84, leaving a net of $8,876.75.
February 27 Claim four hundred and forty-one, for

Arroyo Seco grant, rejected by Land Commissioners.

May 5. Wm. M. Seawell and J. T. King are appointed Justices of the Peace.

May 8. Townships No. 5 and 6 organized.

1855.

May 9. E. B. Yates appointed Justice of the Peace for Township No. 6.

May 15. William M. Seawell, Justice of the Peace, resigned, and F. G. Hoard appointed in his place.

May 16. Four dollars road tax assessed on persons between twenty-one and fifty.

May 19. Board of Supervisors allowed J. C. Shipman five hundred dollars for acting as County Auditor, which he declined taking, deeming it insufficient.

June 21. Supervisors ordered the building of a county jail, costing four thousand two hundred and eighty dollars; Craft & Beale, contractors.

August 6. Killing of six persons at Lower Rancheria by banditti.

August 7. Hanging of three Mexicans at the same place.

General disarming of the Mexicans.

August 12. Death of Sheriff Phœnix at Chinese Camp.

Burning of the church and other houses at Drytown.

Samuel A. Phœnix appointed Sheriff, in place of W. A. Phœnix, deceased.

Hanging at Jackson of three Mexicans concerned in Rancheria tragedy—day uncertain.

Manuel Escobar was the last of the party hanged; he was also the last executed on the famous tree.

Supervisor Districts established.

August 24. First railroad train in California placed on the track of Sacramento Valley Railroad.

September. Board of Supervisors organized.

October 27. *Amador Ledger* commenced at Volcano.

November 15. J. C. Shipman allowed three hundred and fifty-two dollars and fifty cents for making out assessment roll and tax list.

December 21. Three professional robbers, camping about three miles below Jackson, were attacked by Sheriff Thorn, of Calaveras, detective Hume, and J. W. Surface of Ione, two being captured. A large amount of burglars' tools found in the camp.

1854 AND 1855.

Legislature set off territory of El Dorado as part of the county of Amador.

1856.

January 8. —— killed by Cottrell, at Volcano.

March. Survey of Arroyo Seco Grant.

April 6. Cottrell re-arrested at Placerville and placed in Amador jail; eventually tried and executed.

May 16. Vigilance Committee formed in San Francisco.

May 22. Casey and Cora hung by Vigilance Committee in San Francisco.

June 3. Governor Johnson issued a proclamation calling out the State militia to suppress Vigilantes.

June 21. Arrest of Judge David S. Terry by Vigilance Committee of San Francisco.

July 29. Hetherington and Brace hung by Vigilance Committee in San Francisco.

October 5. D. L. Wells, of the Gate, thrown from his carriage while riding down the grade between Mokelumne Hill and the river and killed.

October 6. Death of Thomas Hodges, *alias* Tom Bell, the noted highwayman.

1857.

June 15. First stage on the wagon road, completed round trip, Placerville to Carson Valley.

September 18. Death of Chief Justice Hugh Murray.

September 29. State Fair held at Stockton.

November 7. M. V. B. Griswold murdered by Chinamen.

November. Difficulty near Volcano in which two men were killed by Stevenson, who was tried and executed.

1858.

April 16. Three Chinamen hung at Jackson for the murder of M. V. B. Griswold.

July 23. First overland mail *via* Placerville and Salt Lake left Sacramento.

Fraser River excitement.

1859.

Discovery of the Comstock Ledge.

August. Survey made by Mandeville, locating Arroyo Seco ten miles further west.

September 13. State Fair held at Sacramento.

September 14. Terry and Broderick duel. San Mateo county; Broderick mortally wounded.

November. Large fire in Volcano, burning St. George Hotel and twenty-five other buildings.

1860.

April 26. Judge McAllister decided that the Arroyo Seco Grant should be located west of the Lyons and Martin mountains.

April. Pony express established, and first messenger left Sacramento.

May 12. Massacre of the Ormsby party near Pyramid lake.

September. Death of the Indian chief Captain Truckee.

1861.

January 13. State Agricultural Society decided to make Sacramento a permanent location.

Instrumental survey of the route for the Central Pacific railroad over the Sierras made during this year.

February 16. Meeting in Volcano regarding the building of a wagon road to Nevada.

February 19. Joseph Worthy killed by a slide of earth at Irishtown.

February 23. Meeting in Jackson regarding the building of a wagon road to Nevada.

May 15. Corner-stone of State House laid.

June 28. Articles of incorporation of Central Pacific Railroad of California filed with the Secretary of State.

1862.

January 23. Legislature adjourned to San Francisco on account of flood.
July 1. Pacific Railroad Act approved by President.
August 8 and 9. First fair held in Amador county.
August 8 and 9. First bale of hops raised in Amador county on exhibition at the county fair by J. D. Mason.
August 23. Fire at Jackson, destroying the town.
Hanging-tree at Jackson cut down.
August. Mandeville's survey, on appeal from District Court, confirmed by Judge Hoffman.
October. Fire at Volcano destroying the St. George Hotel and other property.
November 4. Earthquake shock felt at Tarr's Mill.
November 14. Fitzgerald killed by the caving of a bank at Lancha Plana.
November 18. William Golman found dead near his residence; cause of death heart disease.
December 13. Western Pacific Railroad Company incorporated.

1863.

January 8. Ground broken for the Central Pacific railroad at Sacramento.
January 20. Beeson's store entered by masked men Beeson "bucked and gagged," and then robbed; names of robbers unknown.
February 3. Appeal to United States Supreme Court from the decision of Judge Hoffman in the matter of locating the survey of the Arroyo Seco Grant dismissed without a hearing.
February 9. Jerry Conley killed at Lancha Plana by the caving of a bank of gravel.
February 11. Harry Hatch, long known in Amador county, died at the residence of D. C. White.
February 22. Construction of the Central Pacific railroad commenced.
Act approved by Governor granting ten thousand dollars per mile to the Central Pacific railroad.
April 25. A colored boy, aged eighteen, fatally stabbed his father.
May. Capp killed on his claim at Pokerville by A. Moore.
June 2. J. S. Porter appointed Justice of the Peace for Township No. 4, vice H. Wood, resigned.
June 5. Conny Mahoney fatally stabbed by Jack Willson.
July 7. Precinct established at Copper Center.
July 7. Precinct established at Elliott's Ranch.
July 14. James H. Allen drowned in Sacramento river.
July 20. House of Edward Dosh, Ione valley, destroyed by fire; loss, two thousand five hundred dollars.
July 21. Philip Morgan fell two hundred feet in a shaft of the Eureka mine, killing him instantly.

August 8. The Amador wagon road opened to the public.
August 17. Fernandino Belliuomini killed at French Bar by the falling of a timber.
September 7. Three prisoners escaped from the jail by making a hole through the brick walls.
September. Child of Sylvester Rogers, near Willow Spring creek, crushed by the displacement and rolling of a rock.
October. A. F. Northrup exhibited an apple weighing thirty and one-half ounces, of the Glori Mundi variety.
November 4. Frederick Fernsner, of Drytown, committed suicide by shooting himself.
November 14. Charles K. Williams killed by a fall in the shaft of the Plymouth mine.
November 15. A heavy wind blew down a tree on the house of B. Henderson, near Volcano, fatally injuring him.
November 17. Stage stopped and express robbed of two thousand dollars between Fiddletown and Drytown.
December 16. Peter McCabe died from injuries received by being thrown from a wagon.
December 31. Two teamsters robbed of five hundred dollars by highwaymen on the Carson grade.
Three cases for murder came before the District Court.
Thomas Hodge found dead in Cook's Gulch. No clue to the murderer.
Thieves were plentiful around Jackson.
Nevada City destroyed by fire. Loss, five hundred and fifty thousand dollars.

1864.

February 13. Samuel's store in Jackson robbed of cash and clothing amounting to seven hundred dollars.
February 21. David Armstrong died at Gold Hill, Nevada Territory.
February 24. The dwelling of George Clark, in New York Gulch, destroyed by fire; loss, three thousand dollars.
April 6. J. R. Blackwell and —— Sturtevant, near Yeomet, got into an altercation in which the first was killed and the latter severely wounded; cause, a woman.
April 14. Chestnut's building and Crosson's saloon, Oleta, destroyed by fire. Mr. Ford, jeweler, lost his tools and a portion of his stock.
June 13. The wire suspension bridge over the Mokelumne river, between Mokelumne Hill and West Point, fell with sixty head of cattle, all of which were killed. The bridge was about fifty feet high.
August 20. Child of Mrs. Lewis, near Newton mine, burned to death by clothes taking fire.
September. Rattlesnake killed near Middle fork, Jackson Creek, measuring eight feet and three inches in length, thirteen rattles.

1864.
October 26. Writs of ejectment at the instance of Benjamin Bellock issued against William Atkinson, J. C. Fithian, Thomas Rickey, and others, by Judge Field.
November 22. E. H. Chase and E. Rickey died at Ione City, as was believed, from small-pox.
November. An elderly man by the name of Merchant killed by Michael Doonan.

1865.
January 6. Daniel Kerrigan was crushed to death in the Oneida mine, near Jackson.
January 8. C. N. W. Hinkson, Drytown, killed in a difficulty with his son-in-law, a Mr. Hudsell.
February 11. Captain Starr, with seventy-five soldiers, come into Ione valley to dispossess the settlers.
February 17. J. C. Fithian, William Scully, Charles Black, Samuel Deardorff, and others, ejected from their homes in Jackson valley, by Captain Starr and a company of United States troops, acting under the directions of Herman Wohler.
February 19. Herman Wohler shot at Ione.
March 6. Second body of soldiers enter Ione valley, making total number three hundred.
April 23. John Gaver arrested by Captain Starr for "exulting over the assassination of Lincoln."
May 5. Fire in Volcano. Loss, twenty thousand dollars.
May 8. L. P. Hall and W. M. Penry arrested by Captain Starr of Company D, United States Cavalry, and conveyed to Fort Alcatraz.
June 6. Chinaman shot by an Indian at Sutter creek, for refusing to clean up his sluices for the Indian's benefit.
June 11. Fire in Amador City, destroying several buildings.
June 18. Herbertville quartz mill, near Amador, totally destroyed by fire. Loss, thirteen thousand dollars.
July 1. Fire in Jackson; Congress Hall, Washington Hotel, and Schlacter's building, being consumed. Two men injured, one fatally, in the Eureka mine, by the falling of a timber. Hayne bled to death in a few minutes.
July 3. William Ritter, owner of ditch property in Amador county, shot near Michigan Bar, by masked persons. Sam. Marshall supposed to be one of the party.
July 17. Lipker killed in the Keystone mine, by the falling of a timber.
July 22. Earthquake shock felt through the county; severest on the junction of the foot-hills and plains.
July 25. Andrew McClure fatally injured by premature explosion of a blast in the Seaton mine.
July. Discovery of rich pocket in the Hinkley mine, Jackson.
August 10. Son of Mr. Raymond of Jackson, aged two years, drowned in Silver lake.
August 20. Quarrel among a party of Mexicans near Aqueduct, in which one Francisco Vedall was killed by Manuel Peralto.
August 31. Azariah Sollers committed suicide, by shooting himself through the head. Cause, financial embarrassment.
August. Central Pacific railroad purchased Sacramento Valley railroad.
October 8. Great fire in Ione, destroying one entire block.
October 12. Explosion of the steamer *Yo Semite*, in which W. A. Rogers, and Senator-elect G. W. Seaton, were killed.
October 26. James Casey, while intoxicated, was run over by the stage in the night, near the summit, and fatally injured.
October 27. Martin Collins killed in the Eureka mine, at Sutter Creek.
October 29. Spaniard killed by Mr. Moore, in a difficulty on Wilson's ranch.
October. J. W. Bicknell vs. Amador County, in District Court. Plaintiff recovered $1,362.19, for acting as clerk of District and Probate Courts.
December 3. James Fagan killed near Drytown, by a cave in the Potosi mine.
December 23. A. H. Rose elected Senator, to fill the vacancy caused by the death of G. W. Seaton.
Cosumnes copper mine shipped four hundred tons of ore during June, July, and August.

1866.
February 1. Attack made on a Chinese mining camp near Upper Rancheria, in which two Chinamen lost their lives. Dan Myers, hearing the firing, ran over to the assistance of the Chinamen, receiving a ball in his knee, after which the robbers left.
February 28. The body of L. L. Leonard found west of the town of Enterprise, accidentally shot by himself.
February. David Robinson, mining near Volcano, picked up a nugget of pure gold, weighing five and three-fourths pounds.
March 18. Nugget found near Clinton, worth six hundred and thirty-five dollars and twenty-five cents.
March. Titus Rowe shot and instantly killed, by M. Tynan, who was acquitted at the June term of the District Court, 1867.
April 2. Mexican, name unknown, found dead in his claim, near Jackson.
April 3. Niel Toland killed near Irish Hill, by caving of bank of earth.
May 16. Dr. Lund of Muletown, near Ione, committed suicide by cutting his throat with a razor. Financial embarrassment.
May 20. Child of Mr. and Mrs. Galavia burned to death at Volcano.
June 2. Report of Supervisors, outstanding warrants, exclusive of interest, $104,094.57¾.
June 24. Anson Perry died from the effect of a pistol shot, by a Chinaman engaged in robbing a chicken roost.

June 25. Hoisting works of the Sorocco mine, near Volcano, destroyed by fire.
June. Bank of California organized.
July 3. J. Weimbach killed by John Fridenburg, with a billiard ball, during a quarrel at Volcano.
July 4. Pedro Roja, a native of Chili, murdered by parties unknown, near Fiddletown.
Santa Nino, a native of Chili, killed at Jackson, by Louis Robinson.
A woman, named Paublo Monaz, killed in her house on Main street in Jackson, by a Spaniard known as Jose G. Froile.
Three men, Fitzgerald, Branahan, and Faulkner, burned to death while asleep, in a house at Copper Hill.
July 7. Precincts under the new registration law established by Board of Supervisors.
July 18. Otto Walther appointed Treasurer in place of L. Rabolt, declared ineligible.
August 16. Harvey Lee, Assemblyman from Amador and Alpine counties, and Judge of the 16th Judicial District, thrown from a wagon and killed, in Sacramento.
August 18. J. H. Hammond robbed, and left tied to a tree near Sutter Creek, where he remained two days before he was released.
August 24. Water-melon brought into Jackson from Chaleur's ranch, Mokelumne river, weighing fifty-six pounds.
August. Wash. Wright, formerly connected with the press in the county, died at San Francisco of *delirium tremens*.
September. Four cases of murder to be tried in District Court.
October 10. M. Bates, near middle fork of Jackson, lost his house and contents by fire.
December 24. Z. H. Denman found a thirty-three ounce lump of gold, near Grass Valley.
December 28. A. B. Crawford died.
December 29. Stage stopped between Forest Home and Ione City, by robbers; no treasure.

1867.

January 5. Mrs. Church and child drowned in Indian creek.
March 15. Nicholas Orleans killed in the Atchison quartz mine.
March 31. Italian stabbed by countryman, at Sutter Creek.
May 5. James Rodda and Samuel Poglaise killed, by falling down the shaft of the Plymouth mine.
June 3. Manuel Timothy killed at Volcano, by the caving of his mine.
July 10. Philip Burger's brewery, near the Gate, consumed by fire. Loss, two thousand dollars.
July 20. John Phillips of Fiddletown, fatally stabbed during a quarrel, by W. T. Gist, formerly Deputy Sheriff of the county.
August 4. Wagstaff, of Volcano, thrown from a wagon going down the Sutter Creek hill, and fatally injured.

August 6. James M. Hanford appointed Justice of the Peace, *vice* H. T. Barnum resigned.
August 30. A. M. Ballard, a forty-niner, and for many years a resident of Volcano, fell from a bridge in Alamo, Contra Costa county, and sustained injuries from which he died in a few hours.
October 10. Amador Mining Company incorporated. Trustees, Alvinza Hayward, L. A. Garnett, F. Sunderland, A. H. Rose, and S. F. Butterworth.
October 22. D. R. Whitman crushed to death in the Eureka mine at Sutter Creek.
October 23. Two men fell one hundred feet in the Seaton mine, Drytown, and sustained no serious injury.
October 31. Large barn owned by O. N. Morse of Q Ranch, with three horses and eleven hogs, totally destroyed by fire. Loss, eight thousand dollars; insured for three thousand five hundred dollars.
November 8. James C. McFarland, a fair-haired, girlish looking boy, convicted of attempting to commit murder by poisoning. A terrible natural depravity was proved. Sentenced to four years in State Reform School.
November 28. James Morgan, of the Oneida mill, broke his leg.
November 30. A. M. Chappelle committed suicide, by tying weights to his feet, and jumping into the water.
December 3. First frost sufficient to kill melon vines.
December 10. Mrs. Foster, a widow lady at Sutter Creek, was killed by a man called "Eureka John," by a blow from his fist.
December 16. R. Bradshaw removed from the office of Assessor and Collector, and James H. Lowrey appointed to fill the vacancy.
December 17. Joseph King killed in the R. R. mine by a cave, which lacerated the femoral artery, producing death in a short time.
December 27. Big Bar bridge nearly destroyed by high water; the loss falling mostly on Mr. Parrish.
December. Stage robbed near Ione of ten thousand dollars, which was recovered by detectives.
Forty-five thousand gallons of wine made in the vicinity of Jackson. Estimate for county, two hundred thousand gallons.

1868.

January 1. Robinson, of Fiddletown, drowned in the Cosumnes river, near Yeomet.
January 4. Body of unknown man found on Endsley's ranch.
January 7. Boundaries of school districts established.
January 18. Brinn and Newman's store at Sutter Creek robbed of goods valued at one thousand dollars.
February 15. Steckler's house at Jackson burned, the inmates barely escaping.
February 25. Owen Fallon, a respectable man,

being mistaken for an escape from Mokelumne Hill jail, was shot by William Boyd.

March 29. Isaac's store at Newtonville destroyed by fire; supposed to be the work of an incendiary. Loss, three thousand dollars.

April 3. First train of cars run on Western Pacific railroad.

April 6. Stage robbed on the Mokelumne Hill road. Wells, Fargo & Co.'s box rifled. Robbers caught the same day.

April 19. Fire at Volcano, destroying Mooney's saloon, and other property. Loss, twenty thousand dollars.

May 16. Fire at Sutter Creek, destroying Sheridan's harness shop, Myer's saloon, Cuppet's tin shop, Grady's saloon, and Sutter Creek bakery. Loss, ten thousand dollars.

May 26. Shoemaker shot in Sacramento by A. B. Courtwright, formerly of Ione.

May 27. Large fire in Jackson, originating in Chinatown. Loss, fifteen thousand dollars; mostly property of A. C. Brown.

June 2. Fire in Volcano, destroying Goldworthy's saloon, Burleson's warehouse, and other property.

June 10. Amador wagon road leased to John Hosley.

June 13. William Moore tried several times for murder; the jury in the cases disagreeing, he plead guilty, and was sentenced for one year to State prison.

June 16. Fire at Volcano, destroying Sorocco's store.

June 17. District Court decided that James Carroll was the lawful Supervisor for District No. 1, thereby ousting C. H. Ingalls.

June 25. A man by the name of Williams fell into the Eureka shaft and was instantly killed.

June 27. Captain Richards shot by Levy Conley at Volcano; did not terminate fatally.

July 12. Ed. Burns falls four hundred feet in the Eureka mine, at Sutter Creek, and is instantly killed.

August 25. Workmen killed in Eureka shaft at Sutter Creek.

September 7. Kennedy mill started.

September 11. D. C. White's house, Jackson, burned.

September 12. Volcano burned from the St. George to Casinelli's store, including Fridenburg's saloon, Nicholas' meat market and stable, George Shaffer's saloon, and other property.

September 23. Death of Mrs. A. H. Rose, at Amador City.

October 21. Earthquake at San Francisco; sharp shock along the foot-hills of Amador county.

November 28. Cuneo's house, about two miles from Jackson, burned.

December 30. Fire in Jackson. Loss, fifteen thousand dollars.

Year of fires at Volcano, five having occurred.

1869.

January 1. Attempted murder of two children and suicide, by J. R. Walker, at Zimmerman's ranch, near Mokelumne river. One child, a son, died January 13.

January 2. Stage robbed by four highwaymen, between Fiddletown and Drytown.

January 21. Isaac Pierce killed by Joseph Damonti, near the Newton copper mine.

February 10. High water; streams as full as in '61, without doing much injury.

February 11. Chinaman found frozen to death on the hill above the Jackson brewery.

March 14. Coblentz's store at Fiddletown partially destroyed by fire.

March 22. Sanguinetti's store-house, at Jackson, burned. Loss, one thousand dollars.

April 6. Stage line established to Galt, connecting with the California Pacific railroad.

April 21. Mexican found dead near Fiddletown, supposed to have been murdered by Chinamen.

April 29. Death of Judge S. W. Brockway, of congestive chills, in San Mateo county, at the house of Alvinza Hayward.

May 10. Union Pacific and Central Pacific railroads met at Promontory Point.

May 30. Frenchman near Volcano committed suicide by shooting himself.

Chinaman near Volcano committed suicide by hanging.

German, name unknown, near New York ranch, committed suicide by taking strychnine.

June 24. Stage line to Galt established.

June 27. John Scandling killed at the Oneida mine, by falling down the shaft.

August 1. Dwelling of A. P. Woods near Fiddletown destroyed by fire.

August 6. Fire at Jackson, destroying Martell's blacksmith shop, Berry's livery-stable, Wells, Fargo & Co.'s express office; supposed to be incendiary.

August 8. Attempted assassination of Phipps, engineer at Keystone mill.

August 21. Fire in Jackson, destroying the shop of Edward Muldoon, and the dwelling-house of Sanguinettti Caminetti.

September 6. John Fitz Simmons' store at Buena Vista entered, safe abstracted and robbed. Loss, slight.

September 11. John Cables, at Indian Diggings, assassinated in the night time by unknown parties.

September 12. J. Foot Turner, of Jackson, attacked with paralysis.

September 19. Sale of the Keystone mine and mill, by A. H. Rose to a San Francisco company, for one hundred and two thousand dollars.

October 8. Charles Curratto found dead near the Court House, with the appearance of having fallen from an upper window.

October 13. Union House at Jackson fired by Julia Dorr, the cook.

November 6. Francis Tibbetts of Sutter Creek died, aged forty-five years.

December 6. Lamb's bridge fell, instantly killing

George Kopp of Sutter, with seven of the eight horses composing the team.

December 19. House of Joseph Zerga, at Clinton, destroyed by fire.

California Steam Navigation Company transferred all their property to the Central Pacific Railroad Company, sometime during the year.

1870.

February 7. Board of Supervisors passed a resolution, requesting our delegation in the Legislature to use their influence to get a law passed authorizing and compelling the Board of Supervisors to set aside sixty cents on each hundred dollars, as a sinking fund for outstanding registered warrants.

March 2. An Italian, name unknown, killed in his claim by a cave of earth.

March 15. Thomas Leach killed by Joseph in a quarrel.

March 18. Act approved to provide for the redemption of outstanding warrants, and to prevent a farther increase of the debt of said county.

April 10. Amador mine took fire on the seven-hundred-foot level, men all escaping.

April 18. Stage robbed between Ione and Fiddletown of two thousand dollars; robbers arrested, and money recovered.

The house of John Kelly, near Jackson, destroyed by fire.

April 30. A son of Mr. Veley, living near Jackson, fell from a tree, and was fatally injured.

May 15. School-house at Sutter Creek burned by an incendiary.

May 20. Isaac Tripp, a highly respected citizen, killed by a cave of earth in his claim at Butte City.

May 28. Fire at Sutter Creek, destroying McHenry's saloon, Byrd's barber shop, Joyce's tin shop, Tibbett's pattern shop, Quinlan's saloon, Harris' variety store; supposed to be the work of an incendiary.

May 29. Snow fell at Pine Grove.

June 4. Hubert Pritchard, formerly a resident of Volcano, committed suicide by shooting himself in the head with a pistol.

June 20. Row in a camp of Indians, resulting in the death of one, and seriously wounding several more.

July 8. Tom Taylor, an Indian desperado, killed with a dose of strychnine by another Indian, on account of wounded honor in family matters.

July 29. Two Chinamen killed at Sutter Creek, by the falling of a bank of dirt.

August 7. Stage stopped near Volcano, and Wells, Fargo & Co.'s treasure box robbed of a bar of gold worth five thousand dollars; four thousand dollars was offered for the apprehension of the robbers.

August 20. Larry Gannon killed in the Eureka mine, by falling out of the bucket.

August. Laborers' Association established at Sutter Creek.

September 8. Robert Buss' house, in Ione City, burglarized of coin to the amount of one hundred and seventy-five dollars.

1871.

March 7. Tax of the Arroyo Seco Grant company reduced from $11,499.67 to $7,287.50. Assessed value, $394,500.

Tax on Oneida mine reduced from the basis of assessment of $100,000, to that of $76,800, making the taxes $2,238.72.

July 23. Shooting affray at Sutter Creek, in which Hugh McMenomy and E. W. Hatch lost their lives.

August 28. Death of J. Foot Turner, County Judge, at Jackson.

September 12. T. M. Pawling appointed Judge in place of J. Foot Turner, deceased.

October 1. Indian killed by members of his tribe, in a drunken row.

October 4. Three Indians near Ione lassoed a Mexican, and dragged him until he was dead.

October 7. House of Chas. Bennett, Sutter Creek, destroyed by fire.

November 11. Giovanni Quirolo fatally injured in the Paugh mine, near Clinton.

December 23. High water and dangerous traveling; roads nearly impassable.

December. J. A. Eagon announced his intention of acting with the Republican party.

1872.

February 5. Lamb's bridge fell, instantly killing Larkin Lamb and John Kirk.

February 13. A Chileno killed a Mexican in Murderers' Gulch, near Drytown.

February 17. L. N. Ketcham, formerly State Senator from Amador county, died at Yreka.

February 23. J. W. Holman fatally shot during a quarrel, by W. Johnson, who was sentenced to State prison for life.

March 1. Austrian killed in the Eureka mine, by the falling of a stick of timber.

March 23. Hoisting works of the Summit mine destroyed by fire; supposed to be incendiary.

March 24. A. McElrath instantly killed in the Mahoney mine, by a swinging stick of timber.

March 25. Severe shock of earthquake felt all over the county, 2:30 A. M.

May 1. Stage robbed between Pine Grove and Volcano, of ten thousand dollars.

May 11. The Marklee mine cleaned up thirteen thousand dollars, after sixteen days' run with twelve stamps.

June 13. Amador mine (Eureka) took fire; Tom Frakes seriously injured during the efforts to control it. Loss, one hundred thousand dollars.

June 15. George Parker, of Plymouth, thrown from a horse while riding in Sutter Creek, and becoming entangled in the stirrups, was dragged to death.

July. Kennedy mine in twelve days' run made nine thousand dollars.

August 25. August McLarnan thrown from a horse and killed, near Jackson.
September 1. W. H. Bledso thrown from his horse and instantly killed.
September 12. Fire in Sutter Creek on Eureka street, destroying several buildings.
September 13. A son of George Pregnall fell from a wagon, near Mace's mill, and broke his neck.
September 19. Italian boarding-house at Sutter Creek burned.
September 20. Fire in Sutter Creek, consuming dwelling-house, and other property.
October 18. House of Clement Zeres, at Volcano, destroyed by fire.
November 15. Richard Jackson thrown into the Amador shaft (Eureka) by the swinging of the hoisting tub, and precipitated to the bottom, thirteen hundred feet, tearing his body to pieces.
November 18. Peiser's clothing store and Peck's butcher shop, at Sutter Creek, burglarized. Loss, one thousand dollars.
November 26. James Burke ran over by his team, and fatally injured.
December 2. Store of S. Hanford, Volcano, destroyed by fire. Loss, forty thousand dollars.
December 5. George Howard's barn with contents, near Jackson, destroyed by fire.
December 21. James Cole found dead in his cabin near the Oneida. Excessive drink.
December 23. J. L. Howard, foreman of the Lincoln Mining Company, Sutter, caught in the machinery, and instantly killed.
December. Phœnix mill, at Plymouth, forty stamps, put in operation.

1873.

January 6. Total indebtedness Amador county, $208,884.58.
January 13. Attempt to poison four men with strychnine, by putting it in the bread; James Avis, John Yates, N. Rodovich, and an Austrian, partaking were made sick, but recovered.
February 1. Shooting affray at the Lincoln mine, on account of strike and change of time. No one killed.
February 16, 17. Heavy snow-storm; several inches at Jackson, two feet at Pine Grove, three feet at Butterfield's.
February 18. Stabbing affray between George Enfield and Cal Dickens, the former being seriously wounded.
February 21. John J. Watkinson, formerly of Ione, shot and killed J. S. Robinson at Vallejo.
Masquerade ball given by the B. B's at Jackson.
February 22. Fred Tardif shot and instantly killed, by Abram S. Wooly.
March 1. Waterman H. Nelson, an old resident of Amador, shot near Los Angeles, by a man named Parker.
March 2. Harker's barn, near Volcano, with fifty tons of hay, burned.
March 7. Shooting affair at Plymouth between Upton and Deakins, wounding Jackson, who undertook to separate them.
March 8. George Chiradelli and Patrick Collier instantly killed in the Mahoney mine, by the breaking of the hoisting rope, and the fall of the bucket on the men who were working in the bottom of the shaft.
March 16. J. S. Tanner's house, near Sutter, destroyed by fire.
March 31. Masquerade ball at Ione.
April 25. B. Traboca mysteriously killed in the Oneida mine, while descending the shaft in a large iron bucket.
April 28. Decision of Secretary of Interior averse to the State of California, in the matter of title to the school sections.
April. Prevalence of epizootic through the county, nearly all the horses in the livery stables being useless.
May 24. D. Maher's barn, two miles from Jackson, burned with the contents, hay, grain, etc.
June 6. The body of John Ker found (formerly working at the Oneida), having been exposed to the weather and depredations of wild animals during the winter. Supposed to have wandered away in a fit of insanity.
June 7. John Everest killed in the Eureka (Amador) mine by falling down the shaft.
June 20. The house of A. Sheakly burned in the night time, the owner barely escaping with his life. Supposed to be an incendiary fire.
John Collins instantly killed in the Amador mine by falling down the shaft two hundred feet.
June. Bryant & Co. commenced the preliminary work of floating lumber and wood in the Mokelumne river.
July 1. Amador Canal Company incorporated; capital stock five hundred thousand dollars.
July 12. George Hosenfelt instantly killed by the explosion of a giant cartridge while fishing in the Mokelumne river.
August 12. Jerry King thrown from his wagon near Jackson and seriously maimed, losing both hands.
August 16. Residence of P. Grady, Sutter Creek, destroyed by fire.
August 17. L. McLaine of Volcano thrown from his carriage, breaking a leg.
August 25. Death of Dr. Wm. Ives, one of the oldest practicing physicians of Amador county.
August 30. Shooting affray between Silas Penry and E. Turner, in Folger's saloon, Jackson.
September 5. Great disaster in Lincoln mine by which nine persons lost their lives, namely, Patrick Frazier, John Collier, Dennis Lynch, William Coombs, W. H. Rule, G. B. Bobbino, Bartholomeo Gazzolo, Antonio Robles, and Nicholas Balulich.
September 8. Death of E. Turner of Jackson from effect of a pistol shot by S. Penry.

September 11. Death of J. H. Bradley at San Buenaventura.
September 15. House of General McMurran destroyed by fire and two men severely burned, at Ham's station.
September 20. House of John Van Dusen, near Mountain Springs, destroyed by fire. Loss, two thousand dollars.
October 3. B. Gardella fell down one of the shafts of the Oneida and instantly killed.
October 18. The house of John Cook, near Lancha Plana, entered by six masked men for the purpose of robbery, failing because they could not keep the children (John has a full dozen) from running out and giving the alarm.
November 28. Mrs. Good's house at Buckeye burned.
December 2. Snow fell to the depth of several inches on the plains around Ione as well as in Stockton and Sacramento.
December 7. Dennis Townsend, school teacher and ex-School Superintendent, pronounced insane and sent to Stockton.
December 9. Daniel O'Donnell killed by the falling of rock in the Amador mine.
December 18. James Cyne murdered by John Canifex near Forest Home, by stabbing with a knife, Canifex being intoxicated.
December 20. George Shonat drowned in Sutter creek, three miles above the town, while intoxicated.
December 21. John Harker, living above Volcano, mysteriously shot while in bed.

1874.

January 1. Estimated population of Amador county ten thousand five hundred. Estimated assessment roll two million seven hundred and thirty-eight thousand seven hundred and seventy dollars.
January 23. Clement Zeres found dead in his room, with the appearance of having committed suicide by shooting himself through the head with a rifle.
January 25. Thomas Filmer found dead in his cabin five miles from Jackson.
February 6. Dwelling-house of E. S. Schultz, near Volcano, destroyed by fire while the family were absent.
February 26. T. A. Springer, State Printer, and founder of the Amador *Ledger*, died at San Francisco after several months' illness.
February 28. School-house at Sutter Creek burned. Supposed to be an incendiary fire.
March 1. Cutting affray at Volcano, between G. Cassinelli and A. Deluchi, in which the former was instantly killed.
Cutting affray between two Chilenos, in which Antonio Lopez was fatally stabbed.
March 2. G. W. Wagner, first Associate Judge of Amador county and formerly a member of the Legislature, died in Jackson.
March 4. R. N. Smith killed by the premature explosion of a blast on the line of the Amador canal.

April 1. A little daughter of James Grello drowned in a flume at Volcano.
April 18. Joseph Largomarcino fell into the shaft of the Lincoln mine and was instantly killed.
April 24. R. P. Gilliland, a native of Alabama, found dead in his cabin.
April 25. Cutting affray between James Sibert and Francis Bergoon, in which the former was instantly killed.
May 28. Stephen Kenton found dead in his cabin four miles above Amador City.
May 30. Terrible accident in Amador mine, caused by the slipping of the reel on the shaft while hoisting the cage containing five men named Frank Fallon, James Moyle, A. A. Corleiss, Samuel James, and ———, all of whom were instantly killed.
June 11. Barn belonging to Mr. Chantelle, Sutter Creek, destroyed by fire.
June 12. Death of James H. Hardy at San Francisco.
June 27. Last issue of the Sutter Creek *Independent*.
August 1. Water turned into the Amador canal.
Contract between H. B. Platt, constructor of I. and S. Railroad, and Arroyo Seco Grant Company filed in county records.
August 22. John Shearer killed by the fall of a rock from the ascending bucket while working in the Phœnix mine, Plymouth.
August 29. J. R. Hardenburg's house at the Casco mine burned by an incendiary.
August. John Ratto killed by John Devoto. Seven hundred and fifty dollars offered for Devoto's apprehension.
September 2. Local option election in Township No. 2. On the same day also was held an election for Supervisor in Supervisor District No. 1, including Township No. 2. M. Murray was elected Supervisor. The election for or against license: Ione, for license, one hundred and seven, against, one hundred and nine ; Lancha Plana, for license, thirty-nine, against, twenty-three.
September 18. Boarding house at the Kennedy mine destroyed by fire.
October 13. Water run through the Amador canal reaching the distributing reservoir.
O. B. Burton thrown from his horse near Butte City, sustaining fatal injuries.
October 16. Barn at Tarr's mill destroyed by fire. Loss, five thousand dollars.
October 25. Heavy snow-storm in the mountains, causing considerable difficulty in getting the cattle and sheep off the Summer pastures.
December 18. John H. Kruger committed suicide at the house of W. Atkinson, Jackson valley, by shooting himself through the head.

1875.

January 12. James Melody killed by falling rock in the Phœnix mine, Plymouth.
January 24. Death of John B. Keyes at Sutter Creek.

March 1. House of J. M. F. Johnston at Muletown destroyed by fire. Loss estimated at ten thousand dollars.
May 1. M. E. Pearson fatally shot by David Ryal, about three miles from Drytown.
May 2. Stage and passengers robbed on the Galt road near Ione, of about one thousand dollars.
May 8. Great robbery of county funds, amounting to fifteen thousand two hundred and forty-eight dollars, most of which belonged to the school fund.
June 17. Special meeting of Board of Supervisors, to consider the matter of the loss of the county funds.
June 20. David Ryal found guilty of murder in the first degree, for killing M. Pearson, April last, near Drytown.
June 21. Death of Rev. S. G. Briggs, for many years Superintendent of Schools.
July 18. The residence of William Smith, in Sutter Creek, destroyed by fire.
Daniel Moon killed while blasting logs, near Amador City.
September 1. Thomas Andrews found dead, partially devoured by hogs, at Bledford's ranch on Amador wagon road, in accordance with a dream to that effect.
September 25. George Lafferty fatally injured by being thrown from his horse, near Plymouth.
September 26. John Devoto acquitted of the charge of murder in killing John Ratto, in 1874.
November 7. Frank Williams killed in a difficulty with Peter Yaoan, near Drytown.
November 27. Thos. McCullough found drowned in Jackson creek, near Filmer's ranch.
December 15. A Cornishman, named Rogers, while ascending the ladder of the Amador mine, fell about two hundred and fifty feet, and was instantly killed.
December 18. Extensive fire in the Amador mine.

1876.

January 1. Masquerade ball by the K. A. C.
January 3. Francisco Viannelli found dead in his cabin, near the Zeile mine.
January 9. Stage robbed between Plymouth and Fiddletown.
January 31. Attempted robbery of stage near Willow Springs.
March 18. Capture of the noted stage robber, Joaquin Murietta,* who escaped from the cabin, below Jackson, when two others were arrested.
March 18. Three persons, Mr. D. B. Baccigalupi, Miss Carrie Payne, and Miss Louisa Poriare, drowned in attempting to cross the Mokelumne river, below Lancha Plana.
April 13. Fire in Amador, destroying G. W. Kling's saloon, W. Burn's drug store, P. Heisch's barber shop, William Payton's saloon, M. Mooney's saloon and dwelling, Kerr's livery-stable.
April 14. Samuel Mugford fell in the shaft of the Garfield mine, and was instantly killed.

*Not the famous bandit of 1852.

May 2. Richard Webb arrested, at the instance of the Board of Supervisors, for libel.
May 19. Mrs. Murphy's saloon and dwelling, near Jackson, burned.
May 20. Snow at Jackson, and other mountain towns, falling five inches deep at Volcano.
May 23. Robbery of safe in Wells, Fargo and Co.'s office in Amador.
May 26. G. W. Arthur, a patient at the hospital, committed suicide by hanging.
June 2. Attempt to murder L. Largomarcini and family, at Sutter Creek, with giant powder, by which the building was seriously damaged, but no lives lost.
June 18. Younglove's barn at Ione burned, with three mules and seventy-five tons of hay. Fire supposed to be incendiary.
June 20. Indian killed by trap gun while robbing Joseph Cuneo's sluices.
July 1. James Welch, Kennedy Flat, died from sun-stroke.
Arnold Slinghaide, Plymouth, died from sun-stroke.
July 4. Paolo Largomarcini, mentally deranged, perished from sickness and exposure in Sailor's Gulch, near Slabtown.
William Baker, of Jackson valley, thrown from his horse near Ione, and fatally injured.
July 18. Barn belonging to Mrs. Westfall, in Jackson, destroyed by fire.
July 20. Edward Going fatally injured by a cave in the Oneida mine.
July 27. Miguel Doranco found dead in his cabin, evidently murdered some days before, by parties unknown.
July 30. Death of Dr. J. A. Brown of Sutter Creek, an old and highly esteemed resident of the town.
July 31. Volcano Tunnel Company broke ground.
August 3. M. W. Gordon announced his return to the Democratic party.
September 11. Stage robbed on the Drytown road near Finn's ranch, by Chas. Thompson and Chas. Tedeman, both of whom were subsequently arrested and convicted.
September 26. Blass Thomas instantly killed in the Oneida mine, by the falling of a timber down the shaft.
October 21. Accident in the Oneida mine, instantly killing two men and wounding two others.
November 3. Tournament at Ione City.
November 11. Samuel Keller, of Sutter Creek, committed suicide by shooting himself with a pistol.
November 26. Major Green's house, between Ione and Jackson, destroyed by fire.
December 7. Trains commenced running between Ione and Galt.
December 11. F. N. Hoss kicked by a horse, from the effects of which he died on the following morning.
December 14. House of Nicholas Radovich destroyed by fire. Insured for sixteen hundred dollars.

Assessment roll of Amador county, two million five hundred and sixty-three thousand three hundred and seventy dollars.

1877.

January 15, 16, 17. Heavy rains, doing much damage to the Galt and Ione railroad, one car-load of passengers having to remain on the road all night.

January 21. Death of Hon. T. M. Pawling, County Judge.

February 1. Butte Basin Mining Company incorporated.

February 2. Incorporation of the Ione Coal Company by Mark Hopkins, D. D. Colton, C. E. Green, F. S. Dougherty, and C. H. Redington.

February 4. Stage robbed of fifteen hundred dollars near Mountain Springs House.

February 23. Boarding-house of Mrs. Hurley, at Sutter Creek, destroyed by fire; adjoining houses, owned by Burns and Hubbel, seriously damaged.

March 6. Wife and three children of A. Liver-edge, formerly of this county, burned to death at Colusi.

March 18. Three children of Jesse Rhodes, of Buckeye valley, aged eight, six, and three years, died of diphtheria about the same hour.

March 21. Coffin warehouse of Songer and Fagan, Sutter Creek, consumed by fire.

March 31. Nichola Rossiggi fatally stabbed by Dominico Caranza.

April 17. Death of William H. Stowers, Superintendent of Schools, at Bartlett Springs, where he had gone for his health.

May 6. A. Norton, of Jackson, appointed to fill the unexpired term of W. H. Stowers, deceased.

May 26. Laying of the corner-stone of the Presbyterian church at Ione.

June 5. Dwelling-house of Antone Silva, Jackson, destroyed by fire. Loss two thousand dollars.

June 10. Charles Cox, of Lancha Plana, found dead near the suspension flume, with the appearance of having fallen over the cliff of rocks, which at that place is one hundred and thirty feet high.

June 13. Dwelling-house of Jones and Angore, Buckeye valley, destroyed by fire.

June 21. New safe put into the County Treasurer's office.

June 22. Dwelling of L. Rabolt, at Sutter Creek destroyed by fire. Loss, three thousand dollars. Dwelling of John Battiste, near Jackson, burned. Loss, two thousand five hundred dollars.

August 7. John Baker, while in a fit of *delirium tremens*, threw himself against a circular saw in rapid motion, at Brannon's mill, receiving fatal wounds.

August 25. Fire at Jackson, destroying Dr. Peter's office.

September 1. Roy Chamberlain, a forty-niner and an old resident of Amador county, found dead in his chair at his home near the Newton Copper mine. Coroner's verdict, "Death from disease of the heart."

September 12. Cars ran off the track below Ione, fatally injuring W. F. Gary.

October 8. House of Jerry Donovan, Sutter Creek, destroyed by fire.

October 17. James McGee, former engineer at the Oneida, while in a condition of mental derangement jumped into one of the shafts of the mine, falling a distance of six hundred feet, being instantly killed.

October 22. Bucket fell in Oneida, killing John Gardner and John Luderman, and wounding James Forchey.

October 31. House of P. Dwyer, Clinton, burned.

December 2. James Arthur fatally injured in the Amador mine by the caving of the drift in which he was at work.

December 7. Edward E. Stitt died at Drytown from injuries received while taking down the old Loyal mill.

December 22. Hon. John A. Eagon and W. L. McKimm thrown out of a buggy near Jackson. The former seriously and the latter fatally injured, Mr. McKimm dying in two or three hours after.

1878.

January 23. Willow Springs school-house burned.

February 15. Death of the Hon. Robert Ludgate, member of the Assembly for Amador county.

February 17. Mequel Vara found dead in his cabin at Butte City.

High water at Ione and all the western part of the county, destroying much property.

Highest water ever known in Amador City, destroying considerable property and flooding some of the mines.

Great flood in Jackson, drowning seven persons and carrying off and wrecking fifteen buildings. Loss, thirty thousand dollars.

February 23. James Tippet killed in the Phœnix mine by falling out of the bucket while ascending.

February 26. High wind, unroofing and blowing down buildings; Catholic church at Butte City blown down, steeple blown off Catholic church at Jackson, trees, fences, barns, flumes, and other things destroyed.

February. The name of Fiddletown changed to Oleta, by Act of the Legislature.

March 20. H. Traub and Louis Dabovich taken to the asylum.

May 3. House of Mrs. Botto, Sutter Creek, destroyed by fire. Loss, two thousand dollars.

Difficulty between E. M. Phibbs and Fred Varvigat, Ione, the latter being killed.

May 12. Big reservoir of the Amador Canal Company blown up and destroyed.

June 5. Body of Giovani Arata found near Jackson.

June 8. Jackson and Sutter Creek united by telephone.

June 14. Largomarcini's hotel at Amador destroyed by fire.

HISTORY OF AMADOR COUNTY, CALIFORNIA.

June 19. Special election for delegates to Constitutional Convention; John A. Eagon and William H. Prouty, elected.
July 3. Barn owned by Mr. Cox, near Whitmore's mill, burned.
July 5. Shooting affray between George Harville and Peter Smith, the latter being instantly killed.
July 10. McDonald's house, at Amador City, destroyed by fire.
August 22. Moore mine started up.
September 22. New York ranch house, blacksmith shop and barn burned, with all the contents.
October 8. Mrs. Joseph Carreau, of Jackson, while in a condition of mental aberration, committed suicide by shooting herself through the head with a shot-gun.
November 8. E. C. E. Vile, of Ione, committed suicide by cutting his throat with a pen-knife.

1879.

January 4. Henry Peck, County Clerk, died of heart disease. He was a "49er," had been an extensive traveler, having visited Australia, the Amazon mines, Nevada, etc.; was a native of New York.
January 6. Little daughter of Mrs. Hudson, near Ione, accidentally shot by a playmate.
February 1. Death of William H. Hooper, in Oakland. He was formerly a proprietor of the Phœnix mine at Plymouth.
February 5. Sorocco's store and adjoining buildings, at Drytown, burned.
February 21. Hugh Ward killed in a hydraulic claim at Irish Hill.
May 6. Johnson drowned in Mokelumne river, near Clinton Bar.
May 10. O. N. Morse's house, at the Q ranch, destroyed by fire. This was one of the oldest houses in the county, the Q ranch having been a noted place since '49. It was originally claimed by members of Company Q, United States Infantry.
May 25. Edward Phibbs killed in a difficulty with Jesus Vailos, near Jackson Gate.
June 18. Ione connected with Jackson by telephone.
June 18. House of Mrs. Zores, at Volcano, burned.
June 25. Amador *Sentinel* started.
September 1. Dr. Morse's fruit dryer, Q ranch, destroyed by fire. Loss, fifteen hundred dollars.
September 4. The house of David Schuler, Jackson, destroyed by fire, with all the contents.
September 19. R. R. Young, of Amador, committed suicide by taking poison.
September 30. Five hundred feet of the Amador Canal Company's pipe, near Clinton, blown up by giant powder; supposed to have been done by parties damaged by the breaking of the reservoir, February 17.
October 15. Boarding-house of Fopiano, at Keystone mine, destroyed by fire.
October 19. Son of Ed. Wiley, at the Wiley station on the Amador wagon road, fell into a deep well and was drowned.
November 6. Two men, Richard Colliet and John Bachi, seriously injured, the latter fatally, by premature explosion of blast.
November 9. Jesus Aguirra killed by S. Higuerra, for alleged seduction of the latter's wife.
November 15. Lodge of I. O. G. T. organized at Amador.
November 17. John Bachi died from the effect of a premature blast in the Oneida mine.
December 6. A. Swithenbank caught in the machinery of the marble mill, near Plymouth, and torn to pieces.
December 12. A Cornishman by the name of Moyle fatally injured in the original Amador mine by the fall of a rock down the shaft.
December 17. J. M. Myers robbed by highwaymen near Jackson.
December 18. House of G. Bardaracco, near Jackson, burned.
C. A. Cordell instantly killed by falling six hundred feet down the shaft of the Phœnix mine.
December. Stewart and Gillick sold their mine for twenty-five thousand dollars.

1880.

February 1. Difficulty in Jackson between C. Genochio, John Mori, A. Galli, Robert Venglio, and John Balles, resulting fatally to the two latter.
February 5. House of Joseph Carrara, Amador City, destroyed by fire.
April 20. Flood at Drytown doing considerable damage to the mines.
Flood in Ione, the main streets being inundated, also many of the ranches in the vicinity, thirteen hundred feet of the railroad track being washed away.
May 1. Last number of the Ione *Times* issued.
May 4. House of William Sutherland, Ione, damaged by fire.
May 6. Attempted robbery of stage near Ione.
May 7. G. Clincinovich instantly killed by falling down the Lincoln shaft.
May 22. Several hundred dollars' worth of harnesses and wagons stolen from A. H. Palmer, Jackson valley, of which no trace was obtained.
May 27. House of William Marshall, Sutter Creek, destroyed by fire. Loss, one thousand dollars.
May 30. Difficulty between William Cook and Charles Tedeman at Buena Vista, the latter person being shot through the body.
June 15. Joseph Anderson found dead near Dane's ranch, Grass Valley.
July 31. A. D. McDonald fatally injured by a fall from the balcony of a hotel at Amador.
August 3. Barn belonging to W. O. Clark, Drytown, destroyed by fire.
August 18. Augustus Feine fatally injured by being caught in the machinery of the Florence mills at Ione.

September 1. Charles Hutz found dead at Ione. Death said to have been caused by heart disease.

September 3. Charles Steckler of Jackson, an old and much respected citizen, committed suicide by hanging.

September 9. Celebration of admission day by the pioneer society and citizens generally.

October 9. Chautauqua literary society organized at Jackson.

November 5. Difficulty between William Frasier and Charles McKinney in Volcano, in which the latter person was fatally stabbed.

November 21. The residence of Mr. Clark, Plymouth, consumed by fire with all its contents.

November 23. Dr. Charles Boarman died of small-pox.

December. Small-pox prevailed extensively in Jackson.

Extraordinary meeting of the Board of Supervisors to consider the situation. Pest-house erected.

PATRONS DIRECTORY.

TOWNSHIP NO 1, AMADOR COUNTY.

NAME.	RESIDENCE.	BUSINESS.	NATIVITY.	Came to State	Came to County	POST OFFICE.	No. Acres.
Aitken, Robert	Jackson	Butcher	Scotland	1850	1858	Jackson	
Andrews, E	Township No. 1	Farmer	England	1856	1856	Jackson	160
Arata, Andrea	Clinton	Farmer	Italy	1853	1853	Pine Grove	320
Arata, Nicholas P.	Clinton	Vineyard & mining	California			Pine Grove	
Askey, A	Jackson	National Hotel	Pennsylvania	1850	1850	Jackson	
Avise, James	Township No. 1	Farmer and miner	New Jersey	1852	1864	Jackson	160
Bartlett, S. H	Township No. 1	Farmer	Massachusetts	1852	1853	Jackson	40
Boarman, Charles M. D.	Jackson	Physician & Surgeon	Virginia	1849	1858	Jackson	160
Boyd, James	AmadorCanal Res'v'r	Superintendent	Canada	1876	1876	Sutter	
Brown, A. C	Jackson	Attorney at Law	Missouri	1851	1851	Jackson	
Brown, C. Y	Jackson	Physician & Surgeon	Amador County, Cal	1855	1855	Jackson	
Brown, J Ward	Butte City	Mining	New York	1853	1859	Jackson	7
Brown, Jasper	New York Ranch	Farmer	California			Jackson	
Caminetti, A	Jackson	District Att'rney	Amador County, Cal			Jackson	
Caplen, Thomas	Jackson	Under Sheriff	Ireland	1851	1854	Jackson	
Cox, John H	Township No. 1	AmadorCanal tend'r	British America	1857	1868	Pine Grove	
Devoto, Antone	Jacks n Gate	Farmer	Italy	1869	1872	Jackson	320
Dewitt, Isaac N	Murphy's Ridge	Miner	Ohio	1866	1875	Jackson	80
Dick, John H	Township No. 1	Farmer	Ohio	1852	1852	Jackson	320
Eagon, John A	Jackson	Attorney-at-Law	Virginia	1851	1851	Jackson	
Evans, Ellis	Jackson	National Hotel	Pennsylvania	1849	1849	Jackson	100
Fontenrose, L. J	Jackson	County Clerk	Pennsylvania	1858	1859	Jackson	
Freeman, E. G	Jackson	Saddlery and harness	New York	1852	1852	Jackson	
Froelich, D	Township No. 1	Farmer	Germany	1853	1853	Jackson	480
Froelich, Ross	Jackson	Retired	Germany	1847	1854	Jackson	
Fallen, George	Township No. 1	Farmer	Ireland	1860	1860	Jackson	160
Fullen, John	Township No. 1	Farmer	Ireland	1852	1852	Jackson	160
Gardner, Eli ††	Clinton District	Farming & teaming	Ohio	1850	1864	Pine Grove	160
Gerdon, Marion W. Sr.	Jackson	Attorney-at-Law	Tennessee	1850	1850	Jackson	8
Heming, D	Township No. 1	Farmer	Ohio	1852	1853	Jackson	480
Hoffman, Frank	Jackson	Livery and ranching	Germany	1850	1852	Jackson	160
Horton, William J	Camp Opera District	Wood Ranch	Kentucky	1854	1854	Lancha Pl'a	160
Hutchins, John W	Clinton	Miner	Maine	1853	1853	Jackson	1
Kay, Wallace	Jackson	Variety Store	Massachusetts	1869	1869	Jackson	
Keeney, L. G	Township No. 1	Farmer	Pennsylvania	1852	1861	Jackson	140
Kent, Mrs. C. S. G.	Jackson		Illinois	1851	1851	Jackson	
Little, M. J	Jackson	Farmer & orchardist	Maine	1850	1854	Jackson	120
Love, Thomas	Jackson	Liquor dealer	Ireland	1850	1850	Jackson	
Loveridge, H. L	Butte City	Ditch Agent	New York	1851	1851	Jackson	5
McKay, Daniel	Township No. 1	Farmer and miner	New Brunswick	1852	1868	Jackson	120
McKinney, Abraham	Jackson	Merchant and miner	New Jersey	1853	1853	Jackson	20
Morhan, J	Jackson	Co. Treas'r & miner	Ireland	1850	1851	Jackson	30
Meek, C. M	Jackson	Postmaster	Missouri	1852	1854	Jackson	20
Moore, George	Jackson	Lawyer	Kentucky	1877	1879	Jackson	
Myers, Oscar	Township No. 1	Farmer	California			Jackson	160
Nichols, J. B	Township No. 1	Mining	Wisconsin	1859	1859	Jackson	320
Penry, William M	Jackson	El AmadorDispatch	Mississippi	1857	1864	Jackson	
Phelps, T. J	Jackson	Attorney-at-Law	Kentucky	1849	1852	Jackson	
Pitt, William	Township No. 1	Farmer	Connecticut	1850	1850	Jackson	160
Reaves, John F	Township No. 1	Foreman Oneida mill	Tennessee	1850	1851	SutterCreek	
Rees, H	Sutter Creek	Forem'n Oneida mine	Wales	1853	1853	SutterCreek	
Richardson, L. C	Township No. 1	Forem'n Oneida mine	Maine	1854	1868	SutterCreek	
Riebmyer, B. F	Jackson		New York	1850	1850	Jackson	
Schacht, B. H	Jackson		Prussia	1869	1877	Jackson	
Simmons, Thomas H	Sutter Creek	Ditch Agent	Wisconsin	1852	1873	SutterCreek	
Spagnoli, D. B	Jackson	Attorney-at-Law	Italy	1854	1854	Jackson	400
Spagnoli, S. G	Clinton	Merchant and miner	Italy	1854	1854	Jackson	300
Turner, C. Helmer	Jackson	Deputy Clerk	Michigan	1852	1856	Jackson	
Vandament, Eli P	Township No. 1	Farmer and miner	Ohio	1855	1855	Pine Grove	170
Vandament, W. B	Township No. 1	Farmer and miner	Ohio	1855	1855	Pine Grove	
Vogan, John	Jackson	Sheriff	Pennsylvania	1849	1852	Jackson	1200
Welsh, Richard	Jackson	Publisher	England	1871	1875	Jackson	
Wiley, William	Township No. 1	Farmer	Maine	1849	1849	Pine Grove	640

*Wells, Fargo & Co.'s agent, telegraph operator, and proprietor of Jackson Water-works.   †Druggist, Coroner and Public Adm't'r.

TOWNSHIP NO. 2. AMADOR COUNTY.

NAME.	RESIDENCE.	BUSINESS.	NATIVITY.	Came to State.	Came to County.	POST OFFICE.	No. Acres.
Amick, A. J.	Dry Creek	Farmer	North Carolina	1849	1850	Ione City	718
Amick, J. S.	Dry Creek	Farmer	Dry Creek, Cal.	1855	1855	Ione City	160
B_mest, Charles	Township No. 2	Merchant & farmer	Germany	1852	1858	Lancha Plana	840
Barnett, Susanna	French Camp	Stock raiser.	Pennsylvania	1858	1858	Lancha Plana	360
Bishop, Edgar	Ione City	Gen. Merchandise	New York	1861	1861	Ione City	
Black, Charles S.	Buena Vista	Farming	Ohio	1856	1856	Ione	40
Blyther, J. C.	Mokelumne River	Farm'r & fruit gr'w'r	Maine	1850	1857	Camanche	200
Brusie, L.	Ione City	Physician & druggist	Connecticut	1850	1850	Ione	
Burris William	Ione Valley	Farming	California	1852	1852	Ione City	144
Button, O.	Ione City	Teaming	New York	1852	1852	Ione	
Clark, J. S.	Lancha Plana	Teacher	California	1856	1874	Ione City	
Coombs, W. S.	Ione City	Carpenter	Pennsylvania	1850	1852	Ione	
Corneal, A.	Ione City	Miner	Kentucky	1853	1853	Ione City	
Crail, W.	Lancha Plana	Blacksmith	Ohio	1852	1855	Lancha Plana	
Dulian, H.	Jackson Creek	Farming	Iowa	1854	1854	Ione	160
Dunlap, G. H.	Ione Valley	Drayman	Wisconsin	1870	1875	Ione	
Earle, S. B.	Ione City	Laborer	Massachusetts	1867	1867	Ione	
Farnsworth, J.	Ione Valley	Farming	Ohio	1854	1855	Ione	150
Fischer, Bernhard	Forest Home	Wine grower	Germany	1858	1858	Forest Home	60
Ford, H. W.	Buena Vista	Teaching	Kentucky	1863	1864	Ione	20
Frates, Frank	Ione Valley	Mangr of Ione Grant & Ione coal & ir n Co	Azores	1852	1876	Ione Valley	33000
Frates, J. C.	Ione City	Engineer	Portugal	1874	1876	Ione City	
Goodding, J. A.	Pat's Bar	Rancher	Missouri	1854	1857	Lancha Plana	250
Gregory, I. B.	Jackson Valley	Farming	Tennessee	1853	1853	Ione	320
Gregory, U. S.	Ione	Sawyer	Texas	1868	1868	Ione	
Heffron, M	Ione Valley	Farming	Ireland	1852	1853	Ione	100½
Hall, H. F.	Ione City	Miller	Connecticut	1852	1855	Ione	
Hemrick, George K.	Ione City	Carpenter	Kentucky	1863	1863	Ione	
Horton, J. Q.	Township No. 2	Farmer	Kentucky	1853	1858	Jackson	480
Johnson, A. H.	Michigan Bar	Teaming	Maine	1868	1878	Michigan Bar	
Jones, W. C.	Ione Township	Hotel	Missouri	1852	1857	Ione	160
Kidd, Stephen	Jackson Valley	Farming & mining	England	1852	1852	Ione	340
Kientz, Christian	Mokelumne River	Farm'r & fruit gr'w'r	Germany	1830	1858	Lancha Plana	145
Kingsley, M. R.	Ione	Hotel	Illinois	1853	1853	Ione	
Le Clair, Joseph	Buena Vista	Blacksmith	Canada	1878	1878	Ione	
Leininger, F.	Jackson Valley	Farming	Ione, Cal	1857	1857	Ione	130
Ludgate, Mrs. Mary H.	Ione City		Indiana	1869	1869	Ione	
Marchant, J.	Ione	Butchering	England	1858	1858	Ione	35
Maroon, W. Q.	Lancha Plana	Fruit grower	Ohio	1853	1858	Lancha Plana	172
Martin, Mrs. George	Jackson Valley	Farming	New York	1849	1849	Ione	300
Martin, J. P.	Sutter creek	Farmer & stock rais'r	Virginia	1847	1848	Ione	1000
McDonald, A. B.	Ione Valley	Farmer & orchardist	New York	1852	1852	Ione	30
McDonald, Silas	Ione Valley	Farming and mining	New York	1855	1858	Ione	30
Moffett, James Albert	Ione Valley	Express messenger	California	1852	1852	Ione	
Moore, James	French Camp	Farm'r & stock rais'r	Ireland	1854	1854	Lancha Plana	320
Murray, Matthew	Lancha Plana	Mining & ditching	Ireland	1855	1858	Lancha Plana	300
Northup, John	Julien District	Fruit grower	New York	1852	1852	Lancha Plana	80
Palmer, J. W. D.	Lancha Plana	Merchant	Vermont	1849	1849	Lancha Plana	
Phillips, George W	Irish Hill	Ditch agent	Kentucky	1852	1878	Ione	
Prichard, F. M.	Buena Vista	Store keeper	New York	1856	1856	Ione	10
Preoty, W. H.	Jackson Valley	Farmer	Ohio	1852	1852	Ione	350
Rhodes, Jessie	Buckeye Valley	Teaming & farming	Missouri	1852	1865	Ione City	240
Richey, J. H.	Buena Vista	Ranching & thrash'g	New York	1854	1859	Ione	340
Ringer, J. H.	Buena Vista	Farming	Missouri	1852	1852	Ione	431
Ronna Haus	Forest Home	Saloon	Holstein, Germany	1852	1870	Forest Home	
Sheakley, Alex	Ione	Farmer	Pennsylvania	1852	1853	Ione	184
Sibole, I. W.	Mt. Echo	Farmer	Virginia	1865	1865	Ione	160
Smith, Fred P.	Ione City	Hotel	New York	1849	1850	Ione Valley	
Spooner, G. A.	Ione City	Painter	Massachusetts	1857	1858	Ione	
Stevens, T. M.	Jackson Creek	Farm'r & stock rais'r	Maine	1853	1866	Ione	3000
Strong, C. B.	Ione	Undertaker	Vermont	1853	1860	Ione	
Surface, John W.	Ione City	Livery, notary public	Missouri	1852	1852	Ione Valley	
Swift, C. B.	Ione City	Justice of the Peace	New York	1849	1855	Ione City	
Umstead, Isaac L.	Sutter creek	Blacksmith	Pennsylvania	1873	1873	Ione	
Van Sandt, A. A	Mokelumne River	Farm'r & fruit rais'r	Ohio	1852	1853	Camanche	600
Violett, J. W.	Ione Valley	Farmer	Kentucky	1850	1851	Ione City	107
Vivian, H. T.	Lancha Plana	Ditching	England	1856	1857	Lancha Plana	
Washtell, Isaac	Lancha Plana	Mining & clerking	Maryland	1850	1854	Lancha Plana	80
Waters, H. H.	Boston Ranch	Farm'r & stock rais'r	Ireland	1849	1849	Ione	240
Westfall, John C.	Township No. 2	Farmer	Illinois	1854	1854	Jackson	320
Whitlatch, D. H	Ione City	Miner	Indiana	1851	1863	Ione Valley	
Whittle, J. C	Willow Creek	Farm'r & stock rais'r	Canada	1850	1850	Ione	1000
Winship, F. H.	Ione City	Lawyer	Maine	1868	1868	Ione	
Woolsey, Geo.	Ione	Merchant	New Jersey	1856	1858	Ione	240

TOWNSHIP NO. 3, AMADOR COUNTY.

NAME.	RESIDENCE.	BUSINESS.	NATIVITY.	Came to State.	Came to County.	POST OFFICE.	No. Acres.
Adams, R. J.	Aqueduct City	Lumberman	Canada	1868	1875	Pine Grove	
Ames, Serena	Pine Grove		Pine Grove, Cal.	1866	1866	Pine Grove	
Boardman, S. B.	Volcano	Miner and farmer	Indiana	1853	1853	Volcano	30
Boylston, D. S.	Volcano	Druggist	Ohio	1850	1850	Volcano	
Cleveland, F. J.	Volcano	Volcano water-works	New York	1851	1854	Volcano	27
Clough, A. P.	Pine Grove	Fruit grower	New York	1855	1855	Pine Grove	130
Foley, J. M.	Shake Ridge	Ranching & mining	Kentucky	1854	1855	Volcano	140
Foster, John A.	Township No. 3	Farmer	New Hampshire	1849	1854	Volcano	320
Foster, Margaret	Shake Ridge	Public House, Ranch	Illinois	1852	1852	Volcano	260
Goodrich, C. B.	Volcano	Blacksmith	Maine	1859	1859	Volcano	
Hall, James	Township No. 3	Miner	Pennsylvania	1850	1850	Volcano	40
Ham, A. C.	Aqueduct City	Hotel and mining	Kentucky	1855	1855	Pine Grove	500
Harker, J. P.	Harkers Ranch	Farming & timber'ng	Salt Lake, Utah	1850	1855	Volcano	160
Hinkson, J. M.	Volcano	Livery	Missouri	1849	1849	Volcano	
Hinkson, Richard S.	Volcano	Livery	Missouri	1849	1849	Volcano	
Jerome, Alex	Volcano	Ranching	New York	1852	1852	Volcano	160
Jonas, P.	Volcano	Hotel	Germany	1853	1859	Volcano	
Klamann, John	Pine Grove	Miner	Germany	1873	1873	Pine Grove	
Lessley, James	Township No. 3	Ranching & teaming	Missouri	1854	1854	Volcano	240
Mace, F	Pioneer	Lumber & quartz mill	Maine	1851	1851	Volcano	
Marian, Chas. M.	Volcano	Laborer	New York	1850	1880	Volcano	6
Mattice, S.	Volcano	Mining	Canada	1850	1856	Volcano	8
Miller, L.	Volcano	School supt & teach'r	Alabama	1851	1875	Volcano	320
Peck, Palmer N	Volcano	Mining & farming	New York	1853	1858	Volcano	
Petty, A.	Volcano	Hotel	Ohio	1852	1852	Volcano	
Petty, Miss E.	Volcano	Housekeeper	Kentucky	1873	1873	Volcano	
Petty, Solomon	Volcano	Inventor	Missouri	1853	1853	Volcano	
Rank, J. B.	Volcano	Milling and mining	Ohio	1849	1879	Volcano	
Ross, Benjamin	Volcano	County Surveyor	Portland, Maine	1849	1852	Volcano	
Shealor, James W.	Shake Ridge	Milling & ranching	Virginia	1853	1863	Volcano	160
Southiel, L. W.	Pioneer	Logging	Missouri	1856	1873	Volcano	
Stewart. Robert	Volcano	Mining	Ireland	1850	1850	Volcano	
Stolcken, J. D.	Pioneer Creek	Miner	Germany	1870	1870	Volcano	
Tarr, Warren F.	Tarr's Mills	Milling	Maine	1859	1859	Volcano	320
Toop, George W.	Pioneer City	Mining	California	1856	1856	Volcano	20
Wheeler, J. T.	Pine Grove	Merchant and miner	New Hampshire	1849	1849	Pine Grove	40
Whitaker, Jacob	Volcano	Quartz miner	Switzerland	1850	1858	Volcano	
Whitehead, W. H.	Volcano	Carpenter & maner	Ohio	1852	1852	Volcano	
Whiting, Samuel L.	Volcano	Carp'r & millwright	Massachusetts	1854	1854	Volcano	
Whitmore, F. M.	Volcano	Lumberman	Massachusetts	1850	1850	Volcano	480
Whitney, I. W.	Volcano	Mining	New York	1850	1854	Volcano	
Williams. N. C.	Williams Station	Hotel and ranch	Maine	1855	1855	Volcano	164
Wise, E.	Wise Toll Road	Ranching	Pennsylvania	1850	1852	Sutter Creek	160
Zeras, Catherine	Volcano		Missouri		1860	Volcano	

TOWNSHIP NO. 4, AMADOR COUNTY.

NAME.	RESIDENCE.	BUSINESS.	NATIVITY.	Came to State.	Came to County.	POST OFFICE.	No. Acres.
Allen, George	Sutter Creek	Lumber & ranching	New York	1860	1860	Sutter Creek	2700
Bermingham, Rev. P.	Sutter Creek	Catholic pastor	Ireland	1855	1879	Sutter Creek	
Breedlove, W. N.	Sutter Creek	Saloon	Virginia	1852	1862	Sutter Creek	
Brian, Morris	Sutter Creek	Merchant	Germany	1855	1855	Sutter Creek	
Brown, Jno. A.	Sutter Creek	County Surveyor	Missouri	1850	1851	Jackson	
Coolidge, W. S.	Sutter Creek	Supt Amador Canal and Mining Co.	New Hampshire	1849	1851	Sutter Creek	
Culbert, Thos. L.	Amador City	Farmer	Missouri	1854	1854	Amador City	800
Davies, D. T.	Sutter Creek	Supt Con. Amador mines.	England	1862	1862	Sutter Creek	
Deacon, Hiram	Sutter Creek	Amalgamat'r Eureka mill.	England	1858	1858	Sutter Creek	320
De Carolis, R.	Sutter Creek	Catholic pastor	Italy	1878	1878	Sutter Creek	
Downs, R. C.	Sutter Creek	Supt. Down's mine	Connecticut	1849	1849	Sutter Creek	
Dudley, A. K.	Sutter Creek	Prop. American Exchange Hotel	Maine	1859	1860	Sutter Creek	
Dunlap, A.	Amador	Druggist	Ohio	1860	1860	Amador	
Ellis, R.	Township No. 4	Farmer	New York	1849	1849	Amador City	80
Fagan, Peter	Sutter Creek	Livery	Canada	1858	1858	Sutter Creek	140
Furnanzo, Luigi	Township No. 4	Farmer	Italy	1861	1864	Amador City	240
Gabbs, E. S.	Sutter Creek	Dentist	England	1853	1876	Sutter Creek	
Harrington, A. W.	Amador	Prop. Amador House	Massachusetts	1852	1853	Amador	
Herman F.	Sutter Creek	Blacksmith	Pennsylvania	1854	1854	Sutter Creek	
Hewitt, O. C.	Amador City	Supt. Keystone mine	Virginia	1861	1870	Amador City	
Howard F. A.	Sutter Creek	Real estate	Massachusetts	1850	1852	Sutter Creek	
Keeney, W. F.	Amador	Prop. Amador House	Pennsylvania	1855	1863	Amador	
Kerr, Thomas	Amador	Livery	Pennsylvania	1860	1860	Amador	
Kling, G. W.	Amador	Mining	Ohio	1853	1853	Amador	
Lepley, Isaac	Amador City	Builder	Pennsylvania	1864	1864	Amador City	

TOWNSHIP NO. 4, AMADOR COUNTY—Continued.

NAME.	RESIDENCE.	BUSINESS.	NATIVITY.	Came to State.	Came to County.	POST OFFICE.	No. Acres.
Martin, O. E...	Amador	Lumber	Maine	1873	1873	Amador	
Mayon, T H	Amador	Physician & Surgeon	Kentucky	1854	1865	Amador	
McIntire, E. B.	Sutter Creek	Mining	New Hampshire	1849	1850	Sutter Creek	
Mooney, M. G	Amador	Saloon	Ireland	1862	1862	Amador	320
Nickerson, C. J...	Sutter Creek	Supt. Sutter Creek sulphuret works	Massachusetts	1856	1856	Sutter Creek	
Palmer, John	Bunker Hill	Supt. Bunker Hill mine.	Maine	1858	1858	Amador City	160
Palmer, Wilmer	Sutter Creek	Millwright	New York	1853	1857	Sutter Creek	
Parks, J. F	Amador City	Foreman Keystone mine.	Missouri	1855	1873	Amador City	
Peterson Arthur N.	Sutter Creek	Foreman Lincoln mill.	Scotland	1857	1857	Sutter Creek	5
Porter, J. S.	Sutter Creek	Justice of the Peace	Connecticut	1849	1859	Sutter Creek	
Post, J. M.	Township No. 4	Farmer	New Brunswick	1855	1855	Sutter Creek	80
Randolph, I. N.	Sutter Creek	Insurance and collection agent.	Maryland	1846	1853	Sutter Creek	
Sanderson, John.	Township No. 4	Farmer	Ireland	1862	1862	Sutter Creek	160
Stewart, S. D. R.	Sutter Creek	Supt. Lincoln and Mahony mines.	New York	1852	1872	Sutter Creek	
Stone, John T	Sutter Creek	Miner	Vermont	1868	1868	Sutter Creek	
Taylor, B. F..	Sutter Creek	Foreman Amador mine.	Ohio	1859	1859	Sutter Creek	
Taylor, L. J	Bunker Hill	Farmer	Ohio	1859	1859	Amador City	160
Templeton, I. N.	Amador City	Foreman Keystone mill.	New York	1860	1860	Amador City	5
Thompson, A. R.	Bunker Hill	Engine'r Bunker Hill mine.	New York	1875	1875	Amador City	
Towns, H. H.	Sutter Creek	Gen. mangr. Amador Canal & Mining Co.	New Hampshire	1874	1874	Sutter Creek	
Tregloan, J. R.	Amador City	Supt. Spring Hill mine.	Wisconsin	1855	1872	Amador City	
Voorhies, E. C.	Sutter Creek	Supt. Amador Reduction Works.	Michigan	1877	1877	Sutter Creek	

TOWNSHIP NO. 5, AMADOR COUNTY.

NAME.	RESIDENCE.	BUSINESS.	NATIVITY.	Came to State.	Came to County.	POST OFFICE.	No. Acres.
Ball, Reuben	Parson Bar	Ditch tender & ranch	Indiana	1853	1853	Forest Home	120
Bickford A	Forest Home Dis't	Ranch & stock raiser	New Hampshire	1851	1867	Forest Home	320
Cook, H	Willow Springs	Teamster	Illinois			Drytown	
Finn, Catherine	Finn's Ranch	Farm'g, public house and wine grower.	Canada	1853	1853	Drytown	260
Ford, R. M	Township No. 5	Farmer	Kentucky	1853	1853	Amador City	280
Worley, Dan	Township No. 5	Farmer and miner	Pennsylvania	1849	1849	Drytown	160

TOWNSHIP NO. 6, AMADOR COUNTY.

NAME.	RESIDENCE.	BUSINESS.	NATIVITY.	Came to State.	Came to County.	POST OFFICE.	No. Acres.
Aniya, M	Drytown	Saloon-keeper	Italy	1870	1870	Drytown	
Baird, Jefferson	Plymouth	Farming	Pennsylvania	1850	1873	Plymouth	320
Ball, O	Shenandoah Valley	Farmer and miner	Indiana	1854	1857	Plym'nth & Oleta	320
Barney, E. S.	Drytown	Mill superintendent	New York	1849	1873	Drytown	
Bawden, T. P	Plymouth	Mill foreman Empire mine.	Illinois	1872	1872	Plymouth	
Brace, M. T.	Plymouth	Liquors, cigars, etc.	Indiana	1852	1869	Plymouth	
Briggs, Eb. M	Plymouth	Buddler Empire mill	Missouri	1849	1853	Plymouth	
Berner, James	Plymouth	Team'g & butcher'ng	Virginia	1865	1866	Plymouth	160
Bert, James	Oleta	General business	Vermont	1849	1851	Oleta	
Carraro, Joseph	Plymouth	Miner	Italy	1862	1862	Plymouth	
Church, M. B.	Drytown	Justice of the Peace	Connecticut	1849	1850	Drytown	25
Clark, G. W	Oleta	Farming and mining	Kentucky	1850	1860	Oleta	80
Clark, W. O	Drytown	Farmer	Indiana	1850	1850	Drytown	200
Clemens, John.	Plymouth	Miner	England	1866	1879	Plymouth	
Clough, F. W.	Plymouth	Hoisting engineer	Amador Co. Cal	1853	1853	Plymouth	
Coover, Wm.	Plymouth	Teaming & ranching	Ohio	1868	1878	Plymouth	120
Croff, J. W.	Oleta	Farmer and miner	New York	1851	1853	Oleta	120
Dabovich, Andrew	Plymouth	Miner	Austria	1864	1878	Plymouth	
Davis, Jonah	Plymouth	Miner	Wales	1877	1877	Plymouth	
Davis, Thompson	Plymouth	Livery stable	Illinois	1853	1854	Plymouth	
Dingle, James.	Plymouth	Mining	England	1869	1869	Plymouth	
Easton, G. W	Plymouth	Engine'r Empire mill	Wisconsin	1856	1873	Plymouth	

TOWNSHIP NO. 6, AMADOR COUNTY---Continued.

NAME.	RESIDENCE.	BUSINESS.	NATIVITY.	Came to State.	Came to County.	POST OFFICE.	No. of Acres.
Evans, John	Plymouth	Miner	Wales	1850	1872	Plymouth	
Farnham, H. C.	Oleta	Milling and ranching	New York	1850	1853	Oleta	280
Gerle, C. C.	Plymouth	Mason Empire mine	Sweden	1854	1877	Plymouth	
Gilman, John	Plymouth	Mechanic	Maine	1875	1880	Plymouth	
Gilmore, R. M.	Plymouth	Mill machinist	Pennsylvania	1856	1856	Plymouth	
Goff, D. M.	Oleta		Pennsylvania	1853	1853	Oleta	
Green, Charles	Plymouth	Forem'n Empire mill	Ohio	1859	1870	Plymouth	
Gregg, Louisa L.	Plymouth		Plymouth, Cal	1865	1865	Plymouth	
Gregg, S. W.	Plymouth	Teaming	Plymouth, Cal	1855	1855	Plymouth	
Hanks, Louis	Plymouth	Blacksmith Empire mill.	Bavaria	1852	1854	Plymouth	
Hinkson, N. C.	Plymouth	Livery stable	Missouri	1849	1849	Plymouth	
Holman, J. H.	Plymouth	Ranching & Teaming	Indiana	1852	1856	Plymouth	160
Inskeep, Sarah	Plymouth	Farming	Virginia	1854	1860	Plymouth	50
Jennings, Geo. C.	Drytown	Book-keeper	California			Drytown	
Jones, W. T.	Plymouth	Foreman	Wales	1867	1867	Plymouth	
Kephart, George	Plymouth	Lawyer	Pennsylvania	1859	1859	Plymouth	
Keyes, William	Plymouth	Bucket-luoler	Canada	1861	1879	Plymouth	
Lawson, P.	Plymouth	Painter and general workman.	Denmark	1849	1854	Plymouth	
LeMoin, Geo. W.	Drytown	Blacksmith	Drytown, Cal.	1857	1857	Drytown	
Miller, J. H.	Drytown	Blacksmith	Missouri	1849	1849	Drytown	
Mitrovich, Michael	Plymouth	Miner	Austria	1868	1868	Plymouth	
Morris, James	Plymouth	Fireman	Utah	1852	1852	Plymouth	
Mudge, Wm. Hodge	Plymouth	Miner	England	1866	1873	Plymouth	
Page, Michael	Plymouth	Miner	Austria	1870	1876	Plymouth	
Perry, Jno. W	Plymouth	Mining	New York	1873	1873	Plymouth	
Pettitt, I. E.	Plymouth	Farmer	Ohio	1854	1854	Plymouth	224
Potter, E. S.	Plymouth	Ranch'ng and lumber merchant.	Connecticut	1852	1852	Plymouth	141
Puriston, C. A.	Oleta	Ditch owner	Maine	1850	1855	Oleta	
Russell, T. N.	Drytown	Mining	England	1866	1867	Drytown	
Sallee, Jonathan	Plymouth	Farmer	Missouri	1871	1871	Plymouth	320
Schairer, Fred	Plymouth	Farmer	Bavaria	1853	1853	Plymouth	160
Thoms, F. H.	Plymouth	Salesman	Michigan	1860	1862	Plymouth	
Townsend Mrs. E.	Oleta	Public house	Illinois	1852	1852	Oleta	
Vanderpool, Corrinne	Plymouth	School teaching	Iowa	1873	1873	Plymouth	
Venn, Charles	Plymouth	Miner	Wales	1873	1875	Plymouth	
Venn, Wm.	Plymouth	Miner	Wales	1873	1875	Plymouth	
Votaw, C. J.	Williams District	Ranching & teaming	Missouri	1852	1877	Plymouth	155
Wells, Matthew H.	Central House	Farming	New York	1849	1852	Drytown	700
Wheeler, Stephen C.	Plymouth	Farmer	Indiana	1852	1852	Plymouth	165
Whitacre, I. W.	Whitacre Branch	Ranching	Pennsylvania	1853	1858	Plymouth	200
Whitney, N. P.	Plymouth	Mining	Boston, Mass.	1852	1877	Plymouth	20
Williams, Benjamin C.	Williams District	Farming and teaming	Mississippi	1853	1853	Plymouth	160
Williams, J. C.	Drytown	Merchant	New Hampshire	1849	1850	Drytown	320
Wilson, A.	Shenandoah Valley	Farmer	Wisconsin	1850	1850	Plymouth	50
Woolford, Joseph	Plymouth	Blacksmith	England	1862	1862	Plymouth	
Yates, E. R.	Oleta	Farmer	Virginia	1849	1850	Oleta	156

MISCELLANEOUS.

NAME.	RESIDENCE.	BUSINESS.	NATIVITY.	Came to State.	Came to County.	POST OFFICE.	No. of Acres.
Dohrm, C.	San Francisco	Miner & machinist	Paris	1852	1880	San Francisco	
Gaffney, Thos.	Michigan Bar	Potter	New York	1875	1875	Michigan Bar	
Hill, Samuel	Ventura County	Stock raiser	England	1850	1850	Springville	7000
Knox, Israel W.	Oakland	Foundry and mining	Massachusetts	1852		237 First st. S. F.	
Monson, H. H.	Coyoteville	Farming and fruit raising.	Hanover	1857	1854	Oleta	320
Wirts, G. D.	Galt	Farming	Ohio	1859	1859	Galt	
Wrigglesworth, Joseph	Bridgeport District	Ranching & teaming	New York	1859	1859	Oleta	760

www.ingramcontent.com/pod-product-compliance
Lightning Source LLC
Chambersburg PA
CBHW051846300426
44117CB00006B/277